D0350726

THE RUINS
AND EXCAVATIONS
OF ANCIENT ROME

RODOLFO LANCIANI

With a New Foreword by
Richard Brilliant

*Professor of Art History
and Archaeology,
Columbia University*

Bell Publishing Company
New York

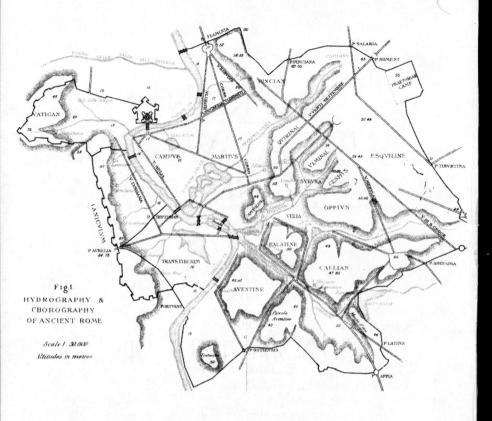

Fig. I.
HYDROGRAPHY &
CHOROGRAPHY
OF ANCIENT ROME

Scale 1:30.000
Altitudes in metres

This book was first published in 1897 and reissued in 1967.
Special material copyright © MCMLXXIX by Crown Publishers, Inc.
All rights reserved.
This edition is published by Bell Publishing Company,
a division of Crown Publishers, Inc.,
by arrangement with Arno Press, Inc.
a b c d e f g h
BELL 1979 EDITION
Manufactured in the United States of America

Library of Congress Cataloging in Publication Data
Lanciani, Rodolfo Amedeo, 1847-1929.
The ruins and excavations of ancient Rome.
Reprint of the 1897 ed. published by Houghton Mifflin, New York.
Includes bibliographies and indexes.
1. Rome (City)—Antiquities. 2. Italy—Antiquities.
I. Title.
DG63.L25 1979   937'.6'01   79-16060
ISBN 0-517-28945-8

FOREWORD

Rudolfo Lanciani's study of *The Ruins and Excavations of Ancient Rome,* lives on with undiminished vitality, because the subject of his research remains as one of the great cities of the world, capital of Italy and of Catholic Christendom. Rome still offers a wealth of visual and historical experiences, referring to her glorious past, within the context of a modern, flourishing city, not frozen into the museum-like entombment of Pompeii or Ostia Antica. Even more, Rome provides the historian of classical antiquity, of the Medieval Papacy, of the Renaissance, of Mediterranean civilization, an opportunity to examine the relationship between the city in her physical, demographic character and her symbolic and political role within a larger context. That there are many Romes contained within the singular Rome on the Tiber has long been known to scholars and to all those who treasure the continuous affecting force of the past upon the present human condition. The willful alienation from tradition, once so avid in the twentieth century, has been currently replaced by a search for roots, thus giving new value to that continuous connection between modern and previous states sustained by Rome.

Lanciani's activity as archaeologist, topographer, historian, and writer has been instrumental in uncovering Rome's past and demonstrating her life in the present. He was a distinguished member of a very distinguished company of scholars of Rome in the late nineteenth century, including most notably Heinrich Jordan, Christian Huelsen, Samuel B. Platner, and Thomas Ashby. Platner and Ashby's *Topographical Dictionary of Ancient Rome* finally appeared in 1929 ; it has been succeeded but not replaced by *Pictorial Dictionary of Ancient Rome* (1961) by E. Nash. Jordan's *Topographie der Stadt Rom im Altertum* (1878–1907) remains useful, although considerably modified by modern research, especially by the work of G. Lugli in the 1930s and 1940s, by A.M. Colini and F. Castagnoli in the

1940s and 1950s, by G. Carettoni, G. Gatti, and F. Coarelli in
the 1960s and 1970s, and by many European and American
scholars since 1945. All topographers of Rome since the Renaissance have depended on ancient textual sources, on Medieval
and Renaissance guidebooks and descriptions of the city, on
maps, and on excavations. Lanciani himself relied heavily on
these materials, but our knowledge of them has improved greatly since his time: beginning in 1953, G. Lugli published many
volumes of ancient texts on Roman topography; from 1940 to
1953 Valentini and Zuchetti presented the Medieval and Renaissance texts *in extenso;* the *Forma Urbis Romae*, once published by Lanciani, was newly edited in 1960 by Carettoni and
others; maps and views of Rome, assiduously studied by Huelsen and Ashby, have been under constant examination—witness
the great collection of *Le Piante di Roma* issued by A.F. Frutaz
(1962); the ongoing issuance of the *Carta Archeologica di
Roma* correlates the results of all finds at each specific site.

Lanciani's *Ruins and Excavations* can no longer serve as a
guidebook, because excavation and modern development have so
greatly changed the historical and physical reality of the city.
Much better for that purpose are the guidebooks of the Touring
Club Italiano, Coarelli's guide to archaeological Rome (1974),
and the limited guides to specific sites or monuments written by
scholars. But Lanciani's book was always intended to be read
before the direct experience of the ancient monuments, so that
with this preparation the educated tourist might better appreciate both the original character of the ruins and how they came
to be known. Nothing has superseded this classic effort of the
greatest of all historians of the excavations of Rome, of the rediscovery of its antique forms. With the decline of Classical
education most of those who are interested in Rome are tourists
who can profit from reading Lanciani. His book, therefore, retains its value as a resource and is enjoyable because the
author's infectious curiosity about Rome and his delight in her
remains have been so successfully served by his friendly, un-
pedantic style. If Rome has so clearly built on the past, our
knowledge of that past still depends very much on Lanciani.

RICHARD BRILLIANT

Columbia University

PREFACE

In writing the present volume the author does not intend to publish a complete manual of Roman Topography, but only a companion-book for students and travelers who visit the existing remains and study the latest excavations of ancient Rome. The text, therefore, has been adapted to the requirements of both classes of readers. Students wishing to attain a higher degree of efficiency in this branch of Roman archæology will find copious references to the standard publications on each subject or part of a subject; while the description of ruins and excavations will not be found too technical or one-sided for the ordinary reader. Special attention has been paid to tracing back to their place of origin the spoils of each monument, now dispersed in the museums of Rome, Italy, and the rest of Europe. The reader, being informed what these spoils are, when they were carried away, and where they are to be found at present, will be able to form a more correct idea of the former aspect of Roman monuments than would otherwise be possible. The volume also contains some tables, which will be found useful for quick and easy reference to the chronology of buildings, to events in the history of the city, and to the various aspects of Roman civilization. It may be observed, in the last place, that the illustrations of the text are mostly original, from drawings and photographs prepared expressly for this work.

The publications of the author to which reference is constantly made are : —

Ancient Rome in the Light of Recent Discoveries. Boston, 1889, Houghton, Mifflin, & Co. London, Macmillan. — *Pagan and Christian Rome.* Boston and London, 1893. — *Forma Urbis Romæ,* an archæological map of the city, in forty-six sheets, scale 1:1000, published under the auspices of the Royal Academy dei Lincei, by Hoepli, Milan. Twenty-four sheets already issued.

The remains of ancient Rome can be studied in books or on the spot from three points of view, — the chronological, the topographical, and the architectural. The chronological brings the student into contact, first, with the remains of the Kingly period, then with those of the Republic, of the Empire, of the Byzantine and Mediæval periods. The topographical takes into consideration, first, the main lines of the ancient city, and then each of the fourteen wards or regions into which Rome was divided by Augustus. The architectural groups the monuments in classes, like temples, baths, tombs, bridges, etc.

Each system has its own advantages, and claims representative writers. The chronological order helps us to follow the progress of Roman architecture, from the rude attempts of Etruscan masons to the golden centuries of Agrippa and Apollodorus; as well as the evolution of architectural types, from the round straw hut where the public fire was kept to the marble temple of Hestia, roofed with tiles of bronze; from the *Casa Romuli* to the *Domus Aurea* of Nero.

Dyer's *History of Rome* is founded mainly on this system. Compare also chapters iii. and iv. (pp. 24–59) of Richter's *Topographie*, Parker's *Chronological Tables*, and Lanciani's *Vicende edilizie di Roma*.[1]

The topographical system, which divides the city into regions and suburbs, is represented by Nardini and Canina.[2] They describe first the fundamental lines, — site, geology, climate, hydrography, the seven hills, the Kingly and Imperial walls, the Tiber, the aqueducts, the military roads radiating from the gates; and

[1] Thomas H. Dyer, *A History of the City of Rome: Its Structures and Monuments.* London, Longmans, 1865. — Rodolfo Lanciani, *Sulle vicende edilizie di Roma*, reprinted from the *Monografia archeologica e statistica di Roma e campagna.* Rome. Tipogr. elzevir. 1878. — John Henry Parker, *A Chronological Table of Buildings in Rome, with the Chief Contemporary Events, and an Alphabetical Index*, reprinted from the *Archæology of Rome.* — Otto Richter, *Topographie der Stadt Rom.* Sep.-Abdr. aus dem Handbuch der klassischen Alterthumwissenschaft, Bd. iii. Nördlingen, Beck, 1889, ch. iii., "Entwicklungsgeschichte," and ch. iv., "Zerstörungsgeschichte der Stadt."

[2] Famiano Nardini, *Roma antica di Famiano Nardini*, fourth edition, revised by Antonio Nibby, and illustrated by Antonio de Romanis. Rome, de Romanis, 1818 (four vols.). — Luigi Canina, *Indicazione topografica di Roma antica*, fourth edition. Rome, Canina, 1850.

then the monuments pertaining to the fourteen regions. Their accounts are founded mainly on official statistics of the fourth century, of which we possess two editions (*Redaktionen*). The first, known by the name of *Notitia regionum urbis Romœ cum breviariis suis*, dates from A. D. 334; the second, called *Curiosum urbis Romœ regionum XIV cum breviariis suis*, must have been issued in or after 357, because it mentions the obelisk raised in that year in the Circus Maximus.

Literature. — Ludwig Preller, *Die Regionen der Stadt Rom.* Jena, 1846. — Theodor Mommsen, *Abhandlungen der sachs. Ges. d. W.*, ii. 549; iii. 269; viii. 694. — Heinrich Jordan, *Topographie d. Stadt Rom in Alterthum.*, Berlin, 1871, vol. ii. p. 1. — Ignazio Guidi, *Il testo siriaco della descrizione di Roma*, in Bull. com., 1884, p. 218. — Christian Huelsen, *Il posto degli Arvali nel Colosseo*, in Bull. com., 1894, p. 312. — Rodolfo Lanciani, *Le quattordici regioni urbane*, in Bull. com., 1890, p. 115.

The two documents give the number and name of each region, the names of edifices or streets which marked approximately its boundary line, the number of parishes (*vici*), of parish magistrates (*vico magistri*), the number of tenement houses (*insulæ*), palaces (*domus*), public warehouses (*horrea*), baths, fountains, bakeries, and the circumference of each regio in feet. For instance : —

"Regio V, the Esquiliæ, contains: the fountain of Orpheus, the market of Livia, the nymphæum of (Severus) Alexander, the (barracks of the) second cohort of policemen (firemen), the gardens of Pallans, the (street named from the) Hercules Sullanus, the Amphitheatrum Castrense, the campus on the Viminal, the (street called) Subager, the (street called) Minerva Medica, the (street named from) Isis the patrician. The Esquiliæ contain 15 parishes, 15 street-shrines, 48 parish officials and two higher officials (*curatores*), 3,850 tenement houses, 180 palaces, 22 public warehouses, 25 baths, 74 fountains, 15 bakeries. The Esquiliæ measure 15,600 feet in circumference."

Comparing these statistics with texts of classics, inscriptions, existing remains, accounts of former discoveries, plans and drawings of the artists of the Renaissance, and other sources of information, we are able to reconstruct, with surprising results, the topography of the whole city.

The system, therefore, is highly commendable, and I follow it myself, in my university course of lectures, as the one best calculated, from its simplicity and clearness, to make the student conversant with this branch of Roman archæology.

The third, or architectural, system takes each class of buildings separately, and groups temples, theatres, fora, baths, etc., by themselves, irrespective of their position and their relation to other buildings. It might be compared with the study of a museum, like the Museo Nazionale of Naples, in which statues are arranged by subjects, one room containing only Venuses, another only Fauns, etc. The system facilitates the comparison of types and schools, and the study of the origin, progress, and decline of art among the Romans.

The representative works of this kind are Nibby's *Roma nell' anno 1838*, and Canina's *Edifizii di R. A.*[1]

It is impossible to deny that a system which may be useful for university work, and for a limited number of specialists, cannot also suit the student or the traveler who does not visit our ruins by regions, but according to the main centres of interest and of actual excavations. Were we to follow the architectural system in the strict sense of the word, we should be compelled to study the Forum with no regard to the temples, basilicas, and triumphal arches which lined its border or covered its area, because they belong to another class of structures. Suppose, again, we were bound to proceed in our study strictly by regions : we should be compelled to separate the Coliseum from its accessory buildings, in which gladiators, athletes, wild beasts, and their hunters were quartered, fed, and trained ; from the armories, in which gladiatorial and hunting weapons were made, kept, and repaired ; from the barracks of the marines of the fleet of Ravenna and Misenum, to whom the manœuvring of the velaria was intrusted ; from the "morgue," whither the spoils of the slain in the arena were temporarily removed, — simply because the *samiarium*, *spoliarium*, and *armamentarium* belonged to the

---

[1] Antonio Nibby, *Roma nell' anno* MDCCCXXXVIII. Parte prima antica, vols. i., ii. Rome, 1838. — Luigi Canina, *Gli edifizi di R. A. e sua campagna*, in six folio volumes. Rome, 1847–1854.

second regio ; the amphitheatre itself, the *Castra Misenatium*, the *Summum Choragium* to the third; the *Amphitheatrum Castrense* to the fifth ; the *vivarium* to the sixth.

To avoid these difficulties, the compilers of the *Beschreibung*, as well as Becker, Burn, Jordan, Richter, Gilbert, Middleton, and others,[1] have adopted a mixed system, taking the best from each of the three methods described above. They have divided and described the city in large sections, more or less connected by topographical or historical relationship. Richter, for instance, cuts ancient Rome in four parts : " das Zentrum," which embraces the Palatine and Capitoline hills, the Velia, the Circus Maximus, and the great Fora of the Empire ; " die Stadttheile am Tiber," which comprises the Aventine, the market, the Campus Martius, and the transtiberine quarters ; " der südosten Roms," made up of the Cælian and of the suburbs on the Appian Way ; and lastly " der osten Roms," with the Esquiline, Viminal, Quirinal, and Pincian hills. Richter's scheme is plainly arbitrary, and might be varied *ad libitum* without interfering with the spirit or diminishing the importance of his work. The same criticism applies to the other manuals of the same type.

Considering that " facile est inventis addere," and that the experience of others must teach us how to find a better solution of the problem, I propose to adopt the following scheme : —

In Book I. the fundamental lines of Roman topography will be described, — site, geology, configuration of soil, malaria, climate, rivers and springs, aqueducts and drains, walls and roads.

The Palatine hill, on which the city was founded and the seat of the Empire established in progress of time, will be visited next (Book II.).

In Book III. a description of the Sacra Via will be given, from its origin near the Coliseum to its end near the Capitolium. The

---

1 Platner, Bunsen, Gerhard, Rostell, Urlichs, *Beschreibung der Stadt Rom*. Stuttgart, 1830–1842. — Adolf Becker, *Handbuch der Römischen Alterthümer*. Erster Theil. Leipzig, 1843. — Robert Burn, *Rome and the Campagna*, London, 1871; *Old Rome*, 1880. Second edition, 1895. — Heinrich Jordan, *Topographie der Stadt Rom in Alterthum*, vol. i., i.², ii. Berlin, 1871. — Otto Gilbert, *Geschichte und Topographie der Stadt Rom*. 1883–1885. — Otto Richter, *Topographie der Stadt Rom*. Nördlingen, 1889. — J. Henry Middleton, *The Remains of Ancient Rome*. Two vols. London, 1892.

Sacra Via, the Forum (with its extensions), and the Capitoline hill contain the oldest relics of Kingly and Republican Rome. They are lined or covered by the grandest monuments of the Empire; they have been largely if not completely excavated since 1870; and every inch of ground they cross or cover is connected with historical events. Beginning, therefore, from such centres of interest as the Palatine and the Sacra Via, we follow the chronological and topographical systems.

The rest of the city will be described in Book IV. by the regions of Augustus in the following order : —

1. The ruins of the Cælian hill and its watershed towards the river Almo (Regions I and II).

2. The ruins of the Oppian (Regio III).

3. The Viminal, the Cespian, the Subura, and the Vicus Patricii (Regio IV).

4. The Esquiline (Regio V).

5. The Quirinal and the Pincian, and their watershed towards the Tiber (Regions VI and VII).

6. The Campus Martius (Regio IX).

7. The markets, the docks, the warehouses, the harbor on the left bank of the river.

8. The Circus Maximus (Regio XI).

9. The Aventine (Regions XII and XIII).

10. The Trastevere (Regio XIV).

Each of these sections has a characteristic of its own. The Cælian may be called the region of barracks, the Esquiline the region of parks, the Quirinal and Aventine the abode of the aristocracy. The Coliseum and its dependencies occupied the greater portion of the Oppian. The Trastevere was the popular quarter *par excellence.* Their description, therefore, from a topographical point of view, is not only rational but lends itself to the grouping of edifices built for the same object, and sometimes by the same man and at the same time.

At all events, as it may suit the reader to study the monuments in a different order, I have added two indexes, in the first of which the existing remains of Ancient Rome are named alphabetically in architectural groups, and in the second according to their chronology. The name of each is followed by the number of the page or section in which it is described.

Before closing this brief preface, I must warn students against a tendency which is occasionally observable in books and papers on the topography of Rome, — that of upsetting and condemning all received notions on the subject, in order to substitute fanciful theories of a new type. They must remember that the study of this fascinating subject began with Poggio Bracciolini and Flavio Biondo early in the fifteenth century, and that in the course of four hundred and fifty years it must have been very closely investigated. In the preface to the *Indicazione topografica*, pp. 4–25 (1850), Canina registers 124 standard authorities, whose books would make a library of a thousand volumes. Since 1850 the number of such volumes has doubled. See in Enrico Narducci's *Bibliografia topografica di Roma* a list (imperfect) of those published between 1850 and 1880. The same bibliographer has given us a list (also imperfect) of over 400 works on the Tiber alone.[1] In the fourteenth volume of the *Archivio della Società romana di storia patria*, 424 publications on the history and topography of the city are catalogued for 1891 alone. How is it possible that, in four hundred and fifty years' time, the antiquaries of the Italian, German, and English schools, working harmoniously, should not have discovered the truth? This does not exclude the possibility that new researches, either on the ground or in libraries and archives, may reveal new data and enable the student to perfect the system of Roman topography in its details, but great innovations are hardly to be expected. Yet there are people willing to try the experiment, only to waste their own time and make us lose ours in considering their attempts. Temples of the gods are cast away from their august seats, and relegated to places never heard of before ; gates of the city are swept away in a whirlwind till they fly before our eyes like one of Dante's visions ; diminutive ruins are magnified into the remains of great historical buildings ; designs are produced of monuments which have never existed. Let each of us be satisfied with a modest share in the work of reconstruction of the great city,

1 *Saggio di bibliografia del Tevere* di Enrico Narducci, Rome, Civelli, 1876.

remembering that both the *Roma sotterranea Cristiana* and Rome the capital of the Empire have long since found their Columbus.

The periodicals and books most frequently quoted in this work are : —

(Bull. com.) *Bullettino della Commissione archeologica comunale di Roma,* 1872–1895. 23 vols., superbly illustrated. — (Not. Scavi) *Notizie degli Scavi di antichità pubblicate per cura della r. accademia dei Lincei,* 1876–1895. 20 vols., illustrated. — (Bull. Inst.) *Bullettino dell' Istituto di corrispondenza archeologica,* 1829–1885. 57 vols. — (Ann. Inst.) *Annali dell' Istituto di corrispondenza archeologica,* 1829–1885. 54 vols. — (Mittheil.) *Mittheilungen des kaiserlich Deutschen archaeol. Instituts,* Roemische Abtheilung, 1886–1895. 10 vols., illustrated. — (Jahrbuch) *Jahrbuch des k. D. archaeol. Instituts,* 1886–1895. 10 vols., illustrated (Denkmäler). — (F. U. R.) *Forma Urbis Romæ, consilio et auctoritate R. Academiæ Lyncæorum . . . edidit Rodulphus Lanciani Romanus,* in 46 sheets. — (C. I. L.) *Corpus Inscriptionum Latinarum,* vols. i., vi. 1, 2, 3, 4, xiv., and xv. 1.

CONTENTS

Book I.—General Information

Book II.—The Ruins and Excavations of the Palatine

Book III. — A Walk through the Sacra Via from the Coliseum to the Capitoline Hill

BOOK IV. — URBS SACRA REGIONUM XIV

APPENDIX.

INDEXES.

LIST OF ILLUSTRATIONS

Note: In this edition, eleven illustrations have been repositioned and are marked by asterisks.

THE RUINS OF ANCIENT ROME

BOOK I

GENERAL INFORMATION

I. SITE — GEOLOGY — CONFIGURATION OF SOIL. — During the sub-Apennine or quaternary period a powerful stream came down from the mountains, on the line of a rent or fissure which separated the Ciminian from the Alban volcanoes. The stream, from 1000 to 2000 metres wide and 30 deep, emptied itself into the sea between Ponte Galera and Dragoncello. By the combined action of the main flood and of its tributaries, portions of the tableland on the east or left bank became detached and formed small islands, while the edge of the bank itself was furrowed and serrated into promontories and inlets. Such is the origin of the isolated hills, since called Capitoline, Palatine, Aventine, and Cælian; and of the promontories projecting from the tableland, called Pincian, Quirinal, Viminal, Cespian, and Oppian. The Vatican and the Janiculum on the west or right bank are less irregular, because they had to withstand the action of the main stream alone, and not of side tributaries.

When men first appeared in these lands the quaternary river had diminished almost to the size and volume of the historical Tiber, and the hills had been reduced to a definite shape ; but the bottom of the valleys remained swampy, so as to be easily flooded by freshets. The marshes of the Velabra, the Capræ palus, the Decenniæ, and other ponds are evidence of this state of things. The mouth of the river was still near Ponte Galera, 12 kilometres farther inland than the present one. The first human settlement, " dove l' acqua di Tevere s' insala," called *Ficana*, stood on the hill of Dragoncello, opposite Ponte Galera. The dim remoteness of these events is shown by the fact that when Ancus Marcius, the

fourth king, founded Ostia, as a substitute for Ficana, the mouth
of the river had already advanced seawards 5310 metres.

Fig. 2. — The Cliffs of the Capitoline Hill above " La Consolazione."

It is difficult to reconstruct in one's mind the former aspect of
the site of Rome, as hills have been lowered, valleys filled up, and
cliffs turned into gentle slopes. By means of borings made in

1872,[1] and of my own investigations into the depths of the foundations of modern buildings, I have ascertained that the promontories and the isolated hills were faced — at least on the river side
— by sheer walls of rock, of which there are a few specimens left
at the southwest front of the Capitoline, and on the west sides of
the Palatine and Aventine. In other words, the site of Rome was
like that of Veii and Faleria, with narrow dales inclosed by craggy
cliffs, shadowed by evergreens, and made damp and unhealthy
by swamps and unruly rivers (Fig. 2).

The other hills, the Quirinal, Viminal, Pincian, etc., were not
different in shape, as shown by the following section taken across
the Quirinal, from the Piazza Barberini to the corner of the Via
Nazionale : —

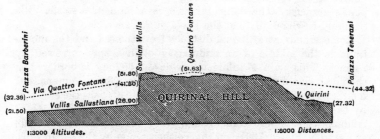

Fig. 3. — Section of the Quirinal Hill.

Within the limits of the old city there were seven hills, of which
those isolated were called *montes* (Palatine, Capitoline, Aventine,
and Cælian), those connected with the tableland were called
colles (Quirinal and Viminal). The Esquiline is an exception to
the rule, being counted among the montes, although connected
with the tableland. In regard to altitude above sea-level they
stand in the following order : —

	Metres.
Quirinal, Porta Pia .	63.05
Viminal, railway station	57.48
[Oppian, the Sette Sale .	55.02]
Esquiline, S. Maria Maggiore	54.43
[Cespian, Via Quattro Cantoni	50.86]
Palatine, S. Bonaventura .	50.00
Cælian, Villa Mattei .	47.85
Capitoline, the Aracœli	46.00
Aventine, S. Alessio .	45.92

---

[1] Raffaele Canevari, *Atti Accademia Lincei*, serie ii. vol. ii. p. 429.

Other summits on the left bank : —

	Metres.
Pincian Hill at the Villa Medici	56.33
Pincian Hill at the Porta Pinciana	63.05
The so-called pseudo-Aventine by S. Saba . . .	43.00
Monte d' Oro, above the Porta Metroni	46.00
Monte Citorio	24.34

Before the construction of the central railway station, the highest point on the left bank was an artificial hill called the Monte della Giustizia, the work of Diocletian and of Sixtus V. It rose to the height of 73 metres, and bears the name of "altissimus Romæ locus" in Bufalini's map (1551). On the other side of the river, the ridge called the *mons Vaticanus* rises to the height of 146 metres at the fort of Monte Mario, of 75 metres at the top of the pope's gardens. The Janiculum measures 89 metres at the Villa Savorelli-Heyland, 81.73 at the Porta di S. Pancrazio.

Rome stands at an equal distance from the sea and the mountains, in the middle of an undulating plain deeply furrowed by ravines. This plain, 47 kilometres wide and 60 long, is bordered on the north side by the Sabatine volcanic range (Rocca romana, 601 metres; Monte Calvi, 590; Monte Virginio, 540) ; on the east side by the limestone pre-Apennines (Monte Gennaro, 1269; Monte Affliano, 598; Monte Guadagnolo, 1218; the citadel of Præneste at Castel S. Pietro, 766) ; on the southeast side by the Alban hills, the highest summit of which is not Monte Cavo (940), as generally supposed, but the Punta delle Faette, 950 metres.

Students who visit Rome for the first time would do well to take at once a general survey of the seven hills, of the plain, of its border of mountains and sea, from the dome of S. Peter's, from the campanile of S. Maria Maggiore, or from the tower of the Capitol, which is easier of access and has a more interesting foreground (open every day from ten to three). The landmarks of the panorama can be singled out by referring to —

Henry Kiepert's *Carta corogr. ed archeol. dell' Italia centrale*, 1 : 250,000. Berlin, Reimer, 1881. — Enrico Abate's *Guida della provincia di Roma*. Rome, Salviucci, 1890. Map in two sheets. Second ed. 1893. Maps of the Istitute geografico militare, 1 : 100,000 and 1 : 50,000. (The map 1 : 10,000 is not in the market.) The best for use is the *Carta topografica dei dintorni di Roma*, in 9 sheets, 1 : 25,000.

The highest peaks visible from Rome are the Monte Terminillo, above Rieti, 2213 metres high, and the Monte Velino, above Avezzano, 2487 metres. They usually keep their shining coat of snow till the middle of May.

LITERATURE. — Giovanni Brocchi, *Dello stato fisico del suolo di Roma.* Rome, 1820. — Raffaele Canevari, *Cenni sulle condizioni altimetriche ed idrauliche dell' agro romano.* Rome, 1874. (Annali Ministero agricoltura.) — Felice Giordano, *Condizioni topografiche e fisiche di Roma e Campagna.* (Monografia della città di Roma, 1881, pp. i.-lxxxvi.) — Paolo Mantovani, *Descrizione geologica della Campagna romana,* Rome, Loescher, 1874 ; and *Costituzione geologica del suolo romano,* 1878. — Murray's *Handbook of Rome,* ed. 1875, p. 349. — Antonio Nibby, *Roma antica,* vol. i. pp. 1-65, 207-300. Rome, 1838. — Adolf Becker, *Topographie der Stadt Rome,* p. 81. (Lage, Weichbild, Klima.) Heinrich Jordan, *Topographie d. S. R.,* vol. i. pp. 117-152. (Lage, Boden, Klima.) — Otto Richter, *Topographie d. S. R.,* p. 18. (Lage und Formation.)

There are two museums of geology and mineralogy — one in the University (della Sapienza), consisting of the collections of Belli, Brocchi, and Spada, and of a bequest of Leo XII. ; the other in the former convent della Vittoria, Via S. Susanna, second floor : open Tuesdays, Thursdays, and Sundays.

II. GEOLOGY. — There are four geological formations in the district of Rome, with which the student must become familiar if he wishes to understand at once some important peculiarities of Roman masonry and architecture. They are the secondary or limestone, the tertiary or argillaceous, the volcanic, and the quaternary or diluvial formations.

The limestone is best examined at Monticelli, the ancient Corniculum, the fourth station on the Sulmona line. The rock, slightly dolomitised, is white at the base of the hill, with *terebratulæ* in great numbers ; reddish in the middle, with a dozen varieties of *ammonites;* and white again at the summit, with *terebratulæ* and traces of the anomalous fossil *aptychus.* The lime of Monticelli, from the Caprine kilns, mixed with pozzolana, makes Roman masonry "ære perennius." The argillaceous formation is conspicuous in the Vatican and Janiculum ridges, the *monti della creta* (clay hills) of the present day. A walk through the extensive quarries of the Valle dell' Inferno and the Valle del Gelsomino will show the student the details of the formation, rich in pteropodous molluscs, and will make him appreciate the vastness of the work of man, since bricks were first accepted as an essential element of Roman masonry As the Valle di Pozzo Pantaléo has been bodily excavated through the hills of Monteverde by the quarrymen supplying tufa for the "opus quadratum" and the "opus reticulatum," so the valleys of the Gelsomino, delle Fornaci, delle Cave, della Balduina, and dell' Inferno have been hollowed out of the clay hills by the ancient, Renaissance, and modern bricklayers. (See Bull. com., 1892, p. 288, and § xi. on Building Materials.) The pliocene marls of the Vatican ridge abound in fossils; they can easily be gathered along the Via

Trionfale opposite the Croce di Monte Mario, or in the cuttings of the Viterbo railway, at the top of the Valle dell' Inferno.

The volcanic formation is represented in or near Rome by three kinds of tufa — the red or lithoid, the yellowish or granular, the grayish or lamellar ; and by two kinds of pozzolana — the red and the black. The surface of tufa beds, soft and unfit for building purposes, is called "cappellaccio." The tufa quarries of S. Saba, the largest within the walls, were abandoned in 1889 ; the largest still in use are those of Monteverde, outside the Porta Portese, and of S. Agnese, outside the Porta Pia. The best kind of pozzolana is quarried near the Tre Fontane. Diluvial or quaternary deposits abound on each side of the Tiber. The cliffs of the Monti Parioli, between the Villa di Papa Giulio and the Acqua Acetosa, as well as the gravel pits of Ponte Molle and Ponte Nomentano, are best adapted for the study of this late formation, so rich in fossil mammalia, like the *Elephas*, the *Rhinoceros tichorinus*, the *Bos primigenius*, the hippopotamus, the lynx, etc. It is well to remember that the flint arrowheads found in the gravel at Ponte Molle do not belong to a local race, but were washed down from pre-Apennine stations by the flood.

Travertine, the king of Roman building materials, is best studied at the Cava del Barco, near the *stazione dei bagni* of both Tivoli railways.

Pietro Zezi, *Indice bibliografico delle publicazioni riguardanti la mineralogia, la geologia e la paleontologia della provincia di Roma.* (Monografia di Roma, vol. i. p. clxiii.)

III. MALARIA. — The Romans did not deny the unhealthiness of the district in the midst of which their city was built. Cicero calls it "a pestilential region," and Pliny likewise calls the Maremma "heavy and pestilential." The hills were comparatively healthy ("colles in regione pestilenti salubres, colles saluberrimi," Livy, v. 54) ; still, the effects of malaria, increased by ignorance or contempt of sanitary rules, must have been felt also by the settlers on the Palatine, Esquiline, and Quirinal. Under Tiberius there were three temples of Fever left standing — one on the Palatine, one near the church of S. Eusebio, the third near the church of S. Bernardo ; but they represented the memory of past miseries rather than actual need of help from the gods, because, long before the time of Tiberius, Rome and the Campagna had been made healthy in a large measure ; and when Horace (Epist., i. 7, 7) describes Rome as half deserted in the summer months, he refers to the habit of the citizens of migrating to their hill farms or seacoast villas, to escape depressing heat rather than malaria. This summer emigration *en masse* is still characteristic of Rome. Sixty thousand citizens left in 1893 for an average period of forty days : one seventh of the whole population.

Sanitary reform was accomplished, firstly, by the draining of marshes and ponds ; secondly, by an elaborate system of sewers ; thirdly, by the substitution of spring water for that of polluted wells ; fourthly, by the paving and multiplication of roads ; fifthly, by the cultivation of land ; sixthly, by sanitary engineering, applied to human dwellings ; seventhly, by substituting cremation for burial ; eighthly, by the drainage of the Campagna ; and lastly, by the organization of medical help. The results were truly wonderful. Pliny says that his villeggiatura at Laurentum was equally delightful in winter and summer, while the place is now a hotbed of malaria. Antoninus Pius and M. Aurelius preferred their villa at Lorium (Castel di Guido) to all other imperial residences, and the correspondence of Fronto proves their presence there in midsummer. No one would try the experiment now. The same can be said of Hadrian's villa below Tivoli, of the villa Quinctiliorum on the Appian Way, of that of Lucius Verus at Acqua Traversa, etc. The Campagna must have looked in those happy days like a great park, studded with villages, farms, lordly residences, temples, fountains, and tombs (see " Ancient Rome," chs. iii. and x.).

The cutting of the aqueducts by the barbarians, the consequent abandonment of suburban villas, the permanent insecurity, the migration of the few survivors under cover of the city walls, and the choking up of drains, caused a revival of malaria. Mediæval Romans found themselves in a condition worse than that of the first builders of the city ; and being neither able nor willing to devise a remedy, as their ancestors had done, they raised their helpless hands towards heaven, and built a chapel in honor of Our Lady of the Fever (see " Ancient Rome," p. 53).

The present generation has once more conquered the evil, and has made Rome the best drained, the best watered, the healthiest capital of Europe, except London. This statement may not be agreeable to those who systematically and deliberately condemn whatever has been done by us since 1870 ; but they would do well to accept facts as they are. Comm. Luigi Bodio, Director of the State Department of Statistics, has favored me with the following official declaration : —

" Rome, 10 *Nov.* 1894.

" From 1st January, 1860, to 31st December, 1869, in an average population of 205,229, there were 5477 average annual births, 5946 deaths. Rate of births, 26.70 per thousand; of deaths, 29 per thousand.

"Between 1890 and 1893, in an average population of 437,355 souls, there were 11,678 births, 9791 deaths per annum. Rate of births, 26.70 per thousand; of deaths, 22.38. This last figure includes the floating population, and, above all, the peasants who come down from their mountains to cultivate the Maremma, and furnish the heaviest percentage to the hospital lists. *The rate of deaths among the resident population is only* 19.45 *per thousand*, while in London it rose to 20.37, in Vienna to 21.53, in Berlin to 23.09, in Paris to 23.80." [1]

LITERATURE. — Pietro Balestra, *L' igiene nella città e campagna di Roma.* 1875. — Guido Baccelli, *La malaria di Roma.* (Monografia di Roma, 1881, vol. i. p. 149.) — Giovanni Brocchi, *Discorso sulla condizione dell' aria di Roma nei tempi antichi.* 1820. — Stefano Ferrari, *Condizioni igieniche del clima di Roma.* (Monografia di Roma, 1881, vol. i. p. 316.) — Rodolfo Lanciani, *Di alcune opere di risanamento dell' agro romano.* Atti Lincei, 1879. "The Sanitary Condition of Rome:" *Ancient Rome*, p. 49. — Lanzi-Terrigi, *La malaria e il clima di Roma.* Rome, 1877. — Francesco Scalzi, *Malattie predominanti in Roma.* Rome, 1878. — Angelo Secchi, *Intorno ad alcune opere idrauliche antiche rinvenute nella campagna di Roma.* — Corrado, Tommasi Crudeli, *The Climate of Rome and the Roman Malaria.* (Translated by Charles Cramond Dick. London, Churchill, 1892.) *L' antica fognatura delle colline romane.* Atti Lincei, vol. x., 1881. *Alcune riflessioni sul clima dell' antica Roma.* Mittheil., 1877, p. 77. *L'ancien drainage des collines romaines.* Mélanges de l'Ecole française, 1882. — Charles Edmund Wendt, *The New Rome and the Question of Roman Fever.* New York, 1892. — Philippe Tournon, *Etudes statistiques sur Rome.* Paris, 1855, vol. i. pp. 223, 230.

IV. CLIMATE. — The climate seems to have been more severe in ancient times than now. Dionysius (Fragm., l., xii. 8) describes a blizzard which covered the ground with seven feet of snow. Men died of cold, sheep and cattle were frozen, and many houses fell under the weight of their snowy pall. He speaks probably of the year 401 B. C., which Livy (v. 13) calls "insignis hieme gelida ac nivosa," when even the Tiber became a mass of ice. In 271 snow lay on the Forum for forty days.[2] On 12th January 67 B. C. the meeting of the Senate was adjourned on account of the cold

---

[1] Death-rate in 1886 — London, 19.8; Rome, 20.0; Paris, 24.6; Berlin, 25.8; Vienna, 26.2; Petersburg, 30.6; Buda-Pest, 39.4.

[2] See Augustine, *De civitate Dei*, iii. 17.

which prevailed in the *Curia*.[1] The severity of another winter, perhaps that of 19 B. C., is described by Horace (Od., i. 9). Martial's epigram, iv. 18, commemorates the fate of a youth transfixed by an icicle. Such excesses of temperature are not recorded in modern days. Between 1828 and 1877 the lowest registered was 8.25° Centigrade (February, 1845), the highest 42°, a most extraordinary case, which happened on July 17, 1841. The mean annual temperature is 16.40°. In the course of the day the mercury rises quickly in the morning and falls slowly after noon. In summer there are two maximums — one from twelve to one o'clock, the other towards nine P. M. The temperature is always lowest at sunrise.

Rain is most frequent in November, heaviest in October. There are 155 cloudless days in the year, 122 misty, 83 cloudy. Maximum rainfall (1872), 1050.30 millimetres; minimum (1834), 319.45. In summer time the land breeze blows from early morning to nine A. M., the sea breeze from eleven to six. These refreshing winds make Rome more comfortable in summer than other cities of much higher latitudes.

V. HYDROGRAPHY — RIVERS, SPRINGS, PONDS, MARSHES. — The Tiber rises from the Monte Coronaro, at the height of 1167 metres above the sea, and reaches Rome after a winding course of 373 kilometres, through Etruria, Umbria, and Sabina. The mean breadth of the river in the city district *was* 80 metres (now 100 metres between the embankments), its average depth 3 metres, total length from springs to sea 393 kilometres. Below Rome it expands into a channel 120 metres wide, navigated by steamers and coasting-vessels of 100 tons burden. Ceselli's observations, from March, 1871, to February, 1872, state the daily average outflow of the river at 1,296,000 cubic metres. During the same year 8,582,333 tons of sand and mud were washed down to the sea, a volume of over 4,000,000 cubic metres. This state of things and the prevalence of southwesterly winds makes the coast advance westwards at a considerable rate. We have just seen that Ficana, the oldest human station near the bar of the river, is now 12,000 metres inland, and kingly Ostia 6600 metres. The Torre di S. Michele, built in 1567 by Michelangelo on the edge of the sands, stands 2000 metres away from the present shore; the Torre Clementina at Fiumicino, built in 1773, "in ipso maris supercilio,"

---

[1] Cicero, *Ad Quint. fratr.*, ii. 12.

stands 690 metres inland.[1] The average yearly increase of the coast at the Ostia mouth is 9.02 metres, at the Fiumicino mouth 3.10 metres.

LITERATURE. — Giuseppe Ponzi, *Storia geologica del Tevere.* (Giornale arcadico, vol. xviii. p. 129.) *Dell' Aniene e de suoi relitti.* (Ibid.) — Aubert, *Roma e l' inondazione del Tevere.* (Giornale arcad., vol. lxvi. p. 142.) — Alessandro Betocchi, *Del fiume Tevere.* (Monografia di Roma, vol. i. p. 197.) *Effemeridi del Tevere,* published yearly by the Accademia dei Lincei. — Marco Ceselli, *Bullettino nautico e geografico di Roma,* vol. vi. n. 3. — Carlo Fea, *Storia delle acque.* Rome, 1817. — Rodolfo Lanciani, *I comentarii di Frontino intorno le acque e gli acquedotti.* Rome, Salviucci, 1880, pp. 3–28. — Alessandro Narducci published, in 1876, an essay on the bibliography of the Tiber (*Saggio di bibliografia del Tevere,* Rome, Civelli), in which over 400 works are registered. Their number may be stated now at 700. The best library for consultation on the subject is the Biblioteca del Ministero dei Lavori publici, Piazza di S. Silvestro. There is a special department in Rome for the works and embankment of the Tiber, with a good collection of maps and diagrams (Ufficio tecnico speciale per la sistemazione del Tevere. Via di Ripetta, n. 222 c).

The inundations are the great historical feature of the Tiber.

From the traditional flood, in the course of which Romulus and his twin-brother were exposed to the waters under the rocks of the Palatine, to the beginning of the Christian era, twenty-six inundations are recorded; thirty from 1 to 500 A. D.; twenty-one from 500 to 1000; twenty-three from 1000 to 1500; thirty-two from 1500 to the present day; a total of one hundred and thirty-two. The worst of which we have the measurement reached the following altitudes at the hydrometer of Ripetta (ordinary level of water, 6.70 metres) : —

	Metres.
December, 1280	16.02
November, 1376	17.02
December, 1495	16.88
October, 1530	18.95
September, 1557	18.90
DECEMBER, 1598	19.56
January, 1606	18.26
February, 1637	17.55
November, 1660	17.11
November, 1668	16.00
December, 1702	15.41
February, 1805	16.42
December, 1846	16.25
December, 1870	17.22

[1] The coast has increased about 390 metres since 1st April, 1857, when an official survey was taken by the local collector of customs.

The flood of 1598, the highest recorded in history, began on Christmas eve; at noon the next day there were 6.50 metres of flood in the Via di Ripetta, 6.58 metres at the Pantheon, 5.28 metres at the Piazza Navona, 4.56 metres on the Corso by S. Lorenzo in Lucina. A boat went ashore in the Piazza di Spagna, where the Fontana della Barcaccia was erected by Bernini to commemorate the event; two arches of the Pons Æmilius were overthrown at three P. M. on the 24th, a few seconds after Cardinal Pietro Aldobrandino had crossed it to rescue some families surrounded by the foaming waters. Houses were washed away by hundreds; 700 persons were drowned in the city, and 800 in the suburbs, besides thousands of cattle. As usual, famine and pestilence followed the flood.

In the flood of 1702, which rose to only 15.41 metres, fifty-two streets and squares were submerged on the left bank, north of the Capitol, eighty-five south of that hill, and sixty-two on the other side of the river.

The last flood, on December 28 and 29, 1870, which gave rise to King Victor Emmanuel's first visit to his new capital on a merciful errand, marks another important date in the history of the city, because to it we owe the construction of the new embankments, which, when finished, will have cost the state, the county, and the city over 200,000,000 lire. The curve of the flood of 1870 is represented in this diagram : —

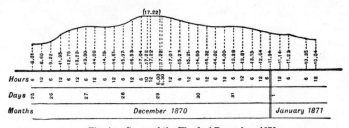

Fig. 4. — Curve of the Flood of December, 1870.

The event is too recent to require a description. It brought to our minds the floods so often mentioned by the "Liber Pontificalis," when the waters, breaking through the walls at the Posterula sancti Martini (Ripetta), would dash against the cliffs of the Capitol, *ita ut in via lata* (Corso) *amplius quam duas staturas* (3.30 metres) *fluminis aqua excrevisset* (A. D. 772).

LITERATURE. — Leone Pascoli, *Il Tevere navigato.* Rome, 1740. — Gasparo Alveri, *Delle inondazioni del Tevere.* (Roma in ogni stato, vol. i. p. 571.) — Antonio Grifi, *Il fiume Tevere nelle sue più memorabili inondazioni.* Album, vol. iv. pp. 29, 390. — Philippe Tournon, *Etudes statistiques sur Rome,* vol. ii. p. 207. — Gaetano Moroni, *Dizionario di erudizione ecclesiastica,* vol. lxxv. p. 125. — Filippo Cerroti, *Le inondazioni di Roma.* Florence, 1871. — Raffaele Canevari, *Tavola delle principali inondazioni del Tevere.* Rome, 1875. — Michele Carcani, *Il Tevere e le sue inondazioni dalle origini di Roma sino ai giorni nostri.* Rome, 1875. — Alessandro Bettocchi, *Monografia della città di Roma,* 1881, vol. i. p. 243. — Ludovico Gomez, *De prodigiosis Tiberis inundationibus.* Rome, 1531.

The earliest project for restraining the Tiber from overflowing its banks dates, as far as we know, from the time of Julius Caesar, who moved in the House a bill for the cutting of a new bed from the Pons Molvius to the Trastevere, along the base of the Vatican hills.[1] The merit of having placed the unruly river under the management of a body of conservators, selected from the highest consular ranks, belongs to Augustus according to Suetonius (37), to Tiberius according to Tacitus (Ann., i. 76) and Dion Cassius (lvii. 14, 8).

Augustus gave the posts of chief conservators to C. Asinius Gallus and C. Marcius Censorinus in the year 7 B. C., when the bed of the river was cleared "ruderibus et ædificiorum prolapsionibus," deepened and widened, and its banks were lined with terminal stones, marking the extent of public property which the conservators had rescued from private encroachment. Scores of these stones are still in existence. After the inundation of A. D. 15, which had caused what Tacitus describes as "ædificiorum et hominum stragem," Tiberius referred the subject to Ateius Capito and L. Arruntius, the first of whom was a great authority on such matters. They suggested, and the Emperor sanctioned, the institution of a permanent committee of five senators, to be called *curatores riparum.* This institution lasted until the reign of Vespasian or Domitian, when we hear for the first time of one conservator only, a patrician, assisted by two *adiutores* of equestrian rank. In or about A. D. 101 the care of the sewers was added to that of the Tiber, and this important branch of the city administration received the title of *statio alvei Tiberis et cloacarum.* About 330 the chief conservator exchanged his classic title for that of *consularis,* and about 400 for that of *comes.* Archæologists have been

---

[1] Cicero, *Ad Attic.,* xxxiii. 3. Cæsar's project was brought forward again in 1879. See Zucchelli, *Di una nuova inalveazione del Tevere.* Rome, Forzani, 1879.

able to draw an almost complete chronology of these officers from
the terminal stones on which their names are engraved.

Literature. — *Corpus Inscr.*, vol. i. p. 180; vol. vi. p. 266. — Theodor
Mommsen, *Staatsrecht*, ii[3], p. 1047. — Giuseppe Gatti, *Bull. comm. arch.*, vol.
xv., 1887, p. 306. — Thédenat, *Dictionn. antiq. grecques et rom.* de Saglio,
vol. i. p. 1623. — Luigi Cantarelli, *Bull. comm. arch.*, vol. xvii., 1889, p. 185;
vol. xxii., 1894, pp. 39 and 354. — Dante Vaglieri, *Bull. comm. arch.*, vol.
xxii., 1894, p. 254.

Two means were adopted in imperial times to protect the city
from floods — an embankment on either side, and the shortening
of the bed between the city and the sea.

First, as to the embankment. We have seen how the Tiber is
subject to differences of level, which reached to 12.86 metres in
the flood of Clement VIII., increasing fourteen times the volume
of its waters. To give such a capricious river a regular outlet,
modern engineers have built a uniform bed 100 metres in width,
which has to serve both for droughts and for floods. Their pre-

Modern embankment

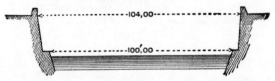

Fig. 5.

decessors, on the other hand, had adopted a triple section, the
narrowest to serve in time of drought, the second in moderate,
the third in extraordinary floods, as shown in the following
diagram : —

Ancient embankment

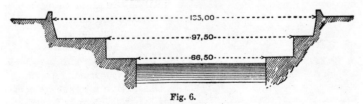

Fig. 6.

The advantages of the old over the modern system are obvious.
With the old the river was obliged to run in every season of the
year within limits well defined, and proportioned to its volume,

without raising sandbanks and depositing silt and mud. The moderate height of each of the three receding steps allowed the river to preserve its pleasing aspect, as is the case in many of the modern capitals of Europe; while the huge walls between which we have imprisoned the stream have transformed it into a deep and unsightly channel, with nothing to relieve the monotony of its banks.

Side outlets to relieve the flood and shorten its course towards the sea were first cut open by Claudius. An inscription discovered at Porto in 1836 contains the expression: FOSSIS DVCTIS VRBEM INVNDATIONIS PERICVLO LIBERAVIT (see Corpus Inscr., vol. xiv. n. 85). Trajan changed the course of the channels. Another fragmentary inscription, now in the cloisters of S. Paul outside the Walls, says of him: FOSSAM *fecit* QVA INVN*dationes Tiberis* aDSIDVE V*rbem vexantes . . . arcerentur.* This subject has been exhaustively treated by —

Pietro Ercole Visconti, *Dissertazioni Accad. archeol.,* vol. viii. (1838), p. 213. — Luigi Canina, *Ibid.,* p. 259. — Antonio Nibby, *Dintorni di Roma,* vol. ii. p. 612. — Reifferscheid, *Bull. inst.,* 1863, p. 8. — Charles Texier, *Revue gén. d'Architecture,* vol. xv. p. 306, pls. 31, 32. — Rodolfo Lanciani, *Ricerche sulla città di Porto* (in Ann. Inst., vol. xl., 1868, p. 144.) *Corpus Inscr. Lat.,* vol. xiv. p. 22, n. 88.

The following cut represents the mouth of the navigable arm of the river at Fiumicino, which is the modern representative of the fossa Traiana : —

Fig. 7. — The Mouth of the Tiber at Fiumicino.

The characteristics of the Tiber are, first, the supposed wholesome qualities of its water, the favorite beverage of Clement VII.,

Paul III., and Gregory XIII. This simply proves that the three pontiffs were proof against typhoid, for the river was then, as it continued up to 1890, the true Cloaca Maxima of the city. The second is the abundance and regularity of its feeding springs, in consequence of which the river has never changed in volume and level within historical times. There is a tendency to believe that the Tiber was much lower in old times, because Pliny (xxxvi. 24, 2) speaks of Agrippa being rowed into the Cloaca Maxima, the mouth of which it is now impossible to enter. Observations made in 1869 by Padre Secchi at the marble wharf (Marmorata), and by the engineers of the embankment, prove that since the fall of the Empire the bed of the river has hardly risen three feet. While this fact is absolutely certain, it gives rise to problems which are difficult to solve.

In the spring of 1879 a Roman house was discovered on the right bank, in the gardens of la Farnesina, the paintings and stuccoed panels of which have become famous in the artistic world, and form the best ornament of the Museo delle Terme.

The pavements of this noble mansion were only 8 metres and 20 centimetres above the level of the sea, and about 3 metres above that of the river. During the four months employed by us in removing the frescoes and the stucco panels, the Tiber entered the house five times. Taking ten times as a yearly average, the paintings and the stuccoes must have been washed by ordinary floods four thousand times, from the age of Augustus, to which the house belongs, to the fall of the Empire; and yet frescoes and stuccoes were in perfect condition, and showed no sign of having been spoilt by water. I have not yet found a satisfactory solution of the problem ; because, even admitting the existence of an embankment between the house and the river, drains would always have provided a way for the flood.

Literature. — *Notizie degli Scavi*, 1880, p. 127, pls. 4, 5. — *Monumenti inediti dell' Instituto*, Supplemento 1891. — Wolfgang Helbig, *Collections of Antiquities in Rome*, vol. ii. p. 220. — Rodolfo Lanciani, *Pagan and Christian Rome*, p. 263.

The Tiber was celebrated for its fish. There is a work on this subject by Paolo Giovio, translated from Latin into Italian by Carlo Zangarolo. Macrobius, Pliny, and Juvenal praise above all the *lupus*, when caught " inter duos pontes " (in the waters of S. Bartolomeo's island), where he fed on the refuse of the Cloaca Maxima. The *lupus* has been identified by some with the "spigola" or *Perca lebrax*, by others with the " laccia " or *Clupea alosa,* better known by the name of shad, the best Tiberine fish of the present day. There is a bas-relief in the Capitol, representing a sturgeon 46 inches long, with the text of an edict of 1581 providing that any sturgeon caught in Roman waters exceeding the statute size would be considered the property of the city magistrates.

VI. BRIDGES.

LITERATURE.— Gio. Battista Piranesi, Opere, vol. iv., *Ponti antichi,* etc.— Stefano Piale, *Degli antichi ponti di Roma.* Rome, 1832. — Adolf Becker, *De muris,* p. 78; and *Topographie,* p. 693. — Theodor Mommsen, *Berichte der sächs. Gesellschaft der Wiss.,* 1850, p. 320. — Heinrich Jordan, *Die Brücken.* (Topographie, vol. i. p. 393.) — Mayerhoefer, *Die Brücken in alten Rom,* 1883.— Zippel, *Die Brücken in alten Rom.* (Jahrbuch für klass. Phil., 1886, p. 81.) — Otto Richter, *Die Befestigung des Janiculum.* Berlin, 1882.

PONS SUBLICIUS, the oldest of Roman bridges. — Its antiquity is proved not so much by the tradition which attributes it to Ancus Marcius, as by the fact that no iron was used in its original construction, or in subsequent repairs. Pliny (H. N., xxxvi. 15, 23), ignorant as he was of " Pre-history," gives a wrong explanation of the fact when he introduces the story of Horatius Cocles, whose followers experienced so much difficulty in cutting it down in the face of the enemy. Such was not the case. Iron was proscribed from the structure for the same reason which prevented masons or stonecutters from using tools of that metal in repairing some of the oldest temples ; for instance, that of the Dea Dia (see " Ancient Rome," p. 41). At that time the Romans lived still " morally " in the age of bronze, and felt a religious repulsion for the new metal.

The bridge was carried away by a flood in 23 B. C., perhaps the same mentioned by Horace (Od., i. 2) ; and again in the time of Antoninus Pius. On either occasion it was restored according to the old rite.[1] It seems almost certain that, if the frame and the roadway were of timber and planks (*subliciæ*), the foundations in mid-stream must have been of solid masonry.[2] The piers were prominent enough above the water-mark to make the memory of the bridge last through the Middle Ages, when we hear very often

---

[1] See Dionysius, iii. 45 ; Pliny, xxxvi. 5, 23 ; Macrobius, i. 11; and *Vita Antonin.,* viii.

[2] Servius, *Æn.* viii. 646, says of Porsenna: *cum per sublicium pontem, hoc est ligneum qui modo lapideus dicitur, transire conaretur ;* but his words deserve little credit. (See Æthicus, *Cosmogr.,* in Jordan's *Topogr.,* i. 393, n. 1.)

of a "pons fractus iuxta Marmoratam." They were destroyed to the water's edge under Sixtus IV. "On July 23, 1484," says the Diary of Infessura, "Pope Sixtus sent into camp 400 large cannon-balls, made of travertine, from the remains of a bridge at La Marmorata, called 'il ponte di Orazio Cocles.'" The last traces were blown up in 1877 to clear the bed of the river.

LITERATURE.— Carlo Fea, in Winckelmann's edit. Prato, 1832, vol. xi. pp. 379–400.— Antonio Nibby, *Roma antica*, vol. i. p. 199.

PONS FABRICIUS (Ponte Quattro capi). — The island of Æsculapius must have been joined to the left bank by a wooden bridge

Fig. 8. — The Æmilian, Fabrician, Cestian Bridges, and the Island in the Tiber.

as early as 192 B. C. (see Livy, xxxv. 21, 5); another structure of the same kind is supposed to have joined the island with the Trastevere and the fortified summit of the Janiculum. In the year 62 B. C. Lucius Fabricius, commissioner of roads, transformed the first into a solid stone bridge. The inscriptions which commemorate the event, engraved below the parapets on either side, are followed by a declaration signed by P. Lepidus and M. Lollius, consuls in 21 B. C., that the work had been duly and satisfactorily executed. From this declaration we learn one of the wise principles of the Roman administration — that the contractors and builders of bridges were held responsible for their solidity for forty years, so that they would regain possession of the deposit which they made in advance only in the forty-first year after it had been made. Nothing speaks more highly in favor of the bridge than the fact that it is the only one which has survived intact the vicissitudes of 1957 years. It has two arches and a smaller one in the pier between them; a fourth is concealed by the modern embankment on the left.

The student must remember that the streets of ancient Rome were from three to five metres lower than the present ones, while the bridges have remained the same; the inclines which gave access to them were, therefore, much longer and steeper than they are now, and offered space for several more openings or arches, which have since been buried by the accumulation of the soil. These steep inclines were called *pedes pontis,* and *coscice* in the Middle Ages.

The Pons Fabricius took the name of Pons Judæorum when the Jewish colony settled in the neighboring quarter. It is now called dei Quattro Capi, from the four-headed *hermæ* which once supported the panels of the parapet. There are only two left *in situ.* The river, unfortunately, no longer flows under this most perfect of Roman bridges; by a miscalculation in the plan of the new embankment the channel has been dried up, and the Ship of Æsculapius has stranded on a mudbank.

Literature. — Luigi Canina, *Edifizii di Roma antica,* vol. iv. tav. 242. — *Corpus Inscr.,* vol. i. p. 174, n. 600 ; vol. vi. n. 1305.

Pons Cestius, Pons Gratianus, Ponte di S. Bartolomeo, between the island and the Trastevere. — Its construction is attributed to Lucius Cestius, one of the six magistrates whom Cæsar entrusted with the government of Rome on leaving for Spain in 46 B. C. It was rebuilt by L. Aurelius Avianius Symmachus, prefect of the city, in A. D. 365, and dedicated in the spring of 370 to the Emperor Gratianus. (See *Corpus Inscr.,* vol. vi. p. 245, n. 1175.) Its third restoration took place in the eleventh century in the time of Benedict VIII.; the inscription which commemorates it describes the bridge as FERE DIRVTVM in those days. In 1849, the followers of Garibaldi threw one of the inscriptions of Gratianus into the stream. The bridge was altered completely in 1886-89, so that of the three arches only the central one is ancient. In the course of the last work it was found that the blocks of travertine used by Symmachus in the restorations of 365-370 had been taken away from the theatre of Marcellus, mainly from the lower (Doric) arcades of the hemicycle. He had also made use of stones bearing historical inscriptions of the time of Trajan.

The two bridges made an architectural and pictorial group with the Ship of Æsculapius.[1] It is not known when and by whom the island was turned into this form. As far as we can

Fig. 9. — The Stern of the Ship of Æsculapius.

judge from the fragment of the stern, represented in the cut above, the imitation must have been perfect in every detail. The ship, however, did not appear as if it was floating on the river, except in time of flood, because it rested on a platform 2 metres above low-water mark. It was entirely built of travertine, and measured 280 metres between the perpendiculars, with a beam of 76 metres. An obelisk, pieces of which are now preserved in Naples, represented the main-mast.

A fanciful copy of this island exists in the Villa d' Este at Tivoli as a part of the plan, or rather model in full relief, of the city

---

[1] Literature on the Island of Æsculapius. — *Cod. Vat.*, 3439, f. 42; Jordan, *Forma Urbis*, ix. 42; *Corpus Inscr.*, vol. vi. n. 9–12, 9824; *Accad. Rom. Arch.:* sessione 20 genn. 1881; Becker, *Topogr.*, p. 651; Richter, *Topogr.*, p. 158; Gamucci, *Antich. di Roma*, iv. p. 279; Nibby, *Roma antica*, ii. 291.

of Rome which Pirro Ligorio added to the curiosities of that delightful place. A stream, derived from the Anio, represents the Tiber, on which the ship appears to be floating, with the obelisk in the place of the mast and the coat-of-arms of Cardinal Ippolito instead of the emblems of the " merciful God."

LITERATURE. — Gio. Battista Piranesi, *Antichità di Roma*, vol. iv. pls. 23, 24. — Antonio Nibby, *Roma antica*, vol. i. p. 167. — P. Bonato, *Annali Societa archit. italiani*, vol. iv., 1889, p. 139. — *Notizie degli Scavi*, 1886, p. 159; 1889, p. 70.

PONS ÆMILIUS. — In the early days of Rome there was but one line of communication with the Janiculum and with the cities on the coast of Etruria : the road that passed over the Sublician bridge, crossed the plain of Trastevere by S. Cosimato, and ascended the Janiculum by the Villa Spada. Livy (i. 33; v. 40) and Valerius Maximus (i. 1, 10) describe it, on the occasion of the flight of the Vestals to Veii; and Fabretti (De Aq., i. 18, p. 43) speaks of its rediscovery in the seventeenth century. He saw a long piece of the pavement between the bridge and S. Cosimato ; and where the pavement was missing, as between the Villa Spada (de Nobili) and the church of S. Pietro Montorio, its course was marked by a line of tombs on either side. The ascent up the hill was exceedingly steep, and hardly fit for carriage traffic. Things, however, were improved in the sixth century of Rome, when a new bridge and a new and better road were built. M. Æmilius Lepidus and M. Fulvius Nobilior, censors in B. C. 181, founded the piers; the arches were added and the bridge was finished thirty-eight years later. The new road, the Lungaretta of the present day, was then traced across the low swampy plain of Trastevere, partly on an embankment, partly on viaducts built of stone. One of these viaducts was discovered in 1889 near the Piazza di S. Grisogono, and is described in the Bull. arch. com., 1889, p. 475, and 1890, pp. 6, 57.

The Pons Æmilius, owing to its slanting position across the river and to the side pressure of the floods against its piers, has been carried away at least four times : the first during or shortly before the reign of Probus (about A. D. 280) ; the second in 1230, when it was rebuilt by Gregory IX.; the third on September 27, 1557 (rebuilt by Gregory XIII.) ; the fourth on December 24, 1598, after which it was never repaired. There is but one arch left now in mid-stream, the two on the right having been destroyed in 1887.

LITERATURE. — Heinrich Jordan, *Topographie*, i. p. 420. — Pietro Lanciani, *Del ponte senatorio*. Rome, 1826. — Gio. Battista de Rossi, *Le prime raccolte*, etc., p. 57. — Filippo Bonanni, *Numism. pontif.*, vol. i. p. 323, n. 38, 39.

BRIDGE OF AGRIPPA. — A stone cippus, discovered in August, 1877, behind the church of S. Biagio della Pagnotta, near the Strada Giulia, has revealed the existence and the name of a bridge of which nobody had ever heard before, either from classic writers, or from inscriptions, coins, or other such sources of information.

The inscription reads as follows : " By order of Tiberius Claudius

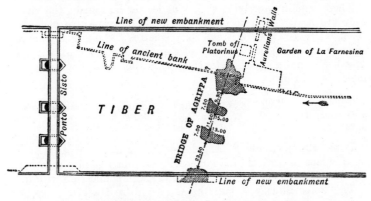

Fig. 10. — Foundations of Bridge (?) above the Ponte Sisto.

Cæsar, etc., we, Paullus Fabius Persicus, C. Eggius Marullus, C. Obellius Rufus, L. Sergius Paullus, L. Scribonius Libo, chief conservators of the Tiber and its banks, have marked with cippi the limits of public property (on the left bank) from the *Trigarium* to the Bridge of Agrippa (*ad pontem Agrippæ*)."

The Trigarium was an open space, near the Strada Giulia, for the breaking in and training of horses, for which purpose the ancients availed themselves of the *triga*, the untamed animal being harnessed between two trained ones. As regards the Bridge of Agrippa, all our science is at a loss to explain the mystery. It seems impossible that there should have existed in Rome a large bridge, thrown across the Tiber by such a man as Agrippa, in the golden age of Augustus, and yet that not a trace should be left of it *in situ* or in written or engraved documents. Two solutions are more or less acceptable. The first is that the bridge now called Ponte Sisto may have been originally the work of Agrippa. Its history is unknown. From the name of Pons Aurelius or

Pons Antonini, given to it in the third century, its construction has been attributed to Caracalla. Caracalla, however, may have been simply a restorer, as we know that Roman bridges used to change their names after every restoration. The second theory is that Agrippa's bridge was swept away by a flood soon after the accession of Claudius, and that its remains were carefully removed to restore free navigation up and down stream. This surmise seems justified by the discovery made, 100 metres above the Ponte Sisto, of what appear to be the remains of sunken piers, as shown in Fig. 10.

These remains are lying so low under the bottom of the river, they are so irregular in shape and in their respective distances (9.30 metres, 11.50 metres, 23.50 metres), their construction shows such a curious mixture of large stones and rubble work, that I still hesitate to consider them to be the remains of Agrippa's mysterious bridge.

LITERATURE. — Luigi Borsari, *Notizie degli Scavi*, 1887, p. 323; and *Bull. arch. com.*, 1888, p. 92. — Christian Huelsen, *Mittheilungen*, vol. iv., 1889, p. 285.

PONS ÆLIUS (Ponte S. Angelo). — A volume could be written on this most historical of Roman bridges; but I confine myself to the mention of the latest discoveries made in connection with it.

The Pons Ælius was built in A. D. 136 by Hadrian, together with the mausoleum to which it gave access. The construction was recorded by two inscriptions (Corpus Inscriptionum, vi. 973), — copied by Giovanni Dondi dall' Orologio in the jubilee of 1375, — which fell into the river in the catastrophe of 1450. There were six arches visible before the transformation of the bridge in 1892; two more have been discovered since in the long incline of the left bank, making a total of eight, of which three only served in the dry season. When the mausoleum was transformed into a fort or *tête de pont* in 403, the bridge was closed with two gates, one at each end. The gate facing the Campus Martius is called Αὐρηλία by Procopius;[1] the other, facing the Vatican, was named Porta S. Petri in Hadrianic, " Hadrianium " meaning the fort.

The access to the bridge from the Campus Martius is represented in the following remarkable photograph taken in July, 1892. The incline is 40 metres long, with a gradient of eleven per cent. The roadway is paved in the ordinary Roman fashion, the side pavement being of slabs of travertine. The holes on the outer edges of the sidewalks mark the line of the parapets, frag-

[1] *Goth.* i. 19. See Becker, *De Muris*, p. 113.

ments of which have been found *in situ*. They were composed of pilasters and panels, very neatly carved. On December 19,

Fig. 11. — The Incline to the Ælian Bridge from the Campus Martius (Left Bank).

1450, while great crowds were returning from S. Peter's, where Nicholas V. had been showing the Sudarium, a mule belonging to Cardinal Pietro Barbo became restive and caused a panic. The parapets gave way under the pressure, and one hundred and seventy-two pilgrims fell into the river. To prevent the recurrence of such a calamity, Nicholas V. opened the modern Piazza di Ponte (enlarged 1854) ; he also built two expiatory chapels at the entrance to the bridge, from the designs of Bernardo Rossellino. During the siege of the castle of S. Angelo in 1527, Clement VII. and his garrison were much exposed to shots fired by outposts concealed in the chapels. After his liberation the pope caused them to be demolished, and raised in their place two statues, of S. Peter by Lorenzetto and of S. Paul by Paolo Romano. The other statues, representing angels with the symbols of the Passion, were added by Bernini in 1668. In the course of the works of 1892 it was ascertained that the foundations of the chapels of Nicholas V. had been built with pieces of statuary and architectural marbles (described by Visconti in Bull. arch. com., 1892, p. 263).

LITERATURE. — Gio. Battista Piranesi, *Antichità*, vol. iv. — Antonio Nibby, *Roma antica*, vol. i. p. 159. — Rodolfo Lanciani, *Itiner. di Einsiedlen*, p. 15 ; and *Bull. com.*, 1893, p. 14. — Luigi Borsari, *Notizie degli Scavi*, 1892, p. 411. — Christian Huelsen, *Mittheilungen*, 1894, p. 321.

A hundred metres below the Ponte S. Angelo the remains of another bridge appear at low water. It is probably the work of Nero, who did so much to beautify and enlarge the gardens in the district of the Vatican, which he had inherited from Agrippina the elder. The classic name of the bridge is not known, although many have been suggested (Neronianus, Vaticanus, Triumphalis). In the Middle Ages it was called *Pons ruptus ad S. Spiritum in Saxia.* See —

Gio. Battista Piranesi, *Antichità*, vol. iv. pl. 13 ; vol. i. p. 13, n. 91 ; and *Camp. Mart.*, pl. 45. — Stefano Piale, in Venuti's *Roma antica*, vol. ii. p. 190. — Antonio Nibby, *Roma antica*, vol. i. p. 205.

PONS VALENTINIANUS (Ponte Sisto). — The bridge of Valentinian I., represented by the modern Ponte Sisto, was one of the noblest structures spanning the river. It was rebuilt in 366 and 367 by the same Symmachus whom I have mentioned in connection with the Pons Gratianus, with the spoils and on the site of an older one (of Agrippa? or Caracalla?), and was dedicated to Valentinian and Valens. Overthrown by the inundation of 797 (?), it was repaired by Sixtus IV., in 1475, from the designs of Baccio Pontelli. In 1878, the branch of the river which flows under the first arch on the left having been diverted, the corresponding arch of Valentinian's bridge was found lying bodily on the bottom of the stream in such good order that the pieces of an inscription, which ran from one end to the other of the south parapet, were discovered in their proper succession. A triumphal arch which decorated the approach from the Campus Martius [1] had fallen also into the river, with the bronze statues and groups by which it was crowned. The pieces, recovered in 1878, are now exhibited in the Museo delle Terme, except a head which found its way into the

Fig. 12. — Bronze Head found in the Tiber.

antiquarian market and was bought, many years later, by Alessandro Castellani. This remarkable head is of the highest im-

[1] As in classic times triumphal arches were raised on the Sacra Via leading to the Capitolium, so in the Christian era they were raised on the roads converging towards S. Peter's; and especially *ad pedes pontium*, at the foot of the bridges which the pilgrims crossed on their way to the Apostle's tomb. That of Gratianus Valentinianus and Theodosius stood in the Piazza di Ponte S. Angelo ; that of Arcadius, Honorius, and Theodosius at the approach to the Pons Vaticanus ; that of Valentinianus and Valens by the Ponte Sisto.

portance in regard to the controversy whether the bronze statues placed on this and other monuments of the end of the fourth century were contemporary works, or simply spoils from earlier edifices which were considered to answer the new purpose more or less satisfactorily; and also whether the head was changed or not into a new likeness. Experts consider this head to be of better style than that prevalent in the second half of the fourth century.

The parapets were divided into panels by projecting pilasters. Each panel contains six or eight letters of an inscription which ran the whole length on either side, and each pilaster an inscription of its own regarding the statue placed upon it. One of the pedestals found in 1892 is dedicated " to the august Victory, faithful companion of our lords and masters, the S. P. Q. R., under the care of Avianius Symmachus, ex-prefect of the city." Near it was lying the right wing of the statue of Victory. It is evident, therefore, that if a proper search were made in the bed of the river nearly all the bronzes of the bridge could be recovered.

The fragments of the Pons Valentinianus are dispersed in various corners of the Museo delle Terme. The inscriptions of Sixtus IV. are in the Museo Municipale al Celio (Orto botanico).

LITERATURE. — *Bull. arch. com.*, 1878, p. 241. — Rodolfo Lanciani, *Ancient Rome*, p. 257. — Theodor Mommsen, in *Ephem. epigr.*, vol. iv. p. 279. — Christian Huelsen, *Mittheilungen*, 1892, p. 329.

VII. TRAIECTUS (ferries). — The traffic between the two banks of the Tiber was carried on also by means of ferries, known by the name of *traiectus*, the *traghetti* of the present day. Each had a name of its own : like the traiectus Luculli, Marmorariorum, Togatensium at Ostia (Corpus Inscriptionum, xiv. 254, 403, 425). The sites of the ferries at Rome are marked by corresponding posterns in the walls of Aurelian, along the banks of the Campus Martius : there was one at the Porto di Ripetta, others at the Porto della Tinta, at the Posterula Domitia, at the Porto dell' Armata, etc. The ferries of the Armata and Ripetta lasted till 1887.

LITERATURE. — *Bull. arch. com.*, 1889, p. 175 ; and Nolli's *Pianta di Roma*, 1748.

VIII. OBJECTS OF VALUE IN THE BED OF THE RIVER. — The belief in their existence dates from the Middle Ages. Leaving aside the old stories of the seven-branched candlestick and of the gold-plate of Agostino Chigi, which rest on no foundation of truth, the dredging works carried out since 1877 prove that the bed of the Tiber contains a marvelous quantity of objects of value, from bronze statues, masterpieces of Græco-Roman art, down to the smallest articles of personal wear, from flint arrowheads of prehistoric times to the weapons used in fighting the French in 1849. The dredging, unfortunately, has been only superficial, its purpose being to give the stream a uniform depth of 9 feet; while the objects of value have been absorbed to depths which vary from 3 to 35 feet below the bottom of the river. Twice only the maximum depth has been reached (Ponte Garibaldi, Ponte Sisto), and on either occasion a great mass of works of art or antiquity has been gathered.[1] By comparing these discoveries with those made in the foundation of the embankment walls, we have satisfied ourselves on several points : —

1. That, however great the absorbing power of mud and sandbanks is, the objects are not so deeply hidden as to be beyond the reach of man.

2. That the power of the current to wash heavy objects down stream, even in time of flood, is moderate. A fragment of the annals of the *Salii palatini*, which fell or was thrown into the river at the Sponda della Regola towards the end of the fifth century, was recovered in 1881, 550 metres below that point. The fragment had traveled, therefore, at the slow rate of 39 metres per century.

3. That there is a certain chronological regularity in the strata of sunken objects, each stratum corresponding to one of the revolutions, sieges, and political disturbances so frequent in the history of Rome. The higher strata are contemporary with the siege and capture of the city by General Oudinot, when thousands of "improvised" war weapons were thrown into the river to avoid detection. There are traces of the disturbances of 1831, of the French Revolution, and of the Napoleonic wars. These objects are more curious than valuable. The real wealth begins with the layer corresponding to the Sacco di Roma of 1527, not to speak of mediæval or barbaric invasions. For two or three years the average of coins dredged up amounted to twelve hundred per month, mostly coppers of the last two centuries, even of popes whose reigns were peaceful and undisturbed. How did they happen to be there? The solution of the mystery lies, perhaps, in the fact that the dirt collected from the streets or from private houses was thrown daily into the river at two points, "la Penna" above Ripetta, and S. Giovanni dei Fiorentini. To lose money in the streets is a rare occurrence, but at home it hap-

[1] See *Ancient Rome*, p. 257.

pens very easily : coppers may drop on the carpets and roll under

Fig. 13. — Statue found in the Tiber.

pieces of furniture, and when servants sweep the rooms the coins may get mixed up with the dust. Such refuse has been thrown into the river for many centuries.

4. That the objects sunk in the river are recovered in good condition, whether of terra-cotta, or marble, or metal, iron excluded. Iron not only gets rusty and almost dissolved in water, but imparts to marble — if in contact with it — a deep reddish hue, which is quite characteristic of the Tiberine sculpture. Brass Imperial and Republican coins are splendidly preserved, but without " patina," which makes them less valuable in the market.

I can give no better evidence of the care which Old Father Tiber has taken of the works of art intrusted to him than by reproducing here one of the marble statues found in his bed not long ago. This archaic Apollo, a copy of a bronze original, is now exhibited in a cabinet of the Museo delle Terme on the south side of the quadrangle. A short notice of the find is given in the " Mittheilungen " of 1891, p. 302. Compare " Notizie degli Scavi," 1891, pp. 287 and 337; Helbig's " Guide," vol. ii. p. 214, n. 1028.

IX. CLOACÆ (drains). — The hills of the left bank, from the Pincian to the Cælian, follow one another so as to make three valleys, each having its own outlet for spring, rain, and waste waters. The northern basin, between the Pincian and the Quirinal, was drained by the river Petronia, which collected the Sallustian springs, and fell into the Tiber a little above our Ponte Garibaldi; the middle basin, between the Quirinal and the Esquiline, by a river probably called Spinon, which collected the waters of the Vicus Longus, Vicus Patricius, and the Subura, crossed the Argiletum, the Forum, and the Velabrum, and joined the Tiber at the

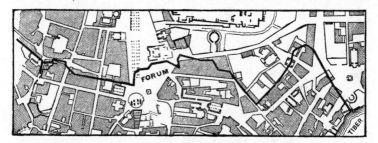

Fig. 14. — The Course of the Cloaca Maxima.

present mouth of the Cloaca Maxima; the southern basin, between the Esquiline, the Cælian, and the Aventine, by a third river (Nodinus), 3600 metres long. After receiving eight tributaries from the springs of Apollo, of the Camœnæ, of Mercury, of the Piscina Publica, etc., it emptied itself into the Tiber a little below the mouth of the Cloaca Maxima. (See map, Fig. 1.)

The first step towards the regulation of these three rivers was taken even before the advent of the Tarquins. Their banks were then lined with great square blocks of stone, leaving a channel about 5 feet wide, so as to prevent the spreading and the wandering of flood-water, and provide the swampy valleys with a permanent drainage; but, strange to say, the course of the streams was not straightened nor shortened. If the reader looks at the map above (Fig. 14), representing the course of the Cloaca Maxima through the Argiletum and the Velabrum, he will find it so twisted and irregular as to resemble an Alpine torrent more than a drain built by skillful Etruscan engineers. The same thing may be repeated for the other main lines of drainage in the valleys Sallustiana, Murcia, etc. When the increase of the population and the extension of the city beyond the boundaries of the Palatine made it necessary to cover those channels and make them run underground, it was too late to think of straightening their course, because their banks were already fixed and built over.

The Roman cloacæ have been overpraised. It is certainly a marvelous fact that some of them were still in use a few years ago, after a lapse of twenty-six centuries; but they bid defiance to modern sanitary principles. First of all, they served to carry off the sewage and the rain-water together. This double employment made it necessary to have large openings along the street, which exposed the population to the effluvia of the sewers. In the third place, the sewers emptied themselves directly into the Tiber, thus polluting its waters, which were used not only for bathing but also for drinking purposes. Only six years ago did the Tiber cease to be the cesspool of Rome. It must also be borne in mind that the "latrina" of Roman houses was inconveniently placed next the kitchen, and the same cloaca was used for the sinks. Against such great dangers to public and private health the Romans had but two protections : the masses of water by which the drains were constantly flushed, and the hilly nature of the city ground, which allowed them to give the drains a steep gradient.

Drains dating from the time of the Kings or of the Republic are built of blocks of peperino and lapis Gabinus (sperone), those of the Imperial period of bricks. Two tiles, placed against each other in a slanting position, form the roof; the floor is made of a large tile slightly convex. There are no sluices or flood-gates.

The Cloaca Maxima and that of the Vallis Murcia (described in Ancient Rome, p. 54; and Bull. arch. com., 1892, p. 279) are by no means alone in respect of their size, length, and magnificence of construction. There is a third, discovered by Enrico Narducci in the plain of the Circus Flaminius, equal, if not superior, to them. The section which Narducci explored in 1880 begins at the corner of Via Paganica with the Piazza Mattei, and runs in a straight line to the Tiber, by the Ponte Garibaldi. Its side walls are built of blocks of lapis Gabinus, some of which measure 45 cubic feet; the arched roof is made of five blocks only, wedged together; the floor is paved like that of a Roman road. It runs at the considerable depth of 9.53 metres under the modern city. (See Bull. Inst., 1881, p. 209.)

We must remember that these great sewers were built through marshes and ponds, and generally through a soil soaked with spring-water. Rome may be said to be floating over this subterranean alluvium even now. In the sixty days required to build the sewer of the Via del Babuino in 1875, 650,000 cubic metres of water were absorbed by seven steam pumps. The inundation of the Coliseum in 1878 could not possibly be got under control : powerful engines only lowered it by a few inches, and it cost the city nearly one million lire to provide the Coliseum with a regular outlet.

The level of the subterranean flood has risen since Roman times. In the foundations of the Banca di Roma and of the Palazzo Canale, on either side of the Via Poli, the pavement of a street was found under two feet of water. The cellars of the wine docks, discovered in 1877 in the gardens of la Farnesina (*cellæ vinariæ Nova et Arruntiana*), were flooded up to the key of their vaulted roofs. The chefs-d'œuvre of Saitic art, discovered by Tranquilli in 1858 in the sacred area of the Iseum, near the apse of la Minerva, were lying on the floor of the peristyle three feet under water. An excavation made by Parker in 1869 in Caracalla's Baths, by SS. Nereo and Achilleo, in the Via di Porta S. Sebastiano, had to be given up, although successful, in consequence of the invasion of spring-water.

In the many hundred antique drains discovered in my time, I have never seen a sign of communication with the houses lining the streets through which the drains passed. All the side channels which empty into the Cloaca Maxima, from the Forum Augustum to the Tiber, belong to streets or public buildings — none to private dwellings. The same observation has been made with regard to the sewers of the Esquiline, Viminal, etc. This fact would lead us to believe that cesspools, or *pozzi neri*, were more popular in Rome than the latrina, communicating directly with the public sewer. Yet only one *pozzo nero* has been found in our excavations. It is described in the Bull. arch. com., 1892, p. 285. In the same periodical, 1873, p. 243, pl. ii., 3, there is a description and the design of a latrina discovered in the drilling grounds of the Prætorians, Via Magenta, No. 2. Fig. 15 (next page) represents the latrina annexed to the guest-rooms of the Villa Adriana.

LITERATURE. — *Antike Denkmäler* of the German Arch. Inst., vol. i., 1889, taf. xxxvii. — *Bull. arch. com.*, 1872, p. 279; 1890, p. 95, pls. 7, 8. — Pietro Narducci, *Fognatura della città di Roma sulla sinistra del Tevere*, Rome, 1884; and *Roma sotterranea, illustraz. della cloaca massima*, 1885. — *Codex* lxxv. 68, in the King's Library, B. M., p. 15. — Theodor Schreiber, *Berichte der sächs. Gesellschaft der Wiss.*, 1885, p. 78. — Rodolfo Lanciani, *Ancient Rome*, p. 54.

Fig. 15. — The Latrina annexed to the Guest-Rooms of the Villa Adriana.

X. THE QUARRIES FROM WHICH ROME WAS BUILT. — The materials used in Roman constructions are the *lapis ruber* (tufa); the *lapis Albanus* (peperino); the *lapis Gabinus* (sperone); the *lapis Tiburtinus* (travertino); the *silex* (selce); and bricks and tiles of various kinds. The cement was composed of pozzolana (0.67) and lime (0.33). Imported marbles came into fashion towards the end of the Republic, and became soon after the pride and glory of Rome.

A. TUFA (lapis ruber). — The only material which the first builders of Rome found at hand was the volcanic conglomerate called tufa. The quality of the stone used in those early days was far from perfect. The walls of the Palatine hill and of the Capitoline citadel were built of material quarried on the spot — a mixture of charred pumice-stones and reddish volcanic sand. The quarries of the Palatine will be described in the proper place. Those used for the fortifications of the Capitol were located at the foot of the hill towards the Argiletum, and were so important as to give their name, *Lautumiæ*, to the neighboring district. It is probable that the prison called Tullianum, from a jet of water, *tullus*, which sprang from the rock, was originally a portion of this quarry. The tufa blocks employed by Servius

Tullius for the building of the city walls, and of the agger, appear to be of three qualities — yellowish, reddish, and gray; the first, soft and easily broken up, seems to have been quarried from the Little Aventine, near the church of S. Saba. The galleries of this quarry, much disfigured by mediæval and modern use, can be followed to a considerable distance, although the collapsing of the vaults makes it dangerous to visit them. I have entered these recesses only twice, with the late Mr. J. H. Parker, while trying to rediscover the channel of the Aqua Appia, first seen and described by Raffaello Fabretti about 1675. I am not able to say where Servius found the reddish tufa (Cervara?). The quarries of the third quality were, or rather one of them was, discovered on February 7, 1872, in the Vigna Querini, outside the Porta S. Lorenzo, near the first milestone of the Vicolo di Valle Cupa. It was a surface quarry, comprising five trenches 16 feet wide, 9 feet deep. Some of the blocks, already squared, were lying on the floor of the trenches, others were detached on two or three sides only, the size of others was simply traced on the rock by vertical or horizontal lines. (See illustration in Bull. arch. com., 1888, pls. i., ii., figs. 3–6.) This tufa, better known by the name of *cappellaccio*, is very bad. The only buildings in which it was used, besides the inner wall of the Servian agger, are the platform of the temple of Jupiter Capitolinus, in the gardens of the German Embassy, and the *puticuli* in the burial-grounds of the Esquiline. Its use must have been given up before the end of the period of the Kings, in consequence of the discovery of better quarries on the right bank of the Tiber, at the foot of the hills now called Monte Verde. A description of these last, still in use, can be found in the —

Notizie degli Scavi, 1886, p. 454; 1888, p. 136; 1889, pp. 71 and 243. — *Bull. arch. com.*, 1892, p. 288. — *Mittheilungen*, 1891, p. 149.

They cover a space about one mile in length and a quarter of a mile wide on each side of the valley of Pozzo Pantaléo. In fact, this valley, which runs from the Via Portuensis towards the lake of the Villa Pamphili, seems to be artificial; I mean, produced by the extraction of the rock by millions of cubic metres in the course of twenty-four centuries. If the work of the ancient quarrymen could be freed from the loose material which conceals it from view, we should possess within a few minutes' drive from the Porta Portese a reproduction of the famous mines of El Masarah, with beds of rock cut into steps and terraces, with roads

and lanes, shafts, inclines, underground passages, and outlets for
the discharge of rain-water. The cuttings on either side show two
strata of tufa : the upper, 8 metres thick, is a very hard ash-col-
ored rock resembling in texture the pudding-stone ; the lower, of
a light red color and less compact, is fractured by seams and veins,
so that it cannot be obtained in large blocks ; and as the purpose
of the Romans was to obtain cubes from 3 to 5 feet long, as shown
by a few left on the spot, they used the lower or reddish stone
only to make prisms for reticulated masonry. The galleries of
the quarry vary in size from 10 to 20 feet, and their floor is leveled so as to conduct the rain-water to one central outlet, running
towards the brook of Pozzo Pantaléo. When a quarry had given
out, its galleries were filled up with the refuse of the neighboring
ones — chips left over after the squaring of the blocks ; so that, in
many cases, the color and texture of the chips do not correspond
with those of the quarry in which they are found. This layer of
refuse, transformed by time into humus, and worked upon by human and atmospheric forces, has given the valley a different aspect,
so that it looks as if it were the work not of quarrymen, but of
nature. Some of the abandoned galleries were transformed into
tombs and columbaria. One raised by Aurelius Niketa to his
daughter Ælianetis contains the following inscription : *Fossor, vide
ne fodias! Deus magnus oculos habet. Vide, et tu filios habes.*
Which means, " Quarryman, do not approach this tomb: the
great God watches thee ; remember that thou also hast children."
These words prove that tombs and quarries were contemporary
and not very far apart.

Tufa may be found used in many existing monuments of ancient Rome, such as the drains of the middle and southern basin
of the left bank, the channels and arches of the Marcia and Anio
vetus, the Servian walls, the temples of Fortuna Virilis, of Hercules Magnus Custos, the Rostra, the embankment of the Tiber,
etc. The largest and most magnificent quarries in the suburban
district are the so-called Grotte della Cervara. No words can
convey an idea of their size and of the regularity of their plan.
They seem to be the work of a fanciful architect who has hewn
out of the rock halls and galleries, courts and vestibules, and imi-
tated the forms of an Assyrian palace. The quarries of La Cervara, at the fifth milestone of the Via Collatina, are described
by Strabo (lib. v.).

B. PEPERINO (lapis Albanus). — For the study of the peperino
mines, which contain a stone special to the Alban district, formed

by the action of hot water on gray volcanic cinders, the reader should follow on foot the line of the new Albano railway, from the place called Il Sassone to the town of Marino. Many of the valleys in this district, now made beautiful by vineyards and oliveyards, owe their existence to the pickaxe of the Roman stonecutter, like the valley of Pozzo Pantaléo. The most curious sight is a dolmen or isolated rock 10 metres high, left in the centre of one of the quarries to certify the thickness of the bed of rock excavated. In fact, the whole district is very interesting both to the archæologist and to the *paysagiste*. The mines of Marino, still worked in the neighborhood of the railway station, would count, like the Grotte della Cervara, among the wonders of the Campagna, were they known to the student as they deserve to be.

If the discovery of a piece of "æs grave signatum" in a seam of peperino near the Ponte di S. Gennaro, between Civita Lavinia and Velletri, could be proved true (by the exhibition not of the piece alone, but of its mould on the rock itself, which has not been done yet), the stone would appear to be of modern formation.

The principal Roman buildings in which the lapis Albanus has been used are : the Claudian aqueduct, the Cloaca Maxima, the temples of Antoninus and Faustina, of Cybele, of the Eventus Bonus, of Neptune, the inclosure wall of the Forum Augustum, Forum Transitorium, and Forum Pacis, the Porticus Argonautarum, Porticus Pompeii, the Ustrinum of the Appian Way, etc. The sarcophagus of Cornelius Scipio Barbatus in the Vatican museum, and the tomb of the Tibicines in the Museo Municipale al Celio are also of this stone.

C. TRAVERTINO (lapis Tiburtinus). — Quarried in the plains of Tivoli at places now called Le Caprine, Casal Bernini, and Il Barco. This last was reopened after an interval of many centuries by Count G. Brazza, brother of the African explorer. Lost in the wilderness and overgrown with shrubs, it had not been examined, I believe, since the visit of Brocchi. It can be reached by stopping at the station of the Aquæ Albulæ, on the Tivoli line, and following the ancient road which led to the works. This road, twice as wide as the Appian Way, is flanked by substructures, and is not paved, but macadamized. Parallel with it runs an aqueduct which supplied the works with motive power, derived probably from the sulphur springs. There are also remains of tombs, one of which, octagonal in shape, serves as a foundation to the farm-house del Barco.

The most remarkable monument of the whole group is the

Roman quarry from which five and a half million cubic metres of travertine have been extracted, as proved by the measurement of the hollow space between the two opposite vertical sides. That this is the most important ancient quarry of travertine, and the largest one used by the Romans, is proved, in the first place, by its immense size. The sides show a frontage of more than two and a half kilometres; the surface amounts to 500,000 square metres. The sides are quite perpendicular, and have the peculiarity of projecting buttresses, at an angle of 90°. Some of these buttresses are isolated on three sides, and still preserve the grooves, more or less deep, by means of which they could be separated from the solid mass; these grooves vary in depth from 50 centimetres to 2 metres, and look fresh and sharp, as if the quarry had been abandoned only a short time ago. The second argument is furnished by the indirect traces of the work of man, which show that the excavation must at least be many centuries old. In order to keep the bottom of the works clean and free for the movement of the carts, for the action of the cranes, and for the manœuvres of the workmen, the chips, or useless product of the squaring of the blocks, were transported to a great distance, as far as the banks of the Anio, and there piled up to a great height. This is the origin of that chain of hills which runs parallel to the river, and of whose artificial formation no one, as far as I know, had the least suspicion. One of these hills, visible from every point of the neighboring district, from Hadrian's villa as well as from the Sulphur Baths, is elliptical in shape, 22 metres high, 90 metres long, and 65 metres wide. It can with reason be compared with our Testaccio. It is easy to imagine how immense must have been the number of blocks cut from the Cava del Barco during the period of the formation of this hill alone. Another proof of the antiquity of the quarry, and of its abandonment from Imperial times down to our own day, is given by this fact. The Aquæ Albulæ, the most copious sulphur springs of central Italy, collected into canals by the Romans and subjected to a scientific hydraulic régime, were allowed free play from the first barbaric invasion up to the sixteenth century, when Cardinal Ippolito d' Este gathered them again into the channel which takes its name from him, and which is in use at the present day. In this long period of abandonment it seems that the principal branch of the wandering waters directed its course towards the Cava del Barco, leaping from the rim of the north vertical side into the chasm below. This fall of water, saturated with carbonate and sulphate of lime, and lasting for many centuries, produced the following effect. The north wall was concealed under a hard chalky incrustation, and transformed into a slope with an inclination of 45° or 50°. This stratum of recent formation is, on an average, 8 metres wide at the base, and only a few centimetres at the top. Stonecutters in the quarry are now obliged to remove this crust before reaching the ancient walls of travertine, which still preserve the traces of the blows of the Roman pickaxe. At the bottom of the quarry we meet with another phenomenon. The stratum of chips which covers it has been cemented and pasted over by chalky sediments, forming beds and layers of a hard breccia resembling the pudding-stone. The southern walls of the quarry, on the contrary, are free from incrustations, as they have never been in contact with the sulphur water.

The system now followed in quarrying the blocks is the same as that which prevailed in old times. The foreman ascertains

Fig. 16. — The Quarries of Travertine, Cava del Barco.

the weak point of the rocky mass, and the vertical or horizontal line of the seams, and directs his men to place steel wedges along the weak line, and hammer them simultaneously, the movement being timed to the rhythm of a song. This illustration, from a photograph which I took in December, 1893, explains the process better than any description could do. The large block in the foreground has already been detached on four sides, and the men are busy placing the steel wedges on the weak seam at the bottom. I need not say that as many men are required to hammer as there are wedges. Sometimes the task is accomplished at the first stroke, sometimes it requires half an hour's work.

D. SILEX (selce). — Used for rubble-work in small fragments, and for paving streets and roads in larger pieces of pentagonal shape. The stone was quarried from four lava streams which had flowed from the Alban volcanoes in the direction of Rome (Capo di Bove, Acqua Acetosa, Borghetto, and Monte Falcone), and from one stream of the Sabatine range (S. Maria di Galera). The working of the quarries, the cutting and shaping of the paving-stones, the laying in and repairing of pavements, was intrusted to a large body of trained men, organized in companies and directed by government officials.[1] The material was kept in store in a great state building named Castra Silicariorum, which may have served also as barracks for the Silicarii. The institution is still flourishing under the name of "Magazzino dei Selci." The present works occupy a large tract of land north of the Protestant cemetery in the plains of Testaccio.

Pumice-stone was used occasionally by Roman masons to diminish the weight and lateral pressure of great vaulted ceilings, as in the baths of Caracalla.

LITERATURE. — The introductory chapters of Middleton's *Remains of Ancient Rome* (2d ed. 1892), dealing with the site and general features of the city, with the materials of which it is built, and with the methods of construction, are the best ever written on the subject. The author shows himself a specialist of unrivaled knowledge. So thoroughly has he mastered the technicalities of ancient masonry and stonework that he makes clear and almost agreeable a subject which students have usually avoided as dry and difficult to understand. An abridged memoir on the same subject, issued by the same author, is to be found in vol. xli. of the *Archæologia*, 1888: "On the Chief Methods of Construction used in Ancient Rome."

Compare also, Giovanni Brocchi, *Dello stato fisico del suolo di Roma*, 1820, p. 109; Antonio Nibby, *Dei materiali impregati nelle fabbriche di Roma, delle costruzioni, e dello stile* (in Roma antica, vol. i. p. 234); Faustino Corsi, *Delle pietre antiche*, Rome, 1845, pp. 11-76.

XI. BRICKS. — There are three collections of brick-stamps in Rome : one, of little value, in the Kircherian museum ; the second

---

[1] The *procurator ad silices,* or *procurator silicum viarum sacræ urbis,* subject to the authority of the Minister of Public Works. (See *Corpus Inscriptionum,* vi. 1598; and Orelli-Henzen, n. 6519.)

in the last room of the Vatican Library, past the "Nozze aldo-brandine;" the third and best in the Museo Municipale al Celio. This last contains over a thousand specimens, and a unique set of the products of Roman kilns. In fact, the first hall of the Museo is set apart exclusively for the study of ancient building and decorative materials.

Roman bricks were square, oblong, triangular, or round, the latter being used only to build columns in the Pompeian style. The square species comprises the *tegulæ bipedales*, of 0.59 metre × 0.59; the *tegulæ sesquipedales*, of 0.45 metre × 0.45; and the *laterculi bessales*, used in hypocausts, of 0.22 metre × 0.22. Arches were built of a variety of the *bipedales*, of the same length, but only 0.22 in width, and slightly wedged. The triangular bricks were obtained by cutting diagonally a *tegula bessalis* with a wooden rule or a string before it was put into the kiln. The largest bricks discovered in my time measure 1.05 metre in length. They were set into an arch of one of the great stairs leading to the avenue or boulevard, established in Imperial times on the top of the agger of Servius (railway station).

Roman bricks are very often stamped with a seal, the legend of which contains the names of the owner and manager of the kilns, of the maker of the tile, of the merchant intrusted with the sale of the products, and of the consuls under whose term of office the bricks were made. These indications are not necessarily found all in one seal.

The most important of them is the consular date, because it helps the student to determine, within certain limits, the date of the building itself. The rule, however, is far from being absolute, and before fixing the date of a Roman structure from that of its brick stamps one must take into consideration many other points of circumstantial evidence.

When we examine, for instance, the grain warehouses at Ostia, or Hadrian's villa at Tivoli, and find that their walls have never undergone repairs, that their masonry is characteristic of the first quarter of the second century, that their bricks bear the dates of Hadrian's age and no others, we may rest assured that the stamps speak the truth. Their evidence is, in such a case, conclusive. But if the bricks are variously dated, or bear the names of various kilns, and not of one or two only, then their value as an evidence of the date of a building is diminished, if not lost altogether.

The following case, derived from personal experience, will explain the point. Professor Jordan, in a remarkable speech deliv-

ered on April 25, 1884, at the German Institute, attributed the
house of the Vestals to the age of Hadrian, because he had found
a stamp of Domitius Tullus (A. D. 59–95) on the south wing of
the atrium; three of Cn. Domitius Clemens (111–123) in the stairs
leading to the first floor; two of Rutilius Lupus (110–122) in one
of the cells of the first floor; and so on.[1] Yet there was no doubt
in my mind that the building was renewed from the foundation,
and on a different plan, by Septimius Severus and Julia Domna,
and that Hadrian had nothing to do with it. I was able to prove
the case so clearly [2] that Jordan's theory was abandoned, and my
contention as to the date was adopted. The presence of bricks of
Hadrian's time can be easily explained. When Severus undertook
the reconstruction of the house of the Vestals and of the whole
adjoining quarter, which had been devastated by the fire of Commodus, he began by leveling to the ground the remains of the
buildings which had partly withstood the violence of the flames.
The materials so saved were put aside and used in the reconstruction of the Atrium Vestæ.

The circular seals have often a symbol in the centre — a figure
of a god or a goddess, a leaf, a fruit, etc. Sometimes the symbol
has a phonetic value. Thus we find the image of the wolf impressed on the tiles of M. Rutilius Lupus; of the wild boar on
those of Flavius Aper; of the eagle on those of Aquilia Sozomena;
the wreath (στεφάνη) on those of C. Julius Stephanus, etc.

The name of the building for which the bricks were destined
appears only in three seals : *Castris Prœtoris*, "for the prætorian
camp;" *Portus Augusti*, "for the Claudian harbor at Ostia;" and
Portus Traiani, "for the harbor of Civitavecchia."

Brick-kilns were called *figlinœ*, their sections or workshops
officinœ. The kilns were named either after their owner, *Acilia-
nœ, Fulvianœ*, etc.; from their being situated in a district, *Sala-
renses, de via Aurelia*, etc.; or from the street on which they were
placed, *a Pila alta, ab Euripo, ad Mercurium felicem*. It is possible, however, that some fanciful name might have been selected
without any reference to the owner or to the site of the works.
The sheds under which the materials were kept ready for sale or
for shipment were called *horrea* and *portus* respectively.

The legends sometimes show curious mistakes of spelling : *opup*
for *opus; phig*(linæ) for *fig*(linæ) ; *pradia* for *prœdia*, etc.

The bricks, again, occasionally bear curious signs, such as foot-
marks of chickens, dogs, or pigs, which stepped over them while

[1] See *Bull. Inst.*, 1884, p. 92.   [2] *Ibid.*, p. 145.

still fresh, impressions of coins and medals, words or sentences scratched with a nail, etc. A bricklayer, who had perhaps seen better times in his youth, wrote on a tegula bipedalis the first verse of the Æneid, " Arma virumque cano," etc.

Names of murdered Emperors were sometimes struck off the stamp, like that of Commodus in No. 541, *b* (Corpus Inscriptionum, xv. 1). After the murder of Geta, the seal AVGGG NNN, which meant "of our three Emperors, Severus, Caracalla, and Geta," was changed into AVGG*IIINNIII* by the erasure of the third G and of the third N.

Antiquarians have discussed the question whether the seals were cast in metal or carved in hard wood, or whether they were made up of movable types, incased in a metal frame. The fact that letters upside down are not uncommon (like SACCESSI for SVCCESSI) has been adduced to prove that the types were movable; but, on the other hand, we have specimens of seals cast bodily in lead or bronze, such as those found in the Tiber in 1879 (Visconti, Bull. arch. com., 1879, pp. 197, 212). There is a stamp (No. 1440, *a*) in which the name of the consul BALBIN has been changed into that of BRTTIO (Brittio) so imperfectly that both can be read at the same time. In another (No. 68, *d*) the letter S in the name RAVSI, omitted by the engraver of the

seal, has been added so, T·RA͆VI. This expedient shows that the missing letter could not have been wedged into its proper place. We must discredit, however, the idea that movable types were not known to the ancients. Albert Dumont (Inscriptions céramiques de Grèce, pp. 46 and 395) brings strong evidence in favor of it; and A. Milchhoefer (Ann. Inst., 1879, p. 90) has traced the use of such types in an Etruscan sarcophagus.

The great manufacturing centre of Roman bricks was the district between the viæ Triumphalis, Cornelia, and the two Aureliæ, now called the Monti della Creta, which includes the southern slopes of the Vatican ridge and the northern of the Janiculum. Here also, as at Pozzo Pantaléo, the traces of the work of man are simply gigantic. The valleys del Gelsomino, delle Fornaci, del Vicolo delle Cave, della Balduina, and a section of the Val d' Inferno, are not the work of nature, but the result of excavations for "creta figulina," which began 2300 years ago, and have never been interrupted since. A walk through the Monti della Creta will teach the student many interesting things. The best point of observation is a bluff between the Vicolo della Cave and

the Vicolo del Gelsomino, marked with the word " Ruderi " and
with the altitude of 75 metres, in the military map of the suburbs.
The bluff rises 37 metres above the floor of the brick-kilns of the
Gelsomino.

There were other important establishments in the plains of
the Tiber (Prati di Castello, Monti della Creta beyond S. Paolo)
and of the Anio (Ponte Salario, Civitas Figlina), to which the
alluvial marls furnished the "materia prima."

Roman bricks were exported to all the shores of the Mediterranean : they have been found in the Riviera, on the coasts of
Venetia, of Narbonensis, of Spain and Africa, and in the island
of Sardinia. One brick from Syria (No. 2415) and two from the
gulf of Genoa (Nos. 2412, 2413) have been picked up in Rome,
but they must have been transported here incidentally by ships in
ballast.

The brick-making business must have been very remunerative,
if we judge from the rank and wealth of many personages who
had an interest in it. Many names of Emperors appear in brick-
stamps, and even more of Empresses and princesses of the Imperial
family. (See index to de Rossi's Iscrizioni doliari, pp. 525, 527.)

LITERATURE. — Gaetano Marini, *Iscrizioni doliari publicate dal comm. G. B.
de Rossi, con annotazioni di Enrico Dressel.* Rome, 1884. — Descemet, *Mar-
ques de briques relatives à une partie de la gens Domitia* (Bibl. des Ecoles fr.
d'Athènes et de Rome, vol. xv. p. 2); and *Inscriptions doliaires.* — C. Ludovico
Visconti, *On Brick Stamps* (in Parker's Archæology of Rome, vol. or part iv.
p. 41. London, 1876). — Heinrich Dressel, *Alcune osservazioni intorno ai bolli
dei mattoni urbani* (in Bull. Inst., 1885, p. 98). — *Untersuchungen über die
Kronologie der Ziegelstempel*, 1886. — *Corpus Inscriptionum Latinarum*, vol.
xv. 1. Berlin, 1891. — Gio. Battista Lugari, *Sopra l' età di alcuni bolli di
figuline* (in Bull. arch. com., 1895, p. 60).

XII. MARBLES. — It would not be consistent with the spirit of
this present work to enter, even superficially, on the question of
Roman marbles. From the topographical point of view (marble
wharves, warehouses, and sheds, places of sale, offices of administration, artists' studios, and stonecutters' shops) it will be illustrated in Book IV. § vii. I refer the reader, in the mean time, to
the following standard works : —

Faustino Corsi, *Delle pietre antiche*, 3d ed., Rome, 1845. — The Rev. H. W.
Pullen, *Handbook of Ancient Roman Marbles*, London, Murray, 1894. — Luigi
Bruzza, *Iscrizioni dei marmi* (in Annal. Inst., 1870, p. 106).

The perusal of these three volumes must go hand in hand
with the study of the marbles which they describe, so as to enable
the student to tell them apart. For this purpose splendid collec-

tions have been placed at our disposal: one at Oxford, which numbers 1000 tablets; one in the geological museum in Jermyn Street, London; a third in the University of the Sapienza in Rome, consisting of 600 large and about 1000 smaller slabs. The best of all is the set bequeathed by Baron Ravenstein to the museum of the Porte de Hal, Brussels. It contains 764 specimens, which were arranged and catalogued by Tommaso and Francesco Belli. The variety and richness of Roman marbles may be estimated from the fact that there are 43 qualities of bigio, and 151 of alabaster. The rarest marbles known are the breccia d' Egitto, the breccia di Villa Adriana and the breccia di Villa Casali. There are specimens of these exhibited in the first hall of the Museo Municipale al Celio. The churches of S. Maria in Aracœli, della Minerva, and della Vittoria, and the Capella Borghesiana in S. Maria Maggiore, are noted for their wealth in rare marbles.

XIII. METHODS OF CONSTRUCTION. — For this subject also I must refer the student to the works quoted on page 38. The Romans have built in *opus quadratum, incertum, reticulatum, lateritium, lateritio-reticulatum,* and in concrete. An excellent set of phototypes explaining these various styles of masonry can be found in vol. i. part ii. of Parker's " Archæology of Rome," Oxford, London, 1874: *The Historical Construction of Walls.*

The following rules are useful to the student for determining the age of a Roman building: —

1. In Rome there are no traces of the so-called Pelasgic or polygonal style of masonry.[1] The oldest remains, like the walls of the Palatine and of the Capitol, are built in *opus quadratum* in the Etruscan style, with the blocks of tufa placed lengthwise in one tier and crosswise in the next. This rule was followed through the Republican period. I know of very few exceptions: one is the great wall upon which the Constantinian basilica of S. Clement is built, where the blocks are all placed lengthwise.

In Imperial times the exception becomes the rule. The inclosure walls of the Forum Augustum, of the Forum Transitorium, etc., and the cellæ of many temples, show the blocks placed in one direction only.

The opus quadratum was given up (except in case of restorations) in the third century after Christ, and imitations in plaster were substituted for it. The façade of the Senate-house, rebuilt by

[1] Rodolfo Fonteanive, *Avanzi detti Ciclopici nella provincia di Roma.* Rome, Sciolla, 1887.

Diocletian, the Thermæ of Constantine, and his Basilica Nova, the Thermæ of Diocletian, and parts of the Sessorian palace, were plastered in this style. (See plates, Nos. 2, 26, 30, etc., in Stefano du Perac's "Vestigi dell' antichità di Roma" and "Atti Lincei," an. 1883, vol. xi. serie iii. pl. 3.)

2. The *opus incertum*, of which Fig. 17 gives a specimen from the Porticus Æmilia, 176 B. C., marks a transition from the polygonal to the reticulated work. The Romans must have im-

Fig. 17. — The Opus Incertum.

ported it from Tibur, where it was in great favor. Besides the Porticus Æmilia, there are (or were in 1872) other remains built in this style under the cliff of the Viminal, opposite S. Vitale. Photographs of them are given by Parker in " Archæology of Rome," vol. i. 1874, *Construction of Walls*, pl. vi. 2. The opus incertum was given up about the time of Sulla, and replaced by the opus reticulatum, made of regular tufa prisms in imitation of network. There are three kinds of opus reticulatum: in the oldest the prisms are small, and the intersecting lines of the network slightly irregular; it marks the infancy of the new style. A specimen may be found on the Palatine, on the left-hand side of the path which ascends from the foot of the Scalæ Caci to the Temple of Jupiter Propugnator.

In the second stage the prisms become larger, and the cross lines of the network perfectly straight, while the angles of the walls are strengthened with rectangular pieces of tufa resembling large bricks. The house of Germanicus on the Palatine is the best specimen of this style, which seems to have lasted until the time of Trajan.

The last period, from Trajan to the first Antonines, marks a decided improvement in the solidity of the work. The angles and arches are built of bricks, and the wall itself is strengthened by horizontal bands of the same material (Fig. 18). The network, therefore, does not cover the whole face of the wall, but is divided into panels from four to five feet high. At the end of the second century the opus reticulatum was given up altogether. I have never discovered what its advantages were. It did not contribute certainly to the solidity of the building, and it demanded more skill and time from the mason than the brickwork. In the last place, its elegance and beauty were generally concealed by a coating of plaster. Yet builders and architects like Trajan and Hadrian preferred it to any other kind of masonry. The extensive warehouses of Ostia, the substructures of the Thermæ Traianæ, Hadrian's villa near Tibur, the inner harbor and docks at Porto, and a hundred contemporary edifices, are built in this style. (See Fig. 18, p. 46.)

3. *Opus lateritium.* — The fundamental rule for the chronology of brick structures is this: the thinner the bed of cement between the layers of bricks, the older the structure. In other words, in the opus lateritium of the golden age the bricks are so close together that the line of cement is hardly visible; while at the end of the third century the layer of cement is even thicker than the line of bricks. The rule is obviously subject to exceptions, especially when the brick facing was destined to be seen and not to be plastered over. In such cases we are apt to find excellent specimens of brick "cortina," even in times of decadence.

The most perfect specimens of brickwork in Rome are some portions of the Prætorian camp (the Porta Decumana, Porta Principalis Sinistra), the Amphitheatrum Castrense, and the Arcus Neroniani on the Cælian. The decline in the style can be followed

almost year by year from the time of the Flavians to that of
Constantine. I suggest as representatives of periods, more than
years, the Domus Augustana for the time of Domitian; the so-
called "baths of Titus" for the time of Trajan; the Pantheon
and the spiral staircase of the Mausoleum for that of Hadrian;
the Villa Quinctiliorum for that of Commodus; the Thermæ Antoninianæ for that of Caracalla; the substructures of the Temple
of the Sun in the Villa Colonna for that of Aurelian; the Baths
of Diocletian, the Basilica Nova, the Senate-house, for the end of
the third century and the beginning of the fourth. These types
of construction are carefully illustrated in vol. i. of Parker's
" Archæology of Rome."

Fig. 18. — The Opus Reticulatum.

I have said that when the brickwork was intended to remain
exposed to view, and not to be concealed by plaster, it is always
more perfect than we should expect from the general style prevailing at the time.

The best period for ornamental brick-carving in three shades of
color — yellow, red, and brown — includes the second half of the
second century and the beginning of the third   The tomb attributed to Annia Regilla (Pagan and Christian Rome, p. 291), the
tombs of the Via Latina, the door of the Excubitorium Vigilum
at the Monte de' Fiori, Trastevere (Ancient Rome, p. 230), the

door of the Catacombs of Prætextatus, the temple at S. Urbano alla Caffarella (Pagan and Christian Rome, p. 294) are the best specimens of this kind of work.

There is another peculiarity of the opus lateritium which may help the student to determine the age of an edifice in doubtful cases. The brick facing of a wall is sometimes interrupted by parallel horizontal lines of tegulæ bipedales of a different hue, from three to six feet apart. These lines appear for the first time, I believe, in the Pantheon and in the spiral staircase of Hadrian's tomb, and are most conspicuous in the buildings of the time of Severus and Caracalla.

XIV. AQUEDUCTS.*— One of the praises bestowed by Cicero on the founder of the city is *locum eligit fontibus abundantem,* "he selected a district very rich in springs." A glance at the plan (Fig. 1) will at once prove the accuracy of the statement. Twenty-three springs have been described within the walls, several of which are still in existence; others have disappeared owing to the increase of modern soil. "For four hundred and forty-one [442] years," says Frontinus (i. 4), "the Romans contented themselves with such water as they could get from the Tiber, from wells, and from springs. Some of these springs are still held in great veneration on account of their health-restoring qualities, like the spring of the Camœnæ, that of Apollo, and that of Juturna."

The springs of the Camœnæ were just outside the Porta Capena, in the slope of the Cælian, behind the church of S. Gregorio, and under the wall of the Villa Mattei. The remains of the temple described by Juvenal (Sat., iii. 11) were discovered and delineated by Pirro Ligorio about 1560.

Nothing is known of the springs of Apollo. Those of Juturna are described at length in Book II. p. 125. The celebrated fountain of Egeria remained visible in the lower grounds of the Vigna Bettini (between the Via di S. Stefano Rotondo and the Via della Ferratella) until 1882, when the vigna was buried under an embankment 11 metres high; but although the nymphæum itself has disappeared, the waters still seem to find their way to another fountain lower down the valley of Egeria. This graceful building of the Renaissance stands in the grounds of the Villa Mattei (von Hoffman), at the corner of the Via di Porta S. Sebastiano and delle Mole di S. Sisto, and the water which inundates its lower floor has some medicinal power. Another famous spring, that of the Lupercal, has been identified with our Sorgente di S. Giorgio,

*See Figure 19 facing page 58.

which bubbles up in the very bed of the Cloaca Maxima, near the church of that name. The identity is uncertain. The Tullianum still flows in the lower crypt of the prison of that name; the Aquæ Fontinales in the Cortile di S. Felice, Salita della Dateria, and in the house No. 25 Salita del Grillo; the Aqua Damasiana in the Cortile di S. Damaso of the Vatican palace, in the foun-

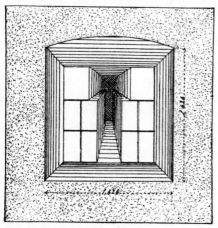

Fig. 20. — The Channel of the Aqua Appia under the Aventine.

tain modeled by Algardi by order of Innocent X. (1649); the Aqua Lancisiana in front of the Palazzo Salviati alla Lungara, where there is a basin with three jets, designed by Lancisi in the time of Clement XI. (1720).

The first aqueduct, that of the AQUA APPIA, is the joint work of Appius Claudius Cæcus and C. Plautius Venox, censors in 312 B. C. The first built the channel, the second discovered the springs 1153 metres northeast of the sixth and seventh milestones of the Via Collatina. They are still to be seen, much reduced in volume, at the bottom of some stone quarries near the farmhouse of La Rustica. The channel followed the Via Collatina, entered Rome *ad Spem Veterem* (Porta Maggiore), crossed the valley of the Piscina Publica (Via di Porta S. Sebastiano) close to the Porta Capena, and ended on the left bank of the Tiber at the foot of the Clivus Publicius (S. Anna, Via della Salara); length of channel, 16,445 metres; volume of water discharged in twenty-four hours, 115,303 cubic metres. The aqueduct of the Appia has been discovered thrice : by Fabretti, in the Vigna Santoro at the corner of the Via di Porta S. Paolo and the Vicolo di S. Balbina (an. 1667); by Parker in 1867, in the tufa quarries of S. Saba; and by myself in 1888, under the remains of the palace of Annia Cornuficia Faustina in the Vigna Maciocchi, Via di Porta S. Paolo. It differs in shape from all other Roman aqueducts, as shown in Fig. 20.

ANIO VETUS. — The second aqueduct was begun in 272 B. C. by

Manius Curius Dentatus, censor, and finished three years later by Fulvius Flaccus. The water was taken from the river Anio 850 metres above S. Cosimato, on the road from Tivoli to Arsoli (Valeria). The course of the channel can be traced as far as Gallicano; from Gallicano to Rome it is uncertain. It entered the city ad Spem Veterem, a little to the right of the Porta Maggiore, where Piranesi, Nibby, and myself have seen and delineated the remains of the *substructio supra terram passuum ccxxi* mentioned by Frontinus (i. 6).[1] From the Porta Maggiore to the Arch of Gallienus (Porta Esquilina) the aqueduct can be followed step by step, having been laid bare at least twenty times during the construction of the railway station and of the Esquiline quarter. Length of channel, 63,704 metres; volume of water discharged in twenty-four hours, 277,866 cubic metres. The Anio Vetus was set apart for the irrigating of gardens and for the flushing of drains.

MARCIA. — In 144 B. C. the Senate, considering that the increase of the population had diminished the rate of distribution of water (from 530 to 430 litres per head), determined that the old aqueducts of the Appia and the Anio should be repaired, and a new one built; the appropriation for both works being 8,000,000 sesterces, or 1,760,000 lire.

The execution of the scheme was intrusted to Q. Marcius Rex. He selected a group of springs at the foot of the Monte della Prugna, in the territory of Arsoli, 4437 metres to the right of the thirty-sixth milestone of the Via Valeria; and after many years of untiring efforts he succeeded in making a display of the water on the highest platform of the Capitol. Agrippa restored the aqueduct in 33 B. C.; Augustus doubled the volume of the water in 5 B. C. by the addition of the Aqua Augusta; in A. D. 79 Titus *rivom aquœ Marciœ vetustate dilapsum refecit et aquam quœ in usu esse desierat reduxit* (Corpus Inscriptionum, vi. 1246); in 196 Septimius Severus brought in a new supply for the use of his Thermæ Severianæ; in 212–213 Caracalla *aquam Marciam variis kasibus impeditam, purgato fonte, excisis et perforatis montibus, adquisito fonte novo Antoniniano, in urbem perducendam curavit* (*ibid.* 1245), and built a branch aqueduct, four miles long, for the use of his baths; in 305–306 Diocletian did the same thing for his great thermæ; and, finally, Arcadius and Honorius devoted to the restoration of the aqueduct the money seized from Count Gildo, the African rebel.

[1] Piranesi, *Antichità*, vol. i. pl. 10. — Nibby, *Roma antica*, vol. i. p. 339. — Lanciani, *Acquedotti*, p. 50, pl. iv. fig. 7.

The Marcia followed the right bank of the Anio as far as S. Cosimato, and the left as far as Tivoli, where it turns round the slope of the Monte Ripoli towards S. Gericomio and Gallicano. Here begins a line of viaducts and bridges, the most magnificent of any that can be found in the whole district of Rome. The course of the Marcia (and of her three companions, Anio Vetus, Claudia, and Anio Novus) being perpendicular to that of the valleys by which this part of the land is thickly furrowed, and their level running halfway between the *thalweg* and the summit of the intervening ridges, the engineers were obliged to alternate bridges and tunnels, some of which are still perfect.

A visit to these beautiful highlands will prove most satisfactory

Fig. 21. — Ponte Lupo.

to the student. It can be made in a day, from the station of Zagarolo on the Naples line, thence by diligence to Gallicano, and on foot (guide necessary) to the ruins. The bridges are seven in number.

Ponte Lupo, in the Valle dell' Acqua Rossa, for the transit of four waters, Marcia, Anio Vetus, Anio Novus, and Claudia, besides a carriage-way and a bridle-path. Originally it was built for the Anio Vetus alone, and its dimensions were 11.20 metres in height, 81.10 metres in length, 2.75 metres in thickness. After the addition of the Marcia, side by side and above it, the structure became 16.60 metres high, 88.90 metres long, 12 metres thick. Lastly, after the addition of the Claudia and Anio Novus, it became 32 metres high, 155 metres long, 14 metres thick, without counting the buttresses, which are clearly visible in the illustration opposite (Fig. 21). All ages, all styles of masonry are represented at Ponte Lupo, and in the four tunnels which converge towards it or radiate from it.

Ponti dell' Inferno in the Valle dell' Inferno, for the transit of the Claudia and of the Anio Novus; and

Ponti delle Forme Rotte, for the same, in the Valle del Fosso di S. Gregorio.

Ponte di S. Pietro, in the Valle delle Forme Rotte, for the transit of the Aqua Marcia.

Ponte di S. Giovanni, in the same valley, for the transit of the Anio Vetus. The bridge was rebuilt by Augustus in reticulated work, and again repaired in brickwork by one of the late Emperors (first arch on the left).

From Gallicano to the sixth milestone of the Via Latina the Marcia runs underground; from the sixth milestone to the Porta Maggiore, Porta S. Lorenzo, and to the present railway station it was borne on almost triumphal arcades, built of tufa with mouldings of travertine. The same arcades were afterwards used to carry the Aqua Tepula and the Julia. The following photograph gives the section of the channel at a point where it emerges from the ground in the farm of Roma Vecchia. A. The channel of the Marcia. B. Remains of that of the Tepula above it. C. A buttress, probably of the time of Hadrian. D. Another, probably of the time of Severus. E. The channel of the Acqua Felice, built by Sixtus V. FF'. The arcades of the Claudia and of the Anio Novus.

The aqueduct reaches Rome at the Porta Maggiore (the meeting-point of ten waters, Appia, Appia Augusta, Anio Vetus, Marcia, Tepula, Julia, Claudia, Anio Novus, Alexandrina, Felice), and follows the line of the walls of Aurelian as far as the Porta S. Lorenzo. The course beyond this gate is so complicated that I think it well to refer the student to sheets xvii. and xviii. of the "Forma Urbis," in which all particulars are carefully mapped, rather than describe it here.

AQUA TEPULA — AQUA JULIA. — The veins, so named from their almost tepid temperature of 17° Cent., and now called Sorgenti dell' Acqua Preziosa, were collected at the foot of the Alban hills (Valle Marciana) in 125 B. C. by the censors Cn. Servilius Cæpio and L. Cassius Longinus. For ninety-two years the Tepula reached Rome by its own channel; but in 33 B. C. Agrippa, after he had collected the springs of the Aqua Julia — higher up the same valley at a place now called "Il Fontanile degli Squarciarelli di Grottaferrata," which were much colder and purer, and double in volume — determined to mix the two and obtain a com-

Fig. 22. — The Aqueducts at Roma Vecchia.

pound water superior in quality to the Tepula, though slightly inferior to the Julia. The Julia was admitted accordingly into the channel of the Tepula at the tenth milestone of the Via Latina, and the amalgamation allowed to proceed for the space of four miles. At the sixth milestone the compound water was again divided in two conduits, proportioned to the volume of the springs (400 quinariæ for the Tepula, and 1206 for the Julia). The temperature of the Tepula being 17° Cent., that of the Julia 10°, and their volumes 1 : 3, the mixture must have marked at the Piscina a temperature of about 12°, which is the best for drinking purposes. Length of channel for the Tepula, 17,745 metres ; for the Julia, 22,853 metres. Volume of the first, 28,115 cubic metres in twenty-four hours ; of the second, 76,195. Both were borne on the same arches which carried the Marcia.

AQUA VIRGO. — The springs, located at the eighth milestone of the Via Latina, above the farmhouse of Salone in the Val del Ponte di Nona, were drawn into a canal by Agrippa, and reached the city on June 9, 19 B. C. Length of channel, 20,697 metres ; volume in twenty-four hours, 158,203 cubic metres.

AQUA ALSIETINA. — " I cannot conceive," says Frontinus (i. 11), " why such a wise prince as Augustus should have brought to Rome such a discreditable and unwholesome water as the Alsietina, unless it was for the use of the naumachia " (an oval pond 531 metres long, 354 metres wide, for naval sham fights). It was destined afterwards for the irrigation of the Transtiberine orchards. Length of channel, 32,848 metres ; volume, 24,767 cubic metres per day. (See Notizie degli Scavi, 1887, p. 182.)

AQUA CLAUDIA. — None of the Roman aqueducts are eulogized by Frontinus like the Claudian. He calls it " opus magnificentissime consummatum ; " and after demonstrating in more than one way that the volume of the springs collected by Claudius amounted to 4607 quinariæ, he says that there was a reserve of 1600 always ready.

The works, begun by Caligula in A. D. 38, lasted fourteen years, the water having reached Rome only on August 1, 52 (the birthday of Claudius). The course of the aqueduct was first around the slopes of the Monte Ripoli, like that of the Marcia and of the Anio Vetus : Domitian shortened it by several miles by boring a tunnel 4950 metres long through the Monte Affliano. (See Ancient Rome, p. 63.) Length of channel, 68,750 metres, of which 15,000 on arches ; volume per day, 209,252 cubic metres. The Claudia was used for the Imperial table : a branch aqueduct, 2000 metres long, left the main channel ad Spem Veterem (Porta Maggiore), and following the line of the Via Cælimontana (Villa Wolkonsky), of the Campus Cælimontanus (Lateran), and of the street now called di S. Stefano Rotondo, reached the temple of

Claudius by the church of SS. Giovanni e Paolo, and the Imperial palace by the church of S. Bonaventura.   (See Book II. § xxv.)

ANIO NOVUS. — The Anio Novus, like the Vetus, was at first derived from the river of the same name at the forty-second milestone of the road to Subiaco, great precautions being taken for purifying the water by means of a piscina limaria.   The works were begun by Caligula in A. D. 38, and completed by Claudius on August 1, 52, on a most magnificent scale, some of the arches reaching the height of thirty-two metres above ground ; and there were eight miles of them.   Yet, in spite of the purifying reservoir, and of the clear springs of the Rivus Herculaneus (Fosso di Fioggio), which had been mixed with the water from the river, the Anio Novus was hardly ever drinkable.   Whenever a shower fell on the Simbruine mountains, the water would get troubled and saturated with mud and carbonate of lime.   Trajan improved its condition by carrying the head of the aqueduct higher up the valley, where Nero had created three artificial lakes for the adornment of his Villa Sublacensis.   These lakes served more efficiently as *piscinæ limariæ*, or "purgatories," than the artificial basin of Caligula, nine miles below.   The Anio Novus reached Rome in its own channel after a course of 86,964 metres, but for the last seven miles it ran on the same arches with the Aqua Claudia. The Anio Novus was the largest of all Roman aqueducts, discharging nearly three hundred thousand cubic metres per day.

There are two places in the suburbs of Rome where these marvelous arches of the Claudia and Anio Novus can be seen to advantage : one is the Torre Fiscale, three miles outside the Porta S. Giovanni on the Albano road (to be reached also from the Tavolato station, on the upper Albano railway) ; the other is the Vicolo del Mandrione, which leaves the Labicana one mile outside the Porta Maggiore and falls into the Tusculana at the place called Porta Furba.   A walk through the Vicolo del Mandrione will make the student more familiar with the aqueducts of ancient Rome, their structure and management, their respective size and importance, than many books written on the subject. He must remember that the higher of the two lines of arches carried the Claudia and the Anio Novus, the lower carried the Marcia, Tepula, and Julia.   The ugly channel of the Acqua Felice takes advantage of the remains of both ; the Alexandrina, Anio Vetus, and Appia run underground (see Fig. 23).

AQUA TRAIANA. — A rule was strictly followed under the Empire, that no one should be allowed to build and open thermæ for public use unless a special supply of water was secured at the same

Fig. 23. — The Seven Aqueducts at the Porta Maggiore.

time. The Aqua Virgo served for Agrippa's thermæ and Euripus, the Alsietina for the naumachia of Augustus; Titus repaired and increased the volume of the Marcia for the use of his baths, and so did Severus, Caracalla, and Diocletian. The construction of the Thermæ Alexandrinæ is contemporary with the canalization of the Aqua Alexandrina, etc. That of the Aqua Traiana seems to be also connected with the construction of the Thermæ Surianæ, which Trajan had built on the table-land of the Aventine in honor of his friend and supporter Licinius Sura. An inscription discovered in 1830 at la Conetta, on the Bracciano road (Corpus Inscriptionum, vi. 1260), and the medal (Cohen, Imper., ii. 49, n. 305) give the date of A. D. 109 for the completion of the aqueduct. Its sources were on the western shore of the Lago di Bracciano, along the chain of hills between Oriolo and Bassano. The various branches met at a central reservoir near Vicarello, where the true aqueduct begins. It was 57,000 metres long, and discharged 118,127 cubic metres per day.

The Aqua Paola of the present day is not at all so good as the Traiana, since Paul V., the restorer of the aqueduct, mixed up the good springs with the inferior water of the lake.

The last water brought into Imperial Rome is the AQUA ALEXANDRINA. Its springs, at the foot of Monte Falcone, on the Via Prænestina, were collected in 226 by Severus Alexander, for the use of his baths. The aqueduct, most minutely described by Fabretti (De Aquis, dissert. i.), was about 22 kilometres long, and increased the daily supply of the city by 21,632 cubic metres. Its most conspicuous remains are to be seen in the Valle di Acqua Bollicante (Via Labicana).

The Roman waters were not equally good. In the scale of perfection the Marcia and the Claudia occupy the first place, the Virgo comes next, followed by the Appia, Julia, Traiana, Anio Novus, Alexandrina, Tepula, Anio Vetus, and Alsietina.

The Traiana reached Rome at the considerable height of 71.16 metres above the sea, the Anio Novus at 70.40, the Claudia at 67.40, the Julia at 63.73, the Tepula at 60.63, the Marcia at 58.63, the Anio Vetus at 48, the Alexandrina at about 43, the Virgo at 20, the Appia at 20 (?), the Alsietina, "*omnium humilior*," at 16.50.

At the time of Constantine there were in Rome 11 great thermæ, 926 public baths, 1212 public fountains, 247 reservoirs, a "*stagnum Agrippæ*," without speaking of private houses, of public and private gardens, of docks and warehouses, each well provided with water.

Some of the fountains were of monumental character, and rich in works of art. Agrippa, while ædile, decorated those existing at the time with three hundred marble and bronze statues and four hundred columns. We know of one work of art only, — an "*effigies Hydræ*" which he placed on the Servilian fountain "*ad Serviliam lacum.*" The fountains of Prometheus, of the Shepherds, of Orpheus, of Ganymede, of the Four Fish (Scari), of the Three Masks, etc., must have been so named from the statues and marbles with which they were decorated.

One only of the great fountains has escaped destruction, that popularly called "I Trofei di Mario," in the Piazza Vittorio Emmanuele on the Esquiline. Its ancient name is not known for certain : Lenormant has suggested that of Nymphæum Alexandri ; I prefer that of Lacus Orphei. Its mediæval name was Cimbrum Marii, a recollection of the monument erected here in memory of the victory of the Campi Raudii ; while in the early Renaissance it was called "Le Oche Armate." The trophies which adorned it were removed to the Piazza del Campidoglio under Sixtus V.

Gio. Battista Piranesi, *Il Castello dell' Acqua Giulia;* and *Trofei di Ottaviano Augusto.* Rome: R. Calcografia. — François Lenormant, *Mémoire sur la véritable désignation du monument connu sous le nom de Trophées de Marius.* (Révue Numism., 1849.) — Rodolfo Lanciani, *I comentarii di Frontino,* p. 173.

Supposing the inhabitants of Rome to have numbered, suburbs included, one million, there was a daily water supply of 1800 litres per head. In modern Rome, for a population of half a million, there are about 760 litres per head.

The volume of water which supplied Rome may be estimated by comparison with the Tiber, which discharges only 1,296,000 cubic metres per day, while the old aqueducts carried not less than 1,747,311 cubic metres.

LITERATURE. — Raphael Fabretti, *De aquis et aquæductibus veteris Romæ,* 2d-ed. Rome, 1788. — Alberto Cassio, *Corso delle acque antiche.* Rome, 1757-59. — Carlo Fea, *Storia delle acque di Roma.* — John Henry Parker, *The Aqueducts of Ancient Rome.* Oxford, London, 1876. — Alessandro Bettochi, *Le acque e gli acquedotti di Roma antica e moderna.* (Monografia della città di Roma, vol. ii. ch. xix. 1881.) — Rodolfo Lanciani, *I comentarii di Frontino intorno le acque e gli acquedotti.* Rome, Salviucci, 1880.

An interesting collection of objects connected with the supply and distribution of water in ancient Rome is exhibited in Hall No. VI. of the Museo Municipale al Celio.

The following table concerning the Roman aqueducts may be useful to the student : —

SUPPLY OF WATER IN ANCIENT ROME.

Name.	Date.	Author.	Length of Course. Metres.	Volume per day in Cubic Metres.	Altitude of Springs above Sea-level.	Level in Rome.
Appia	312 B.C.	Appius Claudius Cæcus, censor	16,444.60	115,303.50	30.00 cᵃ	20 (?)
Anio Vetus	272–269	Manius Curius Dentatus } censors Fulvius Flaccus	63,704.50	277,865.60	280.00	48.00
Marcia	144–140	Q. Marcius Rex, prætor	91,424.10	296,314.20	318.00	58.63
Tepula	125	Cn. Servilius Cæpio } censors L. Cassius Longinus	17,745.40	28,115.10	151.00	60.63
Julia	33	M. Vipsanius Agrippa, ædile	22,853.60	76,195.10	350.00	63.73
Virgo	19	M. Vipsanius Agrippa	20,696.60	158,202.70	24.00	20.00
Alsietina	?	Cæsar Augustus	32,847.80	24,766.60	209.00	16.50
Claudia	38–52 A.D.	Caligula, Claudius	68,750.50	209,252.20	320.00	67.40
Anio Novus	38–52	Caligula, Claudius	86,964.00	299,346.80	400.00 cᵃ	70.40
Traiana	109	Trajan	57,700.00	118,126.80	300.00 cᵃ	71.16
Alexandrina	226	Severus Alexander	22,000.00	21,632.80 (?)	65.00	43.00
Marcia Severiana	196	Septimius Severus	?	26,440.80 (?)	...	?
Marcia Antoniniana	212–213	Caracalla	6,000.00	95,749.30 (?)	...	40.00
Marcia Jovia	305–306	Diocletian	1,500.00	?	...	...
		Total	Kl. 508,631.10	1,747,311.50 c.m.		

SUPPLY OF WATER IN MODERN ROME.

Name.	Date.	Author.	Length of Course. Metres.	Volume per day in Cubic Metres.	Altitude of Springs above Sea-level.	Level in Rome.
Vergine	1570, Aug. 16	Pius V.	20,546.00	155,271.20	24.00	17.00
Felice	1587, June 15	Sixtus V., Felice Peretti	32,592.60	21,632.80	65.00	59.00
Paola	1611	Paul V.	51,851.90	80,870.40	200–160	67.00
Marcia-pia	1870, Sept. 18	Società dell' acqua Marcia-pia	53,649.00	121,305.60	318.00	70–148
		Total	Kl. 158,639.50	379,080.00 c.m.		

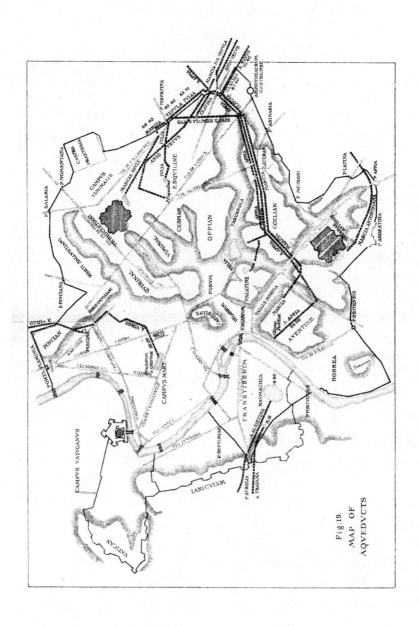

Fig. 19.
MAP OF
AQVEDVCTS

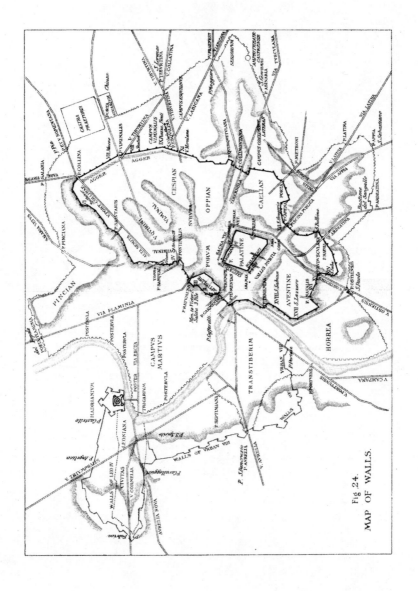

Fig 24.

MAP OF WALLS.

XV. Muri Urbis (the Walls). — Rome has been fortified seven times, with seven lines of walls : by the first King, by Servius Tullius, by Aurelian, by Honorius, by Leo IV., by Urban VIII., and by the Italian government.

The literature on this point of Roman history and topography is very copious. The works in which the subject is treated from a general point of view are —

Antonio Nibby, *Le mura di Roma, disegnate da Sir W. Gell.* 1820. — Stefano Piale, Six Memoirs, reprinted from the *Atti della pont. Accademia rom. d'Archeologia.* 1820-35. — Adolf Becker, *De Romæ veteris muris atque portis.* Leipsic, 1842. — Rodolfo Lanciani, *Le mura e le porte di Servio* (in Annal. Inst., 1871, p. 40) ; and *Bull. arch. com.*, 1876, pp. 24, 121 (1888, p. 12). — Heinrich Jordan, *Topographie*, vol. i. p. 200, Beschreibung der servianischen Mauer ; p. 340, die aurelianische Mauer. — Cesare Quarenghi, *Le mura di Roma.* Rome, 1882.

XVI. Murus Romuli (Walls of the Palatine). It is probable that the Alban colonists of the "hill of Pales," protected by marshes and cliffs, contented themselves with raising a palisade and cutting a ditch at the only weak point of their natural fortress, viz. across the neck of the Velia. After coming in contact with their more advanced neighbors, like the inhabitants of the *turrigeræ Antemnæ*, they thought it more expedient to follow their example, and wall in and fortify their village, which was at the same time the fold of their cattle.

The text most frequently quoted in reference to the Murus Romuli is that of Tacitus (Ann., xii. 24), according to which the furrow ploughed by the hero — the *sulcus primigenius* — started from a point in the Forum Boarium, marked in later times by the bronze Bull of Myron ; and followed the valley between the Palatine and the Aventine as far as the altar of Consus, the valley between the Palatine and the Cælian as far as the Curiæ Veteres, the east slope of the hill as far as the Sacellum Larum. The same historian says that the Ara Maxima of Hercules was included within the furrow, and Dionysius states that Vesta's temple was outside it. The furrow followed the foot of the cliffs or slopes of the Palatine, its course being marked with stone cippi. Others affirm that the city of Romulus was *square* (τετράγωνος — Roma Quadrata). The truth is that neither the walls nor the pomerium of Romulus can be said to make a square ; that a line drawn from beyond the Ara Maxima to the Ara Consi cannot be said to go "along the foot of the cliffs of the Palatine" (*per ima montis Palatini*) ; that the valley in those days was covered with water, deep enough to be navigated by canoes, so that neither a furrow could be ploughed through it, nor stone *cippi* set up to mark the line of the furrow. Moreover, the same marshes extended on the southeast side as far as the Curiæ Veteres, on the northwest as far as the Temple of Vesta; and the shape of the Palatine walls was rather trapezoid, like that of a *terramara* of the valley of the Po, than square like an Etruscan *templum;* while, lastly, the name of Roma Quadrata did not belong to the city on the hill, but to the altar described in " Pagan and Christian Rome," p. 70, which stood in front of the Temple of Apollo.

There is manifestly a chronological error in speaking of places and things, not as they were in the earliest days of Rome, but as they appeared after the draining of the marshes. A confusion is also to be observed in ancient and modern writers with regard to the line of the walls and the line of the *pomerium* marked by stone *cippi.* The two are almost independent, and wide apart. The existing remains of the walls, at the west corner of the hill, are 220 metres distant from the site of the Ara Maxima, which was itself within the *pomerium.* The walls of Romulus have been discovered in six places, marked A, B, C, D, E, F in the annexed map. They will be described in Book II. § viii.

XVII. OTHER WALLS OF THE KINGLY PERIOD. — Although we find in classic texts mention of what may have been fortifications, independent of those on the Palatine, — like the Murus Terreus Carinarum, the Capitolium Vetus, and the arx or citadel on the Araceli summit of the Capitoline hill, — yet there is but one existing relic which can possibly be considered as such: a fragment of a wall in a garden, Via dell' Arco di Settimio, No. 1. It is identical in material and style of masonry with the walls of the Palatine.

LITERATURE. — Stefano Piale, *Del secondo recinto di Roma fatto da Numa, e delle aggiunte degli altri re.* Rome, 1833. — Rodolfo Lanciani, *Annali Instituto,* 1871, p. 42. — Arthur Schneider, *Aus Roms Fruhezeit.* (Mittheil., 1895, p. 160.)

XVIII. THE WALLS OF SERVIUS TULLIUS. — In the eulogy of Bartolomeo Borghesi the late Comm. de Rossi remarks justly that we know more on some points of Roman history, institutions, religion, etc., than the ancients did. The same thing may be repeated as regards some points of Roman topography. Dionysius, for instance, says that the walls of Servius Tullius had become δυσεύρετοι [1] in the Augustan age, on account of the structures of

1 Difficult to trace.

every description, public and private, which had been built against, across, and above them. Owing to discoveries made since 1860 we can trace the line of the Servian walls and of the agger,

describe its structure, and locate its gates more exactly than Dionysius could have done.

SECTION OF WALLS

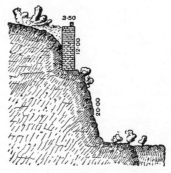

Fig. 25.

The walls run against the face of the cliffs (of the Capitoline, Quirinal, Oppian, Cælian, and Aventine) at two thirds of their height above the plain, and cross the intervening valleys at their narrowest point.

They are built of blocks of tufa, exactly 2 feet high (0.59 metre), placed alternately lengthwise and crosswise, the tufa being of an inferior quality and yellowish gray in color. The thickness of the wall varies from 2 to $3\frac{1}{2}$ metres; the maximum height yet discovered is 12.98 metres (Vigna Torlonia, Aventine, Fig. 29). The blocks are not cemented, at least not in the original structure. I have only once found traces of lime, in a joint of one of the buttresses (corner of Via Volturno and Gaeta); but, as a rule, the use of cohesive substances seems to have been unknown to or despised by the engineers of Servius. The blocks which form the face of the wall are well squared, and fit into each other so that the joints are rendered almost invisible, but they are irregularly cut inside. On the Aventine, however, and especially in the space between the church of S. Saba and that of Il Priorato di Malta, the walls, instead of resting against the live rock of the cliffs or the earth of the slopes, have an inside lining of concrete, the thickness of which equals or exceeds that of the *opus quadratum* itself. This part of the fortifications is not original, but seems to have been rebuilt or strengthened by Camillus.

Across the valleys or tablelands the system of defense varies altogether. There is a ditch, and an embankment made with the earth excavated from the ditch. The embankment is supported on the outer side by a strong wall, fortified with buttresses, while on the inner side it slopes down at an incline of 35° or 40°. Sometimes there is a second supporting wall on the inner side, weaker and much lower than the outer one. Two roads run parallel with the fortification, one at the foot of the inner wall, one on the outer edge of the ditch. This system of defense was called an *agger.*

Topographical books state that in the circuit of the Servian city there was but one agger, between the Colline and the Esquiline gates; but recent discoveries prove that all weak points of the circuit were fortified in that way. We have found the agger in the higher part of the Esquiline, near the Palazzo Field, Via Merulana; on the Smaller Aventine, near S. Saba; and on the Quirinal, by the Piazza di Magnanapoli, etc. Yet there is no denying that the one between the Colline and Esquiline gates, for strength, size, elevation, and length, is the agger *par excellence*, from which a street (*subager*) and a promenade (*nunc licet aggere in aprico spatiari*) were named in classic times, and a whole district (Mons Superagius) in the Middle Ages.

I shall point out to the reader now which of the remains of this

SECTION OF AGGER

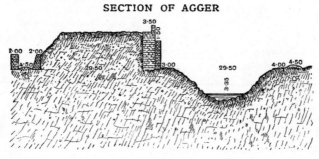

Fig. 26.

venerable fortification deserve a visit, and which are the sites of its historical gates. (See map of Walls.) First, as to the river-front, Livy (ii. 10) and Dionysius (v. 23) distinctly assert that the bank was unprotected, because the river itself, with its wide bed and swift current, was considered to afford a sufficient protection. Yet there is no portion of the whole circuit of the Servian city at which the fortifications are more evident or better preserved than at the river-front. I made designs of every fragment of them before the construction of the modern quays, and I do not think there is a break of 50 metres between the two extreme points (marked approximately by the Pons Fabricius and the Pons Sublicius). The construction is the same everywhere : a foundation-wall about 2 metres high above low-water mark, forming a step or a landing 3 metres wide, and a wall 6 metres high supporting the bank. I have found traces of cement in the upper layers of stones, as well as traces of an inner lining of concrete. Both may pertain to later restorations.

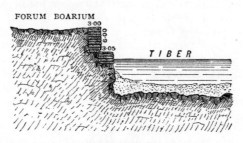

Fig. 27.

The walls left the river halfway between the churches of S. Maria Egiziaca and S. Nicola in Carcere, and reached the rocks of the Capitol at the Via della Bufola. Three gates opened in this short tract : the Flumentana by the river (Via della Fiumara, destroyed 1882), the Triumphalis (Via della Bocca della Verità), and the Carmentalis (Via della Bufola). Consult —

Adolf Becker, *De muris*, p. 81. — Emil Braun, *Monument. Inst.*, 1854, p. 78, tav. x. — Alessandro Donati, *De urbe Roma*, p. 79.

The Capitoline was strongly fortified on the side facing the Campus Martius. Remains of the wall can be seen on the edge of the rock which supports the Caffarelli palace (I) ; on the ascent to the Piazza del Campidoglio, called " La salita delle tre Pile " (II) ; and in the substructures of the monument to Victor Emmanuel (III). They intersected the Via di Marforio between Nos. 81[C] and 81[D], where the Porta Ratumena must be located. The direction of the Via Flaminia, which issued from this gate, is marked by the tomb of C. Poplicius Bibulus on one side, and the so-called tomb of the Claudii on the other.

From the Porta Ratumena to the Porta Fontinalis, under the Palazzo Antonelli, Piazza Magnanapoli, the walls must have been destroyed by Trajan when he cut away the spur of the Quirinal to make room for his forum. The Porta Fontinalis is the only one left standing in the whole circuit (IV). Other remains are to be seen in the beautiful Villa Colonna (V), upon which rest those of the Temple of the Sun; others under the Villa Spithoever, Via delle Finanze (VI). Two gates opened in this tract: the Sanqualis, the approximate site of which is shown by the tomb of the Sempronii, discovered in 1866 near the top of the Salita della Dataria; and the Porta Salutaris, under the Palazzo Crawshay, Via delle Quattro Fontane. The agger began at the junction of the Via di Porta Salaria with the Via venti Settembre, crossed the Treasury buildings, the Via Volturno, the railway station, the Piazza Fanti, the Via Carlo Alberto, and ended near the conservatory of the gardens of Mæcenas in the Via Merulana. It was almost intact before the construction of the new quarters and of the railway station; now there are scanty remains to be seen (VII) in the Piazza del Maccao; in the goods station, Via di Porta S. Lorenzo (VIII); in the gardens of the Acquario Romano (IX); and in the Via Carlo Alberto (X). The Porta Collina, discovered in 1873 at the junction of the Via Goito and the Via venti Settembre, was destroyed for the erection of the northeast pavilion of the Treasury buildings. (See map in "Ancient Rome," p. 145.) Traces of the Porta Viminalis are visible in the goods station, while the Porta Esquilina is represented by the arch of Gallienus, Via di S. Vito.

The annexed cut (Fig. 28) represents an excavation made in 1877 at the foot of the agger to determine the breadth and depth of the great ditch. It seems that when the agger itself was transformed into a public walk, the ditch was filled up, and turned into building lots. Traces of a private house can be seen at the bottom of the trench.

Beyond the last fragment visible in the Via Merulana (XI) we lose sight of the fortifications, although their course and the site of the gates Querquetulana, Cælimontana, and a third near the Piazza della Navicella, can be distinctly traced from discoveries made in times gone by.

The famous Porta Capena, which marks the beginning of the Appian Way, seems to have been discovered twice: by Orazio Orlandi in the latter part of last century; and by Mr. J. H. Parker in 1867, in the slope of the Cælian, behind the apse of S. Gregorio. Parker gives a view of his excavation in Plate xviii. of the "Aqueducts of Ancient Rome" (London, Murray, 1876). The site of the gate can be determined to-day by means of a remarkable fragment of the walls (XII) visible in the wine-cellar of the Osteria della Porta Capena, in the gardens of S. Gregorio, Via di Porta S. Sebastiano, No. 1.

On the other side of the valley the walls appear again, in front and under the old abbey of S. Balbina, now a house of refuge for

Fig. 28. — The Ditch of the Agger of Servius.

women (XIII); at a corner of the Via di S. Saba and the Via di Porta S. Paolo (XIV); on the Via di Porta S. Paolo itself, where the road bifurcates, one arm descending towards the gate, the other towards the Monte Testaccio (XV). This is the finest ruin of all, because it shows the restorations of the time of Camillus resting on the original structure of Servius. Fig. 29 represents the present state of the ruin, but more than half of it is concealed by the accumulation of modern soil. I had the good fortune to see it completely exposed to view in 1868, when I made the drawing a facsimile of which is here given.

There is another fragment to be seen in the adjoining Vigna Maccarani-Torlonia (XVI), some stones of which were removed by Padre Secchi, the astronomer, to the Observatory of the Collegio Romano, to serve as a pedestal for the great Merz equatorial. The walls appear again against the cliff of the Aventine, at the Arco di S. Lazzaro, Via di Marmórata (XVII); and lastly, under the convent of S. Sabina, where they were laid bare in 1856 (XVIII). There is absolutely no trace of Servian fortifications on the opposite or Transtiberine side of the river.

Four gates opened in the walls between the Porta Capena and the Tiber: the Nævia, on the Via Aventina, from which issued the Via Ardeatina; the Rudusculana, on the Via di Porta S. Paolo, from which issued the Via Ostiensis; the Navalis, on the Via di S. Maria Aventinese; and the Trigemina, on the Via di Marmorata.

Many stones built into the original wall of Servius are marked with signs or letters, which have given rise to much speculation. Consult —

Luigi Bruzza, *Sopra i segni incisi nei massi delle mura, etc.* (Annali Inst., 1876, pls. i, k.) — Heinrich Jordan, *Topographie*, vol. i. p. 250, pls. 1, 2. — Otto Richter, *Ueber antike Steinmetzzeichen*, 1885.

LITERATURE. — Adolf Becker, *De Romæ veteris muris atque portis*, p. 81; and *Topographie*, p. 92. — Thomas Dyer, *History of the City of Rome*, p. 47. — R. Bergau, *Die Befestigung Roms durch Tarquinius Priscus und Servius Tullius.* Göttingen, 1867. — Rodolfo Lanciani, *Sulle mura e porte di Servio* (in Ann. Inst., 1871, p. 40) ; and *Bull. arch. com.*, 1876, pp. 24, 121. — Heinrich Jordan, *Topographie*, vol. i. p. 200. — Otto Richter, *Die Befestigung des Ianiculum.*

XIX. WALLS OF AURELIAN AND PROBUS, A. D. 272. — We have no account of the construction of the walls of Aurelian. We only know, in a general way, that the Emperor was compelled to fortify the capital by the barbarian invasion of A. D. 271, in the course of which the enemy had reached the banks of the Metaurus ; that, during the respite between the Marcomannic and the Pal-

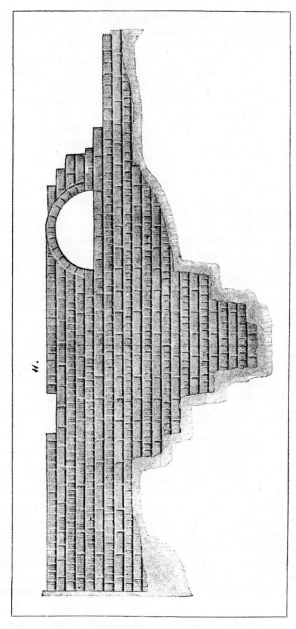

Fig. 29. — Walls of Servius on the Aventine.

myrene campaigns, he inclosed the city *muris quam validissimis,* and that the great undertaking, begun in 272, was finished by Probus about seven years later.

The circuit of the walls, which I have measured inch by inch for the construction of the " Forma Urbis," measures 18,837 metres. The strip of land occupied by these fortifications is 19 metres wide : five of which are taken by the inner " *chemin de ronde,*" four by the walls themselves, ten by the outside road ; 358,000 square metres were consequently expropriated by Aurelian ; and, as the land was thickly covered with villas, houses, gardens, and tombs, the cost of purchase must have been considerable. At 20 lire the square metre it would reach 7,000,000 lire.

The walls consist of a solid foundation of concrete from 3.50 to 4 metres thick, faced with triangular bricks ; of a covered way with loopholes on the outside, and a gallery or arcade in the inner side ; and a terrace or balcony above, lined with battlements (Fig. 30). There are towers at an interval of 100 Roman feet (29.70 metres), projecting from four to five metres. Each tower contains a staircase giving access to the lower corridor and to the terrace above. According to the survey made by Ammon, after the restoration of the walls by Arcadius and Honorius in 403, there were 381 towers in all, exclusive of those of the mausoleum of Hadrian (Hadrianium), which had been converted into a *tête du pont,* to prevent the approach of the enemy from the Via Triumphalis and the Prata Neronis. Of these 381 towers only one has come down to us in a perfect state — the sixth to the left of the Porta Salaria. We can judge from its elegance and good construction that the builders of the walls had tried to disfigure the monumental city as little as possible ; we can judge also how much damage the walls must have suffered in the course of centuries, to be reduced to their present state of decay !

These noble walls, which have so often saved the city from pillage and destruction, on the face of which our history is written almost year by year, and so carefully preserved even in the darkest period of the Middle Ages, are now doomed to disappear. State and city have with equal promptness declined to undergo the expense of keeping them in repair. A section of them, 70 metres long, between the Porta S. Giovanni and S. Croce in Gerusalemme, fell in 1893. The only measure taken was a warning given to passers-by that another portion would soon share the same fate.

The volume of masonry employed in the construction of the walls is estimated at 1,033,000 cubic metres. The cost at the present day would have exceeded 26,000,000 lire, but we cannot make any calculation for Aurelian's time, because we do not know what

Fig. 30. — The Covered Way of the Walls of Aurelian, Vigna Casali.

were the price of labor and the cost of building-materials in his day. As a rule the walls are built with the spoils of the edifices which stood on their line and were demolished to clear the space; only the surface and the arches are coated with bricks made for the occasion. Two recent discoveries illustrate this point; they also bear evidence to the hurry with which the work was done, and therefore to the greatness of the peril from which Rome had escaped.[1]

A piece of the walls was cut away in November, 1884, between the third and the fourth tower on the right of the Porta S. Lorenzo, for the opening of the new Viale del Camposanto. An older construction had been embedded there in the thickness of the masonry, viz., a garden wall incrusted with shells, enamel, and pumice-stones, with niches worked in a rough kind of mosaic, and crowned by a cornice covered with sheets of lead. When Aurelian's engineers met with this obstacle, they did not lose time in demolishing it, but embedded it in their own masonry. So far, this is not remarkable; but what remains inexplicable is that the statues were not removed from their niches.

We have found them one by one in their original places, and they are not the work of an ordinary chisel, but delicate pieces of Græco-Roman sculpture, so much so that Professor Petersen has not disdained to give illustrations of them in the "Bull. arch. com.," vol. xvii., a. 1889, p. 17, tav. 1, 2. The statues and the whole front of the garden wall were not damaged by the new construction because the engineers had taken care to protect them with a coating of clay. Traces of this nymphæum are still to be seen on the left of the new Barriera di S. Lorenzo. The second discovery was made in February, 1892, on the line of the Via Montebello, between the garden of the English Embassy and the Prætorian Camp. Here a private house of the first century stood on the line of the walls. One would have expected the house to be leveled to the ground, and the walls raised on the space left free by the demolition; but the engineers, in their haste, satisfied themselves with filling up the space between the sides of each room, leaving intact mosaic pavements, marble stairs, lintels, thresholds, and frescoes. This done, as soon as their own masonry was sufficiently hardened, they

---

[1] The victory of Aurelian on the banks of the Metaurus must have been so decisive that the whole Empire rejoiced at it. It is recorded even in the formulæ of contemporary gaming-tables (*tabulæ lusoriæ*). One of these, discovered in 1892 in the catacombs of Priscilla, contains the words, "hostes · victos · Italia · gaudet · ludite · Romani;" another, discovered almost at the same time, in the cemetery of S. Eucharius at Trèves, says, "virtus · imperi · hostes · vincti · ludant · Romani."

shaved off, as it were, whatever projected on either side, and went on with their work.

We come now to an important, and altogether new, point of research. For what cause, and from what military, technical, or financial reasons, was this special course of the walls selected? and why were some important districts of the city left out, others included which contained nothing but tombs? The answer is easily given. The course selected was that of the octroi, which followed closely that of the pomerium, or in other words, the line of separation between the city proper (*continentia ædificia*) and the suburbs (*expatiantia tecta*). Much has been written about the octroi line by —

Theodor Mommsen, *Berichte d. sächs. Gesellsch.*, 1850, p. 309. — Gio. Battista de Rossi, *Archaeol. Anzeiger*, 1856, p. 147 ; and *Piante di Roma*, ch. vii. p. 46. — *Corpus Inscr.*, vol. vi. n. 1016, *a, b, c.* — *Ephemeris Epigr.*, vol. iv. p. 276. — Rodolfo Lanciani, *Bull. arch. com.*, vol. xx., 1892, p. 93.

It was marked by stone cippi, five of which have been described by epigraphists. The first was found, at the time of Andrea Fulvio, on the landing-place of the Tiber, under the Aventine. It bore this inscription : —

QVICQVID VSVARIVM INVEHITVR ANSARIVM NON DEBET,

which proves that duties were levied also on some kind of merchandise and provisions which came by water. The other four belong to the reorganization of the octroi made by M. Aurelius and Commodus about the year A. D. 175, and they are all inscribed with the same regulations : " These terminal stones have been set up, in consequence of the quarrels which often arise between the importers and the tax-receivers, to show which is the exact line of the octroi according to the ancient custom."

The place of discovery of the first stone is uncertain ; the second was found near the Porta Salaria ; the third near the Porta Flaminia ; the fourth near the Porta Asinaria. They stood, therefore, on the very line followed a century later by Aurelian's walls. Now it is evident that whoever establishes a financial barrier round an open city must try to take advantage of every existing natural or artificial obstacle to prevent smuggling and fraud. Another obvious precaution is to reduce to a minimum the number of openings, so as to save the expense of a large staff of officers. Between two openings, viz., between two toll-houses, they must have raised palisades, stone walls, hedges, or excavated ditches, unless the obstacles offered by the undulations of the ground or by public edifices afforded sufficient protection against smuggling. This was exactly the case with Rome, where one sixth of the whole octroi line had been found ready-made by the substructure of the Horti Aciliani on the Pincian (550 metres) ; by the inclosure wall of the Horti Sallustiani (1200 metres), and of the Prætorian Camp (1050 metres) ; by the arcades of the Marcian (800 metres) and of the Claudian aqueducts (475 metres) ; and lastly, by the Amphitheatrum Castrense (100 metres). The octroi line, therefore, of the time of M. Aurelius and Commodus comprised an inclosure built on the principles of financial strategy, with first-class gates and custom-houses on the main roads and river landings, and with posterns and small pickets on the smaller lanes and landings of ferry-boats. From such financial fortifications to the walls of Aurelian the step is very short. Aurelian simply changed into a strong bulwark the octroi inclosure, respecting its gates, posterns, and ferries.

REFERENCES. — Adolf Becker, *De muris atque portis.* Leipsic, 1842. — Antonio Nibby and William Gell, *Le mura di Roma,* 1820. — Eugene Müntz, *Les arts à la cour des Papes,* passim. — G. Battista de Rossi, *Bull. arch. crist.,* serie v., anno ii., 1891, p. 35. — Rodolfo Lanciani, *Le mura di Aureliano e di Probo:* Bull. arch. com., xx. p. 87.

The late John Henry Parker prepared illustrations of the walls of Aurelian by numerous drawings and photographs, the first by Cicconetti, the second by Lucchetti. The collection of drawings belongs now to the Commissione Arch. comunale di Roma ; the negatives of the photographic collection were destroyed by fire in July, 1893.

XX. RESTORATION OF THE WALLS BY HONORIUS. — The restoration of the walls by Arcadius and Honorius was commenced, according to Claudianus, " audito rumore Getarum," from the fear of an advance of the Goths under Alaric, and was completed in January, 402, under the direction of Stilicho. The great undertaking was celebrated by several inscriptions engraved above the gates, of which three only have survived destruction : those of the portæ Tiburtina, Prænestina, and Portuensis. (See Corpus Inscriptionum, vol. vi. n. 1188–90.)

These inscriptions speak of " instauratos urbi æternæ muros portas ac turres, egestis immensis ruderibus," Macrobius Longinianus being the prefect of the city. The catastrophe, however, was not avoided, but deferred. Alaric crossed the Alps from Illyria towards the end of 402, and showed himself before the walls of Milan, while Honorius was intrenching himself at Ravenna. Stilicho, by a miracle of energy and bravery, collected an army, reached the Goths at Pollenzo, and defeated them in the spring of

403. The victory was celebrated by Honorius in the following year, with the last triumph witnessed in Rome, the last spark of a noble light about to vanish forever. The pageant marched along the walls just restored, and ended at the triumphal arch raised to the glory of the Emperor and his associates —

QVOD GETARVM NATIONEM IN OMNE AEVVM DOCVERE EXTINGVI.[1]

Six years later, on August 24, 410, Alaric and the Getarum Natio entered Rome by the Porta Salaria !

Without entering into particulars concerning this restoration of the walls and gates, I shall only dwell a moment on the tale it tells about the fate of Rome at the beginning of the fifth century. Stilicho and Honorius found the walls almost buried under a mass of rubbish and refuse (*immensa rudera*) ; and as they had neither time nor means to clear the rubbish away they leveled it on the spot, and raised at once the level of that strip of city land from nine to thirteen feet. The thresholds of the portæ Flaminia, Tiburtina, Prænestina, Ostiensis of Honorius are as much as this above those of the time of Aurelian. And what destructions were accomplished for the sake of providing materials ! It is enough to quote the instance of the Porta Appia, the bastions of which were rebuilt of solid marble, from the celebrated Temple of Mars which stood outside the gate.

XXI. GATES OF AURELIAN AND HONORIUS. — The gates of the city of Rome have seen more historical events during the 1624 years of their existence than any other monuments of the ancient world. Considering that even the volume of Gell and Nibby is far from being exhaustive on this point of historical topography, I could hardly enter into the subject myself. The student will find detailed information in the works mentioned below.

Starting from the left bank of the Tiber, above the Ponte Margherita, we must mention, first, the corner tower of great strength, which was considered by the Romans to be haunted by the ghost of Nero : *ubi umbra Neronis diu mansitavit.* Later it was called Lo Trullo.

C. Ludovico Visconti, *Bull. arch. com.*, 1877, p. 195. — Rodolfo Lanciani, *Forma Urbis*, pl. 1. — Constantino Corvisieri, *Archivio Società storia patria*, vol. i. p. 92, n. 1.

Between the river and the Porta Flaminia (del Popolo) there

[1] See *Corpus Inscriptionum*, vol. vi. n. 1196. The inscription of the arch refers also to the victory gained by Stilicho over Radagaïsus in 405.

was a beautiful tomb, upon which the third tower left of the gate is planted.

Ludwig Urlichs, *Codex topogr.*, p. 243. — *Bull. arch. com.*, 1891, p. 140.

The Porta Flaminia of Honorius, flanked by two round towers, was discovered in 1877 during the demolition of the two square bastions of Sixtus IV.

C. Ludovico Visconti, *Bull. arch. com.*, 1877, p. 209. — Constantino Corvisieri, *Archivio Società storia patria*, vol. i. p. 79, n. 1. — Pasquale Adinolfi, *Roma nell' età di mezzo*, vol. i. p. 81. — Giuseppe Tommasetti, *Archivio Società storia patria*, vol. vi. p. 173.

Behind the apse of S. Maria del Popolo the walls reach the northeast corner of the Pincian hill, the substructures of which, built by the Acilii Glabriones, were so gigantic in size and height that no extra works of defense were added to them by Aurelian. At the opposite or northeast corner of the hill we find the " muro torto," a piece of the substructure which is inclined outwards at an angle of six or seven degrees. Procopius (Goth., i. 23) describes it exactly as we see it now. In the Middle Ages women of ill fame were buried at the foot of the inclined wall, and in more modern times men and women who died impenitent.

The Porta Pinciana, originally a modest postern, was transformed into its present shape by Belisarius. It opens on the Via Salaria vetus, which took the name of Pincia or Pinciana at the end of the fourth century. This gate will always get a share of the interest we feel for the gallant defender of Rome in 537. The Goths of Vitiges were encamped on the Monti Parioli, watching the Porta Pinciana; and on the site of the Villa Albani, watching the Porta Salaria. The best feat of the siege was the sally made by Belisarius, in the course of which the barbarians were driven back as far as the Anio. The Byzantine leader rode a white charger named Φάλιον by Procopius, and *Balan* by the Goths; but in spite of prodigies of valor, his men began to waver, and he was obliged to retreat. The garrison of the Porta Pinciana, not recognizing the leader, covered as he was with dust and blood, obliged the retreating party to face the enemy again and drive them away from the walls. Belisarius at last entered the gate amidst frantic cheering, and his name was given to the gate itself (Porta Belisaria) in memory of the eventful day.

From the Pinciana to the Salaria the walls of Aurelian are in splendid preservation. A tower, the sixth before reaching the Salaria, is the only perfect one in the whole circuit. The Porta

Salaria of Honorius, injured by the bombardment of September 20, 1870, was rebuilt in the present form by Vespignani. The discoveries made on this occasion are described by —

C. Ludovico Visconti, *Il fanciullo Q. Sulpicio Massimo.* Rome, 1871. — Wilhelm Henzen, *Sepolcri antichi rinvenuti alla porta Salaria* (in Bull. Inst., 1871, p. 98.) — Giovanni Ciofi, *Inscript. . . . Q. Sulpicii Maximi.* Rome, 1871. — J. H. Parker, *Tombs in and near Rome,* Oxford, 1877, pl. 10. — Rodolfo Lanciani, *Pagan and Christian Rome,* p. 280.

The Porta Pia, a work of 1561, by Matteo da Castello, stands 75 metres to the left of the ancient gate of the time of Honorius. It was first called Nomentana, and later on, Porta S. Agnetis and Porta della Donna. Its two round towers are built, as usual, over classic tombs. The one on the right was excavated in 1827 by Zamboni. It belonged to Quintus Haterius, called by Tacitus " *senex fœdissimœ adulationis.*"

After passing two posterns in the portion of the walls which surround the garden of the English Embassy, we meet with the Prætorian camp, described in Book IV.; and, on the other side of it, with the Porta Chiusa, which gave access to the Vivarium or imperial menagerie, where wild beasts were kept in readiness for the games of the amphitheatre. The walls on this part of the city have been largely restored with blocks of stone, from the inclosure wall of the Vivarium.

The Porta S. Lorenzo, spanning the Via Tiburtina, was one of the most remarkable before 1869, when Pius IX. caused it to be demolished, to make use of the stones of which it was built for the foundations of the Colonna del Concilio on the Janiculum. The gate was double: the outside arch, dating from the time of Augustus, carried the Marcia, Tepula, and Julia over the road; the inside formed part of the fortifications. Fig. 31 (following page), from a photograph taken in 1868, shows the rise in the level of the city from the time of Augustus to that of Honorius, as the threshold of the gate of the fourth century is on the same level with the spring of the arch of Augustus.

Between the Porta Tiburtina (S. Lorenzo) and the Prænestina (Maggiore) the walls follow the line of the arcades of the Marcia, Tepula, and Julia, beautiful remains of which can be seen in the inner side, near the new barriera.

The Porta Prænestina, a magnificent work of Claudius in the so-called rustic style, served originally for the transit of the Claudia and Anio Novus over the roads leading to Præneste and Labicum. Honorius walled up one of the archways, and fortified the other with towers resting on tombs.   The towers and the gate were destroyed in 1838, when the *panarium* of the baker M. Vergilius Eurysaces and of his wife Atistia were laid bare.

Fig. 31. — The Porta S. Lorenzo.

Luigi Canina, *Sul luogo denominato la Speranza vecchia.*   Rome, 1839. —*Bull. Inst.*, 1838, p. 144. — *Ann. Inst.*, 1838, p. 221. —*Corpus Inscr.*, vol. i. pp. 222, 223 ; vol. vi. n. 1958.

The next piece of the wall, from the Porta Maggiore to S. Croce in Gerusalemme, must be visited from the garden annexed to this church. It appears like a combination of aqueducts and fortifications, of classic, mediæval, and modern structures, ivy-clad and exceedingly picturesque. The entrance is from the first gate on the left of the church.

After passing the Amphitheatrum Castrense, described in Book IV. § xv., the great breach produced by the collapse of the walls in 1893, and the Porta S. Giovanni, built by Gregory XIII. in 1575, we reach the Porta Asinaria, which, although sunk deep in the ground, is one of the best preserved of Roman gates. Through it Belisarius entered on December 9, 536, while the Gothic garrison was escaping by the Porta Flaminia. We can follow the progress of one and the retreat of the other army, and the vicissitudes of the war, by the way contemporary inscriptions are dated. In the lands belonging to or reconquered by the Byzantines the epitaphs of 536 are dated "post consulatum Belisarii;" in those occupied by the Goths, "iterum post consulatum Paulini iunioris." There was, however, in Rome an obscure man whose faith in the liberation of the city from the barbaric rule, at the hand of Belisarius, was never shaken. His tombstone, now in the "Sacre Grotte Vaticane," says that John, the book-keeper of the tavern of Isidorus, had died on May 23, 536, CONSVLATV VILISARI VIRI CLARISSIMI. It was engraved six months before the retreat of the Goths. Ten years later the same gate was thrown open to Totila by the treachery of a body of Isaurians.

There is a postern under the Lateran palace, and farther on, where the Marrana of Calixtus II. enters the city, a gate now closed, the classic name of which seems to be Porta Metroni. An inscription inside it mentions the restoration of this stretch of the walls made in 1157 by the S. P. Q. R., R(egnante) D(omino) N(ostro Friderico) S(emper) A(ugusto). The erasure of the name of Barbarossa must have taken place in 1167, when the city was besieged by the allied forces of the Tusculans and of the Empire.

The next gate, the Latina, is beautifully preserved, but closed like the Porta Metroni. There is the Christian monogram above the arch between the mystic letters A and Ω.

Antonio Nibby, *Roma antica*, vol. i. p. 148. — Giuseppe Tommasetti, *La via Latina*, p. 6. Rome, 1886.

The Porta S. Sebastiano, the Appia of Aurelian and Honorius,

was rebuilt by the latter with the spoils of the Temple of Mars
"*extra muros*." I am sure that if the blocks of marble could be
examined from the inside of the two bastions, they would all be
found sculptured or engraved like those of the Porta del Popolo
of Sixtus IV. On the right post of the gate, and concealed by
the wooden folding frame, is engraved the figure of an angel, with
the inscription, "In the year of our Lord 1327, xi. indiction, Sept.
29, in the feast of S. Michael, a foreign army [that of King Robert
of Naples] tried to force its way into the city, but was repulsed
by the people of Rome led by Jacopo de' Ponziani."

Orazio Marucchi, *Silloge di alcune iscrizioni,* etc., p. 100, n. 47.

On the right of the Porta S. Sebastiano opens one of the posterns used only in jubilee years, and walled up since the Napoleonic times. Others are to be seen on the side of each gate
leading to great places of pilgrimage, like the Salaria (Forma
Urbis, pl. iii.), the Tiburtina, and the Ostiensis. After the tenth
tower there is a fine specimen of brickwork of the time of the
Antonines, a door flanked by half columns of the Corinthian order,
with finely cut capitals and frieze. It does not belong to a tomb,
as Nibby and others have suggested, but to a private villa discovered at the beginning of this century in the Vigna Volpi, within
the walls.

The Bastione del Sangallo, a few steps farther on, carefully kept
in repair up to 1870, is now abandoned to its fate, and its brick
facing is spoilt by vegetation which almost hides it from view.
Huelsen has discovered in the Uffizi the original design of Antonio
da Sangallo, which shows the portion of the wall destroyed by
Paul III. to make room for this bulwark, which was 400 metres
long, with nine towers and one gate. The gate is undoubtedly the
Ardeatina, on the subject of which consult —

Antonio Nibby, *Dintorni di Roma,* vol. iii. p. 560. — Gio. Battista de Rossi,
Roma sotterranea, vol. ii. p. 8. — Heinrich Jordan, *Topographie,* vol. i. pp.
233, 368. — Giuseppe Tommasetti, *Archivio Società storia patria,* 1879, p. 385;
1880, p. 135. — Christian Huelsen, *Mittheil.,* 1894, p. 320, pl. 9.

The Porta Ostiensis, now di S. Paolo, the last on the left bank,
dates from the time of Honorius, its level being nearly four metres
higher than that of the pyramid of Cestius. The treacherous
Isaurians threw it open to the Goths in 549. King Ladislas entered it in 1407, and caused it to be walled up, but the Romans
reopened it in 1410.

The walls did not end at their junction with the Tiber, but

turned inwards, following the left bank for 780 metres, until they

Fig. 32. — Door of the First Century built into the Walls of Aurelian.

met with those of the opposite shore. There were two great towers to protect the entrance to Rome by water, a chain being drawn at night between them. The towers are represented in the accompanying sketch by Van der Aa (Fig. 33).

The walls on the Transtiberine side, still perfect in the sixteenth century, have now disappeared, except for a short space on either side of the Porta Septimiana. There were three gates: the Portuensis, on the road to the Portus Augusti; the Aurelia, on the top of the Janiculum; and the Septimiana, on the road towards the Vatican district.

The Portuensis stood 453 metres in front of the present one, built in 1644 by Innocent X. Its site is indicated in Nolli's plan. It had a double archway, and on the frieze above was engraved the inscription of Honorius (Corpus, vi. 1190). The Aurelia had changed its classic name into that of S. Pancratius since the time of Procopius. Urban VIII. rebuilt it in 1644, and Pius IX. after

Fig. 33. — The Two Towers at the Entrance to the Harbor of Rome.

the French bombardment of 1849. The Septimiana was reduced to its present state by Alexander VI. in 1498.

XXII. Walls of Leo IV., Leopolis, Johannipolis, Laurentiopolis. — The construction of the walls of Leo IV. for the defense of the Vatican suburb and of the basilica of S. Peter is a consequence of the first Saracenic invasions. From Palermo and Cape Lilybæum, which had already been named Mars-allah (Marsala, the Harbor of God), the fleet of the Infidels sailed for the Bay of Naples in 845, and after a long stay at Misenum, advanced towards the mouth of the Tiber in 846. The feeble garrison of Gregoriopolis (Ostia, recalled to life and fortified by Gregory IV.) was easily overcome, and the barbarians were prevented from taking possession of Rome rather by the strength of its walls than by the valor of its defenders.

To revenge themselves for their repulse, the Saracens wrecked the two suburban churches of S. Peter and S. Paul, and carried away the inestimable treasures which the faithful had accumulated in the course of centuries over the tombs of the Apostles. The sight of the burning ruins caused the death of Pope Sergius II., and the panic-stricken citizens elected Leo IV. as his successor.

A curious discovery was made some years ago by Signor Pietro Rocchi in connection with one of these Saracenic inroads. While excavating the remains of a temple, in the farm of La Valchetta, six miles below Rome on the road to Ostia, he discovered traces of one of their camps, consisting mainly of daggers and poniards with curved blades of Oriental make. The Saracens had overthrown the temple, but columns, frieze, and capitals were found lying *in situ*, together with a statue of Bacchus in Pentelic marble. The statue, slightly restored by Fabi-Altini, adorned the studio of the late Mr. W. W. Story in 1892.

Leo IV. lost no time in relieving the fortunes of Rome: he made an alliance with Gaeta, Amalfi, and Naples, organized a fleet, and, taking the command of the allied forces, attacked the Infidels at Ostia, near the mouth of the Tiber, and gained a complete victory over them.[1]

To prevent, however, the repetition of the same occurrence, the pope determined to surround S. Peter's and the Borgo with a fortified inclosure, the remains of which are still to be seen in the gardens of the Vatican and in the so-called Corridojo di Castello.

The study of this work of mediæval military engineering is instructive, and shows how carefully Leo IV. had tried to imitate the structure of the Aurelian walls. For those who have not the opportunity of examining the Leonine walls in the gardens of the Vatican — where the best preserved portion, including two round-towers, is to be seen — the most favorable point of observation is the courtyard adjoining the church of S. Angelo dei Corridori. The wall is 12 feet thick, and has, or rather had, a double gallery, — one in the thickness of the wall, supported by open

[1] This naval battle has been described by Guglielmotti in chap. xi. of the *Storia della marina pontificia*, and illustrated by Raphael in fresco No. IV. of the *Stanza dell' Incendio di Borgo*.

arcades on the inward side, and one on the top, level with the battlements. The lower gallery was afterwards transformed into a passage, Il Corridojo di Castello, connecting the palace of the Vatican with the fortress of S. Angelo. Many popes and cardinals have escaped either from death or from servitude by means of this corridor, one of the leading historical events in connection with it being the flight of Pope Clement VII. from the hordes of Charles V. led by the Constable de Bourbon.

The length of the wall is about 3000 metres ; the height varies from 15 to 22 metres; the most exposed angles are protected by round-towers, two of which are still in existence, and form a conspicuous landmark of the Vatican landscape. The work does credit to Leo IV., considering the poverty of the means at his disposal. Two inscriptions in the arch which spans the Via di Porta Angelica give important details of the scheme adopted to obtain speedy work and cheap labor.

The first says : " In the time of our Lord the Pope Leo IV., the *Militia Saltisina* has built these two towers and the intermediate wall (*pagina*) ; " the other, likewise : " In the time of our Lord the Pope Leo IV., the *Militia Capracorum* has built this tower and the wall which connects it with the next." It appears from these inscriptions that the citizens of Rome being unequal to the task of completing the fortification in the required time, the colonists of the *domus cultœ* (fortified farms of the Campagna) were called upon to take a share in the work. Each section of the walls was assigned to a company of soldier workmen ; and here we find the mention of two: the company from Capracorum, that is to say from Veii (Isola Farnese), whose silent ruins had been recalled to life by Hadrian I.; and the company from Saltisina, a colony on the road to Ardea, fifteen miles from Rome. Both of them declare that they have finished their special part of the construction under the direction of a certain Agatho, who seems to have been the designer and chief engineer of the walls. The new city was solemnly styled CIVITAS LEONIANA, and tables inscribed with its name were fixed on each gate.

Other records of this work have been collected by De Rossi in his memoir entitled " Le prime raccolte di antiche iscrizioni " (Giornale arcadico, 1850). See also "Inscriptiones christianæ Urbis Romæ," vol. ii. pp. 324–326.

There were three gates and two posterns in Leopolis. The first, called Porta S. Petri, opened on the Ælian bridge under the bastions of the Castle (S. Angelo). The second, called Posterula

S. Angeli, corresponds approximately with the present Porta Castello. The third, called Sancti Peregrini (near the Angelica of Pius IV.), opened under the pope's residence towards the Via Triumphalis. The fourth, Porta in Turrione, corresponds with the Porta Cavalleggeri of the present day. The fifth, named Posterula Saxonum, was transformed by A. da Sangallo into the monumental Porta di Santo Spirito.

Fig. 34. — Tower of Leo IV. in the Vatican Gardens. Bastions of Pius IV. in the foreground.

JOHANNIPOLIS. — John VIII. in 880 did for S. Paul's what Leo IV. had done for S. Peter's, with this difference, that while the Vatican Basilica and the Borgo Vecchio were included in the city, the Basilica Ostiensis remained a detached fort, communicating with the city by means of a portico over a mile long. We must acknowledge that the Romans did not show the same zeal and reverence towards the two Apostles. S. Paul's tomb was allowed to be profaned and to remain abandoned for over ten years, until the pontificate of Benedict III. (855–858), who "sepulchrum, quod a Sarracenis destructum fuerat, perornavit." The fortifications were begun only in or about 880, and consisted of walls and towers, like those of Borghetto, Castel Savello, etc., including a considerable space of ground on either side of the road to Ostia, and on the left bank of the Tiber. An inscription in seven distichs, above the gate facing Rome, contained the following words: —

> PRÆSVLIS OCTAVI DE NOMINE FACTA IOHANNIS
> ECCE *IOHANNIPOLIS VRBS* VENERANDA CLVIT.

The fortress was of considerable strength, as we can argue from the vigorous defense which Stefano Corsi made in it against Pope Paschal II. in 1099. A document of 1074 speaks of the *castellum S. Pauli quod vocatur Iohannipolis* as still in good condition; but the so-called Anonymus Magliabecchianus, who wrote between 1410 and 1415, says that it had disappeared long before his time. I have gone over the ground covered by Johannipolis many times, without finding a trace of the fortifications, except perhaps on the river-side, where I saw in 1890 ruins of what appeared to be a landing-stage.

LITERATURE. — Muratori, *Antiqq. med. œvi*, vol. ii. diss. xxvi. p. 403. — Gio. Battista de Rossi, *Inscr. christ. Urbis Romæ*, vol. ii. p. 326. — Rodolfo Lanciani, *Leopolis and Johannipolis*, the Esquiline, June, 1892. — Louis Duchesne, *Liber pontificalis*, vol. ii. p. 298. — Giuseppe Tommasetti, *Archivio storia patria*, a. 1896, fasc. i.

LAURENTIOPOLIS. — A second detached fort was built about the same time for the protection of the basilica of S. Lorenzo fuori le Mura, but no historical document mentions the fact. S. Lawrence was held by the Romans almost in the same veneration as the two Apostles, and a portico was built for the convenience of pilgrims from the Porta Tiburtina to his grave, exactly like those which led from the Ælian bridge to S. Peter's and from the Porta Ostiensis to S. Paul's. A document of the time of Urban VIII. (1623–44), discovered by Armellini, says: "There are yet considerable remains of the wall which once surrounded the basilica of S. Lorenzo like a castle; they are better preserved on the side of the Via Tiburtina." Laurentiopolis has now completely disappeared, but I am able to reproduce here a sketch of its fortifications drawn about 1534 by Martin Heemskerk.

XXIII. THE FORTIFICATIONS OF PAUL III., PIUS IV., AND URBAN VIII. — The horrors which Rome suffered at the time of the Sacco del Borbone, in 1527, were still fresh in the memories of the

Court and of the population when Cardinal Farnese was elected pope with the title of Paul III. One of the first thoughts of this great and generous man was to secure the city from a repetition of the occurrence, and Antonio da Sangallo was commissioned to draw up a plan for the fortifications. The survey he made of the ground and the sketches of his plan of defense are preserved in the Uffizi at Florence. (Disegni 301, 1015, 1019, 1431, 1514, etc.) These drawings show his proposal to reduce the circuit of the walls (on the left bank) by one third at least, in-

Fig. 35. — The Fortifications of Laurentiopolis. By M. Heemskerk.

closing at the same time in the line of defenses the Borgo Vaticano, which was very inefficiently protected by the crumbling walls of Leo IV. Bastions with double wings were to be raised at intervals of 500 metres, the centres of defense being the castle of S. Angelo for the right bank and the Lateran for the left.

The works were begun at once with great determination, but, as time passed and the recollections of Bourbon's atrocities faded quietly away, they were given up altogether. There remain as specimens of Antonio da Sangallo's engineering skill — (1) the bastione di Belvedere; (2) the bastion of the Priorato or Aventino; (3) the bastion of the Vigna Cavalieri or Antoni(ni)ano; (4) the foundations of a third bastion under S. Saba. Many plans of Rome of the time of Paul IV. give the whole system of defenses as finished; others represent the earthworks thrown up

in haste at the approach of the duke of Alva.   The best of all
was engraved in 1557 by Lafreri, under the title: "Recens . . .
topographia cum vallis, fossis, et aggeribus cæterisque quæ ad
hostium impediend(as) irruptiones per universum urb(is) am-
bitum . . . fieri curavit Paul(us) IIII. dum bello parthenop(eio)
premeretur."   Pius IV. fortified the Borgo Nuovo in 1562.

Urban VIII., fearing the hostile action of the duke of Parma,
began in 1642 a new line of walls on the ridge of the Janiculum,
which are still kept in repair for military purposes.   They start
from the Porta Turrionis of Leo IV. (Cavalleggeri), and reach the
Tiber at Ripa Grande.   Among the works of art discovered in
building these bastions, Bartoli mentions "many statues, one of
which, of bronze, is now in the Barberini palace, a bisellium or
magistrate's chair of bronze inlaid with silver, and several objects
of curiosity."   The bronze statue represents Septimius Severus,
and was probably set up in the garden of his son Septimius Geta.
It was lately in the possession of Prince Sciarra, and must have
shared the fate of the rest of his valuable collections.   Urban
VIII. built but one gate, the Porta S. Pancrazio, ruined by the
French guns in 1849.   The scarce engraving of the time, reproduced on the opposite page, shows the entry of the invaders on July
4th of that year.

REFERENCES. — Vincenzo de Marchi, *Architettura militare*, p. 2 A, ed.
1590. — Maggi, *Fortificazione*, p. 115, Venice, 1564. — Scamozzi, *Architettura
universale*, p. 108, Venice, 1615. — Alberto Guglielmotti, *Storia delle fortifi-
cazioni della spiaggia romana*, viii. 2, p. 320. — Mario Borgatti, *Le mura di
Roma*, in Rivista di Artiglieria e Genio, 1890, p. 391. — Christian Huelsen,
Mittheilungen, 1894, p. 328.

XXIV. MODERN FORTIFICATIONS. — Eighteen outlying forts
and batteries have been raised by the Italian government for
the protection of the capital of the kingdom against a *coup de
main* from the sea.   They follow each other in this order, going
from left to right: I. Monte Antemne; II. Batteria Nomentana;
III. Pratalata; IV. Tiburtino; V. Prenestino; VI. Tusculano;
VII. Porta Furba; VIII. Appia Pignattelli; IX. Appia Antica;
X. Ardeatino; XI. Ostiense; XII. Portuense; XIII. Bravetta
(Villa Troiani); XIV. Aurelia Antica; XV. Boccea, on the Via
Cornelia; XVI. Casal Braschi, on the Via Traiana; XVII. Trionfale; XVIII. Monte Mario.   No objects or ruins of archæological
interest have been discovered in building forts numbers III, V,
VIII, XVI, and XVII; the construction of the others has given
occasion for valuable finds.   They are described most carefully in
the "Notizie degli Scavi" from 1876 to 1884.

XXV. THE FOURTEEN REGIONS OF AUGUSTUS. — Whoever
undertakes to separate into a certain number of wards a city,
not new or young, but many centuries old, and already divided
roughly by the undulations of the ground, by popular habits, by
relationship of neighborhood, must, if he wants to succeed, pay
attention to all these elements. Augustus, in attempting this
reform between 10 and 4 B. C., must have felt embarrassed in
the selection of fundamental lines, because the city had no *cardo*

Fig. 36. — The French Army entering the Porta S. Pancrazio, July 4, 1849.

or *decumanus*, and its plan was "magis occupatæ urbis quam
divisæ similis." He selected as a cardo or meridian a line which
started from the banks of the Almo, beyond the first milestone
of the Appian Way, followed northwards this way to the Porta
Capena, and thence the east side of the Circus Maximus (Via de'
Cerchi), the Vicus Tuscus (di S. Teodoro), the Clivus Argentarius (di Marforio), and the Via Flaminia (Corso) to the first
milestone. On this basis (ancient maps and geodetic operations
in general started from the south instead of the north) he divided
the ground on the left bank of the river into thirteen wards or
regiones, and made the fourteenth out of the Trastevere. The
elements of the division are — (1) The meridian line just alluded

to; (2) the Palatine hill, selected as a centre; (3) the line of the Servian walls; (4) the main thoroughfares leading from the centre of the city to the gates of Servius. However, as in the Augustan age the city had extended far beyond the line of the Servian walls, and populous suburbs had sprung up along the main consular roads, six regions were established "extra muros" (I, V, VII, IX, XII, XIV), eight "intra muros" (II, III, IV, VI, VIII, X, XI, XIII).[1] This simple and practical operation is illustrated by the sketch-map on the opposite page.

In Constantine's time the fourteen regions bore the names of I. Porta Capena, II. Cælimontium, III. Isis et Serapis, IV. Templum Pacis, V. Esquiliæ, VI. Alta Semita, VII. Via Lata, VIII. Forum Romanum, IX. Circus Flaminius, X. Palatinum, XI. Circus Maximus, XII. Piscina Publica, XIII. Aventinus, XIV. Transtiberim. Some of these names cannot be original, because at the time of Augustus there was no temple of Isis and Serapis on the Oppian, no temple of Peace near the Carinæ, and probably no Via Lata at the foot of the Quirinal. The original wards were probably distinguished by a number from I to XIV, counted from right to left.

We have two documents on the statistics of each region, the *Notitia* and the *Curiosum*, about which the reader may consult Preller's "Regionen" mentioned below, and Jordan, "Topographie," vol. ii. (Untersuchungen über die Beschreibung der XIV Regionen), pp. 1-312 and pp. 539-582.

Both documents are of the fourth century, and therefore their statistics cannot be made use of in speaking of the Augustan reform; still they may help us in a great measure, because many regions bounded by fixed barriers, like the Tiber and the Servian walls, could not expand with the increase of the population like those "extra muros." Regions II, III, IV, VI, VIII, X, XI of the fourth century, fettered since their first institution by such immovable boundaries, are essentially the same as in the first century. The fact which strikes us most forcibly in examining their statistics is the effort made by the surveying officers of Augustus to equalize the divisions. They adopted as an average measure for each ward a circuit of 12,000 to 12,500 feet (12,270), with the exception of the sixth, to which, for local reasons,[2] was given a

[1] Claudius afterwards (A. D. 47) doubled the extent of the thirteenth, taking in the plains of Testaccio, with their quays, wharves, arsenals, granaries, warehouses, sheds, corn-exchanges, etc.

[2] The great projecting buttress of the Servian walls in the gardens of Sallust.

circuit of 15,700 feet. The others agree so well that there are only 150 feet of difference between the second and the third, 67

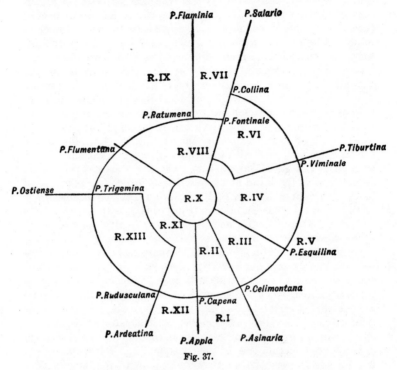

Fig. 37.

between the fourth and the eighth, 10 between the tenth and the eleventh, as shown in the following table : —

Regions.	Circuit.	Parishes.	Tenement Houses.	Private Palaces.
	Feet.			
II.	12,200	7	3600	127
III.	12,350	12	2757	60
IV.	13,000	8	2757	88
VI.	15,700	17	3403	146
VIII.	13,067	34	3480	130
X.	11,510	20	2692	89
XI.	11,500	20	2550	89

Not less remarkable is the uniformity in the number of tenement-houses (*insulæ*). The third and fourth regions have each 2757 insulæ; the difference between the sixth and the eighth is only 77; between the third and the tenth 65. As far as palaces (*domus*) are concerned, it is obvious that the surveying-officers could not even approximately assign an equal number to each ward, and therefore we find a difference of 86 between the maximum and the minimum. In spite of that, the fourth, tenth, and eleventh have the same number (88–89) of palaces; the second, sixth, and eighth almost the same (127–146). These statistics help us to determine which parts of the city were the favorite ones with the aristocracy. The sixth comes foremost, with 1 palace to every 23 houses; last comes the third, with 1 to 46. These results agree very well with the results of our excavations. However, all is not gold that glitters. The *Curiosum* and the *Notitia* do not deserve the blind and implicit faith which has been placed in them by topographers, and we have reason to believe their statistics either incorrect originally or made so by copyists. I cite one or two instances. We may perhaps be mistaken in attributing to the word *domus* the meaning of palace, and to the word *insula* the meaning of tenement-house, and in this case their true significance remains to be found out.[1] But if their meaning is certain,[2] how can we crowd into the Palatine hill 2692 tenement-houses and 89 private palaces, when we know that the palaces of the Cæsars alone occupied nine tenths of its surface? Again, we may believe to a certain extent that the geodetic experts of Augustus, turning their compass over and over again on the map of the city, could have found a circuit line of nearly equal length for each ward; but how is it possible that they could have placed exactly 2757 tenement-houses within the third and the fourth, and 2487 within the twelfth and the fourteenth, although these regions are so different in many other respects? It is impossible, therefore, to accept the statistics, as has been done up to the present day, some of their inaccuracies being patent. They assign, for instance, to

[1] REFERENCES (for *insulæ* and *domus*). — Pietro Visconti, *Atti Accad. Archeol.* vol. xiii. p. 254. — Francesco Bianchini, *Columbar. Liviæ*, p. 49. — Gaetano Marini, *Arvali*, p. 399. — Otto Richter, *Insula* (in Hermes, 1885, p. 91). — Friedländer, *Sittengeschichte Roms*, vol. i. p. 12. — Eyssenhardt, *Römisch und Römanisch*, p. 92. — Pöhlmann, *Die Uebervölkerung der antiken Grossstädte.* Leipsic, 1884. — Attilio de Marchi, *Ricerche intorno alle insulæ.* Milan, 1891.

[2] Cf. the decisive passage of Tacitus, *Ann.* xv. 41: *Domorum* et *insularum* et templorum, quæ amissa sunt, numerum inire haud promptum fuit.

the tenth or Palatine region a circuit of 3418 metres (11,510 feet). I have measured it twice over in designing Sheets xxix. and xxxv. of my "Forma Urbis," obtaining an average length of 2080. There is an exaggeration of 1338 metres.

A remarkable study has just been published on this question by Huelsen in Bull. arch. com., 1894, p. 312. According to his calculations the Coliseum could accommodate only from 40,000 to 45,000 seated spectators, the Theatre of Marcellus from 9000 to 10,000, the Circus Maximus about 150,000. These figures are very far from the 87,000 places (*loca*) which the catalogues attribute to the first, from the 17,580 given to the second, from the 385,000 given to the third. I bring this chapter to a close with the statistics of the regions "extra muros:" —

Regions.	Circuit.	Parishes.	Tenement Houses.	Private Palaces.
	Feet.			
I.	12,214.5	10	3250	120
V.	15,600	15	3850	180
VII.	14,500	15	3805	120
IX.	22,500	35	2777	140
XII.	12,000	17	2487	113
XIII.	18,000	17	2487	130
XIV.	33,194	78	4405	150

Comparing the two tables, we find that the aristocratic quarter *par excellence* was the thirteenth (Aventine), with 1 palace in 19 houses, followed closely by the ninth (Circus Flaminius), with 1 in 20. Last comes the third (Isis et Serapis), with 1 in 46. The patricians evidently preferred the quarters more distant from the centre.

LITERATURE. — Heinrich Jordan, *Topographie*, vol. ii. p. 72. — Ludwig Preller, *Die Regionen d. St. Rom.* Jena, 1846. — Wilhelm Henzen, *Corpus Inscr. Lat.*, vol. vi. p. 86, ad n. 454. — G. Battista de Rossi, *Piante di R. anteriori al ` sec. XVI.* p. 39. — Joachim Marquardt, *Staatsverwaltung*, iii. pp. 204, 205. — Giuseppe Gatti, *Bull. arch. com.*, vol. xvi. p. 224. — Rodolfo Lanciani, *Ricerche sulle XIV regioni:* ibid. vol. xviii. p. 115.

XXVI. THE POPULATION OF ANCIENT ROME. — There is no instance in the history of the world of so rapid and magnificent a growth as that of Rome from its first foundation on the Palatine

by a mere handful of shepherds. Whether by wisdom or by
power or by valor, they were destined from the beginning to
become the rulers of the world. And even now the civilized
nations are governed by their laws, travel by their roads, and
speak or understand their language. During the twenty-six centuries of its existence the population of Rome has had much to
suffer — changing customs, habits, opinions, forms of government,
and religion. No other city has been besieged, taken, robbed, and
burnt so often, and yet the vitality of the root could never be im-
paired. Even in the worst period of the Middle Ages, when temporarily dethroned by Avignon, Rome and its name never lost
their influence and prestige, but while in the first centuries of the
Republic the reality was in advance of reputation, at the end of
the Middle Ages reputation was ahead of true facts.

Roman history is represented with astonishing precision by the
fluctuations in the number of its inhabitants, because men rush
where they can find food, work, luxury, health, power, fame, se-
curity, and fly when such advantages are difficult or impossible to
obtain. Political power alone, without the comforts of life, is
not sufficient to stimulate immigration into a city: Rome was at
its lowest under the most powerful of mediæval popes, Innocent
III.

Three attempts have been made lately to estimate the number
of the inhabitants of ancient Rome: one by Pietro Castiglione,
" Della popolazione di Roma dall' origine sino ai nostri tempi "
(Monografia di Roma, vol. ii. p. 187) ; the second by myself, in a
memoir on the " Vicende edilizie di Roma antica," published in
the same work, vol. i. p. 1 ; the third by Prof. Julius Beloch, " Extrait du Bulletin de l'Institut international de Statistique," Rome,
Botta, 1886.

The question is worth investigation, on account of the amazing
estimates made by older writers. Lipsius mentions 4,000,000,
Vossius 14,000,000 ! Gibbon gives the city 1,200,000 souls at the
time of Constantine, and although his calculations rest on no scientific basis, yet his exquisite historical intuition made him strike
almost the right figure. Bunsen's standard measure — the number
of those to whom grain was gratuitously distributed under Augustus — is the right one, but he is greatly mistaken in reckoning
the number of slaves. At all events his statement — 1,300,000 as a
minimum, 2,000,000 as a maximum — has been accepted by German writers : by Nietersheim (1,500,000), Marquardt (1,600,000),
Friedländer (1,000,000 for the first, 2,000,000 for the second cen-

tury), and others. Again, those who have taken as a basis the area of the city inclosed by walls (nine million square metres), compared with the density of population in modern capitals, have fallen into the other extreme. Dureau de la Malle assigns to fourteen wards of the imperial city a population of 562,000, Castiglione assigns 584,000. The results attained by Beloch are expressed in the closing paragraph of his memoir as follows: " Taking into consideration the number of those who had a right to the free distribution of grain at the beginning of the Empire, the population of Rome, of the Campagna, and of some of the surrounding hills must have amounted to from 950,000 to 1,035,000 souls; that of the city alone from 760,000 to 920,000. Again, calculating the habitable space within the walls of Aurelian, we have found out for the city alone a population of from 800,000 to 850,000 souls. The approximation of these figures reached by different ways shows that we cannot stray very far from the truth if we adopt for Rome and the Campagna the number of about 1,000,000, for Rome inclosed by walls that of 800,000. However modest the number may seem, compared with former ideas, we must remember that it was never reached by a modern capital up to the beginning of the present century."

From the end of the third century downwards the population diminished with appalling rapidity. Castiglione says that in 335 B. C. it was reduced to 300,000, but his estimate is evidently too low. Pillage after pillage, barbarian inroads, famine, insecurity, bad government or no government at all, earthquakes, and inundations did the rest; and we are told that in the year 1377, on the return of the popes from Avignon, there were only 17,000 survivors in the ruinous waste.[1] Whether the figure be exact or not, these few men who held firm and faithful to their native soil deserve the gratitude of mankind. Without them, the site of Rome would now be pointed out to the inquiring stranger like that of Veii, of Fidenæ, of Ostia, and of Tusculum. There are three works on Roman statistics of the sixteenth and seventeenth centuries full of new and interesting information.

Mariano Armellini, *Un censimento della città di Roma sotto il pontificato di Leone X.* Rome, 1882. — Domenico Gnoli, *Descriptio urbis, o censimento della popolazione di Roma avanti il sacco borbonico.* Rome, 1894. — Francesco Cerasoli, *Censimento della popolazione di Roma dall' anno 1600 al 1739.* Rome, 1891.

Here are a few facts. In Pope Leo X.'s time the number of

[1] Compare Domenico Gnoli, *Descriptio urbis.*

the *cortesane* was equal to about one third of the total of single
women or widows within the walls of the city. Their number
had diminished to 604 in 1600, to rise up again steadily until
the maximum of 1295 is reached in 1639. A century later, in
1739, they were reduced to 100 (?).

In 1527, the population being 55,035, some of the cardinals had
the following retinue of servants and officers (*corte cardinalizia*):
Farnese, 306 persons; Cesarini, 275; Orsini, 200; del Monte, 200;
and so on in decreasing numbers, until we reach the figure of 60
for Cardinal Numalio, and 45 for de Vio.

In 1639, in a population of 114,256 souls, there were 24 bishops,
1786 priests, 3539 monks, 2496 nuns, 2180 *famigliari* of cardinals,
— a clerical nucleus over 10,000 strong. There were 975 registered beggars, 13 Moorish slaves. Of 88,144 persons capable of
satisfying the Pascal precept 77,471 took the holy communion.
There were only 238 inmates of public prisons.

At the beginning of this century the population numbered
153,004 souls. The French invasions and the Napoleonic wars
brought a decline, which culminated in 1812 with 117,882 inhabitants. But the ascending movement began again with the
Peace of Vienna, and has continued uninterruptedly to the present
day. When Rome became the capital of Italy in 1870, there
were 226,022 inhabitants; the number has doubled since, as shown
by this table: —

Year.	Popula-tion.	Deaths.[1]	Death-rate.	Births.	Excess of Births.
1885	345,036	8,599	25 per 1000	9,872	1,273
1886	364,511	9,297	26 "	10,484	1,187
1887	382,973	10,641	28 "	11,537	896
1888	401,044	10,293	26 "	12,336	2,043
1889	415,498	10,394	25 "	12,870	2,476
1890	423,217	9,731	23 "	11,956	2,225
1891	436,185	10,099	23 "	12,294	2,195
1895	450,000	....	....	....	....

XXVII. THE MAP OF ROME ENGRAVED ON MARBLE UNDER
SEVERUS AND CARACALLA. — Under the pontificate of Pius IV.
(1559–65), while the architect Giovanni Antonio Dosio da San
Geminiano was excavating at the foot of the back wall of the

[1] Including the Campagna and the floating population.

church of SS. Cosma e Damiano, he found ninety-two pieces of marble slabs, upon which was engraved the map of the city, restored and rebuilt by Severus and Caracalla after the fire of Commodus. A few of the fragments were still fixed against the wall (Fea, Miscell., lii. n. a), but the greater part had fallen on the pavement of the Forum Pacis, each slab being broken into many pieces. Had the discoverer taken care to collect them carefully, and to join the fragments of each slab there and then, the value of the discovery would have been inestimable; but we have reason to believe that they were thrown negligently into baskets and removed to the palace of Cardinal Alessandro Farnese. Here the pieces were sorted even more negligently, the larger and more valuable were exhibited in the museum, the smaller bits were thrown away in the cellars of the palace. Some years later a mason made use of them in restoring the wall of the garden on the river-side. Many of them were rediscovered in 1888 when that garden wall was demolished to make room for the Tiber embankment. (See Notizie degli Scavi, 1888, pp. 391, 437, 569.) Pope Benedict XIV., to whose liberality the Capitoline museum owes so many treasures, asked King Charles III. of Naples, the heir to the Farnese estate, to present the "Forma Urbis" to the city. The request was complied with, and the fragments were arranged in a somewhat disorderly manner on each side of the staircase of the museum. The star which marks some of the pieces tells another tale in the odyssey of the precious relics: those pieces, having been lost in the journey from the Farnese palace to the Capitol, were reproduced from original drawings in Cod. vatic. 3839.

In the year 1867 Augusto Castellani and Effisio Tocco tried fresh excavations in the garden of SS. Cosma e Damiano, and they were rewarded by the find of the celebrated piece containing the plan of the Porticus Liviæ (Fig. 38). In 1882 another piece, containing the plan of the Vicus Vestæ, was discovered under my supervision; a third of no importance in 1884.

Lastly, in 1890 the state undertook to make a final and exhaustive search at the foot of the wall of the Templum Sacræ Urbis, which led to no result, for reasons which it would be out of place to discuss. The origin of the plan may be briefly described as follows: —

The last census of Rome, taken in strict accordance with the old rules, was begun by Vespasian in A. D. 73, and finished two years later. The Flavian dynasty, to use the expression of Suetonius, had found the capital of the Empire "*deformis veteribus incendiis* [the fire of Nero] *atque ruinis* [the disasters caused by the faction of Vitellius]." Vespasian reorganized the city from the material as well as from an administrative point of view : the lands usurped by Nero for his Golden House were given back to the people ; the burnt quarters rebuilt, on a new *piano regolatore ;* the limits of the metropolitan district enlarged ; public property on the line of the Tiber, of the aqueducts, of the pomerium was redeemed from the encroachments of private individuals ; a new map of the city was drawn, and the *cadastre* of public and private property revised. These documents were deposited in a fireproof building, an oblong hall 42 metres long, 25 metres wide, constructed expressly on the west side of the Forum Pacis, between it and the Sacra Via. On the epistyle, above the main entrance, the following words were engraved : "[This building has been raised by] Vespasian in his eighth consulship [A. D. 78]." The map of the city, drawn in accordance with the last official survey and the results of the census, was exhibited on the side of the hall facing the Forum of Peace. We do not know whether it was simply drawn in colors on plaster, like the celebrated maps of Agrippa in the Portico of Vipsania Polla, or engraved on marble.

The city was again half destroyed by fire in the year 191, under Commodus, the centre of the conflagration being precisely the neighborhood of these archives. The house of the Vestals, the jewelers' shops on the Sacra Via, the imperial warehouses for Eastern spices (*horrea piperataria*), and the Forum and Temple of Peace were leveled to the ground. The archives, surrounded by this mighty blaze on every side, must have been turned into an oven in spite of their fireproof inclosure, their bronze roof melted, their contents injured by heat or by water.

Septimius Severus and his son Caracalla undertook, with the reconstruction of the city, the reëstablishment of the archives of the *cadastre*, and, in memory of their work (which was begun in A. D. 193 and completed in 211), they caused a new and revised edition of the plan of the city to be engraved in marble and exhibited in the same place, that is to say, on the front of the building facing the Forum of Peace. The building itself, magnificently restored and decorated in *opus sectile* (a kind of Florentine mosaic), was dedicated under the name of Templum Sacræ Urbis. It exists still in a good state of preservation, thanks to Pope Felix IV., who, in 526, turned it into a church, under the invocation of SS. Cosma e Damiano. The wall, on the marble facing of which the plan of Rome was engraved, measures twenty-two metres in length, fifteen metres in height, and is remarkably

Fig. 38. — The Fragment of the Marble Plan discovered by Castellani and Tocco in 1867.

well preserved. There is a good drawing of it in Jordan's "Forma Urbis Romæ," plate xxxi. fig. 1.

The orientation or meridian line of the plan seems to have been directed from the southwest to the northeast. The scale, save a few exceptions, seems to be 1 : 250.

REFERENCES. — Bernardo Gamucci, *Antichità di Roma*, ed. 1580, p. 36. — Pietro Bellori, *Fragm. vestigii U. R.* Rome, 1673 (2d edition, 1773). — Effisio Tocco, *Annal. Inst.*, 1867, p. 409. — Trendelenburg, *Annal. Inst.*, 1872, p. 75. — Heinrich Jordan, *Forma Urbis Romœ Regionum XIV*. Berlin, Weidmann, 1874. — Anton Elter, *De Forma U. R. deque orbis antiqui facie.* Bonn, 1891. — Christian Huelsen, *Mittheil. des Archaeol. Instituts*, 1889, p. 79; and *Bull. arch. com.*, 1893, p. 130. — Otto Richter, *Göttingen gelehrten Anzeigen*, 1892, p. 130 ; and *Topographie der Stadt Rom*, 1889, p. 3. — Gio. Battista Piranesi, *Antichità romane*, vol. i. tav. 2-6.

XXVIII. The Burial of Rome. — The question most often asked by persons not well acquainted with the details of the downfall of Imperial Rome is, " How came the city to be buried under a bed of earth to a depth which ranges from five to sixty-five feet?" The question is more easily put than answered. The accumulation of modern soil depends upon so many causes, great and small, that it is very difficult to bring them all together and set them before the student in the proper light.

To begin with, I will relate a personal experience which took place in 1883-84, during the excavations made by my late friend Luigi Boccanera, in the villa of Q. Voconius Pollio at Marino, the ancient Castrimœnium. We had been wishing for years to try an excavation in virgin soil, where no one should have disturbed the strata of the ruins corresponding to the pages of history. Here all chances were in our favor, because the Villa Voconiana, so rich in works of art, had not been destroyed by fire, or by earthquake, or by the violence of man, but had been left to decay by itself, piece by piece and atom by atom. The palace, moreover, contained but one floor, the ground floor, no suspicion of staircases leading to upper stories having been found anywhere. Now, as the position of the building was such that the strata of its ruins could not have been altered by the action of water or atmospheric forces, and the volume of the same ruins could not have been either augmented or diminished, it was easy to calculate, with almost mathematical precision, what is the material product of the crumbling of a Roman house.

The results of the careful calculation are these. A noble Roman house, one story high, produces a stratum of loose material and rubbish one metre, eighty-five centimetres high ; or, in other words, a building about ten metres high, crumbling down under the circumstances which caused the ruin of the villa of Voconius Pollio, produces 1.85 cubic metres for each square metre of surface.

Now if a building of very modest proportions has created such a volume of ruins, it is easy to imagine what must have been the results of the destruction of the private and public monuments of ancient Rome.

At the beginning of the fourth century after Christ, Rome, as we have just seen, contained 46,602 tenement-houses, 1790 palaces, not to speak of a thousand public buildings like thermæ, temples, basilicas, theatres, amphitheatres, circuses, porticoes, etc. The height of these edifices was always considerable, sometimes excessive. Strabo mentions a law made by Augustus against the raising of private houses above seventy feet. Trajan tried to reduce the maximum to sixty feet. Tertullian describes the house of a Felicles as reaching the sky. Houses built in the plain of the Circus Flaminius against the Capitoline hill reached the platform of the Temple of Jupiter, and enabled the followers of Vespasian to take the place by storm from the Vitellians. The palace of Septimius Severus at the Septizonium towered fully seventy metres above the arena of the Circus Maximus; the pediment of the Temple of the Sun rose eighty metres above the Campus Martius. Considering that hardly the ten thousandth portion of this mass of buildings has escaped destruction, all the rest having crumbled into dust and rubbish, we cannot wonder that ancient Rome should now lie buried so deep. If the Forum of Trajan, excavated by Pius VII. in the heart of the modern city, was not cleaned or swept once a week, as is the case now, at the end of each year it would be covered by an inch of dust, by one hundred inches at the end of a century; and I speak of matter accumulated there simply by the action of rain and wind. But if the Forum of Trajan should be selected by the living generation as a receptacle for the daily refuse of the city, its disappearance would take place in a few years: and this has been the case with the Forum Romanum, the Coliseum, the Forum Augustum, the Palatine, the Vicus Patricius, and so on. At all events, the increase of the Roman soil begins with the age of the Tarquins, and with the drainage and filling up of the Velabra. An inscription discovered at the first milestone of the Appian Way (Corpus, vol. vi. n. 1270) describes how the steep incline leading from the river Almo to the Temple of Mars had been made easy by the removal of large masses of earth. The ruins of the buildings destroyed by the great fire described by Livy (xxiv. 47) were leveled on the spot, and the pavement of the Forum Boarium and of the surrounding streets was at once raised several feet. Horace (Sat. i. 8; v. 15) describes how Augustus and Mæcenas caused the burial-grounds of the Esquiline to be covered with great masses of earth, and a public park laid out on their site. While building in 1877 the sewer of the Coliseum along the Via di S. Gregorio, we discovered the city of the time of Nero buried under the ruins of the fire of A. D. 65. Here also the level of the streets was raised at once several feet. Frontinus (i. 18) says that the seven hills had gained in altitude: " colles excreverunt rudere."

The 700,000 or 800,000 cubic metres of earth and rock removed by Trajan to make room for his forum were laid over the public cemetery between the Via Pinciana and the Via Salaria (Salaria Vetus and Nova). The baths of Trajan and Titus are founded on the remains of the Golden House of Nero; the baths of Caracalla on the remains of many edifices, of which the engraving on the next page (Fig. 39) represents a small section.

Diocletian began the construction of his own thermæ by demolishing two temples and many other public or private buildings to the extent of 136,000 square metres. The products of the demolition were heaped up in a hillock 20 metres high in the neighborhood of the present railway station. The threshold of the arch built by Augustus over the Via Tiburtina for the transit of the Marcia, Tepula, and Julia lies three metres below the threshold of the gate (Porta S. Lorenzo) built by Arcadius and Honorius in 402 (Fig. 31). These figures give us a yearly average of $7\frac{1}{2}$ millimetres of rise for the surrounding district, during the 406 years which elapsed between Augustus and Honorius. The inscriptions engraved on the same gate of S. Lorenzo describe, among the works undertaken by Honorius toward the strengthening of the fortifications of Rome, the removal of the rubbish accumulated along the line of the walls (" egestis immensis ruderibus; " see p. 73).

I have sometimes discovered four different buildings lying one under the other. The mediæval church of S. Clement was built in 1099 by Paschal II. above the remains of another basilica built seven and a half centuries earlier. This latter rests upon the walls of a noble patrician house of the second century after Christ, under which the remains of an unknown Republican building are to be seen.

When the new Via Nazionale was cut in 1877 across the Aldobrandini and Rospigliosi gardens, on the Quirinal hill, we met, first, with the remains of the Baths of Constantine; then with the remains of the house of Claudius Claudianus; thirdly, with the house of Avidius Quietus; and lastly, with some constructions of early reticulated work.

Fig. 39. — The Remains of a Private House discovered under the Baths of Caracalla by G. B. Guidi, 1867.

These proofs, which I have quoted at random from monuments and writers, show that before the fall of the Empire the ground rose in the same way on the hills and on the plains. However, after the barbarian invasions, twelve out of the fourteen quarters (*regiones*) of the city having been abandoned and turned into farms and orchards, the rise of the hills diminished, and that of the valleys and plains increased, at a prodigious rate; a fact which can be explained, to some extent, by the natural fall of materials from the heights, and by the action of atmospheric forces. The greatest difference between ancient and modern levels which I have yet ascertained in Rome is 72 feet. It was found in excavating the inner courtyard of the house of the Vestals at the foot of the Palatine hill. The foundations of the northeast corner of the new Treasury buildings were sunk in 1874 to a depth of 41 feet, before the stratum of *débris* was passed through. The foundations of the house which forms the corner of the Via Cavour and the Piazza dell' Esquilino were sunk likewise to a depth of 53 feet. At that level the remains of some baths, built by Næratius Cerialis, were discovered, with statues, busts, bronzes, inscriptions, etc.

The rise of the hills after the fall of the Empire was absolutely artificial. I mean to say that if there was a rise in the level of the soil, it was the work of man, and as a consequence of the building of palaces, churches, and villas. I shall here quote a curious illustration of the theory I am trying to explain. The soil which covers (or rather covered) the northern half of the palace of the Cæsars, and more especially the palaces of Germanicus, Tiberius, Caligula, and Domitian, has not been created wholly by the crumbling or destruction of those palaces, but is mostly soil removed from the low lands of the Campus Martius to the top of the Palatine hill by Cardinal Alessandro Farnese, when digging the foundations for his palace and for the church of the Gesù. After remaining there for nearly three centuries, the great mass of material has again been removed, and carted away into the valley between the Aventine hill and the church of S. Balbina, in order that the remains of the Imperial buildings should be laid bare. The district stretching between the Porta Pia and the Porta Salaria has been lately raised to a considerable height with the soil extracted from the foundations of the Treasury buildings and of the royal mews. Without quoting any more instances, I wish only to observe that, if these cases were not known, how could we explain the unexpected rise of the places above named, on the Quirinal and on the Aventine?

When we consider that the archæological stratum, the formation of which I have tried to describe, is at least nine square miles in extent, we wonder how it has been possible to excavate, and search, and actually sift it, since the Renaissance of classical studies. Yet this has actually been done.

During my long experience of Roman excavations, and especially since the building of the new city began in 1871, about four square miles have been turned up. Leaving out of consideration works of art and objects of archæological interest, found scattered here and there in small secluded spots — mere crumbs fallen from the banqueting-tables of former excavators — I have found three places only of any considerable extent, which had absolutely escaped investigation.

The first is the district now occupied by the Central Railway Station, on the border line between the Quirinal and Viminal hills, excavated during 1871 and 1872. It was occupied in classic times by a cluster of private houses built in the so-called Pompeian style. It seems that, being threatened by a conflagration, their inhabitants had collected hurriedly all their valuables and most precious works of art, and heaped them up in confusion in a hall opening on a side street, which they considered as a comparatively safe place. The roof of the hall, however, caught fire, and in its fall carried down the walls in such a way as to shelter the heap of bronzes and marbles placed in the middle of the pavement. We discovered the place in February, 1871, and were able to remove to the Capitoline Museum the artistic bronze furniture of two or three Roman houses, the marketable value of which was calculated at about £6000.

The second virgin spot was discovered on Christmas Eve, 1874, near the southwest corner of the Piazza Vittorio Emmanuele, on the site of the Horti Lamiani (gardens of Ælius Lamia), which had been incorporated by Caligula into the Imperial domain. During the previous days we had been excavating a portico, 200 feet long, with a single line of fluted columns of *giallo antico* (yellow Numidian marble) resting on pedestals of gilded marble. The pavement of the portico was inlaid with Oriental alabaster, and the walls were covered with slabs of a certain kind of slate, inlaid with festoons and groups of birds and other delicate designs in gold leaf. At the foot of the wall, but concealed from view, ran a water-pipe, with tiny jets, two feet distant one from the other, which were evidently used to keep the place cool in summer. At the northern extremity of the portico the floor sank into a kind of chasm, at the bottom of which we discovered, during that memorable eve, a bust of Commodus, under the attributes of Hercules, the most elaborate piece of work which has been found in Rome in our time; another bust of the same Emperor, of smaller size; a statue of the muse Polyhymnia; a statue of the muse Erato; a statue of the Venus (Lamiana); two statues of Tritons; a bust of Diana; and several other works of art, such as legs, arms, and heads formerly set into bronze draperies. (See Book IV. § xxiv.)

The third and last spot which we have been the first to investigate since the early Renaissance is the southern half of the house of the Vestals. However, as I have given a minute account of this charming discovery in chapter vi. of my " Ancient Rome," it is needless to enlarge upon it here.

I must mention two particulars which explain to some extent our success in bringing to light, almost daily, new monuments and works of art and curiosity. The first is, that the pioneers of archæological research, that is to say, the excavators who preceded us, have stopped in many cases at the wrong level. Finding mosaic and marble pavements, or pavements of streets and squares, they thought they had reached the end of their undertaking, and turned their energy in other directions. From what I have said about the superposition of Roman buildings, it is easy to see how wrong they were. Here also I must be allowed to quote a personal experience. In 1879, when the new boulevard connecting the Piazza Vittorio Emmanuele with the Porta Maggiore was cut (Viale Principe Eugenio), we discovered a portion of the palace of Licinius Gallienus, already excavated by Francesco Belardi and Giovanni Battista Piranesi more than a century before. These two men, having gone as far down as the level of the drains running under the pavements, considered their task finished, and all hope of further discoveries vanished; and yet under those pavements and those drains lay buried at a great depth nine columbaria, particularly rich in cinerary urns, inscriptions, and objects of value. The columbaria are designed and their contents illustrated in the Bull. arch. com., 1880, p. 51, pls. 2, 3.

The second remark refers to the foundation walls built with fragments of statuary, to which very little attention was paid by early excavators. The value of this mine may be estimated from the following facts. In 1874 a bath was discovered near the church of SS. Pietro e Marcellino, from the foundations of which we extracted 95 statues, busts, torsos, basins of fountains, pieces of columns, and bas-reliefs. In December, 1873, the group of Hercules capturing the mares of Diomedes, now in the Palazzo dei Conservatori, was found broken in 72 pieces in a wall near S. Matteo in Merulana. Three thousand fragments of sculptured marbles, and 130 inscriptions or pieces of inscriptions were discovered likewise in 1873 in the substructures of the gardens of Prætextatus on the Esquiline. Consult "Monografia archeologica," Rome, 1878, vol. i. p. 40.

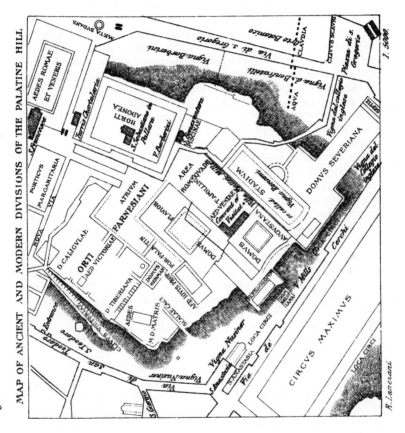

Fig. 41. MAP OF ANCIENT AND MODERN DIVISIONS OF THE PALATINE HILL.

BOOK II

I. Hints to Visitors. — The Palatine hill is the property of the Italian nation, with the exception of the southeast corner, which belongs to the Barberini. The first portion rescued from private hands was the Vigna Nusiner, which the crown of Russia gave up to Pius IX. in 1851 in exchange for some works of art. The same pope purchased the Vigna Butirroni in 1852, the Vigna del Collegio Inglese, formerly Ronconi, in 1862, and the Vigna de' Benfratelli in 1866. In 1860 Napoleon III. bought the Farnese gardens from the house of Naples, and began regular excavations under the management of the late Comm. Pietro Rosa. After the fall of Napoleon in 1870, the national government redeemed this portion of the hill, and took possession of the convents of S. Bonaventura and the Visitation (Villa Mills) and of their gardens. The latter convent is still inhabited by the nuns, while that of S. Bonaventura is partially occupied by the Guardie degli Scavi.

The Palatine is under the management of the Minister of Public Instruction, represented by a local board, or Ufficio degli Scavi. The excavations may be visited every day : entrance fee, one lira, which is not charged on Sundays. Artists, professors, and students of archæology are exempted from the fee, on application to the Ufficio degli Scavi. The restrictions on photographing are most complicated, the heads of the various boards having different views on the subject.

The Palatine cannot possibly be studied in one day : two days at least are required to become acquainted, in a certain degree, with the labyrinth of ruins. A modest literary preparation is needed, to lessen the difficulties of the task, and also a knowledge of the main lines of the map of the hill. Many students on their first attempt come away more discouraged by the intricacies of the topography of the Palatine than pleased with the beauty of its ruins. They have been hurried through so many palaces, — those of Augustus, Tiberius, Caligula, Domitian, Severus, — they have crossed so many halls, cryptoporticoes, stadiums, galleries, basilicas, passages, cellars, etc., that they feel sometimes inclined to give the thing up as hopeless. Yet the fundamental lines of the residence of the Cæsars are simple, and can be understood and remembered even by non-professional men. The main points are these : —

I. The Palatine hill originally was almost square in shape, each side measuring about 450 metres in length. The addition of the palace of Septimius Severus at the southern corner, raised on an artificial platform, the foundations of which are level with the bottom of the valley, altered the shape from square to trapezoid. The fall of the Imperial buildings and the work of human hands have changed the abrupt cliffs into slopes, and given the whole place a new aspect. Vegetation and cultivation have done the rest, by uprooting and crushing and splitting enormous masses of masonry, which, mixed with earth brought from afar, and leveled into flower or vegetable beds, have covered the rocky foundation of the hill with a layer of rubbish from 6 to 67 feet thick. They have hidden from view some of its historical features ; for instance, the valley between the Velia (by the Arch of Titus) and the Circus Maximus, by which the Palatine was divided into two summits — the Cermalus on the north, the Palatium on the south. In its present form the hill measures 2080 metres in circumference, and is 51.20 metres above the sea [1] and 32 above the level of modern Rome.

II. The platform of the hill was entirely occupied by the palaces of the Cæsars, with the exception of a space 175 metres long and 106 wide, at the west corner (above S. Anastasia), where some relics of Kingly Rome were preserved down to the fall of the Empire.

III. The Palatine was selected for the Imperial residence by Augustus, who built over the space now called the Villa Mills (convent and garden della Visitazione — Domus Augustana).

IV. Tiberius, born probably in the house afterwards owned by Germanicus, and still existing in good condition, built a new wing, the Domus Tiberiana, in the centre of the Cermalus, connecting it with that of Augustus by means of underground passages which are still visible (Orti Farnesiani).

V. Caligula extended the house of Tiberius over the remaining portion of the Cermalus in the direction of the Forum (Orti Farnesiani — Domus Caiana).

[1] By S. Bonaventura.

VI. Nero occupied the southeast corner (Villa Barberini) over-looking his artificial lake. After his death and after the suppression of his Golden House, the plot of ground was converted by Domitian into the gardens of Adonis (Horti Adonæa).

The Flavians began to give a unity of plan and architecture to the existing sections of the palace, raising new structures in the free spaces by which they were separated. The valley across the hill was filled up to the level of the platform of the Cermalus, and upon it were built the state apartments (Ædes Publicæ). The house of Augustus, destroyed by the fire of Titus, was rebuilt in harmony with its surroundings; a Stadium [1] (Vigna Ronconi, del Collegio Inglese) and a garden, Horti Adonæa (Vigna Barberini), were added.

Hadrian and Antoninus satisfied themselves with keeping the property in repair, as proved by the bricks inscribed with the names of their kilns, which are found everywhere. Hadrian's principal work — as far as we know — is the exedra of the Stadium (Vigna Ronconi, del Collegio Inglese).

Septimius Severus, after repairing the damages of the fire of Commodus (191) added an immense range of buildings on the edge of the hill facing the Cælian and the Appian Way. A section was occupied by the Imperial Thermæ, called in later documents Balneum Imperatoris, while the front of the palace, decorated with many rows of columns, received the name of Septizonium (Vigna del Collegio Inglese). The same Emperors brought a large volume of water from the Cælian, crossing the intervening valley with a viaduct 36 metres high and 300 metres long, remains of which are seen in the Vigna de' Benfratelli. The channel ended with a reservoir or *piscina* on the site of S. Bonaventura. Other additions are attributed to Severus Alexander and Heliogabalus (Diætæ Mammæiana, Templum Heliogabali, etc.), which have not yet been identified with any of the existing ruins.

Such is the classic topography of the hill in its main lines. With the help of the plans annexed (Figs. 40, 41)* the visitor hardly needs that of a *cicerone* or of a *guardia degli scavi* to make himself at home on the Palatine, or to find his way through the ruins and investigate each section, either by itself or in its relation to the other wings of the Ædes Imperatoriæ.

I must confess, however, that it is impossible to suggest to the student any itinerary which shall combine the topographical and

---

[1] On the correctness of this denomination see § xxi.

*Figure 40 faces page 112. Figure 41 appears on page 105.

chronological interest of the buildings. These are scattered over the hill in a desultory way. Once across the entrance gate, for instance, the visitor is confronted by three monuments, the Murus Romuli, the Templum Divi Augusti, and the church of S. Teodoro, separated by a gap of seven and fourteen centuries respectively. The area containing the hut of Romulus is surrounded by buildings of the first century of our era. It is impossible to cross over from the Domus Augustana to the Tiberiana, as required by chronology, without crossing the οἰκίαν Δομιτιανοῦ, which is three quarters of a century later. These things being so, I have given preference to the chronological order; in other words, my description is written for the use of visitors not pressed for time, who can devote three or four days at least to the systematic and rational study of the Palatine. Those who have no leisure can adopt the following itinerary, the best I can suggest, taking the various sides of the problem into consideration : —

1st day — Walls of Romulus, described § viii.
Altar of Aius Locutius, § ix.
Steps of Cacus, § x.
Hut of Romulus, § xi.
Temple of the great Mother of the Gods, § xiii.
Paternal house of Tiberius (and Germanicus) § xvii.
House of Tiberius, § xvi.
House of Caligula, § xviii.

2d day — Temple of Augustus, § iv.
Clivus Victoriæ, § vi.
Palace of Domitian, § xix.
Palace of Augustus, § xv.
So-called Stadium, § xxii.
Palace of Septimius Severus, § xxiii.
House of Gelotius, § xxvi.
S. Teodoro, § vii.

The visitor must bear in mind one fundamental rule : that many of the existing ruins belong to the substructures, and cellars, and underground rooms built for but one purpose, — to level the undulating surface of the hill, and to extend and protract the level platform over the slopes, and even over the plain below, as is the case with the Palace of Severus and the Septizonium. Their plan is most irregular ; they have no light and very little ventilation ; architecturally speaking they count for nothing. This is the reason why existing maps of the Palatine are so difficult to understand : we find marked in them with the same degree of importance apartments of state and crypts which were destined never to be seen. I have tried to remedy this defect in Sheets **xxix.** and **xxxv.** of the " Forma Urbis," where the apartments alone are depicted in full, while the substructures are simply traced in outline.

Special permission is required to visit the Palace of Augustus (see § xv). The Convent of the Visitation and its grounds are practically inaccessible. The Vigna Barberini and the chapel of S. Sebastian are opened on payment of a fee (see § xxxiii). The Palatine during the winter months ought to be visited in the morning; during the spring and autumn in the afternoon. There is always a great, and sometimes a dangerous, difference of temperature between the sunny and the shady side of the ruins. The Palatine, with its groves of ilexes and green lawns and glorious views, affords a delightful promenade even to those who are not attracted by archæological interests.

GENERAL REFERENCES. — Carlo Fea, *Miscellanea antiquaria*, vol. i. p. 86, n. 76 ; p. 87, n. 77 ; p. 223, n. 5, 6, 7. — Francesco Bianchini, *Il palazzo dei Cesari*, opera postuma. Verona, 1738. — Luigi Rossini, *I sette colli*. Rome, 1827. — Constantino Thon and Vincenzo Ballanti, *Il palazzo dei Cesari*. Rome, 1828. — De Agostini and Brofferio, *Il palazzo dei Cesari*. Vercelli, 1871. — Ippolito Ruspoli, *Avanzi e ricordi del monte Palatino*. Rome, 1846. — Fabio Gori, *Gli edifizi palatini dopo gli ultimi scavi*. Rome, 1867. — Heinrich Jordan, *Die Kaiserpaläste in Rom*. Berlin, 1868. — Wilhelm Henzen, *Annali dell' Instituto*, 1865, p. 346 ; 1866, p. 161. — Pietro Rosa, *Relazione sulle scoperte archeologiche negli anni 1871-72*, p. 75 ; and also *Plan et peintures de la maison de Tibère*, mai, 1869. — Visconti and Lanciani, *Guida del Palatino*, con pianta delineata da A. Zangolini. Rome, Bocca, 1873-93. — A. Preuner, *Das Palatium im alten Rom*. Greifswald, 1875. — Gaston Boissier, *Promenades archéologiques*. Paris, 1882. — Constantino Maes, *Topografia storica del Palatino*. Rome, 1883 (unfinished). — Deglane, *Le palais des Césars* (in Gazette archéologique, 1888, pp. 124, 145, 211). — Otto Richter, *Die älteste Wohnstätte des römischen Volkes*. Rome, Berlin, 1891. — John Henry Middleton, *The Remains of Ancient Rome*, vol. i. chap. iv. p. 158. — Rodolfo Lanciani, *Il palazzo maggiore* (in Mittheilungen, 1894, p. 1). *Forma Urbis Romæa*, plates xxix., xxxv.; and *Ancient Rome*, chap. v. p. 106. — Christian Huelsen, *Untersuchungen zur Topographie des Palatins* (in Mittheilungen, 1895, p. 3).

II. THE ORIGIN OF THE PALATINE CITY. — Two discoveries have illustrated from a new point of view the origin of Palatine Rome, that of the city of Antemnæ, and that of the Terramara di Fontanellato.

According to tradition [1] Antemnæ was a flourishing settlement when a colony of Alban shepherds occupied the Palatine. The distance between the two places being less than four miles, and their bartering trade very active, as they were located on the same (left) bank of the Tiber and on the same road (Salaria Vetus), we

[1] Antonio Nibby, *Analisi dei dintorni di Roma*, vol. i. p. 161. — Dennis, *Cities and Cemeteries of Etruria*, vol. i. p. 44. — William Gell, *Topography of Rome*, p. 64. — Smith's *Diction. geograph.*, vol. i. p. 139.

may assume that manners, habits, stage of civilization, etc., were about the same in Rome and Antemnæ. Antemnæ died a sudden death a few years after the foundation of Rome. It is evident, therefore, that a search made on the site of the former corresponds practically to a search made in the lower strata of Kingly Palatine. The search was made in 1882–83, while the hill was crowned by a fort.[1] The facts ascertained were these (see Fig. 42).*

The city occupied the platform of the hill, protected by cliffs or rivers (ante amnes) on every side, except where a neck or isthmus connected it with the tableland (Monti Parioli, Villa Ada). The natural strength of the site had been increased by a wall built of blocks of local stone, each two feet (0.59 metre) high and three (0.89) long. There were three gates, one leading to the river to the springs, one to the highroad (Salaria), the third to the cemetery and pasture-lands. The Antemnates lived in round or square huts, with a framework of timber and a thatched roof, the site of which is marked by a hard-trodden, coal-colored floor within a ring of rough stones. Their public buildings, like the temple and the curia, were of better style, and probably all of stone. The cattle were driven at night into the inclosures or sheepfolds adjoining each hut. The area inclosed by walls was therefore much larger than was required by the number of inhabitants.

In times of peace the Antemnates drank from the springs at the foot of the hill; for times of war they had provided themselves with cisterns and wells under shelter of the fortifications. One of the wells still in use is 54 feet deep; and one of the cisterns, covered by a triangular roof (destroyed 1883), could hold 5000 gallons of water (see Fig. 43).

The civilization of the Antemnates when their city ceased to exist was in the "bronze" stage. One third of their pottery and domestic ware was of local make, and baked in an open fire; the rest was of Etruscan importation. There were traces of the stone period, such as arrow-heads and lance-spears of polished flint, clay beads, and fragments of the roughest kind of pottery.

This description answers word for word to that of the city on the Palatine. Here again we have the isolated hill protected by cliffs, by water, and by a circuit of walls; the neck of the Velia connecting it with the tableland of the Esquiline; the gate leading to the river and springs (romanula), that leading to the pasture fields and cemeteries (mugonia), and a third descending to the Vallis Murtia: the wells and cisterns within the fortifications;

[1] Notizie degli Scavi, 1882, p. 415; 1883, p. 16; 1886, p. 24; 1887, p. 64.

*Figure 42 faces page 113.

and other such characteristics of the age. The description we have of the Casa Romuli, kept in its prehistoric simplicity as late as the fourth century after Christ, shows that the Romans, like the Antemnates, lived in straw huts; and furthermore, the discoveries made in the cemeteries of the Viminal and of the Esquiline prove

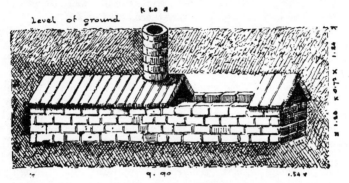

Fig. 43. — Reservoir at Antennæ.

that their civilization was in the "bronze" stage. (See Ancient Rome, chap. ii. p. 26). Roman archaic pottery was half of local (or Alban) make, half of Etruscan importation.[1] Cattle were driven in at night, each family being provided with an *agellus* and a sheepfold.

What has been said about Rome and Antemnæ must be applied to other contemporary settlements like Collatia, Fidenæ, Labicum, Ardea, Gabii, Veii, etc., the sites of which, excepting that of Veii, have not yet been scientifically investigated. They were all organized on the same system: their walls inclosed an area ten times as large as that required by the number of inhabitants, because they shared it with their flocks, and each hut had its own sheepfold and orchard. The highest and strongest point within the walls was occupied by the citadel, containing the temple, the curia, the ærarium, and the reservoir for rain-water. After the Roman conquest the scanty surviving population was concentrated on the site of the citadel, and the rest of the city cut up into farms and allotted to Roman colonists. The Roman municipia of Veii

---

[1] The archaic κειμήλια discovered in the cemeteries of Kingly Rome were removed in September, 1895, from hall No. II. of the Museo Municipale al Celio to two rooms of the Palazzo dei Conservatori, where the want of light and space makes their examination almost impossible.

SKETCH MAP OF EXCAVATIONS OF PALATINE.

Fig. 40.

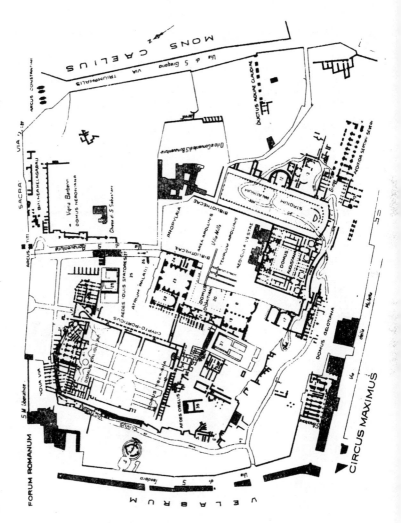

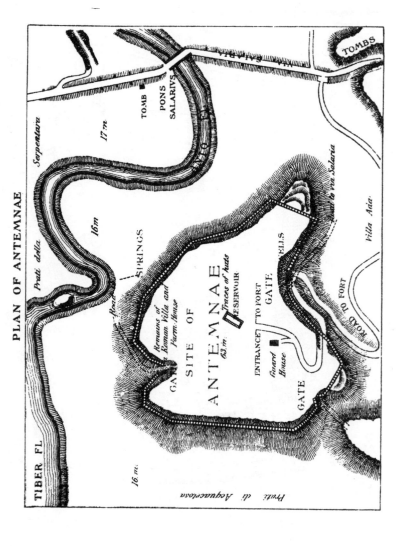

Fig. 42.

PLAN OF ANTEMNAE

TIBER FL

Prati della Serpentara

PONS SALARIVS

TOMB

17.m

16.m

SPRINGS

Road

Remains of Roman Villa and Farm-House

GATE

16.m.

SITE OF ANTEMNAE
63.m.

Traces of huts

RESERVOIR

ENTRANCE TO FORT

Guard House

GATE

TO FORT GATE

WELLS

ROAD TO FORT

to via Salaria

Villa Ada

Prati di Aquacetosa

TOMBS

(Piazza d' Armi), of Fidenæ (Monte di Villa Spada), of Gabii (farmhouse of Castiglione) are all that mark the place of the respective citadels of the time of the independence, while the area once inclosed by the city walls was put into cultivation. For this reason it is almost impossible to recognize the site of the huts and the extent of the piece of ground pertaining to each of them; in other words, to decide whether the old Sabine, Etruscan, and Latin cities in the lower valley of the Tiber had a *cardo* and a *decumanus*, and were planned, according to the principles of the *agrimetatio*, in square plots or *heredia*.

My opinion is that they were not. In the excavations made in 1889 within the walls of Veii,[1] I have seen traces of primitive habitations which were not "oriented," and the same thing was observed at Antemnæ. It is to be regretted that no proper search has yet been made in the lower strata of the Palatine, where the excavations stop generally at the wrong level, leaving most of the problems unsolved;[2] but I believe that the shepherds who occupied the hill in 753 B. C. had no idea whatever of gromatic or astronomical rules of their own, so that the *sulcus primigenius* had to be traced according to a foreign rite. Rome and its neighboring settlements on either side of the " Rumon " must have looked like the temporary villages which the peasants of the present day build in the Pomptine marshes or in the Agro Romano, when they come down from their mountains for the cultivation of the maize-fields. The prototype of these prehistoric contemporary settlements is the village constructed every autumn on the borders of the (now drained) lake of Gabii, at the twelfth milestone on the Via Prænestina, and inhabited by a half-savage tribe of two hundred mountaineers. I never fail to take our students to this remarkable village during the university term, to give them an object-lesson more impressive than any which can be found in the whole of the Campagna.

The populations of the *Terramare*,[3] on the contrary, seem to

---

[1] Described in *Notizie degli Scavi*, 1889, pp. 10, 29, 60, 154, 238.

[2] Goettling (*Geschichte der Römisch. Staatsverw.*, pp. 49, 202, 235) believes the Sacra Via to have been the *decumanus* marking the boundary between the Sabine and the Roman city; but the Sacra Via of those days was but a *winding* path *outside* the Palatine, to which alone my considerations refer.

[3] The name *Terramara* is a corruption of that of *Terra marna*, given till 1862 to the special kind of earth, rich in organic qualities, which the peasants of upper Italy dug from prehistoric stations, and used as a fertilizer. When Pigorini and Strobel began their study of these stations they adopted the corrupted name " Terramara " in preference to " Terra marna," to avoid the confusion which the epithet " marl " might produce in scientific treatises.

Fig. 45. — A Village of Straw Huts near Gabii (Castiglione).

have been familiar with the principles of the *agrimetatio.* The startling discoveries made by Pigorini in the terramara at Castellazzo di Fontanellato, in the province of Parma, are described in the following papers: —

Notizie degli Scavi, 1889, p. 355; 1891, p. 304; 1892, p. 450; 1895, p. 9. — *Monumenti inediti Accademia Lincei,* vol. i. (1889), p. 123. — *Bullettino di paleoetnologia italiana,* vol. xix. (1893), tav. viii. — Friedrich von Duhn, *Neue Heidelberger Jahrbücher,* vol. iv. (1894), p. 143.

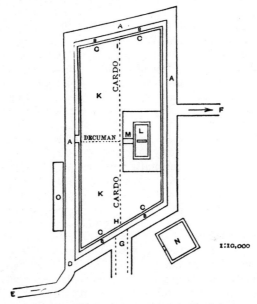

Fig. 46. — Plan of the Terramara di Fontanellato.

This primitive settlement of immigrants in the " Poebene "[1] forms an oblong 230 metres wide between the parallel sides, 480 metres long, and covers an area of 19½ hectares (195,525 square metres). Its fortified inclosure comprises a ditch (A) 100 Roman feet wide, 12 deep (30×3.50 metres), and an *agger* or embankment (B) formed with the earth excavated from the ditch, sloping towards the water and supported by a perpendicular palisade (C) on the inner side. The adoption of a trapezoid form in the Terramare, instead of the square or parallelogram, is explained by

[1] The valley of the Po and of its affluents.

the fact that the sharp corner (D) always faces the river (E), from which the supply of water for the ditch is derived, so as to divide it into two equal streams, which meet again at the outlet (F). There was but one gate, approached by a bridge 30 metres wide (G), the axis of which is in a line with the *cardo* or high street (H, I), cutting the village in two halves. The quarter (K) west of the high street was entirely occupied by huts built on palisades ; on the opposite side we find the central portion occupied by a square of solid ground (L) 100 metres long and 50 wide, protected by a ditch 30 metres wide and 6 deep, and approached by a bridge (M) on the line of the *decumanus*. This fortified terrace represents the *templum* in the primitive sense of the word, or, to use the expression of Helbig, the fundamental idea of the *arx* of Italian towns and of the *prœtorium* of Roman camps. There were two cemeteries outside the fortifications (N, O), also inclosed by a ditch and made accessible by a bridge. The cremated remains of the Terramaricoli were kept in clay urns, placed in rows on a wooden platform supported by palisades.[1]

If the reader refer to the map of the Palatine, Fig. 44,[*] he will find that nature had done for early Rome nearly all the work that human labor and ingenuity had done at Fontanellato. The marshes of the two Velabra and the pond, which Nero transformed afterwards into the lake of the Golden House, represent the water defenses ; the neck of the Velia represents the bridge ; the cliffs answer for the embankment. Other points of resemblance are the square form, the angle facing the stream (Nodinus?) which fed the greater Velabrum, and the area of about seventeen hectares. The Romans, however, did not wait long to make themselves familiar with the *agrimetatio* and to adopt the *pes* (.297 metres), with its multiples and fractions, as the standard national measure. When Servius Tullius built the great agger for the protection of the city on the east side, he simply copied in the minutest details the fortifications of the Terramare. The agger of Servius comprises a ditch exactly one hundred pedes wide and thirty deep; an embankment made with the earth of the ditch, sloping towards the city and supported by a wall on the outside. The three gates, Collina, Viminalis, and Esquilina, were approached by bridges. The ground on the other side of the ditch was occupied by cemeteries.

The history of the Palatine, from the foundation of the city

---

[1] In the campaign of last summer (1895) Pigorini discovered side streets parallel with the *cardo* and the *decumanus*. The Terramara, therefore, was divided into regular squares or parallelograms.

*Figure 44 is on page xii.

to that of the Empire, is not known. At the time of Tarquinius Priscus (616–578) it was still honored by the kingly residence, a *casa* of more elaborate construction than the ordinary citizens' huts, placed near the Porta Mugonia and the Temple of Jupiter Stator (Solinus, i. 24). The hill was not above the reach of fever, even after the drainage of the lesser Velabrum, accomplished by Tarquinius by means of the Cloaca Maxima, as the worship of the Dea Febris was never intermitted, and her temple and altar were not abandoned for centuries after. Beside the Fever's shrine, there were others to the Dea Viriplaca, a protectress of domestic peace; to Orbona, the evil genius of blindness; an altar to Aius Locutius (described § ix.); temples to Victory (§ vi.); to the great Mother of the Gods (§ xiii.); and to Jupiter Propugnator (§ xiv.).

Towards the end of the Republic the Palatine became one of the most aristocratic quarters of the city, resorted to by the great orators, lawyers, and political men of the age on account of its proximity to the Curia, the Rostra, and the Forum. The following palatial residences are recorded in classic texts : —

1. House of M. Fulvius Flaccus, destroyed by order of the senate, after his execution for his share in the conspiracy of the Gracchi. The space left vacant, area Flacciana, was occupied soon after by a wing of the Porticus Catuli.

2. House of Q. Lutatius Catulus, consul B. C. 102, with Marius, with whom he gained the victory over the Cimbri, near Vercellæ. With his share in the spoils of war he enlarged his house and connected it with a portico, the Porticus Catuli, where thirty-one flags taken from the enemy were exhibited.

3. House of M. Livius Drusus, tribune of the plebs in B. C. 91, the great reformer of social laws, whose murder by Q. Varius was immediately followed by the social war, which his policy would have averted. The house was inherited by Crassus the orator, who, having ornamented its impluvium with four columns of Hymettian marble, the first ever seen in Rome, was nicknamed the "Palatine Venus." Cicero bought it in December, 62, for a sum corresponding to $155,000. The peristyle was shaded by six marvelous lotus-trees, which perished one hundred and seventy years later in the fire of Nero. It passed afterwards into the hands of C. Marcius Censorinus, another great orator and Greek scholar; of L. Cornelius Sisenna, annalist historian, translator of the Milesian tales of Aristides; of A. Cæcina Largus, probably the author of the book on the "Etrusca Disciplina;" and finally it was absorbed into Caligula's palace.

4. House of Quintus Cicero, near the one of his brother Marcus, but lower down the slope of the hill. It was wrecked and burnt to the ground by Clodius.

5. House of Clodius, the notorious enemy of Cicero, — composed of two portions: one belonging to Cicero himself, which he had bought at the time of the banishment of the orator; one to C. Seius, which he had obtained by poisoning the owner on his refusal to sell. The domus Clodiana was magnificent, and commanded a glorious view.

6. House of M. Æmilius Scaurus, stepson of Sulla, the dictator, perhaps the richest of all Palatine residences. When Cicero was restored to the possession of his own, he tried to take a revenge on the usurper Clodius by raising one or two floors so as to cut off the view of which his enemy was so proud. To avoid this danger Clodius purchased the palace of Scaurus for a sum of $4,425,000 (?), having already spent $655,000 on his own.

All these residences were in the district of the Clivus Victoriæ, at the corner of the hill commanding the Forum, and must have disappeared when Caligula extended the Imperial Palace as far as the Nova Via and the Temple of Castor and Pollux.

7. The paternal house of Augustus, in the lane called the "Oxen-heads," at the east corner of the hill. (See § xv.)

8. The house of Quintus Hortensius, first the rival, then the associate of Cicero; a man of immense wealth, and endowed with a memory so retentive that he could repeat the auction-list backwards on coming out of sale-rooms. He was also the first to include peacocks in Roman dinner *ménus*. Hortensius's residence was purchased by Augustus, and inclosed in the Imperial Palace together with

9. The house of L. Sergius Catilina. Both were on the edge of the hill facing the Circus Maximus.

It is now time for us to enter the precincts of the famous hill, and examine one by one the remains which bear evidence on so many points of the political and monumental history of the "queen of the world."

III. Vigna Nusiner. — The strip of land between the north-western cliffs of the Cermalus and the Vicus Tuscus, by which we enter the excavations, is known to topographers by the name of Vigna Nusiner, and is represented in the following fragment of the marble plan of Rome, published by Trendelenburg in the "Archaeologische Zeitung," 1875, vol. xxxiii. p. 52; and by myself in the " Bull. com. arch.," vol. xiii. (1886), p. 159. (See Fig. 47.)

The Clivus Victoriæ, cut in the live rock along the foot of the cliffs, bounds the triangular space on one side, the Templum Divi Augusti on the second, the Vicus Tuscus on the third. The ground contains, besides, the Springs of Juturna, the Murus Romuli, the Altar of Aius Locutius (the Lupercal), and the church of S. Teodoro. All these monuments and landmarks, excepting the temple and the church, belong to the earliest period of Roman history, so that we could not begin our visit to the Palatine in more regular order.

The Vigna Nusiner has been excavated oftener than any other part of the Palatine, and yet we know very little about it for want of proper accounts. The Frangipani owned it at the end of the fifteenth century, together with a fortified house called " Lo Palazzo de Frigiapani." I have found two deeds in the records of that family : one dated January 21, 1516, by which the brothers Giambattista and Marcello Frangipani give permission to the rector of the church of S. Lorenzo ai Monti to open *cavam seu fossuram lapidum* in their vineyard *iuxta sanctum Theodorum;* the second, dated October 23, 1535, relates to a controversy between Antonino Frangipani and Camilla Alberini over the produce of the excavations which a stone-cutter named Giuliano was making at that time.

In 1549–1550 the contractors for the supply of building materials to S. Peter's found the pavement of the Vicus Tuscus, the pedestal of the statue of Vortumnus, and the remains of a temple with columns, capitals, entablature, and a frieze ornamented with griffins and candelabra. The plunder was so considerable that no fresh excavations were attempted for a lapse of a century and a half. The land was turned into a kitchen-garden, famous for its artichokes. In a contract of March 11, 1649, the spring harvest of them is valued at 140 scudi.

A new search was made in 1720, between the churches of S. Teodoro and S. Anastasia. It led to the discovery of a portico with pilasters of travertine (one of the three marked in the fragment of the marble plan), of pieces of columns, and of a row of rooms filled with objects of metal and scoriæ, to which Venuti gives the name of *fonderia palatina*, or imperial brass-foundry.

Giovanni Battista Visconti opened the ground for the fifth time at least; but his progress was stopped by the house of Naples under the plea that he was undermining the walls that held up the Farnese gardens.

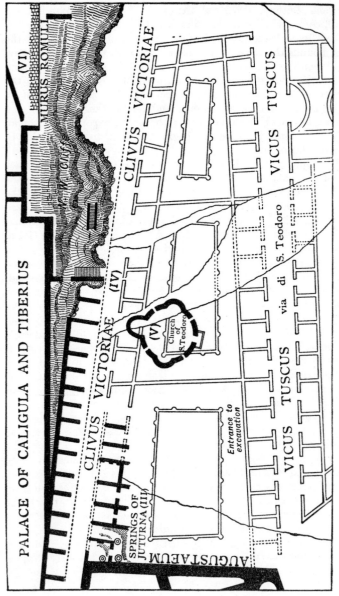

Fig. 47. — A Fragment of the Marble Plan with Clivus Victoriae and Vicus Tuscus.

In June, 1845, the antiquarian Vescovali, acting on behalf of the Emperor of Russia, who had purchased the Vigna for the sake of excavating, discovered the remains of the Domus Gelotiana (see § xxvi.); in December, 1846, he came upon those of the Murus Romuli; and in April, 1847, upon the remains of a private house on the Vicus Tuscus, decorated with columns of porphyry and *giallo antico*.

In 1869 Pius IX. laid bare the pavement of the Clivus Victoriæ and the alleged site of the Porta Romanula. The Italian government began the last and general excavation of the place in 1876 (and again in 1884), but the work was soon given up without results.

On entering the Palatine by the S. Teodoro gate we are confronted with the Augustæum on the left, with the Clivus Victoriæ and the Fons Juturnæ opposite the gate, with the church of S. Teodoro and the Murus Romuli on the right.

IV. TEMPLUM DIVI AUGUSTI (Temple of Augustus). — The temple in honor of the deified founder of the Empire was begun by his widow Livia and by Tiberius, his adopted son, and completed by Caligula. Domitian restored it after the fire of Titus. Pliny (xii. 19, 42) describes, among the curiosities of the place, a root of a cinnamon tree of great size placed by Livia on a golden plate, the sap of which was hardened into globules every year; and also a famous picture of Hyacinthus by Nikias the Athenian, which Augustus had brought from Alexandria. The plan and design of the building are different from the recognized type of a Roman temple, the front being on the long side of the parallelogram instead of the short. The shape seems special to the Augustæa, perhaps on account of the large number of statues which had to be placed on the *suggestum* opposite the door, the deified Emperor being generally surrounded by other members of the family. The temple is mentioned in connection with Caligula's bridge, which is supposed to have crossed the valley of the Forum at a great height, so as to enable the young monarch to walk on a level from his palace to the Temple of Jupiter on the Capitol. The bridge never existed in the strict sense of the word. Caligula passed from roof to roof of the intermediate buildings, spanning the gaps of the streets with temporary wooden passages. Suetonius and Flavius Josephus mention among these buildings, first, the Templum divi Augusti, then the Basilica Julia. There is no doubt, therefore, that these noble ruins, placed between the Basilica and the Emperor's palace, belong to the Augustæum.

The back wall of the temple, the *murus post œdem divi Augusti ad Minervam*, was used for the posting of state notices and imperial decrees. Two attendants of the Augustæum are mentioned in epigraphic documents: a Bathyllus, *œdituus templi divi Augusti et divœ Augustœ quod est in Palatium* (Corpus, vi. n. 4222), and a

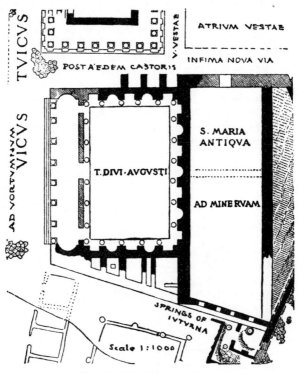

Fig. 48. — Plan of the Augustæum.

T. Flavius Onesimus, *œdituus templi novi divi Augusti* (n. 8704). The temple has been excavated at least five times. I have found in the state archives an Act of October 2, 1526, by which Jacopo de' Muti gives back to a poor widow, Lucrezia Collino, the caution deposited by her before she began the excavations in the garden of S. Maria Liberatrice.

Pirro Ligorio was able to draw the plan of the structure about 1549, in consequence of the excavations described in Book III.

§ xxi. (See Middleton, The Remains of Ancient Rome, vol. i. p. 275, fig. 35.)

In 1702 a contractor named Andrea Bianchi gained permission from Sister Costanza di Santacroce, abbess of the monastery of Torre de' Specchi, to search for building materials within and near the temple. He found the church of S. Maria Antiqua, that is to say, that inner hall of the Augustæum which had been adapted to Christian worship at the end of the fourth century, and dedicated to the Virgin Mary, in opposition to the worship of Vesta, the headquarters of which were on the other side of the street. There are two descriptions of the find: one by Galletti in the Vatican Library (Chron. miscell. xxxiii.); another by Valesio in Cancellieri's "Solenni possessi," p. 370. The church was level with the floor of the Augustæum, and ended with an apse, with frescoes representing the Saviour and some saints, among which was prominent the figure of Paul I. (757–767), with the square nimbus and the legend *Sanctiss. Paulus Romanus Papa.* The frescoes on the walls of the aisles represented scenes in the life of the Saviour, with texts from the Gospel in Greek and Gothico-Latin letters. The figure of the crucifix showed the feet nailed apart. Benedict XIV. ordered the church to be roofed over and kept open for inspection, but the order was never executed.

In 1735 Antonio Vanni excavated the plot of ground near the temple known as the Caprareccia.

The last excavation took place in 1885. It was discovered then that the church of S. Maria Antiqua behind the Augustæum had been put in communication with the Augustæum itself, by cutting an irregular passage through the partition wall seven feet thick. The sides of the passage were covered with figures of saints painted in the eleventh century, with the name appended to each of them: those of the Eastern Church, led by Scs. BASILIVS, on one side; those of the Western, led by Scs. BENEDICTVS, on the other. The two images are connected with the Basilian and Benedictine brotherhoods and convents which at that time flourished on the Palatine (S. Cesario in Palatio and S. Sebastiano in Pallara).

LITERATURE. — Pirro Ligorio, Bodleian MSS., fol. 33. — Henry Parker, *The Forum Romanum*, London, 1876, plates 21 and 24. — *Notizie degli Scavi*, 1882, April, pl. 16. — Henry Middleton, *The Remains of Ancient Rome*, 2d ed., vol. i. p. 275, fig. 35. — Gio. Battista de Rossi, *Bullettino cristiano*, 1885, p. 143. — *Pagan and Christian Rome*, p. 101.

V. FONS JUTURNÆ (the Springs of Juturna). — The Temple of Augustus is built against the live rock of the Palatine, masses

of which appear all along the Clivus Victoriæ, above and under
the pavement of the street. Opposite the gate by which we have
entered the excavations, and right under the west wall of the
temple, the rock is perforated with wells and channels, cut for
the purpose of reaching and regulating the springs with which
the lower or quaternary clay strata are here saturated. This is
the celebrated Fons Juturnæ, placed by Dionysius, Ovid, Florus,
etc., at the north corner of the Palatine, the waters of which, on
reaching the plain, expanded into a deep pond (*profunda palus*)
called the Lacus Curtius. Here the apparition of the Dioscuri
took place, to announce to the Romans the victory of Lake Regillus : they were seen washing and watering their horses "at the
spring which made a pool near the Temple of Vesta," [1] between it
and the temple raised to the celestial messengers themselves in
memory of the event. The pond was drained after the opening
of the Cloaca Maxima, and the only trace left of it was a well
and a *puteal* inscribed with the name of DIVTVR; perhaps the
very one now preserved in the Vatican Museum, Galleria Lapi-
daria, No. 164.

Although the accumulation of modern soil and ruins conceals
these springs from view, they have never ceased to flow, and to
find and force their way towards the Cloaca Maxima. In Crescimbeni's "History of S. M. in Cosmedin," p. 14, we find this
report by Angelo Maffei, dated September 25, 1715: "I remember
to have seen, in my early youth, the ground open and sink into
a chasm fifty cubits deep near the three columns [of Castor's
temple], and a mass of water rush at the bottom of it." The
accident, caused by the erosion of subterranean springs upon the
earth, must have happened at other times, because this corner of
the Palatine was known in Middle Ages under the name of "the
Hell" (l' Inferno) ; hence the name of the church above, *S. Maria
libera nos a poenis Inferni*. The traditional adventure of Q.
Curtius may have originated from a like phenomenon in the
fourth century B. C.

Another powerful jet of water appeared in May, 1702, in the
excavations of the church of S. Maria Antiqua mentioned above;
another in March, 1816, at the foot of the three columns of the
Castores. In 1818 Carlo Fea found water all around the temple,
to the depth of 3.34 metres under the pavement of the Vicus
Tuscus. I remember myself having seen the same place suddenly
inundated in January, 1871, when the excavations had come

[1] Plutarch, *Coriol.*, 3; Dionysius, vi. 13, etc

accidentally in contact with one of the underground channels. The works were suspended for a week or two, until the waters were given an outlet towards the Cloaca Maxima.

REFERENCES. — Rodolfo Lanciani, *Bull. Inst.*, 1871, p. 279; and *I comentarii di Frontino intorno le acque e gli acquedotti.* Rome, 1880, p. 13. — Giuseppe Tommasetti, *Bull. Inst.*, 1871, p. 137. — Francis Nichols, *The Roman Forum*, p. 74, London, 1877.

VI. THE CLIVUS VICTORIÆ. — The Porta Romanula, or "river gate" of the Palatine, could be approached from two sides: from the Forum by a short cut, or steps, used by women in bringing up their load of water from the pool of Juturna; and from the Velabrum, by a carriage-road cut along the base of the cliff at a steep incline. The road is marked (IV) in the fragment of the marble plan, Fig. 47. It was named from an altar of Victory dating from the earliest days of the city, and transformed into a temple 293 B. C., by the consul Lucius Postumius. On April 4, 203, the meteoric stone from Pessinus, which the Romans called the Great Mother of the Gods, was deposited in this sanctuary, pending the erection of the temple described in § xiii. Eleven years later Cato the Censor dedicated a shrine *Victoriæ Virgini*, by the side of the temple, and this is the last mention we find of it in the classics. The temple was discovered by Bianchini in 1728, on the edge of the hill above the road, inside a court or τέμενος, between the palaces of Tiberius and Caligula. There were splendid fragments of its marble decorations: a frieze ornamented with the emblems of a naval victory; columns of *giallo* belonging to the peristyle, capitals, bases, the pedestal of a statue (the same one, probably, dedicated by Cato the Censor in 192); and two pieces of the inscription of the temple itself, which commemorate a restoration by Augustus: —

imp . CAESAR . DIvI . F . aedem . vICTORIAe . refec.

These fragments were kept for a long time on the spot, near the Uccelliera; in 1836, however, they were dispersed: a few went to the Museo Nazionale, Naples; others to the Palazzo Farnese, Rome.

On ascending the Clivus Victoriæ from S. Teodoro towards the Porta Romanula, we pass on the right the remains of thirteen rooms, the walls of which were of *opus quadratum*, strengthened at a later period with *opus lateritium*. These remains, dating from the last century of the Republic, are attributed to the Porticus Catuli. No trace is left of the private palaces of Catulus, Scaurus, Clodius, Cicero, etc., described in § ii.

REFERENCES. — Rodolfo Lanciani, *Il tempio della Vittoria* (in Bull. arch. com., 1883, p. 206). — Christian Huelsen, *Mittheil.*, 1895, pp. 23, 269.

VII. THE CHURCH OF S. TEODORO. — This round structure belongs to the cycle of Byzantine churches and chapels by which the Palatine was surrounded after the fall of the Empire, and is dedicated to an officer who suffered martyrdom at Amasea in the Pontus during the persecution of Maximian. The present rotunda dates from the time of Nicholas V. (1447–55), except the apse and its mosaics, which seem to belong to the time of Hadrian I. (772–795). The level of the church, halfway between that of the Vicus Tuscus and that of the modern road, shows how rapid has been the rise of the soil in the last four centuries. The pieces of serpentine with which part of the court is paved were discovered at the time of Clement XI. in the marble wharf of the Emporium at La Marmorata.

VIII. MURUS ROMULI. — These venerable remains of the primitive fortifications, which we meet with on turning the west corner of the hill towards S. Anastasia, are built of blocks of local tufa, the work of Etruscan masons, as is shown by the way the stones are placed, lengthwise in one tier and crosswise in the next above. The tufa of the walls is characteristic of all works done in Rome before Servius Tullius, such as the fortifications of the Arx in the garden of the Aracœli, and can easily be identified by means of the black scoriæ which it contains, the texture and softness of which resembles that of charred wood. This special tufa, hardly fit for building purposes, was quarried on the spot from the *lautumiœ* near the Temple of Jupiter Propugnator. Other quarries have been discovered in the very heart of the Capitoline hill and at Fidenæ (Villa Spada, Via Salaria).

The walls of the Palatine were discovered on January 26, 1847, but the government commissioners, Visconti, Canina, and Grifi, did not at once realize the importance of the find. They call them in their official report " a monument built of large blocks of tufa, forming two wings 20 palms long, with an arch cut in the live rock between them." The walls are visible at two other points, near the gardener's house and near the so-called Domus Gelotiana. Students wishing to get more information about these early fortifications of the Palatine may consult —

Thomas Dyer, *History of the City of Rome*, London, 1865, p. 14. — Rodolfo Lanciani, *Sulle mura e porte di Servio* (in Ann. Inst., 1871, p. 41). — Visconti and Lanciani, *Guida del Palatino*, Rome, 1873–93, p. 73. — Heinrich Jordan, *Topographie*, vol. i. p. 172. — Otto Richter, *Ann. Inst.*, 1884, p. 189.

Behind the wall and under the northwest corner of the hill there is a reservoir of water, a rough design of which is given by Middleton. Formerly it was deep under ground, the water being drawn from above by means of a well of conical shape; but a land-slip having carried away a portion of the cliff behind the wall, the reservoir can now be entered on a level. There is a basin or cavity right under the well towards which slope all the galleries of the cistern, so as to allow the besieged to draw the last drop in case of water-famine.

IX. The Altar of Aius Locutius. — This remarkable altar was first noticed by Nibby in 1838, on the spot where we see it standing now, on absolutely modern ground, thirty feet at least above the ancient level; but, although not *in situ*, it must have been found not very far off. Nibby and Mommsen consider it as a restoration made in 125 B. C. of the one raised in the Infima Nova Via — in the "lower new street" — behind the Temple of Vesta, in memory of the mysterious voice which, in the stillness of night, warned the citizens of the approach of the Gauls. The voice was attributed to a local genius, whom the people named Aius Loquens or Locutius; but, as Roman religion refrained from mentioning in public prayers the name and sex of unknown local genii, lest the ceremonies should be vitiated by a false invocation, or else the true name of these tutelary gods should be made known to the enemies of the commonwealth, so the altar raised in memory of the event bears the vague dedication —

SEI · DEO · SEI · DEIVAE · SAC(*rum*) —

"sacred to a Divinity, whether male or female." Servius describes likewise a shield dedicated on the Capitol to the Genius of Rome with the legend —

GENIO VRBIS ROMAE SIVE MAS SIVE FEMINA.

The altar of Locutius was restored by Caius Sextius Calvinus, mentioned twice by Cicero as a candidate for the prætorship against Glaucias in 125 B. C. The monument cannot fail to impress the student on account of its connection with one of the leading events in history, the capture and burning of Rome by the Gauls in 390 B. C.

REFERENCES. — Antonio Nibby, *Analisi . . . dei dintorni di Roma*, vol. i. p. 321. — *Corpus Inscr. Lat.*, vol. i. n. 632, p. 185. — *Pagan and Christian Rome*, p. 72. — Carlo Pascal, *Bull. com.*, 1894, p. 188.

Fig. 49. — General view of West Corner of Palatine Hill.

The corner of the hill above the Murus Romuli, towards which we are now ascending by a winding path shaded by ilexes, contains monuments dating from the early days of the city. I have said already that the Palatine was divided into two summits, the "hill of the Twins," or Cermalus, on the north ; the "hill of Pales," or Palatium, on the south. This last is entirely covered by Imperial buildings, which have swept away or concealed whatever monuments there were left of the Kingly and Republican ages, while on the Cermalus the later constructions have avoided the ground made sacred by tradition or by existing remains of bygone days. This historic space overlooking the Velabrum, left free by the Cæsars, measures 175 metres in length, and 106 metres in depth, and contains the steps of Cacus, the hut of Romulus, the old stone quarries, the Temple of the Great Mother of the Gods, and the Temple of Jupiter Propugnator. A section of the space is represented in Fig. 49 (on the opposite page). The background is formed by the arched substructures of the palace of Tiberius, the foreground by the steps of the Temple of Cybele, and by the foundations of the fifth chapel of the Argæi, which Varro places *apud œdem Romuli.* The space is strewn with architectural fragments from the temple of Cybele.

X. Scalæ Caci (Steps of Cacus). — We have seen before that the Palatine city could be entered from three sides : through the Porta Romanula from the northwest, by the Mugonia from the northeast, and by the Steps of Cacus from the side of the Circus. At a very early date these steps took the place of a dangerous path connecting the primitive village with the spring and cave of Faun Lupercus.[1] They are called βαθμοὺς καλῆς ἀκτῆς ("the steps of the beautiful shore") by Plutarch, and Scalæ Caci by Solinus. The first name owes its origin to the picturesque inlet formed by the waters of the greater Velabrum near the Lupercal ; the other

[1] The Lupercal opened at the foot of the cliffs between the Velabrum and the Circus Maximus in the direction of S. Anastasia. Its entrance was once shaded by the Ficus Ruminalis, marking the spot where the cradle containing the infant twins had been washed ashore by the flood. The memory of the miraculous event was perpetuated by a bronze group of Tuscan workmanship, representing the twins nursed by the wolf. This is probably the same as the one preserved in the Conservatori Palace and restored by Guglielmo della Porta (?). The Lupercal was discovered in the first half of the sixteenth century. Ulisse Aldovrandi, quoted by Fea (*Miscell.*, i. 206, n. 4), says: "There was a temple of Neptune (of Faun Lupercus) built by the Arcadians near the Circus Maximus, and I believe it to be the same chapel discovered lately under the cliffs of the Palatine, near S. Anastasia, all encrusted with marine shells."

to the hut of a certain Cacus, a friend of Hercules, who lived near the Ara Maxima, on the shore of the same pool. The Scalæ were shaded by the sacred cornelian tree, believed to be the spear of Romulus, which, being thrown by the hero from the opposite heights of the Aventine, had struck the ground with such force as to take root and grow up again into a beautiful tree.

Two historical events are connected with the steps. First, their restoration by Caligula, in consequence of which the roots of the cornelian tree were cut off and the tree was killed; secondly, the escape of Vitellius in December, 69, when, after the capture of the city by the generals of Vespasian, he fled " per aversam partem Palatii " to the Aventine. The steps have nearly all disappeared, but the walls of *opus quadratum,* by which they were inclosed, and the pavement of the upper landing are tolerably well preserved. There was a gate at the top of the ascent, the site of which is marked by travertine jambs.

REFERENCES. — Ludwig Preller, *Die Regionen,* p. 152. — Karl Bethmann, *Bull. Inst.,* 1852, p. 40. — Ampère, *Histoire romaine à Rome,* vol. i. p. 292. — Wecklein, *Hermes,* vol. vi. p. 193. — Otto Richter, *Annali Inst.,* 1884, p. 189. — Wolfgang Helbig, *Guide,* vol. i. n. 618, p. 459.

XI. CASA ROMULI (the hut of Romulus). — Tradition tells us that at the top of the steps just described there was the hut of Faustulus the shepherd, in which Romulus and Remus had found shelter and food and received their early education. History shows that down to the middle of the fourth century after Christ the hut had been preserved in its primitive shape by the periodical renewal of its thatched roof and wooden framework. The foundations of this " memorial " are still in existence. They are made of blocks of yellowish granular tufa, and form a parallelogram 30 feet long and 17 feet wide. When discovered in 1872, the parallelogram was perfect, but the quality of the tufa is so soft, and the blocks are so easily disintegrated by atmospheric agencies, that it will soon disappear, unless protected by a roof. The cut (Fig. 50) represents a prehistoric hut, modeled from nature by an Alban shepherd, about the time of the foundation of Rome. It was discovered in the necropolis of Alba Longa by Carnevali in 1817, and it is now owned by Michele de Rossi.

We might consider this clay hut-urn[1] as a perfect model not

[1] REFERENCES. — Michele-Stefano de Rossi, *Annali Inst.,* 1871, p. 242, tav. v. — Pigorini and Lubbock, *Notes on Hut-urns,* p. 11. — Rodolfo Lanciani, *Ancient Rome,* chap. i.

only of the Casa Romuli (also called Tugurium Faustuli), but also of the other Casa Romuli on the Capitol, sacred to his memory as a hero and demi-god, of the *focus* of Vesta, of the chapels of the Argæi, and other such prehistoric dwellings, which are all described as *vimine texti, stipula tecti,* and made *de canna straminibusque.* Their type was never forgotten : in the inscriptions of Lella Marnia in Africa a tomb in the shape of a *casa* or *tugurium* is called " Domus Romula." (See Corpus, viii. p. 1123.)

Fig. 50. — Hut-urn from Alba Longa.

The foundations of the Casa Romuli are surrounded by other remains of the Kingly period which cannot be identified. There is a square mass of stones, with a gutter around the base, which may possibly mark the site of the fifth *sacrarium* of the Argæi. (See Fig. 49.)

REFERENCES. — Scheidewin, *Philologus,* vol. i. p. 82. — Ludwig Preller, *Die Regionen,* p. 180. — Francesco Cipolla, *Rivista di Filologia,* 1878, p. 47. — Heinrich Jordan, *Hermes,* vii. p. 196 ; and *Topographie,* i. p. 292. — Theodor Mommsen, *Hermes,* xiii. p. 527. — Gio. Battista de Rossi, *Piante di Roma,* p. 4. — Otto Richter, *Topographie,* p. 100. — *Notizie degli Scavi,* 1896, p. 291.

XII. THE OLD STONE QUARRIES. — An underground passage

between the Temple of Jupiter Propugnator and the Palace of
Domitian, which can be entered by a slope under the coffee-house
of the Farnese Gardens, gives access to a network of tufa quarries
extending over an acre.   They cannot be explored now on account
of their dangerous state, but I remember going over them in every
direction when they were first discovered in 1867.   The section
which runs under the Temple of Jupiter is comparatively recent,
and must have been excavated by a *vignaiuolo* before the laying
out of the Farnese Gardens, or when these were again put under
cultivation in the first half of the last century.   The section approaching the house of Germanicus and Tiberius is very ancient,
perhaps contemporary with the first colonization of the hill.   There
is something impressive and solemn in the aspect of these old
lautumiæ, which at a later period were turned into a water-tank.
There were several wells communicating with the ground above,
but only one is kept open, at the turn of the street called (probably) " Victoria Germaniciana." The puteal or mouth of the well
is of modern restoration; the shaft is ancient and lined with slabs
of Alban stone, with holes to make the descent into the reservoir
easy.   A conical heap of terra-cotta ex-votos was found at the
bottom of this well.   This find reminded us at the time of the
passage of Frontinus : " In the present abundance of water (brought
to Rome by eleven aqueducts) we have not forgotten the historical
springs from which drank our forefathers " (fontium memoria cum
sanctitate adhuc extat et colitur).   Suetonius says that under Augustus all classes of citizens (*omnes ordines*) threw ex-votos into the
well of Juturna.   The Fontinalia, or Feast of Springs, was celebrated in Rome on October 13th.   (Another well was found July
10, 1896.)

There are in this public space of ground two more monuments,
independent of the Palace of the Cæsars, which, although raised
long after the Kingly period, must be described before we enter the
Imperial grounds, — the Temple of the Great Mother of the Gods,
and that of Jupiter Propugnator.

XIII.   Ædes Magnæ Deum Matris (Temple of Cybele). —
Livy (xxxvi. 35) relates that during the second Punic war in 206
b. c. an embassy was sent by the senate to Pessinus, after consult-
ing the Sibylline books, which brought back to Rome a famous
relic, called (by Servius, Æn. vii. 188) the *acus Matris Deum.*
This was a small meteoric stone of siliceous texture, brown in
color, pyramidal in shape, set, instead of the face, in a silver

statue of Cybele. Great was the veneration of the Romans for this image, and a temple was raised in its honor in 192 B. C., rebuilt by Augustus in A. D. 3, after a fire. The phrase "ædem Matris Magnæ in Palatio feci," which Augustus uses in his autobiography, has been interpreted as if the temple was in the opposite part of the hill called strictly " Palatium," but we must remember that the autobiography was written long after the name had been assigned to the whole tenth region.

The most noticeable event in the history of the sanctuary is the sacrilege committed by Heliogabalus, who removed to his own private chapel the great object of popular worship. (See Ancient Rome, p. 127.) The description which Herodianus gives of it is identical with that of Servius. " The stone," he says, " is large, shaped as a cone, and black in color. People think it a stone fallen from heaven," etc. When Bianchini excavated in 1725–30 the imperial chapel or *lararium*, he found " a stone nearly three feet high, conical in shape, of a deep brown color, like a piece of lava, and ending in a sharp point." I have no doubt that it was the celebrated " needle of Cybele." No attention was paid to the find.

The last mention we have of the Great Mother of the Gods belongs to the end of the fourth century, when Nicomachus Flavianus and a few surviving champions of polytheism tried to stir up the old popular superstitions. During the revolution against Theodosius II., which ended with the defeat of Eugenius, September 7 to 9, 392, Nicomachus and his followers indulged in the most fanatic display of long-forgotten pagan superstitions, like the Isia, the Floralia, the Lustrum, and the Megalesia, the mysterious worship of Cybele. After being baptized in blood, they carried through the main streets of the city the chariot of the goddess with lions of solid silver.

It is not certain whether the temple, the scattered remains of which appear in Fig. 49, belongs to the Great Mother of the Gods, because its columns and entablature are of Alban stone (*peperino*) coated with stucco, and therefore cannot presumably be the work of Augustus, who used only marble. I do not dare to express any definite opinion on the subject, because there are other circumstances in favor of the supposition which must be taken into consideration. The first is the discovery made in January, 1872, near the *pronaos* of the temple, of a semi-colossal statue of the goddess (Fig. 51, p. 134). The statue is headless, but has been identified by means of the *suppedaneum* or footstool which the ancients gave to Cybele as a symbol of the stability of the earth.

The second is the discovery of several altars inscribed with her name, made at various times in this part of the Farnese Gardens. The one marked No. 496 in vol. vi. of the " Corpus Inscriptionum " was raised at the expense of three attendants of the temple, named

Fig. 51. — Headless Statue of Cybele, found near her temple on the Palatine.

Onesimus, Olympias, and Briseis.   A second, No. 3702, came to light in 1873 near the south wall of the temple.   See also the inscription, No. 513, belonging to a statue offered to the goddess by Virius Marcarianus, and the fragment in " Notizie degli Scavi," 1896, p. 186.

There are about sixty fragments of columns, capitals, entabla-

ture, and pediment lying scattered in confusion, which, if properly
put together in their former position, as Huelsen has done in
design (Mittheilungen, 1895, pp. 10–22), would make this temple
one of the most beautiful ruins of the Palatine. The foundation-
walls of the *cella* and *pronaos* are still intact. The statue itself is
lying aside, in a slanting position.

There is a valuable marble in the Capitoline museum connected
with the history of the temple, viz., an altar with bas-reliefs representing the ship on which the goddess came from Pessinus to
Rome, and the Vestal Claudia Quinta hauling it up the Tiber,
with her *infula* tied to the prow. There is written underneath:
" Matri Deum et Navi-Salviæ voto suscepto, Claudia Synthyche
d(ono) d(edit)." Maffei and Preller think that the surname of
Navisalvia was given to the Vestal Claudia because she had
brought the ship safely to her moorings; Orelli and Mommsen
attribute it to the ship herself (Navis Salvia), or rather to her pro-
tecting genius (see Corpus, n. 495). The altar can be seen in the
gallery of the Capitoline museum, where it is used as a pedestal to
the statue No. 25 (Jupiter found at Antium).

Greek and Greco-Roman artists have always given Cybele a
type of majestic beauty. One of the finest representations of the
merciful goddess, " who gave fruitfulness alike to men and beasts
and vegetation," was discovered not long ago at Formiæ (Mola di
Gaeta), together with the remains of her temple of the Ionic
order. The statue, which would have formed the pride of the
Naples museum, has been allowed to migrate to foreign lands.
When I stood before her the first time, and felt the influence of
her wonderful beauty, I easily understood why she remained a
favorite deity to the very end of pagan worship in Rome. I am
sure it will please my readers to become acquainted with this wonderful work of art known only to a privileged few (Fig. 52, p. 136).

REFERENCES. — Francesco Cancellieri, *Le sette cose fatali*, Rome, 1812,
p. 22. — Visconti and Lanciani, *Guida del Palatino*, Rome, 1873, pp. 29, 134. —
Theodor Mommsen, *Res gestæ divi Augusti*, 2d ed. 1883, p. 82. — Christian
Huelsen, *Untersuchungen zur Topographie des Palatins* (in Mittheilungen,
1895, p. 3). — *Ancient Rome*, p. 126.

XIV. ÆDES IOVIS PROPUGNATORIS IN PALATIO (Temple of
Jupiter Propugnator). — Between the house of Germanicus and
the Nymphæum of the house of Domitian stands the platform of
a temple, the mass of which is built of concrete with chips of tufa
and silex, inclosed in a frame of *opus quadratum*. The temple,

which is 44 metres long, and 25 wide, faces the southwest, but not
a fragment of its decorations has escaped the cinquecento lime-

Fig. 52. — The Cybele from Formiæ.

burners. Probably it was octostyle peripteral, viz. surrounded by
a colonnade which had 8 shafts in the front, 16 on the sides.
Rosa, who discovered the platform in 1867, identifies it with the

Temple of Jupiter Victor, a memorial building of the victory gained by the Romans over the Samnites in 294 B. C. We prefer to see in it the Temple of Jupiter Propugnator, connected with the residence (*schola collegii*) of a priesthood ranking in nobility with that of the Quindecemviri, of the Arvales, and other kindred religious corporations, of which the Emperor was a *de iure* member. The remains of a building in *opus quadratum* of the late Republic, remarkably suited for the use of a *schola*, have actually been discovered side by side with the temple itself.

Many fragments of the *fasti cooptationum*, or registers of the elections to this priesthood, have been found, not *in situ*, however, but employed, after the prohibition of pagan worship, in the restoration of the pavements of the Basilica Julia and of the Senate-house. (See Corpus, n. 2004, 2009, etc.) They are all worded this way : " In the year nine hundred and forty-two of Rome," (A. D. 190) for instance, "under the consulships of the Emperor Commodus, for the sixth time, and of Petronius Septimianus, on the 15th day of October, in the Temple of Jupiter Propugnator on the Palatine, Lucius Attidius Cornelianus has been elected." Sometimes they add the name of the deceased member whose place was vacant : " Claudius Paternus cooptatus in locum Attidi Corneliani vita functi " (A. D. 198).

On the top of the steps of the temple there is a fragment of an altar inscribed with the words, " Domitius Calvinus, son of Marcus, high priest, consul for the second , time and [victorious] general [has built or repaired or ornamented this building, or raised this monument] with the spoils of war." (See Ephemeris epigraphica, 1872, p. 215.)

Cneus Domitius Calvinus, consul in 53 and 40 B. C., is the gallant general of Julius Cæsar who led the centre at the battle of Pharsalos. Later he carried on a successful campaign in Spain, for which he was rewarded with the triumph in 36 B. C. With the spoils of war — *aurum coronarium* — he restored the Regia by the house of the Vestals, as related by Dion Cassius (xlviii. 42). The altar, therefore, has nothing to do with the Temple of Jupiter Propugnator, having been found in January, 1868, at some distance from it, in the excavations of the Forum Palatinum. It ought to be put back in its place by the Regia. The four pieces of fluted stone columns placed by Rosa at the top of the stairs belong likewise to another edifice, perhaps to the Temple of Cybele. Pirro Ligorio pretends to have seen a fragment of the colossal statue of the god, measuring eight feet from shoulder to shoulder. It was

sold by Cristoforo Stati to a stone-cutter named Leonardo Cieco
"per farne opere moderne." His statement (Bodleian MSS. p. 138)
deserves no credit.

REFERENCES. — *Corpus Inscr. Lat.*, vol. vi. p. 450, n. 2004–2009. — Adolf
Becker, *Topographie*, p. 422. — Ludwig Preller, *Röm. Mythologie*, p. 177.

XV. DOMUS AUGUSTANA (house of Augustus). — An irregular
opening made in March, 1893, through the left wall of the Stadium
(Fig. 53, BB.) leads — for the time being — into the house of
Augustus. This newly cut passage seems to be calculated to
mislead the visitor at once: it occupies the site of a staircase
connecting the two floors of the house, the remains of which were
likewise obliterated in 1893, leaving only the marks of the steps
against the side walls. The following plan (Fig. 53), although
defective in two or three points, which cannot be made good unless
the excavations are completed, will enable the visitor to find his
way without difficulty.

The Palatine hill, so near the Forum and the Capitol, the centres of Roman political and business life, had always been the
favorite place of residence with statesmen, eminent lawyers, and
orators, and wealthy citizens in general. Augustus made it the
seat of the Empire. Born near the east corner of the hill, in
the lane named "ad capita bubula,"[1] he selected it again as the
Imperial residence, after the victory of Actium, which had made
him master of the world. The ambitious plan was not carried
into execution at once. He began, 44 B. C., by purchasing the
modest house of Hortensius the orator, the columns and pavements
of which were of common stone. After the conquest of Egypt in
28, he bought other property, including the house of Catilina.
The Imperial residence was then rebuilt on a larger scale and in
more becoming style, the whole estate being divided into three
sections. The first, from the side of the Velia, was occupied by
the Propylaia, the Temple of Apollo, the Portico of the Danaids,
and the Greek and Latin libraries; the middle section by the
Shrine of Vesta; the last, on the side of the Circus, by the Imperial house.[2] This magnificent set of buildings was crowded

[1] "Ox-heads." The tomb of Metella is actually called "Capo-di-Bove"
from the ox-skulls of its frieze. The lane where Augustus was born was close
to the "street of the old Curiæ," ad Curias veteres.

[2] "Phœbus habet partem: Vestæ pars altera cessit — quod superest illis, ter-
tius ipse tenet" (Ovid, *Fast.*, iv. 951). References for the Temple of Apollo,
and the Portico of the Danaids: Rodolfo Lanciani, *Il tempio di Apolline palatino*
(in Bull. arch. com., vol. xi. 1883, p. 185, pl. 17); and *Ancient Rome*, p. 109. —
Christian Huelsen, *Mittheilungen*, 1888, p. 296; and 1895, p. 28.

with the masterpieces of Greek, Tuscan, and Roman art, as minutely described in "Ancient Rome," p. 109. The building of a shrine of Vesta near the house was a necessity of state, since Augustus had been elected pontifex maximus after the death of

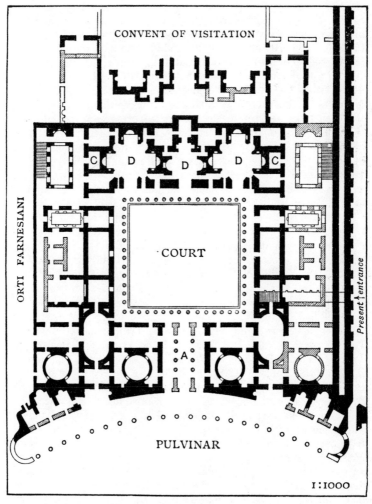

Fig. 53. — Plan of the Domus Augustana, Ground Floor.

Æmilius Lepidus in 12 B. C. On this occasion the old pontifical palace was presented to the Vestals, to increase the accommodation provided by their own.

The Domus Augustana was destroyed by the fire of Nero, with the exception of the room in which the founder of the Empire had slept for forty years. It was rebuilt by Domitian towards A. D. 85, never to suffer any more by the violence of man or at the hand of Time, until the vandal hand of the Abbé Rancoureuil ruined it in 1775. The Temple of Apollo and its libraries were destroyed in the night, between the 18th and 19th of March, A. D. 363, the fury of the flames being such that only the Sibylline books were saved from the wreck. We hear no more of the monumental group until the time of Fra Giocondo da Verona († 1520), when the beautiful ruins, set in their frame of evergreens, began to attract the attention of architects and archæologists. Dosio, Palladio, Heemskerk, Ligorio, Panvinio have left important memoranda of the state of the "palazzo maggiore" in the sixteenth century. Palladio mistook the palace for a public bath — *terme di palazzo maggiore* — but his plan is none the less important. I found it in the Burlington-Devonshire collection and published it in the "Mittheilungen" of 1894, plates i.–iii. Comparing the various accounts, maps, drawings, sketches, acts of notaries, etc., of the cinquecento, we gather the following information : —

The ground occupied by the Augustan buildings belonged, towards the middle of the sixteenth century, half to Alessandro Colonna, half to Cristoforo Stati. Duke Paolo Mattei purchased both properties about 1560. We do not know whether Alessandro Colonna had searched the ground : the two other gentlemen did. They came across (and destroyed) the Propylaia, described by Pliny (xxxvi. 4, 10); the Portico of the Danaids, described by Propertius (ii. 31); and the Temple of Vesta. No mention is made of the Temple of Apollo, unless we can consider as such the notice given by Pietro Sante Bartoli (Memorie, n. 7) of the discovery of a hiding-place inlaid with precious stones, where the Sibylline books were probably kept. The Portico of the Danaids numbered fifty-two columns of *giallo antico*, many of which have been recovered from time to time, probably because they were considered unfit for the lime-kiln. "On October 29, 1664," says an eye-witness, "in the gardens of Duke Mattei, a portico was discovered of extraordinary richness, with columns of *giallo antico*, and two bas-reliefs representing Romulus, the Wolf, the Lupercal, Faustulus, the Tiber, and other subjects connected with the foundation of Rome." Winckelmann speaks of two other panels representing Dædalos and Ikaros, and a young Satyr drinking from a cup. A fifth, described by Matz, represents Theseus and the Minotaur, a sixth Ulysses and Diomedes.

In 1728 Count Spada, who had bought the villa from the Mattei, discovered seven rooms "ornamented with precious marbles, gilt metal, stucco bas-reliefs on a golden ground, and arabesques." In one of the rooms, which was used for bathing purposes, there was a marble *cathedra,* and a basin of lead before it. The two columns of oriental alabaster, which stood on each side of the *cathedra,* were removed to the chapel of Prince Odescalchi in the church of SS. Apostoli. Count Spada found also "several broken statues of marble and bronze."

In 1825 Charles Mills found another column of *giallo* 2.25 metres long, lying on a marble pavement, at a depth of 1.56 metre. Other pieces of fluted shafts of *giallo* came to light in 1869 and 1877, in the excavations of the so-called Stadium, where they had rolled down from the portico, together with the eighteen or twenty torsos of the Danaids described by Flaminio Vacca (Mem. 77).

In March, 1849, Colonel Robert Smith, who had succeeded Charles Mills in the ownership of the grounds, destroyed a portion of the Pulvinar (see Fig. 53), to make room for a carriage road between the gate on the Via de' Cerchi and the Casino. In the same year he discovered the drain connecting the Area Apollinis with the main sewer of the Vallis Murcia.

The blame for having destroyed to a great extent the house of Augustus rests with the Frenchman Rancoureuil, who excavated the Villa Spada in 1775, and sold even the bricks and stones of the historical sanctuary to a stonecutter in the Campo Vaccino named Vinelli. I have heard it related that the abbé was so anxious to keep his proceedings secret, that besides preventing any one from seeing the excavations by daylight (except his friend Barbèri), he kept a fierce mastiff to watch the place at night. Roman archæologists, however, did not give up the contest, and a young man named Benedetto Mori, an assistant of Piranesi, volunteered to sketch the plan of the ruins *coûte qui coûte.* He began by making advances to the dog, tempting him with food, until after many nocturnal meetings the two became so friendly that the beast helped the architect to accomplish his mission. It appears from his designs — although rather imperfect — that the front of the palace followed the curve of the Pulvinar or state balcony from which the games of the Circus were seen, and that there were five windows on either side of the entrance door. This door was still visible in 1829, but it is concealed now by the gardener's house. Inside the building first came the *atrium* (A) with a colonnade on each side, giving access to apartments of elaborate shape and design; farther on was the court of honor, with a peristyle of 56 fluted marble columns of the Ionic order, on which opened other private apartments. One of the most elegant chambers was the *sterquilinium* (CC), with three recesses supported by finely carved brackets. Its pavement and walls were incrusted with polychrome marbles; of marble also were the water-pipes connected with the basins. The lead pipes found in other parts of the building bore the name of Domitian. No trace seems to have been found of the tower or "belvedere" named Syracuse or τεχνόφυον, to which Augustus retired when worn with the care of governing the world. From this *locus in edito*, as Suetonius calls it, he must have watched day by day the transformation of the capital, which he had found built of bricks and wanted to leave a city of marble. Just opposite the west windows of the palace, his friend L. Cornificius was rebuilding with great magnificence the old federal Temple of Diana on the Aventine, and Augustus himself the three temples of Minerva, Juno Regina, and Jupiter Libertas on the same hill. Turning to the other points of the horizon, he could see the transformation of the Campus Martius made by Agrippa and by himself, the Portico and Temple Herculis Musarum built by Marcius Philippus, the Atrium Libertatis by Asinius Pollio, the Temple of Saturn by Munatius Plancus, a theatre and a portico by Cornelius Balbus, an amphitheatre by Statilius Taurus, and scores of other edifices, masterpieces of architecture and museums of fine arts.

Of the Domus Augustana nothing except a few bare walls is left standing, and three underground rooms of graceful design, marked DDD in the plan (p. 139). The shimmering light which falls through masses of ivy from an opening in the middle of the ceilings makes these ruins very picturesque. As a contrast to the loneliness of the spot, there is above our heads an artistic gem of the cinquecento, a small portico designed and painted by Raffaellino del Colle. The subjects of the graceful frescoes are: Cupid showing the arrow to Venus; Venus lacing her sandals; Jupiter in the form of a Satyr pursuing Antiope; and other such mythological scenes. The frescoes, injured by neglect, were restored by Camuccini in 1824 at the expense of Charles Mills.

It is probable that the works of art, discovered at various times in the adjoining Stadium, have fallen there from the Domus Augustana and from the Portico of the Danaids (see § xxii.).

The two columns of alabaster found in 1728 have been used in the decoration of the Odescalchi chapel. The two bas-reliefs symbolic of the foundation of Rome (Monumenta Mattheiana, vol. iii. pls. 37 and 45) are now set into the wall of the courtyard of the Palazzo Mattei. The third, with Dædalos and Ikaros (Winckelmann, Monum. inediti, n. 95), belongs to the Villa Albani; the fourth, with the young Satyr (Visconti, Museo Pio Clement, vol. iv. pl. 31), to the Galleria dei candelabri. The fifth, of Theseos and the Minotaur, is broken in two, one part belonging to the British Museum (Ancient Marbles, xi. 48), one to the Museo delle Terme in Rome. The latter also owns the sixth panel, with the figures of Ulysses and Diomedes. How interesting it would be to the student if plaster-casts of this unique set of panels were exhibited in the place to which the originals belong! The capital of the Corinthian order with the acanthus leaves bending from right to left (Guattani, Monum. ined., vol. ii. 1785, p. 94, tav. ii. fig. 6) is now in England. The exquisite frieze of the *sterquilinium* was divided between the architect Barbèri and the Venetian ambassador Andrea Memmo. One of the two Ledæ discovered by Rancoureuil went to England, and the Apollo Sauroktonos, also discovered by him, was purchased by Pius VI. for the Museo Vaticano (Galleria delle statue, No. 264). The Apollo Cithorœdos by Scopas, which stood in the temple, between the images of Latona and Diana, is represented in some brass medals of the time of Augustus; there are also several reproductions in marble. The one (No. 516) in the Hall of the Muses was found in 1774 in the Pianella di Cassio near Tivoli. A second replica (No. 495 in the same hall), known as "Bacchus in Female Attire," and very much restored, was removed from the Villa Negroni. There is a third subject in the hall of the Greek Cross, No. 582, known as the "Muse Erato," which does not deserve the name of Apollo Palatinus attributed to it in official catalogues. The last replica, discovered in the Villa of Quintus Voconius Pollio near Marino, March, 1885, was purchased by Leo XIII., and largely restored by Galli. It now occupies the place of the Faun of Circæii, No. 41 Braccio nuovo.

In all these works of art "Apollo appears in a costume which at first sight surprises us. We seem to have before us one of those exalted females who were mistresses of the lyre and of song, and we require circumstantial evidence to convince us that these splendid robes envelop the form of a slender youth." [1]

REFERENCES. — Giuseppe Guattani, *Roma descritta ed illustrata*, vol. i. p. 48, tav. viii.-xiv. ; and *Monumenti inediti*, vol. ii. 1785, pp. 1 and 29. — Luigi Canina, *Edifizii di Roma antica*, vol. iv. pl. 108. — Henry Deglane, *Gazette Archeol.*, 1888, p. 145. — *Bullettino arch. com.*, vol. xi. 1883, p. 185. — Visconti and Lanciani, *Guida del Palatino*, Rome, 1873, pp. 33 and 98. — Rodolfo Lanciani, *Pagan and Christian Rome*, chap. v. ; and *Il palazzo maggiore*, in Mittheilungen, 1894, pp. 3–36.

XVI. DOMUS TIBERIANA (house of Tiberius), Fig. 54. — We now cross the valley which separated, before Domitian's time, the house of Augustus from the Cermalus, and visit the wing of the Imperial residence which owes its existence to Tiberius and Caligula. This part is not yet laid bare, the underground floor alone having been made accessible here and there. As we have observed in the introductory remarks, the substructures are most irregular in their plan, because they were intended to serve but one purpose : to support an artificial platform, upon which the palace was built on its own independent design. At the same time we must acknowledge that the irregularity of the substructures is less apparent here than in any other section of the hill, so that we can almost foresee what would be the general outline of the Domus Tiberiana and of the Domus Gaiana if the living apartments were laid bare. The two buildings now form a rectangle 150 metres long and 115 metres wide, limited by the Forum Palatinum on the south, by the area containing the prehistoric monuments on the west, by the Clivus Victoriæ on the north and east. It contains the following places of interest : (XIV) the Domus Tiberiana ; (XV) the House of Germanicus ; (XVI) the wing added by Caligula, which we shall call Domus Gaiana ; (XVII) the Forum Palatinum, a public square between the palaces of Caligula and Domitian. Apropos of the last-named place, the reader must remember that the Imperial buildings of the Palatine did not form a mass inaccessible to the public, like the Vatican palace and gardens of the present day; the hill was crossed by streets and passages, through which the citizens could probably pass without restriction at all hours of the day. The gates with which these streets and passages are provided were probably closed at night, and had a guard posted by them.[2] This is certain for the Porta

---

[1] Emil Braun, *Ruins and Museums*, p. 236.

[2] At the time of Caligula's murder the watch at the main gate was probably kept by the *Germani corporis custodes* (Suetonius, 58). There were also porters (*janitores*) assisted by a watch-dog (Suetonius, *Vitellius*, 16).

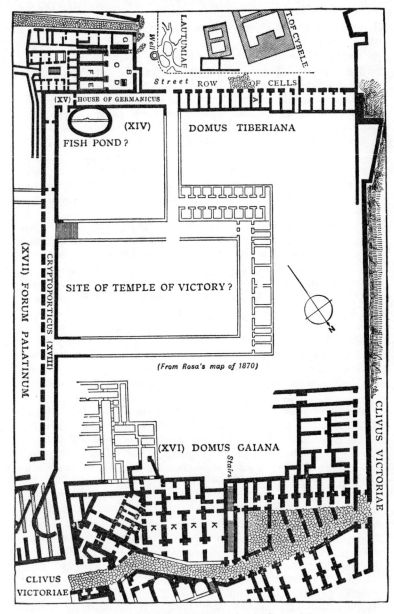

Fig. 54. — Plan of the Domus Tiberiana and of the Domus Gaiana.

Romanula and the Clivus Victoriæ, and for the grand state entrance in front of Domitian's palace; it is probable for the steps of Cacus, at the top of which the jambs of a travertine gate are still to be seen. For other streets of access to the Palatine we must await the results of further excavations.

Tiberius Claudius Nero, father of the Emperor, owned a modest house (XV) on the Palatine, which afterwards came into the possession of Germanicus. Tiberius the Emperor raised a noble palace next to it, known in classic documents as the Domus Tiberiana. It formed a square, the south side of which opened on the street called "Victoria Germaniciana," whilst the west towered above the valley of the Velabrum at the height of 50 metres, the north touched the Temple of Victory and Caligula's palace, and the east opened on the Forum Palatinum.

Tacitus (Hist., i. 27) says that Otho, wishing to join the conspirators against the life of Galba, who were about to meet in the Forum, descended to the Velabrum through the Domus Tiberiana (probably by the steps of Cacus, or by one of the private stairs which are still to be seen behind the gardener's house and the walls of Romulus). The same historian describes Vitellius glutting himself in the banqueting-room of the palace, while his partisans, who were fighting against Flavius Sabinus, had set the Capitol ablaze. The fire could be seen from the Imperial table. On receiving the news of his defeat, which left no hope for his crown or for his life, he rushed to the Aventine *per aversam partem palatii,* viz., by the same steps which Otho had descended a few months before.

The great attraction of the palace was the library, Bibliotheca Tiberiana, which seems to have contained state papers and documents more than books. The passage of Dion Cassius about the fire of Commodus very probably refers to it : " The flames pervaded the palace with such suddenness and force that nearly all the registers and records of the Empire were lost."

The only portion now visible is the arched substructures of the south front, with a row of cells very poorly lighted, ventilated, and ornamented (see Fig. 49). They must have been occupied by soldiers or slaves. One of them (A) protected by a wooden railing, is very rich in graffiti, lately published and explained by Professor Correra in "Bull. arch. com.," 1894, p. 95, plates 2–4. There are many names, followed by the specification *castre[n]sis,* "from the prætorian camp," or *miles,* "soldier." One of them writes in tolerably good Greek, "Many have written many things

on this wall, I nothing;" to which another hand subscribes
" Bravo ! " Per-
haps the most
curious graffito
is a rough TVLLIVSROMANVS MILES
sketch of the
head of Nero made by a soldier named
Tullius Romanus.

Rough sketches and bona-fide carica-
tures of Imperial heads are not unknown
on the Palatine. One was found in
March, 1876, by an English lady, graffito on a slab of *giallo antico* with the
semi-barbaric legend " Caxir Nero" (*Nero
Cæsar*), the work of one of the Teutonic
body-guard.[1] This also is a specimen of
the artistic propensities of another soldier, who perhaps had just seen the Emperor walking in front of the *corps-de-
garde* of the Domus Tiberiana. Several
officers from the Domus Tiberiana are
recorded in Roman epitaphs : a *balam-
belus acuarius*, or plumber (Corpus, n.
8653) an *albanus a supelectile*, or keeper

Fig. 55. — A Graffito of the
Domus Tiberiana.

of plate (n. 8654) ; a *jucundus vilicus*, or caretaker (n. 8655), etc.

XVII. HOUSE OF GERMANICUS (Fig. 54, XV.). — This beautiful edifice was discovered in the spring of 1869, and I well remember the excitement created among artists and archæologists
by the appearance of its celebrated paintings. It is the only Roman private house now existing, the one discovered by Azara in
the Villa Montalto, near the present railway station, having been
destroyed in 1777, and its paintings cut away from the walls and
sold to Lord Bristol.[2]

The house has but one entrance (B), not from the streets, which
go round three sides of it, but from the *cryptoporticus* of the

---

[1] Published in facsimile, *Bull. arch. com.*, 1877, p. 166.

[2] The house discovered by Azara was illustrated by Angelo Uggeri,
Iconografia degli edifizi di Roma antica, vol. iii. pls. 14–17, p. 53; vol. ii.
pl. 24. — Raffaele Mengs and Camillo Buti, *Pitture trovate l' anno 1777 nella
villa Negroni*. 13 plates. — Camillo Massimi, *Notizie della villa Massimi*,
Rome, 1836, p. 214. — Luigi Canina, *Edifizi di Roma antica*, vol. iv. tav. 192.

palace of Tiberius and Caligula, in which the murder of the latter took place on January 24, A. D. 41. The historians who describe the event say that the murderers, not daring to retrace their steps for fear of the guards posted at the main entrance by the Velia, ran away in the opposite direction and concealed themselves in the house of Germanicus. This statement leaves no doubt as to the identity of the building, which, besides, abounds in hiding-places, crypts, and underground passages running in the direction of the house of Augustus. The intense love felt by the Romans for the unhappy prince, and the veneration for his memory, which lasted for centuries, explain the fact that this house alone, among so many public and private buildings, altars, shrines, temples, palaces, etc., destroyed by the Cæsars, was kept as a national relic down to the fall of the Empire. Evidence of the care taken of, and of repairs made on, the house from time to time is to be found in the legends of its water-pipes. One bears the name "Ivliae·Avg" (Julia, the daughter of Titus, or Julia Domna); the second, "Domitiani Caesar[*is*] Avg[*usti*]"; the third has the name of a plumber, "L[*ucius*] Pescennivs Eros," probably a contemporary of Septimius Severus.

The fore portion of the house, sunk below the level of the street, is built of reticulated work with small prisms of yellowish tufa. The angles and arches are of the same material, without any mixture of bricks, a style of masonry which came into fashion towards the end of the Republic. Like all Roman private residences, it is divided into two sections: one for the reception of friends and clients, one for domestic use. We enter the first by an inclined vestibule paved with fine mosaic. The *atrium* (C) was probably *testudinatum*, viz. covered by a roof with no *impluvium* in the centre. The pavement is of fine mosaic; and there are remains of the altar of the domestic gods (D). Three halls open on the side opposite the vestibule; the first on the left (E), damaged by the sinking of the outer wall, has some good decorative panels divided by slender columns, with ivy and vines woven around their shafts.

The central hall or *tablinum* (F) has a similar decoration of composite columns, but the panels contain frescoes far superior to the others in interest, design, and execution. They have been reproduced many times and by various processes by Rosa, Perrot, and the German Institute; the best copies in facsimile, made at the time of the discovery by M. Layraud, were presented by Napoleon III. to the Library of the Ecole des Beaux Arts.

The one in the back wall represents Polyphemus the giant, half merged in the waters of the sea, who, having crushed his rival Akis under a heavy rock, turns toward Galatea with an expression of cruelty mingled with tenderness. The Nymph glides over the water on the back of a sea-horse, followed by two Nereids. The passion by which the giant was mastered is represented by a Cupid, who stands upright on his left shoulder and guides him with a ribbon.

On the right, and above the frieze, there is a smaller panel representing a scene of private initiation. The picture which follows, on turning to the right wall, belongs to the landscape order, and shows a street scene with houses many stories high on either side. A woman, followed by her attendant, knocks at one of the doors, and four or five figures appear at the windows or on the balconies to make sure who is seeking for admittance. The second small panel, above the frieze, seems to indicate the preparations for a domestic sacrifice.

The last and best picture pertains to the myth of Io, loved by Jupiter and persecuted by Juno. The fair daughter of Inachus is kept prisoner in the sacred wood by Mycenæ, and sits at the foot of a pillar surmounted by the image of the jealous goddess. The all-seeing Argos, armed with lance and sword, gazes intently at the girl in his custody. Behind the rock, on which he is leaning with the right elbow, Mercury appears to advance cautiously, waving the caduceus as a symbol of his mission from the father of the gods for the deliverance of Io. The name ΕΡΜΗΣ is written in white letters under the Messenger's feet, and there is no doubt that the other personages were likewise indicated by their proper names ΙΩ, ΑΡΓΟΣ.

The dining-room or *triclinium* (G) opens on the west side of the court. Its frescoes have suffered very much from exposure and damp, the apartment being sunk four metres below the street. The walls have been found coated with flange tiles, with the rim turned inwards, so as to leave a free space for the circulation of air and the evaporation of moisture. A curious vase of glass filled with fruit is painted above the entrance door. The panels have a vermilion ground, except two which show fanciful groups of birds, animals, trees, etc., on a white surface, the work of a very inferior artist.

Admittance to the inner (and higher) rooms is gained by a narrow wooden staircase (H) on the west side of the *atrium*, near the door of the *triclinium;* but they hardly deserve a visit, having been despoiled of every bit of ornamentation.

REFERENCES. — Pietro Rosa, *Plan et peintures de la maison paternelle de Tibère*, s. l. — Lanciani and Visconti, *Guida del Palatino*, Rome, Bocca, 1873, p. 132. — Georges Perrot, *Mémoires d'archéologie*, Paris, Didier, 1875, p. 74. (Les peintures du Palatin.) — J. H. Middleton, *The Remains of Ancient Rome*, vol. i. p. 175. — *Monumenti dell' Instituto*, vol. xi. pls. 22, 23.

XVIII. DOMUS GAIANA (house of Caligula), Fig. 54, XVI. — Suetonius (Calig. 22) and Dion Cassius (lix. 28; lx. 6) say that Caligula protracted the Imperial Palace as far as the Forum (*ad Forum usque*), making use of the Temple of Castor and Pollux for a vestibule. He must have thus occupied and built over the ground once covered by the houses of Clodius, Cicero, and other wealthy citizens, described in § ii., and crossed by the Clivus Victoriæ. The front of the palace opened on the Nova Via, towering above its pavement to the height of 150 feet. This façade is represented in its present ruinous state by the following plate (Fig. 56).

Starting from the foreground — the Clivus Sacer by the Arch of Fabius Allobrogicus — we first see the house of the Vestals, with the statues of the priestesses lining the south side of the peristyle; and above it the Nova Via, by which the house was separated from Caligula's palace. The whole mass of arched masonry which rises above the street, and which appears crowned by a clump of ilexes, represents only the substructures built by Caligula to raise the slope of the hill to a level with its summit. The palace itself, with its state apartments and halls and porticoes, began where the ruins actually stop, not a particle being left above ground to tell the tale. The substructures, at all events, are well worth visiting : we gain by them the true idea of the human *fourmillière* of slaves, servants, freedmen, and guards, which lived and moved and worked in the substrata of the Palatine, serving the court in silence and almost in darkness. It is difficult to understand or to explain how the greater portion of these underground dens were lighted and ventilated. I believe that, in the original design, they were well provided with such essential elements of light and comfort : the *cryptoporticus*, where the murder of Caligula took place, received light from the Forum Palatinum (Fig. 54, XVII.) by means of skylights opening under each intercolumniation ; the rooms KK had a skylight in the middle of their vaulted ceiling, and so forth. In progress of time, and on the occasion of the repairs and changes which every Emperor considered it his duty to make, no regard was paid to the original plan : staircases, windows, and corridors were condemned, intercepted, or closed; rooms subdivided into two or four apartments; free spaces built over; and streets turned into dark passages.

Fig. 56. — The Remains of the Palace of Caligula, seen from the Sacra Via.

The student's most perplexing labor on the Palatine is to single out which parts are architecturally essential and pertain to the

original plan, and which are later changes deserving no consideration. His task is made even more troublesome by the fact that all
maps of the hill, from that of Zangolini, which I published in
1873,[1] to the latest of Richter (1889), Middleton (1892), and Burns
(1895), mark existing remains with the same shade of color,
no matter whether they belong to the great banqueting-hall of
the masters of the world, or to a cellar sunk deep in the ground.
I have tried to avoid this mistake in Sheets xxix. and xxxv. of
the " Forma Urbis," where only the living apartments and public

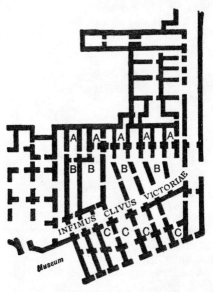

Fig. 57. — A Corner of the Palace of Caligula according to Rosa's Map.

buildings are marked in full tint, the substructures and cellars
in lighter color or in simple outline. The results obtained by this
process of sifting are in many cases remarkable. The following
from Caligula's house might serve for all.

The portion of the house which spans the Clivus Victoriæ is
represented in guide and topographical books as above (Fig. 57).

According to this accepted plan, none of the rooms marked AA,
BB, CC had light or air, the whole space — the street included —
being vaulted over. Now, as " several rooms . . . are richly

---

[1] The same that I have made use of in *Ancient Rome*, pp. 106, 107.

decorated with a combination of colored stucco reliefs and paintings on the flat, very gorgeous in effect, but almost invisible for
want of light, except that of lamp," [1] and others have an elaborate
mosaic floor, as is suitable for rooms inhabited, not by slaves, but
by officers of superior rank, we were trying to find the proper explanation of these facts, but in vain. It came in the most satisfactory way when I adopted the system of distinguishing, in color
or in outline, the original walls from later additions.

By glancing at the map made with this caution, Fig. 58, we see
at once that when the palace was built by Caligula, the apartments

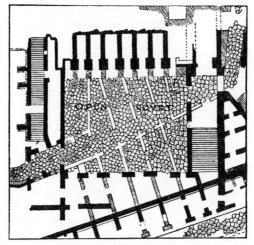

Fig. 58. — The Same, according to Sheet xxix. of the "Forma Urbis."

now plunged in darkness received light and air from a court 32
metres long and 26 wide, through which passed the Clivus Victoriæ.
The rooms on the southwest side opened on a balcony "supported
on stone corbels carrying a series of arches." These and the
front of the balcony "are richly decorated with delicate reliefs,
modeled in stucco, of figures and foliage, once covered with gold
and colored decoration, and designed with great skill and beauty
of effect" (Middleton). The marble railing or parapet is an
addition by Rosa.

The rooms under the balcony, on a level with the court, were
used as a *corps de garde*. The walls of one (now protected by a

[1] Middleton, i. 194.

wooden railing) are covered with graffiti. There are names like "Philaromvs," "Annaevs," "Aprilis;" the impression of a coin repeated five times; and the phrase, written perhaps in the hour of the siesta in a hot summer day: "Somnvs clavdit ocellos." (See Bull. arch. com., 1895, p. 195.)

Another portion of the building, the *cryptoporticus*, marked XVIII, Fig. 54, has been identified beyond any shade of doubt with the "solitary and obscure corridor" in which the assassination of Caligula took place on January 14, A. D. 41. The event is described at some length on pp. 117–119 of "Ancient Rome."

Near the bend of the *cryptoporticus* towards the house of Germanicus, there is an oval basin, which Rosa calls a fish-pond (*vivaio di pesci*). I doubt whether it is ancient, or the work of a mediæval farmer. It marks the place in which the Renaissance lime-burners established their kilns. One of these was discovered by Rosa in 1866, filled to the brim with exquisite works of art, some of which had by an accident escaped the effects of fire. The objects formerly exhibited in the local Museo Palatino, where they attracted intense interest, and now scattered in various rooms of the Museo delle Terme, comprise a veiled head of the Emperor Claudius; a head of Nero; three caryatides or *canephorai* of *nero antico* of an archaistic type; an exquisite statue of an *ephebos* in green basalt, with the arms and lower portion of the legs missing;[1] head of Arpokras, and several fragments of less importance.

The last place deserving of a visit is the long and well-preserved staircase which leads from the Clivus Victoriæ to the top of the ruins, where a charming little grove of evergreens now casts its shade. The grove is known in literary history as the first place of meeting of the Accademia degli Arcadi.

The palace, or whatever remained of it in tolerable preservation after the barbarian inroads, was taken possession of and sometimes inhabited by the popes, as a practical evidence of their political power in Rome. The palace was put under the care of an officer styled *a cura palatii*. One of them named Plato, whose epitaph was seen by Pietro Sabino in the pavement of the church of S. Anastasia, rebuilt or repaired about 680 the long staircase which I have just mentioned as descending from the top of the ruins to the Clivus Victoriæ and the Porta Romanula. His son, having been elected pope in 705 under the name of John VII.,[2]

[1] The statue has been recently illustrated by F. Hauser in the *Mittheilungen* for 1895, pp. 97–119, pl. 1. (Basalt statue vom Palatin.)

[2] John VII. was buried in S. Peter's before the altar of the Sudario, which

conceived the plan of making the palace of the Cæsars the permanent and official residence of the Bishops of Rome; and accordingly "super ecclesiam sanctæ Dei genitricis quæ antiqua vocatur [above the church of S. Maria Liberatrice] episcopium construere voluit," [1] and established brick-kilns for the purpose, the produce of which is marked by the stamp shown in Fig. 59.

Fig. 59. — A Brick Stamp of John VII.

John VII. did not live to see his project accomplished: his successors did not care for it, and they repaired to the convents or strongholds of the Palatine only in case of necessity. Celestinus II. died in 1144 *apud Palladium* (in the monastery of S. Cesario); Lucius II. in 1145 *apud ecclesiam S. Gregorii* (in the fortress of the Septizonium); Eugenius III. was elected pope in 1145 *apud monasterium S. Cesarii;* Gregory IX. in 1227 *apud septemsolium.* They were simply chosen as places of refuge in times of popular disorder, which once quelled, the popes resumed their habitual residence at the Lateran.

Caligula's palace has not been excavated since the sack by the Duke of Parma in 1725-27; and we do not know whether there are still traces left of the work of John VII. or of his Imperial predecessors.

XIX. The Palace of Domitian (οἰκία Δομετιανοῦ). — One of the first thoughts of Vespasian, after his election in A. D. 69, was to reduce the Imperial residence to its old limits on the Palatine,

he had built and endowed. His portrait, a miniature in a golden ground, is given by Giacomo Grimaldi, *Cod. Barb.*, f. 93.

[1] References. — *Liber pontificalis,* in Johann. VII., ed. Duchesne, vol. i. p. 385. — G. Battista de Rossi, *Notizie degli Scavi,* dicemb. 1883. — Rodolfo Lanciani, *L' itinerario di Einsiedlen,* p. 63. — Louis Duchesne, *Bulletin critique,* 1885, p. 417 *sq.;* and *Mélanges de l'Ecole française de Rome,* 1896, fasc. ii. — Grisar Hartmann, S. J., in *Civiltà Cattol.,* May, 1896.

and give back to the people the immense tract of land which
Nero had usurped for his Golden House. At the same time he
could not abstain from raising himself a new palace, to be used
for state receptions and banquets. This great structure, called by
Nerva *œdes publicœ populi Romani*, was brought to perfection by
Domitian, who lavished upon it all the costliest productions of
contemporary art. Hence Plutarch (Poplic., 15) calls it οἰκία
Δομετιανοῦ, and compares Domitian to Midas, who turned into gold
whatever fell under his touch. See also the eulogy of Statius
(Sylv., iv. 11, 18). It stands between the palaces of Tiberius and
Caligula on one side, and that of Augustus (with its temples and
porticoes) on the other, in the line of the valley which runs from
the Arch of Titus to the Circus. The valley was still occupied at
that time by private mansions, and by one or two shrines; they
were not destroyed, but made use of to support the platform on
which the palace stands. Some of these older buildings are still
visible, and will be described below. The plan of the palace is
that of a private Roman house, but it is of a size and magnificence
becoming the ruler of the world. Little or nothing is known of
its history; in fact, it seems never to have required repairs on
account of the solidity of its construction. The Emperors did
not live in it, but held their levees, delivered their judgments,
presided over councils of state, received foreign envoys, and gave
official banquets in the various apartments set apart for such
purposes. The last Emperor seen in the palace was Heraclius,
whose coronation took place in the throne-room A. D. 629. We
hear of it again nine centuries later, when the northern half of the
Palatine was bought by the Farnese. To this family we owe the
first excavations of the Palatine. They took place in 1536, when
the avenue now called di S. Gregorio was cut open between the
Septizonium and Constantine's Arch for the triumphal progress of
Charles V. In the legal deeds for the acquisition of property on
the hill, the Farnese, and above all the glorious Cardinal Alessandro, always betray their inclination for archæological discoveries.
One of them, dated January 17, 1542, contains these words :
"Marco Antonio Palosio sells to the cardinal, etc., his vineyard
on the Palatine, adjoining that of Virginio da Mantaco, with its
crypts, ruins, edifices, marbles, and statues, whether visible above
ground or covered yet by the accumulation of soil." The result
of the Farnese excavations is not known; but considering that
the front walls of the gardens (destroyed in 1881) cut the house
of the Vestals right in two, that the Uccelliera (now the Uffizio

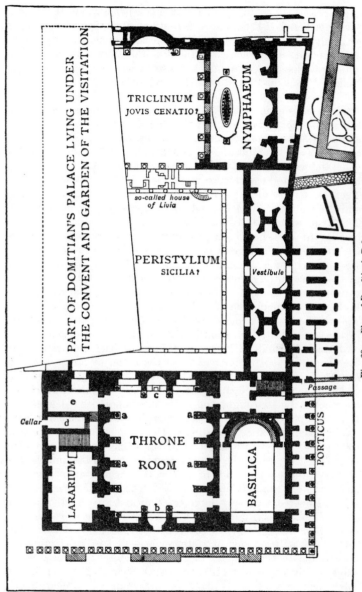

PART OF DOMITIAN'S PALACE LYING UNDER
THE CONVENT AND GARDEN OF THE VISITATION

TRICLINIUM
JOVIS CENATIO?

NYMPHAEUM

so-called house
of Livia

PERISTYLIUM
SICILIA?

Vestibule

Passage

Cellar

e

c

d

a

a

THRONE

ROOM

a

a

LARARIUM

b

BASILICA

PORTICUS

Fig. 60. — Plan of Domitian's Palace.

degli Scavi) was founded on Caligula's palace, and the Casino (described on p. 164) on that of Domitian, something of value must certainly have come to light. The only monument mentioned by contemporary archæologists is the pedestal (Corpus Inscr., vi. 456) which marks approximately the site of the Ædes Penatium in Velia. It was discovered near the Arch of Titus.

Three halls open on the front of Domitian's palace : the throne-room, *aula regia*, in the centre; the chapel, or *lararium*, on the left; and a *basilica*, or court-room, on the right. The throne-room, built of bricks from the kilns of Flavia Domitilla, is 160 feet long and 120 wide, and was decorated with sixteen columns of pavonazzetto (aa), having bases and capitals exquisitely cut in ivory-colored marble. There were three niches on either side for colossal statues or groups, and each of them was flanked by smaller columns of porphyry. The two statues of black basalt, discovered in the adjoining basilica in 1724, had been probably removed from these niches. On either side of the great door (b), opening on the front portico, stood two columns of giallo antico, which the Duke of Parma sold to the stone-cutters Perini and Maciucchi for 3000 scudi. The threshold was made of a block of Greek marble so large that the high altar of the church of S. M. Rotonda has been cut out of it. The throne (c), or *augustale solium*, was placed opposite the door, in the apse where Bianchini in 1726 set up his mendacious praise of Francis I., Duke of Parma and Piacenza, the last destroyer of the Palatine. Bianchini has given the name of *lararium*, or domestic chapel, to the room on the left, on account of the altar which he found built against the back wall. The altar, which was approached by two flights of stairs, has since been demolished. Here took place the remarkable find described in " Ancient Rome," p. 127. Heliogabalus, according to Herodianus, had attempted to collect into the chapel attached to the palace of the Cæsars the most famous relics of the Roman world — the Palladium, the fire of Vesta, the ancilia, and, of course, the Acus Matris Deum or meteoric stone from Pessinus, described in § xiii. The stone, it may be remembered, was very large, of conical shape, and brown in color. Monsignor Bianchini, who excavated the *lararium* in 1725, seems to have positively discovered the relic. " I am sorry," he says, " that no fragment of statue or bas-relief or inscription has been found in the chapel; . . . the only object discovered was a stone nearly three feet high, conical in shape, of a deep brown color, looking very much like lava, and ending in a sharp point. I do not know what became of it."

If my surmise is well founded, and the identity between the Acus Matris Deum and Bianchini's stone probable, if not certain, we can better understand the passage of the " Vita Heliog.," iii. The *templum Heliogabali iuxta œdes imperatorias,* which he mentions, must have been close to the *lararium,* unless the *lararium* itself was transformed into a temple.

Behind the chapel is the only staircase (d) yet discovered in these apartments. It led to the upper galleries, from which the great ceremonies of state could be witnessed by invited guests. Another flight of steps, now buried again, leads to the wine-cellars, where Bianchini discovered, in 1721, rows of amphoræ marked with the label *liquamen excellens L. Purelli Gemelli* (Bianchini, p. 260). The walls of the staircase and those of the room (e) were covered with exquisite fresco paintings, of which not a square inch has been spared destruction. Fortunately they were copied in time by Gaetano Piccini and Francesco Bartoli. Piccini's album is to be found now in the Museum of the Hofburg, Vienna; Bartoli's plates in the Topham collection at Eton. These last number 58, of which 16 are of great size. They represent campestrian scenes, sacrifices, and Bacchic dances, crowded with graceful figures.[1]

Some of the subjects have also been engraved on copper. They are to be found in Cameron's " Baths of the Romans from the Restorations of Palladio " (London, 1772) ; in Morghen's appendix to the " Picturæ antiquæ Cryptarum Romanarum " of Bartoli ; and in the " Collection of Ancient Paintings after the Originals at Rome, with Critical, Historical, and Mythological Observations upon them," by George Turnbull, LL. D. (London, 1741, folio, 54 plates). When we think that these exquisite specimens of the golden art of Domitian's age were found intact in the first quarter of last century, under the eyes of such men as Cardinal Alessandro Albani, Pier Leone Ghezzi, Francesco Bianchini, and Francesco Bartoli, and that the very walls which they covered were demolished for the sake of the bricks, we may indeed ask by what right we continue blaming the Middle Ages or the barbarians for deeds which are not as disgraceful as those here recorded.

The hall on the opposite side of the throne-room is thought to have been a *basilica,* or court-room, where the prince delivered judgment in cases pertaining or submitted to the crown. There

---

[1] See *Disegni di antichità nella Biblioteca di S. Maria di Eton* (in Bull. arch. com., 1894, p. 164). — *Picturæ antiquæ Cryptarum Romanarum* (*ibidem,* 1895, p. 182). — *Il palazzo Maggiore* (in Mittheilungen, 1894, p. 26).

are still traces of the *suggestum* or platform on which sat the Imperial judge and his assessors, and of the staircases which led to it. The fragment of a marble screen, dividing the apse from the space reserved for the audience, and the columns by which the hall would be divided into aisles and nave, are "restorations" of Commendatore Rosa, resting on no sufficient evidence. The *basilica* was excavated for the first time (?) in 1724. There is an account of the results in MSS. p. 248 of the queen's library at Windsor, from which we gather that the two colossal statues of Bacchus and Hercules in black basalt, now in the Museo at Parma, were found lying on the floor on April 20 of the same year.

Behind the three front halls opens the inner court or peristyle, the area of which amounts to 3600 square metres. The columns were of porta santa, with columns, capitals, and entablature cut in white marble like lace-work. Suetonius says that this was a favorite haunt of Domitian, who could walk under the colonnades away from the crowd and secure from danger. The biographer adds that the side walls had been incrusted with slabs of phengite marble, reflecting the images like a mirror, so as to allow the prince to see whatever might take place behind his shoulders. The two sides of the peristyle are occupied by a set of nine rooms of various shapes, the use of which it is not easy to imagine. Considering, however, that the middle room, octagonal in shape, forms a vestibule through which personages driving to the palace by the Forum Palatinum were admitted into it, it is obvious that they were used for cloak and waiting rooms, porter's lodge, etc.

Before proceeding any farther in our description, it is necessary to remember that below the halls we have visited, and even below the peristyle, there are other splendid apartments, galleries, cryptoporticuses, and bathrooms, the existence of which has remained unknown to the modern excavators of the Palatine. I only discovered it myself in 1892, while examining Bianchini's manuscripts in the Biblioteca Capitolare at Verona, and the Topham collection of drawings at Eton. The subject is so curious and new that a few words of explanation will not be out of place.

In 1720, the Marchese Ignazio de' Santi, Minister of Parma to the Pope, asked leave for his master, the Duke Francis, to excavate the Palatine Gardens which he had inherited from the Farnese. Cardinal Patrizi, in giving consent on behalf of Innocent XIII., imposed two conditions : that if the value of gold and silver coins, engraved stones, and medals should eventually exceed the sum of 10,000 scudi, the Pope's treasury should share the profits ; secondly, that life-size statues and architectural marbles should not be removed from Rome. Duke Francesco rebelled against these fair conditions, and his agent in Rome gave so much trouble that, on April 4, 1720, Cardinal Albani gave him *carte blanche* to do what he pleased on the Palatine. He did not hesitate about it. The acts of vandalism committed by this Ignazio de' Santi and his successor Count Suzzani, with the tacit consent of Monsignore Francesco Bianchini, who had been appointed superintendent of the excavations, have no parallel in the history of the destruction of Rome. The words *ladronecci infami*, used by Guattani in referring to them, are comparatively mild. The prelate was the only one to suffer. While watching the works one day, the ground gave way under his feet, and although the drop was hardly fourteen feet, the shock was ultimately the cause of his death. His posthumous volume, " Il palazzo dei Cesari," is almost worthless, both in the text and in the plates, which an eye-witness of the excavations, Pier Leone Ghezzi, denounces as "impostures." The discovery of an underground floor is not mentioned nor illustrated by Bianchini, and I had to make a pilgrimage to Verona, Eton, and Paris to collect information about it.[1] Without entering into particulars already published in the " Mittheilungen " of 1894, I will merely mention the discovery of a bathroom 21.30 metres long and 11.50 metres deep, the richest and most beautiful apartment, as far as we know, in the whole palace of the Cæsars. The walls were incrusted with " Florentine " mosaic work in pietra dura, alternating here and there with marble bas-reliefs set in a richly carved frame, and with niches for statues. A colonnade of porphyry shafts, each two feet in diameter, ran along three sides of the hall ; while on the fourth side five lions' heads of gilt bronze threw jets of water into a marble basin. Each fountain was flanked by ten columns of porphyry, serpentine, giallo, verde, and pavonazzetto, with capitals and bases of gilt bronze. The roof (fragments of which lay scattered on the pavement inlaid with crusts of the rarest breccias) seems to have been divided into panels, some of which contained mythological groups in fresco painting, others figurines of white stucco on a heavily gilt ground.

All these treasures were destroyed in May, 1721. An English artist, E. Kirkall, who has left two rare colored prints of this hall, says in the footnote, " The plan of Augustus's (Domitian's) bath,

[1] The memory of the find was lost altogether by the houses of Parma and Naples and by their diplomatic agents in Rome, so much so that in 183ε another search was made in the same spot, naturally without results.

found underground on the east side of the Palatine hill in Rome in the year 1721, and barbarously defaced and broken in pieces during the conclave of that year, and the broken pieces sent to Parma."

It is to be regretted that this underground portion of Domitian's palace, without which we shall never be able to understand the working and mechanism of Roman Imperial state life, should be still buried under a mass of rubbish. The only rooms now visible (under the west wing of the peristyle — very damp and chilly) have nothing to do with it: they belong to a private mansion of the late Republic, which Domitian left undisturbed because it lay below the level of his artificial platform. The discoverers of 1726 misnamed it the Baths of Livia (see Fig. 60). The first room at the foot of the (modern) stairs was decorated with arabesques and festoons on a ground of gold; the second with groups of figurines on a blue ground; the ornaments of the ceilings were also worthy of the golden age of Augustus. Owing to the neglect in which this gem of Roman domestic architecture has been kept since 1726, the decorations have nearly disappeared.

The *triclinium*, or great state banqueting-hall, opens on the south side of the peristyle. Nardini has identified it with the *Iovis Cenatio*, in which the murder of Pertinax took place, as described in the "Vita," ch. xi. The biographer says that the three hundred rebels from the Prætorian camp entered the palace by the vestibule opening on the Forum Palatinum, and rushed through the *locus qui appellatur Sicilia* to the Iovis Cenatio, where they met with their Imperial victim. If the Iovis Cenatio is the name of the dining-room, that of Sicilia must belong to the peristyle. Nothing remains to tell us how this hall was decorated save two fragments of granite columns, of which there must have been sixteen. The pavement of the apse, where the table of honor was set, is well preserved, but the administration is compelled to keep it covered, to save it from frost, rain, and the hands of tourists. It is made of crusts of porphyry, serpentine, giallo, and pavonazzetto in imitation of geometrical patterns. The small triangular cabinet, on the left of the apse, was probably a *latrina*. The dining-room was necessarily connected with kitchens and pantry, haunted by hundreds of *coci;* but here again we are left in the dark because the excavations have stopped at the wrong level. The tombstones of members of the Imperial household, collected in vol. vi. part ii. pp. 1150–1204 of the "Corpus Inscriptionum," mention among other officers several members of the

collegium cocorum Cæsaris (No. 8750); a grand chef, *præpositus
cocorum* (No. 8752); cooks that the Emperors had purchased or
obtained from the Cornufician and Sestian families (Nos. 8753,
8754); a butler *a cena centurionum* (No. 8748), viz., for the service
of the officers of the bodyguard on duty at the palace; a superintendent of the wine-cellars (No. 8745); a Gemellus *præpositus
argenti potorii*, keeper of silver drinking-cups (No. 8729); an
Ulpius Hierax, keeper of gold plate and cups (No. 8733); a *triclini-
archa* or chief butler (No. 1884); a keeper of lamps (No. 8868);
keepers of table-linen, bakers, pastry-cooks, and *prægustatores.*
Princes and princesses of the Imperial family had their own
special cooks like the Zethus, No. 8755, who calls himself *cocus
Marcellæ minoris.*

In the portion of the Imperial palace or palaces visible to us
there is no room for the lodging and keeping of such a powerful
army of servants as we know to have been attached to the court.
The *columbaria* of servants and freedmen of Augustus and Livia
on the Appian Way — described in " Ancient Rome," p. 130 — contained about six thousand cinerary urns. The number must have
been doubled under the extravagant rule of Nero and Caligula;
and yet not half of the Palatine was built over in those days.
There are many mysteries to be solved before we gain a satisfactory knowledge of the material organization and working of the
Imperial Court.

There is one more hall of the οἰκία Δομετιανοῦ to be visited on
the right of the *triclinium.* It was used as a *nymphœum*, where
the water, playing in various ways, the light, filtering through
bushes of exotic plants, the perfume of rare flowers, and the
balmy air admitted through Cyzicene windows, made the post-
prandial siesta most agreeable. The fountain is elliptical in
shape, with niches and recesses for flower-pots and statuettes.
The pavement is inlaid with the most rare bits of oriental alabaster. Upon it were lying at the time of the discovery (1862)
two pieces of fluted columns of giallo brecciato, and a statue of
Eros with large wings, restored by Karl Steinhauser, and removed
to the Louvre. Froehner (Musée National du Louvre, Sculpture
antique, p. 311, No. 325) describes it as " un torse grec d'une
exquise délicatesse de ciseau. De la main droite levée, Eros ado-
lescent versait du vin dans une coupe." The statue has been illustrated by Froehner himself in the " Illustration," 1867, p. 152, and
by Henzen in the " Bull. Inst.," 1862, p. 227.

It is hardly necessary to remind the reader that the palace of

Domitian is symmetrical in all its parts, and that a room of the same style and size as this Nymphæum is lying buried under the Convent of the Visitation (Villa Mills).

On the edge of these ruins Cardinal Alessandro Farnese raised a casino, the north portico of which was painted in arabesques by a pupil of Taddeo Zuccari. The panels represent Æneas visiting Evander, Cacus stealing the oxen of Hercules, Evander sacrificing to Hercules, the grotto of the Lupercal, the foundation of Rome, subjects drawn from the Virgilian reminiscences of the Palatine.

The works of art discovered in the Palace of Domitian are scattered to the four winds. The basalt statues of Hercules and Apollo, found in 1724, are in the Museo di Antichità at Parma, together with other architectural and ornamental marbles; more pieces were removed to the Palazzo Farnese at the end of last century. Napoleon III. presented to the Louvre the most rare and beautiful results of his excavations (November 4, 1861, to April, 1870); even the small but highly interesting local museum founded by Commendatore Rosa (catalogued in the Guida del Palatino, p. 52) has been dispersed, and its contents have lost their individuality in the great collections of the Museo Nazionale alle Terme.

As to the fate of the fresco paintings discovered behind the *lararium* in 1721–25, I quote this passage from Winckelmann's "Storia delle Arti," ed. Fea, vol. iii. p. 105, § 26 : " A hall forty feet long, with the walls entirely covered with frescoes, was unearthed on the Palatine in 1724. The panels were separated by columns (in the so-called grotesque style) very thin and long. The panels detached from the walls went first to Parma, then to Naples, together with other rare objects inherited from the Farnese. But as they were kept in their boxes for twenty-four years, the mildew and damp effaced every trace of them, except in the case of a small Caryatid, which is now exhibited at Capo di Monte."

All writers on the Palatine describe some exquisitely carved marbles, spoils of the excavations of 1725, which had been laid aside by the Uccelliera; and Luigi Rossini has illustrated them in one of the best plates of his work " I Sette Colli." Twenty-four pieces were shipped to Naples in 1787, by order of Carlo Paniceri, agent of the king; the others were removed to the Palazzo Farnese about 1830. In May, 1834, Count Ludolf, the Neapolitan envoy, asked leave of Gregory XVI. for the removal to the Museo Borbonico of this last remnant from the Palatine. The government had not courage to refuse, and tried to throw the responsibility on a committee of experts. The commissioners in this case gave the government a good lesson. Their report, signed by Carlo Fea, the veteran defender of our archæological patrimony, contains these words: "Carlo Fea begs to be excused for not giving his consent to the removal, because these marbles are essential parts of the Imperial palace, and must be left where they belong for the use of archæologists, historians, and artists, who could never understand the architecture and the ornamentation of those noble ruins without them. We must not renew the example of Absyrtus and Orpheus, whose limbs were torn to pieces and scattered far and wide."

A last observation about the Palace of Domitian and the Farnese gardens in general. The rubbish or newly made ground which covers the ruins is not entirely local, but has been brought there from various parts, from the foundations of the Chiesa del Gesù, built by the same cardinal (1575) and by the same architect (Vignola), from those of the Palazzo Farnese, etc. Under the rule of the French invaders, 1809–14, the earth from the excavations of the Temple of Venus and Rome was deposited in the strip of land between the Nova Via and the Palace of Caligula.

REFERENCES. — Francesco Bianchini, *Il palazzo dei Cesari*, Verona, 1738, chap. v. p. 48. — Wilhelm Henzen, *Ann. Inst.*, 1862, p. 225; 1865, p. 346. — Friedlaender, *Mœurs Romaines*, vol. i. p. 156. — Wilhelm Froehner, *L' Illustration*, 1867, p. 152.

XX. THE GARDENS OF ADONIS (Horti Adonæa — Vigna Barberini). — Domitian added to the comfort and luxury of the state apartments gardens laid out in Oriental style, and called "Horti Adonæa." [1] He had borrowed the idea from the Assyrians, who dedicated such places to Adonis, as the representative of the Sun and the promoter of vegetable life. Amongst their specialties were the κῆποι ʾΑδώνιδος, large pots of clay, sometimes of brass and silver, in which fennel, lettuce, and other special plants were sown on the approach of the anniversary feast of the god. The Palatine gardens are represented in a fragment of the marble plan, Jordan's "Forma," pl. 10, n. 44, reproduced on the next page (Fig. 61).

Where were the *horti* located? The answer is not so easily given: perhaps they were laid out in the corner of the hill above the Coliseum, which had already been incorporated in the Impe-

1 Philostratus, in the *Life of Apollonius of Tyana*, vii. 32, mentions not gardens but αὐλὴν ʾΑδώνιδος, which means either a hall or a villa: in the first case the indication of Philostratus might be referred to the hall designed in Fig. 61 in the middle of the gardens; in the second case it refers to the gardens themselves.

rial domain by Nero, and which is the only one that the plan fits. This rectangular space, supported by great substruction walls, is the property of the Barberini, and is called either the Vigna di S. Sebastiano or Vigna dell' Abbadia.

A visit to this lovely spot is necessary to complete our study

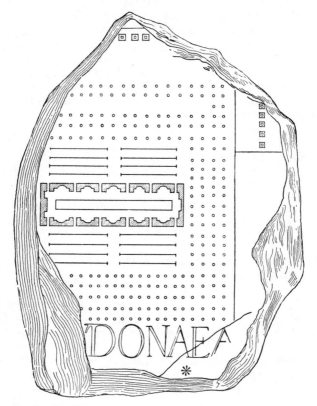

Fig. 61. — The Horti Adonæa, a Fragment of the Marble Plan of Rome.

of the Palatine. No special permission is required, and the gate — Via di S. Bonaventura, No. 3 — is usually kept open ; but the gardener has acquired the habit of asking exorbitant fees. It is better to address one's self to the keeper of the Cappella di S. Sebastiano, on the left of the entrance.

The topographers of the Renaissance have given this Vigna

Barberini the name of Foro Vecchio, derived obviously from the Curiæ Veteres, which were located at this very corner of the hill. Lucio Fauno (Antichità, p. 106) says " in molti istromenti antichi

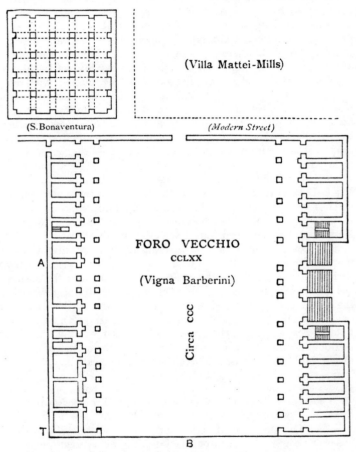

Fig. 62. — Plan of the Horti Adonæa (?), according to Ligorio.

di notai si truova questo luogo cognominato alla Curia Vecchia." [1] Ligorio (Bodleian, f. 55) gives the plan of the ruins here presented (Fig. 62), stating at the same time that their condition was such

[1] In deeds and records of notaries of the fourteenth and fifteenth centuries.

that he could not vouch for the exactness of his survey. Flavio Biondo (Rom. Inst., i. 76), who visited the place at the time of Eugenius IV. (1431–39), speaks of it as one of the best preserved and most imposing parts of the Palatine: "Remarkable ruins they are, with marble doors in the circuit of the walls, finer and more perfect than any others to be found in Rome." In chap. ix. part i. of "Fabiola," Cardinal Wiseman gives a charming description of this spot, where he supposes that his hero Sebastian was quartered; and in chap. xxv. part iii. describes his martyrdom in the "court of the palace near his own dwelling, planted with rows of trees and consecrated to Adonis," and "that ancient chapel which stands in the midst of the ruined Palatine, to mark the spot on which he fell." The Acts of Sebastian are not altogether trustworthy, having been written in the fifth century, but their topographical indications are genuine. They place the scene of the martyrdom *in hippodromo palatii;* [1] and we know from other sources that this was precisely the name given to the present Vigna Barberini from the fall of the Empire to the tenth century, when it was transferred to the so-called Stadium.

In the appendix to the "Piante di Roma," the late Comm. de Rossi has published a curious description of the Palatine, written at the foot of a map, in twelve numbers, corresponding to those marked in the map itself. It is a document of the Byzantine period. After describing the *atrium*, the throne-room, the basilica, the banqueting-hall, etc., of the Palace of Domitian, it passes to the house of Augustus (VII), to the great baths of the Palace of Severus (VIII), to the *stadium* or *gymnasium* (IX), to an unknown *coquina* (X), to the great reservoir of the Aqua Claudia at S. Bonaventura (XI); and beyond it, viz. at the corner of the hill above the Meta Sudans, it places the *hippodromum*.

REFERENCES. — Pirro Ligorio, *Cod. Bodl.*, f. 55. *Cod. Turin.*, xiv. — Francesco Bianchini, *Palazzo dei Cesari*, p. 139, *sq.* — Heinrich Jordan, *Forma Urbis Romæ*, tab. x. n. 44, p. 59. — Gaston Boissier, *Promenades archéol.*, p. 132, n. 1. *Mélanges de l'Ecole française*, avril 1893, pp. 101–104.

XXI. The presence of a memorial to Sebastian, the gallant officer who gave his life for his faith, in the very gardens (the hippodrome of later days) in which church traditions place the scene of his execution, proves how well founded is the tradition. The chapel, the earliest mention of which dates from the eleventh century, was restored in 1636 by Prince Taddeo Barberini. We

[1] Bolland, *Acta SS.*, ii., Jan., p. 278. — Mabillon, *Mus. ital.*, ii. pp. 161, 574. — Jordan, *Topographie*, ii. 384.

could not make our study of the Palatine complete without noticing the three ecclesiastical buildings which made this corner of the hill famous in the Middle Ages.

A. Ecclesia S. Cæsarii in Palatio (the Imperial Christian oratory and Christian representative of the classic Lararium). — It is first mentioned in the time of Phocas (603), but it may be older. The titular saint is believed to be Cæsarius, an African deacon, who suffered martyrdom at Terracina; but it is evident that, whoever he may be, his name was selected to suit the place to which the chapel belonged. Such coincidences, which almost amount to *jeu de mots*, are by no means fortuitous. The remains of the villa near Velitræ, where Augustus passed his youth, are actually called S. Cesario.[1] The images of the Byzantine

Fig. 63. — The Church of S. Cæsarius in Palatio.

Emperors were exhibited in this chapel, as a mark of the power they still claimed over the ancient capital of the Empire; and their keeping was intrusted to Greek monks *ordinis saccitarum*, a name perhaps derived from the ample frocks they wore. Saint Saba junior, sent on a diplomatic mission from Amalfi to Otho

1 The following distich was engraved on the door of the church of *S. Martina*, built on the site of the *Martisforum* (Marforio): *Martyrii gestans virgo* Martina *coronam, Eiecto hinc* Martis *numine templa tenes.*

III. in 989–991, died while a guest of these monks, and his funeral was attended by Otho's Empress Theophania. "The monks," says Anselmus of Avelbury, "use the fermented bread for the Holy Communion, instead of the azym, without the pope or the Roman Catholics taking offense at it." The last mention of S. Cesario occurs in the fourteenth century, when there was but one officiating priest left.

The site of this historical sanctuary, seen and described only five centuries ago, is not known to us; but I am inclined to place it among the remains of the so-called baths of Heliogabalus on the Sacra Via, represented in the cut above.

Whatever may have been the object of this edifice in classic times (third century after Christ), there is no doubt that it was transformed into a church at the end of the fifth century. At the time of its discovery in 1872 many particulars could be traced which have now disappeared: patches of Byzantine mosaic in the floor, traces of inscriptions and paintings, not to speak of the secretarium and of the baptistery. The apse and the presbyterium are still discernible, as well as many rooms and cells suited for the abode of monks. No name has yet been given to this church: that of S. Cæsarius in Palatio seems the most appropriate, especially if we consider how close it is to the Turris Chartularia, the great mediæval stronghold of the popes.

B. MONASTERIUM QUOD PALLADIUM DICITUR (chapel and monastery, variously called, of S. Maria in Pallara; of SS. Sebastiano and Zotico; of S. Sebastiano alla Polveriera; of S. Andrea in Palladio, etc.). — The first mention occurs in documents of the year 1001,[1] but it may belong to the Constantinian era, that is to say, to the group of memorials raised under that Emperor to the heroes and heroines of the last persecution of Diocletian.

The monastery was fortified, or, to speak more exactly, was included in the Palatine fortifications of the Frangipani. In describing the election of Pope Gelasius II. (1118), the "Liber pontificalis" (ed. Duchesne, vol. ii. p. 313) calls it *locum tutissimum infra domos Leonis et Cencii Fraiapane.*[2] Later on it became the official residence in Rome of the abbots of Monte Cassino. Under Urban V. (1362–70) we find it intrusted to the care of a single clergyman, Angelo Riccardelli. The ruins of the church, on the walls of which the history of the martyrdom of S. Zoticus

---

[1] Pertz, *Monumenta Germaniæ historica,* vol. iv. p. 768.

[2] Cencio Frangipane is the same to whom the monks of S. Gregory leased the Septizonium and the tower of the Circus Maximus in 1145.

was painted, are described by Baronio. At the time of Urban VIII. the building was entirely profaned and turned into a farmhouse. Michele Lonigo saw on the spandrils of the front of the tribune two remarkable figures : one representing a certain Petrus *illustris medicus*, a mediæval restorer of the church, offering a model of it to S. Sebastian; the other his wife Giovanna offering other gifts to S. Zoticus.

Pope Barberini and his nephew Taddeo restored the chapel in 1636, destroying at the same time all traces of the frescoes, except those of the apse. They had been copied, however, in 1630 by Antonio Ecclissi; but he failed to catch the spirit and the meaning of the subjects, as we can ourselves judge from the facsimiles which are now exhibited in the chapel.

The frescoes of the apse represent the Saviour between SS. Lawrence, Stephen, Sebastian, and Zoticus, the last two wearing the costume of the court officers of the fifth century. There is a lower belt of figures painted in the eleventh century at the expense of the monk Benedictus.

The two columns of breccia corallina on the altar were probably removed from the upper cloisters of the house of the Vestals. The *balaustri* in front of it are cut in the rarest kind of lumachella.

The monastery had its own cemetery, where burial was carried on in the Roman fashion, the corpses being protected by a double row of tiles placed in a slanting position. The cemetery was discovered on May 24, 1879.

C. The Turris Chartularia (the centre of the fortifications of the Frangipani, in which the archives of the church were kept for a long time). —The foundations, built of chips of marble, silex, and travertine, rest on an ancient bed of concrete, and are flanked by huge blocks of peperino, belonging to the temple of Jupiter Stator. (See Book III. § viii.) The date of its construction is not known. In 1167 Pope Alexander III., persecuted by the partisans of Barbarossa, found shelter in it. The name of Chartularia is derived, according to Marini, from a manufacture of papyrus-paper ; according to Cancellieri from the archives which it contained. The cut (Fig. 64) shows the state of the tower in the sixteenth century, to which it had been reduced by Brancaleone in 1257. Valadier destroyed the rest in 1829. A detailed account of it is given by Nibby, " Roma Antica," vol. ii. p. 471.

References. — Louis Duchesne, *Bulletin critique*, 1885, p. 417. — Gio. Battista de Rossi, *Bullet. crist.*, 1867, p. 15 ; and *Notizie Scavi*, December, 1883. —

Enrico Stevenson, *Il cimitero di Zotico*, Modena, 1871, p. 71 ; and *Bull. arch. com.*, 1888, p. 295. — Mariano Armellini, *Chiese di Roma*, 2d ed., pp. 517, 524. — Heinrich Jordan, *Topographie*, vol. ii. p. 609. — Pasquale Adinolfi, *Roma nell' età di mezzo*, vol. i. pp. 392–397.

Fig. 64. — The Torre Cartularia in the Sixteenth Century.

XXII. The so-called Stadium (Xystus). — The name of Stadium has been given to the circus-like edifice, 160 metres long and 47 wide, which separates the house of Augustus from the Baths of Septimius Severus. The giving of this name seemed justified first by the oblong shape of the place, with a slightly curved end ; secondly, by the measure of 160 metres, which comes very near that of a stadium (177.40) ; thirdly, by the two fountains which occupy the place of the goals. Professor Marx, on the other side, thinks the name to be wrong, and that the place was a garden, a *xystus* with a *gestatio*, etc., attached to the house of Augustus. The question is too technical and minute to be treated in these pages. One theory does not absolutely exclude the other. For the sake of clearness I shall follow the old denomination, without taking any responsibility for it.

The foundation of the Stadium is attributed to Domitian while rebuilding the Domus Augustana. The style of the brickwork is the same in both, and so are some of the brick stamps from the kilns of T. Flavius Clonius and T. Flavius Hermes, freedmen of the Emperor. By a close examination of the structure in its present state we can reconstruct its history from the time of Domitian (if not of Augustus) to that of Theodoric. Originally it was nothing but a level space of ground, perhaps laid out in grass and flower-beds, inclosed by a wall slightly curved at the western end. There was no portico, no seats, no steps, nothing characteristic of a place of public meeting. Hadrian probably built the two-storied portico, as shown by the style of masonry and by the brick-stamps of the years 123–134, found in great numbers in the excavations of 1871 and 1893. Septimius Severus improved the aspect of the Stadium by the addition of an Imperial tribune or hexedra. The lower arcades of the portico rest on half columns coated with slabs of portasanta, the bases of which are hollow, and fit into the masonry like half-rings. One of the capitals discovered in 1868 by Visconti is cut out of a block quarried A. D. 195 under the consulship of Scapula Tertullus and Tineius Clemens. The portico, therefore, was included by Septimius Severus in his general reconstruction and embellishment of the place. A prefect of the city of the fourth century made other restorations, if we may believe the words of a fragmentary inscription discovered in 1878. Last of all, King Theodoric tried to stop the ruin and the fall of this part of the Imperial buildings. His name has been read many times on bricks discovered by Visconti in 1868 and by myself in 1877. Theodoric seems to have propped with buttresses the walls which threatened to collapse, and to have also transformed the plan and the destination of the building. The arena, once used for athletic sports or for flower-beds, was then occupied by a large oval basin, which we would call a swimming-bath were it not for the absence of a water-tight floor; probably it was meant for a small amphitheatre. It is highly interesting to the student of the decline and fall of Imperial Rome to examine the work of Theodoric in its details. First of all, when the basin was built, the floor of the Xystus was already covered with a bed of rubbish from two to three feet thick, as we can certify by comparing the level of the original marble pavement with that of the foundations of the oval. These foundations are built of chips and blocks of porphyry, serpentine, giallo antico, and, above all, of pieces of cipollino columns, belonging to the second floor of the portico. The Stadium therefore must have been half ruined in Theodoric's age, probably in consequence of the earthquake mentioned in the contemporary inscriptions of the Coliseum.[1] Another circumstance deserving notice is that on either side of the entrance to the ring there are two marble pedestals removed from the house of the Vestals, and inscribed with the name of Cœlia Claudiana, virgo vestalis maxima. In adapting them to their new object, Theodoric's masons did not even take time and care to erase the name of the illustrious abbess.

Nothing is known of the fate of the building in the Middle Ages. The document of the eighth century produced by De Rossi (Piante di Roma, p. 127), of which mention has been made above, describes it as a *gymnasium*, viz. *locus diversis exercitationum generibus deputatus.* In the tenth or eleventh century it was occupied by a colony of stone-cutters and lime-burners, whose sheds and workshops were seen and described in the excavations of 1877. The floor around the sheds was covered with chips and fragments of statues and architectural marbles. When we recollect that there were on each tier of the portico eighty-six columns, and over a thousand feet of richly carved marble cornice, and marble roofs, and marble parapets, floors, and incrustations, and numberless statues and bas-reliefs, of which hardly a trace is left, the magnitude of the work of destruction needs no comment. There is an altar left standing in the middle of the arena, which they had begun to hammer and split, when, for a reason unknown to us, the work of destruction was suddenly given up. To one object only they seem to have paid respect, namely, the beautiful statue of Juno, discovered March 3, 1878, and now exhibited in the Museo delle Terme. We found it lying on two supports (*cuscini*) of stone, on which it had been placed so carefully that not even the most delicate folds of the peplum had suffered damage from the operation. The photograph of this masterpiece is given in the " Notizie " for 1879, pl. 1, n. 2. A regular search for plunder was opened in 1552 by Alessandro Ronconi. Julius III. being engaged at that time in building his famous Villa Giulia, outside the Porta del Popolo, a campaign was opened against the antique monuments of the city by all those wishing to please the pope, or to make money by dealing with him in marbles for the palace, or in statues and inscriptions for the ornamental grounds by which it was surrounded. The tombs of the Via Flaminia at

[1] *Corpus Inscr.*, vi. 1716, *a, b.*

Torre di Quinto, the remains of the gardens of Domitia in the Vigna of Bindo Altoviti (Prati di Castello), the Baths of the Aquæ Albulæ near Tivoli, the Baths of Agrippa behind the Pantheon, the Villa of the Acilii on the Pincian, the ruins of Porto and

Fig. 65. — Headless Statue of a Muse discovered in the so-called Stadium.

Ostia, the Temple of the Sun in the Villa Colonna, and the stadium of the Palatine were put to ransom. Between May and July, 1552, Alessandro Ronconi sold to the pope columns of cipollino, pedestals and bases, and even the gutter of white marble which carried off the drippings from the roof of the portico.

Francesco Ronconi, son or nephew of Alessandro, was more successful in his excavations of 1570. Their results are thus described by Flaminio Vacca (Mem. 77) : " I remember the finding in the Vigna Ronconi of eighteen or twenty mutilated statues of Amazons (Danaids), somewhat larger than life-size. In the same place, and exactly under the wine-press, which Ronconi was repairing at the time, the Hercules of Lysippus was discovered." The fate of the Danaids is unknown, except that in the account books of Cardinal Ippolito d' Este the following entry has been discovered by Professor Venturi : " March 5, 1570 : To expense for statues, seventy-five scudi to Francesco Ronconi and Leonardo Sormano for a life-size statue of an Amazon."

Pius IX. in 1868, Commendatore Rosa in 1872, and the Italian government in 1877, 1878, and 1893, have liberated the Stadium once for all from its heavy pall of ruins. No other part of the Palatine impresses us more vividly. There is no break in the inclosure wall, nor in the colonnade of the lower portico, although many of the shafts are only a few feet high : the remains of the Imperial hexedra tower at the height of 120 feet. The east end of the portico is especially well preserved and so are the metæ in the shape of fountains, and some of the monuments which mark the middle line of the arena.

The exedra deserves a few words of description. There is a ground floor, level with the arena, with a middle hall of good size, and a smaller room on each side of it. The pavement, the marble incrustations, and the paintings of the hall have been destroyed, with the exception of the frescoes in the lunette of the vault. They would hardly be noticeable, owing to their bad style and imperfect preservation, were it not for a rare and perhaps unique representation of a terrestrial globe fixed to the circle of the horizon, which rests on three pegs. This globe shows how wide-spread in Roman schools was the theory, known and supported since the time of Aristotle, that the earth was a sphere.

This hall formed part of the castle of the Frangipani, facing the monastery of SS. Andrea e Gregorio in Clivoscauri. In the excavations of 1871 some thirty skeletons of men who seem to have perished in their youth were found at the foot of the wall on the right ; some of the skulls bore marks of blows and cuts from battle-axes or swords. We thought, while gazing at these remains, that, during one of the bloody contests which every now and then marked the election of a pontiff, these young warriors had lost their lives in the defense of the stronghold of the Septizonium, and had been buried in haste under the Imperial tribune. The vaulted ceiling of the hall must have been intact at that time, because the skeletons were found covered by great masses of masonry.

The small room on the right was never finished and its floor never paved; the other one, on the contrary, is nicely painted and

Fig. 66. — Female head of Greek workmanship discovered in the so-called Stadium.

has a mosaic floor with festoons and birds in black and white. There are graffiti on the plaster to the left of the entrance, among which is a roll of names followed by a cipher. The names may be of athletes or sportsmen, and the figures may refer to their contests or to the victories won.

The Imperial box occupied the whole hemicycle on the upper floor. A colonnade of syenite granite decorated its front, another of pavonazzetto the curve of the apse. Shafts, capitals, bases, and fragments of the entablature cover the floor in front of it. It is probable that the Hercules of Lysippus discovered by Ronconi in 1570, and bought by Cosimo III. for the Pitti Palace, belonged to one of the eleven niches of the exedra.

This statue is the only one pertaining to the Stadium which has been taken away from Rome. I have already spoken of the fate of the Danaids discovered by the same Ronconi. The Muse found by Visconti in 1868 and the Juno of 1878 are exhibited on the west side of the quadrangle in the Museo delle Terme. In the excavations of 1893 several remarkable works of art came to light, namely, a headless statue of another Muse (March 29), which has been left on the spot, at the east end of the north portico ; a bust of Antoninus Pius ; a torso of a Faun ; and a superb female head of pure Greek workmanship, of which I give a reproduction (Fig. 66). It is the work of a great master of the fifth century B. C., and may belong to one of the Muses by which the image of Apollo Citharœdus was surrounded in the neighboring temple. These marbles are preserved in the Museo delle Terme.

REFERENCES.— Carlo Ludov. Visconti, *Di un nuovo graffito palatino* (in Giorn. arcad., vol. lxii.).— Visconti and Lanciani, *Guida del Palatino*, p. 87.— Pietro Rosa, *Relazione sulle scoperte archeologiche*, p. 78, Rome, 1873.—Fabio Gori, *Archivio Storico*, vol. ii. p. 374. — Henry Deglane, *Gazette archéologique*, 1888, p. 216 ; and *Mélanges Ecole franç. de Rome*, ix. 1889, pp. 184–229.— *Notizie degli Scavi*, 1878, p. 66 ; 1879, tav. i. n. 2 ; 1893, pp. 31, 70, 117, 162 ; 1894, p. 94.— Joseph Sturm, *Das kaiserliche Stadium*, Würzburg, 1888.— *Monumenti antichi pubblicati per cura della r. Accademia dei Lincei*, vol. v., 1895, p. 17.— Friedrich Marx, *Das sogennante Stadium* (in Jahrbuch des deutschen Instituts, 1895, p. 129).— Rodolfo Lanciani, *Mittheil.*, 1894, p. 16.— Christian Huelsen, *Ibid.*, 1895, p. 276.

XXIII. THE PALACE OF SEPTIMIUS SEVERUS (ædes Severianæ). — Between the two summits of the Palatine, the Cermalus and the Palatium, there is a marked difference in shape. The first was, and is still for the most part, surrounded by cliffs which made it inaccessible ; the second slopes down more gently towards the Cælian and the Piscina Publica ; and while the Imperial buildings stop with the edge of the precipice on one side, they descend to the bottom of the slope and to the level of the valley on the other. Immense substructures were raised here by Septimius Severus and Caracalla to reach the average level of the other palaces, as shown by the following engraving from a photograph, taken from the

Aventine. The letters A A′ mark the level of the platform; B marks the remains of the Palace of Severus, built on the platform; C, the curved end of the Stadium; D, the remains of the palace of Augustus.

Fig. 67. — Substructures of the Palace of Septimius Severus, as seen from the Aventine.

No other section of the Palatine has suffered as much as this one from the action of time and from the hand of man. By measurements on the spot, compared with descriptions and documents left by those who saw the ruins in a better state, I have ascertained that the Ædes Severianæ must have covered an area of 24,500 square metres, and must have reached the height of fifty metres above the pavement of the streets which inclosed them on two sides. This gives a volume of one million and a quarter cubic metres, a perfect mountain of masonry, of which only a few traces are left standing to tell the tale. The edge of the substructures, marked A' in the illustration, is celebrated for its fine view, which extends over hills and dales as far as the coast of Ostia and Laurentum. (See Ancient Rome, chap. v. p. 126.) In gazing at it from his lofty point of vantage the reader must remember that he is only level with the ground floor of the palace, which rose from twenty-five to thirty metres above his head. The ruins were granted in 975 to the monks of S. Gregorio by Stephen of Hildebrand, then ruler of Rome. We gather from the act of donation that there were at that time thirty-eight arches still standing on the side of the Circus, which were popularly called the "Porticus Materiani;" others were visible in the adjoining property of John de Papa de Septem Viis. Above this line of crypts and arcades there was a strip of cultivated land, and still higher up the bathing apartments of the palace (*ubi dicitur balneum imperatoris*).

On March 18, 1145, the ruins, or at least the portion of them between the stronghold of the Septizonium and the tower which had been raised over the triumphal Arch of Titus at the entrance to the Circus Maximus, were leased to Cencio Frangipane. A century later the monks thought it best suited to their interests to break up the property and lease the crypts and arcades one by one. Between 1215 and 1218 twenty-one were rented individually for various purposes, which in progress of time were reduced to one, for a hay-loft (*ad retinendum fenum*)! One of the conditions in these contracts obliged the tenant to paint the coat-of-arms of S. Gregory above the gate of the crypt, and keep it fresh and bright. The abuse was suppressed in 1862 after the terrific fire which consumed in one night thousands of bales of hay, and threatened to destroy the whole mass of buildings.

This corner of the Palatine is connected with two well-known names, that of Tommaso Inghirami da Volterra, surnamed Fedra, a famous poet, orator, and scholar of the sixteenth century, and that of Marcello Venusti, a painter and a pupil of Michelangelo, like Sebastiano del Piombo and Daniele da Volterra. The first owned the part of the palace called BALNEUM IMPERATORIS, which he sold to Marcello Crescenzi, auditor of Clement VII., on January 22, 1533; the second owned the vigna (marked " dei Benfratelli " in the plan facing p. 110), which he had bought on April 24, 1560, from Concordia Maccarani, widow of Francesco Cecchi.

The only work of art found — as far as I know — among these ruins is a torso of Minerva with the ægis dotted with stars. Paolo Biondi discovered it by accident on June 5, 1823, and it was removed soon after to the Museo Vaticano. I may mention also a precious gold fibula, a piece of Byzantine work of the sixth century, discovered by Mr. Bliss at the top of the stairs leading from the Stadium to the exedra. It is now exhibited in one of the ground rooms of the Museo delle Terme, together with the " tesoro " of Castel Trosino.[1]

XXIV. THE SEPTIZONIUM. — Few remains of the Imperial palace, or indeed of the whole city, are as widely known as the Septizonium, and yet archæologists are still discussing what the name means and what was the real nature of the edifice. Visconti (Guida del Palatino, pp. 49 and 93) thinks that " Septizonium " was the name of the front of the Palace of Severus facing the south, which was ornamented with seven rows (*septem zonæ*) of columns, symbolizing the seven bands or atmospheres of heaven.[2] He supports the theory by two arguments: first, that the hebdomadal cycle in honor of the seven planets came into fashion and practical use about the time of Septimius Severus; second, that even in the Middle Ages the Septizonium was connected with the sun and the moon. Jordan and others, on the other hand, deny that there were seven tiers of columns: they fix the maximum at three, which is the number represented in the earliest designs of this noble ruin. Now as the word *septifolium* indicates a plant with seven leaves, and the word *septimontium* indicates a group of seven hills, so the word *septizonium* must indicate, in the present case, an edifice with seven bands or horizontal lines; in other words, with seven entablatures supported by rows of columns one above the other. It is also possible that the rows were only six, if we reckon among the horizontal bands the basement and

[1] REFERENCE. — Benedetto Mittarelli, *Ann. Camaldul.* (Mittheilungen, 1894, vol. ix. p. 4).

[2] Rawlinson, *The Five Great Monarchies*, vol. ii. pp. 269, 547.

the steps of the structure. Visconti also remarks that we actually have a bona fide septizonium in the Campanile of Pisa, the tiers of which were only seven in the original design of Wilhelm and Bonanno. The eighth was added about a century later. We must remember in the last case that the three rows of columns, of which the Septizonium was composed, reach only the height of 25.64 metres above the level of the Via Triumphalis. The existing remains of the Palace of Severus are at least 55 metres high ; there-

Fig. 68. — The Remains of the Ædes Severianæ and of the Septizonium, from a Sketch by du Cerceau.

fore if the Septizonium was built, as we believe, to screen the confused mass of structures behind, and to serve as a monumental façade to the Palace of Severus, it must have been higher than we supposed. This condition of things appears evident in the above sketch by Jacques Androuet du Cerceau, which I borrowed from his volume of 1560, marked E, *d*, 26 in the Cabinet des Estampes, Paris.

As we have seen above (pp. 178, 179), the line AA′ marks the top of the substructures and the beginning of the palace. Supposing the Septizonium to have been only three stories high, it would hardly have masked even the substructures.

The Septizonium was already in a ruinous condition at the end of the eighth century. The inscription engraved in the frieze of the lower colonnade numbered 280 letters, of which 118 were copied by the so-called Einsiedlensis on the extreme left, towards the Circus Maximus; 45 by the anonymous Barberinianus (Cod. xxx. 25) on the extreme right, towards the Arch of Constantine. There was consequently a gap of 117 letters between the two ends of the ruins, which were respectively called " Septem solia maior " and " Septem solia minor." The total length of the building being 90 or 95 metres, two fifths of it had already collapsed in the eighth century. On July 22, 975, John, abbot of S. Gregory, was allowed to destroy the minor portion; but he did not take advantage of the permission. In the year 1084 Henry IV., while besieging the fortress of Septem Solia, in which Rusticus, nephew of Gregory VII., had sought refuge, caused the fall of many columns (quamplurimus columnas subvertit). In 1257 the larger portion was destroyed by Senatore Brancaleone. The last remnants disappeared in the winter of 1588–89 by order of Sixtus V., and at the hand of his favorite architect Domenico Fontana. The destruction cost the pope 905 scudi, but he recovered more than his money's worth by making use of the materials, whether blocks of peperino and travertino or columns of rare marbles.

Thirty-three blocks of stone were used in the foundations of the pedestal of the obelisk in the Piazza del Popolo; 104 of marble in the restoration of the column of Marcus Aurelius, including the base of the bronze statue of S. Paul; 15 in the tomb of the pope in the Cappella del Presepio at S. Maria Maggiore; and an equal number in that of Pius V. The staircase of the Casa dei Mendicanti, or workhouse, by the Ponte Sisto; the washing-house, or *lavatore*, in the baths of Diocletian; the door of the Palazzo della Cancellaria; the north façade of the Lateran Palace, its court and staircases; and the church of S. Girolamo degli Schiavoni, had all their share of the spoils of the Septizonium.

REFERENCES. — Heinrich Jordan, *Bullettino dell' Instituto*, 1872, p. 145; and *Forma Urbis Romœ*, pp. 37–41, tab. viii. n. 38. — Antonio Bertolotti, *Artisti Lombardi*, vol. i. p. 87: Libro xix. del cav. Fontana per la disfattura della scola di Vergilio. Milan, Hoepli, 1881. — Christian Huelsen, *Das Septizonium*, etc.: xlvi. Programm zum Winckelmannsfeste der archaeologischen Gesellschaft zu Berlin. 1886. — Enrico Stevenson, *Il settizonio Severiano* (Bullettino comm. arch., 1888, p. 269, tav. xiii.). — Rodolfo Lanciani, *Il Palazzo Maggiore* (in Mittheilungen, vol. ix., 1894, p. 4).

XXV. The Water Supply and Reservoirs of the Palace.
— Nothing is known of the water supply of the Palatine before
the time of Domitian.   The fact that Augustus would take his
siesta in summer months " by the fountain of the peristyle," proves
that his house was well provided with water from the time of its
first construction.   After doubling the extent of the Imperial
domain on the hill, Domitian carried a powerful siphon from the
reservoir of the Arcus Cœlimontani (Aqua Claudia) by the temple
of Claudius, to the highest point of the hill by S. Bonaventura.
The pressure must have been enormous, as the siphon crossed
the valley between the two hills at a point 41 metres (41.16) below the feeding reservoir.   It must have reached four atmospheres.
Remains of Domitian's hydraulic work were discovered in 1658
and 1742.   The pipe, made of solid sheets of lead, and oval in
shape, measured about a foot in diameter, and could carry 276
unities (*oncie*) of water.   The laying of the siphon had been
intrusted to the care of M. Arrecinius Clemens, the brother-in-law
of Titus and consul A. D. 73, and its construction to a plumber
named Postumius Amerimnus.   We have been able to follow the
course of the water not only across the valley, but through the
various sections of the Imperial palace.   The pipe supplying the
house of Augustus bore the inscription *dom*vs AVGVSTANÆ and
the name of Evhodas, the *procurator aquarum;* that supplying
the house of Germanicus, the names of Eutychus, procurator, and
Hymnus, plumber; that of the Stadium the names of Epagathus,
procurator, Martialis and Alexander, plumbers, and so forth.

Domitian's siphon is thrown into the shade by the exploit of
Septimius Severus.   After rebuilding, repairing, and connecting in

Fig. 69. — The Aqueduct of the Palatine across the Valley of S. Gregorio.

one mass the various sections of the palace, damaged by the fire
of Commodus; after raising another palace of his own, to which
the Septizonium served as a façade; after providing the Imperial

residence with thermæ of great size and magnificence, he carried the channel of the Claudia from the top of the Cælian to the top of the Palatine, making it span the valley at a prodigious height. The viaduct, composed of four lines of arcades, measured at least 425 metres in length and 42 metres in height. The sketch on the opposite page represents the portion above the modern Via di S. Gregorio. The five arches on the left on the road, shaded in black, are still in existence; the six on the other side were destroyed, on November 14, 1596, by Caprizio Cornovaglia (Cornwall), the owner of what is now called "Orto Botanico."

The water was stored in the great reservoir, afterwards turned into a refectory for the monks of S. Bonaventura. Among the discoveries made when the convent was built, Bartoli mentions a spigot of Corinthian brass weighing ninety pounds.

REFERENCES. — Rodolfo Lanciani, *I comentarii di Frontino*, etc., Rome, Salviucci, 1880, pp. 211, 234. — Ridolfino Venuti, *Roma antica*, vol. i. p. 38.

XXVI. Two more edifices, or rather two parts of the same edifice, remain to be examined before we leave the Palatine : the PÆ-DAGOGIUM and the DOMUS GELOTIANA.

The Domus Gelotiana was purchased and embodied in the crown property by Caligula, not for want of additional space and accommodation, but to satisfy his passion for the races of the circus, and his affection for the squadron of the greens, *factio prasina*, in whose stables (by SS. Lorenzo e Damaso) he used to spend days and nights indulging in all kinds of excesses. The

Fig. 70. — Plan of the Domus Gelotiana.

house adjoined the Circus and the Carceres, where the riders were massed on race days, so that it was easy for the young prince to join his friends without leaving the Imperial palace.   The Domus Gelotiana is composed of two parts: one adjoining the Circus, which is still in private hands, and is entered from the gate No. 45 Via dei Cerchi.   It contains the vestibule, the atrium, the tablinum, and the triclinium.   The inner part, which is Government property, contains many smaller apartments opening on a second courtyard or peristyle, and it has become famous for the graffiti

Fig. 71. — One of the Walls of the Pædagogium with Greek and Latin Graffiti.

which cover its walls.   We learn from them that, after the death of Caligula, the Domus Gelotiana, or, at least, this inner part of it, was turned into a training-school for court pages, under the name of Pædagogium.   The name occurs very often in the graffiti: *Corinthus exit de pædagogio!   Marianus Afer exit de pædagogio!* as if the boys wanted to chronicle their liberation from the rod of the master on the walls which had long imprisoned them.   There was another amusing allusion to the hardships of school life, composed of a vignette and its explanation.   The vignette represented a donkey turning the mill, and the legend said, *Labora, aselle, quomodo ego laboravi et proderit tibi.* "Work, work, little donkey, as I have worked myself, and thou shalt be rewarded for it." This graffito was destroyed by an unscrupulous tourist in 1886. The most interesting of the set is the one representing a caricature of the Crucifixion of our Lord, discovered at the beginning of the year 1857, and removed soon after to the Kircherian Museum of the Collegio Romano.

The front part of the house, entered by the Via dei Cerchi, No. 45, was partially excavated in 1888, when a remarkable set of fresco paintings was discovered in the dining-hall, marked A in Fig. 70.

The figures, varying in height from 1.60 metres to 1.80, represent butlers and waiters in the act of leading the guests to the banqueting table. The tricliniarch with a rod in his hand stands by the entrance door, whilst other men are carrying napkins, wreaths, silver plate, etc. It is to be regretted that such an interesting place should not be accessible to the public, and that the front and back sections of this historical house should not be excavated at one and the same time. The discovery of the triclinium has been illustrated by Marchetti in the "Notizie degli Scavi," 1892, p. 44; and by Huelsen in "Mittheilungen," 1894, p. 289.

LITERATURE on the graffiti of the Pædagogium. — Raffaele Garrucci, *Il crocifisso graffito nella casa dei Cesari.* Rome, 1857; and *Graffiti di Pompei,* p. 97, plates 30, 31. — Ferd. Becker, *Das spottcrucifix d. röm. Kaiserpaläste.* Breslau, 1866. — Franz Xaver Kraus, *Das spottcrucifix vom Palatin.* Freiburg im Breisgau, 1872. — G. Battista de Rossi, *Bull. Inst.,* 1857, p. 275; *Bull. crist.,* 1863, p. 72; 1867, p. 75. — C. Ludovico Visconti, *Di un nuovo graffito palatino* (in Giornale arcadico, vol. lxii.); and *Sulla interpretazione della sigle V. D. N. dei graffiti palatini.* Rome, 1868. — Visconti and Lanciani, *Guida del Palatino,* p. 78. — Fabio Gori, in *Giornale arcadico,* vol. lii. p. 45. — Rodolfo Lanciani, *Ancient Rome,* p. 119. — Luigi Correra, *Graffiti di Roma* (in Bull. com., 1893, p. 245; 1894, p. 89).

BOOK III

I. THE SACRA VIA. — The line and direction of the Sacra Via
in Imperial times is no longer a matter for discussion, because,
since April 21, 1882, its pavement has been laid bare from one
end to the other, together with the remains of the edifices which
bordered it, of the monuments in honor of different worthies
which decorated its pavement, and of the drains which ran under
it. The topography of this "queen of streets" was, however, very
different in Kingly or early Republican times. It can be made
out in two ways: from the remains of Kingly or Republican
buildings which appear here and there, below the level of the
Imperial ones (for instance, under the house of the Vestals and
under the Basilica Julia), or from the configuration of the ground.
Geological analysis proves, among other things, that the primitive
road crossed the ridge of the Velia, not by the Arch of Titus, as
it did afterwards, but fifty metres north of it, where the church of
S. Francesca Romana now stands. The furrow followed by the
road was discovered by Nibby in 1827–32 by means of borings
through the clay and marl strata of which the ridge is composed.
The same archæologist found remains of private houses under the
pavement of the present or Imperial road. From these pieces of
evidence we can conclude that the primitive Sacra Via left the
hollow of the Coliseum at a point equidistant from the Colossus
(I in plan) and the Meta Sudans (II), — I mention these monuments to give the reader some "points de repère;" crossed the
depression between the Palatine and the Oppian on the line of the
axis of the Templum Romæ et Veneris (IV); descended the northern slope towards the Forum along the Porticus Margaritaria
(XII); then turned diagonally towards the Vicus Tuscus (XXIX),
passing between the Temple of Vesta (XIX) and the habitation of
the Pontifex Maximus (Regia, XVIII). From the junction of the

*See Figure 72 following page 189.

Vicus Tuscus to the Capitoline hill no changes seem to have taken place. The whole course of the primitive Sacra Via was irregular and winding as becomes a much frequented path over undulating ground not encumbered by buildings or obstacles of any kind; but as soon as buildings began to rise on either side, it took a definite shape, and angles were substituted for curves until the street was made to turn at a right angle no less than five times. The transformation was obviously accomplished by degrees: first in 42 B. C., when the Temple of Cæsar was raised on the spot where his body had been incinerated, secondly after the fire of Nero, thirdly after that of Commodus, and lastly after that of Carinus. Each of these calamities gave rise to a new "piano regolatore."

After the fall of the Empire, when traffic was practically reduced to its primitive state, and the glorious monuments of this "celeberrimus urbis locus " crumbled into dust, the bend round the Temple of Cæsar was abandoned, and the traffic resumed the ancient line, which was the easiest and shortest. This late path is still marked by bits of rough pavement made up with old worn-out paving-stones, blocks of marble, and architectural fragments.

The primitive path was named Sacra Via (*infima, summa, clivus sacer*) because three very sacred hut temples stood on its border: the hut for public fire, or Temple of Vesta, that in which the Penates brought from Troy were kept, and a third inhabited by the high priest. The people adopted the form Sacra Via, instead of Via Sacra, and its inhabitants were called Sacravienses. In the early days of Rome it was divided into three sections, the first from its origin near the Sacellum Streniæ (site unknown, but near the Giardino delle Mendicanti) to the house of the "rex sacrificulus " on the top of the ridge; the second from this house to the Regia or habitation of the Pontifex Maximus; the third from the Regia to the summit of the Capitoline hill. In Imperial times the ascent to this hill was called *clivus Capitolinus*. Its total length from the Meta Sudans to the foot of ascent was 790 metres. The street retained its name at least up to the ninth century after Christ, as certified by the "Liber Pontificalis " in the Life of Paschal I. (817–824, "ecclesia Cosmæ et Damiani in Via Sacra "), but its classic meaning was altogether forgotten. The church of S. Cosma and that of S. Adriano were called "in Via Sacra " because they were on the line of the great pontifical processions, which entered the Forum by the Via di Marforio and left it in the direction of the Arch of Titus.

MAP OF SACRA VIA Fig. 72.

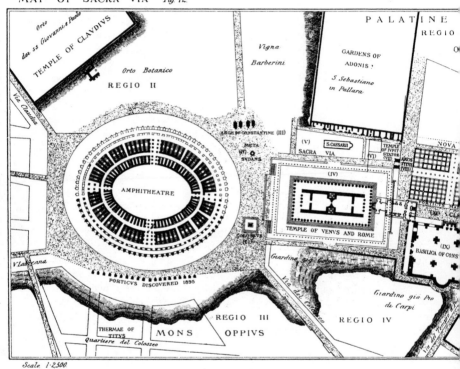

Scale, 1:2500.

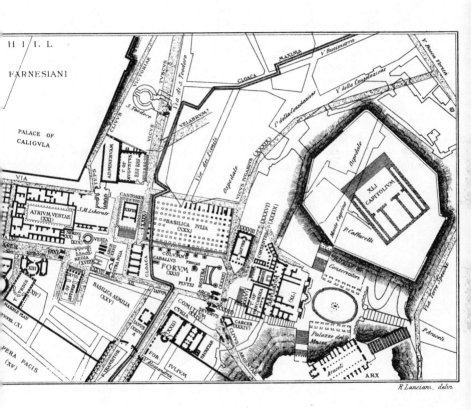

R Lanciani, delin.

LITERATURE. — Ambrosch, *Studien und Andeutungen.* Breslau, 1839. — Adolf Becker, *De Muris,* p. 23; and *Topographie,* pp. 219–243. — Antonio Nibby, *Roma nell' anno 1838,* part i. vol. i. p. 49. — Luigi Canina, *Descrizione del Foro.* Rome, 1845. — Heinrich Jordan, *Capitol, Forum und Sacra Via,* Berlin, Weidmann, 1881; and *Topographie,* vol. i. p. 155. — J. Francis Nichols, *The Roman Forum,* pp. 277–299. — J. Henry Parker, *The Via Sacra in Rome,* London, 1876.

II. THE COLOSSUS (colossal statue of the Sun) (I in plan). — The platform of the Velia, from the " summa Sacra Via" to the site of the amphitheatre, was occupied by the vestibule of the Golden House of Nero, a square portico with a colossal bronze statue in the centre.   The statue had been cast in Rome by Zenodorus in the likeness of Nero; but after the death of the tyrant the head had been changed into that of the radiant Sun, the face bearing a resemblance to that of Titus. Vespasian generously rewarded the artist who had thus served the interests of the Flavian dynasty.   When Martial wrote the second epigram, " De spectaculis," about A. D. 75, the Golden House had already been pulled down, and the ground near the Colossus seems to have been occupied by scaffoldings connected with the work of the new amphitheatre.   The statue remained in its place until 121, when Hadrian, having chosen the site for his Temple of Venus and Rome, caused it to be placed nearer to the Coliseum.   The displacement was effected by the architect De(me)trianus with the help of twenty-four elephants, the statue remaining all the while upright and suspended from the movable scaffolding.   The difficulty of the operation may be estimated by the fact that the bronze mass was 30.5 metres high.   The seven rays round the head, each 6.68 metres long, were a later addition.   The " Vita Comm." affirms that the head was changed once more by Commodus to bear his own likeness.   It is represented in coins of Alexander Severus and Gordianus.   The last classic mention occurs in the Chronicon of Cassiodorus; the first mediæval record (?) in a document of A. D. 972 (" domus posita Romæ regione quarta non longe a Colosso ").   The pedestal of the Colossus (I in plan) was discovered by Nibby in 1828.   It is built of concrete with brick facing, once covered with marble slabs.

LITERATURE. — Antonio Nibby, *Roma nell' anno 1838,* part i. vol. ii. p. 442. — Fr. Morgan Nichols, *The Roman Forum,* p. 294. — J. H. Parker, *The Via Sacra in Rome,* London, 1876, plate 38. — Donaldson, *Architectura numism.,* n. 79. — De Rossi, *Piante di Roma,* p. 76, n. 1.

III. META SUDANS (II in plan), a fountain called *meta* from its shape like a goal of the circus, or from its location at the meeting point of four regions, II, III, IV, X, and *sudans* from the playing of its water in sprays and cascades. The Chronicon of Cassiodorus names Domitian as its founder, and the year 97 as the date of its construction. Perhaps Domitian only enlarged and embellished a fountain already existing, because a *meta* of pyramidal shape appears in the medal struck in the year 80 for the dedication of the Coliseum ; and besides Seneca, who died in 65, mentions the neighborhood of the fountain as the place where people would try new bugles and flutes, and make an unbearable noise (Ep. lvi. 5). The round basin of the present day dates from the time of Constantine. When Ficoroni excavated it for the first time in 1743, there were six metres of rubbish around the *meta*. It is represented in the marble mouth of the well of the Vatican museum, Corridoio delle Iscrizioni, compartment XIII., right side, the photograph of which is marked No. 4671 in Parker's collection. Nibby, however, declares that this *meta* is the work of a modern restorer. A church of S. Maria de Meta is mentioned by Armellini (Chiese, 2d ed. p. 522).

LITERATURE. — Cohen, *Monn. imp.*, vol. i. p. 362, n. 184; p. 359, n. 163. — Donaldson, *Arch. numism.*, n. 79. — Ficoroni, *Vestigie di Roma*, vol. i. p. 36. — Alberto Cassio, *Corso delle acque*, vol. ii. p. 194. — Antonio Nibby, *Roma nell' anno 1838*, part i. vol. i. p. 370.

IV. THE ARCH OF CONSTANTINE (III in plan). — The origin of this noble monument is described in " Pagan and Christian Rome," p. 20. It was raised in A. D. 315 to commemorate the victory of the first Christian Emperor over Maxentius, with marbles taken at random from other public and private monuments. The bas-reliefs of the Attic, the statues of the Dacian kings, the eight medallions above the side arches, the eight columns of giallo antico, and the greater part of the entablature were removed from a triumphal arch of Trajan, probably from the " Arcus divi Traiani " which spanned the Via Appia near the Porta Capena. A piece of the inscription, probably from the same arch, is to be found in the Coliseum.[1]

The two bas-reliefs on each side of the middle passage are attributed by Nibby to the time of Gordianus the younger, all the rest to the time of Constantine. The inside of the structure is also built with a great variety of materials taken from monuments belonging to the Fabii and to the Arruntii, the carvings and

[1] *Bull. arch. com.*, 1880, 217, n. 9.

inscriptions of which are still perfect. The bricks alone are contemporary with Constantine, and are stamped with the well-known
seal OF(*ficinæ*) S(*acræ*) R(*ationis*).

The name of the pious Emperor saved the arch from destruction
in the darkest period of mediæval history. A little church dedicated to the Saviour also shielded it from damage; it was called
S. Salvatore de Trasi from the name of Arcus Traseus, or Arco
de' Trasi, given to the monument in the twelfth century, perhaps
from the statues of the Thracian (Dacian) prisoners which stand
on the attic.

Giovio and others have accused Lorenzino de' Medici, the murderer of Duke Alessandro, of having decapitated the statues and
some of the bas-reliefs of the arch. He was capable of the deed, but
the charge is not proved. The heads were not removed to Florence : in fact, no one has ever traced them; one only was found
buried deep in the ground at the foot of the arch about 1795.
The state of the sculptures in the sixteenth century is most carefully reproduced in a drawing of the Laing collection at Edinburgh (vol. xi. pl. 24). Paul III. removed the earth which covered
the arch up to the plinth of the columns, to prepare the way for
the triumphal entry of Charles V. Clement VIII. laid hands on
one of the columns of giallo antico, to make it pair with another
from the Forum of Trajan, and placed both under the organ in the
transept of the Lateran.

LITERATURE. — *Corpus Inscr.*, vol. vi. n. 1139. — De Rossi, *Bull. crist.*, 1863,
p. 49. — Rohault de Fleury, *L'arc de Constuntin* (in Revue archéol., Sept.
1863, p. 250). — Wilhelm Henzen, *Bull. inst.*, 1863, p. 183. — Antonio Nibby,
Roma nell' anno 1838, part i. vol. i. p. 443. — *Beschreibung der Stadt Rom*, iii.
1, p. 314. — Antonio Guattani, *Roma descritta*, i. p. 41. — Theodor Schreiber,
Berichten der k. sächs. Gesellschaft der Wissenschaften, April, 1892, p. 121. —
Eugen Petersen, *Mittheil.*, 1889, p. 314.

The "conservatori" of Rome and Clement XII. ordered a general restoration of the arch in 1731. The works were superin-
tended by Marchese Alessandro Capponi, who made use of a colossal piece of the marble entablature of the Neptunium which
had just been found near the Piazza di Pietra. The missing column
was replaced, although of different marble; the heads of nine
Dacian kings and one of the statues (the third on the S. Gregorio
side) were replaced. The position of the latter was occupied by a
fragment which is now kept in the Capitoline museum. The words
"ad arcvm" are engraved on its plinth, an address for the porters
who had to remove it from the sculptor's studio to the arch.

Fig. 73. — The Arch of Constantine in Botticelli's "Castigo del fuoco celeste," Sistine Chapel.

The Arch of Constantine has been a favorite subject for artists since the early Renaissance. It appears many times in the background of famous pictures, like the " Dispute of S. Catherine," by Pinturicchio, in the Appartamento Borgio ; or in the " Castigo del Fuoco Celeste," by Sandro Botticelli, in the Sistine Chapel, of which I give a reproduction.

When I first visited the staircase and the rooms in the attic story, on February 27, 1879, the first signature of a visitor which struck me at the first landing was that of Michelangelo, dated 1494 (genuine ?). Antonio da Sangallo the elder and Cherubino Alberti have also left accounts of their exploration of those rooms.

V. ÆDES ROMÆ ET VENERIS (Temple of Venus and Rome) (IV in plan), designed and built by Hadrian on the site of the vestibule of the Golden House. — As the Temple of Castor and Pollux was named in progress of time from Castor alone, so that of Venus and Rome is called simply *templum Urbis* by the " Vita Hadriani," *Urbis fanum* and *delubrum Romœ* by others. The foundation stone was laid on the birthday of Rome, April 21, A. D. 131, and the dedication solemnized in 135. Antonio Nibby, who led the excavations of the temple from November, 1827, to December, 1829, found many brick stamps of 123, and a few of 124. Dion Cassius relates that, when the work was already in progress, Hadrian submitted his drawings to Apollodorus of Damascus, the illustrious architect of Trajan's Forum, whom in a fit of jealousy he had already banished to a remote island. The architect did not disguise his opinion : the statues, he said, were too large for their niches, and the temple ought to have been raised much higher so as to be seen to greater advantage from the side of the Clivus Sacer. This arrangement, besides, would have permitted the construction of caves and vaults under the foundation, useful both for storing the machinery of the amphitheatre and for preparing it out of sight for immediate use. It is related that the great man paid for his criticism with his life.

The temple was brought to perfection by Antoninus Pius, on whose medals it appears with the legend ROMAE AETERNAE VE-NERI FELICI, perhaps the very one engraved on either front of the structure. Having been greatly injured by fire in 307, it was restored by Maxentius, whose brick stamps, OFF(*icina*) S(*ummae*) R(*ei*), F(*ecit*) DOM(*itius*), are found in great numbers in the walls of the double cella. Ammianus Marcellinus includes it among the

[1] Nichols, *The Roman Forum*, p. 294.

marvels of Rome (A. D. 356). In 391 it was closed and abandoned to its fate, but the solidity of the building was such that, two centuries later, we find it still intact. Pope Honorius I. (625–640)

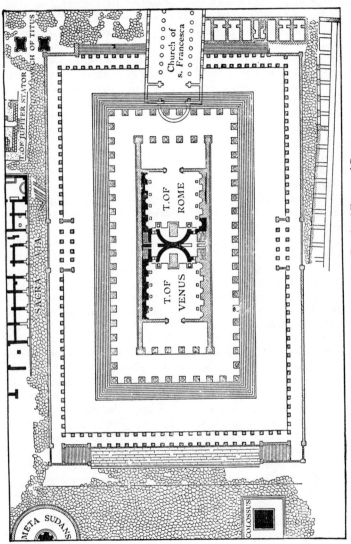

Fig. 74. — Plan of the Temple of Venus and Rome.

obtained from the Emperor Heraclius the gilt-bronze tiles of the roof, which he removed to that of S. Peter's. Many of these were carried off by the Saracens in the loot of 846; those left on the roof of the nave, seen and described by Grimaldi in 1606, must have been melted by Paul V., together with the other bronzes of the fountain of Symmachus. (See Pagan and Christian Rome, p. 136.) Paul I. (757–767) built a church in honor of SS. Peter and Paul on the vestibule of the temple facing the Forum, where the fall of Simon the Magician was believed to have taken place.   Two small cavities in one of the paving-stones of the Sacra Via were shown to the faithful, as the marks left by the knees of the prince of the Apostles, while praying for the discomfiture of the impostor. The stones are still kept in the present church of S. Francesca Romana, on the right of the tomb of Gregory XI. The chapel of Paul I. did not last long: at the time of Leo IV. (847–855) its place was occupied by the church of S. Maria, called Nova, in opposition to that of S. Maria Antiqua, still existing, behind the remains of the Augustæum. The present edifice, dedicated to S. Francesca Romana, dates from the time of Paul V., 1612.

All these chapels and churches were built at the expense of the temple. Nibby says that the bed of rubbish immediately above the antique pavement was composed of architectural fragments, split and charred; that he found in 1810 a lime-kiln near the Arch of Titus, bordered by pieces of precious columns of porphyry — a material refractory to fire — and filled with sculptured fragments; and that, while restoring the church of S. Francesca in 1828 and 1829, he found the walls built with pieces of marble; yet enough plunder was left among the ruins of the temple to satisfy the greed of scores of modern excavators. Flaminio Vacca could purchase about 1575 slabs of Greek marble from the pavement of the cella facing the Coliseum, which he describes as a "cosa stupenda." Ligorio says that pieces of columns and of the entablature found by the monks of S. Maria, in adding a wing to their convent, were made use of in the "fabbrica di S. Pietro." Other beautiful marbles are described and designed by the Gobbo da Sangallo. An oval basin of a fountain of oriental granite, 5.57 metres in diameter, discovered also in the sixteenth century, was "ruinato dalle scellerate mani" of the excavators. At last, when these vandals thought that nothing was left to plunder above ground, they attacked the foundations of the portico and temple, which were built of blocks of travertine or peperino! Not one is left *in situ*. The

annexed plan explains the form and architecture of the building.
The portico inclosing the temenos had columns of gray granite,
seventy-two pieces of which have escaped destruction, simply
because they were unfit for the lime-kiln, and too hard to be made

Fig. 75. — Bas-relief with the Temple of Venus and Rome.

use of. If these columns were raised into their former position,
as has been done with those of the Basilica Ulpia, the Temple of
Venus and Rome would become the most picturesque ruin of this
classic district. The peristyle of the double cella was made of
shafts of cipollino, six feet in diameter. There is one fragment
lying on the northeast side of the platform, which the stone-cutters engaged in the repairs of S. Paolo fuori le Mura had begun

to saw, to make discs for the pavement of that church. This last act of destruction was stopped by Carlo Fea, then Superintendent of Antiquities, who broke the saw and put the stone-cutters to flight.

The drains which run parallel with the wings of the portico are beautifully preserved; they are 2.70 metres high and 0.90 wide, and the tiles of their roofs are marked with the consulates of Pætinus and Apronianus (A. D. 123), and Servianus III. and Varus (125). The north corner of the platform is built over the remains — still visible through a trap-door — of a private mansion. They include part of the atrium with the impluvium paved with pieces of blue, green, and white enamel.

The temple is represented in a bas-relief, formerly in the Muti house, Piazza della Pescheria, and now half in the Museo delle Terme, half in the Lateran! An illustration of it was given by Professor Petersen in the "Mittheilungen" of 1896. (See Fig. 75.)

LITERATURE. — Dion Cassius, lxix. 5. — Amm. Marcellin., xvi. 10. — Flaminio Vacca, *Memorie*, n. 73. — Carlo Fea, *Miscellanea*, vol. i. p. 85, note (*a*); *Varietà di Notizie*, p. 137. — Nibby, *Roma antica*, vol. ii. p. 723. — J. H. Parker, *Archæology of Rome*, vol. ii. p. 86. — Rodolfo Lanciani, *L' itinerario di Einsiedlen*, pp. 62–67; *Mélanges de l' Ecole française de Rome*, 1891, p. 164, pl. 3. — F. M. Nichols, *The Roman Forum*, p. 293.

VI. So-called BATHS OF HELIOGABALUS, and CHURCH OF S. CESARIO IN PALATIO (V in plan). See p. 169.

VII. TURRIS CHARTULARIA (VI in plan). See p. 171.

VIII. THE TEMPLE OF JUPITER STATOR (VII in plan). — The Turris Chartularia marks most likely the site of the Temple of Jupiter Stator, and the blocks of peperino of which its foundations are built belong probably to the cella. The temple vowed by Romulus, during his first encounter with the Sabines in the valley of the Forum, was only built in 296 by M. Atilius Regulus. Classics place it near the Mugonia gate of the Palatine, at the highest point of the Nova Via, near the highest point of the Sacra Via, and within the limits of the fourth region. The four indications concur in locating the temple on the site of the Turris Chartularia, side by side with the Arch of Titus; and in precisely this position do we find it in the famous pictorial bas-relief of the Haterii, exhibited in the tenth room of the Lateran Museum. According to this sculptural sketch, the temple was of the Corinthian order, and hexastyle, the front facing the north. It is hardly necessary to remind the reader that a certain mass of concrete at the entrance of Domitian's palace on the Palatine hill,

Fig. 76. — Arch of Titus — Temple of Jupiter Stator in the Bas-relief of the Haterii.

described in books and shown to visitors as the Temple of Stator, has nothing in common with it. That mass of concrete belongs to the foundations of one of the towers built by the Frangipani to make their Palatine stronghold a *locus tutissimus.*

LITERATURE. — Emil Brunn, *Annali dell' Inst.,* vol. xxi. 1849, p. 370. — Heinrich Jordan, *Topographie,* i², p. 277. — Wolfgang Helbig, *Guide to the Public Collections of Rome,* vol. i. p. 496, n. 671. — *Forma Urbis,* pl. xxix.

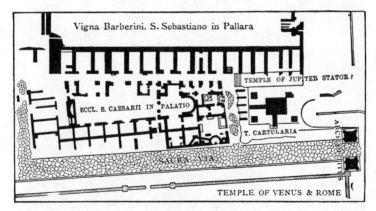

Fig. 77. — Plan of Neighborhood of the Arch of Titus.

IX. THE ARCH OF TITUS (VIII in plan). — It stands at the west corner of the great platform of Venus and Rome at the highest point of the Sacra Via ; it is called, therefore, *Arcus in Sacra Via Summa* in the bas-relief of the Haterii reproduced above.

Fig. 78.   The Summa Sacra Via, with Arch of Titus and Temple of Jupiter Stator.

The title of *divus* (deified) given to the conqueror of Judæa in the inscription of the attic (Corpus, vol. vi. n. 945), as well as the relief of his apotheosis, shows that the monument was finished only after his death. The style is that prevalent in Domitian's time, with a superabundance of carving in the architectural lines. Having been included in the fortifications of the Frangipani, it suffered great damage during the fights of the twelfth and thirteenth centuries. To insure its safety after the demolition of the tower and houses by which it was partly supported, Giuseppe Valadier took down the whole structure piece by piece in 1822, strengthened the foundations, and reconstructed it in its present form, completing the missing parts in travertine so as to make them easily distinguishable from the originals, which are in pentelic marble. The bas-reliefs on the left represent the triumph of Titus, those on the right the spoils taken from the Temple of Zion, like the seven-branched candlestick (from which comes the name of *Arcus Septem Lucernarum* given to the arch in the Middle Ages), the golden table, the silver trumpets, etc. These spoils were deposited in the Temple of Peace in A. D. 75, five years after the conquest of Judæa, together with a marvellous collection of works of art, which included a statue of Naukides from Argos, a figure of the Nile surrounded by the sixteen infants all cut in a single block of *basalte ferrigno*, the Ialysos, a celebrated picture of Protogenes, the Scylla of Nikomachos, the Hero of Parrhasios, and many other masterpieces. All these, except the Jewish relics, perished in the fire of 191. They ultimately fell the prey of Genseric and were landed safely at Carthage in 455, where, eighty years later, Belisarius recaptured them and sent them to Constantinople.

LITERATURE. — *Corpus Inscr.*, vol. vi. n. 945 (943). — Flavius Josephus, *Jud.*, book vii. 17. — Antonio Nibby, *Roma antica*, vol. i. p. 490. — Rodolfo Lanciani, *Ancient Rome*, p. 291.

Nearly opposite the arch, at the corner of the Porticus Margaritaria on the Nova Via, is a shapeless mass of concrete, believed to be the pedestal of the equestrian statue of Clœlia, described by Livy, Seneca, Plutarch, and Servius. The surmise is not improbable, especially as we know that the group was still existing *in Sacra Via Summa* at the time of Servius, viz., at the beginning of the fifth century. A century later Cassiodorus mentions as yet visible in the same place a group of bronze elephants.

LITERATURE. — Becker, *De muris atque portis*, p. 38. — Nichols, *The Roman Forum*, p. 311.

X. BASILICA NOVA (Basilica of Constantine) (IX in plan). — The space of ground covered by this vast building was probably occupied at an early age by the Macellum or Forum Cupedinis, a market for the sale of fruit, honey, flowers, and wreaths, the last mention of which occurs under Augustus. Domitian built on part of the ground the Horrea piperataria, warehouses for Oriental spices, which were burnt down in the fire of 191, together with many private houses, one of which, discovered in 1811 under the right aisle, is described by Fea (Varietà di Notizie, p. 24). I have myself seen traces of other buildings, on the occasion of repairs made to the water-pipe which supplies the fountains of the Palatine and which crosses the basilica diagonally. The basilica was begun by Maxentius and finished by Constantine, partly with materials

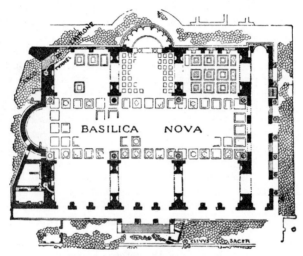

Fig. 79. — Plan of Constantine's Basilica.

found on the spot, partly with bricks made expressly in one of the *officinæ summæ rei*. Hundreds of these were found in the excavations of 1880. It seems that when Maxentius lost his life in the battle of October 27, 312, the basilica was very nearly completed, as is shown by the discovery of a silver medallion — bearing the legend MAXENTIUS P(*ius*) F(*elix*) AUG(*ustus*) — in 1828, in a block of masonry fallen from the highest point of the building.

The basilica had a nave and two aisles. The noble vaulted ceiling of the nave, eighty-two metres long and twenty-five broad, was supported by eight fluted columns of Proconnesian marble, of which only two appear in the vignettes and designs of the Renaissance. Such is, for instance, a sketch by Bramante in the Uffizi collection (No. 1711), which shows one between the first and second arches, with its capital and entablature, and another without capital between the second and third. This last must have disappeared at the time when Sangallo the elder was directing the works of S. Peter's; certainly he made use of its base, which is described by

Fig. 80. — The Basilica of Constantine at the time of Paul V.

Dosio as "larga piedi 8 dita 7 . . . ed è la basa d'una delle colonne . . . che fu portata (a S. Pietro) a tempo che era architetto el Sangallo." The other pillar, so conspicuous in the vignettes of the sixteenth century — among which I may mention the one painted by Raphael's pupils in the last room, first floor, of the Farnesina —

was removed to the Piazza di S. Maria Maggiore by Paul V. in 1613, and set up in honor of the Virgin, as described in "Pagan and Christian Rome," p. 136. We can account also for the fate of a third base. It supplied the material for the statue of Alexander Farnese, now in the Sala dei Capitani, Palazzo dei Conservatori.

The basilica, in its original construction, faced the east, and was entered from the side of the Temple of Venus and Rome by a clumsy portico out of proportion with the rest of the edifice. Later on, a new entrance was opened on the south side facing the Sacra Via, and a new tribune built in harmony with it. The entrance was decorated with four large columns of porphyry, pieces of which were found in 1487, 1819, and 1879, and restored to the place to which they belong. Here also were discovered the fragments of the colossal marble statue of Domitian, now in the Cortile dei Conservatori.

The collapse of this ungraceful structure must date from a comparatively recent time, because Nibby asserts that he saw traces of a Christian fresco painting of the thirteenth century in the north apse. Perhaps the ceiling of the nave fell in the earthquake of 1349, described by Petrarch (Epist. x. 2), carrying down with it the greater portion of the south aisle. The roof of the north aisle, still perfect, was granted by the city in 1547 to Eurialo Silvestri, who laid out a garden on the top of it and filled it with antiques. The basilica itself was used as a cattle-shed until 1714, when it was granted to Marchese Emilio de' Cavalieri for a riding-school. Ten years later I find it used as a hay-loft by the architect Barigioni. The French invaders began excavating it in 1812, and Pius VII. continued their work in 1818–19. In 1828 Nibby laid bare the pavement, which remained in good condition till the second French invasion of 1849. The basilica having been selected as a drilling-place for French recruits, the last trace of the pavement was destroyed about 1854 by the treading of feet.

Literature. — Carlo Fea, *La basilica di Costantino sbandita dalla via Sacra*, Rome, 1819; *Prodromo di nuove osservazioni*, 1816, p. 24; *Miscellanea*, vol. ii. p. 47. — Antonio Nibby, *Della via Sacra*, etc., p. 189; *Del tempio della Pace e della basilica di Costantino*, Rome, 1819; *Roma antica*, vol. ii. p. 238. — Nicola Ratti, *Su le rovine del tempio della Pace*. Rome, 1823. — Bunsen, *Beschreibung*, vol. iii. p. 291. — *Notizie degli Scavi*, 1879–80. — Rodolfo Lanciani, *Bull. com.*, 1876, p. 48.

The basilica was freed from the granaries and factories and ironworks which concealed its northern apse between March, 1878, and February, 1880, when the tunnel known in the Middle Ages as the Arco di Latrone was again made accessible (X in plan).

Before the construction of the basilica direct communication existed between the Sacra Via and the region of the Carinæ, the cross street passing between the Forum of Peace and the warehouses for Oriental spices (Horrea piperataria). Maxentius brought his building into contact with the Forum of Peace and obstructed the passage. To obviate the consequences of the obstruction and to save the citizens a long detour, a subway was opened under the northeast corner of the basilica. The subway is about four metres wide and fifteen long; it is paved with tiles inscribed with the stamp of the Imperial kilns, OFF . S . R . F . OCEN; the side walls

Fig. 81. — The Arco di Latrone under the Basilica of Constantine.

are worn with longitudinal grooves to the height of cart-wheels. When the adjoining Temple of the Sacra Urbs was dedicated by Pope Felix IV. (526–530) to SS. Cosmas and Damianus, one end of the passage was walled up and the passage itself turned into a sepulchral cave. Loculi resembling those of the catacombs are still to be seen in the upper part of the walls, and two or three appear in the illustration above. At a much later period hogsheads of wine took the places of the dead.

This passage was known in the Middle Ages as the Arco di Latrone. Pirro Ligorio (Bodl., f. 15) speaks of it as follows: "The subway which we now call Latrone runs between the church

of S. Cosma and the Temple of Peace (the Basilica of Constantine). After it had served as a burial-place at the time of the
destruction of Rome, traffic was restored through it; but it was
a lonely, dark place, and murders and robberies were freely committed in it. To atone for these crimes, and to bring about a
better state of things, the Arco di Latrone was included in the
itinerary of the famous procession of mid-August, when the image
of the Saviour is removed from the Lateran to S. Maria Maggiore."
The procession of "mezzo agosto," to which Ligorio refers, was
one of the great events of mediæval Rome; the contest for prece-
dence among the popular corporations afterwards degenerated
into open fights and bloodshed. The magistrates of the city
issued regulation after regulation, the last of which, engraved on
marble in the antique style, is still to be seen in the vestibule of
the Palazzo dei Conservatori at the foot of the stairs. The regulations did no good: the pageant was preceded or followed by so
many struggles that it left a bloody trail upon its path. It was
suppressed in 1566 by Pope Pius V.

LITERATURE. — Vincenzo Forcella, *Iscriz. delle chiese di Roma*, vol. i.
n. 60, p. 37. — Giovanni Marangoni, *Istoria dell' oratorio appellato Sancta
Sanctorum*, p. 112. Rome, 1747. — Rodolfo Lanciani, *Archivio della Società
di storia patria*, vol. iii. p. 378; *Itinerario di Einsiedlen*, p. 119.

XI. THE CLIVUS SACER, or gradient of the Sacra Via by the
Basilica of Constantine (XI in plan). — This tract, excavated
between March and June, 1878, is the noblest and widest of the
whole line. It measures 23 metres across from building to building, and 12.35 metres between the sidewalks. Under the roadway
runs a cloaca 2.10 metres high, and 0.90 wide, built of bricks and
vaulted over, with side embranchments to collect the waters from
the north slope of the Palatine and from Constantine's Basilica.

The left-side pavement, along the Porticus Margaritaria and
the House of the Vestals, is 8.20 metres wide, and entirely encumbered by monuments in honor of different people, dating mostly
from the time of Septimius Severus and his successors. There
are pedestals of single or equestrian statues, shrines, fountains,
hemicycles, etc., which, found in a good state of preservation in
1879 and 1882, have been since greatly injured by frost and neglect.
The most important are: (*a*) the pedestal of a statue, probably of
a Greek masterpiece, set up by Fabius Titianus, prefect of the
city in A. D. 339–341, together with many others (see Corpus
Inscriptionum, vi. 1653); (*b*) that of a statue raised to Constantius, by Flavius Leontius, prefect of the city in 355–356; (*c*) that

of a statue of Titus; (*d*) an altar dedicated to the *Lares augusti*;
(*e*) a shrine dedicated to Gordianus the younger by the people of
Tharsos, together with his equestrian statue. This graceful ædi-

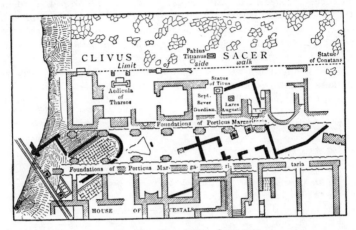

Fig. 82. — Plan of Clivus Sacer.

cula was supported by two columns of portasanta; the letters
ΤΑΡϹΕΩΝ on the epistyle were of gilt metal. It could be reconstructed almost in a perfect state.

LITERATURE. — *Notizie degli Scavi*, 1879, p. 14, tav. vii., and p. 113 ; 1882,
p. 216, tav. xiv.-xvi. — *Bull. com.*, 1878, p. 257 ; 1880, p. 80.

On the side opposite the Basilica Nova stood the

XII. PORTICUS MARGARITARIA, an arcade for jewelers and
goldsmiths (XII in plan). — The parallelogram between the Sacra
and the Nova Via, the Arch of Titus and the House of the Vestals,
remained a *terra incognita* to the topographer until the excavations
of 1878–79. Instead of the *œdes Penatium*, of the house of the
Tarquins, of the Temple of Jupiter Stator, and other such edifices
crowded into it by the fancy of modern students, it was found to
contain a portico, supported by ten or eleven rows of stone pilasters (twenty-two in each row), similar in every respect to the Porticus Septorum under the Palazzo Doria, and to the Porticus
Vipsania under the (now demolished) Palazzo Piombino. The
stone pilasters stand four metres apart, and the covered galleries
must have been lighted by openings in the vault. The classic
name of this portico is easily found by referring to the Almanac

of 354, which mentions, among the edifices near to the Forum, a Porticus Margaritaria, viz., a portico occupied by jewelers and goldsmiths. Considering that the jewelers and goldsmiths of the Porticus Margaritaria call themselves *de Sacra Via*, it is evident that the arcades opened on that very street. Part ii. of volume vi. of the "Corpus Inscriptionum" contains scores of epitaphs of these tradesmen of the Sacra Via: there are *unguentarii*, perfumers; *aurifices*, goldsmiths; an *auri vestrix*, weaver of gold cloth (?); *cœlatores*, engravers also in repoussé work; *coronarii* or wreath-makers; *flaturarii*, metal-casters; *gemmarii* and *margaritarii*, dealers in jewels and pearls; *pigmentarii*, makers of cosmetics; *tibiarii*,

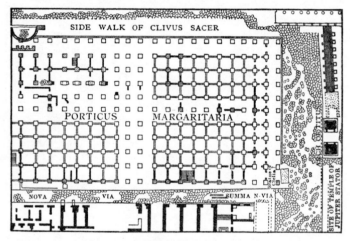

Fig. 83. — Plan of Porticus Margaritaria.

flute-makers; and *negotiatores* in general. Originally they must have exhibited their precious merchandise in booths and screens and desks under the shelter of the portico; later on, the portico was cut up into regular shops by means of brick walls raised between each pair of stone pilasters, exactly as was done with the Septa and with the Porticus Vipsania. The space was cut up also vertically by means of wooden floors, so as to secure an office or a bedroom above the shop.

The visitor who looks at the apparently barren site of the portico may wonder how and where the subtle eyes of the topographer can see all these details. The explanation is this. When the excavators, in search of building-materials, attacked the ruins of the

portico at the time of Alexander VII., under the leadership of
Leonardo Agostini, they removed only the blocks of travertine of
which the pilasters were built, and left alone the partition walls
of brick.   The portico, therefore, is gone, except a few blocks
which remain *in situ* here and there, especially on the side of the
Nova Via, but we can judge of its shape and size and aspect from
the brick walls, which still show the marks of the blocks stolen
away under Pope Chigi.   Many brick stamps found in the excavations of 1879 mention the kilns of Domitia Lucilla, wife of Lucius
Verus.   The shops, therefore, must date from the second quarter
of the second century, probably from the year 134.   The whole
building was not level, but followed the slope of the ground, like
the inclined wings of Bernini's portico at the end of the piazza of
S. Peter's.

LITERATURE. — *Notizie degli Scavi*, 1882, p. 228. — Ludwig Preller, *Die
Regionen der Stadt Rom*, p. 154. — *Forma Urbis Romæ*, pl. xxix. — Sante
Bartoli Pietro, *Mem.* 50 (in Fea's *Miscellanea*, vol. i. p. 234). — *Corpus inscr.*,
vol. vi. n. 1974, 9207, 9212, 9214, 9221, 9283, 9418, 9434, 9545, 9662, 9775.

Continuing our descent of the Clivus Sacer, after passing on the
right the street leading to the Carinæ, described in § x., we find
on the same side the monumental group of SS. Cosma e Damiano,
which comprises a round vestibule, once the Heroon Romuli, and a
square hall, once the Templum Sacræ Urbis.

XIII.   THE HEROON ROMULI (Temple of Romulus, son of Maxentius) (XIII in plan). — When this young prince died in 309, a
coin was struck with the legend DIVO ROMVLO, on the reverse of
which is represented a round monument erected to his memory.
The "Liber Pontificalis," John the deacon, and others mention the
site of SS. Cosma e Damiano as that of a templum Romuli (meaning the founder of the city), and this tradition has lasted to our
own time.   (See Nibby, Roma nell' anno 1838, part i. vol. ii. p. 710.)
Commendatore de Rossi, with the help of a fragmentary inscription which still remained affixed to the building towards 1550, has
been able to prove, first, that the round vestibule of SS. Cosma e
Damiano and the Heroon Romuli are one and the same thing;
secondly, that the Heroon was still unfinished when Maxentius
lost his life at the battle of Saxa Rubra on October 27, 312.   The
Senate completed the rotunda, and dedicated it, together with
the basilica, to Constantine.   Pope Felix IV. (526–530) cut open a
communication between the rotunda and the Templum Sacræ
Urbis behind it, and dedicated both to SS. Cosmas and Damianus,
physicians and martyrs.

The style of the Heroon shows a decided decline in taste and elegance. Instead of a round marble cella surrounded by a peristyle of fluted Corinthian pillars, as we see in the Temple of Matuta, of Hercules Magnus Custos, etc., we are confronted with a clumsy mixture of curved and straight lines, a round hall between two rectangular ones, a front with a hemicicyle between the middle columns, and two doors between each side couple.

Fig. 84. — The Portico of the Heroon Romuli.

Two columns (of cipollino) are left standing; a third was removed at the time of Urban VIII.; the site of the fourth is only marked by its socle. The most conspicuous portion of the building is the entrance door, with bronze folds and an elaborate entablature supported by two columns of porphyry. The door and its ornaments were raised to the level of the modern city by Pope Barberini about 1630. The Italian government restored it to its ancient site in 1879. I may add that when Urban VIII. repaired the roof of the cupola, the cupola itself was in imminent danger of collapsing. We found wedged in its cracks roots of ilexes over ten centimetres in diameter, the remains of an *hortus siccus* many hundred years old.

LITERATURE. — Gio. Battista de Rossi, *Bull. crist.*, 1867, p. 66. — Rodolfo Lanciani, *Bull. com.*, 1882, p. 29, pl. 9. — *Corpus Inscr.*, vol. vi. n. 1147. — Mariano Armellini, *Chiese di Roma*, pp. 152 and 155. — *Notizie degli Scavi*, 1879–1880.

XIV. TEMPLUM SACRÆ URBIS (archives of the Cadastre) (XIV in plan). The inner rectangular hall, back of the Heroon Romuli, was built by Vespasian in 78.

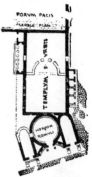

When this wise prince took the reins of empire after the great disasters which had befallen the capital under Nero and Vitellius, the city was still "deformis veteribus incendiis atque ruinis." Its state may be compared with that of Paris after the Commune as far as public buildings are concerned, but we must go back to the Chicago fire of 1871 to find a parallel for the thousands of palaces, tenement houses, temples, and shrines destroyed, the ruins of which covered ten regions out of fourteen. Between 73 and 75, the high priests, magistrates, architects, surveyors, and military engineers, under the

Fig. 85. — Plan of SS. Cosma e Damiano.

leadership of the censors, attended to the reorganization of the city both materially and from an administrative point of view. The last Roman census in the antique fashion was taken in 74, the city area and limits were defined, the ground surveyed, the line of the Servian walls and that of the octroi measured, together with the length of the streets radiating from the golden milestone towards the gates, the fourteen wards divided into many hundred "compita larum" (parishes?), the cadastre of public and private property revised and brought up to date, the pomerium enlarged, the streets straightened and repaved, the temples rebuilt, and a new and revised map of the city made. All the documents connected with these geodetic and financial operations were deposited in a fire-proof building erected for the purpose on the southwest side of the Forum of Peace, between it and the Sacra Via. The hall had two entrances, one from the northwest, decorated with a portico of six columns, on the epistyle of which the following inscription was engraved: —

imp · *caes* · *ve*SPASIAN*us* · AVG · PONT · MAX · TRIBVN · *pot* ·
viii imp · XVIII · P · P · CENSOR · COS · VIII

---

impp · *caess* · *s*EVERVS · ET · ANTONINVS · PII · AVGG · FELICES
RESTITVERE

(This epistyle was broken, with the fall of the portico, into four pieces. Two are missing; one was found about 1530 in the Piazza della Consolazione; the last, in 1612, near the steps of S. Francesca Romana.) The second entrance, still perfect, opened on the street described in § x. This monumental gate has been designed and illustrated by Middleton in the "Remains of Ancient Rome," vol. i. p. 41. The last two lines of the inscription, which contain the names of Severus and Caracalla, refer to the restorations made by these Emperors to the edifice, considerably damaged by the fire of Commodus. Their work can be easily recognized from the fact that while Vespasian's hall was of opus quadratum, of tufa strengthened with blocks of travertine at the corners, the restorations of 211 are of bricks. When Panvinio and Ligorio described and sketched the building towards the middle of the sixteenth century it was practically intact, the only changes made when it was Christianized by Felix IV. being the introduction of the apse and the altar. They described the hall as lighted by fifteen large windows (three

Fig. 86. — The Church of SS. Cosma e Domiano in the Middle Ages.

still visible, see Fig. 86). The walls were divided into three horizontal bands by finely cut cornices. The upper band was occupied by the windows, as in our old churches; the lower was simply lined with marble slabs covered by the bookcases and screens which contained the papers and records and maps of the cadastre; the middle one was incrusted with tarsia-work of the rarest kinds of marble, with panels representing panoplies, the Wolf with the infant founders of Rome, and other such allegorical scenes. A particular that may surprise the reader is that a large percentage of the tiles of the present roof are ancient, their dates varying from the time of Caracalla to that of Theodoric. After the restoration of Cara-

Fig. 87. — The Church of SS. Cosma e Damiano at the end of the sixteenth century.

calla the place took the name of Templum Sacræ Urbis. This most perfect of the buildings in the classic district of the Sacra Via was mercilessly mutilated by Pope Urban VIII. in 1632. He raised the level of the church by 24 feet, destroyed the stone walls which made it fire-proof, and sold or gave up the stones to the Jesuits for their Church of S. Ignazio. The bronze gates of the Heroon were wrenched from their sockets and rebuilt out of place in symmetry with the axis of the church; the historic inscription of Constantine was destroyed, and the precious incrustations of the nave were obliterated.   The Christian decorations of the edifice had no better fate.   There was a ciborium in the apse, made about 1150 by Guy, cardinal of SS. Cosma e Damiano, a masterpiece of the school of Paolo Romano, signed by four of his son's pupils: IOHanneS, PETRVS, ANGELVS, SASSO, FILII PAVLI HVIVS OPERIS MAGISTRI FVERVNT.   It was leveled to the ground, together with the ambones of Sergius I. (695).   The frescoes in the lower portion of the walls were whitewashed.   Pope Barberini laid his hands also on the mosaics of the apse, mutilating those of the arch as well as those of the calotta.   Lastly, he called the monks to help in the work of destruction, and a brief dated 1630 (discovered by Armellini in the Archivio dei Brevi) gave "licentiam effodiendi lapides" as they pleased.

The fame of the Templum Sacræ Urbis comes, however, from another cause.   When Agrippa and Augustus surveyed the city in 6 B. C., the result of their labors, viz. the plan, or Forma Urbis, was publicly exhibited in the Porticus Vipsania on the Via Flaminia (Aug. 1, 7 B. C.).   Vespasian, likewise, must have exhibited the plan of the city reconstructed, after the fire, by Nero and by himself, in this building of SS. Cosma e Damiano.   The third edition of the map, representing the city rebuilt and reorganized by Severus and Caracalla after the fire of Commodus, was certainly affixed to the outside wall of the building, looking on the forum of Peace. This celebrated "Forma Urbis," engraved on marble at an approximate scale of 1 : 250, the fragments of which are exhibited in the Capitoline museum, has been described at length in Book I. pp. 95-98.

LITERATURE on the Heroon Romuli and the Templum Sacræ Urbis. — Gio. Battista de Rossi, *Bull. arch. crist.*, 1867, p. 66 ; and 1891, p. 76, n. 3 ; *Musaici delle chiese di Roma*, part iv. — Rodolfo Lanciani, *Bull. com.*, 1882, p. 29, tav. iii.-x. — Mariano Armellini, *Chiese di Roma*, 2d ed. p. 152. — Leone Nardoni, *Di alcune sotterr. confessioni nelle antiche basiliche.* Rome, 1881. — *Notizie degli Scavi*, 1879-80, *passim*; and *Bull. com.*, 1881, p. 8.

On the names *Urbs Æterna* and *Urbs Sacra* consult F. G. Moore in *Transact. Amer. Philol. Association*, 1894, 34.

The back wall of the temple covered by the marble plan formed at the same time part of the inclosure of the Forum of Peace (XV in plan), the pavement of which is inlaid with slabs of portasanta.   The pavement has been uncovered both at the foot of the wall, where it is still to be seen, and under the house Via del Tempio della Pace, No. 11, where it lies buried under thirty-eight feet of rubbish.   I have already mentioned (§ ix.) some of the famous ornaments of this forum; we may add to the list a gallery of statues of famous athletes from Greece, of which we heard the first time in March, 1891, when a marble pedestal was discovered at the corner of the Via del Sole and the Salara Vecchia, bearing the inscription ΠΥΘΟΚΛΗΣ · ΗΛΕΙΟΣ · ΠΕΝΤΑΘΛΟΣ · (πο-) ΛΥΚΛΕΙΤΟΥ · (᾽Αργε)ιοΥ. It refers to the celebrated statue of Pythokles, a work of Polykletos, the original of which was erected at Olympia, in memory of exploits of the former in the pentathlon. There the statue was seen by Pausanias (vi. 7, 10), and there also its pedestal was rediscovered by the Germans in 1879 between the temples of Juno and Pelops. The original figure must have been leaning on the right leg, as shown by the marks on the plinth, whereas the Roman copy seems to have been leaning the opposite way, unless the pedestal has been made use of twice, before and after the first barbaric invasion. The loss of the Roman replica is deeply to be regretted because we have no specimen of the work of the second Polykletos. The pedestal is exhibited in the Museo Municipale al Celio.

A little below the Temple of Romulus, the Sacra Via was spanned by the

XV. FORNIX FABIANUS (the Arch of Q. Fabius Allobrogicus) (XVI in plan). — On the left footway of the Sacra Via, nearly opposite the street which divides the Temple of Faustina from the Heroon Romuli, are lying several blocks of travertine, with mouldings, cornices, and capitals of very simple design. They were discovered in 1882 in the middle of the street, not one standing in its original site. Ancient writers place at this exact point the fornix or archway erected by Q. Fabius Maximus Allobrogicus, consul 121 B. C., in memory of his successful campaign against the Allobroges and Arvernes. The monument was celebrated more from its location than for architectural value or size. Crassus the orator used to say of Memmius that he thought himself so great that he could not enter the Forum without stooping his head at the Arch of Fabius. Cicero places it at the foot of the Clivus Sacer.

The remains of the arch were certainly dug up in 1543, but the statements of contemporary writers are so contradictory that it seems impossible to make out the truth. Some assert that the stones inscribed with the name of the conqueror of Savoy were found built in the vault of the Cloaca Maxima! Others describe not only the exact spot where the arch stood, but also its decorations, trophies, victories, etc. Judging from the existing fragments, it was a very simple structure, worthy of the austerity of Republican times. The diameter of the archway measured 3.94 metres. It was built of travertine on the outside, with the core of tufa and travertine. Near or upon it were statues of L. Æmilius Paullus and of P. Cornelius Scipio Africanus.

LITERATURE. — Cicero, *De orat.*, ii. 66; and *Pro Plancio*, 7. — *Corpus Inscr.*, vol. i. p. 178; and vol. vi. n. 1303, 1304. — Gio. Battista de Rossi, *Dell' arco Fabiano nel Foro* (in Annal. Inst., 1859, vol. xxxi. p. 307). — *Notizie degli Scavi*, 1882, p. 224, tav. xvi. — Nichols, *The Roman Forum*, p. 126. — Thédenat, in Daremberg and Saglio's *Dictionnaire*, p. 1302, n. 28.

The last building on the right side of the Sacra Via, before reaching the Forum, is the

XVI. ÆDES DIVI PII ET DIVÆ FAUSTINÆ, or Temple of Antoninus and Faustina — church of S. Lorenzo in Miranda (XVII in plan). — When Antoninus Pius lost his wife, Faustina the elder, in A. D. 141, the Senate voted a temple to commemorate her apotheosis, with priestesses attached to it, with gold and silver statues, etc. On the architrave of the temple this simple inscription was engraved : —

DĪVAE · FAVSTĪNAE · EX · S · C.

The same divine honors were given to Antoninus after his death in 161; and his name was added to that of Faustina on the frieze, with little consideration for the laws of epigraphic symmetry. (See Corpus Inscriptionum, vol. vi. n. 1005.) The edifice was named from the last occupant, Ædes divi Pii. It is prostyle, with six columns on the front and three on the sides. The columns are of Carystian or cipollino marble, which had come into great fashion since the time of Hadrian. The frieze, with its griffins, vases, candelabra, and festoons, is considered a marvel of art.

In the wide space covered by the pronaos there were statues of friends or relatives of the Antonines, like those of Vitrasius Pollio (Corpus Inscriptionum, 1540), husband of Annia Faustina, governor of Asia and of lower Mœsia, consul A. D. 138 and 176; and of Bassæus Rufus (*ibid.*, 1599), one of the victorious leaders in the Marcomannic campaign. The temple is represented in contemporary medals, as well as in a bas-relief of the Villa Medici. (See Bull. Inst., 1853, p. 141.) Its remains, most beautifully preserved, were dedicated to S. Lawrence in the seventh or eighth century, probably by a devout lady named Miranda (compare the names of S. Lorenzo in Formoso, in Damaso, in Lucina, etc.). This saved them from destruction until the time of Urban V., 1362–1370, who allowed the temple to be reduced to the present state, to provide stones and marbles for the reconstruction of the Lateran. Martin V. granted the church in 1430 to the corporation

Fig. 88. — The Frieze of the Temple of Faustina.

of apothecaries, who built shrines and chapels in the intercolumniations of the portico, protected by a roof the slanting traces of which are still visible. Roof and chapels were demolished by Paul III. on the occasion of the entry of Charles V. Fra Giocondo da Verona mentions more than once excavations made round the temple at the end of the fifteenth century, by which he and Peruzzi were enabled to take measurements of the substructures and basement; but no further spoliation seems to have been committed until the temple was again given up by the same Paul III. to the deputies for the Fabbrica di S. Pietro.

The results of the loot of 1540 are described as follows by Ligorio (Bodl., p. 28) : " I shall now describe some marbles found at the foot of the temple, when they were searching for, and removing to S. Peter's, the beautiful steps, an act of vandalism

which I cannot condemn too strongly. There was a bas-relief
representing Nereids riding on dolphins; a portion of the figure
which stood on the top of the pediment; a square pedestal with
low relief, in a style like the Egyptian; and many fragments of
statues, capitals, and friezes, half burned in a lime-kiln. There
was also the base of a statue dedicated to Antoninus by the corpora-

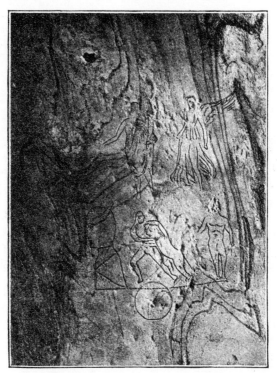

Fig 89. — Graffiti on the Carystian Columns of the Temple ot Faustina.

tion of bakers, which became the property of the Mattei." There
were twenty-one steps, as ascertained in the course of the excavations made in 1811 by the French prefect of the Département du
Tibre. The same excavations brought to light the threshold of
the door leading to the crypt below the stairs. M. Lacour Gayet
discovered in 1885, and published in the "Mélanges de l'Ecole
française de Rome" of that year, p. 226, a set of graffiti scratched

on the lower portion of the columns of the pronaos, after their surface had been softened by the fire of Commodus. They represent Hercules and the lion of Nemea, a Lar, the Victory, etc. The inscriptions date from the Christian era, as if some one was hastening the "purification" of the building. There are salutations like EVTICIANE VIVAS and the monogram

$$\omega \; \text{✗} \; \text{A}$$

which must have been sketched by some one of Eastern extraction, as the Latins always made the Alpha precede the Omega.

The ground in front of the temple was cleared in January, 1876. Among the objects recovered on this occasion were a fragment of the fasti consulares from the year of Rome 755 to 760; a pedestal of a statue which, having been overthrown by an earthquake (fatali necessitate collapsa), was replaced on its pedestal by Gabinius Vettius Probianus, a prefect of Rome, at the beginning of the fifth century, well known for the care he took for the preservation of works of art, injured in one way or another during those eventful years; and the pedestal of an equestrian statue raised by the policemen to Geta. The ground in front of the temple is called in the inscription of Probianus CELEBERRIMVS VRBIS LOCVS.

LITERATURE. — *Vita Pii*, 6. — Eckhel, *Doctrina num. vet.*, vii. 39. — Pɪrro Ligorio, *Cod. vat.*, 3374, f. 168; and *Cod. Torin.*, xv. f. 100. – Fra Giocondo da Verona, *Uffizi*, n. 202. — Tournon, *Etudes statist. sur Rome*, vol. ii. p. 264. — Valadier et Visconti, *Raccolta delle più insigni fabbriche di Roma*, tav. ii., iii. — Antonio Nibby, *Foro romano*, p. 181. — Angelo Pellegrini, *Scavi di Roma* (in Buonarroti, February, 1876). — Armellini, *Chiese di Roma*, p. 157.

We must now cross to the opposite side of the Sacra Via, and examine, before entering the Forum, the group of Vesta, which comprises the Regia, the temple, the shrine, and the house of the Vestals.

XVII. THE REGIA (XVIII in plan). — The now vacant space of ground between the Temples of Vesta and Faustina was occupied by the Regia, the official residence of the Pontifex Maximus, and the centre of his administration, the foundation of which was attributed to Numa. It contained a chapel where the lances of Mars were kept; another sacred to Ops Consiva, which could be entered only by the Vestals and by the "sacerdos publicus;" spacious archives for the safe keeping of the annals, commentaries, and books of the Supreme Priesthood; and a meeting hall where religious conventions were held (like that of the Fratres Arvales of May 14, 14 B. C., for the cooptatio of Drusus Cæsar, son of Tiberius). The Regia was burnt to the ground not less than four times : first in 210 B. C.; then in 148, when only the chapel of Mars and the laurel-trees shading the entrance were saved from the flames; and again in 36, when it was rebuilt by Domitius Calvinus in solid marble, and ornamented with statues obtained from Julius Cæsar, much against his will. Pliny (Natural History, xxxvi. 18, 8) says that two of the four statues which once had supported the tent of Alexander the Great were placed before the Regia, the other two being before the Temple of Mars Ultor.

In 1883 I expressed the opinion (Notizie Scavi, p. 479) that

Fig. 90. — The Regia, as sketched by Pirro Ligorio.

the graceful little edifice (once more attacked by the flames in the conflagration of Nero) never rose from its ashes; but after reading the account of its discovery and outrageous treatment by the deputies of the Fabbrica di S. Pietro in 1543–46, I wish to correct this statement. The illustration, which I have photographed from an original sketch by Ligorio, who was present at the discovery, speaks better than any other argument. The design is more a restoration of that fanciful architect than a picture of the real state of the building when first discovered (August 15, 1543?); but many of the particulars are genuine, as any one can see by comparing them with the existing fragment, reproduced by Huelsen and Nichols, with Michelangelo's reconstruction in the Sala dei Fasti, Palazzo dei Conservatori, and with Panvinio's designs. Ligorio labored under the delusion that the edifice discovered was a "Janus," and so he gave it four entrances, while in reality there were but two. At any rate all those present at the find, Palladio, Metello, Panvinio, Ligorio, agree that there was a considerable portion of the Regia standing above ground, and that very many lines of the Fasti triumphales et consulares were found *in situ*, engraved on its marble walls and pilasters; the first between 18 and 12 before Christ, the consulares in 36. Ligorio says that it took thirty days to demolish the exquisite ruins down to the level of the foundations, some of the blocks being split for the lime-kiln, others handed over to the stone-cutters of S. Peter's. Cardinal Alessandro Farnese came finally to the rescue: the fragments of the Fasti were piously collected by him, and removed to the Capitol, and the ground was tunneled in various directions in search of stray pieces. Michelangelo for the architectural part, and Gentile Delfino for the epigraphic, were deputed to arrange them in one of the halls of the Palazzo dei Conservatori. Other fragments have been discovered since 1870.

Literature.— *Corpus Inscr.*, vol. i. p. 415; second edition, pp. 10–12, pl. 1*a*. — Fea, *Frammenti d. Fasti.* — Adolf Becker, *Topographie*, p. 234. — *De Muris*, p. 23. — F. M. Nichols, *The Roman Forum*, pp. 118–125. — Heinrich Jordan, *Forma Urbis*, pl. 3, n. 21. — *Notizie degli Scavi*, 1882, p. 226. — The discoveries of 1886 were illustrated by Nichols, *The Regia and the Fasti Capitolini* (in Archæologia, vol. l., 1887, p. 227); by the same in Mittheil., 1886, pp. 94–98; by Jordan, *Gli edifizi fra il tempio di Faustina, e l' atrio di Vesta* (in Mittheil., 1886, p. 99, pls. 5–7); and by Huelsen, *Die Regia* (in Jahrbuch Arch. Inst., 1889, p. 228).

XVIII. The Temple of Vesta (XIX in plan). — " In prehistoric times, when fire could be obtained only from the friction caused by rubbing together two sticks of wood or from sparks of flint, every village kept a public fire burning day and night in a central hut for the use of each family. The duty of watching the precious element was intrusted to young girls, because girls, as a rule, did not follow their parents or brothers to the pasture grounds, nor did they share with them the fatigues of hunting or fishing expeditions. In course of time this simple practice became a kind of sacred institution, especially at Alba Longa, the mother country of Rome; and when a party of Alban shepherds settled on the banks of the Tiber, the worship of Vesta — represented by the public fire and the girls attending to it — was duly organized at the foot of the Palatine, on the borders of the marketplace " (Ancient Rome, p. 135).

It seems that the original hut built by Numa perished in the invasion of the Gauls in 390 B. C. The Vestals, on being warned of their approach, concealed the Palladium and other relics in two earthen jars, buried them near the house of the flamen Quirinalis — the place was henceforth called *doliola* — and took refuge at Cære. A second fire in 241 destroyed the temple. While the Vestals tried to save their lives, Cæcilius Metellus, the high priest, threw himself into the flames, and saved the Palladium at the cost of one eye and one arm, which was charred to the bone. The valor of thirteen slaves saved the temple from being gutted for the third time in 210, and for this action they were at once liberated. The architecture of the temple of those days can be seen in the coins of the gens Cassia, dating from the commencement of the seventh century.[1] The round structure is covered by a conical roof surmounted by a statue, and fringed around with dragons' heads. Horace describes an inundation of the time of Augustus, by which the temple was seriously damaged. Nero restored it after his own fire. Lastly, the terrible conflagration which swept over the valley of the Forum in 191 A. D., under the Empire of Commodus, destroyed with the temple the house of the Vestals, the Temple of Peace, etc. The Vestals fled to the Palatine, carrying with them the Palladium, which was thus seen for the first time by profane eyes. The reconstruction by Julia Domna, the Empress of Septimius Severus, and the mother of Caracalla, is the last recorded in history. The " vignettes " of her medals (ap. Cohen, Méd. imp., 2d ed. n. 239) give an exact idea of its architecture and style ; it is also represented on several bas-reliefs, reproduced by the authors and in the works quoted at the foot of this section. After the defeat of Eugenius in 394, Theodosius II. shut the gates of the temple and extinguished forever the mysterious fire which had been kept burning for over a thousand years.

A shapeless mass of concrete of the foundations is all that is left of the famous shrine. The responsibility for such a great loss

[1] Babelon, *Monnaies de la républ. romaine*, vol. i. p. 331, n. 8, 9.

Fig. 91. — Temples of Vesta and Castores (Auer's Reconstruction).

falls not on the would-be barbarians, but, as usual, on the genial masters of the Renaissance. When first discovered, at the time of Fra Giocondo da Verona in 1489, it was practically intact, and had suffered only slight damage. The Fabbrica di S. Pietro destroyed it in 1549, removing or burning into lime not only the marble blocks of the cella, the entablature, and the peristyle, but even the tufa blocks which strengthened and surrounded the concrete of the foundations, like a ring. Thirty-five pieces only escaped by a miracle, and we found them scattered over a large area in the excavations of 1877. With their help, and by comparison with the designs of medals and bas-reliefs, architects and archæologists have attempted the reconstruction of the temple. The one I suggest is represented on pp. 159 and 160 of "Ancient Rome." Compare it with Jordan's "Der Tempel," pl. 4; and Auer's "Der Tempel," plates 6–8. This last is reproduced in the preceding cut.

LITERATURE. — Wolfgang Helbig, *Bull. Inst.*, 1878, p. 9. — Rodolfo Lanciani, *L' atrio di Vesta* (in Notizie Scavi, December, 1883); and *Ancient Rome*, chaps. vi. and vii. — Heinrich Jordan, *Der Tempel der Vesta*. Berlin, Weidmann, 1886. — Hans Auer, *Der Tempel der Vesta*. Vienna, Tempsky, 1888. — Christian Huelsen, *Mittheil.*, vol. iv., 1889, p. 245. — J. Henry Middleton, *The Remains of Ancient Rome*, vol. i. p. 298. — H. Thédenat, in Daremberg and Saglio's *Dictionnaire*, p. 1285, n. 7.

XIX. THE SHRINE (XX in plan). — The ancient practice of placing shrines of domestic gods at the corners of the main streets of each ward of the city, was raised to the dignity of a public institution by Augustus.[1] Four hundred and twenty-four of these popular chapels were numbered in Rome under Constantine. The Christians accepted the institution, and developed it to such an extent that not less than three thousand two hundred and forty-six were registered in Rome in 1853. Although many inscriptions belonging to the "ædiculæ larum" have been found from time to time, only two may be said to exist now : the shrine of the Vicus Sobrius near S. Martino ai Monti, and that of the Vicus Vestæ. The latter stands behind the temple on the right of the entrance door to the cloisters. The entablature was supported by two columns of the composite order. The frieze contains the following inscription, in letters of the golden age : SENATVS POPVLVSQVE ROMANV(S) · PECVNIA · PVBLICA · FACIENDAM · CVRAVIT. Underneath there was, very likely, a statue of Mercury, a socle inscribed

[1] See *Pagan and Christian Rome*, p. 62 ; and Suetonius, *Octav.*, 13, "compitales Lares ornare bis in anno instituit vernis floribus et æstivis."

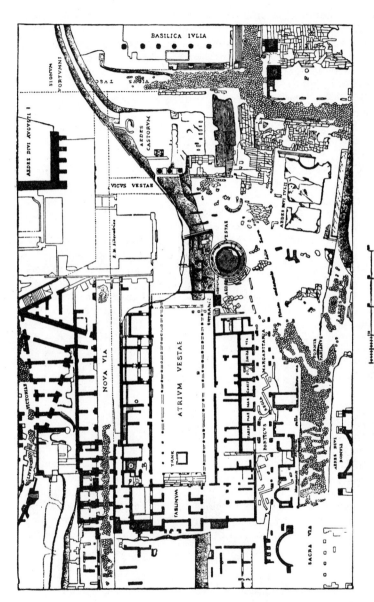

Fig. 92. — Plan of Atrium and Temple of Vesta.

DEO · MERCVRIO having been found not far away. An inscription discovered in June, 1878, at S. Paolo fuori le Mura tells us the name and the history of this monument. It says that in A. D. 223, Severus Alexander being Emperor, the street magistrates of the eighth region (Forum) had rebuilt ÆDICVLAM · REG · VIII · VICO VESTÆ. Vesta's Temple is separated from that of Castor and Pollux by a lane, which is evidently the Vicus Vestæ mentioned above.

This beautiful shrine could be reconstructed in its entirety, but the attempt has not yet been made.

XX. ATRIUM VESTÆ (House of the Vestals) (XXI in plan, and Fig. 92). — The House of the Vestals is an oblong brick building, of the time of Septimius Severus and Julia Domna, surrounded by streets on every side : by the Sacra Via on the north, by the Vicus Vestæ on the west, by the Nova Via on the south, and by an unknown lane on the east. The most prominent feature of the building is the Atrium ; in fact, its size and magnificence were so great that the whole building was named from it, Atrium Vestæ. The building itself is 115 metres long, 53 wide ; the Atrium 67 metres long, 24 wide. The surface of the house amounts to 6095 square metres, of which not less than one fourth (1608 square metres) is occupied by the Atrium. Its architecture can be compared with that of our mediæval and Renaissance double-storied cloisters, which, being the abode of people seldom or never allowed to go out, must necessarily be very airy and spacious to give the inmates the chance of taking bodily exercise. The portico on the ground floor has, or rather had, forty-eight columns of cipollino marble, of the Corinthian order. Of this stately colonnade not a piece is left standing. The site and the number of the shafts are marked only by the foundation stones (cuscini) of travertine. Not a trace has been found of the capitals and of the entablature, which was 146 metres long ; and I do not know any other instance of such a wholesale destruction of an ancient building. The second or upper story had an equal number of columns, smaller in size and of the precious breccia corallina. Two whole columns and many fragments have been recovered. They have escaped destruction because the breccia corallina cannot be burnt into lime.

The Atrium is surrounded by state apartments on the ground floor. On the upper it was surrounded by the private apartments of the Vestals. Of course, we cannot give their right name to the single pieces, or state one by one their former use and place. At the east end of the cloisters there is a large hall, twelve metres long and eight metres wide, which corresponds to the tablinum of a Roman house. Its pavement is laid out in colored marbles, such as giallo, porfido, serpentino, etc., and the pattern belongs to the style brought into fashion under Septimius Severus. The walls were incrusted also with rare marbles framed by a cornice of rosso antico. On each side of this hall there are three smaller rooms, making a total of six, a figure corresponding to the number of the Vestals. Their destination is doubtful; certainly they were not used as bedrooms, in the first place because the bedrooms have been traced in the upper story, and secondly, because the dampness of these low cells is such that they were absolutely unfit for human habitation.

The position of the house, as regards health and health-giving sunshine, is most unfavorable. Being built against the cliff of the Palatine, at the bottom of an artificial cutting, its ground floor lies thirty feet below the level of the Nova Via; this street is actually supported by the back walls of the state apartments on the west side of the Atrium. No wonder that these walls should be saturated with damp, which must have told severely on the health of the sisters. They did their best to fight the evil. Double walls were set up against the buttress of the Nova Via, with a free space between them to allow of the circulation of air. Ventilators and hot-air furnaces are to be seen in every corner. Another precaution taken by the Vestals against rheumatism was the raising of the pavements of every room subject to damp, and the establishment of hot vapor currents in the free space between the double floors. This was done rather awkwardly. Instead of the terra-cotta cylinders or brick pillars which were commonly used by the Romans to support the upper floor of these hypocausta, the Vestals of latter days made use of large amphoræ sawn across and cut into two portions of equal length. These half jars are placed in parallel rows and very near each other, and made to support the large *tegulæ bipedales* over which the pavement is laid. Hot air was forced to circulate in the interstices between the jars by means of terra-cotta pipes from a furnace. In spite of all these precautions, the house must have remained unhealthy, especially from want of sunshine. Even now it is cast into the shade of the surrounding ruins of the imperial palace at an early hour of the day; imagine what must have happened when that palace was towering in all its glory fully 150 feet above the level of the Atrium. These unfavorable hygienic conditions allow us to explain, with a certain degree of probability, a remarkable change in the rules of the order made towards the beginning of the fourth century. Physicians were not allowed in former times to enter the Atrium. As soon as the first symptoms of a case of sickness made their appearance the patient was at once removed from the nunnery and put under the care of her parents, or else under the charge of a distinguished matron. In the fourth century we hear for the first time of an *archiater* or physician attached to the establishment.

When the excavations began in October, 1883, we were in hope of discovering some kind of fasti which would tell us the names of the Vestal virgins, the dates of their coöptation and death, and, above all, the list of the abbesses of the monastery. The expectation was disappointed; and when we consider that amongst the forty thousand inscriptions discovered in Rome since the early Renaissance there is not a line, not a fragment, which can be attributed to the above-named fasti, we may confidently assert that they never existed. It is difficult to explain this fact. The parallel religious corporations of the Fratres Arvales, of the Salii Palatini, of the Augurs, took care that the fasti of their order, year after year, should be engraved in marble; and these marbles, more or less injured by time, have come down to us, and they are considered as the most precious documents of Latin epigraphy and chronology. Perhaps it was not customary that female corporations should have special annals; perhaps these annals were only permitted to true collegia, and the Vestals, like the Curiones, were not considered as such. At any rate, the want of the fasti is compensated for, as regards the Atrium, by the magnificent set of pedestals, with statues and eulogistic inscriptions, raised in honor of the Vestales maximæ. The fashion of these dedications seems to have come in with the Empire, and was kept until the fall of the pagan superstition. The Atrium Vestæ must have contained more than one hundred "honorary" pedestals, not because there were as many abbesses during the last four centuries of Vesta's worship, but because many statues represented and many pedestals bore the name of the same lady. The stone-cutters and the lime-burners of the Middle Ages have destroyed more than four fifths of this series. We possess actually the originals or the copies of thirty-six inscriptions bearing names of Vestales maximæ of these, twenty-eight were found in the Atrium itself, two on the Palatine, six in various other quarters of the town. Comparing the information given by these marbles with the accounts of classical writers, we can put together an important section of the *fasti maximatus* (the word *maximatus* has appeared for the first time in one of the new inscriptions).

1. Occia. She presided over the sisterhood from the year 38 B. C. to A. D. 19. (Tacitus, Ann., ii. 86.)

2. Junia Torquata, daughter of Silanus, the noblest of the noble Roman ladies; *maxima* between A. D. 19 and 48.

3. Vibidia, the generous protector of Messalina when the long story of her infamies was disclosed to Claudius. (Tacitus, Ann., xi. 32.)

4. Cornelia Maxima, murdered by Domitian. (Pliny, Ep., iv. 11.)

5. Prætextata. Her name appeared for the first time on a pedestal discovered December 29, 1883: "Prætextatæ Crassi Filiæ Virgini Vestali Maximæ, C. Iulius Creticus a Sacris." Her mother, "Sulpicia Crassi uxor," is mentioned by Tacitus (Hist., iv. 42).

6. Numisia Maximilla, A. D. 200. Two pedestals mention her name — one found three centuries ago, one discovered on December 29, 1883, "Numisiæ Maximillæ V.V. Maximæ, C. Helvidius Mysticus devotus beneficiis eius."

7. Terentia Flavola, A. D. 215, whose name is engraved on four pedestals, was the great-granddaughter of Lollianus Avitus, consul in A. D. 114; the granddaughter of L. Hedius Rufus Lollianus Avitus, consul in A. D. 144; the daughter of Q. Hedius Rufus Lollianus Gentianus, Salius Palatinus and consul of uncertain date. She had, moreover, two brothers, Lollianus Plautius Avitus, husband of Claudia Sestia Cocceia Severiana, and Terentius Gentianus, husband of Pomponia Pætina.

8. Campia Severina, A. D. 240.

9. Flavia Mamilia, A. D. 242.

10. Flavia Publicia, A. D. 247. This lady was undoubtedly the most famous and venerable chief of the order. Her eulogies and her pedestals have been discovered in vast numbers. Judging from the appearance of the exquisite statue discovered, together with one of her pedestals, on December 20, Flavia Publicia was a lady of tall, queenly appearance, of noble demeanor, of a sweet and gentle, if not handsome face. Seven pedestals have been found, — one in 1497, one in 1549, five in our own excavations. Of these recent ones the first was dedicated on July 11, 247 A. D., by her niece Æmilia Rogatilla, and by Minucius Honoratus, son of Æmilia; the second by two captains of the army, Ulpius Verus and Aurelius Titus; the third was dedicated on September 30,

A. D. 257, by a certain Bareius Zoticus, with his wife Flavia Verecunda; the fourth by a M. Aurelius Hermes; the last by T. Flavius Apronius, a sub-intendant of the monastery.

11. Cœlia Claudiana, A. D. 286. This abbess was already known from five inscriptions discovered at various times. The two others lately found tell nothing remarkable, except that she is said to have ruled over twenty years.

12. Terentia Rufilla, A. D. 300.

13. On November 5th, a pedestal was discovered bearing the following inscription: "Ob meritum castitatis, pudicitiæ, atque in sacris religionibusque doctrinæ mirabilis . . . [name erased] virgini Vestali maximæ, Pontifices viri clarissimi, pro magistro Macrinio Sossiano viro clarissimo, pro meritis." Then follows the date of June 9, A. D. 364: "dedicata quinto idus Iunias, divo Ioviano et Varroniano consulibus." Now, why should the name of this highly praised priestess have been erased? Two reasons only can be given: either she happened to forget the vows of chastity, or she was converted to Christianity. The first explanation does not seem satisfactory, not only because she was most probably a mature, if not an old woman, when the crime and the *memoriæ damnatio* took place, but also because the fall of a Vestal would certainly have been noticed and registered and proclaimed to the four winds by contemporary Christian writers. Conversion to the Gospel seems more probable; one of these conquests of the new faith in Vesta's Atrium seems to be mentioned by Prudentius (Peristeph., hymn 2).

14. Cœlia Concordia, the last *Vestalis maxima*, or the last but one. She was a great friend of the great champion of polytheism, Vettius Agorius Prætextatus. Some of her exploits have been revealed by the discovery of a pedestal in the house of Prætextatus himself, which house stood where is now the Convento dei Liguorini, formerly the Villa Caserta, at the corner of the Via Merulana and the Via dell' Arco di S. Vito. Cœlia Concordia had raised a statue in honor of Prætextatus in the Atrium itself; she received the same distinction in the house of that nobleman. The statue of Prætextatus was discovered in the Atrium the last day of 1883.

In the four months during which the excavations lasted, 36,000 cubic metres of earth were carted away and the following objects discovered: Marble pedestals with inscriptions, 13; inscriptions on marble slabs, 12; brick-stamps, 102; silver coins, 835; gold coin, 1; pieces of jewelry, 2; busts and heads, 15; statues, 11; important pieces of statues, 7; columns or pieces of columns of breccia corallina, cipollino, and bigio, 11.

The most remarkable find was that of a *ripostiglio*, or hidden treasure of Anglo-Saxon coins, made on November 8, 1883, under the remains of a mediæval house built within the northeast corner of the Atrium. About a metre and a half above the ancient pavement our men found a rough terra-cotta jug containing 832 silver coins, one of gold, and a piece of jewelry inscribed "Domno Marino Papa."

The gold coin, a solidus, shows on one side the head and the name of the Byzantine Emperor Theophilus (827–842), on the other side the busts of Michael and Constantine VIII. The piece proves only that the treasure was not buried before the first half of the ninth century, and proves nothing else, as Byzantine solidi have been used both in the East and in the West for centuries; in fact, a few of them were still current not many years ago in some Turkish provinces. In the Middle Ages they were the standard international currency; the Merovingian kings even struck a certain number of these coins with the effigies and names of Justinus, of Justinian, and so forth. Of the 832 silver denarii, 828 are Anglo-Saxon, one from Ratisbon, one from Limoges, two from Pavia. The Anglo-Saxon group is subdivided as follows: Coins with the legend AELFRED REX, 3; with EADVVEARD REX, 217; with AETHELSTAN REX, 393; with EADMVND REX, 195; with ONLAF (Anlaf, Anlef) REX or CVNVNC, 6; with SITRICE CVNVNC, 1; with the name of archbishop PLEGMVND, 4; uncertain, 10; total, 829. Of Æthelstan's coins, 2 were struck at Bath, 1 at Canterbury, 1 at Chichester, 1 at Dartmouth, 4 at Derby, 20 at Dorchester, 6 at Exeter, 16 at York, 2 at Hertford, 1 at Lewes, 2 at Longport, 25 at Leicester, 66 at London, 1 at Maldon, 14 at Norwich, 9 at Oxford, 7 at Shrewsbury, 1 at Shaftesbury, 3 at Stafford, 14 at Winchester, 13 at Wallingford, 3 at TOLIE (?). The names of the *monetarii* are nearly as numerous as the coins themselves. The piece of jewelry is a kind of fibula or brooch, with silver designs and letters inlaid on copper. It is a unique piece, not only as a work of art of a Roman goldsmith of the tenth century, but because fibulæ inscribed with the name of the living pope are not to be found. It was certainly used to fasten on the shoulder the mantle of some high official belonging to the court of Marinus II., a pontiff otherwise obscure, who occupied the chair of S. Peter from 942 to 946; Albericus being then the *Princeps romanorum* and Edmund the King of England. This official must have been in charge of the pope's episcopium, which nestled among the ruins of the palace of Caligula (see

p. 155), and must have been paid with "Peter's pence" from
England. His small house, destroyed in 1884, rested on the three
pedestals of Cœlia Claudiana, of the condemned Vestal, No. 13,
and of Flavia Publicia, which one finds on the right-hand side of
the entrance (letter A in plan).

The foundations of an octagonal shrine, purposely and deliberately leveled to the ground, appear in the centre of the cloisters.
This shrine contained probably the "sacra fatalia," the sacred
tokens of the Roman commonwealth, like the Palladium, intrusted
to the care of the Vestals. We believe that the destruction of
this innermost sanctuary was accomplished by the Vestals themselves in the last days preceding the suppression of the order and
their banishment from the cloisters, A. D. 394.

In a room near the southeast corner, marked B in the plan, is
the mill used by the Vestals to grind meal with which the "mola
salsa," a most primitive kind of cake, was prepared on February
15 of each year, during the celebration of the Lupercalia.

The House of the Vestals has lost much of its fascinating
interest since the best works of art, busts, statues, portraits, and
inscriptions, pertaining to it, have been removed to the baths of
Diocletian.

LITERATURE. — Rodolfo Lanciani, *L'atrio di Vesta, con appendice del comm.
de Rossi.* Rome, Salviucci, 1884. — Costantino Maes, *Vesta e Vestali.* Rome,
1883. — Heinrich Jordan, *Der Tempel der Vesta und das Haus der Vestalinnen.*
Berlin, 1884. — Hans Auer, *Der Tempel der Vesta und das Haus der Vestalinnen.*
Vienna, 1888. — J. Henry Middleton, *The Remains of Ancient Rome*, vol. i. p.
229. — Joachim Marquardt, *Staatsverwaltung*, vol. iii. p. 323. — *Bull. Inst.*,
1884, p. 145. — *Mittheil.*, 1889, p. 245; 1891, p. 91; 1892, p. 287. — *Atti Accad.
archeol.*, 1890, p. 407.

THE ROMAN FORUM.

XXI. FORUM ROMANUM MAGNUM (XXII in plan, and Fig. 93).
— We have now come to the most interesting part of our walk,
to the chief attraction of this attractive district, to the Forum
Romanum Magnum, where for so many centuries the destinies of
the ancient world were swayed.

At the time of the foundation of Rome the bartering trade
between the various tribes settled on the heights of the left bank
of the Tiber was concentrated in the hollow ground between the
Palatine, the Capitoline, and the Quirinal. Around this elemen-
tary marketplace, bordering on the marshes of the lesser Velabrum,
were a few conical straw huts, such as the one in which the public
fire was kept, afterwards the Temple of Vesta. There were also
clay pits on the north side, from which the neighborhood took

the name of Argiletum, and stone quarries under the Capitoline called Lautumiæ, afterwards transformed into a state prison. The market-place was well supplied with drinking-water from local springs, like the Tullianum (which tradition has transformed into a miraculous feature of S. Peter's prison),[1] and the spring of Juturna, described on p. 124.

According to the Roman legend, Romulus and Tatius, after the mediation of the Sabine women, met on the very spot where the battle had been fought, and made peace and an alliance. The spot, a low, damp, grassy field, exposed to the floods of the river Spinon (p. 29), took the name of "Comitium" from the verb *coire*, to assemble. It is possible that, in consequence of the alliance, a road connecting the Sabine and the Roman settlements was made across these swamps; it became afterwards the Sacra Via. Tullus Hostilius, the third king, built a stone inclosure on the Comitium, for the meeting of the Senators, named from him Curia Hostilia; then came the state prison built by Ancus Marcius in one of the quarries (the Tullianum). The Tarquins drained the land, transformed the unruly river Spinon into the Cloaca Maxima, gave the Forum a regular (trapezoidal) shape, divided the space around its borders into building-lots, and sold them to private speculators for shops and houses, the fronts of which were to be lined with porticoes.

These shops, so closely connected with the early life of Rome, were at the beginning of the commonest kind: butchers' stalls (afterwards replaced by the Basilica Sempronia) and butchers' shops, from which Virginius took the knife to stab his daughter. Other tabernæ were occupied by schools for children, where Appius Claudius first saw Virginia reading. As the dignity of the place increased, ordinary tradesmen disappeared and their shops were occupied by goldsmiths, silversmiths, money-changers, and usurers. Hence the name "tabernæ argentariæ," applied, as a general rule, to all the shops; as a distinctive name, to those on the north side. On the occasion of the triumph of L. Papirius, dictator in 308 B. C., the gilt shields of the Samnites were distributed among the owners of the argentariæ to decorate their shop fronts. There were two rows of them, on either of the longer sides of the Forum: one called the *tabernæ veteres* (*septem tabernæ*) on the shady or south side; one called the *tabernæ novæ* or *argentariæ*

---

[1] See *Der mamertinische Kerker u. die römischen Traditionen vom Gefängnisse und den Ketten Petri*, von H. Grisar, S. J., in *Zeitschrift für kath. Theologie*, xx. Jahrgang, 1896, p. 102.

on the sunny or north side. The same were designated concisely with the formula "sub veteribus, sub novis."

It does not come within the scope of the present chapter to follow stage by stage the development of the market-place into a magnificent forum surrounded by stately edifices. The chronology of its monumental transformation up to the time of Augustus may be found in the following table. Compare the "Geschichte des Forum Comitium und der Sacra Via" in Jordan's "Topographie," i², p. 315.

Year of Rome.	B. C.	
257	497	September 17. — Temple of Saturn dedicated by the consuls A. Sempronius and M. Minicius.
258	496	Apparition of the Dioscuri by the spring of Juturna.
270	484	January 27. — Dedication of the Temple of the Dioscuri.
364	390	Temple of Vesta burnt by the Gauls and rebuilt.
387	367	Erection of the Temple of Concord voted by the Senate.
391	363	The legendary chasm at the northwest corner of the Palatine.
416	338	Rostra decorated with beaks from the fleet of the Antiates.
450	304	Chapel of Cn. Flavius on the Græcostasis.
490	264	Tabula Valeria painted on the east side of the Curia.
491	263	First sun-dial erected by M. Valerius Messala.
494	260	Columna rostrata of C. Duilius.
513	241	Temple of Vesta burnt and rebuilt.
544	210	Regia destroyed by fire and rebuilt.
570	184	The first Basilica or court-house, built by M. Porcius Cato the elder (Basilica Porcia).
575	179	Basilica Fulvia, by M. Fulvius Nobilior.
585	169	Basilica Sempronia, by T. Sempronius Gracchus.
590	164	Second sun-dial, by L. Marcius Philippus.
595	157	First clepsydra, by P. Scipio Nasica.
606	148	Regia destroyed by fire and rebuilt.
633	121	Reconstruction of the Temple of Concord by L. Opimius, voted by the Senate.
633	121	Basilica Opimia, by L. Opimius.
633	121	Fornix Fabianus, by Q. Fabius Allobrogicus.
637	117	Temple of Castor rebuilt by L. Cæcilius Metellus Dalmaticus.
676	78	Basilica Fulvia (Æmilia) restored by M. Æmilius Lepidus.
680	74	Tribunal Aurelium, by L. Aurelius Cotta.

It is evident that a forum dating from the time of the Kings must soon have become inadequate for its purpose, and for the requirements of an ever-increasing population; its area, besides, was so crowded with statues, tribunes, altars, putealia, and obstacles of every description that we wonder how public meetings could be held within its precincts. In 159 B. C. P. Scipio and M. Popilius, censors, ordered the removal from the Forum of all statues of magistrates unless they had been erected by decree of the S. P. Q. R.; and yet we hear, at the Rostra alone, of the statues of the four Roman ambassadors murdered by the Fidenates in 438 B. C.; of the two Junii Coruncanii, murdered by Tenta, queen of the Illyrians, in 229; of Cn. Octavius, assassinated at Laodicæa in 162 while on a mission to the Syrian court; of Servius Sulpicius the jurist, who died in the camp at Mutina in 43; of Camillus the dictator, who, as an example of the ancient simplicity of dress, was clothed in a toga without tunic; of C. Mænius (equestrian), who conquered the Latins in 338; of Sulla; of Pompeius; of Lepidus; of Julius Cæsar; of young Octavianus; and lastly, of the three Sibyls, which Pliny classifies among the earliest works of the kind in Rome.[1]

Besides these obstacles, the Forum and its vicinity were crowded by certain classes of people, not very distinguished, who so constantly haunted certain points and corners of the place that they were nicknamed from them. Thus we hear of the Subrostrani, lawyers without employment, keeping themselves by the Rostra in search of prey; of the Canalicolæ, described by Paul the Deacon as " homines pauperes qui circa canales fori consistebant; " and in a general way of the forenses, so graphically described by Plautus (Curculio, iv. 1).

One of the first steps to reform this state of things was taken in the seventh century of Rome by the construction of a fish-market (*forum piscatorium*), in consequence of which the fishmongers, who poisoned the clients of the court-houses with the offensive smell of their merchandise, were driven away from the porticoes of the basilicæ. These basilicæ, — the Porcia, oldest of all, built by the elder Cato in 184 near the Curia; the Sempronia, erected in 169 on the line of the tabernæ veteres; the Opimia, in 121, by the Temple of Concord; and the Fulvia Æmilia, 179–178, by the Via Argiletana, — as they were surrounded by porticoes accessible both by day and by night, increased the public accommodation to some extent.

The grand era of transformation begins with the year 700 (54 B. C.), when L. Æmilius Paullus bought private property on the north side and built his superb Basilica Æmilia. The reason for

[1] See Nichols, *The Roman Forum*, pp. 79, 86–89, 203, 217; and Thédenat, in Daremberg and Saglio's *Dictionnaire*, p. 1281.

such a costly undertaking (about 12,000,000 francs) is given by
Cicero: *ut forum laxaremus*, to enlarge the Forum. The work of
Æmilius Paullus was continued by Julius Cæsar, who purchased
other private property and built an extension — the Forum Julium — at a cost of 20,000,000 francs. This happened between
the years 700 and 708 (54 and 46 B. C.). Augustus followed the
example of Cæsar, and, in continuation of the two fora, built a
third one named Forum Augustum or Forum Martis, from the
Temple of Mars the Avenger, which stood at one end of it. Augustus himself explains in his "Res gestæ" the necessity of this
work, by the inadequacy of the two existing fora for the transaction of business and the administration of justice. It took him
forty years to finish the structure, from 712 to August 1, 752 (42
to 2 B. C.). During this lapse of time the old Forum Romanum
had been, in its turn, vastly improved, as is shown by the following summary : —

Year of Rome.	B. C.	
702	52	The Curia, the Basilica Porcia, and several houses burnt down by the Clodians. The Temple of Felicitas built on the site of the Curia in 705. Substituted once more by the Curia Julia in 710. Dedicated by Augustus in 725.
708	46	First Basilica Julia dedicated by Julius Cæsar ; Sub Veteribus rebuilt and enlarged by Augustus in 742.
708	46	Lacus Servilius embellished by Agrippa.
710	44	The Rostra Julia built at the other (east) end of the Forum.
712	42	Temple of Saturn rebuilt by L. Munatius Plancus.
718	36	The Regia rebuilt by Domitius Calvinus. Fasti consulares engraved the same year, fasti trium-phales between 736 and 742.
725	29	August 18. — Temple of Cæsar dedicated by Augustus, and triumphal arch of Augustus dedicated near the temple by the S. P. Q. R.
745	9	Altar of Vulcan dedicated by Augustus on the Volkanal.
747	7	Temple of Castor and Pollux restored by Tiberius.

We can add to the list the restoration of the Temple of Concordia by Tiberius in 763 (10 A. D.) ; that of the state prison by C.
Vibius and M. Cocceius about the same date ; the erection of an
altar to Ops by the Temple of Saturn, August 10, 760 (A. D. 7) ;
and that of a triumphal arch of Tiberius in 769 (A. D. 16).

From the age of Tiberius to that of Constantine the history of the Forum is represented by four great fires followed by three great restorations, in the course of which the space for the accommodation of the crowds is vastly increased, new buildings are added, new art collections formed, etc. The first is the fire of Nero, A. D. 65, which lasted six days and seven nights, destroyed three regions of the city, and damaged seven more. The Regia, the temples of Vesta and of Jupiter Stator, the Curia, the Græcostasis, the Temple of Janus, and the region of the Argiletum as far as the Carinæ, were devastated by the flames. The second is the fire of Titus, A. D. 80.

Vespasian and Domitian repaired the damages of both, and in doing this they added two fora to the three already existing, the Forum Pacis and the Forum Transitorium.

Vespasian began by clearing and repairing the streets " deformes veteribus incendiis atque ruinis," [1] and the temples, for which he was rewarded with the title of " Restitutor Ædium Sacrarum." [2] Then he took up a large section of the burnt land between the Sacra Via and the Carinæ, and erected on it a splendid temple to Peace, surrounded by a large open space, which must have served, like the fora of Julius and Augustus, to relieve the Forum Romanum. He also rebuilt the temples of Jupiter Capitolinus and of Claudius on the Cœlian hill, and began the construction of the amphitheatre.

In a short reign of two years Titus (A. D. 79–81) could do little more than complete the buildings which his father had left unfinished, like the amphitheatre, which he dedicated in the year 80. At the same time another frightful conflagration, which raged for three days and three nights, stopped all work. The fire of Titus was particularly destructive in the region of the Circus Flaminius, lying under the Capitoline hill, as well as on the hill itself.

Domitian, youngest son of Vespasian, rebuilt a large area on the north and west sides of the Forum, under a new piano regolatore, the orientation of which is parallel with the Via Argiletana (and the fora of Augustus, of Cæsar, and of Peace), not with the Sacra Via. The copious list of his buildings comprises the transformation of the Via Argiletana into the Forum Transitorium ; the reconstruction of the Temple of Janus, of the Curia Julia, of the Græcostasis, of the Regia and the House of the Vestals,[8] of the Meta

---

1 Suetonius, *Vespas.*, 8 ; and *Corpus Inscr.*, vol. vi. n. 931.

2 *Ibid.*, n. 934.

8 Thédenat, in Daremberg and Saglio's *Dictionnaire*, p. 1290, n. 12–14.

Sudans; the construction of the horrea piperataria, of the Temple of Vespasian and Titus on the Clivus Capitolinus, of the Arch of Titus on the Summa Sacra Via; and the completion of the amphitheatre. In memory of these architectural exploits, an equestrian statue was raised to him in the middle of the Forum, the description of which by Statius (Silv., i. 1) is a fundamental text for the topography of this classic district.

Shortly before the end of the reign of Commodus, A. D. 191, another fire, which lasted several days, swept over the region of the Sacra Via. It began in a house near the Temple of Peace, after a slight shock of earthquake. The temple was leveled to the ground; hence the fire spread to the spice-warehouses of Domitian, and from them, over the Sacra Via and the Atrium and Temple of Vesta, to the Palace of the Cæsars, a great part of which was destroyed, together with the archives of the Empire. "It was on this occasion that Galen's shop on the Sacra Via was burnt down, when, as he tells us himself, he lost some of his works of which there were no other copies in Rome. The fire was extinguished at last by a heavy fall of rain." [1]

The damages were repaired by Septimius Severus, by his Empress, Julia Domna, and by his son, Caracalla, with the adoption of a new piano regolatore, in consequence of which the orientation of edifices on the Clivus Sacer was shifted by 33°. This change appears most evident in the map of the Clivus Sacer (p. 207, Fig. 82), in which the ruins anterior to the fire of 191 are marked in black, those from 191 downwards in a lighter tint. It is necessary to remind the reader that the excavations of the Forum and of the Palatine have nowhere been carried to the proper depth. We have satisfied ourselves with laying bare the remains of the *late* Empire, without taking care to explore the earlier and deeper strata. The foundations of the triumphal arch of Augustus were discovered in 1888 hardly ten inches below the level at which the excavations of 1872 had stopped. The water-tank of Mykenean shape discovered on the Palatine while this book was in the press (August, 1896) had actually been seen in 1876, but not excavated because it lay lower than the surrounding ruins. We are still discussing the exact location of the Arch of Fabius, when it could be ascertained *de facto* by scraping away a few inches of ground.

Severus and Caracalla repaired or rebuilt *a fundamentis* the Temple of Vesta, the House of the Vestals, the Templum Sacræ

---

[1] Thomas Dyer, *A History of the City of Rome,* ed. 1865, p. 263.

Urbis, that of Vespasian, the Porticus Margaritaria, and the front of the palace on the Nova Via. Their names are commemorated forever in the Forum, in the triumphal arch erected in 203 on the border-line of the Comitium.

We have no definite account of the fire of 283 under Carinus. Judging from the works of repair which it necessitated, it must have raged from the foot of the Capitoline to the top of the Sacra Via, from the Vicus Jugarius to the Temple of Venus and Rome.

Diocletian repaired the Basilica Julia, the Græcostasis (?), and the Forum Julium, and rebuilt the Senate-house from its foundations. Maxentius repaired the Temple of Venus and Rome, and built the heroon of his son Romulus, and the great basilica afterwards named from Constantine. The monumental columns which stand on the edge of the Forum, opposite the Basilica Julia, date also from the beginning of the fourth century.

The first incident in the history of the destruction of the Forum is the abolition of pagan worship. In 383 Gratianus did away with the privileges of temples and priests, and confiscated their revenues. In 391 Valentinian and Theodosius prohibited sacrifices, even if strictly domestic and private. This brought the pagan faction to open rebellion, as related at length in "Ancient Rome," p. 173. After the defeat of the rebel leader Eugenius, which took place on September 6, 394, temples were closed forever; but this measure contributed, for the time being, to the embellishment more than to the spoliation of the Forum and its surroundings, because the beautiful statues of the gods, removed from their altars, were set up again, as mere works of Greek art, in public places like law-courts, fora, baths, main thoroughfares, etc. Information on this point is supplied by —

G. B. de Rossi, *Bullettino di arch. crist.*, 1865, p. 5 ; and *Bull. della comm. arch. com.*, 1874, p. 174. — *Corpus Inscr. Lat.*, vol. vi. p. 356, n. 1651–72. — *Notizie degli Scavi*, 1895, p. 459.

The Forum was tolerably well preserved at the beginning of the sixth century. In 500 King Theodoric addressed the people from the Rostra, promising to maintain the privileges granted by his predecessors, and the words of his promise were engraved on a bronze tablet, hung probably in front of the Senate-house. The Anonymus of Valesius,[1] in mentioning these events, gives to this corner of the old Forum the name *ad Palmam*, about which have written —

[1] Quoted by Nibby, *Roma antica*, vol. ii. p. 58.

H. Jordan, *Topographie*, ol. i², p. 259, n. 91. — Ferdinand Gregorovius, *Geschichte*, vol. i. p. 276. — G. B. de Rossi, *Bull. com.*, 1887, p. 64 ; 1889, p. 363.

The former name of the corner was *in tribus fatis*, or *tria fata*, from the statues of the three Sibyls mentioned by Pliny (xxxiv. 11) *iuxta Rostra*, and considered to rank among the earliest works of the kind in Rome.   The new denomination *ad Palmam* originated from a statue of Claudius Gothicus, wearing the palm of victory (*statua Palmata*), which stood near the Arch of Severus.   It soon extended to the whole neighborhood.   The promulgation of the *Codex Theodosianus* is said to have taken place in 438, in the house of Anicius Glabrio Faustus, *quæ est ad Palmam*, viz., near the Senate-house.   The same house is called *domus palmata* in a letter of King Theodoric.[1]   The meeting of a committee of bishops with a committee of senators, which took place here in 502 to discuss the schism of Lawrence, is called *palmaris*, for the same reason.

The first solemn transformation of an historical building near the Forum into a Christian place of worship took place about 526, when Pope Felix IV. dedicated to SS. Cosmas and Damianus the Templum Sacræ Urbis, or Record Office.   In 630 the Senate-house was dedicated to S. Hadrian by Honorius I.; in 731 Gregory III. rebuilt the oratory of SS. Sergius and Bacchus by the Temple of Concord and the chapel ðf the Mamertine Prison; in 760 Paul I. rebuilt the church of S. Maria Antiqua in the inner hall of the Augusteum, and raised a new one to S. Peter in the vestibule of the Temple of Venus and Rome (transformed in 850 by Leo IV. into that of S. Maria Nova).   The Temple of Antoninus likewise was placed under the patronage of S. Lawrence, that of Janus under that of S. Dionysius, the offices of the Senate under that of S. Martina, the Basilica Julia under that of S. Maria de Foro, the Ærarium Saturni under that of the Saviour.   The Heroon of Romulus, son of Maxentius, became the vestibule of SS. Cosmas and Damianus; the so-called Baths of Heliogabalus on the Sacra Via became the church and convent of S. Cæsarius in Palatio; the Basilica of Constantine was christianized under a name unknown to us.   (See Pagan and Christian Rome, p. 162.)

The buildings mentioned by Procopius, about 537, are, besides the Forum itself, the Senate-house, the Temple of Janus, etc. He also states that many statues by Pheidias and Lysippos could

---

[1] Cassiodorus, *Var.*, iv. 30.

still be seen in Rome, after it had been so often sacked. In 546 the barbarians of Totila looted the city once more; still the Forum, free of ruins, continued to be used as the meeting-place of the remaining population. In 608 the last "honorary" monument, the column of Phocas, was erected in the middle of it, with marbles taken from some neighboring edifice. A few years later Pope Honorius I. (625–640) stripped the roof of the Temple of Venus and Rome of its bronze tiles, which could not but hasten the destruction of that glorious building. In 663 a Christian emperor, Constans II., held the starving and ruined city to ransom for twelve days, inflicting upon it more damage than it had suffered at the hands of the Goths and Vandals. In 768 Stephen III. was elected pope in a popular meeting, held *in tribus fatis* by the Comitium.

If the so-called "Itinerary of Einsiedlen" dates really from the time of Charlemagne, it gives us a very detailed account of the state of the Forum at the beginning of the ninth century. The monuments registered in this document are: the arches of Severus, of Titus, and of Constantine; the umbilicus Romæ, a "pendant" to the golden milestone; the equestrian statue of Constantine; the Curia (S. Adriano); the Augusteum (S. M. Antiqua); the Templum Sacræ Urbis (SS. Cosmas and Damianus); the Temple of Venus and Rome (Palatium Traiani); and the Meta Sudans. This is the last evidence we possess of the Forum retaining its original level.

An examination of the state of its pavement shows that in former times carriages could not cross it, on account of police regulations and of the steps (and occasional palisades) by which the travertine floor was surrounded. However, all obstacles were removed after the fall of the Empire. Vehicles were then allowed to cross the Forum diagonally from the Argiletum (by S. Adriano) to the Vicus Tuscus (by S. Teodoro) and vice versa, coming in and out between the first and second pedestals of the "honorary" columns on the Sacra Via, where the pavement is deeply furrowed by the friction of wheels. A curbstone, made of a broken column of African marble, is set up at the corner of the first pedestal at the turn of the Sacra Via.

What happened to the Forum from the ninth to the fourteenth century it is exceedingly difficult to say. It is unnecessary to remind the student how negligently excavations were made up to a recent date. Their purpose was to reach and lay bare the classic remains of the Empire, and if mediæval or decadence monuments barred the way, they were mercilessly sacrificed. We have careful descriptions of the objects discovered in these excavations, — inscriptions, pedestals, statues, bas-reliefs, columns, etc., — but not a word is said about the way they were lying in their bed of ruins, at what depth, whether *in situ* or overthrown, whether belonging to the place of discovery or brought from some distance to be used as building-materials, etc. The archæologists and the excavators of the Napoleonic period, Fea, Nibby, and Amati, were far more careful in noting these particulars, the only means we have of reconstructing the history of the decline and fall of the city.

Take the Basilica Julia, as an illustration : what is left of the noble building to tell the tale of its downfall? The steps leading to it are modern for the greater part, and so are the pavement, the pilasters of the nave and aisles, the brick arches towards the Vicus Jugarius, the marble pillars of the Doric order on the Sacra Via, the opening of the Cloaca Maxima, etc. Even the fragments arranged on the pilasters are not all found on the spot. But we do not complain of restorations so much as of destructions. I have just said that part of the Basilica was dedicated to S. Maria de Foro ; the elegant little church was found almost intact in 1880 in the northern aisle on the Vicus Jugarius, with its double row of columns, apse, presbyterium, marble transennæ, fresco paintings, main and side doors, etc. The only trace left standing by accident is one of the columns of the presbyterium. The remaining portion of the Basilica had been taken possession of by the Roman marmorarii of the eleventh century, who prepared there the *materia prima* for their cosmatesque cloisters, ambones, pavements, etc. They had provided themselves with booths and workshops by closing with mud walls the spaces between the pilasters of the western aisles. There were about twenty such shops. The great nave was covered with a layer of chips and fragments of historical marbles, destined to feed the lime-kilns, two of which were discovered full of half-charred blocks. The east aisles towards the Sacra Via were found unencumbered by mediæval partition walls, and we know the reason why. They were used as rope-walks, from which the place derived its name of Cannaparia. The upper strata of rubbish was composed mostly of human bones ; because, after the last devastations of Cardinal di Corneto, the site had been turned into a burial-ground for the Ospedale della Consolazione. The chain of historical events which made the building pass from the hand of the Roman magistrates into that of the priests of S. Maria de Foro, and then of ropemakers, of marmorarii, of lime-burners, of the guardians of the Ospedale della Consolazione, was thus illustrated by actual remains. They have all been sacrificed to the desire of bringing into evidence one period only in the history of the building, the classic. Another subject of discussion about this place was the roof. Was the Basilica vaulted over, like that of Constantine, or roofed with tiles supported by a wooden framework? The answer was given materially, by the huge blocks of the vault with panels and lacunaria in stucco, which lay scattered on the floor of the aisles. They were destroyed for fear that they would obstruct the view.

The Forum has had the same experience. The southeast side of it, facing the Temple of Cæsar, was found in 1872 closed by a line of shops of the beginning of the fifth century, and of the utmost importance for the history of the place. They were mistaken for a mediæval fortification (see Bull. Inst., 1872, pp. 234, 235) and destroyed. The same mistake was made with regard to the walls which supported the platform of the Rostra. The pedestal of an equestrian statue in the middle of the Forum — wrongly attributed to Domitian — was likewise dismantled for the sake of some blocks of giallo antico used in its masonry. If such errors were committed in so recent an age, it is easy to understand what must have happened in centuries gone by, and what opportunities of reconstructing the Forum have been lost.

The accumulation of soil began, as far as we can judge, after the visit of Charlemagne (800). When an officer of Pope Marinus II. built in 946 a small house within the cloisters of the Vestals, there were already five feet of rubbish above the old pavement. After the fire of Robert Guiscard in 1084, the Forum and its surroundings disappeared altogether from the sight, and almost from the memory, of the living. The Frangipani and other turbulent barons occupied the ruins of temples and arches, crowning and surrounding them with battlemented towers, many of which were in their turn leveled to the ground in 1221, 1257, and 1536. See, also, upon this point —

Ferdinand Gregorovius, *Geschichte*, iv. 376; v. 316. — Heinrich Jordan, *Topographie*, ii. 480; and *Ephemeris epigr.*, 1876, p. 238.

The Forum was then turned into a vegetable garden. In the inventory of the possessions of the Lateran basilica, written by Nicolo Frangipani about 1300, we find mentioned: " Two small houses near the image of Phocas (*foce magina*), with their orchards ;

two orchards near the arch by the image of Phocas; others near the church of SS. Cosma e Damiano; one near S. Adriano, where stand the four columns," etc. The "Res gestæ" of Innocent III. mention, vol. ii. p. 102, an orchard behind the church of SS. Sergio e Bacco, and another "among the columns" in the direction of the Mamertine prison. The ground was still cultivated in the middle of the sixteenth century, when we hear of the inscription of Nævius Surdinus found "in the gardens of the columna Mænia," viz., of Phocas; and of the pedestal (Corpus, 1458, *a*) found "in the gardens by the three columns," viz., of Castor and Pollux. The area of the House of the Vestals was occupied by a *harundinetum*, or bamboo shrubbery.

It has been said that the earth and rubbish from the foundations of public and private buildings were regularly thrown into the area of the Forum, from the time of Eugenius IV. (1431–47), but no documents have been produced to prove this. I have found one — the first within my knowledge — in the account-books of Pope Paul II. (1464–71). It appears from them that the earth and rubbish excavated from the foundations of the Palazzo di Venezia were regularly thrown out "ad tres columnas," viz., in the neighborhood of the Temple of Castor and Pollux. Considering the state of the city in the fifteenth century, the want of police regulations, and the freedom of building, destroying, and excavating which every one enjoyed, it is no wonder that rubbish was thrown out in the nearest convenient place, and no place was more convenient than the hollow of the Forum. I have collected many data about the periodical increase of its level; but two instances will give the reader an idea of them. It appears that, after the obstruction of the Cloaca Maxima,[1] the only outlet for rain and spring water in the district of the fora was a channel or furrow cut by the rushing stream through the bed of rubbish, on the line of the Via di S. Teodoro, passing right in front of this church. Communication between the banks of this ditch was assured by means of a bridge, called *il ponticello*. Albertini speaks of a discovery made about 1510 *ad ponticulum*, between S. M. Liberatrice and S. Teodoro. Martin Heemskerk made a sketch of the bridge in 1534.[2] The last mention of it occurs in 1549 (Corpus, vi. 804) apropos of the discovery of the Vortumnus *prope ponticulum ante*

---

[1] The Forum of Augustus could not have been turned into a marsh — il Pantano — unless the Cloaca Maxima, which runs under it and drains it, had ceased its functions.

[2] See *Mittheilungen*, 1894, p. 10, n. 1.

ædificium quadratum, " near the ponticello in front of the Temple of Augustus." Bridge and ditch had disappeared under the ever increasing deposits of rubbish in 1593, when Cardinal Alessandro Farnese made a present of the ground to the S. P. Q. R. for the erection of a fountain and of a watering-trough for cattle. We have the evidence of these facts to the present day in the church of S. Teodoro, built in the sixth (?) century at the level of the Vicus Tuscus; and rebuilt in 1450 by Pope Nicholas V. ten or twelve feet higher. In the vignette of Martin Heemskerk, just mentioned, the threshold of the church appears still above the street (1534). In 1674 it was considerably below it. Finally, to save the building from filtering waters and from the pressure of earth, Pope Clement XI. was compelled to cut a ditch round and to open a court before it, to which we now descend by a flight of steps.

Such has been the fate of all ancient churches in this region. Built originally ten or twelve steps higher than the Forum, by the end of the fifteenth century they had sunk deep in the ground, and many were deserted by their attendants. The third vignette of Etienne Duperac shows people descending to the Church of S. Adriano, the ground being almost level with the architrave of the door. A strong remedy alone could save the buildings from destruction, and that of raising them to the level of the new city was decided upon. The thing was done, but in a reckless way, so that the present churches have nothing but their name in common with their predecessors. Those who know what the word "restoration " means with reference to the seicento will understand what those venerable buildings must have gone through at the hands of their restorers.

The second instance I propose to quote is this. The greatest centre of traffic in ancient times was the Argiletum, a thoroughfare which ran along the bottom of the valley between the Quirinal, Viminal, and Esquiline, and entered the Forum between the Curia and the Basilica Æmilia.[1] It retained its importance throughout the centuries until Cardinal Michele Bonelli cut through the Curia the street which bears his name (Via Bonella), and led the traffic into a new thoroughfare, better leveled, paved, and drained. A search made in 1869 at the point where the Argiletum fell into the Comitium showed the existence of four pavements, one above the other, viz., the stone floor of the Comitium; another, 9 feet higher,

---

[1] The lower section of the Argiletum was transformed by Domitian into the Forum Transitorium.

dating probably from the time of Robert Guiscard (1084); a third, 7 feet higher still, with mediæval walls on each side and a curb-stone at the corner made out of a broken column; the fourth and last pavement, at the present level, dates from the time of Paul III., who, on preparing the ground for the triumphal entry of Charles V. (1536), did not remove the materials of the several churches, houses, and towers demolished for the occasion, but leveled them on the spot. In the excavations made by Nibby between 1827 and 1834 many coins of Paul III. were discovered at a considerable depth on the line of the Sacra Via.

I have mentioned above the fountain and water-trough estab-lished by the S. P. Q. R. about 1593, near the three columns of Castor and Pollux, on a piece of ground granted by Cardinal Ales-sandro Farnese. The fountain consisted of a large granite basin, 23 metres in circumference, placed on a high pedestal of travertine. The basin had been discovered opposite the Mamertine prison, together with the Marforio, in the fifteenth century. When the architect Antinori suggested to Pius VII., in 1816, the removal of the basin to the Piazza del Quirinale (where it was actually placed at the foot of the obelisk two years later), the basin was sunk in the earth, so that carters used to drive their teams right across it, to refresh them in the heat of the summer. I have myself seen a portion of the area of the Forum increase by two metres at least in 1868, when Baron Visconti, then engaged in discovering the site of the Porta Romanula, deposited the earth on the site of the House of the Vestals, instead of carting it away.

As regards the search for antiquities, we can safely say that, from the time of Urban V. (1362-70) to the end of the last cen-tury, every year is marked by a plunder of some kind or other, the worst deeds of destruction being connected with the golden age of the cinquecento. The history of these excavations has not been written yet. Materials for such a history, however, have been collected by —

Heinrich Jordan, *Sylloge inscript. fori romani* (in Ephem. epigr., 1876, pp. 238-248). — Charles Bunsen, *Le forum romanum*, 1835, pp. 4-6. — A. Zahn, *Bullettino Instituto*, 1867, p. 189. — Eugène Müntz, *Les arts à la cour des Papes*, vols. i. -iii.; and *Revue archéol.*, 1876, p. 158. — Orazio Marucchi, *Des-crizione del foro romano.* Rome, Befani, 1883.

But they hardly cover one tenth of the ground. Students will find a complete chronology of the facts in the "Storia degli Scavi di Roma," which I hope soon to publish as a companion text to the "Forma Urbis."

The oldest official record dates from the year 1364, when Urban V. granted the materials of the Temple of Antoninus and Faustina to the rebuilders of the Lateran, provided they would not touch the chapel of S. Lorenzo in Miranda, which had been set up in the portico. As an account of excavations is appended to the description of each building, I need not enter into many particulars. In general, however, let us distinguish three periods. In the first, from Urban V. to July 22, 1540, the popes grant to building contractors or lime-burners the destruction of such and such a monument, one third of the profits being reserved for the Apostolic Chamber. Thus in 1431–62 the great travertine wall separating the Senate-house from the Forum of Cæsar was legally destroyed by permission of Eugenius IV. and of his successors; in 1461–62 the same fate befell the Templum Sacræ Urbis or Record Office; in 1450 the Temple of Venus and Rome; in 1499 the House of the Vestals, etc. If the government treated the antique remains in this fashion they could certainly not expect mercy from private hands. In reading the contracts signed between the owners of ruins and their excavators, one is reminded of the expression of Pirro Ligorio, that "ruins were sold like oxen for the meat-market." What I may call "excavation fever" had seized every class of citizens, from the cardinals and noblemen, who wanted to link their name to a museum or a villa, to the poor widow, who sought to relieve her miseries by some unexpected find. Excavations may be called the "lotto" of the sixteenth century.

Sentence of death on the monuments of the Forum and of the Sacra Via was passed on July 22, 1540. By a brief of Paul III. (Farnese) [1] the privilege of excavating or giving permission to excavate is taken away from the Capitoline or Apostolic chambers, from the "magistrates of streets," from ecclesiastical dignitaries, etc., and given exclusively to the "deputies" for the Fabbrica di S. Pietro. The pope gives them full liberty to search for ancient marbles wherever they please within and outside the walls, to remove them from antique buildings, to pull these buildings to pieces if necessary; he orders that no marbles can be sold by private owners without the consent of the Fabbrica, under the penalty of excommunication *latæ sententiæ*, of the wrath of the pope, and of a fine of 1000 ducats. No pen can describe the ravages committed by the Fabbrica in the course of the last sixty

---

[1] Published by Müntz, *Revue archéol.*, mai, 1884, from the original of the Vatican archives. The importance of the document has not yet been fully appreciated by archæologists.

years of the sixteenth century. The excesses roused the execration of the citizens, but to no purpose; on May 17, 1580, the conservatori made an indignant protest to the town council, when a portion of the Palace of the Cæsars had fallen, in consequence of its having been undermined by the searchers for marble. A deputation was sent to Gregory XIII. to ask for the revocation of all licenses ("ad perquirendos lapides etiam pro usu fabricæ Principis apostolorum"). We may imagine what answer was given to the protests of the city when we learn that by a brief of Clement VIII., dated July 23, 1598, the archæological jurisdiction of the Fabbrica was extended over the remains of Ostia and Porto! The Forum Romanum was swept by a band of devastators from 1540 to 1549; they began by removing the marble steps and the marble coating of Faustina's Temple (1540), then they attacked what was left standing of the Arch of Fabius (1540). Between 1546 and 1547 the Temple of Julius Cæsar, the Regia, with the Fasti Consulares et Triumphales, fell under their hammer. The steps and foundations of the Temple of Castor and Pollux were next burnt into lime or given up to the stone-cutters, together with the Arch of Augustus. The Temple of Vesta, the Augustæum, and the shrine of Vortumnus, at the corner of the Vicus Tuscus, met with the same fate in 1549.

The chronology of subsequent excavations is given by Charles Bunsen, "Le forum romanum expliqué selon l'état des fouilles," Rome, avril 21, 1835, p. 4; Antonio Nibby, "Roma antica," vol. ii. p. 178; Heinrich Jordan, "Topographie," vol. i², p. 154, n. 1; and "Sylloge inscript. fori Romani" (in Ephem. epigr., 1876, p. 244); Orazio Marucchi, "Descrizione del foro romano," Rome, Befani, 1883, ch. ii. p. 9; but their accounts are only summary sketches. A great many unknown documents will be published in volumes iii. and iv. of "Storia degli Scavi di Roma," the publication of which has been announced above.

From the end of the sixteenth century downwards the more noticeable events are, first of all, the raising of christianized pagan edifices to the level of the modern city, by which they suffered great damage. Urban VIII. is responsible for the modernization of the Heroon Romuli, of the Templum Sacræ Urbis (SS. Cosma e Damiano), of the Secretarium Senatus (S. Martina), and of the Senate-house (S. Adriano); Paul V. and the architect Carlo Lombardo for that of S. Maria Nova in 1615; the corporation of apothecaries and their architect Torriani for that of S. Lorenzo in Miranda (Temple of Antoninus and Faustina) in 1602; Cardi-

nal Marcello Lante and his architect Onorio Longhi for that of
S. Maria Antiqua (S. M. Liberatrice) in 1617; the trustees of the
Ospedale della Consolazione for that of S. Maria in Cannapara
(S. M. delle Grazie) in 1609.

Under Alexander VII. (1655–67) Leonardo Agostini excavated
and destroyed the greater part of the Porticus Margaritaria. In
1742 a trench ten metres deep was cut across the Forum to put
in order the Cloaca Maxima, which had become choked. The
Chevalier Frédenheim excavated the Basilica Julia between November, 1788, and March, 1789.

The end of the eighteenth century marks also the end of the
era of destruction in the valley of the Forum. Pius VII., whose
memory is dear to all lovers of art and antiquities, seconded by
Carlo Fea, his "commissario per le antichità," determined that
the historical monuments from the Capitol to the Coliseum should
be laid bare and their foundations strengthened if necessary. His
work, interrupted by the French invasion of 1809, was continued
by Comte Tournon, the préfet of the Département du Tibre.
Leo XII. began in 1827, and Gregory XVI. completed in 1835,
another section of excavations from the Basilica Julia to the
Clivus Capitolinus. The Republicans of 1848–49 extended the
belt of discoveries along the north side of the Basilica Julia, and
Pius IX. completed their work between 1851 and 1852.

The Italian government undertook the general excavation of
the ground crossed by the Sacra Via from one end to the other a
few weeks after Rome was made the capital of the united kingdom. Thirteen years' untiring labor and a sum of 2,000,000 lire
were required to accomplish the task. The progress of the works
can be followed by referring to the dates appended: —

1870, December; 1871, November. — Basilica Julia.
1871. — Streets adjoining the Temple of Castores, steps of temple, monumen-
    tal columns on the south side of the Forum, Cloaca Maxima.
1872. — Space between temples of Castores and of Divus Julius, Rostra Julia,
    shops on the east side of the Forum (destroyed in 1874).
1873. — Area of the Forum, sculptured plutei, pedestal of Caballus Constan-
    tini, Temple of Vesta.
1874. — The neighborhood of Temple of Julius, site of Regia.
1876. — Steps of Temple of Antoninus, and neighborhood.
1877–1879. — The Clivus Sacer from the Heroon Romuli to the Arch of Titus,
    Basilica Nova, Arco di Latrone, front of Porticus Margaritaria, etc.
1882. — The Sacra Via by the Arch of Fabius, Arch of Fabius, shops of the
    House of Vestals, shrine of the Vicus Vestæ.
1883–1884. — House of Vestals, Nova Via.

We shall first study the area of the Forum, and the various monuments which it contains; then the edifices on the north side (Senate-house, Temple of Janus, Basilica Æmilia); those of the east side (Temple of Julius Cæsar, Arch of Augustus, Temple of Castores); those of the south side (Basilica Julia between the Vicus Tuscus and the Vicus Jugarius); and lastly, those of the west side (Temple of Saturn, Rostra, Arch of Severus, Tullianum) and of the Clivus Capitolinus (Temple of Concord and of Vespasian, Porticus Deorum Consentium, Tabularium, Capitolium, Arx).

The bibliography of the Forum is particularly rich. There is no book connected with Roman archæology without a reference to it. The works must be divided into three classes: (*a*) accounts of discoveries of single buildings, sculpture, inscriptions, etc., with no attempt at a general reconstruction of the Forum; (*b*) attempts at a general reconstruction of the Forum before the final excavations of 1870–84; (*c*) works published after the excavations of 1870–84.

In the first class we find a precious source of information. The series begins with an "Exposé d'une découverte de m. le chev. Frédenheim faite au Forum romanum en janvier, 1779," published by Oberlin at Strassbourg in 1796, and ends with Pietro Pericoli's "Storia dell' Ospedale della Consolazione di Roma," 1879, where the history of the destruction of the Basilica Julia is related from unedited documents. Works of this class will be quoted in connection with the single discoveries or monuments which they throw light upon.

The second class has lost much of its importance, its elements being necessarily rather speculative than founded on fact; yet students will find in works of this kind wonderful erudition, and copious references to classic texts. Consult, among others —

Antonio Nibby, *Del foro romano, della via sacra*, etc., Rome, 1819; and *Roma nell' anno* 1838, part i. vol. ii. p. 277. — Stefano Piale, *Del foro romano, sua posizione e grandezza*, Rome, 1818 (1832); *Della basilica Giulia*, 1824 (1833); *Dei tempi di Giano*, etc., 1819 (1833). — Auguste Caristie, *Plan et coupe d'une partie du forum romain.* Paris, 1829, fol. — Luigi Canina, *Descrizione storica del foro romano e sue adiacenze.* Rome, 1834. — Charles Bunsen, *Les forums de Rome restaurés et expliqués.* Rome, 1837; and *Beschreibung d. St. Rom*, vol. iii. B. — Ravioli and Montiroli, *Il foro romano.* Rome, 1852. — Emil Braun, *Das Forum* (in Philologus, suppl. ii., 1862, p. 381, *sq.*). — Effisio Tocco, *Ripristinazione del foro romano.* Rome, 1858.

The excavations of 1870–84 have called forth a number of works. Leaving aside those that refer to single discoveries or to

single monuments, mention of which will be found in the proper
place, the few of a general character are —

Heinrich Jordan, *Capitol, Forum, und Sacra Via*, Berlin, Weidmann, 1881;
Die überreste des Forum (in Topographie, vol. i², p. 154); and *Sylloge inscript.
fori romani* (in Ephem. epigraph., vol. iii., 1876, p. 237). — Edoardo Brizio,
Relazione . . . sulle scoperte archeologiche della città . . . di Roma, 1873. —
Ferdinand Dutert, *Le forum romain et les forums de Jules César*, etc. Paris,
1876. — John H. Parker, *The Roman Forum* (in Archæology of Rome, vol. ii.
1876). — Francis M. Nichols, *The Roman Forum.* London, 1877. — Orazio
Marucchi, *Descrizione del foro romano e guida per la visita dei suoi monumenti.*
Rome, 1883. French edition. — John H. Middleton, *The Forum Romanum,
and its Adjacent Buildings* (in Remains of Ancient Rome, vol. i. chap. vi. p.
231). London, 1892. — Levy and Luckenbach, *Forum romanum.* Munich, 1895.

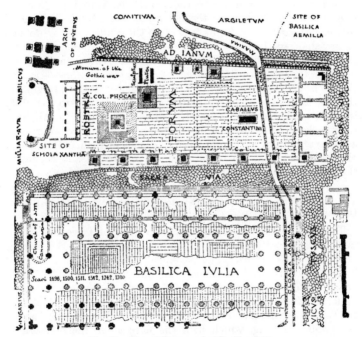

Fig. 93. — Map of Forum and of Basilica Julia.

XXII. AREA OF THE FORUM. — The Forum is not rectangular,
as prescribed by Vitruvius (v. 1), but in the form of a trapezoid.
Before the construction of the Temple of Cæsar, on the site where
his body had been cremated, it was 160 metres long. After the

temple was built, its area was severed from that of the Forum, and the Sacra Via made to pass between them; by which measure the Forum was reduced to a length of 102 metres. The breadth varies from a maximum of 45 metres on the west side to a minimum of 36 metres at the east end.[1] It is surrounded by streets on three sides : by the Street ad Janum on the north, by the Sacra Via on the east and south, while the Area Concordiæ and the winding Clivus Capitolinus constitute its western boundary line.

The Sacra Via has been already described in the opening section of this Book. The Street ad Janum took its name from the temple of that god which stood at the entrance to the Via Argiletana, between the Senate-house and the Basilica Fulvia-Æmilia. It extended from the Comitium to the Temple of Antoninus, limiting the area of the Forum on the north side. At the beginning of the seventh century of Rome it became the rendezvous of brokers, money-changers, bankers, and usurers, who could find shelter from rain or sun under the porticoes of the basilica. Cicero and Horace describe the centre of the street — ad Janum medium — as the Bourse or Exchange of ancient Rome. Modern writers, forgetting that the adjectives " summus, medius, imus," applied to a slightly inclined road, mean its highest, middle, and lowest point, have imagined the existence on this road of three " jani " or four-faced archways, and have even produced drawings of them. Bentley on Horace (Epist., i. 1, 54) is the first to have found and suggested the true meaning of those adjectives.

LITERATURE. — F. M. Nichols, *The Roman Forum*, p. 240. — H. Jordan, *Una rettificazione alla pianta del foro* (in Bull. Inst., 1881, p. 103). — Rodolfo Lanciana, *La cloaca maxima* (in Bull. com., 1890, p. 98).

The Forum is paved negligently with slabs of travertine which must date from the time of Diocletian, who repaired the ravages of the fire of Carinus. The pavement was edged with a raised border also of travertine, which, being only 0.72 metre wide, cannot be called sidewalk, *semita*, but simply *margo*, or border. Its most noticeable feature consists of a series of square holes, which line the edge (letter A) and look like the sockets in front of our palaces and public buildings which held the fiaccole on the occasion of festivities. Such holes are also to be found at Pompeii in the street which runs along the so-called " Scuola al foro." Schoene thinks they may have served to hold a wooden fence, to direct and contain

[1] According to Varro the Forum originally measured *septem jugera* = 17,539.20 square metres ; its actual surface does not exceed 4131 square metres.

the crowd in election days ; but such cannot have been their purpose in Rome, because they are to be found also in front of the
temples of Julius Cæsar and of Castor and Pollux. It is more

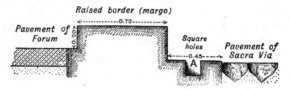

Fig. 94. — The Margo of the Forum.

probable that the poles around our Forum and its neighboring
temples were used to support awnings during the summer months.
The situation of the Forum is such that, while it is exposed to the
full violence of the rays of the sun, the Capitoline and the Quirinal
shelter it from the north, and shut off refreshing breezes. In
summer the temperature is often above 100° in the shade. To
save the citizens from sunstroke, and to make it possible for judges
and advocates to discuss their cases, and for orators to address
their audience, the *velaria* were brought into use towards the end
of the Republican period. The merit of the invention seems to
belong to Julius Cæsar, who "totum forum romanum intexit,
viamque sacram." Marcellus, the nephew of Augustus, while ædile
in 23 B. C., "velis forum inumbravit, ut salubrius litigantes con-
sisterent." [1] The same thing occurred in A. D. 39, as related by
Dion Cassius (lix. 23). At all events, we must not picture the
Forum to ourselves as being always a grave and solemn place, only
fit for legal discussions, for criminal prosecutions, popular indigna-
tion meetings, and so forth. The Forum could be also a gay and
festive place. Religious ceremonies and pageants occasionally took
place in it; sacrifices were offered on temporary altars; statues of
gods moved round in processions among the smoke of incense and
the singing of hymns; military reviews, hunting-scenes, gladiatorial
fights, and games of every description were scenes in the drama of
this great stage. Thousands of citizens would sometimes sit down
in it at political or funeral banquets. Works of art and curiosities
were also exhibited in the Forum. L. Hostilius Mancinus, for
instance, the first Roman who entered Carthage, had a grand
panorama of the siege and capture of the Punic capital set up here,
while he would describe *viva voce* to the crowd the details of the

[1] Pliny, *Hist. Nat.*, xv. 20 ; xix. 6.

assault. Famous pictures and bronze or marble statues brought over from Greece were also shown to the multitudes; and such wonders of nature as the serpent fifty cubits long, described by Suetonius (Aug., 43). On the occasion of triumphs or processions, private citizens would lend their artistic treasures and draperies and carpets for the decoration of the Sacra Via. At night the Forum was brilliantly illuminated.

LITERATURE. — Thédenat, in Daremberg and Saglio's *Dictionnaire*, p. 1280. — F. M. Nichols, *The Roman Forum*, pp. 85–93.

The area of the Forum was encumbered with monuments of various kinds. Leaving aside those of early Republican times, which disappeared under the Empire (the *columna Mœnia*, the *pila Horatia*, the *Venus Cluacina*, etc.), I shall only mention the few the remains of which have been or can still be traced in our days.

XXIII. COLUMNA ROSTRATA, or Columna Duilia, a marble pillar ornamented with beaks of war-ships, erected in memory of the naval victory gained by C. Duilius over the Carthaginians in 260 B. C. A fragment of its inscription was discovered in July, 1565, between the Arch of Severus and the Column of Phocas, and removed to the vestibule of the Palazzo dei Conservatori, where it is to be seen at the foot of the stairs, under a more or less fanciful model of the column. The inscription, although dating from the time of Claudius, is not a copy of the original one. It is prolix, slightly incorrect, and seems to have been made up by a grammarian from passages of early annalists. (See Corpus Inscr., vol. i. pp. 37–40.)

XXIV. THE SCULPTURED PLUTEI. — Between the Column of Phocas and the Street of Janus, one of the most interesting monuments was brought to light in September, 1872. It consists of two screens or *plutei* of white marble, with bas-reliefs on either side, surmounted with a richly carved cornice. Each screen, composed of several pieces of marble (a few missing), stands on a foundation of travertine, and a plinth of marble, which is a modern and doubtful addition. The exact state in which the bas-reliefs were found in September, 1872, is shown in the following cut (Fig. 95). The inside panels represent the three animals sacrificed in the great lustral ceremony of the *suovetaurilia* — the sow, the ram, and the bull — all adorned with ribbons, and all moving in the direction of the Basilica Julia. The outer reliefs represent historical scenes, with a view of the Forum itself on the background. Their meaning has given rise to much controversy. Consult —

Wilhelm Henzen, *Rilievi di marmo scoperti nel f. r.* (in Bull. Inst., 1872, p. 273). — Edoardo Brizio, in *Annal. Inst.*, 1872, p. 309, pl. 47. — Camillo Ravioli, *Il soggetto esposto nei bassorilievi del f. r.* (in Corrispondenza scientifica, 1872, anno 25, n. 14, 15). — C. Ludovico Visconti, *Deux actes de Domitien en qualité de censeur*, etc. Rome, 1873. — F. M. Nichols, *The Roman Forum*, pp. 60–68. — J. H. Parker, *The Forum* (in Archæology of Rome, vol. ii. pl. 13). — Orazio Marucchi, *Importanza topografica dei bassorilievi del f. r.* (in Gli studi in Italia, 1880, i. p. 678); and *Bull. Inst.*, 1881, pp. 11, 33. — Heinrich Jordan, *Topographie*, i², p. 220. — Luigi Cantarelli, *Osservazioni sulla scene nei bassorilievi del f. r.* (in Bull. com., 1889, p. 99).

It seems almost certain that the scene facing the Capitol alludes to the provision made by Trajan for the education and maintenance of children of poor or deceased citizens ("pueri et puellæ alimentarii"). The Emperor is seated on a *suggestum* addressing a female figure, a personification of Italy, who carries an infant on the left arm, while another child probably stood on her right. On the opposite side of the same picture the Emperor

Fig. 95. — The Fragments of the Marble Plutei, discovered in September, 1872.

is represented addressing the crowd from the Rostra. The second bas-relief, facing the south, represents the burning of the registers in which the sums due to the Fiscus by negligent tax-payers were recorded. This act of generosity of Trajan is praised by Ausonius.

The importance, however, of these panels rests in the view of the background, which represents the scene that was in reality before the spectator, the Forum and its surroundings.

The view begins on the left with the Rostra Julia, from which the Emperor is addressing the crowd; behind him we see (*a*) the Arch of Augustus, (*b*) the Temple of Castor and Pollux, (*c*) the

Fig. 96. — One of the Marble Plutei, after Restoration.

opening of the Vicus Tuscus, (*d*) the Basilica Julia. The design
of the latter is continued on the second bas-relief facing the Capitol. Next comes (*e*) the Temple of Saturn, (*f*) a fragment of the
Tabularium (?), (*g*) the Temple of Vespasian, (*h*) the Rostra
Vetera, represented in a conventional form. The statue of Marsyas and the Ficus Ruminalis, which appear in both panels, sym-
bolize the Forum and the Comitium. (See Jordan's Marsyas auf
den Forum. Berlin, 1883.)

Opinions differ very much as to what purpose — beyond a commemorative object — these two screens served. Nichols suggests

Fig. 97. — The Rostra as represented in a Bas-relief of the Arch of Constantine.

that they "formed a sort of an avenue leading to an altar and
statue of the Emperor, in whose honor the monument may have
been erected after his deification." Middleton supposes "that they
formed a sort of gangway through which voters had to pass to
reach the ballot-boxes on the Comitium, in order to facilitate the
onward movement of the crowd of citizens in an orderly stream."
It is almost certain, however, that the plutei are not in their
original place ; so that all speculation about their scope is useless.
They must have been placed on their rough travertine socles by
Diocletian in his restoration of the Forum after the fire of Carinus.

Thédenat seems to attribute them to the Rostra Vetera (Dictionnaire, p. 1305).

XXV. Monumental Columns on the Sacra Via. — Near
and along the *margo* which limits the pavement of the Forum
on the south side stand eight square pedestals of monumental
columns, the shafts of which, varying in size and quality, are lying
close by. The first column near the southeast corner was covered
with ornaments of gilt bronze, as shown by the holes of the clamps
to which they were riveted. Other shafts are of gray or red granite, and one is of white marble. Professor Jordan has been able to
date the erection of these pillars by means of brick-stamps which
can still be seen at the foot of the first and third pedestals:
they belong to the age of Constantine. Five pillars of this kind
are represented in a bas-relief of the triumphal arch of that Emperor, the background of which is almost as interesting for the
topography of the Forum as that of the plutei described above.
The first building on the left is the Basilica Julia; the second is
the Arch of Tiberius (?); then come five monumental columns,
supporting statues, and last of all the Arch of Severus. The
Emperor is delivering a speech from the Rostra Vetera. If these
columns were raised on their pedestals the picturesqueness and
interest of the Forum would be greatly enhanced.

LITERATURE. — Carlo Fea, *Varietà di Notizie*, p. 71. — Francesco Ficoroni,
Memorie, n. 80. — Heinrich Jordan, *Bull. Inst.*, 1881, p. 106; *Ann. Inst.*, 1883,
p. 49; and *Ephemeris epigraphica*, p. 259. — Otto Richter, *Die römische Rednerbühne* (in Jahrbuch, 1889, pp. 8–14).

XXVI. The Caballus Constantini (Equestrian Statue of
Constantine). — In 1873 an official announcement was given to
the archæological world of the discovery of the "pedestal of
Domitian's equestrian statue" in the middle of the Forum. (See
Pietro Rosa, Relazione, p. 71.) They did not hesitate to identify
as a famous work of art of the golden age a rough and ugly bit of
masonry, resting, without foundations, on the travertine pavement
of the time of Diocletian; they did not recollect that the equestrian statue cannot have survived the "memoriæ damnatio" of
Domitian; that it must have perished the very day of his death;
and that, if it had not been described accidentally by a contemporary poet (Statius, Silv., 1), no one would ever have had a suspicion of its existence. The pedestal belongs very likely to the
Caballus Constantini, mention of which occurs in documents of
the seventh and eighth centuries. The equestrian group was

raised in 334, and its commemorative inscription is given by the
" Corpus," vol. vi. n. 1141.

References. — Carlo Fea, in Winckelmann's *Storia dell' arte*, vol. iii. p.
410. — Charles Bunsen, *Forum*, p. 15. — Heinrich Jordan, *Ephem. epigr.*, vol.
iii. p. 256. — Gio. Battista de Rossi, *Inscript. christ.*, vol. ii. 5. — Rodolfo Lanciani, *Itinerar. Einsiedlen*, p. 20.

XXVII. Unknown Building on the east side, opposite the
Temple of Julius. — Three buildings of the late Empire, not later
at all events than the end of the sixth century, were rashly destroyed in 1872–74, under the pretext that they did not belong to
the classic age. Jordan has described them carefully, p. 252 of
vol. iii. of the " Ephemeris epigraphica," and considers their disappearance as a "maximum detrimentum" to the study of the
Forum. The first stood near the marble plutei, the second near
the Column of Phocas, the third extended over the whole east side
of the Forum, from the Vicus Tuscus to the Street ad Janum, and
consisted of five large rooms, handsomely decorated with marble
cornices, pieces of which are still left *in situ*. Rather than shops
I would consider them used for a public office like that of the
" scribæ ædilium curulium " at the opposite end of the Forum.
An inscription discovered here on May 13, 1872, engraved on an
architrave 3.44 metres long, relates how Lucius Valerius Septimius Bassus, prefect of the city between 379 and 383, had dedicated the structure to which the architrave belongs, in honor of
Gratianus, Valentinian, and Theodosius. Perhaps this is the date
of the building destroyed by Rosa.

XXVIII. Monuments of the Gothic and Gildonic Wars.
— On the Street ad Janum, opposite the Senate-house, stands an
historical monument, relating to the Gothic wars of the beginning
of the fifth century. The inscription, fifteen lines long, praises
the fidelity and valor shown by the army of Arcadius, Honorius,
and Theodosius, in the mighty struggle which ended with the
defeat of Radagaisus in 405. The victory is attributed to Stilicho,
the Roman leader : " confectum gothicum bellum . . . consiliis
et fortitudine magistri utriusque militiæ Flavii Stilichonis." The
memorial set up by decree of the S. P. Q. R. under the care of
Pisidius Romulus, prefect of the city in 405, is the meanest and
poorest in the whole Forum, and shows how low Roman pride,
taste, and finance had fallen in those days. It is made of two
blocks — one of travertine, which forms the base, and one of

marble above it. This last had been already used as a pedestal to an equestrian statue of bronze; the statue was knocked off, the pedestal set negligently upright on one of the ends, its cracks readjusted with iron clamps, and the new inscription written across the old one after the latter had been obliterated with care.

The details of the struggles which mark this period of the agony of the Western Empire are copiously described by the monuments found or existing in this corner of the Forum. In August, 1539, two pedestals were found between the Arch of Severus and the church of SS. Sergio e Bacco: one recording the African exploits of Stilicho, the other set up by the same Pisidius Romulus " pro singulari eius (Stilichonis) amore atque providentia." The first was removed to the Palazzo Capranica alla Valle, the second to the Villa Medici. In 1549–65, a few feet from the monument of 405, Cardinal Farnese found the base of an equestrian group raised to Arcadius and Honorius, in commemoration of their victory over Count Gildo, the African rebel of 398. The inscribed slabs of this monument are still lying abandoned in disorder in this vicinity. In the same year 405 a triumphal arch was raised to the three Emperors, " because they had wiped off from the face of the earth the nation of the Goths." Four years later Rome was stormed by the very barbarians whom they boasted to have annihilated.

LITERATURE. — Christian Huelsen, *Il monumento della guerra gildonica sul foro Romano*, in Mittheil., 1895, p. 52. — *Notizie degli Scavi,* 1880, p. 53. — Heinrich Jordan, *Silloge inscr. fori romani,* n. 111, 111a, 122. — *Corpus Inscript.,* vol. vi. n. 1187, 1730, 1731.

XXIX. THE COLUMN OF PHOCAS. — The pedestal of this column, to which the most conflicting names had been given by early topographers, was discovered in the morning of February 23, 1813, with the inscription which tells the tale of its erection. According to this document, the pillar was set up in honor of Phocas by Zmaragdus, exarch of Italy, " pro innumerabilibus pietatis eius beneficiis, et pro quiete procurata Italiæ," and dedicated on August 1, 608. It is the last monument erected in the Forum yet free from the ruins which were to bury and conceal it so soon after : it marks the close of the ancient period and the beginning of the Middle Ages. The brick pedestal is exactly like the eight others which line the Sacra Via; it was concealed from view by a flight of nine marble steps, each 0.36 of a metre high. The inscription is engraved on the marble base which stands at the top of the steps. The column is fourteen metres high, with a diameter of 1.39 metres, and leans considerably towards the southeast. Its style (and that of its capital) is certainly better than

Fig. 98. — The Column of Phocas — The Marble Plutei in the Foreground.

that prevailing in the seventh century; therefore, either the column has been removed bodily from a classic edifice, or else Zmaragdus dedicated to Phocas a monument which, up to his time, had borne another name. I believe that the words of the inscription, "Zmaragdus has placed a gilt statue of his Emperor on the top of this sublime column," must be understood in the latter sense.

REFERENCES. — *Diario di Roma*, 5 marzo, 1817 ; 4 agosto, 1818. — F. Aurelio Visconti, *Lettera sopra la colonna di Foca*. Rome, de Romanis, 1813. — Carlo Fea, *Osservaz. sull' anfiteatro Flavio*, p. 63, n. 3. — *Iscrizioni di monumenti pubblici*. Rome, Contedini, 1813, n. 2. — *Corpus Inscr.*, vol. vi. n. 1200.

BUILDINGS ON THE NORTH SIDE OF THE FORUM.

XXX. Curia Hostilia — Curia Julia — Senatus (XXIII in plan). — The Senate-house was, politically speaking, the most important building in the Roman world. The place where it stands was occupied at an early age by a small wood, by a cave overgrown with ivy, and by a spring, at which Tarpeia was drawing water when she saw Tatius for the first time. The first senators met here, dressed in sheepskins, in a square hut covered by a thatched roof. Tullus Hostilius gave the *patres conscripti* a better seat, an oblong hall, built of stone on the northeast side of the Comitium, raised on a platform above the reach of floods, and accessible by a flight of steps, down which the body of Servius was hurled by Tarquinius. Inside, it contained several rows of benches, the Speaker's chair, a small apartment for the archives, and a vestibule. The outside wall on the Argiletum was decorated in 264 B. C. with a picture representing the victory of M. Valerius Messalla over King Hieron of Syracuse. Hence the name *ad tabulam Valeriam* popularly given to the place. We must remember also that, the Senate being forbidden to vote a measure unless assembled in a temple, their hall was consecrated. Cicero calls it sometimes a *templum inauguratum*, sometimes *templum publici concilii*. So extreme was the frugality and self-denial of Republican senators that they had never allowed their hall to be warmed in winter. On January 6, 62 B. C., Cicero wrote to his brother that the Speaker Appius had summoned the senators to an important meeting, when it grew so cold that he was obliged to dismiss the assembly, and expose its members to the raillery of the populace. Such was the Curia Hostilia.

Sulla repaired and perhaps enlarged it in 80 B. C. Twenty-eight years later, it was burned down by the partisans of Clodius. The revolutionary instincts of the mob having been aroused by fiery speeches from the Rostra, a certain Sextus Clodius, a scribe, broke into the Curia at the head of a band of roughs carrying the body of the murdered anarchist, and, having made a pyre of the benches, tables, books, and shelves, set the building ablaze and destroyed it with the adjoining Basilica Porcia.

The task of reërecting it in a more splendid form was given by the Senate to Faustus, son of Sulla, with the promise that it should be called, from both of them, Curia Cornelia. The works were interrupted a few years later, and Lepidus the triumvir was asked to substitute for the Curia a temple of Felicitas. In 44 B. C., however, Julius Cæsar, who hated to see the name of the Cornelii attached to the Senate-house, obtained for himself the commission

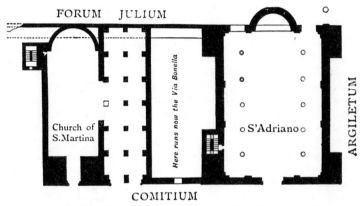

Fig. 99. — Plan of the Senate-House, rebuilt by Diocletian.

to rebuild it under the name of Curia Julia. The works interrupted by the death of the dictator, on March 15, 44, were continued by the triumvirs, and completed by Augustus. The solemn dedication took place in 725 (29 A. D.), a year famous for the three triumphs celebrated by the founder of the Empire, and for the closing of the Temple of Janus *pace terra marique parta.* Augustus added to the Curia Julia a *chalcidicum* (called in later times *Atrium Minervœ*), a court surrounded by a colonnade ; placed in the hall two famous pictures signed by Nicias and Philochares, the statue of Victory from Tarentum, and an altar before it, which was inaugurated on August 28 of the same year, 29. It is needless to state that the Curia Julia occupied absolutely the same consecrated space, the same *templum inauguratum* as the old Curia Hostilia, and that the new inauguration mentioned by Gellius (xiv. 7) refers not to the hall itself, but to the additions made to it.

The Curia Julia suffered great damage from the fire of Nero, and was repaired by Domitian. Another fire burnt it to the ground under Carinus, and Diocletian reconstructed it under the name of *Senatus.* I have found in the Uffizi at Florence and in the Kunstgewerbe Museum at Berlin, a precious set of drawings by Antonio da Sangallo, Baldassarre, Sallustio Peruzzi, and others, in which Diocletian's work is illustrated in every architectural and decorative detail.

LITERATURE. — Rodolfo Lanciani, *L' aula e gli uffici del Senato romano,* Rome, Salviucci, 1883 (Atti Lincei, vol. xi. 28 genn. 1883) ; and *Ancient Rome,* p. 77. — Thédenat, in Daremberg and Saglio's *Dictionnaire,* p. 1293.

The Senate-house formed a rectangle 51.28 metres long and 27.54 metres wide, with the front on the Comitium, and the back resting against the inclosure wall of the Forum Julium, a huge construction of tufa and travertine (see Fig. 99).

On the right side it touched the Argiletum, viz., the open space preceding the Forum Transitorium, in the middle of which stood the Temple of Janus; on the left it bordered on a small square ornamented with a fountain, composed of a river god (the *Marforio* of the Capitoline Museum) from whose urn the water fell into a tazza of granite (now in front of the Quirinal palace). The hall itself was 25.20 metres long, 17.61 metres wide. Its walls were covered with marble incrustations like those of SS. Cosma e

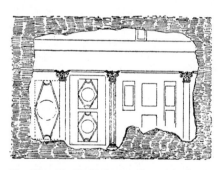

Fig. 100. — The Marble Incrustations of the Senate Hall.

Damiano, of the Hierusalem (S. Croce), of the Basilica of Junius Bassus, etc., and they are described by A. da Sangallo and Etienne du Perac. Cardinal du Bellay destroyed them about 1550. I have discovered a sketch of three panels in a drawing formerly in the Destailleur collection, now in the Kunstgewerbe at Berlin (portfolio f. A. 376, pl. 35). The quality of the marbles is carefully noted : " serpentin, porfide, marmo," etc., and also the position of the panels : " deli dui bande de la nice " on either side of the apse.

The hall was covered by a vaulted ceiling, with heavily gilt lacunaria. On the outside, the building appeared rather shabby: plain brick walls were plastered over in imitation of marble. The cornice was more elaborate, as shown by the following sketch of the Anonymus of Destailleur.

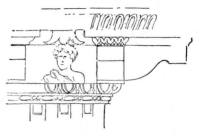

The bas-reliefs of the pediment represented, according to Ligorio (Bodl., p. 7), " certi mostri marini chiamati Tritoni quali suonavano certe bucine. . . . "

Traces of the stucco work can still be seen in the up-

Fig. 101. — Details of Cornice of the Senate Hall.

per part of the façade. The Senate-house was doubly christianized: the hall of assembly at the time of Pope Honorius I. (circa 630), under the invocation of S. Adriano; the offices or *secretarium amplissimi Senatus*, about the same epoch, under the invocation of S. Martina. They kept their classic form and retained their classic adornments until the beginning of the seventeenth century. Cardinal Michele Bonelli under Sixtus V. cut the building in two with his new " Via Bonella." The church of S. Adriano was modernized partly in 1589 by Cardinal Agostino Cusano, partly in 1654 by Alfonso Sotomayor; that of S. Martina by Urban VIII. and Piero da Cortona.

The bronze gates of the Curia were removed to S. Giovanni in Laterano by Alexander VII., but as the folds measured only 5.79 metres in height and 3.56 in width, while the size of the Lateran door was considerably larger, Borromini was obliged to add a band to the ancient metal work. The band is ornamented with the typical stars of the Chigi. Martinelli says that while the bronze folds were thus adapted to their new destination, several coins were discovered hidden between the inside and outside panels, one of which bore the name and the image of Domitian.

LITERATURE. — Giuseppe Bianchini, *Dissertazione sopra la Curia* (in Cod. Vat., 8113, f. 113). — Lucas Holstenius, *De origine ecclesiæ S. Hadriani* (in Fea's Miscellanea, vol. i. p. 306). — Luigi Canina, *Sugli edifici esistenti nel luogo ora occupato dalla chiesa di S. Martina.* Rome, 1830. — Theodor Mommsen, *De Comitio romano, curiis, Janique templo* (in Annal. Inst., 1844, p. 288). — Franz Reber, *Die Lage der Curia Hostilia und der Curia Julia,* 1858. — Detlefsen, *De Comitio romano* (in Annal. Inst., 1860, p. 138). — Auer, *Der Altar der Göttin Victoria in der Curia Julia zu Rom.* Vienna, 1859. — Rodolfo Lanciani, *L' aula 'e gli uffici del Senato romano.* Rome, Salviucci, 1883 (Atti Lincei,

vol. xi. 28 genn. 1883). — J. H. Middleton, *The Remains of Ancient Rome,*
vol. i. p. 239. — Christian Huelsen, *Das Comitium und seine Denkmäler* (in
Mittheil., 1893, p. 279, pl. 4) with the comments of Thédenat, in Daremberg
and Saglio's *Dictionnaire,* p. 1292, n. 7.

XXXI. THE COMITIUM (XXIV in plan). — The space between
the Rostra Vetera and the front of the Senate-house, neatly paved
with slabs of travertine, marks the site of the Comitium.   It must
be remembered that the street passing through the Arch of Septimius Severus, by which the Rostra and the Forum are separated
from the Comitium, is an addition of the third century after Christ.
Before it, the two places were separated only by a few steps.   In
the early days of Rome the Comitium was the centre of civil and
political business, while the Forum was simply used as a market-
place ; but with the increase of the population and with the spread
of democracy the centre was shifted to the Forum, and the Comitium lost forever its importance.   Its main ornaments were the
statue of Atta Navius, the augur who cut the whetstone with the
razor, and the puteal under which whetstone and razor had been
buried; and the *ficus Navia,* a fig-tree which the popular fancy
believed to have been transplanted here from the banks of the
Tiber by the same miracle-working augur.   It was considered to
represent the *ficus ruminalis* which had sheltered with its shade
the infant twins sucking the she wolf ; and this event was recorded
by a bronze group not unlike the one now preserved in the Palazzo
dei Conservatori.   (Compare Helbig's Guide to the Collection of
Antiquities in Rome, vol. i. p. 459, n. 618.)   There were also the
statues of Porsena, of Horatius Cocles, of Hermodoros from Ephesus, who had helped the decemvirs in the codification of the laws,
of Pythagoras, Alcibiades, and others.   Concerning the last mentioned, Ennio Quirino Visconti observes that the noble statue of
the Museo Pio Clementino, known as the " Gladiatore " or the
" Atleta Mattei " (No. 611 sala della Biga), is nothing else than a
marble copy of the bronze figure of Alcibiades in the Comitium,
and corroborates his statement by comparing the features of the
head with those of bust No. 510 in the Hall of the Muses, inscribed
with the name of the Greek hero.   Emil Braun (Ruins and Museums, p. 282, n. 166) says : " It is not impossible that this statue,
originally in the Villa Mattei, is a repetition of that placed upon
the Comitium, although positive proofs are wanting."   Wolfgang
Helbig (Guide, etc., vol. i. pp. 192 and 235) denies any connection
between the marble of the Vatican and the bronze of the Comitium.
The only monuments visible in the narrow ledge of the Comi-

tium yet excavated are two marble pedestals of statues dedicated, one to Flavius Julius Constantius (350–361), by Memmius Vitrasius Orfitus, prefect of the city in 353–354; the other to Arcadius (395–408), by Ceionius Rufius Albinus, prefect in 398. These and other pedestals lined the border of the Comitium towards the Argiletum, the pavement of which has been excavated for a length of ten or fifteen metres only.

REFERENCES. — Brecher, *Die Lage des Comitium*, etc. Berlin, 1870. — H. Dernburg, *Uber die Lage des Comitium und des prätorischen Tribunals* (in Bull. Inst., 1863, p. 38). — Theodor Mommsen, *De Comitio romano*, etc. (in Annal. Instit., vol. xvi., 1844, p. 288). — Franz Reber, *Die Lage der Curia*. 1858. — Detlefsen, *De Comitio romano* (in Ann. Inst., vol. xxxii., 1860, p. 138, pl. D). — Rodolfo Lanciani, *Atti Lincei*, vol. xi. 28 genn. 1883. — Thomas Dyer, *Roma* (in Dictionary of Greek and Roman Geography, vol. ii. p. 775). — Orazio Marucchi, *Descript. du forum romain*, p. 51. — Christian Huelsen (in *Mittheilungen*, vol. viii., 1893, p. 279).

The other two buildings on the north side of the Forum were the Temple of Janus (XXIV A) and the Basilica Æmilia (XXV). Both still lie buried under the modern embankment; and as it is not my scope to write a manual on Roman topography, but simply to guide the student and the traveler in their visit to monuments and ruins which have been made accessible by modern excavations, I shall proceed at once to describe the

BUILDINGS ON THE EAST SIDE OF THE FORUM.

XXXII. ÆDES DIVI IULII (Temple of Julius Cæsar) (XXVI in plan). — The spot where the body of Cæsar had been cremated on March 17, 44, was consecrated by the erection of an altar and of a column of Numidian marble, on which the words *parenti patriæ* were inscribed. The illicit worship was stopped by Antonius; C. Amatius, the leader of the populace, was put to death, and many of his partisans were crucified, if slaves; or, if citizens, hurled from the Tarpeian rock. In 42 B. C., however, the triumvirs decided to erect a temple on the historical spot; Augustus began its construction in 33, and dedicated it on August 18 of the memorable year 725 (29 A. D.). The programme of the ceremony included, among other performances, the Trojan games, gladiatorial and theatrical shows, and an exhibition of wild beasts upon which the Romans had never set eyes before. The temple was enriched with treasures conquered in the Egyptian campaign and with pictures representing the Dioscuri, the Victory, and the Venus Anadyomene. This last, a masterpiece of Apelles, having been injured by damp and age, was removed from the temple by Nero, who substituted in its place another by Dorotheos.

The temple, being in the lowest portion of the Forum and of the Sacra Via, was raised on a high platform to protect it from the inundations of the Tiber. This platform of concrete was strengthened by perimetral and cross-walls made of blocks of tufa and travertine, which were stolen away in the excavations of 1543, so that it is hardly possible to-day to recognize the former shape of the temple. The fragments of its entablature (one of which is lying on the platform) belong to a very late restoration. The following view of the platform was taken in 1872 at the very moment of its discovery.

The remains of a semicircular tribune on the edge of the podium pertain to the celebrated Rostra Julia, ornamented by Augustus with the beaks of the ships captured in the battle of Actium. It

Fig. 102. — The Rostra Julia and the Temple of Cæsar.

was from this tribune that the same emperor pronounced the oration on the death of his sister Octavia. Tiberius likewise spoke from it on the occasion of the funeral of Augustus. A medal struck in the year 119, representing an allocution of Hadrian, from the same rostra, proves that they continued to be used for Imperial communications for a long time.

References. — Babelon, *Monn. de la république*, ii. p. 59, n. 138. — Cohen, *Monn. impér.*, Hadrian, n. 416-419. — Edoardo Brizio, in Rosa's *Relazione sulle scoperte archeologiche*, etc., Rome, 1873, p. 59 ; and *Bullett. Instit.*, 1872, pp. 225, 237. — Heinrich Jordan, *Der Tempel des d. Julius* (in Hermes, ix. p. 342). — Otto Richter, *Die Augustbauten auf dem Forum* (in Jahrbuch Arch. Instit., 1889, p. 140 ; and Mittheilungen of the same Institute, 1888, p. 99).

XXXIII. Triumphal Arch of Augustus (XXVII in plan). — In the same year (725) in which the dedication of the Temple of Cæsar and of the Curia Julia took place, Augustus celebrated three triumphs for his victories in Dalmatia, in Egypt, and at Actium, and the Senate offered him a triumphal arch in the Forum. The same honor was granted to him in 18 b. c. for the recovery of the flags and of the prisoners lost by Licinius Crassus in the Parthian war. Otto Richter discovered the foundations of the arch of 725 in 1888, in the narrow space which separates the Temple of Cæsar from that of the Castores. I myself proved, as far back as 1882, that this arch had been found and destroyed by the workmen of the fabbrica di S. Pietro between 1540 and 1546 exactly in that place, and that the inscription in "Corpus," vol. vii. n. 872, belonged to it. The arch had three openings like the one of Severus.

Literature. — Rodolfo Lanciani, *Notizie degli Scavi*, April, 1882. — Otto Richter, *Mittheil.*, 1888, p. 99; and *Jahrbuch*, 1889, pp. 153-157. — F. Nichols, *The Roman Forum*, p. 140 ; *Bull. com.*, 1888, p. 117. — Theodor Mommsen, *Res gestæ*, 9. — Christian Huelsen, Mittheil., 1889, p. 244.

XXXIV. Ædes Castorum (Temple of Castor and Pollux) (XXVIII in plan). — This was dedicated by A. Postumius on January 27, 482 b. c., on the spot, near the pool of Juturna, where the Dioscuri had appeared in 496 to announce the victory of Lake Regillus. It was rebuilt in 119 by L. Metellus Dalmaticus with the prize money of the Dalmatian war, and ornamented with statues and pictures, among which was the portrait of Flora the courtesan. Al-

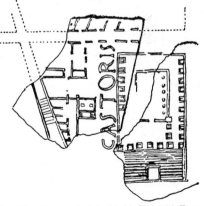

Fig. 103. — Fragment of the Marble Plan with Temple of Castores.

though named officially from both the Dioscuri, it went usually by that of Castor alone, as shown, among other documents, by the fragment of the marble plan discovered in 1882 (Fig. 103).

Bibulus, whose name was never pronounced with that of Cæsar, his more famed colleague in the ædileship, used to say that he shared the same fate as Pollux. It is interesting to follow the story of the extortions of Verres in connection with this temple, as related by Cicero, because it throws much light on the system adopted by the Romans to keep their buildings in repair. The censors had entered into a contract with P. Junius, to take charge of the temple and of its contents for a fixed yearly sum of money. Junius died leaving a son, a minor, in whose name the contract was transferred to a L. Rabonius. Verres, who, as prætor urbanus, had special cognizance of repairs to public buildings, thinking it intolerable that out of so great a temple and so large a contract he should not obtain some plunder, summoned Rabonius before him to declare what could be required from his ward that he had not fulfilled. The answer was that no difficulty whatever had arisen from the contract and that the temple was in perfect repair. Verres goes himself to inspect the building. " The only thing you can do here," suggests one of his accomplices, " is to require the columns to be made perpendicular." In Junius' contract, though the number of columns was specified, not a word was said about the perpendicular; yet, overpowered by Verres, L. Rabonius agrees to do the work at 560,000 sesterces, the sum to be taken out of the minor's estate, and to find its way, for the greater part, into the prætor's hands. The work done, under these circumstances, is thus described by Cicero : " Those columns which you see freshly whitened have been taken down by machinery and erected again with the same stones. Nay, some of them have not been touched at all. There is one from which the old plastering only has been removed, and new stucco applied." We gather from the words of Cicero that the columns of the temple of Metellus were of stone covered with fine stucco, like those of the temples of Fortuna Virilis, of Hercules Magnus Custos, and of Cybele on the Palatine.

The Temple of Castor, with its lofty substructures and commanding situation, was one of the most conspicuous objects of the Forum, and became in turbulent times a rallying-point of great political importance. Popular meetings were often held in front of it, when its pronaos served the purpose of the Rostra. In 88 B. C. Sulla and Q. Pompeius Rufus, his colleague in the consulship, were attacked here by the partisans of Marius. The contest between Cato and Metellus, respecting the recall of Pompeius from Asia, also took place on the terrace before the temple. In 58 B. C., during the troubled consulate of Piso, when Cicero's banishment was discussed, the temple fell into the hands of the partisans of Clodius; its steps were torn up and used as missiles, and the building became, in the words of Cicero, a citadel in the hands of his political enemies.

The present ruins, considered to be a gem of art, date from the reconstruction of Tiberius and Drusus, 7 B. C. Caligula opened a communication between the cella and his palace, pretending he would make the sons of Jupiter and Leda his private doorkeepers. He also used to place himself unobserved between the statues of the divine twins, so as to get a share in the honors paid to them. Claudius restored the temple to its former state.

Two annual celebrations were connected with it, — one on January 27, the anniversary day of the dedication; another on July 15, in memory of the battle of Lake Regillus. The Roman knights, five thousand strong, waving olive branches, clad in purple garments, and wearing the decorations gained on the battle-field, mustered at the Temple of Mars outside the walls, and, after marching through the city, passed in front of the Temple of the Dioscuri, presenting a sight worthy, as Dionysius says, of Rome's Imperial greatness.

No remains of a classic edifice have been studied, sketched, admired by artists as have the three standing columns of this temple. Baldassarre Peruzzi calls them *la più bella e meglio lavorata opera di Roma.* The temple must have fallen at a very early period, because the lane between S. M. Liberatrice and S. M. della Grazie has been called *via trium columnarum* at least since the end of the fourteenth century. The first excavations of which we have positive knowledge date from the end of the quattrocento. They are described by Pomponio Leto and Francesco Albertino. The second date from 1546–49, when, according to Ligorio, two pieces of the entablature were discovered, one of which served Lorenzetto for his Jonah in the Chigi chapel at S. M. del Popolo; the other, Michelangelo for the pedestal of the equestrian statue of M. Aurelius. Ligorio, as usual, tells a falsehood, because the Jonah was finished in the lifetime of Raphael († 1520). In 1773 part of the walls of the cella was destroyed, the marble coating removed, and even some of the foundation walls demolished for the sake of the blocks of stone of which they were built. In consequence of this last spoliation, the size of the substructures is reduced by half, that is to say, it is reduced to only the central mass of concrete; but the impressions left against this mass by the blocks of stone of which the outside wall was built enable us to get an idea of the original size. (See Fig. 104.)

Fig. 104. — The Substructure of the Temple of Castores.

Other excavations took place in 1799, 1811, 1816, and 1818. The temple was finally liberated from the accumulation of modern soil in December, 1871 (on three sides only).

The temple, in common with other religious edifices, was used as a safe or repository for objects of value, which private owners were afraid of retaining at home. There was also a *ponderarium* of standard weights and measures, many of which are found in our excavations inscribed with the words EXAC*tum* AD CASTOR*es*. A fragment of the great inscription of the frieze lies at the foot of the stairs; it contains traces only of two letters, which have been completed by Professor Tomassetti: —

(*Polluci · e*)T · C(*astori*).

LITERATURE. — Maurice Albert, *Le culte de Castor et Pollux en Italie.*

Paris, 1883. — Luigi Canina, *Supplem. al Desgodets*, chap. x. pl. 33. — Antonio Nibby, *Roma nell' anno 1838*, part i. vol. ii. p. 82. — Pietro Rosa, *Relazione sulle scoperte.* Rome, 1873, p. 53. — Rodolfo Lanciani, *Bull. Inst.*, 1871, p. 11. — Giuseppe Gatti, *Annal. Inst.*, 1881, p. 181, pl. N. — Giuseppe Tomassetti, *La epigrafe del tempio dei Castori* (in Bull. com., 1890, p. 209). — Orazio Marucchi, *Guide du Forum.* Rome, 1885, p. 119. — *Notizie degli Scavi*, 1896, p. 290.

BUILDINGS ON THE SOUTH SIDE OF THE FORUM.

XXXV. Between the edifice just described and the Basilica Julia runs the Vicus Tuscus, or street of the Tuscans (XXIX in plan), which led from the Forum to the Circus Maximus. The origin of its name is variously explained by different authors, but there is no doubt that it came from a colony of Tuscans who settled in its vicinity, at the time either of Cæles Vibenna or of Porsenna. The tradition on this point seems justified by the presence of the shrine and statue of Vertumnus, at the entrance to the street, whose worship would have been imported by the Etruscans, as that of Semo Sancus had been imported on the Quirinal by the Sabine colonists, but the Etruscan origin of the god Vertumnus is more than doubtful.

The street vied with the Sacra Via in religious importance, being the route followed by the great procession of the Ludi Romani, in which the statues of the gods placed on *thensæ* (four-wheeled chariots) were carried from the Capitol to the Circus. It was also a busy trade quarter. Horace calls these tradesmen *Tusci turba impia vici*, and alludes to the street as the place to which the works of unappreciated poets were carried, to wrap up parcels of spices or perfumes.

XXXVI. Basilica Julia (XXX in plan), begun by Cæsar about 54 B. C., on the site of the Tabernæ Veteres, of the Basilica Sempronia, and of the house of Scipio the African (?), and dedicated in an unfinished state in the year 46, together with the Forum Julium and the Temple of Venus Genetrix. Augustus rebuilt and enlarged it after a fire, and opened it for public use in the year 12, under the name of his grandsons Caius and Lucius. It consists of a nave and four aisles divided by square pilasters of travertine, once coated with marble. The fronts and sides were built of solid marble, with half columns of the Doric order, projecting out of square pilasters. The half column which stands alone and perfect on the side of the Sacra Via was reconstructed by Rosa in 1873; those on the side of the Vicus Jugarius are genuine, although in a ruined state. The Basilica was destroyed by fire under Carinus and rebuilt by Diocletian, who substituted brick pilasters and arches for the old solid structure of travertine. The mixture of the two styles and epochs is satisfactorily illustrated by the following view, taken at the southwest corner of the Basilica, by the Lacus Servilius. (Fig. 105.)

In March, 1883, a pedestal was found on the edge of the steps descending to the Sacra Via, with the inscription : GABINIVS · VET-

Fig. 105. — The Southwest Corner of the Basilica Julia.

TIVS · PROBIANVS · Vir · clarissimus · PRÆFectus · VRBi · STATVAM QVÆ · BASILICÆ · IVLIÆ · A · SE · NOVITER · REPARATÆ · ORNA- MENTO · ESSET · ADIECIT. Probianus was prefect of Rome A. D. 377, under Valens, Gratian, and Valentinian.   He restored the Basilica and enriched it with works of art and statues removed from temples which were either closed or falling into ruin.   Five pedestals bearing his name have already been found.   The origin of the first is not known, but it was first noticed in the Santa- croce Palace in the fifteenth century.   The second was discovered in 1554 near the Column of Phocas; the third in 1655 by the

Senate-house; the fourth in 1835 on the steps of the Basilica itself; the fifth, a fragment, is kept at S. Clemente. We know that three, at least, of these statues were the work of Polykletos, of Timarchos, and of Praxiteles, these celebrated names being engraved on plinths discovered within or near the Basilica.

LITERATURE. — Gio. Battista de Rossi, *Bull. com.*, 1893, p. 174. — Rodolfo Lanciani, *Bull. Inst.*, 1871, p. 245. — Heinrich Jordan, *Ephemeris epigraphica*, vol. iii. p. 277. — Eugen Petersen, *Notizie degli Scavi*, 1895, p. 495.

The question has been asked whether the Basilica was totally or partially hypæthral, and in case it was not, whether it was vaulted over or covered by a roof resting on trusses. The question was rather complicated by a discovery I made in 1878. During the inundation of that year, which brought the Tiber on a level with the marble floor of the building, I noticed that, while the northeast corner was just lapped by the still waters, the southeast was fifteen centimetres above them, the southwest forty-five centimetres, the northwest thirty-seven centimetres. The floor of the basilica, therefore, is slanting diagonally from the corner by the Lacus Servilius to that by the Temple of Castor; but this fact does not imply that the place was hypæthral, and that its pavement could be rained upon. The floors of our churches of S. Saba and of S. Maria in Aracœli are equally inclined towards the front door, perhaps to facilitate the washing of their mosaic floors. The four aisles of the Basilica Julia were covered by a vaulted ceiling, large masses of which, with stucco mouldings, were discovered in 1852, and destroyed in 1872; the nave was roofed over.

The Basilica Julia was the seat of the court of the *centumviri*, who sometimes were divided into four sections, sometimes sat all together when the case appeared to be of exceptional gravity. Pliny the younger has left an account of the aspect of the Basilica on the day of a great trial. The case was brought before the four united sections of the court. Eighty judges sat on their benches, while on either side of them stood the eminent lawyers who had to conduct the prosecution and defend the accused. The great hall could hardly contain the mass of spectators: the upper galleries were occupied by men on one side, by women on the other, all anxious to hear, which was very difficult, and to see, which was easier. Trajan presided over this court more than once.

The remains of the stairs leading to the upper galleries are yet visible on the south side, together with the shops of bankers and money-changers, known in epigraphic documents as the *nummularii de basilica Julia*. (See Fig. 106.)

Fig. 106. — General View of the Basilica Julia.

The Basilica Julia was partly christianized towards the end of the sixth century, when one half of the outer aisle on the Vicus Jugarius was dedicated to the mother of the Saviour (S. Maria de Foro; later, in Cannaparia). The remains of the church, discovered partly in 1871, partly in 1881, were not treated well, so that, of a neat edifice, with apse, nave, aisles, side and front door, traces of fresco paintings, and considerable remains of the work of Roman marmorarii of the eighth and ninth centuries, only one column is left standing *in situ*. (See Mazzanti, in Archivio storico dell' Arte, 1896, p. 164.)

In the Middle Ages and in more modern times the Basilica Julia has been used first as a rope-walk, *cannaparia*, then as a workshop for stone-cutters, and lastly as a cemetery for the hospital of la Consolazione. (See p. 242.)

The earliest accounts of excavations date from 1496, when Adriano di Corneto, the pope's collector of revenues in England, was planning the construction of his beautiful palace (now Giraud-Torlonia) in the Piazza di Scossacavalli, of which he made a present to King Henry VII. in 1505. All the travertines used by Bramante in the façade of the palace came from the Basilica Julia.

The excavations were resumed in July, 1500, by Gregorio da Bologna and Domenico da Castello, continued in 1511–12 by Giovanni de' Pierleoni, and in 1514 by Jacopo de Margani. In the time of Gregory XIII. a sitting statue of a Roman magistrate was discovered, sold to Ferrante de Torres, and removed to Sicily. Flaminio Vacca restored it to represent Julius Cæsar covering his head at the sight of the murderer Brutus!

In 1742 the portion of the Basilica crossed by the Cloaca Maxima was laid bare, with its pavement of giallo antico, a cartload of which was sold to the stone-cutter de Blasii. The rest of the pavement and many architectural pieces fell a prey to Chevalier Frédenheim in November, 1788 (to March, 1789).

Its final discovery, begun in 1848, was completed in 1872. The pavement of the aisles, of white marble, is covered with tabulæ lusoriæ, gaming-tables of every description, about which consult, among others, Becq de Fouquières' " Les jeux des anciens ; " Friedlaender's " Sittengeschichte," vol. i. p. 376; and Huelsen's " Mittheilungen," 1896, pp. 227–252.

LITERATURE. — Theodor Mommsen, *Res gestæ divi Augusti*, iv. 13, 15. — Heinrich Jordan, *Sylloge inscript. fori rom.* (in Ephemeris epigr., 1877, pp. 275–283); and *Forma urbis romæ*, pl. 3, n. 20–23. — Otto Gerhard, *Sulla basilica Giulia* (in Effemeridi letterarie, 1824). — Oberlin, *Exposé d'une découverte de*

M. le chev. Frédenheim. Strassburg, 1796. — Rodolfo Lanciani, *Bull. Inst.,* 1871, p. 6 ; and *Bull. com.,* 1891, p. 229. — C. Ludovico Visconti, *Il rapporto sulla escavazione della basilica Giulia.* Rome, 1872. — Angelo Pellegrini, *Escavazione della basilica Giulia* (in Bull. Inst., 1871, pp. 225–233). — Thédenat (in Daremberg and Saglio's *Dictionnaire,* p. 1303).

XXXVII. Vicus Jugarius (XXXI in plan), leading from the Forum Romanum to the Forum Olitorium and the Porta Carmentalis, under the cliffs of the Capitoline, known as the Saxum Carmentæ. It corresponds to some extent to the modern streets of la Consolazione and la Bufala. At the point where the Vicus Jugarius touched the Basilica Julia there was a fountain, named Lacus Servilius from the member of the Servilian family who had built it. It acquired a ghastly notoriety during the civil wars as the place where Sulla exposed the heads of the victims of his proscriptions. Agrippa ornamented it with the figure of a hydra. The site of the fountain has not yet been explored.

BUILDINGS ON THE WEST SIDE OF THE FORUM.

XXXVIII. The Rostra Vetera (XXXII in plan). — The date of the erection of this renowned platform, from which magistrates and orators addressed the people, is not well determined; it must be placed, however, between 449 B. C., when the old Volkanal is still described as the speaking platform of Appius Claudius, and 438, when the first mention of the new tribune occurs in Livy (iv. 17). In 338 C. Mænius ornamented it with the (six) beaks of the war vessels captured at Antium, from which it took the name of Rostra. It stood near the border line between the Comitium and the Forum, so that the orators could be easily heard by the patricians and the plebeians at the same time. The orators, when speaking, generally turned towards the Comitium and the Curia, until C. Gracchus or Licinius Crassus introduced the habit of facing the people assembled in the Forum. The proximity of the Rostra to the Senate-house is proved by the fact that the leaders of the mob, on the day of the funeral of Clodius, were chased from them by the flames which were consuming the Curia. These topographic references correspond exactly to the place where the remains of a platform, once ornamented with projecting bronze ornaments, and dating from the fifth century B. C., have actually been found (see Plan, p. 251). It has been the fashion among modern topographers to believe in an alleged displacement of the Rostra from one place to the other in the last years of Cæsar's dictatorship. They seem to forget that the Rostra, having been consecrated by the augurs, were, like the Curia, a *templum* in the strictest sense of the word; so they are called by Livy (viii. 14) and by Cicero (In Vatin., x. 24). As the Curia itself never changed its position, so the Rostra Vetera have never been removed from their old location, nor has the relationship between the two temples been altered or broken. The platform which we behold before us is the same venerable *suggestum* from which the warfare of centuries between aristocracy and democracy was carried on in Republican times, and from which Cicero pronounced two of his orations against Catiline. Here the heads of Antony, of Octavius, of the victims of Marius and Sulla were exposed, as well as the bodies of Sulla himself and of Clodius; and here also the laws of the twelve tables were exposed to view.

I do not pretend to say that Julius Cæsar did not interfere in some way with the old Rostra; he may have enlarged them, lined them with new beaks, and repaired in a general way the damages of the revolution of the Clodians, but he did not change their position. He set up again the statues of Sulla and Pompey, which had been removed after the battle of Pharsalus, and raised an equestrian one to Octavian, then aged only nineteen. We hear also of a magnificent bronze statue representing Hercules expiring under the tunic of Nessus.

The head and the hands of Cicero were shown to the populace from this very seat of his former triumphs. Orations on the death of Cæsar and of Augustus were also delivered from the Rostra.

LITERATURE. — F. M. Nichols, *The Roman Forum*, pp. 197–217. — Ibid., *Notizie dei Rostri*. Rome, Spithoever, 1885. — Heinrich Jordan, *Sui rostri del foro* (in Annal. Inst., 1883, p. 49; and *Monumenti dell' Inst.*, vol. xi. pl. 49). — Otto Richter, *Scavo ai rostri del foro* (in Bull. Inst., 1884, p. 113). — Ibid., *Rekonstruktion und Geschichte der römischen Rednerbühne*. Berlin, Weidmann, 1884. — Ibid., *Die römische Rednerbühne* (in Jahrbuch, 1889, p. 1).

XXXIX. Three monuments connected with the Rostra deserve notice: the *Genius Populi Romani*, the *Milliarium Aureum*, and the *Umbilicus*.

No trace exists of the first monument. It consisted of an ædicula or shrine with a golden statue of the Genius, the gift of the Emperor Aurelian, before which sacrifices were offered on October 9. The statue was still standing in its place at the end of the fourth century, when some one scratched on the pavement of the Basilica Julia the words —

GENIVS . . . . . .
POPVLI . . . . . .
ROMANI . . . . . .

which seem to make the half of a "tabula lusoria" (three words
of six letters in three lines). The small circular shrine of the
Genius (*tempietto di marmo di forma circulare*) was discovered in
1539. The pedestal of the Genius of the Roman armies had already
been found in 1480.

LITERATURE. — Theodor Mommsen, *Corpus Inscr.*, vol. i., Commentarii
diurni, October 9 ; and *Ueber der Chronograph vom Jahre* 354, p. 648. —
Ludwig Urlichs, *Codex U. R. topographicus*, pp. 10, 11. — Heinrich Jordan,
Ephem. epigr., 1876, p. 278, n. 40. — Ligorio, *Cod. Neap.*, xxxiv. p. 145.

Milliarium Aureum (the golden milestone). — A column of gilt
bronze, on the surface of which were noted the distances from the
gates of Rome to the postal stations on each of the main roads
radiating from the metropolis. It was erected by Augustus in 29
B. C., as a record of the *mensuratio totius orbis* on which he and
Agrippa had for many years been engaged. Its position was discovered in 1849–50, together with the remains of its exquisite
marble base. The principal historical interest of the Milliarium
arises from the meeting which Otho had here, A. D. 68, with the
handful of Prætorians who committed the double crime of mur-
dering Galba and of raising Otho to the Imperial throne.[1]

The *Umbilicus Romæ*, the round basement of which still exists
at the other end of the platform, near the Arch of Severus, belongs
to a much later period, probably to the age of Diocletian. It
corresponded to the ὀμφαλός of Greek cities. Ancient documents
place it close to the Temple of Concord and to the church of SS.
Sergius and Bacchus. This last named edifice is so closely connected with the topography of the west end of the Forum and of
the Clivus Capitolinus that, although its remains have long since
disappeared, it seems necessary to have it briefly described here.

XL. THE CHURCH OF SS. SERGIUS AND BACCHUS was the
only one in this classic district which did not occupy the site of an
ancient building, but stood in its own ground. The "Liber pontificalis" mentions it for the first time in 731–741 at the time of
Gregory III., who transformed into a church a small oratory
already existing in the Volkanal. Hadrian I. (772–795) enlarged

---

[1] In his work *Le Piante di Roma anteriori al secolo xvi.*, Commendatore de
Rossi has written some admirable pages on the Milliarium Aureum, and the
mensura totius orbis which it represents (ch. iv. pp. 25–34). Consult also
Luigi Canina, *Sul valore dell' antico piede romano*, Rome, 1853 ; Heinrich
Jordan, *Topographie*, vol. i[2], p. 244; and *Ann. Inst.*, 1883, p. 57; Rodolfo
Lanciani, *Bull. com.*, 1892, p. 95.

and improved the structure, and Innocent III. (1198–1216) added
the front portico facing the Rostra. The exact position of the
church appears from the following unpublished sketch by Martin
Heemskerk (Fig. 107). The three fluted Corinthian columns in
the foreground are those of the Temple of Vespasian. According
to Armellini (Chiese, p. 538) the bell-tower stood on the attic
of the Arch of Severus; but he evidently mistakes it for another
tower, having no connection with the church, which appears in du
Perac's third vignette on the opposite corner of the arch. I have
discovered in the report of the sitting of the city council of September 9, 1636, what was the end of this tower. This sitting
agreed " that the tower
on the Arch of Septimius
be pulled down, and its
materials be given to the
church of Santa Marti-
na, which is in course of
reconstruction."

Paul III. began demol-
ishing the church of SS.
Sergius and Bacchus on
the advent of Charles V.
(1536). Some of its
walls appear still in Do-
sio's twenty - first vig-
nette, dating from 1569;
the last traces of the
apse disappeared in 1812.

Between the Rostra and
the Sacra Via stood a
beautiful little building,
the so-called Schola Xan-
tha, or offices of the *scribæ librarii* (book-keepers)

Fig. 107. — The Church of SS. Sergius and Bacchus,
sketched by Heemskerk.

and *præcones* (heralds) of the Ædiles Curules. Its construction is
attributed by Henzen to C. Avillius Licinius Trosius, a contemporary of Caracalla, and by Huelsen to A. Fabius Xanthus and Be-
bryx Drusianus, who lived in the first century. These personages are all mentioned in inscriptions discovered on the spot in
1539. (See Corpus, vi. 103.) From the words of these documents,
and from the account of the excavations left by Marliano and
Ligorio, we gather that the Schola was built of solid marble, and

consisted of three rooms at least, with a portico in front facing the south; and that Fabius Xanthus and his associates had decorated it with bronze seats, a statue of the Victory, seven silver statues of the gods, etc.   The edifice and its inscriptions were destroyed and the marbles turned into new shapes.   I believe, without being able to prove it, that the Schola Xantha formed the west side of the Rostra, the office-room of the scribes being under its lofty platform.   The pedestal of the statue of Stilicho (Corpus, 1730), which stood *in rostris*, was discovered at the same time with the remains of the Schola.

LITERATURE. — Christian Huelsen, *Il sito. e le iscrizioni della Schola Xantha*, in Mittheilungen, 1888, p. 208.

XLI. THE ARCH OF TIBERIUS stood at the foot of the Clivus Capitolinus, where the Vicus Jugarius diverges from the Sacra Via, between the northwest corner of the Basilica Julia and the Milliarium.   It was erected in 769 (16 A. D.) in memory of the recovery by Germanicus of the eagles and flags which had been lost with the legions of Varus in the battle of Teutoburg.

The name of Germanicus, so dear to the Romans, must have saved the arch from destruction, after the death and the *memoriæ damnatio* of Tiberius.   According to Montiroli, many fragments were discovered in 1848, with one or more pieces of the inscription, in which the Elbe and the Rhine were alluded to, and the recovery of the flags was mentioned.   These pieces now lie scattered all over the Forum.

LITERATURE. — Olaus Kellermann, *Bull. Inst.*, 1835, p. 36. — Giovanni Montiroli, *Il foro romano*.   Rome, 1852. — Theodor Mommsen, *Res gestæ divi Augusti*, ed. 1883, p. 127. — Heinrich Jordan, *Ephemeris epigr.*, 1887, p. 262.

XLII. THE ARCH OF SEPTIMIUS SEVERUS (XXXIII in plan) was dedicated to him and to his sons Caracalla and Geta, A. D. 203, in recognition of the benefits they had conferred on the commonwealth by reforming the administration and extending the boundaries of the Empire.   After the murder of Geta, A. D. 212, his name was suppressed in the inscriptions on either face of the attic; but the holes left in the marble by the clamps of the original bronze letters give us the means of reconstructing the original text; it contained the words (lin. 3) *et* (lin. 4) *Getæ nobilissimo cæsari*, which were substituted by the acclamation *optimis fortissimisque principibus*, addressed to Severus and Caracalla alone.

The arch has three passages connected by a transverse one. There are four columns of the composite order on each front, on the pedestals of which are carved groups of prisoners of war. (See Fig. 108.) On the spandrils of the side archways are figures of River Gods, on those of the middle passage Victories with trophies. The panels above the side arches are covered with bas-reliefs illustrating the campaigns of Severus in the East. The small door on the south side leads to a set of rooms in the attic, some of which have no light.

The arch was erected on the edge of the platform (*Volkanal.— area Concordiæ*), which, being six or seven feet higher than the level of the Forum and of the Comitium, was accessible only by means of steps. The roughly paved road going through the cen-

Fig. 108. — Pedestals of Columns, Arch of Severus.

tral arch dates from the fall of the Empire. Among the materials of which it was built, Fea discovered in 1803 a pedestal of an Imperial statue and pieces of a monumental column. No part of the Forum has been more frequently and more successfully excavated than the neighborhood of this arch. On June 22, 1480, the pedestal of the Genius of Roman armies was found *apud arcum.* In August, 1539, the pedestals of two statues of Stilicho were discovered; in 1547–49 many pedestals were unearthed commemorating the peace restored to the world by the Flavian Emperors, — the victory of the Emperor Julius Constantius over Magnentius, A. D. 353, the feats of Flavius Valerius Constantius Cæsar, etc.; and in 1549 the pedestals of the equestrian statues of Arcadius and Honorius. In 1774, another pedestal of a statue of Diocletian was found; and in 1803 another, dedicated, A. D. 357, to Julius Constantius by Orfitus, prefect of the city, the latter being probably in commemoration of the raising of the great obelisk of the Circus Maximus (now in the Lateran). These historical documents are marked Nos. 196–200, 234, 1119, 1132, 1158, 1161, 1162, 1174, 1187, 1203, 1204, 1205, 1730, 1731, in vol. vi. of the "Corpus Inscriptionum Latinarum."

Fig. 109. — A Fruiterer's Shop under the Arch of Severus.

Nos. 197, 199, 234, 1132, 1174, 1204 have perished. No. 1730 is to be found in the Palazzo Capranica della Valle; No. 1731 in the Villa Medici; Nos. 196, 198, 200, in the Museo Nazionale at Naples. No. 1158 was removed to the Farnese gardens, and brought back in 1875, together with No. 1203. Fragments of No. 1187 are dispersed all over the Forum. No. 1119 is kept in the Vatican Museum with No. 1161. No. 1162 is broken in three pieces: the first is missing, the second is to be found in the Vatican, the third near the Arch of Severus!

Many pages could be written on the history and on the fate of this noble monument in recent times. One incident shall answer for all. The arch, being the property of the S. P. Q. R., was put to ransom in this way. The two side passages were walled in at each end, and turned into shops. I have found in the city archives two leases, one dated May 1, 1721, by which one of the dens is rented to Bonaventura Rosa for four scudi and eighty baiocchi a year; the other dated January 30, 1751, by which both are given up to Battista Franchi for seven scudi and twenty baiocchi. The last occupant, in 1803, was a fruiterer. This odd state of things is represented in the above original sketch by Gianni, made about 1800 (Fig. 109).

LITERATURE. — Suarez, *Arcus L. Septimii Severi anaglypha.* Rome, 1676. — Antonio Guattani, *Roma antica*, vol. i. p. 71. — *Corpus Inscr.*, vol. vi. n. 1033.

XLIII. THE CARCER TULLIANUM (S. Peter's Prison) (XXXIV in plan), is mentioned by Livy as having been built by Ancus Marcius in a place near and a little higher than the Forum: *carcer imminens foro.* It contained an underground cell, formerly a cave named Tullianum, from a *tullus* or jet of water which sprang from the rock. It was used as a place of execution, and Sallust depicts it as a dark, filthy, and frightful den, twelve feet underground, walled in and covered with massive stone walls. The façade is very severe in style, and has an inscription commemorating the repairs to the prison, made at the time of Tiberius by C. Vibius Rufinus and M. Cocceius Nerva. (See Corpus Inscr., vol. vi. n. 1539.) Nichols justly remarks that "the Carcer plays a part in Roman history like that of the Tower of London in English. The Tullianum was, if one may say so, a Secret Tower Hill. One of the first heroes of the long tale of miseries is Pleminius, who, being detained in prison for his excesses at Locri, was convicted of bribing men to set fire to the city, lowered into the Tullianum, and executed. The same fate befell Lentulus, Cethegus, and several other conspirators during the Catilinarian troubles. Cicero, who played such a leading part in them, speaks of the Carcer as having been ordained by the kings as the avenger of heinous and notorious crimes. The jail is also associated with the name of King Jugurtha, starved to death in the lower hole. The body of Seianus, the disgraced minister of Tiberius, was cast on the Scalæ Gemoniæ (steps adjoining the prison), and also those of his innocent children, whose execution was marked by circumstances of frightful atrocity. Here also the headless trunk of

Flavius Sabinus, brother of Vespasian, was thrown by the soldiers of Vitellius, and soon after Vitellius himself met his end on the same spot. The Carcer," Nichols concludes, "like the Tower, had also its literary reminiscences. Nævius is said to have written two of his plays while confined in prison for his attacks on the aristocracy." [1]

The bibliography on the Carcer is given by Cancellieri, "Notizie del Carcere Tulliano." Rome, 1788, pp. 6, 7.

XLIV. ÆDES CONCORDIÆ ('Ομονοεῖον, Temple of Concord), (XXXV in plan). — The approval of the Licinian laws in 367 B. C. was a great event in the history of the Republic, because the alliance between patricians and plebeians, by restoring peace and tranquillity at home, allowed the government to turn its attention to foreign affairs. The laws, however, did not pass without a struggle. During a particularly violent fight in the Forum, Camillus promised to erect a temple to Concord, as soon as peace should be restored; and he kept his word in 367. The temple, a simple and graceful structure of stone, wood, and painted terracotta, was raised at the foot of the Clivus Capitolinus, between the Temple of Saturn and the prison. In B. C. 121, after the death of C. Gracchus, the Senate commissioned L. Opimius with the reconstruction of the temple, to the great distress of the plebeians, who could not tolerate the idea that a monument commemorating a popular victory should be made to represent the triumph of aristocracy, and so the original inscription was changed one night into the words : " Discord raises this temple to Concord." The edifice, scanty fragments of which have come down to us, dates from A. D. 10, when Tiberius reconstructed it for the second time, and dedicated it on January 16 under the title of Concordia Augusta. Designed and executed by the cleverest masters of the golden age, entirely built of white marble, profusely enriched with masterpieces of the Greek school, the Temple of Concord was one of the finest monuments in the valley of the Forum, and one of the richest museums of Rome. The cella contained one central and ten side niches, in which were placed the Apollo and Hera by Baton; Latona nursing Apollo and Diana by Euphranor; Asklepios and Hygieia by Nikeratos; Ares and

---

[1] On the connection of this historical monument with S. Peter, consult *Der mamertinische Kerker u. die römischen Traditionen vom Gefängnisse und den Ketten Petri,* an excellent paper published by H. Grisar, S. J., in the *Zeitschrift für kath. Theologie,* 1896, p. 102.

Hermes by Piston; and Zeus, Athena, and Demeter by Sthenios. Pliny speaks also of a picture by Theodoros representing Cassandra; of another by Zeuxis which portrayed Marsyas bound to the tree; of a third, Bacchus, by Nikias; of four elephants cut in obsidian, a miracle of skill and labor; and of a collection of precious stones. Among these was the sardonyx set in the legendary ring of Polykrates of Samos. I may mention in the last place the statue of Hestia, which Tiberius had taken away almost by force from the inhabitants of Paros.

Like that of Castor, the Temple of Concord played an important part in Roman political life, and was used very often by the Senate as a meeting-place on extraordinary occasions. Cicero delivered in it his fourth oration against Catiline, denouncing the conspiracy and the names of those concerned in it. Other meetings are recorded in Imperial times, under Severus, Alexander, and Probus. The open space in front of the temple, originally called Volkanal, and later on Area Concordiæ, is mentioned several times in connection with the "showers of blood." These were rain mixed with reddish sand from the deserts of Libya, a phenomenon by no means uncommon in Rome, for I have myself observed it on three occasions.

The fate of the building after the barbaric invasions is not known. The Anonymus of Einsiedlen saw (?) it almost perfect in the eighth century, and copied the inscription of the pronaos, which alludes to the restoration made by the S. P. Q. R. after the fire of Carinus. (See Corpus Inscr., vol. vi. n. 89 and 938.) The "Liber Pontificalis" speaks of it as threatening to collapse at the time of Hadrian I. (772–795). When Poggio Bracciolini visited Rome the first time about 1405, the portico was still standing, but he saw it himself, soon after, fall to the ground, and its beautiful marbles were broken and thrown into the lime-kiln.

The excavations of the site of the temple began on May 2, 1817. The fragments of decorative marbles found within the cella are described by contemporary witnesses as "the most delicate, the most perfect productions of ancient art." These fragments are exhibited in the portico of the Tabularium, where dampness and saltpetre corrode their surface, and will soon reduce them to dust; two bases of the side shrines are in the ground floor of the Museo Capitolino; two capitals, with lambs in the place of volutes, are in the Palazzo dei Conservatori. Nibby says that at the time of the discovery half the pavement was perfect; but its slabs of africano, giallo, and pavonazzetto were afterward stolen one by one

.by stone-cutters, and probably made into paper-weights and other
,such marketable articles. The threshold of the cella, one of the
few pieces left on the spot, has the mark of the caduceus engraved
near the left end.

LITERATURE. — *Corpus Inscr.*, vol. vi. n: 89–94. — Ulrichs, *Codex topogr.*,
pp. 220, 238. — Stefano Piale, *Degli antichi templi di Vespasiano e della Con-*
.*cordia.* Rome, (1818) 1834. — Carlo Fea, *Varietà di Notizie*, pp. 93–95.

XLV. THE CLIVUS CAPITOLINUS (XXXVI in plan). — The
end of the Sacra Via which ascended the eastern slope of the Capitoline hill in zigzags was called the Clivus Capitolinus. Its pavement has been laid bare in the lower tract before and between the
temples of Vespasian, of Saturn, and the Porticus Deorum Consentium, as represented in the illustration (Fig. 119); but its upper
course is as yet a matter of speculation. It probably rounded the
Porticus Consentium and emerged on the Area Capitolina, skirting the south side of the Tabularium, as marked (XXXVI) in
the plan.

At the foot of the pronaos of Saturn are the only existing remains of a Roman street pavement of classic times. They owe
their preservation to the fact of having been covered by the steps of
the temple in one of the later reconstructions. The reader hardly
needs to be reminded that all the other pavements that go by the
name of "ancient streets" are a patchwork of the fifth and sixth
centuries after Christ.

XLVI. TEMPLE OF VESPASIAN (XXXVII in plan; Figs. 106
and 110), erected under Domitian in memory of his deified father
(and brother). — There is no doubt that the three columns, standing on a lofty platform between the Temple of Concord and the
Porticus Consentium, belong to this temple, because the dedicatory
inscription, copied by the so-called Anonymus of Einsiedlen when
still intact, ends precisely with the eight letters ESTITVER which
we see engraved in the existing fragment.

divo · uespasiano · augusto · s · p · q · r
impp · cæss · seuerus · et · antoninus · pii · felic · augg · rESTITVER

Of this very elegant edifice only the platform, the altar, and the
three corner columns of the pronaos are left standing. The frieze
is decorated with the instruments of sacrifice — the "albogalerus,"
the "aspergillus," the "urceus," the knife, the "patera," the axe
— in bold relief and in the purest style of art (Fig. 111). The
cornice is remarkable for the tiny rings interposed to the dentels ;

it is a characteristic of ornamental work of the time of Domitian, which occurs also in the cornices of the Flavian Palace, of the Forum Transitorium, of the Albanum, of the Serapæum, of the Horti Largiani — buildings erected or restored by the same Emperor.

Fig. 110. — The Clivus Capitolinus, now concealed by the Modern (1880) Causeway.

When the excavations of the Clivus Capitolinus were begun in 1810, it was observed not only that the three columns were falling out of the perpendicular by over two feet in the direction of the

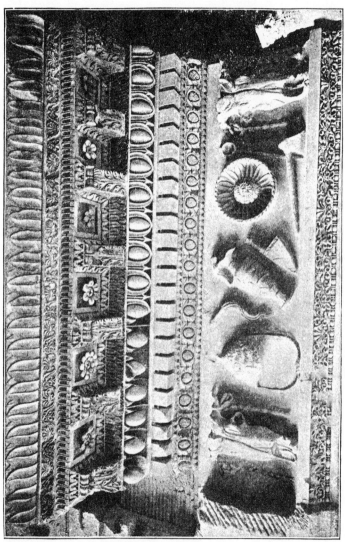

Fig. 111. — The Frieze of the Temple of Vespasian.

Forum, but that their foundations had been uprooted in the excavations of the cinquecento. The architects Valadier and Camporese, after measuring and sketching the ruin stone by stone, took it down, rebuilt the foundations, and set it up straight again. The accumulation of rubbish, which reached nearly to the top of the shafts, was then removed, and the expectant public could see outlined against the sky those capitals and that frieze which, only a few months before, had been trodden by the feet of tourists. This clever operation is described in Tournon's " Etudes statistiques sur Rome," vol. ii. p. 266, pl. 21.

On the opposite side of the street stands a nearly perfect Ionic hexastyle portico, which topographers agree in attributing to the

XLVII. Ædes Saturni (Temple of Saturn) (XXXVIII in plan; Fig. 110). — According to an old tradition the Greek followers of Hercules had raised an altar to Saturn in the " jaws," or " at the foot " of the hill which bore his name (Collis Saturnius), and which was inhabited, even before the Trojan war, by a colony of men called Saturnii. The tradition was founded on the fact that, in much later times, sacrifices were offered to the god in the Greek rite, the worshipers being allowed to keep their heads unveiled. A temple was substituted for the altar in 497 B. C., and dedicated on the day of the Saturnalia, December 17. Lucius Munatius Plancus rebuilt it at the request of his friend Augustus in 42 B. C., the money being taken from the spoils of the Rhætic war.

The fire of Carinus must have damaged the structure, as shown by the inscription SENATVS POPVLVSQVE ROMANVS INCENDIO CONSVMPTVM RESTITVIT engraved on the architrave of the pronaos, and by the patchwork style of the pronaos itself, which betrays an utter decadence of taste and a great poverty of means. The columns on the front are of gray granite, those at the sides of red, and made up of several pieces; some of the bases are Attic, others Corinthian, and without plinth. It has been asked why the name of the S. P. Q. R. should appear on the architrave of the temple instead of the name of an Emperor. The reason is evident: the temple was rebuilt in the fourth century, when Christianity had become, if not the religion of the State, certainly the personal religion of the Emperors; and it would not have become a Christian Emperor to see his name associated with the restoration of heathen temples. I believe, moreover, that the restoration by the S. P. Q. R. was undertaken not from a religious point of view, but as a necessity of public administration, because the temple had been used, since the time of Valerius Publicola, as the civil treasury — Ærarium Saturni, — as that of the temple of Concord was used for military purposes. The Ærarium Saturni was divided into two sections : one for current business, one as a reserve fund (Ærarium sanctius). Appeal was made to this last in 211 during the second Punic war, and again in 49 B. C., on the approach of Julius Cæsar to Rome. There were corresponding strong rooms under the cella, but no attempt has ever been made to discover them. The Ærarium contained also the archives of the quæstors, in which, among other records, the sentences of death were deposited.

A small square opened behind the temple, called Area Saturni. It contained a celebrated altar, raised to Ops and Ceres on August 10, A. D. 7, while the peninsula was suffering from a famine of unprecedented severity.

The lofty platform on which the temple stands was reached from the Clivus Capitolinus by means of a long flight of stairs, designed in fragment iii. 22, 23 of the marble plan of Rome.

LITERATURE. — Theodor Mommsen, *Res gestæ*, 2d ed. iv. 12, 13. — F. M. Nichols, *The Roman Forum*, p. 23. — H. Jordan, *Ephemeris epigraphica*, vol. iii. p. 55. — Orazio Marucchi, *Le forum romani*, p. 139. — Thédenat, in Daremberg and Saglio's *Dictionnaire*, p. 1285.

XLVIII. PORTICUS DEORUM CONSENTIUM (Portico of the Twelve Gods) (XXXIX in plan ; Fig. 112). — At the highest point of the ascent, and under the southeast corner of the Tabularium, there is a line of cells built partly against the cliff, partly against the retaining wall of the Clivus, the front of which is decorated with a portico of the Corinthian order. It was rebuilt in A. D. 367 by Vettius Agorius Prætextatus, on the site of a much earlier shrine of the twelve deities, whose gilded images, six of gods and six of goddesses, are mentioned by Varro as existing in the Forum at a very remote age. The inscription on the architrave discovered in the excavations of 1834 and the remains of the colonnade were set up in 1853 by Canina. " Agorius Prætextatus is known as one of the most obstinate upholders of paganism, already dying out. He persecuted the Christians whenever he could do so without incurring the penalties of law ; restored the abandoned and half-ruined temples ; and, when Pope Damasus remonstrated with him for his cruel and illegal behavior, answered, 'Make me ·Bishop of Rome and I shall at once become a good Christian.' "

Remains of his gardens on the Esquiline were discovered in 1873–74 near the Piazza Manfredo Fanti. The palace connected with the gardens had already been discovered in 1591 in the grounds of Federigo Cesi, near the Arch of Gallienus. It con-

Fig. 112. — The Porticus Consentium.

tained, like the gardens, a valuable set of works of art, among which was the statue of Cœlia Concordia, a Vestalis Maxima, so perfectly preserved that even the insignia of her order, of gilded metal, remained fastened around her neck.

LITERATURE. — Olaus Kellermann, in *Bull. Inst.*, 1835, p. 34. — Luigi Grifi, *Atti accad. pontif. archeol.*, vol. xiv. p. 118. — Adolf Becker, *Topographie*, p. 318. — Rodolfo Lanciani, *Bull. com.*, 1874, p. 83; and *Ancient Rome*, p. 169. — *Corpus Inscr.*, vol. vi. n. 102.

XLIX. TABULARIUM (XL in plan). — This is an immense and well-preserved building, on the slope of the Capitoline facing the Forum, destined for the safe keeping of the deeds of public interest, among which were the decrees of the Senate from the earliest days of the Kings, the plebiscites, the treaties of peace and alliance, and so forth. Bunsen calls the Tabularium "le seul édifice grand qui nous reste de la République, le seul édifice d'Etat de la Rome ancienne;" Emil Braun, likewise, "a grand edifice, one of the most considerable of the brightest epoch of the

Republic, . . . which deserves our fullest admiration; " and yet it is one of the least visited monuments in Rome.

The Tabularium is probably the work of Q. Lutatius Catulus, to whom the task of rebuilding the Capitol after the fire of 83 B. C. had been intrusted by a decree of the Senate in 78 B. C. There are two inscriptions commemorating his work: one seen by Poggio Bracciolini about 1530, which expressly mentions *svbstrvctionem et tabvlarivm;* the other discovered by Canina in 1845, which has been set into the wall of the Tabularium itself on the north side. This last contains only the general expression *de* SENatus SENTentia FACIVNDVm (tabularium?) *coeravit.* (See Corpus Inscr., vol. i. p. 170, n. 391, 392.)

The area of the building corresponds almost exactly with that of the Palazzo del Senatore, the official residence of the Roman municipal administration. The walls of the palace rest on the ancient ones on the north, east, and south sides, as any one can see; but I have discovered a document which proves that the west side, viz., the façade of the palace towards the Piazza del Campidoglio, is likewise built upon ancient foundations. In p. 88 of the Bodleian MSS. Pirro Ligorio asserts that a beautiful "basamento di sasso tiburtino di bella e vaga modanatura " runs under the pedestals of the two River Gods on either side of the fountain, and gives a good outline of it. He also tells the following remarkable story about the fate of the two River Gods. They had formed part of the mediæval museum of statuary on the Piazza di Montecavallo, which comprised the two colossal groups of Castor and Pollux, two statues of Constantine, one of Cybele, and the two reclining figures of the Nile and the Tigris, known by the name of Saturn and Bacchus.[1] When the River Gods were removed to the Capitol for the decoration of the Palazzo del Senatore, an influential person (*un malo consigliere*) suggested that the Tigris should be transformed into a Tiber. The suggestion was adopted; the head of the tiger was changed into that of a wolf, and the two sucking infants were added to the group. Ligorio says that the fingers of the right hand of one of the twins were originally part of the hair of the tiger.

LITERATURE. — Giovanni Azurri, *Descrizione dell' arcata dorica dell' antico Tabulario.* Rome, 1839. — *Beschreibung d. Stadt Rom,* vol. iii. p. 40. — Luigi Canina, *Monumenti dell' Istituto,* vol. v. pl. 31. — Charles Bunsen, *Les forums,* p. 286. — Emil Braun, *Ruins and Museums,* p. 14. — Theodor

[1] See Michaelis, *Le antichità della città di Roma, descritte da Nicolao Muffel,* in Mittheil., 1888, p. 271, n. 23, 24.

Mommsen, *Annal. Inst.*, 1858, p. 211; and *Bull. Inst.*, 1845, p. 119. — Heinrich Jordan, *Il tabulario capitolino* (in Annal. Inst., 1881, p. 60).

The Tabularium comprises a substructure built of gabinian stone, an underground floor, which has long been used for a city jail, and an upper portico of the Doric order, with many halls, passages, corridors, and staircases, all in perfect preservation. The halls were used, as has been said, for state documents, engraved on bronze tablets, "tabulæ æneæ," from which the building was

Fig. 113. — Old Gate of Tabularium blocked by Temple of Vespasian.

named. Three thousand tablets, called by Suetonius "instrumentum imperii pulcherrimum ac vetustissimum," perished in the fire of Vitellius. Vespasian restored the set by means of duplicates kept in other archives.

The Tabularium was accessible directly from the Clivus Capitolinus and from the Ærarium Saturni, by means of a staircase of sixty-seven steps, the preservation of which is truly wonderful. The entrance to it was blocked at the time of Domitian, in consequence of the erection of the Temple of Vespasian, as shown in Fig. 113.

Nibby asserts that the many fragments of columns and capitals of travertine (of the Corinthian order) discovered at the foot of the substructure, and now piled up in front of the Portico of the Consentes, belong to a second or upper arcade of the Tabularium. His opinion is corroborated by documents of the time of Anacletus II. and Innocent III., which mention two Camellariæ, the lower and the upper, "Camellaria" being then the denomination of the Tabularium; and by Poggio Bracciolini, who saw in it *fornices duplici ordine*, a double tier of arcades.

L. CAPITOLIUM (Temple of Jupiter Optimus Maximus) (XLI in plan). — This national sanctuary of ancient Rome, designed by the elder Tarquin and built by his son Superbus, was dedicated by M. Horatius Pulvillus, consul, on September 13, 509 B. C. Writers describe it as raised on a platform 61.62 metres long, and 57.17 wide, in the middle of a sacred area, which was bounded on three sides by precipitous cliffs. There were three rows of columns on the front of the temple, but none at the back; the style of architecture was pure Etruscan, low and heavy, with intercolumniation so wide (areostyle) as to require the use of wooden architraves. The cella was divided into three compartments, the middle one sacred to Jupiter, the one on the left to Juno Regina, the one on the right to Minerva. The pediment was crowned by a quadriga of terra-cotta, in the manner of an acroterium; and the statue of the Father of the Gods was of the same material. It was the work of Turianus of Fregenæ, who had painted the face of the god in vermilion, and dressed his body with the tunica palmata and the toga picta. Considering that the wooden architraves must have been covered likewise with panels of painted terra cotta, the roof lined with antefixæ, etc., we may assume that the old Capitolium did not differ from the contemporary temples of southern Etruria, a splendid specimen of which, discovered at Faleria, is now exhibited in the Villa Giulia outside the Porta del Popolo.

In 386 B. C. the rugged and uneven surface of the hill around the temple was made level by means of gigantic substructures, which rose from the level of the plain to that of the temple itself, a work called "insane" by Pliny, and classed by Livy among the wonders of Rome. The Capitolium was only accessible from the side of the clivus by means of stately stairs, a kind of "scala santa," which Cæsar and Claudius ascended on their knees.

On July 6, 83 B. C., a malefactor, whose name was never discovered, set the building ablaze. Sulla undertook its reconstruction, for which purpose he laid his hands on some of the columns of the Temple of Jupiter the Olympian at Athens. Sulla's work was continued by Lutatius Catulus (the builder of the Tabularium), and finished by Julius Cæsar in 46. A second restoration took place in the year 9 B. C. under Augustus, a third in 74 A. D. under Vespasian, and the last in the year 82 under Domitian. Domitian's temple was of the same length and width as its predecessors, but higher and more *svelte*. It had Corinthian columns of pentelic marble.

For many generations topographers have discussed which of the two summits of the Capitoline hill was occupied by the temple, which by the citadel. A discovery made on November 7, 1875, gave me the first clue to the solution of the difficulty. While building the foundations of the new rotunda in the garden of the Palazzo dei Conservatori (where the works of art dug up on the Esquiline are now exhibited), we discovered the edge of the platform built by the Tarquins, and upon it a fragment of one of the columns of pentelic marble pertaining to the last restoration of Domitian. Such a find, taken by itself, would not have been conclusive; but compared with others made in the course of the last four centuries, it proves beyond doubt that the Capitolium stood on the summit of Monte Caprino, and consequently that the Arx and the Tarpeian rock must be placed on the Aracœli side.

First as to the *insanæ substructiones* which supported the sacred area. They have been seen and described by Flaminio Vacca on the side of the Piazza della Consolazione, by Sante Bartoli on the side of the Piazza Montanara, by Ficoroni on the side of the Via di Torre de' Specchi, their thickness exceeding five metres. The travertine facing of these walls was covered with inscriptions and dedications in honor of the great Roman god by the kings and the nations of the world. One cannot read these historical documents, these messages of friendship and gratitude from the remotest corner of the earth, without acquiring a new sense of the magnitude and power of Rome.[1] These dedications are found only on the side of the Monte Caprino.

[1] See *Bull. com.*, 1886, p. 403; 1887, pp. 14, 124, 251; 1888, p. 138; 1890, p. 57. —

The platform of the Tarquins, built of small grayish blocks of tufa lamellare, without cement, exists still in tolerable preservation under the garden and palace (Caffarelli) of the German Embassy. A sketch in Fabretti's "De Columna traiana" shows that when the Caffarellis enlarged their palace on the Monte Caprino, about 1680, fourteen tiers of stone at least were removed. The following illustration shows the only portion now left visible of this great platform (Fig. 114). It lies under the partition wall between the Caffarelli garden and that of the Palazzo dei Conservatori.

Borings made all over the Monte Caprino in 1876 by Jordan

Fig. 114. — Remains of the Platform of the Capitolium in the Garden of the Caffarelli Palace.

and Schupmann have enabled us to trace three out of four sides of the parallelogram, as well as the size and direction of one of the *favissæ*.

The temple rebuilt by Domitian was plundered in June, 455, by the Vandals of Genseric, who carried off the statues to adorn his

Mommsen, *Zeitschrift für Numismatik*, xv. p. 207. — *Corpus Inscrip.*, vol. i. p. 169.

African residence. From that time the temple, stripped of its roof of gilt bronze tiles, fell into ruin, and became, like so many others, a stone quarry and a lime-kiln. In January, 1545, Giovan Pietro Caffarelli discovered the first relics in the garden behind the Palazzo dei Conservatori. Some of the pieces were sketched and measured by Antonio da Sangallo the younger, and the whole find is described as follows by Flaminio Vacca : " Upon the Tarpeian rock (Monte Caprino) several pillars of pentelic marble were found, with capitals of such size that I was able to carve out of one of them the great lion now in the garden of Grand Duke Ferdinand of Tuscany by the Trinità de' Monti (Villa Medici). The rest of the marbles were used by Vincenzo de Rossi to carve the Prophets and other statues of the chapel of Cardinal Federico Cesi at S. Maria della Pace. . . . No fragments of the entablature were found, but as the building was so close to the edge of the precipice, I fancy they must have fallen into the plain below." The surmise was proved correct by subsequent discoveries. In 1780 great pieces of cornice and frieze, ornamented with bucranii and festoons, were dug up from the foundations of the house No. 13 Via Montanara at the foot of the rock; other fragments in May, 1875, under the house No. 33 Via della Consolazione. The dedications by foreign kings and nations, mentioned above, have also rolled down the hill towards the Piazza della Consolazione, where they were discovered in 1887 under the Casa Moroni. Another piece of a fluted column of pentelic marble was discovered on January 24, 1889, on the slope towards the Tullianum (S. Pietro in Carcere), where it had been dragged and abandoned by a cinquecento stone-cutter.

A careful examination made in 1875 by the late Padre Luigi Bruzza proves that the statues of the Cappella Cesi are really sculptured in pentelic, and so is Flaminio Vacca's lion, in the Villa Medici. The piece of a column discovered in November, 1875, is to be seen in the small garden of the Palazzo dei Conservatori; the one discovered in January, 1889, in the Via di S. Pietro in Carcere has been buried over in the same place. The platform of the temple discovered in 1865 in the garden of the German Embassy (Caffarelli) was buried in 1880 by Baron von Keudell. The dedicatory inscriptions found in the Piazza della Consolazione, instead of being replaced on the Capitol, to which they had been offered by the discoverer, have found their way to the Museo delle Terme ; those found in the sixteenth century (Corpus Inscr. Lat., vol. i. p. 169, n. 589) have perished.

LITERATURE. — *Corpus Inscr.*, vol. i. p. 170 ; and vol. vi. n. 372–374. — Rycq, *De Capitolio romano.* Leyden, 1669. — Bunsen, *Beschreibung d. Stadt Rom*, vol. iiiᵃ, p. 14. — Hirt, *Der capitolinische Jupitertempel* (in Abhandl. d. Berliner Akademie, 1813). — Dureau de la Malle, *Mémoire sur la position de la roche tarpeienne* (in Mém. Académie Inscriptions, 1819). — R. Lanciani, *Il tempio di Giove ottimo massimo* (in Bull. com., 1875, p. 165, pls. 16–18) ; and *Pagan and Christian Rome*, p. 84. — Pietro Rosa, *Annali Instituto*, 1865, p. 382. — H. Jordan, *Osservazioni sul tempio di Giove Capitolino* (in Annali Instit., 1876, p. 145) ; and *Topographie*, vol. i², p. 67. — Fabio Gori, *Archivio storico letterario della città e provincia di Roma*, vol. i. 1875, pp. 285–334. — Christian Huelsen, *Osservazioni sull' architettura del tempio di Giove Capitolino* (in Mittheilungen, 1888, p. 150, pl. 5). — Audollent, *Dessein inédit d'un fronton du temple de Jupiter Capitolin* (in Mélanges de l'Ecole française de Rome, 1889, p. 120, planche 2).

LI.   FORUM JULIUM. — In spite of the construction of so many temples and basilicæ on the borders of the Forum, by which the space accessible to the public had been more than doubled, the Forum itself, dating from the early days of the city, had become absolutely insufficient for the wants of a population which was fast approaching a million.   The first step towards the improvement of this state of things was taken by Julius Cæsar in 54 B. C. He seems to have planned the creation of a new forum while absent from Italy; stimulated perhaps by the example of L. Æmilius Paullus, who had purchased the site of his basilica (Æmilia) at a cost of 1500 talents, or 12,000,000 lire.   Equally large was the sum spent by Cæsar in securing a space for his "extension."   At the date of Cicero's letter (iv. 16) to Atticus, some 60,000,000 sesterces had already been expended.   The total cost of ground, without including the new buildings, is said to have exceeded 100,000,000 sesterces, or about 20,000,000 lire, a sum obviously exaggerated, and which has been reduced by careful calculations to 1,343,750 lire (about 168 lire the square metre). The Forum Julium took the shape of a sacred inclosure around the temple dedicated by the dictator 45 B. C. to Venus Genetrix, the goddess from whom he professed to descend.   Her statue was a masterpiece by Arkesilaos, and a masterpiece also was the statue of the famous charger, which had been foaled in the mews of the Julian house, and whose fore feet were nearly human, the hoofs being split, as it were, into toes.   Appianus speaks of a statue of Cleopatra by the side of that of the goddess ; Ovid of a fountain adorned with figures of nymphs called Appiades ; and Pliny of famous paintings by Greek artists, of six collections of engraved gems, and of a breastplate for the goddess covered with British pearls.

The beautiful temple was discovered at the time of Palladio in the foundations of a house at the corner of the present streets Cremona and Marmorelle. He describes the structure as built of blocks of marble "lavorati eccellentemente." The cornice was adorned with symbols of the sea — dolphins, tridents, etc. ; the temple itself was hexastyle, peripteral, and pycnostyle. This last particular is expressly mentioned by Vitruvius (iii. 3), and Palladio confesses " di non hauer veduto intercolunnii cosi piccioli in alcun altro edificio antico " — never to have seen such small intercolumniation in any other ancient edifice. The temple is now completely hidden from view ; the only remains visible, in an alley, Via del Ghettarello, No. 18, pertain to the tabernæ, or shops which lined the Forum on the (south-) west side. They have been excavated twice at least : first about the end of the fifteenth century, when Fra Giocondo da Verona made a design of them (Uffizi, n. 1537), and again by Parker in 1866. These important remains were called Forum Martis, Martis Forum, *Marforio*, in the Middle Ages. The statue of the River

Fig. 115. — The Venus Genetrix by Arkesilaos — a Fragment in the Museo delle Terme.

God, known as the facetious partner of Pasquino, was discovered at the foot of the street which bears his name, together with the granite basin into which the water fell from the god's urn. The statue was removed to the Capitol by Sixtus V., and placed by

Clement XII., in 1734, in the court of the Capitoline Museum, above the fountain. The basin was removed first to the Campo Vaccino, by S. Maria Liberatrice, in 1594, and again to the Piazza del Quirinale in 1818. The place where both were discovered is marked by a tablet (written by Bartolomeo Marliano) above the door No. 49 Via di Marforio.

There are several copies of the Venus Genetrix of Arkesilaos. The goddess appears clad in a thin, semi-transparent chiton, through which the form of the young and lovely body can be clearly seen; the left breast is bare. There is a replica in the Borghese Museum (Helbig, Guide, vol. ii. p. 141, n. 915); another in the Museo delle Terme, reproduced in Fig. 115 (ibid., p. 213, n. 1027); a third in the Louvre (Froehner, Sculpture antique, vol. i. p. 166, n. 135), etc. Consult Otto Jahn, "Leipziger Monatsberichte," 1861, p. 114; and Wissowa, "De Veneris Simulacris romanis." Wratislaw, 1882.

LITERATURE. — Andrea Palladio, *Architettura*, ed. 1570, lib. iv. c. 31. — Flaminio Vacca, *Mem.* 69 (in Fea's Miscell., vol. i. p. lxxxiii.). — Francesco Cancellieri, *Notizie delle statue dette di Marforio e di Pasquino.* Rome, 1789. — Giovanni Battista Cavalieri, *Antiquar. statuar.* Rome, 1585, pl. 94. — Charles Bunsen, *Bull. Inst.*, 1836, p. 55. — Luigi Canina, *Foro Romano*, 94; and *Edifizii*, vol. ii. pls. xcii.–xcv. — F. M. Nichols, *The Roman Forum*, p. 251. — *Forma Urbis Romæ*, pl. xx.

LII. FORUM AUGUSTUM (plan, Fig. 116). Augustus followed the example of Cæsar and built a third and more magnificent forum in continuation of the two existing ones. Its remains, known by the name of "Arco dei Pantani," rank among the finest of ancient Rome. The most remarkable feature of the place is a wall of blocks of peperino, raised to a great height to screen the view of the mean houses clustered on the slope of the Quirinal, in the neighborhood of the present Via Baccina and Salita del Grillo. The wall is pierced by an original archway, the Arco dei Pantani just named, through which the modern traffic passes at a considerably higher level than the original street which led to the Subura. Against it stand the remains of the beautiful Temple of Mars Ultor, one of the few which have come down to us from the Augustan age without restorations. They consist of three fluted Corinthian columns, of part of the right wall of the cella, and of the roof of the vestibule. They stand on a substructure excavated in 1842, when the inscription in "Corpus," n. 2158, was found, relating to the solemn procession which the Salii Palatini made every year on March 1 (and for several days following), chanting

the *axamenta* or *saliaria carmina*, and dancing sacred war-dances —
whence the name of Salii. The inscription had already been seen
and copied at the time of Sixtus IV. in 1477, and had been used,
later on, in the restorations of the church of S. Basilio of the
Priory of Malta, which occupied the southern hemicycle of the
Forum. Mars (Gradivus) being the god presiding over the Col-

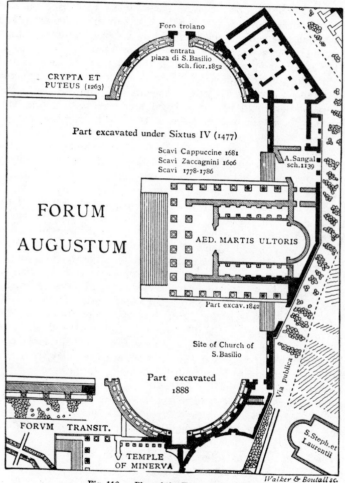

Fig. 116. — Plan of the Forum Augustum.

lege of the Salii, its temple was selected by them as the last halt-
ing-place (*mansio*) after their exhausting progress through the
city.   The splendor of the banquet which terminated the celebration is praised by both Cicero and Horace, and indeed the phrases
"saliares dapes" and "epulari saliarem in modum" seem to have
passed into a proverb.   Suetonius relates that while the Emperor
Claudius was sitting one day on the throne delivering judgment
in this forum, his nostrils were struck by the appetizing odor of
the repast prepared for the Salii.   Adjourning, therefore, the
case which was being argued before him, he rushed into the temple and sat down among the banqueting priests.

The irregular form of the wall at the back of the temple and
of the Forum is accounted for by the circumstance that Augustus
was unable to obtain a symmetrical area, as the owners of the
nearest houses could not be induced to part with their property.
Flaminio Vacca says that a piece of the wall having been demolished, towards the end of the sixteenth century, it was found out
that the blocks of peperino were fastened to each other by means
of wooden clamps shaped like a swallow's tail, and that nobody
could ascertain what kind of wood they were cut out of (probably
box-wood).   Pliny praises the Temple of Mars Ultor as one of
the most beautiful and perfect works of man ever seen on earth,
and places it on the same level with the Forum and Temple of
Peace, and with the Basilica Æmilia.   The great pieces of timber
used in the roof had been cut in the Rhætian Alps, in the dog-
days, a precaution which was considered to make wood indestruc-
tible.   Pliny also mentions among its treasures vases of chiseled
iron, a statue of Apollo cut in ivory, two large pictures representing a battle and a triumph, and four noble works of Apelles, one
of which, representing the victory of Alexander the Great, was
altered in the time of Claudius by substituting the likeness of
Augustus for that of the Macedonian king.   The temple also
contained a set of standard weights and measures, and safes and
strong boxes, where large sums belonging to private citizens
were kept under the guarantee of the priests.   A daring robbery
perpetrated towards the end of the first century, when even the
precious helmet was wrenched from the head of Mars Ultor,
frightened the depositors so that the priests gave up banking, at
least for the time.

The main point of interest of this forum was the gallery of
statues, raised by Augustus to the generals who by their exploits
and victories had extended the boundaries of the Roman Empire.

The rules formulated by Augustus for the giving of so great a distinction were very strict, but his successors soon relaxed their severity, and statues were offered right and left, just like the equestrian orders of nowadays. L. Silanus, although a minor, was given a statue after his betrothal to Octavia, daughter of Claudius. Another was raised in honor of Q. Curtius Rufus, legate of Germany, for having opened a silver mine (near Nassau

Fig. 117. — The South Hemicycle of the Forum Augustum, excavated in 1888.

on the right bank of the Rhine) which brought little profit to the treasury, but caused great toil and hardship to the soldiers. Nero, after the conspiracy of the Pisones was revealed to him, convened the Senate, and obtained the *ornamenta triumphalia* for those who had turned informers. Pliny the younger reproaches Domitian for having given statues to men who had never been in action, not even in camp, and who had never heard the sound of a trumpet except from the stage.

The Forum of Augustus lost its privilege of being the national *protomotheca* with the construction of that of Trajan. The honors were then divided between the two places, as shown by the inscription of M. Bassæus Rufus (Corpus, n. 1599).

Many important discoveries illustrating this point were made in 1888–89, when the municipality of Rome, at my suggestion, pulled down the houses and factories which concealed the southern hemicycle and laid bare its boundary wall and the niches once occupied by the statues of the Roman heroes. I have described the results of these great excavations in the "Bull. arch. com.," 1889, pp. 26 and 73 (compare 1889, p. 481; and 1890, p. 251).

Besides fragments of statues in military attire, columns of giallo antico, capitals, friezes of exquisite workmanship, we brought to light the base of a donarium, for which one hundred pounds of gold had been used, offered to Augustus by the Spanish province of Bætica; a pedestal of a statue dedicated to Nigrinianus, nephew of the Emperor Carus, by a financier named Geminius Festus; and inscriptions — in a more or less fragmentary state — which accompanied the statues of some victorious generals, giving a short account of their exploits. The editors of the first volume, second edition, of the "Corpus Inscript." [1] attribute to Professor Bormann the merit of having made known the fact that these eulogistic biographies, dictated by Augustus, are divided into two parts, — one giving the name in the first case, like —

```
M · AIMILIVS · Q · F · L · N
BARBVLA . DICTATOR
```

engraved on the plinth of the statue; the other giving the account of his career, being engraved on a marble tablet placed below the

---

[1] *Inscriptiones latinæ antiquissimæ*, editio altera, pars prior, Berlin, Reimer, MDCCCXCIII, p. 187, col. a.

niche. I had myself pointed out this important circumstance so far back as February, 1889 (see Bull. com., pp. 73, 77), and I was able to prove thus that many eulogies of illustrious men — the place of discovery of which was not known — belonged to the Forum of Augustus.

The eulogies, or fragments of eulogies, found in 1888–89 are now preserved in the Museo Municipale al Celio. They belong to Appius Claudius Cæcus, the builder of the Via Appia; to C. Duillius, who destroyed the Punic fleet on the coast of Sicily; to Q. Fabius Maximus, dictator; to L. Cornelius Scipio, who led a successful war against King Antiochus in 190 B. C.; to Q. Cæcilius Metellus Numidicus; to L. Cornelius Sulla Felix, dictator, etc.

The area of the Forum of Augustus is covered by a double bed of ruins. The lower one, 2.75 metres high, formed the bottom of the marsh, or pond, called *il Pantano*, where, for want of a proper outlet, the rain-water from the slopes of the Quirinal and the valley of the Subura collected in the Middle Ages. The upper one, 3.25 metres thick, dates from the year 1570, when Pius V. and the commissioner of streets, Prospero Boccapaduli, drained the marsh, found an outlet for the waters, and raised the city to the present level. Needless to say, works of art and objects of archæological value are found only in the lower strata. Marchese Alessandro Guiccioli, syndic of Rome, at the time of the excavations of 1888–89 had formed the project of laying bare the whole extent of the Forum; and certainly no greater benefit could have been conferred on students of ancient Rome, and no greater addition secured to the archæological wealth of our city than by the liberation of these ruins from the ignoble superstructures which hide them from view. An exchange of property between the municipality and the Ospizio dei Convertendi, which owns the place, had already been agreed upon, when the financial crisis of 1889 occurred, and stopped the progress of our work.

LITERATURE. — Theodor Mommsen, *Res Gestæ divi Augusti*, iv. 21–26, p. 126, 2d edit. — *Corpus Inscr.*, vol. vi. 1386; and *Inscr. lat. antiquiss.*, 2d edit. Berlin, Reimer, 1893, p. 186. — Luigi Borsari, *Il foro di Augusto e il tempio di Marte Ultore*, Accad. Lincei, 3 serie, vol. xiii., 1883–84, p. 406. — Rodolfo Lanciani, *Bull. com.*, 1889, pp. 26 and 73. — Giuseppe Gatti, *ibid.*, 1889, p. 481; and 1890, p. 251, pl. 14. — Christian Huelsen, *Mittheilungen*, vol. v., 1890, pp. 247, 305; and vol. vi., 1891, p. 94. — Thédenat, in Daremberg and Saglio's *Dictionnaire*, p. 1311.

LIII. FORUM TRANSITORIUM. — This Forum, commenced by Domitian and finished by Nerva, was called *transitorium* or *pervium* because the great thoroughfare of the Argiletum passed through it; also Forum Nervæ from the founder and Forum Minervæ or Forum Palladium from the goddess to whom it was dedicated. It was a long, narrow inclosure, 117 metres by 39, more like a handsomely decorated street than a square. The inclosure walls, built of peperino and coated with marble, were lined with fluted columns supporting a richly carved entablature, of which one intercolumniation alone remains, known by the name of Le Colonnacce (corner of Via Alessandrina and Via della Croce Bianca). Four hundred years ago it could still be measured in its entirety by Antonio da Sangallo the younger, Baldassarre, and Sallustio Peruzzi and others, whose drawings I have published in the "Atti d. r. Accad. d. Lincei," vol. xi. 1883. The destruction was not accomplished at once, but was the work of many generations, the monks of S. Adriano being foremost in the campaign against the edifice. I have found mention more than once, in deeds of the fourteenth century, of a great lime-kiln established near their church under the name of "calcaria ecclesiæ sancti Hadriani." In November, 1520, a gang of *fossores lapidum* [1] opened a trench at the foot of one of the archways of the Forum, known by the name of Arcus Noe, or Arcanoe (the Arch of Noah), and began to undermine the wall of peperino. Francesco di Branca, one of the city magistrates, caused a member of the gang to be arrested; but Cardinal Scaramuccia Trivulzio, in whose interests perhaps he was working, obtained his prompt release from Leo X. The "vignettes" of the sixteenth century, of Dosio, Du Perac, Koch, Gamucci, etc., represent this Arch of Noah and the adjoining Temple of Minerva in a good state of preservation. The ruins were so striking and picturesque that many artists have selected them as a background to their compositions. The following sketch (Fig. 118) of Boscolo in Laing's collection, Royal Scottish Academy, Edinburgh, represents the meeting of some holy men before the Temple of Minerva; the Arch of Noah appears on the right, and above it the church and belfry of SS. Stefano and Lorenzo (now SS. Quirico e Giolitta).

The destruction of the arch and of the temple is commonly attributed to Pope Paul V., Borghese; but Clement VIII., Aldobrandini, had already laid hands on them. Giacomo Grimaldi says that while walking one day through the Lungara with Giacomo della Porta, they saw a great block of Parian marble being removed from this temple to S. Peter's. The block, belonging to the architrave, measured 11.55 cubic metres, or about 346 cubic feet. Clem-

---

[1] Contractors for the supply of building materials.

ent VIII. made use of it for the high altar of S. Peter's, which he inaugurated on June 26, 1594. The rest of the temple disappeared in 1606. The columns and the frieze were cut in slabs, and made use of for the decoration of the fountain of the Acqua Paola on the Janiculum. The blocks of stone belonging to the cella and to the inclosure wall of the Forum were given by Paul V. to the prior and monks of S. Adriano. The platform of the temple still exists, although hidden from view; the house at the corner of the Via Alessandrina, which faces the Colonnacce on one side and the church of S. Agata on the other, is built upon it. Another house, No. 38 Via della Croce Bianca, may be truly said to rest on a bed of marble. I saw its foundations sunk, in October, 1882, through a mass of broken columns, capitals, friezes, and pedestals. The pavement of the Forum lies here at the depth of 5.50 metres.

Like the Forum Augustum and the Forum Traiani, this one

Fig. 118. — The Forum Transitorium : a sketch by Boscolo.

had also its own gallery of portrait statues. Its institution dates from the time of Severus Alexander; compare "Vita Alex.," 28: "Colossal statues, single or equestrian, were raised by him in Nerva's Forum to deified Emperors or Empresses." Two speci-mens have come down to us: one of them was discovered in the first quarter of the sixteenth century by Angelo de Massimi, and removed, first to the family palace in the Via Papale, and later on to the Capitoline Museum (ground floor, corridor No. 19). The name of King Pyrrhus attributed to it is manifestly erroneous; at the same time we cannot agree with Helbig in identifying it with Mars, on account of the evidence of the biographer, who speaks not of gods but of deified Roman Emperors. The fragments of a second colossal (female) figure, resembling to a certain degree the Thusnelda in the Loggia de' Lanzi, Florence, were discovered by Vitali in 1882.

LITERATURE. — Rodolfo Lanciani, *L' aula e gli uffici del Senato Romano* (in Mem. Accad. Lincei, 1883, p. 23). — Wolfgang Helbig, *Guide,* vol. i. p. 295, n. 405. — H. Blümner, *Annal. Inst.,* 1877, p. 5; and *Monumenti,* vol. x. pl. 11. — Eugen Petersen, *Mittheilungen,* vol. iv. 1889, p. 88. — Thédenat, in Daremberg and Saglio's *Dictionnaire,* p. 1314. — Heinrich Jordan, *Forma,* p. 27.

LIV. FORUM TRAIANI (Forum of Trajan, Plan, Fig. 119). — We must now enter the last and most magnificent of Roman fora, built by Trajan between A. D. 112 and 114 from the designs of Apollodorus of Damascus. It was not only a masterpiece of architecture, but also, if we recollect the difficulties its builders had to contend with to find a suitable space for it, a *chef-d'œuvre* of engineering skill.

The Capitoline, located in the heart of the city, was not an isolated hill, as it is at present: the tide of traffic between the northern and southern quarters could not round it on either side as is now the case. The Capitoline was a spur of the Quirinal, advancing towards the river to within a few hundred feet from its left bank. The obstruction could be overcome in one of two ways: by crossing the ridge connecting the two hills by the Clivus Argentarius, corresponding to our Via di Marforio, only five metres wide with a gradient of ten per cent; or else by rounding the rock on the river-side. The passage was certainly easy and level on the river-side, but three times as long as the cut through the ridge, and obviously insufficient for the traffic of a city inhabited by a million people. To obviate this evil, to relieve the strip of land west of the Capitoline from the pressure of traffic, and to double, at the same time, the extent of the five existing fora (Romanum, Iulium, Augustum, Pacis, and Transitorium) Trajan and Apollodorus conceived the plan of severing the Capitoline from the Quirinal, and of substituting for the narrow and steep gully of the Clivus Argentarius a level space 185 metres wide. Private property on each slope and on the top of the ridge was accordingly bought and destroyed to the extent of over 40,000 square metres, and the ridge was cut, excavated, and bodily carted away. So great was the astonishment created by the great work that the well-known column was erected at a public cost, "ad declarandum quantæ altitudinis mons et locus sit egestus" (Corpus Inscr., vi.

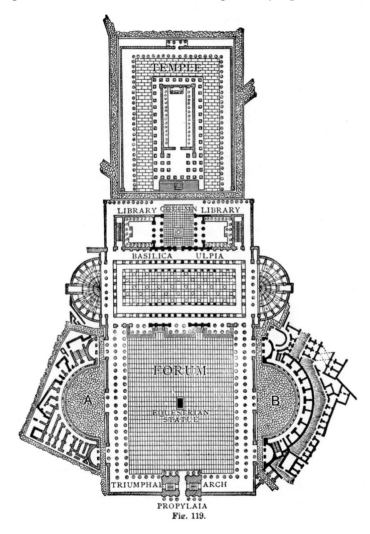

Fig. 119.

n. 960), — "to show to posterity how high rose the mountain leveled to make room for the forum." The pillar, statue included,
is 42 metres high. The 700,000 or 800,000 cubic metres of earth
and rock were carted away outside the Porta Collina, and spread
over the cemetery between the Via Salaria Nova and Vetus. (See
Pagan and Christian Rome, p. 284.)

Trajan's Forum comprised seven parts: the propylaia with the
triumphal arch of the founder, the square itself with the equestrian statue in the middle, the Basilica Ulpia, the Bibliotheca
Ulpia, two hemicycles, the monumental column, and the Temple
of Trajan.

The triumphal arch which formed the entrance to the Forum
was demolished, or at least greatly injured, by the commissioners
of streets in March, 1526. The case was inquired into by Francesco Cenci, the chief magistrate of the city, who made a report
to the town council March 26, but no redress seems to have been
obtained. In the latter part of the sixteenth century (about
1570) other remains were dug up near the church of S. Maria in
Campo Carléo. Flaminio Vacca describes them as "vestigie di
un' arco trionfale con molti pezzi di istorie," viz., with fragments
of bas-reliefs which represented Trajan fording a river on horse-
back, King Decebalus bound in chains, the seizing of the enemy's
cattle, etc. The last discoveries took place in 1863, when the
church of S. Maria in Campo Carléo was demolished to widen
the roadway at the entrance of the Via Alessandrina. The arch,
erected, or at least voted, by the S. P. Q. R. in A. D. 117, a few
months before Trajan's death, is represented with minute details
in the medal ap. Cohen, "Monnaies imper. Trajan," n. 167.

LITERATURE. — Dion Cassius, lxviii. 29. — *Codex vatic.*, 3439, f. 84. — *Codex
Berolin.*, f. 36. — Flaminio Vacca, *Mem.* 9 (in Fea's Miscellanea, vol. i.). —
Angelo Pellegrini, *Bull. Inst.*, 1883, p. 78. — Pasquale Adinolfi, *Roma nell'
età di mezzo,* vol. i. p. 54.

The Forum, 95 metres long and 116 wide, was surrounded by a
double colonnade on three sides, the fourth side, opposite the
propylaia, being occupied by the basilica. The porticoes were
crowded with statues of eminent men, with an account of their
career engraved on the pedestals. Many of these valuable historical documents have already been discovered;[1] they belong mostly
to the fourth century after Christ. The inclosure wall of the
forum was built of blocks of peperino lined with marble, like

[1] *Corpus Inscr.*, 1141, 1679, 1683, 1710, 1715, 1721, 1724, 1725, 1727, 1729,
1736, 1749, 1764, 1783.

those of the Forum Augustum and Forum Transitorium. No trace
of it appears now above ground, but we have a careful description of it in a deed of 1263 quoted by Adinolfi in vol. ii. of " Roma
nell' età di mezzo," p. 54. It was called the " murus marmoreus,"
and crossed the whole extent of the Campo Carléo from the Capitoline to the Quirinal hill. The equestrian statue of the Emperor
rose in the centre of the square. Ammianus Marcellinus (xvi. 10)
describes the impressions felt by the Emperor Constantius at
the first sight of the group. " Having now entered the Forum
Trajanum, *the most marvelous creation of human genius*, he was
struck with wonder, and looked round in amazement at the great
structures which no pen can describe, and which mankind can
create and see but once in the course of centuries. . . . Then he
turned his attention to the equestrian statue in the centre of the
forum, and said to his attendants he would have one like it in
Constantinople, to which Hormisdas, a young Persian prince attached to the court, replied, ' You must first provide your horse
with a stable like this.' " I shall recall to the memory of the
reader only two of the many historical events which have taken
place in this forum. First the burning of the registers of the
arrears due to the Imperial Treasury (*syngrapha* or *tabulæ debito-
rum*) by private citizens, ordered by Hadrian A. D. 118. The sum
was simply appalling : " novies millies centena millia sestertium,"
or about 170,000,000 lire. A fragment of the inscription recording the event, discovered in 1812, has been set up in the modern
wall behind the pillar. (See Corpus Inscr., vi. 967; Eckhel,
Doctr. numm., vol. vii. 486; and Vita Ḥadr., 7.) The other
occurrence is related in the " Vita Marci," ch. xvii. The treasury
being exhausted in consequence of the Marcomannic wars, and
the Emperor being unwilling to burden his subjects with new
contributions (especially as the pestilence was then raging), he
put up at auction all the valuables of the crown. The auction
took place in the Forum of Trajan and lasted two months, a large
sum of money being realized, with the help of which the war was
brought to a successful close. Marcus Aurelius sold the golden
plate and vases of crystal and murrha, even the Imperial drinking-
cups, the state robes set with gems and woven of silk, and also
many marvelous jewels which he had found in a secret drawer of
Hadrian (*in repostorio sanctiore Hadriani*). After the end of the
war he offered to buy back the objects sold, and showed no dis-
satisfaction whatever with those who refused.

To support the deep cuttings on either side of the Forum, Apollodorus raised two hemicycles (Fig. 119, A, B) the design and architecture of which is so complicated that it would be difficult to describe it properly.   There are few traces left of the one towards the Capitol, but the semicircular line of the houses in the Piazza delle Chiavi d' Oro shows it to have been perfectly symmetrical with the one on the opposite side.   This last, very well preserved, bears the traditional name of baths of Æmilius Paulus — Balneapauli, Magnanapoli — and consists of many-storied corridors and shops or rooms, built against the live rock of the Quirinal.   The pavement which extends in front of the building was laid bare during the French invasion (1812).   The place well deserves a visit. Apply to the custode of the Forum, or to the Ufficio dei Monumenti via in Miranda.   The remains, however, are not all accessible.   They cover an immense space under the Palazzo Ceva-Roccagiovane, Palazzo Tiberi, under the barracks and monastery of S. Caterina da Siena, under the house and garden of Prince Ruspoli, and also under the houses of the Via del Grillo.

LITERATURE. — Carlo Fea, *Prodromo di nuove osservazioni*, p. 4 ; and *Iscrizioni di Monum.*, p. 13. — Emil Braun, *Ruins and Museums*, p. 20, n. 8. — Mariano Armellini, *Chiese*, 2d ed. p. 177.   The remains have been measured and sketched by Sangallo the elder, *Cod. Barberin.*, f. 2 ; by Sangallo the younger, *Uffizi*, n. 1187 ; by Sallustio Peruzzi, *Uffizi*, 653, 654, 656, 665, 687; by Gio. Antonio Dosio, *Uffizi*, 2540, 2565; by Martin Heemskerk, *Berlin*, 28, 34; and by Andrea Aleppi and Domenico Cacchiatelli, after the French excavations in 1815.

The Basilica Ulpia, a hall 89 metres long and 54 wide, surrounded by a double line of columns, 96 in all, was excavated in 1813 by the French government after the demolition of the convents dello

Fig. 120. — Frieze from the Basilica Ulpia (Lateran Museum).

Spirito Santo and di S. Eufemia, which occupied its site. On the return of Pius VII. in 1814 the works were resumed, a wall supporting the modern streets was built on the border of the excavations, and the columns of the nave and aisles were set up on their bases, many of which had been found *in situ*. It must be observed, however, that not all the columns were of gray or Psaronian granite; those on either side of the entrance doors were certainly, and those of the nave were probably, of giallo antico, and fluted. One of these last was removed to the Lateran at the time of Clement VIII. and placed under the organ of the nave Clementina; and four went to the transept of S. Peter's. The nave was covered by a roof of bronze, the ὀρόφου χαλκοῦ of Pausanias (v. 12, 4, and x. 5, 5), and

Fig. 121. — Frieze from the Basilica Ulpia (Lateran Museum.).

paved with crusts of the rarest marble, many fragments of which, discovered in 1813, have since been stolen by unscrupulous tourists.

The basilica faced the Forum on its longer side, as the Basilica Julia faced the Forum Romanum. There were three doors, flanked by four columns each, and above them quadrigæ, and trophies of gilt metal, made *ex manubiis*, viz., with the produce of the sale of the spoils of war. The names of the glorious legions who had fought so bravely in both Dacian campaigns were engraved on the

frieze over the doors; we can still read those of the XI Claudia,
of the XV Apollinaris, and of the XX Valeria Victrix. Other
trophies were set up, on the edge of the five marble steps which
descended to the "area fori," on pedestals inscribed with the legend
(Corpus, vi. n. 959), "The S. P. Q. R. to Traian, son of Nerva
. . . consul for the sixth time (A. D. 112), father of the country,
for the great services rendered to the commonwealth in peace and
in war." The marvelous beauty of the marble decorations of the
nave and aisles cannot be properly described. The reader may get
an idea of it from the two fragments which are here reproduced
(Figs. 120, 121). (Compare Helbig's Guide, vol. i. p. 468, n. 627;
and p. 470, n. 629, 630.) The side of the basilica towards the
Forum is represented in two medals ap. Cohen, "Monnaies imper.
Trajan," n. 42, 43, 44; and its plan in a fragment of the "Forma
Urbis," ap. Jordan, 25, 26.

The basilica ended with two hemicycles, one of which was called
"Libertatis." The meaning of the name is not certain, but, as we
know from Sidonius Apollinaris that the formalities attending the
manumission of slaves were accomplished in this Forum, it is
possible that the old name of Atrium Libertatis had been transferred in the second century from the neighborhood of the Forum
Romanum[1] to the hemicycle of the Basilica Ulpia, a portion of
which is still visible under the Palazzo Ceva-Roccagiovane. Mommsen and De Rossi have expressed the opinion that the ceremony of
manumission was again performed in the fourth century in or near
the old site, in the Secretarium Senatus.

Coming out of the basilica from the side opposite the Forum,
we enter a small court or cavædium (24 metres by 16) flanked by
two halls, which have been identified with the libraries mentioned
by Dion Cassius (lxviii. 26). They were called Bibliotheca Ulpia,
and also Bibliotheca Templi Traiani. Nibby, who saw them excavated in 1812–14, gives a good description of their arrangement in
vol. ii. p. 189 of the "Roma antica." Gellius names among their
contents the *edicta prætorum*, and Vopiscus (?) the *libri lintei* or
official registers (*regesta*) of the acts and deeds of each Emperor.
A special license from the prefect of Rome was required to inspect
these records of the history of the world; and when Vopiscus
himself was asked to write the life of Aurelianus on the basis of
official documents, he had to apply to Junius Tiberianus, prefect
A. D. 291, for a permit to consult them. There was another set
called *libri elephantini*, on the leaves of which, made of sheets of

---

[1] Cicero, *Ad Attic.*, book iv. n. 16 ; Servius, *Æneid*, book i. v. 726.

ivory, were transcribed the *Senatus consulta* concerning the person of the Emperor. The documents of state were afterwards removed by Diocletian to his baths.

The great column, *columna cochlis*, 128 feet, or 38 metres, high, without the statue, stands in a court of such diminutive proportions that it could not possibly be seen to advantage, except from the north side, that is, from the steps of the temple. It is composed of 34 blocks of Carrara marble, 8 of which form the pedestal, 1 the base, 23 the shaft, 1 the capital, and 1 the pedestal of the bronze statue. A spiral staircase of 185 steps, lighted by 45 loopholes, leads to the top, viz., to the square platform above the capital. A spiral band of high reliefs describing the fortunes of the Dacic wars covers the column on the outside. The reliefs, containing 2,500 figures, were cut after the shaft had been set up, so as to make the joints of the blocks absolutely imperceptible. The same process was followed with regard to the spiral stairs, which were only roughly hewn out of the block before it was lifted into position, and then finished. Nothing can give a better idea of the exactness and ingenuity with which the great work was accomplished than to ascend the pillar [1] and examine the joints, the development of the steps, and the clever distribution of the loopholes, which, while supplying plenty of light, are so well concealed by the outer relief as to remain almost invisible. On nearing the door, which opens on the platform or balcony above the capital, we see the sides of the stairs covered with graffiti, with historical names among them. The oldest dates from A. D. 663, and refers to the disastrous visit of Constans II., described in " Ancient Rome," p. 294.

There is a current belief that Trajan's ashes were deposited underneath the column in an urn of solid gold. Dion Cassius (lxix. 2) is responsible for this statement, which is confirmed by Eutropius and Cassiodorus ; but if we consider that the column was finished in 113, viz., four years before Trajan's death, that the inscription on the pedestal distinctly asserts that it was raised to mark the height of the hill cut away to make room for the Forum and not as a funeral monument, and that there is no trace of a room, recess, or vault, nor of a door and of stairs leading or descending to it, Dion's statement appears to us more than doubtful. The question could be easily cleared up *de facto* by examining the foundations on which the column rests.

[1] Permission may be obtained at the Ufficio regionale dei Monumenti via in Miranda.

An inscription discovered in Rome in the latter part of the fifteenth century is closely connected with the Emperor's death at Selinus in Cilicia, in August, 117. It mentions likewise the death of one of his faithful servants, a young man of twenty-eight, M. Ulpius Phædimus, a butler, which took place on August 12 of the same year and in the same city. His ashes were also removed to Rome and given a solemn burial: "reliquiæ treiectæ eius ex permissu collegii pontific(um) piaculo facto."

The discovery of the polychromy of the column, viz., of traces of colors (and of gilding?), was made by G. Semper on July 9, 1833, as briefly described in the "Bull. Inst.," 1833, p. 92. P. Morey, one of those who had joined Semper in his perilous expedition,[1] tried to deny the statement in a letter addressed to Bunsen (ibid., 1836, p. 39). Later observations, made when Napoleon III. caused a plaster cast to be taken of the column, have shown Semper's theory to be the correct one.

The pedestal of the column was excavated at the time of Paul III., who caused the church of S. Nicolao de Columna to be demolished. Sixtus V. in 1588 built an inclosure wall round the pedestal, and placed the bronze statue of S. Peter on the top of the pillar. The murder of Hugues Basseville or Basville, the envoy of the French revolutionists, took place at the foot of this column the 23 nivôse, an I. (January 13, 1793). The assassination is represented in a rare engraving by Berthault.

LITERATURE. — *Corpus inscr.*, vol. vi. n. 960. — Antonio da Sangallo the elder, *Cod. Barber.*, f. 18, and other artists mentioned in Ferri's Catalogue of Architectural Drawings in the Uffizi (Rome, 1885), pp. 156 and 167. — Pietro da Cortona, in Dr. Meade's collection of drawings at Eton College. See *Bull. com.*, 1895, p. 182. — Alfonso Ciaccone, *Historia utriusque belli Dacici*, etc. Rome, 1576, fol. — Anton. Francesco Gori, *Columna traiana . . . ab Andrea Morellio delineata*, etc. Amsterdam, 1652. — Raffaele Fabretti, *De columna traiana syntagma*. Rome, 1683. — Gio. Battista Piranesi, *Trofeo o sia magnifica colonna*, etc., in 28 plates. — Platner and Hirt, *Gesch. des Baukunst*, ii. 355. — Carlo Fea, in Winckelmann's *Storia dell' Arte*, vol. iii. p. 355. — Froehner, *La colonne trajane*, in 8° 1865, in fol. 1874. — Salomon Reinach, *La colonne trajane au musée de Saint Germain*, 1886. — Auguste Geffroy, *La colonne d'Arcadius à Constantinople*, extrait des Monuments et Memoires publiés par l'Acad. des Inscr. Paris, Leroux, 1895. In the Cabinet des Estampes, Bibliothèque Nationale, Paris (Rome, volume *Monti*, D), there are over one hundred prints of the column. A silver model carved by Valadier is now in the royal palace at Munich.

The Temple of Trajan closed the monumental group on the

[1] They had been lowered from the capital in a kind of cage held by ropes and pulleys.

north side. It was erected by Hadrian *parentibvs svis* (Trajan
and Plotina), and was noted for its colossal proportions. The
Corinthian capitals six feet high, and the pieces of columns of
granite six feet in diameter which now lie at the foot of the pillar,
have been discovered at various times under the Palazzo Imperiali-
Valentini. Winckelmann describes the removal of one, found
in August, 1765, while five more were left on the spot. I have
myself seen other pieces discovered when the Palazzo Valentini
became the seat of the county council. The curious set of heads
of animals, alluding, perhaps, to the conquest of Arabia made by

Fig. 122. — Heads of Animals discovered in the Forum of Trajan.

Cornelius Palma, formerly in the court of the palace, was removed
in 1878 to the Collegio Romano, and again in 1890 to the Museo
delle Terme. (See Fig. 122.)

LITERATURE. — *Corpus Inscr.*, vi. n. 966. — Winckelmann, in Fea's *Miscellanea*, vol. i. p. cci. n. 7; and *Storia dell' Arte*, vol. ii. p. 372, iii. p. 44. —
Minutolo, in Sallengre's *Suppl. antiq. rom.*, vol. i. col. 159. — Rodolfo Lanciani, *Bull. Inst.*, 1869, p. 237.

The Forum of Trajan has been a favorite subject of study with
the young architects of the French Academy, Villa Medici. A
list of their drawings and restorations has been published by E.
Pourchet, 15 Rue des Beaux Arts, Paris.

BOOK IV

BEFORE giving an account of the rest of the city, I must remind the reader once more that in writing this book I do not intend to produce a manual of Roman topography, but simply a description of its existing remains. In carrying out the scheme I have endeavored, as stated in the preface, to group the buildings in regard to their chronology or destination rather than to the place they occupy accidentally in the various quarters of the city.

THE RUINS OF THE CÆLIAN HILL.

REGIO I. PORTA CAPENA.*

I. The Cælian hill and its southwestern slopes were included by Augustus within the limits of the first and second regions, the line of separation being the wall of Servius Tullius. Regio I, named Porta Capena, extended on the left side of the Appian Way as far as the river Almo (the Acquataccio, or Marrana della Caffarella), a distance of 2107 metres from the gate. Richter calls it appropriately "die Vorstadt der Via Appia" and àlso "die Vorstadt extra Portam Capenam." It was a narrow strip of land, bounded on the side opposite the Appian Way by another road, issuing from the Porta Metroni, the name of which is unknown. A third road, the Latina, crosses it diagonally, skirting the base of a hillock called by Ficoroni "il Celiolo," "Remuria" by others, "Calvarello" in the Middle Ages, and now the "Monte d' Oro." Considering the preference given by the Romans to the borders of the great consular roads for the establishment of public cemeteries, and for the erection of private tombs and mausoleums, no wonder that Regio I, crossed by three of them, the Appia, the Latina, and the one issuing from the Porta Metroni, should be in the main a region of tombs. Some of them date from a remote age, when

*See Figure 123 on page xxiv.

the Via Appia and the Via Latina were mere paths traced by the hoofs of beasts of burden and not leveled or yet paved by the hand of man. Such is the sepulchral cave discovered in May, 1836, in the Vigna Cremaschi, the first on the right of the Porta Latina, a description of which is given in the "Bullett. Inst.," 1836, p. 103. It was found by accident below the pavement of a columbaria of the first century, at a depth of 7.80 metres. It consisted of "a grotto hewn out of the live rock, of irregular shape and without ornaments. It contained several vases of black ware (bucchero?) with rough figures of animals traced on their surface in the Etruscan fashion. One of the vases contained the remains of an incinerated body." Roman tradition and epigraphic documents help us in following the growth and development of this great necropolis, especially after the opening of the Viæ Latina and Appia, which took place between 312 and 297 B. C.[1] The first historical tomb, on leaving the gate, was that of Horatia, which Livy (i. 26) describes as built "saxo quadrato" with blocks of tufa; then followed the family mausoleums of the Catalini, of the Scipios, of the Servilii, of the Metelli, mentioned by Cicero (Tuscul. 1, 7, 13), two of which, those of the Scipios and of the Metelli, are still in existence.

II. HYPOGÆUM SCIPIONUM, discovered partly in 1614, partly in 1780. This venerable monument and the ground which covers and surrounds it were bought, on my suggestion, by the city in 1880. They are entered by the Via di Porta S. Sebastiano, No. 12, and can be visited every day, Sundays excepted. Entrance fee, 25 centimes.

The discoveries of the seventeenth century have been mentioned by one epigraphist alone, Giacomo Sirmondo, in a book entitled "Antiquæ inscriptionis, qua L. Scipionis Barbati filii expressum est elogium, explanatio," Rome, 1617. Two sarcophagi were found: one, of L. Cornelius Scipio, quæstor 167 B. C., was left undisturbed; the other, of L. Cornelius, son of Barbatus, consul 259, was broken and its inscription sold to a stone-cutter near the Ponte Rotto, in

---

[1] The Via Appia was *munita*, that is to say, leveled, straightened, and macadamized by Appius Claudius Cæcus, censor in 312 B. C. (Livy, ix. 29). The brothers Ogulnii, censors in 297, added to it a sidewalk paved with flagstones, which went as far as the Temple of Mars (*ibid.*, x. 23). Lastly, T. Quinctius Flamininus and M. Claudius Marcellus, censors in 188, "viam silice sternendam a porta Capena ad Martis locaverunt" (*ibid.*, xxxviii. 28). If we can believe the same historian, the rest of the road from the temple to Bovillæ had been paved since the year 292 (x. 47).

whose shop Grimaldi saw it on September 25, 1614. Agostini bought it for twenty scudi, and gave or sold it to the Barberini, who set it into the wall of the spiral staircase of their palace, near the door of the library.

The brothers Sassi, owners of the vineyard in which the discoveries of 1614 had taken place, while enlarging their wine-cellar in May, 1780, came once more across the hypogæum, and laid bare its precious contents. In reading the accounts left by Morcelli, Marini, Visconti, and Amaduzzi, we cannot understand how such acts of wanton destruction as the brothers Sassi perpetrated on this most venerable of Roman historical tombs could have been permitted or left unpunished by Pius VI., whose love for antique monuments certainly cannot be questioned.

> "The Scipios' tomb contains no ashes now:
> The very sepulchres lie tenantless
> Of their heroic dwellers!"

The sarcophagi were broken to pieces; their inscribed fronts removed to the Vatican; the aspect of the crypts altered; the

Fig. 124. — Sarcophagus of Scipio Barbatus in the Vatican.

movable objects dispersed; the facsimiles of the original epitaphs affixed to the wrong places; the signet ring of one of the heroes, with the image of the Victory, given away to a Frenchman, Louis Dutens, who in his turn gave or sold it to Lord Beverley. And lastly, the very bones of the illustrious men, which had been respected even by the so-called barbarians, would have been dispersed to the four winds, but for the pious interference of Angelo Quirini, a senator of Venice, who rescued the relics of L. Cornelius Scipio, son of Barbatus, and placed them in a marble urn in the

Villa dell' Alticchiero, near Padua. A remarkable fate indeed, if we recall to mind the words of Livy (xxxviii. 53): "Scipio spent the last years of his life at Liternum, without missing in the least degree the attractions of city life; and, if we are to believe tradition, he left instructions at the point of death to be buried in his farm: monimentumque ibi ædificarine funus sibi in ingrata patria fieret." The same mother country, obdurate in her ingratitude, allowed these remains to be dispersed after twenty centuries of rest.

From the descriptions left by those who witnessed the excavations of 1780, compared with a model in full relief made at the same time [1] and with the present aspect of the place, we learn the following details about the origin and the arrangement of the hypogæum.

The part of the ancient cemetery now occupied by the Vigna Sassi was crossed at an early period by a side road, connecting the Via Appia with the Latina, the pavement of which is still visible at the two ends. The road followed the foot of a rocky ridge ten or fifteen feet high, and passed one or more tufa quarries which had been opened in the face of the cliffs. One of these quarries, probably the property of the Scipios, was transformed into their family tomb at the beginning of the third century B. C., probably on the occasion of the opening of the Via Appia, B. C. 312. The hypogæum, roughly modeled on the Etruscan type, formed a large room, with a flat low ceiling supported by four massive pillars of rock, yet very far from the regularity which it appears to have in Piranesi's drawings (Fig. 125). The first occupant was L. Cornelius Scipio Barbatus, consul in 298 B. C. His sarcophagus, now in the Vatican Museum (Belvedere, No. 2), is the only elaborate piece of work discovered in the tomb. The frieze, which is Doric in style, consists of triglyphs and of metopes adorned with rosettes: the torus of the lid ends with Ionic volutes. The inscription, in the early Italic Saturnine verse, has been translated by Mommsen as follows: —

> Cornelius Lucius — Scipio Barbatus
> son of his father Gnævus — a man as clever as brave
> whose handsome appearance — was in harmony with his virtue
> who was consul and censor — among you, as well as Ædile
> Taurasia Cisaunia — he captured in Samnium
> utterly overcomes Lucania — and brings away hostages.[2]

---

[1] Nibby saw it in 1839 in the house of Signor Vincenzo Titoli.

[2] Wolfgang Helbig, *Guide to the Collections of Antiquities in Rome*, vol. i. p. 75. — *Corpus Inscr.*, vol. i. p. 16, n. 29, 30; vol. vi. n. 1284, 1285. — *Revue de Philologie*, xiv. (1890) p. 119.

The other sarcophagi were made of plain slabs of stone, or cut out of a single block. Their respective positions are marked in the annexed plan.

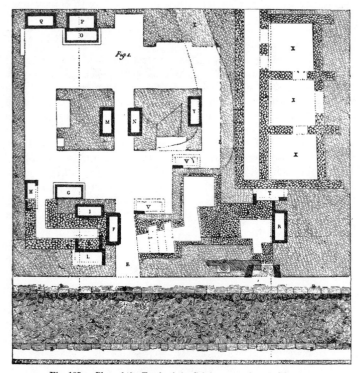

Fig. 125. — Plan of the Tomb of the Scipios, according to Piranesi.

A A, Cross-road between the Via Appia and the Latina. B B, *Margo* or *semita*, raised footway. C, Arched entrance built of rough blocks of pepe-rino. D, Base of one of the columns which decorated the front of the upper story. E, Ancient entrance to the quarry, by which the sarcophagi were introduced into the crypt. F, Sarcophagus of Lucius Scipio, son of Asiaticus, *Corpus*, vol. i. n. 31. G, H, L, T, V, Coffins of unknown personages. I, Coffin of peperino before which the marble tablet of Julius Silanus was found. M, Sarcophagus of L. Scipio, son of Barbatus, n. 32. N, Sarcophagus of L. Scipio, son of Cnæus, n. 34. O, Sarcophagus of Scipio Barbatus, n. 29. P, Sarco-phagus of Cornelia Paula, n. 39. Q, Sarcophagus of Scipio Asiagenes Comatus, n. 36. R, Sarcophagus of Scipio Hispallus, n. 38. S, Marble slab with name of Cornelia Gætulica. X X X, Three rooms, forming part of an edifice of the second century, built of bricks. Y, Sarcophagus of P. Scipio flamen dialis, n. 33. Z, Present entrance to the crypt.

We are not sure how much faith Piranesi's plan deserves, some of the particulars being manifestly fanciful. The gallery, for instance, which runs in front of the sarcophagus of Barbatus (O), has never been finished, and its end on the right is still blocked by a ledge of live rock. The reader may estimate the amount of damage which the hypogæum has suffered since 1780 by comparing Piranesi's plan with the following one, which shows its present state.

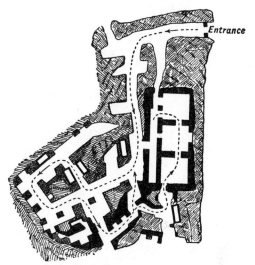

Fig. 126. — Tomb of the Scipios. (Present State.)

There are three more particulars to be noticed. The first is that the crypts of the Scipios were kept accessible as a place of historical pilgrimage up to the fourth century after Christ, as shown by the walls in the so-called "opus maxentianum," built here and there to keep the tomb in repair.

In the second place, the preference shown by the gens Cornelia, of which the Scipios were a branch, for burial as opposed to cremation, is proved by the presence of sarcophagi and by the absence of cinerary urns. (See Cicero, De Leg., ii. 12; and Pliny, vii. 54.) The first Cornelius to give up family traditions on this point was Sulla the dictator, who, having caused the remains of Marius to be exhumed and profaned, ordered his own body to be cremated for fear of retaliation. Sulla's ashes were not deposited in this family vault, — which seems to have been owned only by the three branches of the Scipios called Africani, Asiatici, and Hispalli, — but in a great mausoleum on the Campus Martius described by Plutarch. What seems strange, however, is that none of the leaders of the three branches — Publius Cornelius Scipio Africanus Maior, the conqueror of Carthage, † 183 B. C.; Lucius Cornelius Scipio Asiaticus, his brother; and Cn. Cornelius Scipio Hispallus, consul in 171 — should have found rest in this tomb. Livy (xxxviii. 56) says that no one knew whether the great Africanus had been buried at Liternum or at Rome, because a grave and a statue were shown in both places. Seneca likewise writes to Lucilius from Liternum: "I address this epistle [lxxxvi] to you from the very villa of Scipio the African, after having paid reverence to his memory and to the altar which *I suspect* to be his grave." The monument and statue erected in or near the Roman hypogæum have yet to be discovered.

The third particular refers to the presence of an outsider in the same hypogæum, of Q. Ennius the poet, who was born at Rudiæ in Calabria in 289 B. C., and died in Rome at the age of seventy. Although dwelling in a humble house on the Aventine, and supporting himself by teaching the Greek language and translating Greek plays for the Roman stage, he was the friend of the great, and lived on terms of the closest intimacy with the elder Africanus. Livy (xxxviii. 36) says that "in Scipionum monumento extra portam Capenam" three statues could be seen, one of which was considered to represent the poet, and Cicero adds that the statue was of marble. A laurel-crowned portrait head in peperino was actually found in the tomb in 1780, and is now placed in the Vatican Museum above the sarcophagus of Barbatus. "The un-Roman type of countenance and the presence of the laurel wreath, which might well be worn by a poet," have led many to attribute this head to the statue mentioned by Livy and Cicero. The objection derived from the material in which it is carved (peperino instead of marble) has no great weight. I have no doubt that Cicero is mistaken in mentioning marble, because in the third century B. C. portrait statues and busts were sculptured in Rome out of stone.

LITERATURE. — Giovanni Amaduzzi, *Novelle letter. fiorentine*, 1780–83. — Gio. Battista Visconti, *Antologia romana*, vols. vi.-ix. — Louis Dutens, *Œuvres mélées.* Geneva, 1784. — Enrico Quirino Visconti, in Piranesi's *Monumento degli Scipioni*, Rome, 1785; and *Opere varie*, Milan, 1827, vol. i. pp. 1–70. — Lanzi, *Saggio di lingua etrusca*, vol. i. p. 150. — Gaetani Marini, *Atti Arval.*, p.

117, n. 109. — Carlo Fea, in Winckelmann's *Storia dell' Arte*, i. 30, and iii. 46. — Antonio Nibby, *Roma antica*, vol. ii. p. 561.— *Corpus Inscr.*, vol. i. pp. 11–16, n. 29–39 ; and vol. vi. p. 282, n. 1284–1294. — Wolfgang Helbig, *Guide*, vol. i. p. 75, n. 127; and p. 356, n. 484.

Fig. 127. — Portrait Bust of Scipio the Elder (Capitoline Museum).

At the opposite end of the Vigna Sassi, close to the chapel of S. Giovanni in Oleo and to the Porta Latina, are to be seen —

III. The Columbaria (so-called) of Pomponius Hylas. Keys with the custode of the tomb of the Scipios; open every day except Sunday.

This graceful structure, one of the best preserved of its kind in Rome, was discovered by Pietro Campana in 1831. It is known by the name of "Hylas and Vitaline," because the mosaic tablet inscribed CN · POMPONI HYLAE — POMPONIAE · CN · L VITALINIS occupies the most conspicuous place opposite the entrance; but the fact is that it was built, like so many others of the Augustan age, either by subscription among friends or relatives, or by speculators ready to sell the cinerary urns to the first comer. The crypt itself contains but twenty-two inscriptions, of no special interest. One hundred and seventeen more were discovered in the neighborhood, many of which are set into the modern wall inclosing the tomb. It appears from one of them (Corpus, n. 5631) that the ground where this and the neighboring tombs are located belonged to Cnæus Manlius Hasta, a freedman of the Manlii.

Some of the ædiculæ and niches for cinerary urns have been elaborately decorated by the purchasers, though not often in good taste. The decorations are mostly in bold relief of white stucco on a colored ground, and represent various subjects, such as the education of Achilles by Chiron, Oknos twisting the rope of rushes while the ass eats it up, the tripos of the Delphic Apollo between two griffins (under the mosaic tablet of Hylas), Bacchic scenes and dances, etc.

LITERATURE. — Girolamo Amati, *Codex vatic.*, 9770, p. 3, *seq.* — Antonio Nibby, *Roma antica*, vol. ii. p. 556. — Pietro Campana, *Di due sepolcri romani del secolo di Augusto scoverti tra la via Latina e l' Appia.* Rome, 1840, fol. — Otto Jahn, *Specimen epigraph. in memoriam Olai Kellermann.* Kiel, 1841. — *Corpus Inscr.*, vol. vi. n. 5539–5678.

IV. THE COLUMBARIA OF THE VIGNA CODINI. — The southeast end of the necropolis, between the Vigna Sassi and the walls of Aurelian, is occupied by the Vigna Codini, famous for the columbaria discovered within its limits since the renaissance of classical studies. The first of which we have an account was found towards the middle of the fifteenth century, and seems to have belonged to the freedmen and servants of the sons of Nero Drusus senior, brother of Tiberius, born 38 B. C., died A. D. 9. It contained at least eighty-six inscriptions, which were bought by several amateurs of the age — Giovanni Ciampolini, Paolo Alessi, and Francesco Porcari. They have all perished except a dozen or so which were removed from the Porcari House (Vicolo delle Ceste, No. 25) to the Vatican by Gaetano Marini. Consult the "Corpus Inscr.," vol. vi. p. 899, n. 4327–4413. Other columbaria were excavated and destroyed under Pius IV. (1559–66). Pirro Ligorio designed one of them, belonging to the freedmen of the gens Pompeia; and his drawings have been reproduced by Pietro Sante Bartoli in plates 39–41 of the volume "Gli antichi sepolcri," Rome, 1768. Flaminio Vacca speaks of a "magnifica sepoltura" discovered and destroyed by Cardinal Prospero Santacroce, † 1589,[1] and of some sarcophagi, inscribed *Diis Manibus*, of columns, architectural ornaments, and other fragments which he himself bought in a vineyard near the Porta Latina. Pietro Sante Bartoli likewise mentions the discovery of pagan and Christian cemeteries near the junction of the Appia and the Latina, in a vineyard of a certain Orlandi. Orlandi had collected a very rich harvest in cameos, intaglios, cinerary urns of glass, of marble, and of metal, figurines of bronze and terra cotta, and other "cose bellissime," when Donna Olimpia Pamfili, the omnipotent sister of the reigning Pope Innocent X., seized the whole collection, and carried it in four cartloads to her own palace in the Piazza Navona. Another excavation, described by Bartoli, led to the discovery of a sepulchral room containing the cinerarium of Asinia Fortunata (Corpus, n. 12,547).

In 1726–33 many columbaria (*gran quantità di camere sepolcrali ripiene di colombaj*) were excavated by Francesco Bevilacqua near the boundary line with the Vigna Sassi. Ficoroni speaks of many hundred urns of terra cotta and alabaster filled with incinerated remains, of inscriptions still retaining the red color of the letters, of vases carved in marble, and of frescoes, one of which represented the figure of an architect with the instruments (the graphium, the pes, the square, the plummet) of his profession. This interesting picture would have been destroyed like the others, but for the prompt action of Marchese Alessandro Capponi, who caused it to be removed from the wall, transferred to canvas, framed, and afterwards engraved on copper. The original is now preserved in the Kircherian Museum. Pier Leone Ghezzi adds that the excavations of 1726 were carried on in both vineyards at the same time, — in the Vigna Sassi at the expense of Herr Wenkler of Leipzig, in the Vigna Codini at the expense of Signor Garzia Muggiani, who then owned the property. The quantity of tombs brought to light by these men is described as "prodigious." The reader may appreciate the barbarous way in which antique monuments were treated in those days from the fact that many of the inscriptions discovered in 1726–33 have perished, and the few spared are now dispersed far and wide, at Verona, Venice, Lowther Castle near Penrith, and at Rome itself in the Vatican and Kircherian museums.

[1] Cardinal Prospero is famous for having first introduced into Rome the tobacco leaf, which was named from him *erba santa*, or *erba santacroce*. In memory of this event Roman tobacconists used to put in the signs of their shops a white cross, the coat of arms of the Santacroce family.

LITERATURE. — Francesco Ficoroni, *La bolla d' oro*, p. 47 ; and *Memorie* (in Fea's Miscellanea, vol. i. p. cxxxiv. n. 33). — Pier Leone Ghezzi (in *Bull. arch. com.*, 1882, p. 206, n. 2 ; and p. 222, n. 60). — Theodor Schreiber, *Die Fundberichte des P. L. Ghezzi* (in Berichten der k. sächs. Gesellschaft d. Wissenschaften, 1892, p. 111). — *Corpus Inscr.*, vol. vi. part ii. p. 968, n. 5813-5841.

Excavations were resumed in 1788, near the tomb of the Scipios ; sixty-four inscriptions came to light, of which fourteen have perished ; the others were removed to the Museo Borgia at Velletri (now in the Museo Nazionale, Naples), to that of Palermo, of the Vatican, etc. A few are to be seen on the spot. (Corpus Inscr., vol. vi. part ii. p. 963, n. 5679-5743.)

The three columbaria now visible in the Vigna Codini (entrance Via di Porta S. Sebastiano, No. 13, last door on the left) were discovered respectively in 1840, 1847, and 1852; the first and the second by Pietro Campana, the third by Codini himself. The columbarium opened in 1840 consists of one room deep under ground, and accessible by a flight of twenty steps. It measures 7.50 by 5.65 metres, and has a. massive pier in the centre, to which the weight of the vaulted ceiling was intrusted. The ancient walls, 6.24 metres high, were covered with frescoes and arabesques representing birds and animals. The room contains 450 pigeonholes for cinerary urns, and 297 inscriptions, dating mostly from the time of Tiberius and Claudius. They afford much interest to the student of Roman antiquities, and throw a considerable light on the organization and management of the Imperial household.

The trade in pigeonholes and cinerary urns appears to have been very brisk. The urns passed sometimes through several hands. One, marked n. 4884 in the " Corpus," was sold by Porcius Philargurus to Pinarius Rufus, who in his turn sold it to Sotericus Lucer. Pinarius Rufus is mentioned more than once as an active stock-jobber, selling at a profit what he had purchased at low price. It appears that to facilitate the approach to the upper rows of niches — there are nine in all — the tomb was provided with movable wooden balconies, supported by wooden brackets; this is, at least, the explanation suggested for the square holes visible between the fourth and the fifth row. Inscription n. 4886 commemorates a buffoon of Tiberius, a mute, who tried to divert the gloomy temper of his master by imitating the gesticulations of lawyers pleading in the Forum. Another, marked 5076, contains the fragment of a diary of a journey from the borderland of Cilicia towards Cæsarea in Cappadocia. The dates go from the 12th to the 19th of October, during which time the traveler proceeds from Mopsukrene, a frontier station near the Cilician gates, to Tyana and Andabalis on the side of Cæsarea, a distance of seventy-seven miles, according to the "Itinerary of Antoninus," or of eighty-one miles, according to the Hierosolymitanum.

LITERATURE. — Pietro Campana, *Di due sepolcri romani del secolo di Augusto*, parte seconda. Rome, 1840. — Emil Braun, *Colombario scoperto nella vigna accanto a porta Latina* (in Bull. Inst., 1840, p. 136). — Otto Jahn, *Specimen epigraphicum*. Kiel, 1841, p. 28. — *Corpus Inscr.*, vol. vi. part ii. p. 926, n. 4881–5178.

The second columbarium was discovered by Campana in February, 1847, not far from the preceding one. It consists of a plain square room, with nine rows of pigeonholes in each wall, numbering 295 in all, with over 400 funereal tablets. Four inscriptions (one of which is written on the floor in letters of mosaic) tell the tale of the place. The columbarium was finished and the urns divided among the shareholders of the company which had built the place in the year A. D. 10, under the consulship of Sergius Lentulus Maluginensis and Q. Junius Blæsus. The pavement was a private contribution of two shareholders, one a freedman of Sextus Pompeius, son of Pompey the Great, the other a freedman of C. Memmius. The majority of those whose ashes have found rest in this room belong to the servants and freedmen of Marcella the elder, who married Julius Antonius after her divorce with M. Agrippa (21 B. C.); and of Marcella the younger, who had also married twice, first Paullus Æmilius Lepidus, and then M. Valerius Messalla. Annexed to the columbaria were the *ustrina*, or spaces set apart for the incineration of bodies. The indications on this particular given by the inscribed stones allow us to reconstruct a fragment of the plan of the necropolis, as follows : —

Lane (via, populus).				
(No measure given.)	xiii½ ft.		xviii. ft.	xii. ft.
Ustrinum of the College of Musicians.	xi. ½ ft. Ustrinum of Vitalis and Præpusa.	xiii⅔ ft.	Ustrinum of the corporation of wreath-makers.	xii. ft. Ustrinum of the makers of sacks.
Lane (via, populus).				

LITERATURE. — Wilhelm Henzen, *Bull. Inst.*, 1847, p. 49 ; and *Ann. Inst.*, 1856, p. 9. — *Corpus Inscr.*, vol. vi. part ii. p. 908, n. 4414–4880.

The third and last columbarium was discovered by Gio. Battista
Guidi in May, 1852.   The shape of the edifice differs considerably
from that of the preceding ones, and presents the appearance of

Fig. 128. — The Columbarium discovered in the Vigna Codini, May, 1852.

a corridor the three wings of which follow each other at right
angles.   The stairs occupy the end of the wing parallel with the
Via Appia, while the opposite wing terminates with a crypt exca-

vated in the live rock. The bones and skulls which filled it up at the time of the discovery were considered to belong to slaves of the lowest order, whose remains had been thrown into the den as if they were carrion. The walls of the corridor are divided into compartments by means of pilasters with capitals of the composite order (Fig. 128). The niches for cineraria are not arched, as usual, but square, and contain four urns each. The characteristic of this " coöperative tomb," so evident in our illustration, is a set of marble brackets which project from the walls between the fourth and fifth row of niches, counting from the floor. They were destined to support the temporary wooden balcony by means of which the relatives and friends of the deceased could reach the upper tiers of niches on anniversary days, when the urns were decorated with flowers, libations were offered, and other ceremonies were performed. This sepulchral chamber appears to have been tenanted by a better and wealthier set of people than the other two. Many were freedmen of the Julian dynasty from the age of Augustus and Livia to that of Claudius. The last places seem to have been occupied under the last-named Emperor. The room was entered again under Trajan and Hadrian, and a few liberti Ulpii and Ælii laid to rest on the only vacant space left, viz., on the floor. This has been more or less the fate of all Roman columbaria. It seems that at one time, towards the middle of the second century, no more room could be found within reasonable distance from the city for the erection of sepulchral chambers, or else that the price of land had reached a prohibitory figure above the means of the poorer classes. Old columbaria were therefore reopened, as *res nullius*, and new corpses crammed within their precincts. I remember having seen in the excavations of the necropolis by the Porta Maggiore one or two columbaria of the Statilian family, which had been used again as a burial-place when their pavement was already covered by a bed of rubbish three feet thick. Some of the terra-cotta coffins had been simply laid on this newly made ground, other bodies had been buried in it.

LITERATURE. — Emil Braun, *Bull. Inst.*, 1852, p. 82. — Wilhelm Henzen, *Annal. Inst.*, 1856, p. 18. — *Corpus Inscr.*, vol. vi. part ii. p. 939, n. 5179–5538.

In the triangle between the viæ Latina and Appia and the walls of Aurelian, in fact, in the vigne Sassi and Codini alone, 1559 tombstones have already been found, not counting those of the

Scipios, one twentieth perhaps of the original number. The exploration is far from being complete.

Before leaving this conspicuous section of the Roman necropolis I must mention two monuments which connect it with the early days of Christianity.

While Pietro Campana was searching the ground in his first attempt of 1840, a cubiculum was discovered the paintings of which represented Biblical scenes. The Pastor Bonus was given the place of honor in the middle of the vault, while Moses striking the rock, the feeding the five thousand, the raising of Lazarus, and a fourth uncertain subject were painted on the four lunettes. Three sides of the room were occupied by arcosolia, the fourth by the door. The paintings of the arcosolia represented the " Orante " (a woman praying with hands raised), Daniel in the den of lions, Noah and the ark. The figures of the paralytic and of Job were represented on each side of the door. Two inscriptions were found in front of two arcosolia, one of which, written in a patois half Greek half Latin, bore the name of a Veratius Nikatoras (BHPATIOTΣ NIKATOPAΣ) and ended with the sentence, O BIOΣ TAYTA, " this is life," *vita hoc est!* This Veratius was a Galatian, as is proved by the discovery made by George Perrot near Ancyra of the tombstone of his wife, which ends with the same words, ὁ βίος ταῦτα. Now it seems certain that this particular plot of the necropolis was destined for foreigners who died in Rome. De Rossi discovered here in 1883 the broken epitaph of one of the faithful from Smyrna, and Campana the tombstone of another from the borderland of Cappadocia and Armenia. The importance of the discovery lies in the fact that the crypt adorned with Christian paintings must be older than the walls of Aurelian (272), contemporary, in fact, with some of the pagan mausoleums by which it is surrounded. This remarkable monument is lost. Campana concealed its discovery from De Rossi, and revealed it only many years afterwards, when he had lost the memory of its exact position. De Rossi tried in vain to rediscover it in 1884.

LITERATURE. — Gio. Battista de Rossi, *Bull. crist.*, 1884–85, pp. 57, 58; and 1886, pp. 14, 17. — Raffaele Garrucci, *Monumenti del museo lateran.*, pl. 1, n. 3; and *Arte cristiana*, tav. 484, 10. — Compare, also, Gian Pietro Secchi, *Monumenti inediti d' un antico sepolcro.* Rome, Salviucci, 1843.

The second Christian monument of this region is to be found on the opposite side of the Vigna Sassi, under the farmhouse of the Vigna Pallavicini. Mariano Armellini rediscovered it in 1875, all traces of it having been lost since the days of Agincourt. It is an ancient crypt dedicated to Gabriel the archangel, and also to the memory of the "seven sleepers" of Ephesus. It was entirely covered with frescoes representing Gabriel with his hands raised in the attitude of prayer, the Redeemer among hosts of angels, Greek saints of both sexes, and seven tiny reclining figures under that of the Saviour, which were considered to be the "sette dormienti." The frescoes had been executed in the eleventh century at the expense of Beno de Rapiza and of his wife Maria Macellaria, the same to whom we owe the paintings of S. Clemente and of S. Urbano alla Caffarella. It seems that in those days the Greek legend, which had transformed the "sleep of the just," the "dormitio in Domino," of the seven young Ephesians into an actual state of catalepsy, had already found its way to Rome, and struck the imagination of the people. Their anniversary feast fell on the 27th day of July. The "cavern of the sleepers" is now used as a pig-sty.

LITERATURE. — Alberto Cassio, *Corso delle acque antiche*, Rome, 1757, p. 28. — *Dissertatio de SS. septem dormientibus.* Rome, 1741. — Mariano Armellini, *Scopertà di un' antico oratorio presso la via Appia dedicato all' arcangelo Gabriele.* Rome, 1875.

REGIO II. CÆLIMONTIUM.

V. THE CÆLIAN HILL was named Querquetulanus in the early days of Rome, from the trees (*quercioli*, oaks) which clothed its eastern slope, as the opposite or western slope of the Esquiline was named Mons Fagutalis from the beeches (*fagi*) by which it was shaded. The name of Cælian was subsequently adopted in memory of the Etruscan lucumo Cæles or Cælius Vibenna, who had settled with his followers on the hill at the time of Servius Tullius. An attempt was made under Tiberius to change the name into that of Mons Augustus because, during a terrible conflagration in the year A. D. 27, which destroyed hundreds of houses and palaces, the only object respected by the flames was a statue of the Emperor placed in the vestibule of the palace of the Junii.

A spur of the hill, crowned by a shrine of Diana, was called Cæliolus, or minor Cælius. Topographers disagree as to its position. Ficoroni and others place it at the Monte d' Oro, Canina at the SS. Quattro, Brocchi on the site of the Villa Wolkonsky, Nibby on the site of S. Gregorio.[1] The hill and the spur were included in the first region of Servius, Suburana.

[1] Consult: Stefano Piale, *Delle porte meridionali di Servio, del vero sito*

Augustus in his reform of 10–4 B. C. made of the Cælian the second region of the city. At the time of Constantine it contained 7 parishes (*vici*), 3600 tenement houses, 127 palaces, 85 public baths, 65 public fountains, and 15 bakeries. The most curious feature consisted in the fact of its being at the same time a district of barracks (with the customary annexes, drinking and gambling dens, lupanaria, etc.) and a district of aristocratic palaces.

VI. THE CASTRA CÆLIMONTANA. — The list of barracks includes —

A. THE CASTRA EQUITUM SINGULARIUM, a select body of horsemen, who, like our life-guards, cent-gardes, or cuirassiers du roi, were employed in the personal service of the Emperor. They were lodged in two splendid barracks, the *castra vetera* and the *castra nova*. The first were discovered between 1885 and 1887 in the Via Tasso, in the grounds of the Villa Giustiniani; the second in 1733 and 1734, in the foundations of the Cappella Corsini at the Lateran. Both barracks were magnificently decorated with statues, busts, altars, and works of art of every description, among which were the Bacchus in the Maraini House, illustrated by Visconti in "Bull. com.," 1886, p. 166, pl. 6, and the marble seat in the Corsini Library, considered to have been chiseled by a Greek artist. The *equites singulares* were substituted for the old German bodyguard (*collegium Germanorum, Germani corporis custodes*) about the time of the Flavians, and were likewise recruited among the semi-barbarians of the estuary of the Rhine and of the Lower Danube, the Thracians being preferred to all other nationalities. The regiment, one thousand strong, was placed under the command of the *præfectus prætorio.*

LITERATURE. — Wilhelm Henzen, *Ann. Inst.*, 1850, p. 5; and 1885, p. 235. — Theodor Mommsen, *Ephem. epigr.*, vol. v. p. 233; *Hermes*, vol. xvi. p. 459, 4; and *Korrespondenzblatt der Westdeutschen Zeitschrift*, 1886, pp. 50, 123. — Rodolfo Lanciani, *Bull. arch. com.*, 1885, p. 37; 1886, p. 94; and *Notizie Scavi*, 1885, p. 524; 1886, pp. 12, 48; 1887, p. 139; 1888, p. 566. — Orazio Marucchi, *Bull. arch. com.*, 1886, p. 124. — Carlo Ludovico Visconti, *Bull. arch. com.*, 1886, p. 166, pl. 6. — *Corpus Inscr.*, vol. vi. n. 224–228, and p. 766, n. 3173–3323. — Francesco Ficoroni, *Memorie* (in Fea's Miscellanea, vol. i. n. 46).

B. THE CASTRA PEREGRINORUM. — Whatever may have been

del Celiolo. Rome, 1824. — Buhsen, etc., *Beschreibung*, 3ª, p. 478. — Antonio Nibby, *Roma antica*, vol. i. p. 19.

the original scope of the institution of a special body of men called *milites peregrini* (foreigners) and of their associates the *milites frumentarii* (commissariat), there is no doubt that towards the beginning of the second century after Christ the peregrini performed the duties of the modern gendarmes or carabinieri, while the frumentarii had become secret police agents or detectives. They were employed to carry dispatches, to act as spies and informers, and to make arrests. The biographer of Hadrian says that he knew all the secrets of the Imperial household and of his friends with the help of the frumentarii: "per frumentarios omnia occulta explorabat" (Vita Hadriani, c. 6). They were the chief agents in the persecutions of the Christians, as described by Cyprianus and Jerome. Prisoners of state were also intrusted to their custody; Cnodomer, king of the Germans, made prisoner in the battle of Strasburg and brought to Rome, is said to have died "in castris peregrinis, quæ in Monte Cælio sunt." The frumentarii and the peregrini were commanded by an officer called "princeps." The body was suppressed by Diocletian as "pestilential" and replaced by another called *agentes in rebus*.

The barracks were placed in the neighborhood of S. Maria in Dominica, but we do not know exactly where. In March, 1848, an inscription describing the baths of the barracks was discovered *in situ*, but Matranga, who illustrated it in the "Bull. Inst." of the same year, p. 39, keeps the secret of the find to himself, and only mentions in general terms "una vigna rimpetto S. Maria in Navicella." The barracks were discovered partly about 1550, partly under the pontificates of Innocent X. (1644–55) and Clement X. (1670–76). Ligorio (Torin., vol. xv. p. 127) describes them as divided into two sections or quadrangles (one for the frumentarii, one for the peregrini?), and as occupying the space between the aqueduct of Nero, S. Stefano Rotondo, and la Navicella. Holstenius places them between the aqueduct, S. Stefano Rotondo, and the hospital of S. Giovanni, and describes one of the rectangles as lined with cells, flanked by towers and walls 1.20 metre thick, and containing in the middle of the court a round temple with columns of porphyry and oriental granite. The works of art, statues, and busts discovered in the excavations of 1550 were probably removed to the house of Ascanio Magarozzi, where Ulisse Aldovrandi saw and described them in 1553. The account which approaches nearest the truth, and settles the question of site, is perhaps that of Pietro Sante Bartoli (Mem. 55). He says that under Innocent X. and Clement X. great excavations were made in the garden of

Teofilo Sartori, Via di S. Stefano Rotondo, viz., on the site of the
present military hospital (Villa Casali); that rows of cells (una
filara di botteghe) were uncovered pertaining to the Castra Pere-
grina, as well as great halls and mess-rooms, courts lined with
colonnades, the shafts of which were of "bellissima breccia,"
statues, busts, heads, and various ornaments of metal incrusted
with silver, which Bartoli thinks belonged to a triumphal arch.
Here also was found the pedestal (Corpus, vi. 231) dedicated GENIO
SANCTO CASTRORVM PEREGRINORVM.

LITERATURE. — Pirro Ligorio, *Cod. torin.*, xv. p. 127. — Lucas Holstenius,
Cod. vatic., 9141. — P. Sante Bartoli, *Mem.* 55 (in Fea's Miscell., vol. i. p.
ccxxxv.). — Wilhelm Henzen, *Bull. Inst.*, 1851, p. 113. — Pietro Matranga,
Bull. Inst., 1849, p. 34. — Gio. Battista de Rossi, *Le stazioni delle coorti dei
Vigili*, p. 28; and *La basilica di S. Stefano rotondo*, etc., p. 9 (in Studii e
docum. di storia e diritto, vol. vii. 1886).

C. STATIO COHORTIS V̄ VIGILUM (barracks of the fifth battalion
of firemen and policemen), on the platform of the Villa Celimontana, formerly belonging to the Mattei dukes of Giove, and now
to Baron Richard von Hoffmann.   In January, 1820, two marble
pedestals were found near the gate of the villa, standing in their
original position on a tessellated pavement which formed part of
the vestibule.   The rolls of the battalion, name by name, were
engraved upon them.   The first pedestal had no dedicatory inscription; the second (and the statue upon it) were offered to Caracalla
in the year 210 by C. Julius Quintilianus, prefect of police, M.
Firmius, adjutant-general, L. Speratius Justus, colonel of the fifth
battalion, the captains commanding the seven companies, the four
physicians and surgeons attached to the barracks, etc.   The last
names engraved on the front of the pedestal are those of the captain and of the standard-bearer of the first company, the trustees
of the fund subscribed towards the erection of the statue.   The
importance of these two documents, however, comes from the rolls
of the rank and file.   " In the year 205, which is the approximate
date of the first pedestal, the battalion numbered 113 officers and
sub-officers, and 930 men.   In the year 210 the number of the
former had decreased to 109, the number of the latter had increased
to 1013.   Taking as the average strength of a battalion 1033 men
all told, the whole police of the metropolis must have numbered
7231 men." [1]   The pedestals are still to be seen in the Villa Mattei
at the entrance of the celebrated avenue of ilexes between the
Casino and the obelisk.   Luigi Rossini asserts that in the excava-

[1] *Ancient Rome*, p. 228.

tions of 1820 the prison of the barracks was also found, "as proved by the chains still fixed to its walls." Students are kindly allowed to visit the Villa Mattei on Thursdays.

LITERATURE. — Olaus Kellermann, *Vigilum latercula duo cælimontana.* Rome, 1835. — Gio. Battista de Rossi, *Le stazioni delle sette coorti dei Vigili,* p. 27 (in Annal. Inst., 1858). — *Corpus Inscr.,* vol. vi. n. 221, 222, 1057, 1058. — P. Sante Bartoli, *Mem.* 79 (in Fea's Miscell., vol. i. p. ccxlii.). — Luigi Rossini, *I sette colli,* n. 13. Rome, 1829.

Connected with the barracks of the Cælian hill were the Lupa-naria, mentioned in the catalogues of the second region, probably a state establishment, the site of which corresponds with that of the Vigna Colacicchi, as shown by the discovery of some charac-teristic mosaic pavements made there in 1878.

VII. THE PALACES OF THE CÆLIAN : —

A. DOMUS LATERANORUM — EGREGIÆ LATERANORUM ÆDES (Lateran palace). It is a current opinion that after the execution of Plautius Lateranus in A. D. 66 for his share in the plot of the Pisones, his magnificent palace on the Cælian was confiscated by Nero, and the grounds were added to the Imperial domain of the Domus Aurea. No classic historian speaks of such a confiscation ; on the contrary, we are informed by one of them that T. Sextius Lateranus, consul in 196, was offered large sums of money by Septimius Severus, with the help of which he restored the paternal estate on the Cælian. This account is confirmed by the discovery made in 1595 of water-pipes inscribed with the names of Sextius Lateranus and of his brother Torquatus. Another water-pipe, bearing the name of Mammæa, mother of the Emperor Severus Alexander, found among the ruins of the palace in 1890, seems to prove that the palace had become state property only under the rule of the last (A. D. 222–235). It remained so until the time of Constantine, who offered part, or perhaps the whole, of it to Pope Miltiades in 313 ; this, at least, is the date of a council of bishops convened in the palace under the presidency of the pope. Perhaps it was only a case of a loan, as we find the palace called "Domus Faustæ," the house of Fausta, at a later date.[1] I do not yet under-stand clearly myself what happened in those days, how the trans-ference of property from the Crown to the Church was made, and which portion was transformed into a Christian basilica, "omnium ecclesiarum urbis et orbis mater et caput." The difficulty arises

[1] Fausta, second wife of Constantine, was smothered by her husband's order in 326, and her stepson Crispus was executed on the same day.

from the fact that the area of the basilica is cut in two by a
Roman street, which runs parallel with the transept of Clement
VIII. (*nave Clementina*), passes under the canopy of Urban V.,
and leads to a postern in the walls of Aurelian still visible in the
garden "dei Penitenzieri." The ruins east of this ancient street
are "oriented" with it; those on the other side form an angle of
31°. There were therefore two distinct and independent palaces,—
one on each side of the street. The one on the west was certainly
the palace of the Laterans; the one on the east might possibly be
identified with the "castra nova equitum singularium," epigraphic
records of which have been found under the Corsini chapel. The
nave and aisles of the church would occupy in this case the site of
one of the courts of the barracks; while the transept and the apse
would occupy the site of the atrium of the palace. I need not
remind the reader that the name of St. John the Lateran is comparatively recent, the basilica having been dedicated originally to
the Redeemer alone.

Many discoveries have taken place east of the street mentioned
above. In 1732 Alessandro Galilei, the architect of Clement XII.,
whilst building the new façade, found walls, cells, water-pipes, and
other remains. In the following year the excavations extended to
the site of the cappella Corsini, and to the vacant space between
the chapel and the walls of the city. Splendid remains of the
barracks and of their annexes were found everywhere,[1] with other
sections of the water-pipes mentioned before, bearing the name of
M. Opellius Macrinus, prefect of the prætorium, and Commander-
in-Chief of the equites singulares. Other walls, decorated with
frescoes of no special value, came to light in 1838 in the foundations of the "sala capitolare" behind the Lancellotti chapel. In
style of masonry, in age, and in direction they correspond exactly
to the remains discovered by Rohault de Fleury and by myself in
the cellars of the palace of the pope (Sixtus V.) on the other side
of the church.[2]

More important are the finds obtained at various epochs among
the remains of the "egregiæ Lateranorum ædes," on the opposite
side of the street. Flavio Biondo describes those of the time of
Eugenius IV. (1431–47) on the site of the monastery, west of the

---

[1] LITERATURE. — See p. 336 and Ridolfino Venuti, *Descriz. di Roma*, ed.
1803, p. 179. — Lupi, *Epitaph. sanctæ Severæ*, p. 43. — Francesco Ficoroni,
Gemmæ litteratæ, p. 126. — *Corpus Inscr.*, vol. vi. n. 225, 226.

[2] Emil Braun, *Bull. Inst.*, 1838, p. 6. — Rohault de Fleury, *Le Latran au
moyen âge*. (Plan général.) — Rodolfo Lanciani, *Forma Urbis*, pl. xxxvii.

cloisters of Vassalectus ; and speaks of halls the pavements of which were 5.34 metres lower than that of the church, of colonnades, statues, etc. Flaminio Vacca says that when Clement VIII. removed and destroyed in 1595 the old presbyterium (un certo rialzo innanzi al coro), three large niches were found, pertaining

Fig. 129. — One of the Courts of the Palace of the Laterans, discovered in 1877.

to an "edifizio antichissimo e nobilissimo," the pavements of which were incrusted with porphyry and serpentine. Filippo Martinucci discovered in 1853 the pavement of the street under the canopy of Urban V., as related above. Costantino Corvisieri excavated in 1873 the neighborhood of the Baptistery. Pius IX. and Leo XIII., whilst destroying the Constantinian apse and building the new one, with the sacristry and the chapter-house (1877–90), brought to light other remains, described by Stevenson in the "Annal. Inst.," 1877, pls. R, S, T, and represented in the above view (Fig. 129). I have tried to express as well as I could the results of all these excavations in sheet No. xxxvii. of the "Forma Urbis." The level of this part of the palace was 7.50 metres lower than that of the church.

Nothing is left visible of the old Constantinian Basilica except a few bits of the walls which support the roof of the nave. When Borromini inflicted upon the nave itself the present hideous transformation, and encased the columns dividing the nave from the aisles in a coating of bricks, he left patches of the original walls visible in a set of oval panels between the windows. The ovals are now concealed by indifferent paintings on canvas. However, there is at least one set of precious relics of Constantine's age which has escaped destruction but not transformation : I refer to the four large fluted bronze columns of the Corinthian order which adorn the Altare del Sacramento, at the south end of the transept. The guide-books of Rome have suggested various theories about them, the current belief being that they belonged in days gone by to the Temple of Jupiter Capitolinus. Others contend that they were cast under Augustus with the bronze beaks of the ships captured in the battle of Actium; others that they were removed from Solomon's Temple, etc. The columns are mentioned for the first time under Constantine, who offered them to the Church to be used as "pharocantharoi"[1] on either side of the altar. Clement VIII. and Pietro Paolo Olivieri, his architect, found them seriously injured and without capitals; Orazio Censori, the pope's brass-founder, was asked therefore to make a tour through the cities of southern Etruria and try to collect antique objects of bronze. Hundreds of tombs must have been rifled of their invaluable treasures ; at Corneto alone Censori gathered 665 pounds of metal, and a great deal more at Civita Castellana (Falerii). The treasures were melted together with pieces of the bronze beams of the Pantheon, and the metal was employed in casting three

---

[1] Lighthouses, or pillars supporting a circle of lights on the capitals.

capitals, the whole cornice and pediment of the altar, sixteen
doves, sixteen stars, and two angels. It was lucky that the bronze
masterpieces formerly in the Campus Lateranensis (Piazza di S.
Giovanni) had been removed to a place of safety since the times
of Sixtus IV. and Paul III., otherwise they would probably have
shared the fate of the bronzes from Tarquinii and Falerii.

The mediæval collection of bronzes at the Lateran comprised
the equestrian statue of M. Aurelius, removed by Paul III. to the
Piazza del Campidoglio in 1538; the she-wolf; the colossal hand
with the globe; the Zingara or Camillus; the head of young
Nero (?), removed to the Palazzo dei Conservatori by Sixtus IV.;
and the "lex regia," now in the Capitoline Museum. The following sketch by Martin Heemskerk represents the Campus Lateranensis about 1534, with the statue of M. Aurelius in its proper

Fig. 130. — Campus Lateranensis, about 1534.

place. The four columns in the foreground supported a slab of
marble which was thought to mark the height of the Saviour.
Heemskerk's view has already been published by T. Springer, in
1885.[1]

LITERATURE FOR THE LATERAN PALACE. — Louis Duchesne, *Le liber
pontificalis*, vol. i. *passim.* — Rohault de Fleury, *Le Latran au moyen âge.*
Paris, 1877. — Giovanni Ciampini, *De sacris ædificiis a Constantino magno
extructis.* Rome, 1693. — Cesare Rasponi, *De basilica et patriarchio Late-
ranensi.* Rome, 1656. — Nicola Alemanni, *De Lateranensibus parietinis.*
Rome, 1756. — Eugène Müntz, *Les arts à la cour des papes*, vol. iii. *passim.*
— Rodolfo Lanciani, *Bull. Inst.*, 1870, p. 50 ; and *Itinerario di Einsiedlen*, pp.
70 and 102. — Enrico Stevenson, *Scoperte di antichi edifizi al Laterano* (in

[1] In *Gesammelte Studien zur Kunstgeschichte : eine Festgabe zum 4 Mai* 1885.
Für Anton Springer, Leipzig, 1885.

Annal. Inst., 1877); and *Topografia e monumenti di Roma nelle pitture di Sisto V., etc.*, plate iv. n. 2.

The bronzes formerly in the Lateran are illustrated in *Annal. Inst.*, 1877, p. 381. — *Röm. Mittheilungen*, vol. vi. 1891, p. 14. — *Revue archéol.*, xliii. 1882, pp. 26, 28. — Wolfgang Helbig, *Guide to the Coll. of Class. Antiquities*, vol. i. p. 402, n. 538 ; p. 454, n. 612, etc.

B. DOMUS VECTILIANA, a favorite resort of the Emperor Commodus, whither he used to repair when suffering from insomnia, and where he was strangled in A. D. 192. Its site is not known, but it cannot have been very far from the Lateran. The equestrian statue of Marcus Aurelius, of which we hear for the first time in A. D. 966 (when Peter, prefect of Rome, was hung by the hair from the horse for his rebellion against John XIII.), must have come from this Domus Vectiliana. The house was certainly discovered at the time of Ficoroni, about 1735, by a man named Giuseppe Mitelli, but the site of the excavation is indicated only by the vague formula " nell' estremità del Monte Celio " (at the extreme point of the Cælian hill).

The family of M. Aurelius and Commodus was closely connected with that of the Annii. Annia Faustina the elder, wife of Antoninus Pius ; Annia Faustina the younger, wife of M. Aurelius ; Annia Cornificia, his sister ; Annius Verus, his son ; Annia Lucilla, his daughter, have made the name illustrious in the annals of the Empire. By a singular coincidence we find a DOMUS ANNIORUM on the Cælian, close to the supposed site of the Vectiliana in which Commodus was assassinated. One of the new streets of the Cælian, the Via Annia, has been named from it. The house is distinctly mentioned by the biographer of M. Aurelius, chapter i.: " Marcus was born on the Cælian hill, in the family villa (*horti*) in the year (A. D. 121) in which his grandfather Annius Verus was consul with Augur. . . . He was educated in the villa in which he was born, as well as in the palace of his grandfather, near that of the Laterans." The palace of Annius Verus was discovered for the last time in 1885–87, on the site of the present military hospital (Villa Casali).

LITERATURE. — *Bull. arch. com.*, 1885, pp. 95, 104, 166, 175, 176 ; 1866, pp. 50, 93, 109, 278, 342, 369, 405 ; 1887, pp. 27, 57. — *Notizie degli Scavi*, 1885–89, *passim.* See index, *Villa Casali.*

C. DOMUS TETRICORUM. — C. Pesuvius Tetricus, one of the " thirty tyrants," and the last secessionist ruler of Gaul (A. D. 267–274), was defeated by Aurelian at the battle of Chalons, and obliged to grace the triumph of the conqueror with his presence.

After the triumph he was treated with kindness and distinction by Aurelian. The biographer who wrote the " Tyranni Triginta " in the first decade of the fourth century says, " The palace of the Tetrici, one of the most beautiful in the city, is still to be seen on the Cælian, in the street called 'inter duos lucos,' opposite the Temple of Isis Metellina." The site was indicated in the Middle Ages by a church of S. Maria *inter duo* or *inter duas*, which stood in the valley between the Cælian and the Esquiline (cf. Armellini, Chiese, p. 140).

D. Domus Valeriorum. — There was on the Cælian, between S. Stefano Rotondo and the Lateran, a palace belonging to the descendants of the Valerii Poplicolæ, namely, to Valerius Severus, prefect of Rome in A. D. 386, and to his son Pinianus, husband of Melania the younger. The palace was so beautiful, and contained so much wealth, that when Pinianus and Melania, grieved by the loss of all their children, put it up for sale in 404, they found none willing to purchase it : " ad tam magnum et mirabile opus accedere nemo ausus fecit." Seven or eight years after the capture of Rome by Alaric, August, 410, the same palace was given away for little or nothing, " domus pro nihilo venumdata est," having been " dissipata et quasi incensa " by the barbarians. There must be some inaccuracy in this account, which Commendatore de Rossi has found in a MS. of the library of Chartres. In the first place, a considerable part of the property was transformed into a hospice and a hospital under the title of " Xenodochium Valeriorum " or " a Valeriis," which flourished until the ninth century, and the transformation must have been the work of Pinianus himself and not of an outsider. In the second place, the house was discovered in 1554, 1561, and 1711 in such a wonderful state of preservation that we must exculpate the Goths from the charge of having pillaged and gutted it in 410. The account of the find sounds like a fairy tale. When the workmen entered the atrium of the palace in the first excavations of 1554 and 1561, the deeds and records of the family, engraved on bronze tablets, still hung to the columns of the peristyle. The tablets contained mostly decrees in honor of the Valerii, or treaties of friendship with their house passed by the corporations of Zama, Hadrumetum, Thenæ, and other cities of Africa. Four pedestals of statues dedicated to Valerius Aradius by the corporations of the grocers, bakers, etc., were discovered under the portico. The excavations were stopped perhaps for fear of undermining the church and the monastery of S. Erasmus, or whatever was left standing of this celebrated abbey, the mediæval representative of the old Xenodochium a Valeriis. Under the pontificate of Innocent X. (1644–55), when no traces were left of S. Erasmo, the atrium of the palace was entered again, and seven "bellissime statue" were brought to light, among them two fauns dancing to the sound of the κρόταλα; they were purchased by Monsignor Mazarino. The experiment was tried again under Clement X. (1670–76) with equal success. Bartoli mentions statues and busts, among them two of Lucius Verus bought by Cardinal de Bouillon; the group of Cupid and Psyche, now in the Galleria degli Uffizi; the finest specimens of fresco paintings ever seen in Rome; columns of rare breccias; and the bronze lamp representing a ship with the figure of our Lord at the helm, also in the Uffizi at Florence.

LITERATURE. — *Corpus Inscr.*, vol. vi. n. 1684–94. — Pietro Sante Bartoli, *Mem.* 53, 54 (in Fea's Miscellanea, vol. i. p. ccxxx.). — Pietro Bellori, *Lucerne antiche*, p. 11. — Gio. Batt. de Rossi, *Il monastero di S. Erasmo e la casa dei Valerii sul Celio* (in Studi e docum. di Storia e Diritto, vol. vii. 1886; and *Bull. com.*, 1890, p. 288). — Giacomo Lumbroso, *Notizie di Cassiano dal Pozzo*. Torino, 1875, p. 50.

E. DOMUS PHILIPPI, probably of the Emperor M. Julius Philippus (A. D. 244–249), which he must have acquired while prefect of the Prætorium. The only clue in regard to its position is given by an altar (Corpus Inscr., vi. 150) dedicated by a "servus Philipporum" to a local spring, which was found in the slope of the Villa Mattei, towards the Marrana. Near the same place a statue was discovered in 1747 representing a hunter with a hare in the right hand, which Ennio Quirino Visconti attributes to the age of the Philippi. The statue, signed by the artist (POLYTIMVS LIB), is now exhibited in the Capitoline Museum.

LITERATURE. — Ficoroni, *Mem.* 91 (in Fea's Miscellanea, vol. i. p. clxiii.). — E. Quirino Visconti, *Catalogo del museo Jenkins*, p. 22. — Pierre Aube, *Le Christianisme de l'emp. Philippe* (in Revue arch., vol. ix. 1880, p. 140). — Wolfgang Helbig, *Guide to the Collections of Antiquities*, vol. i. p. 370, n. 506 (27).

F. DOMUS L · MARII · MAXIMI, discovered in February, 1708, in the Villa Fonseca. It contained the pedestals of statues (Corpus Inscr., vol. vi. n. 1450, 1451) dedicated to him, the first by an officer of the third legion, Cyrenaica; the second by a friend, Pompeius Alexander. Other pedestals from the same noble mansion are described by the "Corpus," n. 1452, 1453.

G. DOMUS OF THE SYMMACHI, discovered in 1617 in the garden of Sartorio Teofili, afterwards included in the Villa Casali.

L. Aurelius Avianius Symmachus, the great scholar, statesman, and orator of the latter half of the fourth century, proconsul of Africa in 373, prefect of the city in 384–386, consul in 391, speaks of this paternal house on the Cælian in Epist. 18 of Book vii.: "de Formiano regressus in Larem Cælium." Compare Epist. iii. 12, 88. Although constantly exposed to danger and disgrace, as leader of the pagan side of the Senate, he never diverged from his path. Having been delegated by the House in 382 to remonstrate with the Emperor Gratian on the removal of the altar of Victory from their council hall, and on the curtailment of the sums annually allowed for the maintenance of the Vestal Virgins, he was ordered by the indignant Emperor to withdraw from his presence and to retire to his villa at Formiæ; and yet, two years later, we find him prefect of Rome, and engaged in rebuilding with unusual magnificence the bridge now called Ponte Sisto (see p. 24). Among the objects discovered in the excavations of 1617 we find the pedestal of a statue dedicated to him by his own son, and a second set up in honor of his father-in-law Virius Nicomachus Flavianus, another great leader of the pagan faction. The ruins were searched again in 1885–87.

I do not remember having ever seen such a scene of devastation as that presented by the remains of this palace of the Symmachi and of the Nicomachi. Columns, pedestals, statues seem to have been purposely hammered and ground into atoms. The headless female statue of gray basalt, now in Hall V of the Museo Municipale al Celio, was put together by us in 1896 out of seventy-four pieces. If we remember that basalt was a worthless material to the destroyers of ancient Rome, unfit for the lime-kiln and too hard to be worked anew, we must find another reason for their treating that noble figure so wantonly. The explanation is given, if I am not mistaken, by the discovery of another statue broken into one hundred and fifty-one pieces, which represented the Victory. When the pagan faction was put down forever at the battle of September 6, 394, in which the usurper Eugenius and Nicomachus Flavianus lost their lives, the recollection of the duel fought before Valentinian II. and Theodosius, between S. Ambrose on the Christian and Symmachus on the pagan side, on account of the statue of Victory, was still fresh in the minds of the people. No wonder that, on hearing the news of the battle, and of the decisive collapse of the party led by the Symmachi and by the Nicomachi, the populace should have pillaged their palace on the Cælian and satisfied their desire for vengeance.

From this point of view the statue, which we have recalled to
life out of one hundred and fifty-one fragments, and exhibited in
the Hall II of the above-named museum, is one of the great historical monuments of the fourth century.

LITERATURE.— *Corpus Inscr.*, vol. vi. n. 1699, 1782.— Angelo Mai, *Script.
vett. nova collectio*, vol. i. append. pp. xviii.–xxiv. — Morel, in *Revue archéol.*,
June, 1868. — Rodolfo Lanciani, *Ancient Rome*, pp. 162–173.

H. THE HOUSE OF SS. JOHN AND PAUL. — This house and
the church (Titulus Byzantis, Titulus Pammachii) built upon it
at a later period are given a place of honor in early itineraries of
pilgrims because they contained the only martyr's tomb *within* the
walls of the city. The account of the lives of the two brothers
John and Paul, and of their execution under Julian the apostate,
is apocryphal; but no one who visits the remains of this house
and the records it contains will deny the fact that some one was

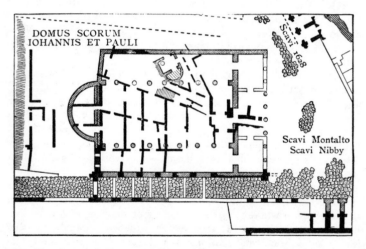

Fig. 131. — Plan of the House of SS. John and Paul, and of the Church built above it.

murdered or executed for his faith here, and that over the apartment in which the event took place a church was built at a later
age. On this occasion the Roman house was left intact with its
spacious halls and classical decorations to be used as a crypt,
while the basilica was raised above the level of the ceilings. The
murder of the saints seems to have taken place in a narrow passage (*fauces*) near the tablinum or reception-room. Here we see

the "fenestella confessionis" by means of which pilgrims were allowed to behold and touch the venerable graves. Two things strike the visitor: firstly, the variety of the fresco decorations of the house, which begin with pagan Genii holding festoons, and end with stiff, uncanny representations of the Passion, of the ninth and tenth century; secondly, the fact that such an important monument should have been buried and forgotten[1] until Padre Germano of the Passionists rediscovered it ten or twelve years ago. Padre Germano has given us a delightful account of his work in a volume entitled " La casa celimontana dei SS. Martiri Giovanni e Paolo scoperta ed illustrata." Rome, Cuggiani, 1894.

This house and another one annexed to the nymphæum of the gardens of Sallust are the only ones in Rome which show the third floor in one case, the fourth in the other. The student walking up the Clivus Scauri, between the house of John and Paul on the left, and the house and library of Agapetus on the right, may fancy himself transported into the midst of a street scene of "declining" Rome towards the end of the sixth century.

I. THE HOUSE OF GREGORY THE GREAT. — The "Liber pontificalis" (vol. i. p. 313, edit. Duchense) leaves no doubt that the present church and monastery of S. Gregorio are built on the site of the paternal house of the great pontiff, son of Gordianus and Sylvia, of the Petronian branch of the Anicii. The transformation of the palace into a cœnobium, where Gregory and his associates lived under the rule of S. Benedict, seems to have taken place in 575. John the Deacon describes it as placed "within the walls of the city, on the Clivus Scauri, close to the church of SS. John and Paul," and as containing an atrium with a fountain of elaborate design in the middle (nymphæum). The spring, called "mirabilis immo saluberrimus," was probably the same known in classic times by the name of Fons Mercurii. The site of the piscina can still be traced on the east side of the present church. There was an inner court within the clausura, around which opened the cells of the monks. The establishment was also furnished with a hostelry for pilgrims and visitors, with stables and granaries, and with a grand triclinium, in which the monks took their siesta during the hot hours of the day.

The name of S. Gregorio given to the abbey is comparatively recent, the old establishment being placed under the patronage of S. Andrew. His chapel was splendidly decorated with paintings and mosaics. There were also other chapels or oratories under

---

[1] *Pagan and Christian Rome*, p. 159.

the invocations of the Virgin Mary (the S. Andrea of the present day) and of S. Barbara (the present triclinium). Save a few bits of antique walls, which appear here and there under the modern plastering, nothing is left visible of the home of S. Gregory and of the monastery " SS. Andreæ et Gregorii ad clivum Scauri," one of the most powerful in central Italy, and the owner of the Circus Maximus, of the Septizonium, and of the palace of the Cæsars. The first blow to the institution was struck in 1573, when the Camaldolese monks took the place of the Benedictines. Cardinal Scipione Borghese and his architect, Giovanni Soria, destroyed the old vestibule and the atrium in 1633; all the rest was modernized in 1725. I have discovered in the Kupferstich Kabinet at Stuttgart a sketch by a contemporary of Martin Heemskerk, representing the Monasterium ad Clivum Scauri before the modern profanation. I give here a facsimile of this rare design.

Fig. 132. — A View of the Church and Monastery of S. Gregorio in the First Half of the Sixteenth Century.

The two leading edifices of the Cælian hill which remain to be described are the Temple of Claudius and the Rotunda of S. Stefano.

VIII. CLAUDIUM (Temple of Claudius), begun by Agrippina the younger, niece and fourth wife of that Emperor. After the

murder of Agrippina, which took place in A. D. 59, Nero her son
took possession of the unfinished temple and turned it into a
nymphæum and reservoir for the Aqua Claudia, joining it to the
main aqueduct "ad Spem veterem" (Porta Maggiore) by means
of the Arcus Cælimontani or Arcus Neroniani, which still forms so
conspicuous a feature of the Cælian hill. After the suicide of
Nero, A. D. 68, the place was restored to its original use by Vespasian under the name of "Templum divi Claudii," which the
people shortened into that of Claudium. A bull of Honorius III.,
dated February 2, 1217, shows that the classic term was still in
use in the thirteenth century (Clodeum). The causes and the
date of its final collapse are not known; but the fact that one of
the travertine capitals from the substructure was made use of in
the reconstruction of the house of SS. John and Paul (first door
on the left on the Clivus Scauri) proves that men had already
laid hands on the noble building in the time of Julian the Apostate (360–363), or else of Pammachius, the builder of the church
(† 410). Flaminio Vacca relates the following discoveries made
at the time of Pius IV.: "In a vineyard between the Coliseum
and SS. Giovanni e Paolo the foundations of a building were discovered, made of 'grossissimi quadri di travertino,' and also two
marble Corinthian capitals, one of which was removed by Pius
IV. to the church of S. Maria degli Angeli, and placed on one of
the columns of the nave. I remember also the discovery of a
marble ship 8.92 metres long, and of a fountain splendidly decorated with marbles, which, however, appeared much damaged by
fire." Etienne du Perac mentions the finding of some fragments
of statues of heroic size, and calls the platform of the temple
facing the Coliseum the "cemetery of the church of S. Gregorio."
No words can convey the idea of the beauty and peacefulness of
the garden of the Passionist fathers which now occupies the platform of the temple, and of its secluded paths, shaded by ilexes on
the west side, and by cypresses on the side of the Coliseum. The
garden, unfortunately, is under the monastic clausura, and ladies
are refused admittance. The only parts of the building visible
to all without hindrance are the substructures of the platform,[1]
which, strange to say, differ in design and style of masonry for
each side of the rectangle. The substructures on the west side,
upon which stands the beautiful campanile of SS. Giovanni e
Paolo, are composed of a double row of arches in the so-called
rustic style so much in favor at the time of Claudius (Fig. 133);

[1] Apply to the sacristan of the church.

those facing the Coliseum appear divided into receptacles for the storage of water required for some of the venationes of the amphitheatre; those on the Via Claudia show a succession of square and semicircular recesses, the object of which it is not easy to imagine, especially as they are separated from the mass of the platform by a corridor or vaulted passage, less than a metre wide, which follows their capricious outline. Two Christian churches or oratories have been found hidden, as it were, in these substructures.

Fig. 133. — The Substructures of the Claudium, West Side.

Ciampini speaks of the first in "Cod. vatic.," 7849. In September, 1689, while the modern vandals were excavating and destroying the northern front of the platform for the sake of building materials, a door was discovered with the sign of the cross on one side, and a star or *crux decussata* on the other. After passing another door on the right, a room was entered, 7.80 metres long, with frescoes in the apse representing the Redeemer giving the scroll of the law not to S. Peter — as *de iure* in early Christian iconography — but to S. Paul. Two smaller figures of Pope Formosus (891) and of Michael, the first converted king of the Bulgarians, were painted at the feet of the Saviour. The figure of Pope Formosus had been carefully obliterated after his *memoriæ damnatio* at the hands of Stephen VII., his successor. This historical monument was very likely destroyed by its discoverers. The second church, called "ecclesia S. Laurentii supra S. Clementem," was established in the fourth recess (a square with an apse) of the east side of the substructures on the Via Claudia. Armellini mentions having seen traces of Christian frescoes in the apse when first cleared of the rubbish in 1881, but he and the late Commendatore de Rossi are mistaken in identifying this second place of worship with Ciampini's oratory, which opened not on the east but on the north side, and among ruins not of brick but of reticulated work.

LITERATURE FOR THE CLAUDIUM. — Heinrich Jordan, *Forma Urbis Romæ*, pl. x. n. 45. — Suetonius, *Vespas.* 9. — Luigi Canina, *Indicazione di Roma antica*, p. 73. — Otto Richter, *Topogr.*, p. 167. — P. Germano di S. Stanislao, *La casa celimontana dei SS. Giovanni e Paolo*. Rome, 1894, p. 19. — Etienne du Perac, *Vedute di Roma*, pl. 14. — *Corpus Inscr.*, vol. vi. n. 10,251a. — R. Lanciani, *I comentarii di Frontino*, p. 152. — Giuseppe Gatti, *Annal. Inst.*, 1882, p. 205.

LITERATURE FOR THE CHRISTIAN ORATORIES. — Mariano Armellini, *Chiese*, 2d edit., pp. 135, 513. — Gio. Batt. de Rossi, *Bull. crist.*, 1868, pp. 59, 60 ; and 1882, p. 98.

IX. MACELLUM (S. Stefano Rotondo). — Commendatore de Rossi, in his splendid volumes " I musaici delle chiese di Roma," and also in the memoir already quoted, " La basilica di S. Stefano rotondo," etc., proposes some architectural and topographical problems in regard to this mysterious structure, which, he thinks, is not a pagan but a Christian edifice of the beginning of the fifth century ; and he brings in support of his theory the authority of Hübsch (Die altchristlichen Kirchen, p. 36) and of Rahn (Ursprung des Christl. Central- und Kuppelbaus, p. 53).

To tell the truth, the theory is strictly Italian, and over a cen-

tury old.   See Valadier in Canina's " Supplementi al Desgodetz,"
p. 15 : " Le défaut de documents ne permet pas d'admettre
l'opinion de Desgodetz, lequel suppose que ce fut un temple dédié
au dieu Faune. . . . Il faut le regarder comme l'ouvrage du pape
Simplicius I., dédié à S. Etienne et restauré depuis par Nicolas V."
Valadier's opinion is proved correct by the general style of the

Fig. 134. — S. Stefano Rotondo, Inner View.

rotunda, by the quality and variety of its columns, capitals and
bases, spoils of older edifices, by the crosses cut in bold relief
on the cushions of some capitals, and above all by the fact that
the present edifice rests on the remains of an earlier one of the
first century after Christ. They were discovered by Valadier in
or about 1814, between the seventh and ninth columns of the
outer circle on the right of the present entrance. Other walls of
the best period, profusely decorated with marbles, were found six
years ago under the adjoining convent and garden of the Theresian
nuns. However strange may appear the fact of great structures
being raised in Rome at the end of the fourth century, when all
resources had given out, and the want was felt not of the luxuries
but of the necessaries of life, and when monuments were collapsing in all quarters for want of repairs, it is certain that the
rotunda of S. Stefano, this alleged Temple of Faun, of Bacchus,
of Jupiter Peregrinus, this alleged Macellum Magnum, or Mica
Aurea of Nero, has lost forever its position among the classic
buildings of Rome. Who was, then, its true founder, and what was
the true object of its foundation ?

The "Liber pontificalis" (i. 249) attributes to Pope Simplicius
(468–482) the dedication "basilicæ S. Stephani in Cœlio monte."
For a long time an exaggerated value has been attributed to the
formulæ of the Papal chancery, "dedicavit, fecit, optulit," etc.,
and accordingly Felix IV. has been called the builder of SS.
Cosma e Damiano, Honorius I. of S. Adriano, Helena of the
"Hierusalem," and Simplicius of S. Andrea on the Esquiline,
while they had simply adapted to the Christian worship edifices
of classic times, — the Templum Sacræ Urbis, the Senate-house,
the hall of the Sessorian Palace, and the basilica of Junius Bassus. This rotunda likewise, built for civil and public use, underwent the same transformation at the hands of Simplicius. Its
architecture has nothing to do with a place of worship, whether
Christian or pagan. It consists of an inner circle of twenty-two
columns supporting a drum pierced by twenty-two windows; of
an outer portico of thirty-six columns and eight pilasters, open to
wind and rain ; of four open courts; of four covered storerooms;
and of an inclosure wall pierced by eight doors. There is no place
for an altar, no apse, no presbyterium (see Fig. 135). The names
of mausoleum and of baptistery have also been suggested, on no
better grounds, because no burial was allowed within the walls,
and no great church existed in this part of the Cælian, to which
the rotunda could be attached as a baptistery. We cannot hope

to tear away the veil of mystery in which this "sfinge celimontana" is wrapped ; at the same time we may accept the following
points as probable, if not certain : —

A.   The rotunda of S. Stefano stands on the remains of a classic
edifice of the same architectural type, probably the Macellum
Magnum or "great market-place" of Nero, which occupied the
middle of a square lined with porticoes and shops.

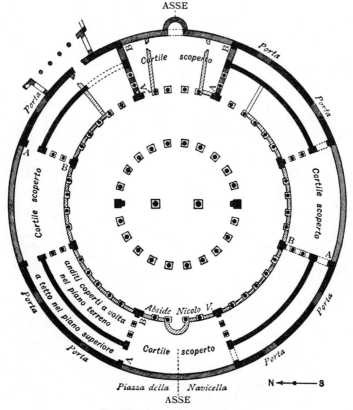

Fig. 135. — Plan of S. Stefano Rotondo.

B.   This edifice of classic times, having come to grief for
reasons unknown to us, was reconstructed at the end of the fourth
century for civic purposes, probably for the same use of a market.

We may cite in support of this idea the contemporary reconstruction of the *Macellum Liviæ* on the Esquiline, at the hands of Valens and Gratianus.

C. After the plunder of the city by Alaric and Genseric, the half-deserted Cælian being no more in need of a public market, Pope Simplicius occupied the edifice and dedicated it — with some slight alterations — to the memory of S. Stephen. This happened about one century after its reconstruction as a market-place.

D. The apse adorned with mosaics, the transformation of one of the open courts into a presbyterium and high altar, the closing of seven doors out of eight, and the porch over the only one left open, are the work of Theodore I. (642–649).

Ruccellai, who visited S. Stefano in the jubilee of 1450, describes the drum and the inclosure wall as inlaid with finely cut crusts of porphyry and serpentine, grapes and leaves of mother-of-pearl, "tarsie et altre gentileze." These beautiful works of art were destroyed in 1453 by Pope Nicholas V.

THE RUINS OF THE OPPIAN.

REGIO III. "ISIS ET SERAPIS." *

X. The third region occupies that portion of the Esquiline ridge which was properly called Mons Oppius. The first and unique inscription mentioning the Oppian, its compital shrines, and its organization as a ward of the city in Republican times, was discovered in September, 1887, in the cellars of the ex-convent of le Cappuccine alle sette Sale — "Mag(istri) et Flamin(es) montan(orum) montis Oppi(i) de pecunia mont(anorum) sacellum claudend(um) et coæquandum et arbores serendas coeraverunt." The name "montani" applies strictly to the inhabitants of the septimontium — even to the present day (*monticiani*) — while those of the surrounding districts were called "pagani." The yearly celebration called by Varro "septimontiale sacrum" was performed on the Palatium, Cermalus, Velia, Fagutalis, Oppian, Cispian, and in the Subura, in memory of the first settlement of the population in those places. The festive groups gathered round the oldest shrine of the ward, led by their own popular magistrates and priests. The shrines were surrounded by clusters of old trees, such as birches (*lucus fagutalis*), oaks (*lucus querquetulanus*), laurels (*vicus Loreti*), and so forth. The inscription found on the Oppian shows how carefully these historical woods were preserved.[1]

[1] LITERATURE. — Giuseppe Gatti, *Bull. com.*, 1887, p. 150.

* See Figure 136 facing page 360.

We do not know what name was given to this third region by
Augustus, that of Isis and Serapis being of a later age. The
temple of the two gods (Isium Metellinum?) stood between the
Via Leopardi, the Via Curva, and the Via Macchiavelli. It was a
magnificent structure, rich in masterpieces of Egyptian, Greek, and
Roman art, and yet the only mention we have of it is a brief passage of Bartoli (Mem. 2) : " An Egyptian temple has been discovered near the church of SS. Pietro e Marcellino, the figures of
which were designed by order of Cassiano dal Pozzo." And so
thoroughly did the seicento excavators destroy it that not one
stone is left *in situ*. Its marble spoils seem to have been scattered
far and wide soon after the prohibition of pagan worship. Many
hundred fragments were discovered in 1888 under the house at
the corner of the Via Labicana and the Via Macchiavelli, having
been used as building-material in a foundation wall of the sixth or
seventh century. They represent Jupiter Serapis; Isis crowned
with poppies and "spicæ;" Isis veiled, with the crescent on the
forehead; three replicas of the same type; and a female figure
wearing the Egyptian head-dress, probably a portrait statue. A
figure of the cow Hathor, the living symbol of Isis, cut in the
rarest kind of spotted granite, was discovered, half in the foundations of the Palazzo Field, Via Merulana, half in those of the convent of the Sœurs de Cluny, Via Buonarroti. A pedestal inscribed
with the name of the goddess came to light in 1889, a few yards
from the Coliseum. I may mention in the last place the find of
another wall in the Via Labicana entirely built of blocks of amethyst, which seemed to belong to one or more columns.

The designs of Cassiano dal Pozzo are in England. Some small
Egyptian figurines are in the Capitoline Museum, ground floor,
first room on the left. The blocks of amethyst are in the Palazzo
dei Conservatori. The altar of Isis is in the Museo delle Terme,
and the marble statues in the Museo Municipale al Celio, Halls II.
and V.; the cow Hathor in the coffee-house of the Villa Field ![1]

The monuments of the third region, which we must take into
consideration in this chapter, are the Golden House of Nero, with
its reservoir called the Sette Sale; the baths of Titus and the
baths of Trajan, built on the remains of the Domus Aurea; and
the Flavian amphitheatre with its annexes.

XI. DOMUS AUREA (the Golden House of Nero). — Of the

---

[1] LITERATURE. — *Forma Urbis*, pl. xxix. — Ludovico Visconti, *Bull. com.*,
1887, pp. 131–136; and 1889, p. 37. — *Athenæum*, n. 3191. — *Notizie Scavi*, 1888,
p. 626.

wonders of the Golden House — a park one mile square laid out by Nero after the fire of July, 64 — it is enough to say that it contained waterfalls supplied by an aqueduct fifty miles long; lakes and ponds shaded by ancient trees, with harbors for the Imperial galleys; a vestibule with a bronze colossus 120 feet high; porticoes 3000 feet long; farms and vineyards, pasture-grounds and woods teeming with game; zoölogical and botanical gardens; sulphur baths supplied from the aquæ Albulæ; sea baths supplied from the Mediterranean; thousands of columns with capitals of Corinthian metal; hundreds of statues removed from Greece and Asia Minor; walls inlaid with gems and mother-of-pearl; banqueting halls with ivory ceilings, from which rare flowers and costly perfumes fell gently on the recumbent guests. More elaborate still was the ceiling of the state dining-hall. It is described as spherical in shape, carved in ivory so as to represent the starry skies, and kept in motion by machinery in imitation of the course of stars and planets.

Remains of this fairy-like establishment have been found during the last four centuries, wherever the proper depth was attained, below the level of the Imperial buildings of a later age in the space between the Palatine and the gardens of Mæcenas on the Esquiline. Some of the apartments are still visible under the Temple of Venus and Rome, and in the gardens formerly of Cardinal Pio di Carpi and of Cardinal Marzio Colonna, now belonging to the Ospizio delle Mendicanti. A nymphæum (Fig. 137) incrusted with shells and enamels has just been found (1895) near the Via della Polveriera in the same Vigna de Nobili in which Pietro Sante Bartoli witnessed the discovery of "diverse stanze sotterranee adornate di marmi, pitture, fontane, e statue." Alberti Giovanni says that in the first half of the sixteenth century a considerable portion of the Golden House (*ruine del appartamento di Nerone*) was excavated in the vineyard of the monks of S. Pietro in Vincoli, at the depth of 9.36 metres, and that there were "most beautiful rooms" with stucco carvings on a golden ground, and paintings; porticoes with columns of the rarest breccias, and capitals of the Ionic order, and other such relics. Another wing of the palace, a corridor on which opened five guest-rooms, with a rich set of mosaic pictures, was excavated in 1668, 55.75 metres east of the Coliseum in the direction of Trajan's baths.[1] The mosaics, the paintings, and some of

---

[1] Literature on discoveries connected with the Golden House : Pietro Sante Bartoli, *Mem.* 3, 51 (in Fea's Miscellanea, vol. i. pp. ccxxii, ccxxxiv). — Carlo Fea, *Varietà di notizie*, p. 124. — Alberti Giovanni, *Cod. Borgo S. Sepolcro,*

the marbles were removed to the Massimi Palace. The collection was sold by the present prince.

Fig. 137. — Nymphæum discovered near the Via della Polveriera.

The principal building of Nero's park lies half buried but almost intact under the baths of Trajan, as shown in the accompanying map (Fig. 138).

It consists of a long row of halls A, A′, A″, opening on one side due north, on a garden B, B′, which is surrounded by a portico C, C′, C″, C‴, and has a fountain D in the centre; and on the other side opening due south, E, E′, E″, on a great court F, surrounded also by a colonnade G, G′. By this arrangement the palace was made equally pleasant in winter or summer. When Trajan determined to erect a great bathing-establishment on the adjoining heights of the Oppian, he made use of this noble house to support the semicircular portion of the platform on the side nearest to the Coliseum. For this purpose he built a series of parallel walls, some at right angles with the masses of buildings already in existence, some sloping towards them, in the manner of buttresses, at an angle of 61°. Trajan's substructures are easily distinguished

40′, 41′; *Bull. arch. com.*, 1895, pp. 174–181. — Christian Huelsen, *Mittheil.*, 1891, p. 289; and 1896, p. 213. — R. Lanciani, *Ancient Rome*, p. 124; and *Bull. com.*, 1895, p. 174.

Fig. 136. MAP OF REGION III ISIS ET SERAPIS.

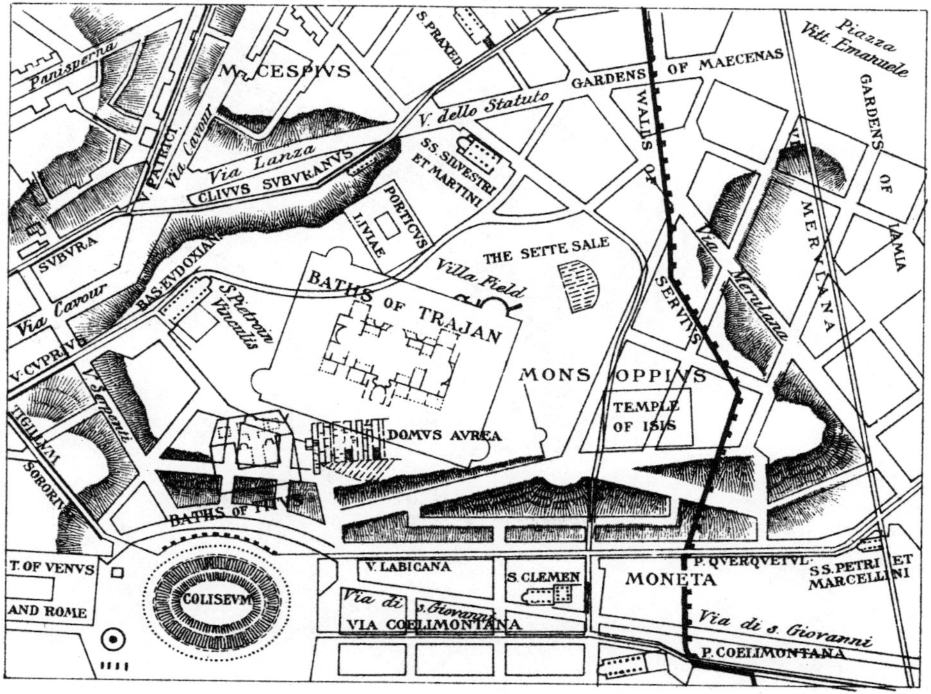

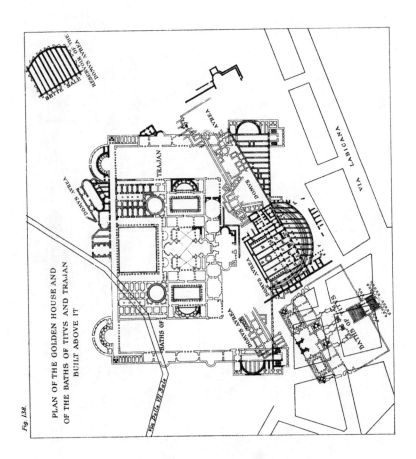

Fig. 138.

PLAN OF THE GOLDEN HOUSE AND
OF THE BATHS OF TITVS AND TRAJAN
BUILT ABOVE IT

by their style of masonry, — a perfect specimen of opus reticulatum divided into panels by bands of bricks, — while Nero's walls are all in opus lateritium, with a coating of plaster.

These ruins were first visited by Giovanni da Udine at the beginning of the sixteenth century.[1] He made a careful study of their fanciful paintings, to which the name of "grottesche," viz., "found in underground ruins or grotte," has since been given.

Fig. 139. — A View of the South Wing of the Domus Aurea.

Giovanni's sketches (the originals of which are now dispersed in various European collections) inspired his master, Raphael Sanzio, to produce the immortal creations of the Loggie Vaticane. Only a few traces of these celebrated frescoes are now visible in the cryptoporticus H, H', on the north side of the garden B, B', and in the halls marked A, A'. They help us to appreciate the power possessed by the ancient house-decorators to increase the apparent extent of a limited space by perspective drawings of this kind. It seems almost certain that these halls were used, or perhaps in-

---

[1] Nibby has found the date 1493 written in one of the rooms by an unknown visitor. On the visit of Raphael and Giovanni Ricamatore to the crypts, see Vasari, *Vita di Giovanni*; and Rodolfo Lanciani, *Rendiconti Lincei*, 1895, p. 3.

habited, even after their conversion into substructures, light and
air being supplied by skylights opening in the terrace of the baths.
Fifteen skylights open on the cryptoporticus H alone.

A point of interest to the modern visitor is the chapel dedicated to S. Felicitas at the beginning of the sixth century (I, in
plan). Its paintings, now much effaced, have been illustrated
by Marulli, Piale, Armellini, and copied in facsimile by Ruspi.
The principal group represented the Saviour offering a crown of
jewels to Felicitas Cvltrix Romanarvm. The heroic woman is
surrounded by her seven sons, four on the left, Silianvs, Martialis,
Philippvs, Felix; three on the right, Vitalis, Alexander, Zenva-
rivs. The names were written twice, once in red, once in black
letters. The side walls are covered with graffiti mostly of the
class of *proscinema*, or devout salutations. One of the legends
began with the words IVSTINVS DOMO . . .; another tells us that
the *domus* was that of an Alexander (ΑΛΕΞΑΝΔΡΟΙΟ ΔΟΜΟΣ); and as
Alexander is the name of one of Felicitas' sons, who shared with
her the glory of martyrdom under Marcus Aurelius, it is highly
probable that this memorial chapel was consecrated after the peace
of the Church in the very house in which he lived.

LITERATURE. — Troiano Marulli, *Lettera sopra un' antica cappella nelle
terme di Tito.* Naples, 1813. — Antonio Guattani, *Memorie Enciclopediche,*
1816. — Girolamo Amati, *Cod. vat.,* 9776, f. 6. — Mariano Armellini, *Chiese di
Roma,* p. 136.

The walls of the Golden House are covered here and there
with graffiti (published by Correra, Bull. com., 1895, p. 197),
which proves that these underground rooms were left permanently
accessible, and were resorted to for purposes not always lawful.
In one of the apartments on the left of the (present) entrance
door there is a latrina, and above it the painting of two serpents
coiled around a tripos, the meaning of which is to be found in the
first satire of Persius, v. 127 : *pinge duos angues : pueri, sacer est
locus !*

Near the entrance to the cryptoporticus H H', at the place
marked K, remains are to be seen of a building, destroyed by the
fire of Nero, and consequently older than his Golden House. The
cryptoporticus itself was discovered for the first time in 1813.
The state in which it was found, with the ceiling most exquisitely
painted on a white ground, while the walls had received only their
first rough coating of plaster, and the work of laying the pavement had not even begun, proves that this wing of the Golden

House was not finished at the time of Nero's death. The arabesques of the ceiling have been published by De Romanis in plates viii. and ix. of the "Camere Esquiline." Neglect, damp, and the smoke of torches have nearly effaced them. Towards the middle of the corridor, on the right hand, there is an altar, and above it another representation of the two snakes, with a legend declaring in the most crude and undisguised form what the symbol of the snakes meant. The text can be found in Nibby (Roma antica, vol. ii. p. 829) and De Romanis (Camere Esquiline, p. 7). Its meaning is, "Commit no nuisance."

Other remains of the Golden House are to be seen in the garden annexed to the Scuola degli Ingegneri (ex-convent of S. Pietro in Vinculis) under the building called "la Polveriera," and also in the Vigna Gualtieri and in the Villa Field. They are practically inaccessible. The Villa Field contains also the magnificent reservoir, known by the name of Le Capoccie or the Sette Sale, divided into nine compartments by eight parallel walls. The nine sections communicate by means of four openings through the cross-walls, placed not opposite each other but diagonally, so as to prevent the violent rush of the water from one receptacle to the next. The reservoir seems to have been kept in use, first for the baths of Titus, and afterwards for those of Trajan.

The Camere Esquiline are entered by the first gate on the left of the (modern) Via Labicana. Open every day, Sundays excepted.

XII. THERMÆ TITIANÆ (Baths of Titus). Classic inscriptions and early ecclesiastic documents mention two great baths on the platform of the Oppian, between the Coliseum, the Sette Sale, and the Basilica Eudoxiana (S. Pietro in Vinculis); namely, the baths of Titus, "Thermæ Titianæ," and the baths of Trajan, "Thermæ Traianæ." Topographers have discussed the question whether the two edifices were really independent and distinct from each other, or whether they were but one and the same establishment, built in haste (*velocia munera*) by Titus, and rebuilt, enlarged, and embellished by Trajan. The supporters of the first theory quoted in their favor the "Notitia," which mentions among the edifices of the third region *Thermas Titianas* ET *Traianas;* and the inscription of Ursus Togatus, the *pilicrepus* or juggler of the time of Hadrian, famous for having played with a light glass ball in *Thermis Titi* ET *Traiani.* Those who believed in the one edifice having had two names, that of the founder and that of the restorer, quoted the case of the baths of Nero by the Pantheon, which became the Thermæ Alexandrianæ after their reconstruction by Severus Alexander. I have myself been a supporter of this second theory, because, in surveying the platform and the slopes of the Oppian for the construction of Sheets xxiii. and xxx. of the "Forma Urbis," I could not find the proper space for two baths of such size in that district. At the beginning of last year (1895) the question stood therefore in these terms. Had the baths of Titus lost their name and their identity through restoration and enlargement by Trajan? There was no doubt that the extensive ruins, known, described, and designed for centuries, between the Coliseum and the Sette Sale, belonged to them. The site of those of Trajan — in case of an independent building — was vaguely pointed out in the neighborhood of San Martino ai Monti.

The question has been since decided theoretically by means of a discovery which I have made among the drawings of Palladio (formerly at Chiswick, now intrusted to the care of the Royal Institute of British Architects, Conduit Street, London), and practically by the finding of the propylaia of the true baths of Titus in the course of the excavations carried on in the spring of 1895 on the northeast side of the Coliseum.

Palladio's drawings prove that on the northeast side of the Coliseum (*per mezo el colixeo*) there were still standing about 1550 remains of baths which he attributes to Vespasian; that their level was 17.50 metres above that of the street surrounding the amphitheatre; that they were approached by stately stairs opening on a piazza or platform; and lastly, that the thermæ were *molto ruinate*, so that in many points his plans and drawings were simply conjectural.

After Palladio's time every trace of them disappeared under the increase of modern soil. Valuable marbles were dug up about 1590 and made use of in decorating one of the chapels of the Chiesa del Gesù, and granite columns were found in 1797.

The excavations for the construction of a new humble quarter — especially calculated to disfigure this classic corner of old Rome — and those made last year by Commendatore Baccelli, minister of public instruction, while confirming in the main lines the exactness of Palladio's drawings, have enabled us to give a definite place to these much discussed baths in the map of the ancient city, and to restore to the adjoining ruins of the Oppian their proper name of Thermæ Traiani.

Towards the end of the fourth century the front portion of the Baths of Titus had already collapsed. An extension of the offices of the prefect of the city was built on its site, remains of which are still to be seen.

LITERATURE ON THE OFFICES OF THE PREFECT. — Rodolfo Lanciani, *Gli edifici della prefettura urbana fra la Tellure e le terme di Tito e di Traiano* (in Bull. com., 1892, p. 19). Compare *Bull. com.*, 1882, p. 161; and *Mittheil.*, 1893, p. 299.

XIII. THERMÆ TRAIANI (Baths of Trajan). — No account of their construction is to be found in classics, except in a brief passage of Pausanias (v. 12), where the baths "which bear Trajan's name," ἐπώνυμα αὐτοῦ, are placed at the head of the list of his works. When the statues of the gods were removed from the temples, in which divine honors had been paid to them, and distributed among the state buildings of Rome as simple works of art, the Baths of Trajan received their full share at the hands of Julius Felix Campanianus, prefect of the city at the beginning of the fifth century. Officers from the staff of the establishment are mentioned in Nos. 8677, 8678 of the "Corpus Inscr.:" a Philetus, "exactor," and an Ireneus, "adjutor thermarum traianarum." The extensive ruins did not lose their identity until a comparatively recent date.

The "Itinerary of Einsiedlen" calls them by their proper name, *thermas Traiani ad Vincula*, and all the artists of the Renaissance adhere likewise to the right denomination. The fault of adopting the wrong one has been attributed to Pope Julius II., who wrote on the pedestal of the granite basin, removed from S. Pietro in Vinculis to the Vatican Belvedere, the words "labrum . . . ab Titi Vespasiani thermis in Carinis . . . in vaticanos hortos advexit;" but the legend is correct, the basin having been seen in 1450 by Ruccellai on the true site of the Thermæ Titi, "in una vigna appresso al coliseo." The change of name took place towards the end of the sixteenth century.

The history of the destruction of this noble edifice, as I have been able to reconstruct it from documents preserved in Roman archives, would fill a volume. The monks of S. Pietro in Vinculis are responsible for it: they sold the marbles to lime-burners, the bricks to master masons, and allowed excavators to tear up the foundations of the frigidarium, tepidarium, and caldarium. While the architects of the sixteenth century were still able to draw their plan and design their shape without difficulty, very little is now left standing above ground, either in the garden of the scuola degli Ingegneri or in the Villa Field. These few remains, a per-

fect specimen of Roman brickwork of the golden age of Apollodorus, are well taken care of, and appear to great advantage in
their frame of evergreens.   Students are allowed to visit the beautiful grounds.   If they wish to single out the various remains
which they contain, they must remember that the Domus Aurea
(and the Baths of Titus) were "oriented" on the meridian line,
while the axis of the Baths of Trajan diverges towards the east
by 30°.

Many works of art have been found in this classic district, but
it is not possible to say exactly where.   The first is the granite
tazza just mentioned, which was seen by Ruccellai, during the
jubilee of 1450, "in una vigna appresso al coliseo," removed by
Julius II. "in vaticanos hortos" A. D. 1504, and buried at the
time of Pius IV. in the "teatro di Belvedere." Its place of con-
cealment was pointed out to Paul V. by a master mason named
Battista.   Paul V. caused it to be restored in 1616 and used it as
a basin to his fountain in the same teatro di Belvedere.   Another
oval granite tazza, twenty palms long, ornamented with rings and
lions' heads, was seen by the Gobbo da Sangallo at S. Pietro in
Vinculis in the first quarter of the sixteenth century.   Its fate is
not known.   Cherubino Alberti speaks of columns of portasanta,
africano, etc., found and broken (*spezzate*) on one of the peristyles
of Trajan's baths; Ligorio of a statue which he calls "imagine
simbolica del mondo; " Vacca of several statues and "infiniti
ornamenti;" Aldovrandi of a statue of Hercules discovered by
Niccolo Stagni near the Sette Sale; Bartoli of twenty-five statues
"di meravigliosa conservazione e bellezza " discovered by Cardinal
Trivulzio in 1547 in the same place; Brunelleschi of an altar
dedicated to Jupiter by Vespasian, discovered also at the Sette
Sale, or Capoccie, on January 8, 1509; Ficoroni of a bronze lamp
in the shape of a human head, with its wick of threads of amianth,
found in 1696.   The Laocoon was found, on June 1, 1506, in the
vineyard of Felice de Fredis at the Sette Sale, in a hall which, according to Pliny (H. N., xxxvi. 4, 11), must have formed part of
the house of Titus (Laocoon, qui est in Titi imperatoris domo,
opus omnibus et picturæ et statuariæ artis præponendum).   The
group must have been removed by Trajan to his own thermæ,
when the site of the Domus Titi was occupied by the new structure; but it is also possible that the Domus should have been
allowed to stand as a historical monument in the space between
the baths and the Sette Sale.   Here, in fact, some exquisitely
adorned apartments were brought to light in 1683, the designs

and description of which I have discovered in the Cabinet des Estampes, Paris, in a volume marked G, d, 2. A statuette of Pluto, of indifferent workmanship, discovered in 1814, before the Chapel of S. Felicita, is now kept in the Capitoline Museum, Room III., on the ground floor.

<small>LITERATURE ON THE BATHS OF TITUS AND TRAJAN, AND ON THE DOMUS AUREA, UPON WHICH THEY ARE BUILT.— Giuseppe Carletti, *Le antiche camere delle terme di Tito, e le loro pitture delineate* . . . *da Lodovico Mirri* (Smugliesviecz and Brenna). Rome, about 1780, folio atlas. — Carlo Fea, *Della casa aurea di Nerone e della Torre cartularia.* Rome, Boulzaler, 1832. — Antonio de Romanis, *Le antiche camere esquiline dette comunemente delle terme di Tito.* Rome, 1822. — Luigi Canina, *Intorno un frammento della pianta marmorea capitolina* (in Memorie romane di Antichità, vol. ii. 1825, p. 119); and *Edifizi,* vol. vi. pls. 202–204. — Stefano Piale, *Delle terme traiane, della domus Aurea e della Titi domus.* Rome, Puccinelli, 1832. — *Vue du palais doré de Néron* (tiré du Spectacle de l'histoire romaine par M. Philippe, gravé par Ransonette), 1776. — Cesare Trivulzio, in *Lettere pittoriche,* vol. iii. n. 196, p. 231; and Francesco Sangallo, in Fea's *Miscellanea,* vol. i. p. cccxxix. — Rodolfo Lanciani, *Picturæ antiquæ cryptarum romanar.* (in Bull. com., 1895, p. 174); and *Gli scavi del Colosseo e le terme di Tito* (ibid. p. 110). — *Corpus Inscr.,* vol. vi. n. 369, 1670, 9797, 12,995. — Heinrich Jordan, *Forma Urbis Romæ,* p. 42, n. 109.</small>

XIV. AMPHITHEATRUM FLAVIUM (the Flavian Amphitheatre — Coliseum). — The name " amphitheatre," although of Greek origin, dates from the last century of the Roman Republic, and was formed and adopted to indicate a new type of public building, strictly national, and used for gladiatorial fights (*ludi gladiatorii*) and fights with wild beasts (*venationes*). Such exhibitions had taken place in former times either in the Forum or in the Circus, or wherever a free space could be found inclosed by higher grounds or buildings from which the spectators could command the view. The idea of a special structure was suggested, as the name itself implies, by the already existing theatre for scenic plays ; in fact, the first amphitheatre, erected by C. Scribonius Curio, the partisan of Cæsar, for the celebration of his father's funeral games in 46 B. C., was essentially a double theatre, viz., composed of two theatres, " placed on pivots, so that they could be turned round, spectators and all, and placed either back to back, forming two separate stages for dramatic exhibitions, or face to face, forming an amphitheatre for the shows of gladiators and wild beasts." [1] It was not, however, till the fourth consulship of

---

[1] William Wayte in Smith's *Dict. of Antiq.,* i. 107. Other passages of this section are quoted from the same excellent article.

Augustus, 30 B. C., that a permanent edifice was erected by Statilius Taurus, in that part of the Campus Martius which is now
called Monte Giordano (Orsini). The mound, about 450 metres
in circumference, and about 20 metres high, formed by the ac-

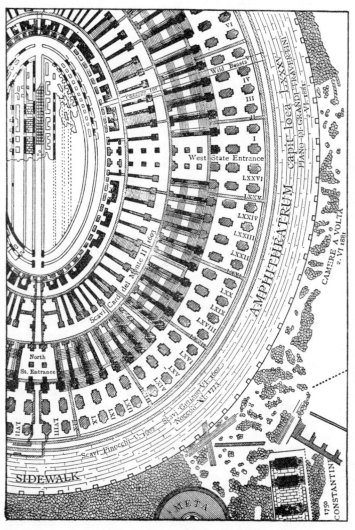

Fig. 140. — Plan of Western Section of the Flavian Amphitheatre.

cumulation of ruins, was crowned in the Middle Ages by a shrine or chapel of Michael the archangel, to whom other conspicuous ruins (the mausoleums of Augustus and Hadrian, etc.) were dedicated; and this chapel was called *De Rota*, a special mediæval denomination for an amphitheatre. That of Statilius Taurus was destroyed in the burning of Rome, A. D. 64, and we argue from this fact that its shell alone was built of stone and marble, while the seats and staircases were of wood.

The second permanent amphitheatre was built by Tiberius (?) at the extreme end of the Esquiline, for the training of the venatores and of "performing" beasts. The design of Augustus, however, that an amphitheatre, proportioned to the magnitude of the capital of the Empire, should be erected in the very heart of the city, was carried into effect only by the Flavians. Nothing can furnish a better example of the prodigal contempt of labor and expense which the Emperors displayed in their architectural works than the selection of its site.

> Hic ubi conspicui venerabilis amphitheatri
> Erigitur moles, stagna Neronis erant.
>
> Martial, *De Spect.*, ii. 3.

The hollow between the Cælian, the Oppian, the Velian, and the Palatine was marshy, damp, unsteady even before Nero's artificial lake, the abundance of the local springs being so great that any accidental stopping of the drains produces an inundation. I have already mentioned the event of 1875–78, when, after the late Commendatore Rosa undertook to excavate the arena without providing in advance an outlet to the flood, the substructures were covered by twelve feet of water, which four powerful engines could lower only by a few inches. We have no account of the means adopted by Vespasian's architect to overcome the difficulty found in getting firm foundations, and to give the soil steadiness. I have seen them explored but once, in 1864–65, by a Signor Testa, while searching for the "Frangipani treasure," which, to the best of our knowledge, had already been found in 1805 by Signor Lezzani, while laying the foundations of the buttress (*sperone*) of Pius VI. Signor Testa discovered the upper belt of the substructures, arched like those of the ambulacra, above ground; and underneath them a bed of concrete which must descend to a considerable depth.

"This wonderful building, which for magnitude can only be compared to the pyramids of Egypt, and which is perhaps the most striking monument at once of the material and the moral degradation of Rome under the Empire," was commenced by Vespasian, and inaugurated by Titus in the year 80, the event being recorded by the medals (Cohen Imper., vol. i. p. 359, n. 163; and p. 362, n. 184 [1]). An entry in the Chronographer of A. D. 354 attributes to Domitian the completion of the edifice; and the phrase "amphitheatrum usque ad clypea (fabricatum est)" has been interpreted as if Domitian had added the whole fourth story, besides the ornamental work. The statement is contradicted by other documents, such as the coins of Titus, mentioned above, and the celebrated passage in the "Acta Arvalium," which describes the *loca adsignata in amphitheatro* (the places assigned) to that brotherhood in the first distribution of places, A. D. 80.[2] The "Acta" speak of the *mœnianum primum, secundum*, and of the *mœnianum summum in ligneis;* the amphitheatre, therefore, had reached its extreme height the very year of its inauguration. The event must have been celebrated by one or more inscriptions, which are now lost. Hübner thought he had found fragments of them on two or three blocks of travertine used by Severus Alexander in the restorations of the upper belt, A. D. 223, but Professor Spinazzola, who climbed to the height of the cornice at the risk of his life (March, 1896), has found the name of Nerva engraved upon the stones; the inscription, therefore, refers to the restorations of *Nerva* Trajanus mentioned by Pausanias in § xii. 4 of the Ἠλιακῶν. Trajan's work is not recorded otherwise; and the "Vita Pii" is the only authority concerning the repairs made at the time of Antoninus Pius.

On August 23, A. D. 217, Macrinus being Emperor, the amphitheatre was repeatedly struck by lightning. The *tabulationes* of the fourth story caught fire and the falling embers set the floor of the arena ablaze. In fact, there must have been more wood and timber in the structure than we generally believe. The seven battalions of firemen, helped by the detachments of marines from the ports of Ravenna and Misenum, and by a waterspout (ἡ τοῦ οὐρανίου ἐπίρροια, πλείστη τε καὶ σφοδροτάτη γενομένη — Dion Cass., lxxviii. 25), did not get the fire under until the stone and marble

---

[1] Compare Donaldson, *Archit. numism.*, n. 79; and Parker, *Colosseum*, pl. 24, n. 1. There is another coin forged by the Padovano.

• [2] LITERATURE. — Gaetano Marini, *Arvali*, p. 224. — Luigi Canina, *Edifizi di R. A.*, vol. iii. p. 26. — Hübner, *Ann. Inst.*, 1856, p. 52. — Theodor Mommsen, *Ann. Inst.*, 1859, p. 125. — Wilhelm Henzen, *Acta Arvalium*, p. cvi. — *Corpus Inscr.*, vol. vi. n. 2059, p. 506. — Christian Huelsen, *Il posto degli Arvali nel Colosseo* (in Bull. com., 1894, p. 388, pl. 15).

work had suffered great damage; so great, indeed, that the amphitheatre was abandoned for many years and the games were celebrated in the circus.

The catastrophe had taken place on August 23, the very day of the "Volkanalia," the celebration of which had been forbidden by Macrinus a few days before. The population was so terror-stricken by the occurrence that the "games of Vulcan" were reestablished at once.

Heliogabalus began and Severus Alexander finished in 223 the work of reconstruction, the funds being taken from what the Italians used to call "fondi segreti del ministero dell' interno." The repairs of Severus and Heliogabalus can be examined to the best advantage from the upper platform; they consist of a patch-work of stones of every description, trunks of columns, pieces of entablatures, lintels, and architraves recovered from the portions damaged by fire or taken away from other buildings. The construction of this upper story is altogether hasty and negligent: the joints of the stones are irregular and the composite pilasters are not all straight nor placed on the same perpendicular as the columns below.

In 240 the Emperor Philippus celebrated the millennium of the city with the secular games, in the course of which all the wild beasts collected by Gordianus the younger in view of his Persian triumph were slain. The biographer mentions among them 30 elephants, 10 elks, 10 tigers, 10 wild lions and 60 tame ones, 30 tame leopards, 10 hyenas, 19 giraffes, 20 wild asses, 40 wild horses, 1 hippopotamus, 1 rhinoceros; there were also 1000 pairs of gladiators. Another great display of *venationes* took place in A. D. 281, on the occasion of the triumph of Probus. One hundred of the finest breed of lions (*iubati*) were let loose in the arena at the same time. Their thundering roars shook the great amphitheatre to its foundations. They were followed by 100 lionesses, 100 leopards from Nubia, 100 leopards from Syria, and 300 bears. The slaughter of these noble animals without offering them fair play and letting them fight for their lives revolted the assembly; the biographer calls the sight "magnum magis spectaculum quam gratum."

From the time of Decius (A. D. 250), who repaired the damages of another fire, to the earthquake of 422 the history of the building is not known. We are well informed, on the other hand, about the campaign undertaken by slowly spreading Christian influence against the gladiatorial shows. In 325, the year of the council of Nicæa, Constantine addressed to Maximus, prefect of the prætorium, the constitution "Cod.ᵗtheod.," xv. 12, 1, forbidding those human butcheries; but it had no effect. Constantius and Julianus on October 16, 357, and Arcadius and Honorius in 397, renewed the injunction with about the same results. They also tried to show a great partiality towards the athletes, whose performances were, to be sure, less cruel. In 365–375 Valentinian and his colleagues raised a statue to a champion fighter named Philumenos; Theodosius did the same in 384–392 to celebrate the deeds of another athlete named Johannes (a Christian or a Jew); [1] yet the old passion could not be uprooted from among the populace. The celebrated mosaic representing the *editiones gladiatoriæ* of the Symmachi (Marini, Arval., 165) belongs to the middle of the fourth century, and so does the great fighting-scene discovered near Torre Nuova in 1834, illustrated by Henzen in 1845 in vol. xii. of the "Atti dell' accademia romana di archeologia," p. 73.

The only provision of the Imperial constitution which seems to have been enforced was that forbidding the magistrates to condemn Christians to fight in the arena. In one of his strongest poems Prudentius urges Honorius to put an end to the "detestable" practice, but the feeble son of Theodosius still hesitated to comply with the request. At last, in 404, seventy-five years after the first decree of Constantine, the self-sacrifice of Telemachus, who threw himself into the arena and was stoned to death by the mob while he attempted to wrench the deadly weapons from the fighting pairs, induced Honorius to suppress forever the gladiatorial shows. [2] After this memorable year the amphitheatre was used occasionally for *venationes* or, perhaps, for boxing-matches, but no further mention occurs of gladiators.

The earthquake of 422, described by Paul the Deacon, must have done the building serious injury. An inscription discovered by Fea in 1813, and now placed in the north vestibule (Corpus, vol. vi. n. 1763), speaks of restorations made by Theodosius II. and Valentinian III. between 425 and 450. There are also copious fragments of three inscriptions, each 70 or 80 metres long, commemorating other work done under the latter Emperor, by Flavius Paulus, prefect of the city in 438. A second *abominandus terræ motus* is mentioned in three inscriptions bearing the name of Decius Marius Venantius Basilius, who repaired its damages

---

[1] *Corpus Inscr.*, vol. vi. n. 10,153, 10,154.

[2] LITERATURE. — Theodoretos, v. 26. — Tillemont, *Histoire des empereurs*, vol. v. 533. — Gio. Battista de Rossi, *Bull. crist.*, 1868, p. 84. — P. T. Meier, *De gladiatura romana*. Bonn, 1881.

about 508 A. D. These inscriptions are to be seen in the same north vestibule.

Eutaricus Cillica, son-in-law of Theodoric, gave the last show but one in the arena, on the occasion of his election to the consulate in 519. Cassiodorus, the king's secretary, says that wild beasts were imported from Africa, the sight of which was a novelty for the living generation. The venationes of Anicius Maximus in 523 are the last recorded in the history of the place. Here I must observe that, while repairing the drains and underground passages of the arena in 1878, we discovered a considerable quantity of bones, which were identified by Professor de Sanctis as pertaining to domestic animals, like bulls, horses, and stags. The discovery shows how insignificant the last shows must have been in comparison with those of the golden age.

The amphitheatre, its shell at least, was intact in the eighth century, when Bede wrote his famous proverb, "Quamdiu stabit Coliseus stabit et Roma: quando cadet Coliseus cadet et Roma." When was it reduced to its present ruinous state? By whom, and under what circumstances, was this done? The possibility of a spontaneous collapse must be rejected. If we look at the Coliseum from the east side, where it appears intact, and consider the prodigious solidity of its structure and the clever way its stones are wedged and fastened into each other, we are led to discard the idea that it could be damaged to any serious extent by age, atmospheric agents, fire, or even earthquakes. Yet it is possible that the shaking of the earth might have produced a crack like that which cuts the back of the Pantheon in the Via della Palombella; and this contingency is even more probable if we recollect that while the drum of the Pantheon is solid, and fifteen feet thick at least, the shell of the Coliseum is pierced by four tiers of arches and windows. The equilibrium once broken, the process of disintegration could not be stopped by human power, especially when shrubs and plants began to take root in the joints of the stones and in the opening of the crack, and to act like powerful levers. At the same time we cannot deny the fact that at a given moment, the date of which has yet to be fixed, the whole of the western half of the shell fell towards the Cælian and gave rise to a hill, or rather to a chain of hills, of loose blocks of travertine and tufa, which supplied Rome of the Renaissance with building-materials for the lapse of five centuries. The following view (Fig. 141) shows the precarious state in which the inner walls of the mæniana were left after the collapse of the outside arcades towards the Cælian. The date of this event must be restricted to the period between 1332 and 1362. On September 3 of the former year the Roman nobility were still able to meet in the arena free from ruins and take part in a bullfight which cost the lives of eighteen young patricians, while nine more were badly mangled.[1] In 1362 the Romans, the legate of Pope Urban

Fig. 141. — The Shell of the Coliseum after the Collapse of the Western Arcades.

V., and the Frangipani were already quarreling over the spoils of the fallen giant, " de faciendo tiburtinam " with the stones of the Coliseum. The collapse, therefore, must be attributed to the earthquake of Petrarch, which ruined so many monuments of ancient and mediæval Rome, September, 1349. A few years later, in 1386, the S. P. Q. R. made a present of one third of the Coliseum to the " Compagnia del Salvatore ad sancta Sanctorum." The event is chronicled to the present day on the walls of the amphitheatre — above the sixty-third arch, towards the Meta Sudans —

---

[1] LITERATURE. — Ludovico Muratori, *Rerum Italic. Scriptores,* vol. xii. p. 332. — Antonio Nibby, *Roma antica,* vol. i. p. 413. — Pietro Ercole Visconti, *Splendore di Roma nel secolo xiv.* Rome, 1867, p. 23.

by a marble bas-relief with the bust of the Saviour between two
burning tapers (Fig. 142); and above arch No. LXV. by the coats
of arms of the Company and of the S. P. Q. R. painted on white
plaster.

The mountain of stone caused by the fall of the western belt —
known in contemporary documents as the Cosa, Coxa, or Coscia
Colisei — ranks first among the *petrale* or stone quarries within
the walls. It has taken four centuries and fifteen generations of

Fig. 142. — The Insignia of the Compagnia del Salvatore on the Coliseum.

stone-cutters and lime-burners to exhaust it. Its history has yet
to be written. A document published by Müntz in the "Revue
arch.," September, 1876, certifies that one contractor alone, in the
space of only nine months, in 1452, could carry off two thousand
five hundred and twenty-two cartloads of travertine. I have discovered a brief of Eugenius IV. (1431–1439) in which he expresses
his regret to hear that the rapacious hand of Roman masons had
been laid even on the standing remains of the amphitheatre; and
while leaving them free "ut de locis subterraneis a Coliseo distan-
tibus lapides evellere possint," he threatens them with his wrath
if they dare to touch "vel minimum dicti Colisei lapidem." There
is a tradition, registered by Vacca (Mem., 74), that the same pope

inclosed the remains within a boundary wall, placing them under
the protection of the monks of S. Maria Nuova; yet Poggio Bracciolini describes the same as "maiori ex parte ad calcem deleta."

The travertines for the palace of Paul II. (Palazzo di Venezia)
and for the Pons Æmilius (Ponte Rotto), restored on the occasion
of the jubilee of 1575, were taken from the same quarry. The
arena was transformed at the beginning of the sixteenth century
into a kind of Ober-Ammergau stage, and Passion plays were performed among the ivy-clad ruins for a number of years. The
perspective plan of Jerusalem, painted above the main entrance
on the side of the Sacra Via, is a recollection of these Passion
plays of the time of Paul III. (?). At the same time the Coliseum
served as headquarters to those who believed in witchcraft, one
of the nocturnal meetings (1532) being described by Benvenuto
Cellini in the second book of his memoirs. Under Sixtus V. the
monument ran the risk of being converted into a manufactory of
woolen goods (1585). The plans prepared by Domenico Fontana,
the pope's architect, are described by Bellori, and by Fontana
himself (Della Transportatione dell' obel. vatic., ii. p. 18). The
Compagnia del Salvatore rented its part, March, 1594, for a
glue-factory; the contractor, however, was put in prison by the
S. P. Q. R. and his lease canceled. On June 28, 1604, the same
S. P. Q. R. made a barter with the Compagnia on these terms:
that the Compagnia would let the municipal administration draw
from the Coscia Colisei as much travertine as was necessary to
finish the building of the Museo Capitolino, while the Compagnia,
in its turn, was allowed to pull down the famous Arco di Basile
(over which the Aqua Claudia crossed the Via Cælimontana) to
use its stones in the building of the Hospital del Salvatore.

In 1639 the S. P. Q. R. transferred to a certain Bramante Bassi
the right of excavating "within the circuit of the Coliseum," one
third of the produce being set apart for the Capitoline Chamber.
On March 2, 1697, the quarry was placed at the disposal of Domenico Ponziani, a contractor for municipal works, on the condition
that the great blocks of travertine should be triturated on the spot,
and the chips used in macadamizing certain streets. Towards the
end of the seventeenth century the supply seemed to be exhausted,
when another accident, the earthquake of February 3, 1703, filled
the quarry with new material. The stones were mainly used in
the construction of the Porto di Ripetta, one of the most graceful
and useful works of Clement XI., destroyed six or seven years ago
to make room for the new embankment. The same pope closed

the lower arches with wooden railings and transformed the glorious monument into a deposit of manure for the production of saltpetre. Benedict XIV. consecrated the arena to the memory of those who had suffered martyrdom in it; the cross which he erected in the centre, and the "stations" or shrines around it, were pulled down by Rosa in February, 1874. Pius VII. in 1805, Leo XII. in 1825, Gregory XVI. in 1845, and Pius IX. in 1852 contributed liberally to save the amphitheatre from further degradation, by supporting the falling portions with great buttresses. The lower floor and a portion of the arena were excavated under the French administration between 1810 and 1814. Other excavations were undertaken by Rosa in 1874, which led to the discovery of many epigraphic and architectural fragments, and made students more closely acquainted with the arrangement of the arena and with the management of the venationes.

The flora of the Coliseum was once famous. Sebastiani enumerates 260 species in his "Flora Colisea," and their number was subsequently increased to 420 by Deakin. These materials for a hortus siccus, so dear to the visitors of our ruins, were destroyed by Rosa in 1871, and the ruins scraped and shaven clean, it being feared by him that the action of roots would accelerate the disintegration of the great structure.

The amphitheatre does not stand in a commanding position: the heights of the Oppian on the east, of the Cælian on the south, of the Palatine on the west, of the Velia on the north, surround it so as to leave but one narrow outlet for the spring and rain water, that of the Via di S. Gregorio. The state of things must have been even worse in classic times, when those heights were respectively crowned by the baths of Titus and Trajan, by the Temple of Claudius, by the Palace of the Cæsars, and by the Temple of Venus and Rome. To mend matters as well as the local conditions would allow, the amphitheatre was surrounded first by a pavement, 17.50 metres wide, and then by a street which expanded into squares at either end of the longest diameter (Fig. 140). The pavement, made with slabs of travertine, was lined by a set of stone cippi, each furnished with two pairs of bronze rings, through which wooden bars were made to slide (Fig. 143). The explanation of this arrangement, and the reason why the amphitheatre was provided with this outer temporary fence, must be found in the necessity of regulating the movement of the crowd on days when there were spectacles. A double control was established on such occasions: one at the gates of this outer fence, at which the holders of tickets were admitted in a general way; another at each of the 80 (76) arches of the ground floor, where the number of the mænianum, of the cuneus, of the vomitorium, and of the step and the seat marked in the ticket were verified.

Fig. 143. — Stone Cippi surrounding the Coliseum.

The numbering of the arches begins from the side of the Cælian, and precisely from the first to the right of the west state entrance. Nineteen arches are numbered on each of the four sectors of the ellipse, making a total of 76, the four state entrances not being numbered. Two of these last were reserved for the Imperial family and grand dignitaries, namely, those between Nos. LXXVI. and I. on the side of the Cælian, and between Nos. XXXVIII. and XXXIX. on the side of the Oppian. They are more spacious and better adorned than the other two ; in fact, the (once) painted and gilded stucco reliefs on the walls and on the vault of the east passage rank among the finest specimens of Roman decorative art, and have been studied with delight by the artists of the Renaissance. I have found copies of them in the Queen's library at Windsor Castle (Cod. Vincenzo Vittoria, f. 24); in vol. xi. f. 29 of the Laing collection in the Royal Scottish Academy, Edinburgh; in box of drawings No. IV. at Chatsworth, the Duke of Devonshire's seat in Derbyshire; and in plates 40 and 61 of Destailleur's album in the Kunstgewerbe Museum, Berlin. Very few visitors of the Coliseum are aware of their existence.

In entering the great building we must direct our investigations, first, to the way in which the vast crowds of spectators were handled, directed, and distributed over the seats on exhibition days; secondly, to the arrangement of the arena and of its substructures.

The official Almanac of 354 says that the amphitheatre could accommodate 87,000 spectators. Professor Huelsen, considering that there is certainly no room for more than 45,000 people, perhaps for 50,000 if we take into consideration the *pullati* who stood looking at the performance from the top of the attic, attributes to the term "locus" (amphitheatrum capit loca lxxxvii) the signification not of "place" or "seat" but of "length in feet." In other words, the Coliseum contained, according to Professor Huelsen, 87,000 feet of seats, each spectator occupying a space of 18 or 20 inches.[1] There was accommodation, therefore, for only 50,000 people. Such a crowd is, at all events, very large and difficult to deal with, and the most minute precautions were taken to direct its movements towards the place of destination, and again towards the exits when the show was over. The entrances, staircases, passages, and vomitories were contrived with such exquisite skill that each person, whether of the senatorial, of the equestrian, or of the plebeian order, could gain his seat without trouble or confusion. An ivory ticket for the amphitheatre of Frusino is said

---

[1] The word "locus," in its genuine signification of *place* or *seat*, is still in use in Rome. The cry of men offering places and seats for hire on the occasion of a public pageant or exhibition of any kind is, "ecco sedie, ecco lochi," "here are chairs, here are places."

to be labeled "the sixth cuneus, lowest row, seat No. 18;" in those for the Coliseum the number of the entrance arch must also have been specified, and, indirectly, that of the stairs leading to the proper mænianum.

The seats of honor were on the ledge above the podium, as the nearest to the arena and the most accessible from the four state entrances. The ledge could contain only three rows of (marble?) thrones, some of which, transformed into episcopal chairs in our mediæval churches, are still in existence (S. Stefano Rotondo, S. Gregorio, the *biga* of the Vatican Museum, etc.). Cushions or *pulvini* had come into fashion since the time of Caligula, before the amphitheatre was built.

No trace is left of the Imperial *suggestum* nor of the *cubicula* connected with it. The balcony or pulpit (*editoris tribunal*) reserved for the magistrate who exhibited the games has also disappeared. We have, on the other hand, many epigraphic records of the places pertaining to senators, knights, high priests, ambassadors, guests of the S. P. Q. R., etc., according to the distribution made in A. D. 80 by the Imperial commissioner, Manius Laberius Maximus, assisted by an officer named Thyrsus. The places were not assigned to individuals, but collectively to the body or college or corporation to which they belonged ; for instance, "to the exconsuls, one hundred and ten feet," or, "to the school-teachers, . . . feet." Towards the middle of the fourth century this division by classes was given up, and spaces for one or more seats were permanently occupied by the same individual, or by the same family, whose name was accordingly engraved on the marble pavement or on the parapet of the podium ; and as families were extinguished in the course of years, and individuals died away, the names were erased, and those of the newcomers engraved. Some of the marble slabs appear to be reduced to half their original size by this process of erasing and substituting names. The following cut (Fig. 144) represents one of the steps from the senatorial ranks (?), with the name of an Insteius most negligently cut upon it. I have published in the " Bull. com." of 1880 one hundred and ninety-three inscriptions of seats, and a few more have been discovered since. The " Corpus inscriptionum " of the Flavian amphitheatre numbers over two hundred and sixty specimens, which, if properly arranged and exhibited on the spot, would revive its history and make us conversant with details which it is difficult to make out from books and manuals. The amphitheatre, in fact, is not so poor in architectural or ornamental marbles as we make it appear to be. It would be an easy and also a most useful and noble undertaking to put back these marbles into their proper places, and fully restore one of the "cunei" of this wonderful structure. There are about forty shafts of columns belonging to the upper loggia, and as many capitals of the Corinthian order, some of the time of the Flavians, others of the fourth century; there are hundreds of marble steps and seats, and many exquisite screens or parapets once placed on the side or above the vomitoria; there are inscriptions making the round of the edifice; and yet all these valuable materials are

Fig. 144. — Step-seat of the Coliseum, with the Name of a Fabius Insteius.

allowed to lie useless and scattered in great confusion, and some pieces have actually been taken away and removed I know not whither.

The arena or central open space, where the shows took place, derived its name from the sand with which it was covered for the purpose of absorbing the blood. Such Emperors as Caligula, Nero, and Carinus showed their prodigality by using cinnabar and borax instead of the common arena. It was composed of a boarded floor supported by beams which rested on a series of walls, some parallel with the main axis, some following the curve of the ellipse (see Fig. 145).   A great piece of wooden floor was discovered in the excavations of 1874 at the bottom of the middle corridor, as shown in the following illustration, but we are not sure whether it did really belong to the arena or to the floor below it.   I am in favor of the second surmise, and I believe that when the substructures of the amphitheatre became damp and wet on account of the

Fig. 145. — Wooden Floor discovered in 1874 in the Substructures of the Arena of the Coliseum.

neglect in keeping the drains in repair, the old floor of opus spica-
tum must have been covered with a floor of wood resting on those
supports of stone, which appear so distinctly in the illustration
above. Every trace of the woodwork has been allowed to disappear
since 1874. In the same excavations of 1874–75 the sockets were
discovered to which windlasses, capstans, or lifts (*pegmata*) were
fixed, by which the cages of wild animals were raised to the level
of the trapdoors of the arena. Lifts, cages, and trapdoors are
represented by Parker in plate xvi. of his work on the Coliseum.
We must not suppose that the animals could be kept for any
length of time in the dark and stuffy dens below the arena or the
podium. They were kept in readiness in the west porticoes of the
Claudium and brought up in rolling cages as they were wanted.
From this point of view, that is, from the point of view of exhibition of gladiatorial or hunting shows, the Coliseum appears to us
as the capital of a kingdom of its own, as the centre of a vast
administration, with branch offices in Syria, in Africa, on the Red
Sea, and head offices in Rome itself, occupying large tracts of the
second, third, fifth, and sixth regions.

LITERATURE. — Justus Lipsius, *De amphitheatro* (in Grævii Thesaur., vol.
ix. p. 1292, chs. xi.–xv.). — Giuseppe Suarez, *Diatriba de foraminibus lapidum
in priscis ædificiis.* Rome, 1651. — Carlo Fontana, *L' anfiteatro flavio descritto
e delineato.* Aia, 1725. — Scipione Maffei, *Degli anfiteatri.* Verona, 1727. —
Giovanni Marangoni, *Delle memorie sacre e profane dell' anfit. flav.* Rome,
1745. — Carlo Fea, *Osservazioni sull' arena e sul podio dell' anfit. flav.,* Rome,
1813; *Nuove osservazioni,* Rome, 1814; and *Notizie degli scavi dell' anfit. flav.,*
Rome, 1813. — Antonio Nibby, *Roma antica,* vol. i. p. 529. — Luigi Canina,
Edifizii di Roma antica, vol. iii. p. 23; and vol. iv. pls. 164–177. — Hübner,
Iscrizioni esistenti sui sedili dei teatri ed anfiteatri (in Annal. Inst., 1856, p. 52,
pl. 12). — Effisio Tocco, *Dell' anfit. flav. e dei gladiatori* (in Buonarroti, 1869
and 1870). — Fabio Gori, *Le memorie storiche dell' anfit. flav.* Rome, 1874. —
J. H. Parker, *The Flavian Amphith.* Oxford, London, 1876. — Joachim Mar-
quardt, *Staatsverwaltung,* vol. iii. p. 462. — Rodolfo Lanciani, *Iscrizioni dell'
anf. flav.* (in Bull. com., 1880, p. 211, pls. xxi.–xxiii.). — Christian Huelsen,
Bull. com., 1894, p. 312.

XV. Connected with the venationes were the Vivarium, the
Amphitheatrum Castrense, and the Claudium; with the gladiato-
rial shows, the Samiarium, Spoliarium, Armamentarium, Ludus
Magnus, Ludus Dacicus, Ludus Matutinus; with athletic sports,
the Curia Athletarum; and lastly, with shows in general, the
Castra Misenatium (and Ravennatium ?).

The Vivarium was a large rectangle built on the type of a Roman camp, on the south side of the Castra Prætoria. (See Forma

Urbis, pl. xi.)   It was composed of an inclosure wall built of great
blocks of stone like that of the barracks of the second legion,
Parthica, at Albano; and of a row of cells against it, where the
menagerie was kept.   A *euripus* or channel, with plenty of flushing water, ran in front of the inclosures.   The barracks of the
venatores and of the *custodes vivarii*, a special detachment of the
Prætorians to which the care of the establishment was intrusted,
occupied probably the centre of the rectangle.

The Vivarium, separated from the Prætorian camp by a street
starting from the Porta Chiusa of the walls of Aurelian, is mentioned very often in mediæval documents, under the name of
"Vivariolum," and its remains appear in plans and perspective
views of Rome of the sixteenth century, as of an edifice of great
importance.   Its last traces disappeared in 1876.   See Procopius,
Goth., i. 22. — *Corpus Inscr.*, vi. 130. — *Bull. arch. com.* 1876, p. 188.
— *Forma Urbis Romæ*, pl. xi.

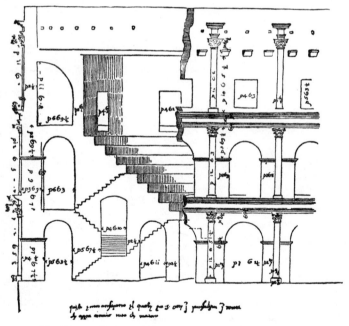

Fig. 146. — Palladio's Diagrams of the Amphitheatrum Castrense.

THE AMPHITHEATRUM CASTRENSE, a small amphitheatre built at the extreme end of the Esquiline for the training of the *venatores*, and also for the taming and training of animals destined to perform special games in the arena. Its construction has been attributed to Tiberius, like that of the Prætorian camp, but considering that at the time of that Emperor there was no state amphitheatre in Rome — that of Statilius Taurus being private property — I am inclined to refer it to a much later period, possibly to the times of Severus and Caracalla. Aurelian and Honorius included part of the edifice in their line of walls. In the sixteenth century Palladio was able to measure it in its entirety, as shown by the drawing in the possession of the Duke of Devonshire, which is here reproduced for the first time. (Fig. 146.)

Since Palladio's time the amphitheatre has suffered great damage. The upper floor has disappeared, and so have the mæniana and the steps which surrounded the arena. The arena has been excavated at least six times. Ficoroni (Roma antica, p. 121) speaks of discoveries made towards 1740 by the prior of Santa Croce, concerning the crypts, which were full of " ossa di grossi animali." Other excavations made in 1828 led to no results.

The present remains of the amphitheatre are seen to the best advantage from the Strada delle Mura, between the Porta S. Giovanni and the Porta Maggiore.

LITERATURE. — Antonio Nibby, *Roma antica*, vol. i. p. 399. — Adolf Becker, *De Muris*, pp. 120, 121. — Rodolfo Lanciani, *I comentarii di Frontino*, p. 217, n. 34, 35.

THE CLAUDIUM. — The Vivarium being one mile and a quarter distant from the Coliseum, the beasts destined to a special *venatio* were removed (I suppose by night) to a place much nearer to the show, viz., to the substructures of the Temple of Claudius by SS. Giovanni e Paolo, which communicated with those of the arena by means of an underground passage. This passage can still be seen ; it enters the amphitheatre by the fifth arch on the right of the west state entrance, and leads to the lifts and to the trapdoors described above. (See Fig. 140.)

THE SAMIARIUM — a name otherwise unknown — is described by some as a temporary hospital where the wounded gladiators were given first aid, and by others as the factory in which the weapons for gladiatorial fights were made or repaired.

THE SPOLIARIUM corresponds to the " Morgue," to which the bodies of those who had fallen in the arena were removed.

THE ARMAMENTARIUM must be understood as the arsenal or armory where the bucklers (*parmæ*) and the short crooked cutlasses (*sicæ*) of the *Threces;* the shields (*scuta*), crested helmets (*galeæ cristatæ*), wadded breastplates (*spongiæ*), and greaves (*ocreæ*) of the *Samnites;* the coats of mail of the *Hoplomachi;* the nets (*iacula*) and three-pointed spears (*fuscinæ*) of the *Retiarii*, were kept. The pedestal mentioned in "Corpus," n. 999, must have been found among the ruins of the Armamentarium. The site of these three buildings is only approximately known.

Regular academies, called Ludi Gladiatorii, or simply Ludi, were instituted for the training of prize-fighters, under the care of a *lanista*. The *tirones*, or undrilled novices, were instructed in the principles of their art, and made to practice with heavy wooden swords called "rudes," while their bodies were brought into condition by regular exercise and special food (*sagina*). Many of these ludi were kept by private speculators, who sold or let out for hire the "paria gladiatorum" exhibited in country towns; but the Roman ludi were a regular Imperial institution, managed by Imperial officers. There were four of them, the Magnus, the Gallicus, the Dacicus, and the Matutinus. The first is represented in fragment i. 3 of the marble plan;

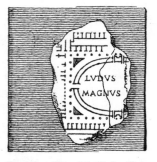

Fig. 147. — Plan of the Ludus Magnus.

its remains were excavated by Reinach in 1875, in the level stretch of ground at the corner of the Via Labicana and the Via delle Sette Sale. (See Forma Urbis, pl. xxx.) It contained an oval ring surrounded by porticoes and by rows of cells. The Ludi Gallicus and Dacicus were named after the nationality of the gladiators trained in them. The Matutinus is not considered by Preller as a school of gladiators, but as a place where the venationes were prepared, because these were exhibited in the morning, whilst the gladiatorial shows took place at a later hour of the day. The Chronicle of Cassiodorus attributes to Domitian the institution of the Ludus Matutinus, whilst the Catalogue of Ekkardt makes him responsible for the institution of all four, as a necessary complement to the great amphitheatre which his father had begun and his brother had continued.

These establishments were under the management of a large staff of officers, like the M. Ulpius Callistus, *præpositus armamentario ludi magni* (Corpus, n. 10,164); Tigris, *cursor* (n. 10,165); Nymphodotus, *dispensator* (n. 10,166) ; M. Calpurnius, *medicus*, etc., directed by a governor or *procurator familiæ gladiatoriæ Cæsaris ludi magni*, selected from the equestrian ranks. We hear also of a *curator Spoliarii*, of a *medicus ludi Matutini chirurgus*, of a *medicus ludi Gallici*, etc.

THE SUMMUM CHORAGIUM, placed between the Castra Misenatium and the Ludus Magnus, was also an annex to the amphitheatre, but nothing is known about its name, origin, and special appointment. Its staff of officers was even larger and of a higher standard than that of the ludi. (See Corpus Inscr., vol. vi. n. 297, 776, 8950, 10,083–10,087.) Canina thinks that it was a repository for the *pegmata* or machinery and scenery required for the venationes.

THE CASTRA MISENATIUM were the barracks of the marines from the fleet of Misenum, called to Rome for the manœuvring of the velarium or awning of the amphitheatre. The site of these buildings, between the Baths of Trajan and the Summum Choragium, was discovered on March 9, 1812. In 1888, however, the whole line of cells forming the south side of the quadrangle was brought to light when the drain of the Via Labicana was opened. (See Forma Urbis, pl. xxx.; Corpus, n. 1091; Kaibel, Inscr. gr. Ital., 956.)

LITERATURE. — *Corpus Inscr.*, vol. vi. 6, 631, 632, 1063, 1064, 1091. — Wilhelm Henzen, *Ann. Inst.*, 1862, p. 64 ; and *Atti Accad. pontif. arch.*, vol. xii. p. 73–157. — Theodor Mommsen, *Hermes*, v. 303. — Heinrich Jordan, *Topogr.*, ii. 116 ; and *Forma*, pl. i. n. 5. — Joachim Marquardt, *Staatsverwaltung*, vol. i. p. 538. — Gaetano Marini, *Inscr. albane*, c. 12. — Ridolfino Venuti, *Marmora albana*. Rome, 1756. — Domenico Scutillo, *De collegio gladiator.* Rome, 1756. — Luigi Canina, *Indic. Topogr.*, p. 112.

THE CURIA ATHLETARUM or ΞΥΣΤΙΚΗ ΣΥΝΟΔΟΣ was discovered in February, 1569, and again in 1660–1661 and 1713–1716, in the garden of S. Pietro in Vincoli, on the northeast side of the Baths of Trajan, where remains of their meeting-hall can still be seen (Villa Hickson Field). These remains, as well as the athletic brotherhood who had here their headquarters, have been illustrated by —

Pirro Ligorio, *Cod. torin.*, xv. 95. — Ottavio Falconieri, *Inscr. athl. Romæ repertæ*. Rome, 1668. — Kaibel, *Inscr. gr. Sicil. et Ital.*, n. 1102–1110. — *Corpus Inscr. Lat.*, 10,153, 10,154, 10,161. — Serafino Ricci, *La curia Athletarum* (in Bull. arch. com., 1891, p. 185, pl. vii.).

THE VIMINAL, THE CESPIAN, THE SUBURA, AND THE VICUS PATRICII.

Regio IV.

XVI. The fourth region of Augustus, named Sacra Via from the historical street which formed its southwestern boundary, extended over the Viminal and the Cespian as far as the present railway station. The "Notitia" and the "Curiosum" give the fourth region a circumference of 13,000 feet (3861 metres), and say it contained 8 parishes, 2757 tenement-houses, 88 palaces, 65 baths, 81 fountains, and 15 bakeries. Its principal edifices, the temples of Venus and Rome, of the Sacra Urbs, of Romulus, of Antoninus and Faustina, the basilicæ Æmilia and Constantiniana, the Colossus of Nero, and the Forum Transitorium have been described already. There are no important remains visible in the other parts of the region, nor excavations of any kind; but a walk through the Argiletum (Via della Madonna de' Monti), the Subura (Via Leonina), the Clivus Suburanus (Via di S. Lucia in Silice), and the Vicus Patricii (Via Urbana) cannot fail to attract the student on account of its classic associations, and also of the great discoveries which have taken place in the adjoining districts.

XVII. The Subura. — The Argiletum was the great book-market, the Paternoster Row of ancient Rome. Here the *librarii* and the *antiquarii* (booksellers and copyists) kept their well-furnished shops, so often mentioned by Martial and Horace. Advertisements giving the title and price of literary novelties were hung on either side of the entrance door. Each of the leading booksellers secured the privilege of the works of a leading author; the Sosii brothers were the agents for Horace, Atrectus and Secundus the publishers of Martial, Tryphon of Quintilian, and Dorus of Seneca. (See Ancient Rome, p. 183.)

The Subura is generally considered to have been the noisiest, the most vulgar and licentious street of the city. Martial calls it " clamosa," and Juvenal says he preferred living in the island of Procida rather than in such a rowdy neighborhood, and yet historical personages did not disdain to live in it, Julius Cæsar (Sueton., 46) and L. Arruntius Stella (Martial, xii. 3) being among them.

The long street was divided into sections. First came the Fauces Suburæ, called also the Prima Subura. Then we hear of a Subura Maior [1] (the rendezvous of pickpockets, who would assemble at the close of the day in its dark alleys to dispose of the produce of their thefts), which seems to call for a Subura Minor. There was also a tract called *ad turrim Mamiliam.* We hear of this place in connection with the contest between the Suburanenses and the Sacravienses for the possession of the head of the horse which was slain in honor of Mars on October 15, at a place called "ad Ciconias nixas" near the Trigarium. If the bloody trophy remained in the hands of the Sacravienses it was to be affixed to the walls of the Regia; if the Suburanenses gained the contest, it was to be affixed to the Turris Mamilia. The steep gradient at the top of the valley, now called Salita di S. Lucia in Silice, is described by Martial as a bad bit of road, with the pavement always wet and slippery, and crowds of beasts of burden dragging heavy loads towards the uplands of the Esquiline.

> alta Suburani vincenda est semita clivi
> et numquam sicco sordida saxa gradu :
> vixque datur longas mulorum rumpere mandras,
> quæque trahi multo marmora fune vides. (V. 22. See x. 19.)

Ancient epitaphs speak of a Q. Gavius, crepidarius de Subura (shoemaker); of a Crescentio, ferrarius de Subura (ironmonger); of a L. Marius, lanarius de Subura (merchant of woolen goods); and of a M. Livius, præco (public crier). The name has survived in the present "piazzetta della Suburra," and in the churches of S. Agata, S. Barbara, S. Bartolomeo, and S. Salvatore.

LITERATURE. — Heinrich Jordan, *Forma Urbis*, pl. ii. 8. — *Corpus Inscr.*, vol. vi. n. 1953 (1956), 9284, 9399, 9491, 9526. — *Bull. arch. com.*, 1883, p. 398. — Fioravante Martinelli, *Diacon. S. Agathæ.* Rome, 1617. — *Corpus Inscr.*, voluminis i. editio altera, 1893, p. 332. — Emiliano Sarti, *Archivio Società storia patria*, vol. ix. p. 20.

Near the top of the ascent, the Clivus Suburanus was crossed by the Vicus Sobrius. The compital shrine which stood at the junction of the two streets was discovered in April, 1888 (corner of Via di S. Martino and Via dei Quattro Cantoni), and I have described and illustrated it in "Pagan and Christian Rome," p. 34. The inscription on the face of the altar, still left standing, says "the Emperor Augustus dedicated this shrine (and statue) to Mercury, in the year of the city 744, from money received as a new year's gift, while absent from Rome." The statue was nicknamed Mercurius Sobrius, "Mercury the teetotaler."

[1] "Donatus qui manet in Sebura (m)aiore ad nimfa(s)." *Corpus Inscr.*, vol. vi. n. 9526. See also the *Schol. Crucq.* ad Horace, *Sat.*, i. 6, 116.

XVIII. The Vicus Patricii. — The Subura bifurcated at the foot of the ascent. The branch on the left ran up the valley between the Viminal and the Cespian, taking the name of Vicus Patricii in the lower tract, and of Clivus Patricius in the upper, between our piazza dell' Esquilino and the railway station. The street, already famous in the classic age, continued to enjoy the same privilege in Christian times, on account of the house of Pudens, in which the first Roman converts had met for prayers. Pudentiana, Praxedes, and Timotheus, daughters and son of Pudens, obtained from Pius I. the privilege of transforming their house into a regular parish assembly (Titulus Pudentis, afterwards Ecclesia Pudentiana). Some pieces of household furniture which had been used

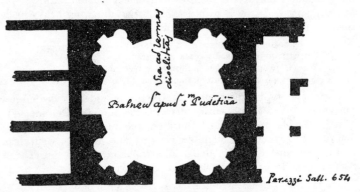

Fig. 148. — Remains of Public Baths near S. Pudenziana.

by the "prince of the apostles" were preserved in it. The "Liber Pontificalis" says that the church occupied part of the baths of Novatus, but the remains of ancient walls which can still be seen under the present church can hardly be attributed to Roman thermæ : they pertain to a building of a more modest nature and dimensions. (See Parker's "plan of the subterranean chambers of the palace of the Pudens family (sic)," and Sheet xvii. of my Forma Urbis.) At the same time there are two documents proving the existence of thermæ in this very district of the Vicus Patricii : the inscription quoted by De Rossi (Bull. crist., 1867, p. 55) MAXIMVS HAS OLIM THERM*as* . . . DIVINAE MENTIS DVCTV CVM . . . and a fragmentary plan by Sallustio Peruzzi (Uffizi, n. 654), of which the above is a reproduction.

Sallustio calls these remains "balneum apud S. Pudentianam," a bath near S. Pudentiana, and says that the street or path leading in the sixteenth century to the baths of Diocletian passed through them. This noble hall or caldarium, with its semicircular recesses, and niches for statues, and strong walls, may well have formed part of the baths of Timotheus or Novatus mentioned in church documents. The connection of this group of buildings with the apostolate of SS. Peter and Paul made it very popular from the beginning. Pope Siricius (384–397), his acolytes Leopardus, Maximus, and Ilicius, and Valerius Messalla, prefect of the city (396–403), contributed to transform the old meeting-place into a handsome church, and to make the Vicus Patricii one of the best streets of the city of the decadence. An inscription discovered in 1850 in the Villa Caserta, Via Merulana, says, "Ilicius, priest, has built at his expense the arcade [represented in the mosaic of the apse of the church, and still existing half buried under the houses to the left of the Via del Bambin Gesù] which you see connecting the Memoria Sancti Martyris Hippolyti with the Ecclesia Pudentiana." The memoria of S. Hippolytus is now represented by the church of S. Lorenzo in Fonte; [1] the arcade of Ilicius was therefore 400 metres long, such being the distance between the two edifices at each end. The work of the worthy priest was not remarkable for its solidity; because a few years later another devout man, a patrician, an ex primicerius notariorum Sacri Palatii, was compelled to rebuild it from the foundations: *detersis* SQVALORIBVS PORTICVM A FVNDAMENT*is* renovavit. (See Corpus Inscr., n. 1790.) It had probably been damaged by the Goths of Alaric in August, 410. Another inscription (ibid., 1775) speaks of other work of embellishment done by Valerius Messalla, prefect of the city, ad SPLENDOREM PVBLICVM IN VICO PATRICIO.

LITERATURE. — Heinrich Jordan, *Forma Urbis*, pl. ii. n. 9. — Gio. Battista de Rossi, *Bull. crist.*, 1867, p. 43, *sq.*; and *Mosaici delle chiese di Roma*, fasc. xiii. xiv. — Rodolfo Lanciani, *Pagan and Christian Rome*, p. 112. — Gaspare Celio, *Memoria dei nomi degli artefici*, p. 81. — Hartmann Grisar, *Un affresco sotto la chiesa di S. Pudenziana* (in Civiltà cattolica, 1896, vol. i. p. 733). — *Bull. arch. com.*, 1891, p. 305, pls. xii. xiii. fig. 1; and p. 311, pls. xii. xiii. fig. 2.

XIX. The characteristic of the fourth region was the predominance of private dwellings over public buildings. It was an essentially popular quarter, the reverse of the eighth and ninth regions, in which we can hardly find room for insulæ and domus. The excavations which have taken place on the Viminal and Cespian

---

[1] The well which gives the name to the church is still accessible. The place deserves a visit.

and in the intermediate valley since the revival of classical studies have always yielded a rich harvest in objects and works of art pertaining to private mansions, the remains of which appear to

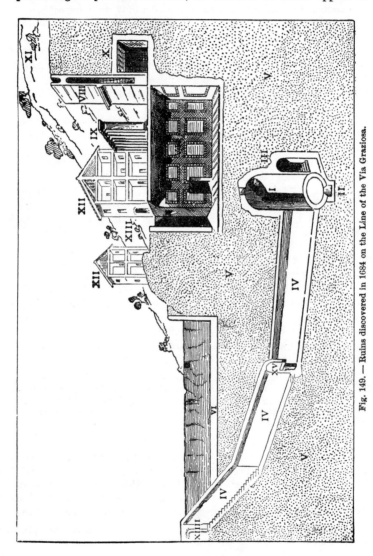

Fig. 149. — Ruins discovered in 1684 on the Line of the Via Graziosa.

be in wonderful preservation. The history of these excavations has not yet been written, and many of the finds are yet unknown to students.

Here is one instance. In 1684 a new street was opened along the north slope of the Cespian, halfway between the Via Urbana, which runs at the bottom of the valley, and the Via Sforza-Paolina, which runs on the edge of the plateau. The street, called Via Graziosa, from the name of Pietro Graziosi, a rich local landowner, was cut right across a group of old Roman houses, beautifully preserved and full of objects of interest. The preceding unpublished sketch, made by Pietro Sante Bartoli at the time of the discovery, shows the state of the remains as they appeared when the street was cut. I have found the original on p. 65 of Bartoli's volume " donné au Cabinet des Estampes du Roi par M. le Comte de Caylus en 1764," which now bears the mark G, d, 2, n. 3871 [1] of the Bibliothèque nationale. The drawing is explained by the following notes : —

(I) Crypt in which S. Lawrence was imprisoned. (II) Spring with the waters of which S. Hippolytus was baptized. The crypt could be reached in two ways, by a spiral staircase (III) and by an inclined corridor (IV) entered by a heavy travertine gate (XV). (The crypt, the well, and the corridor are still to be seen under the church of S. Lorenzo in Fonte.) (VII) Hall with walls and vaulted ceiling covered with mosaic, shells, and enamel. (VIII) Aqueduct. (IX) A colonnade of the Doric order with shafts of travertine coated with stucco. (X) Room with walls of reticulated work. All these remains built on virgin soil (marked V) were covered by a bed of rubbish (marked XI) which had rolled down the slope of the Cespian. No. XIII marks the cutting of the Via Graziosa, and No. XII the new houses in course of construction when Bartoli made his sketch. He speaks of the same excavations in his " Memorie," edited by Carlo Fea. " When a new street was opened (on the slope of the Cespian) opposite S. Lorenzo in Panisperna, remains of ancient edifices were found, and an exquisite fragment of a Venus, which was restored by Ercole Ferrata for Queen Christine of Sweden. Duke Livio Odescalchi bought it with the rest of the queen's marbles, which were ultimately removed to the museum of S. Ildefonso, Spain. There was also a Bacchic flute of Corinthian brass, three palms long, and several other objects, which, for reasons known to me, I must

---

[1] I have described the contents of this volume, one of the most precious in the Cabinet des Estampes, Paris, in the *Bull. com.*, 1895, p. 166.

abstain from mentioning (Mem. 17). . . . A mosaic pavement has been laid bare in the foundations of the house of Signor Pocavena, with birds and arabesques in bright colors " (Mem. 26). On January 8, 1613, the lararium or chapel of the house of L. Crepereius Rogatus was discovered at the foot of the Salita di S. Maria Maggiore;[1] but the most important find by far is that of November, 1848, when the set of frescoes with landscapes and scenes from the Odyssey were discovered in repairing the foundations of the Monastery delle Turchine at the corner of the Via Sforza. Reproductions of the frescoes, which are now preserved in the room of the Nozze Aldobrandine in the Vatican library, have been given by —

Noël des Vergers, *Bull. Inst.*, 1849, p. 17. — Heinrich Brunn, *Ibid.*, p. 129. — Matranga, *La città di Lamo stabilita in Terracina*. Rome, 1852. — Woermann, *Die antiken Odysseelandschaften vom esquilinschen Hügel*. Munich, 1876. — Wolfgang Helbig, *Guide*, vol. ii. p. 175.

The Via Graziosa exists no more. The great Via Cavour runs in its place at a higher level. The building of the Via Cavour, therefore, gave no opportunity of fresh discoveries ; and in fact, if anything lies still at the level of the ancient city it may be truly said to be beyond the reach of man.

THE GREAT PARKS ON THE EASTERN SIDE OF THE CITY.

REGIONS V, VI, AND VII.

XX. No modern capital of Europe can be compared with ancient Rome for the number and extent of public parks and gardens. While the nine larger parks of London, with their aggregate surface of 2,000 acres, represent a thirty-ninth part of the city area, those of ancient Rome, extending over the chain of hills for two miles at least, on either side of the Tiber, represent an eighth part. If such open spaces act as lungs to a city, no city ever breathed more freely than Rome. The accompanying sketch-map (Fig. 150)*may help the student to locate the various *horti* mention of which occur in classics or in inscriptions. The city was not only surrounded and inclosed by them, but intersected in every direction. Those on the eastern chain of hills followed each other (from south to north, as ancient maps are oriented) in this order : —

[1] *Bull. arch. com.*, 1891, pp. 305, 341.

*Figure 150 faces page 428.

Regio V. Esquiline.	Horti	Variani.
,, ,,	,,	Liciniani.
,, ,,	,,	Torquatiani, Pallantiani, Epaphrodotiani.
,, ,,	,,	Tauriani, Calyclanii, Vettiani.
,, ,,	,,	Lamiani, Maiani.
,, ,,	,,	Mæcenatiani.
,, ,,	,,	Lolliani.
Regio VI. Alta Semita.	,,	Sallustiani.
Regio VII. Via Lata.	,,	Luculliani.
,, ,,	,,	Aciliani.

These gardens did not make one continuous stretch of verdure : they were intersected by streets like the Salaria Vetus, the Alta Semita, the Vicus Portæ Collinæ, the Vicus Portæ Viminalis, the viæ Tiburtina, Prænestina, Labicana, etc., by groups of houses and palaces, and by a few public buildings of large area.

I shall describe first the parks, then a few of these prominent buildings set as they were in a frame of green.[1]

XXI. HORTI VARIANI. — The extreme southeast corner of the city, between the line of the Claudian aqueduct and the Amphitheatrum Castrense, seems to have been the property of the Varian family from an early period, and to have been transformed into a park by Sextus Varius Marcellus, father of the Emperor Heliogabalus (Sextus Varius Avitus Bassianus). Heliogabalus enlarged and improved the gardens, which became part of the Imperial domain. Here he retired to conspire against the life of his cousin, Severus Alexander, and here he was found, starting a chariot race, by the prætorians eager to take a revenge for the attempted assassination of the cherished young prince.

The gardens, officially named *horti Spei veteris*, from the old Temple of Hope which stood close by the Porta Maggiore, were cut in two by Aurelian's walls. We do not know whether the part *extra muros* was abandoned; probably it was not, and the communication across the line of the walls may have been kept open by means of posterns. The section *intra muros* continued to be an Imperial garden and residence, and attained great notoriety at the time of Helena and Constantine. Three of the Varian edifices deserve notice : the Circus, the Palace, and the Thermæ.

The approximate situation of the Circus in respect to the neigh-

[1] On Roman gardens in general consult Wüstermann, *Ueber die Kunstgärtnerei bei die alten Römern.* Gotha, 1846. — Woermann, *Ueber landschaftlichen Natursinn der Griechen u. Römer.* Munich, 1871. — *Ancient Rome,* p. 271.

boring monuments is shown in this fragment of a perspective plan of the sixteenth century, and also in Bufalini's map of 1551. When Antonio da Sangallo the younger examined the ruins in the second quarter of the sixteenth century, the obelisk was still lying broken in three pieces (along the *spina?*) in the vineyard of a Messer Jeronimo Milanese, which was then being excavated by a stone-cutter named Rugieri. Sangallo also saw and designed (Uffizi, n. 900) a graceful nymphæum not unlike that still exist-

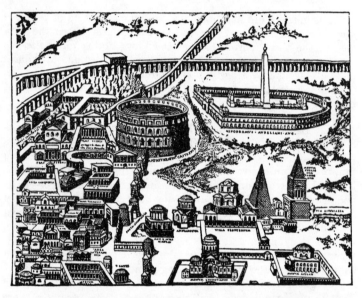

Fig. 151. — Ligorio's Perspective View of the Horti Variani.
(From sheet iv. of the *Antiquæ Urbis Imago.* Rome, 1551.)

ing in the gardens of Sallust. The remains of the Circus were very conspicuous in those days, and bore the name of "Ciercho, Cerchio, Circo Vetere," and also of "lo Girolo." The obelisk was dug out in 1570, and the brothers Curzio and Marcello Saccoccia, who owned the ground, put up a tablet commemorating its discovery, which is still to be seen in one of the arches of the Acqua Felice. The obelisk was removed in the following century to the Barberini garden, Via delle quattro Fontane, where Bernini wanted to raise it in front of the palace. President de Brosses and five other gentlemen from Burgundy asked leave from Pope

Clement XII. to erect it at their expense in front of S. Luigi de'
Francesi. The project luckily failed, but the odyssey of the pillar
did not end then. Princess Cornelia Barberini presented it to
Clement XIV., who caused it to be removed to the Giardino della
Pigna in the Vatican. Pius VI. planned to place it, first, on the
pedestal of the column of Antoninus Pius in the same gardens,
and again on the top of the tower of the Porta Pia. Valadier and
Pius VII. erected it at last in the central avenue of the passeggiata
del Pincio. It is a work of Hadrian's time, cut in memory of his
favorite Antinous.

LITERATURE. — Andrea Fulvio, *Antiqq.*, iv. — Andrea Palladio, *Antichità*,
ed. 1554, p. 9. — Pirro Ligorio, *Circhi*, p. 9. — Gio. Battista Cipriani, *Obelischi*,
p. 21. — Fea Bianconi, *Circhi*, ch. ii. p. ix. — Winckelmann, *Storia delle arti*,
vol. i. p. 96, n. C. — Antonio Nibby, *Roma antica*, vol. i. p. 607. — Christian
Huelsen, *Mittheil.*, 1896, p. 122.

The Palace, inside the walls, is known in documents of a later
age as the Palatium Sessorianum. The origin of the name is
obscure,[1] but the fact that it was an Imperial residence of the
third and part of the fourth century is undoubted. Helena,
mother of Constantine, preferred it to the Palace of the Cæsars,
and the place is full of associations of her. Here were found the
pedestals of statues raised to her by Julius Maximianus, a dignitary of the Constantinian court; and by Flavius Pistus, keeper of
the privy purse (Corpus, n. 1134, 1135); and here also, in the vineyard of Girolamo Muziano the painter († 1550), was found a bust
considered to represent her likeness. I confine myself strictly to
archæological evidence: but Church documents give fuller details
about her works, and about the transformation of the great hall
of the palace into a Christian place of worship under the title
of *Hierusalem.* This hall resembled very closely in shape and
dimensions the Templum Sacræ Urbis turned into a church by
Felix IV., having the same line and number of arched windows
under the roof, and the same wall decorations in "florentine"
mosaic, composed of crusts of porphyry, serpentine, and other
"pietre dure." [2] Constantine left the hall as it was; he only
closed the lower arches opening on the garden, and added an apse
at the east end. The columns by which the hall was divided into
nave and aisles are an addition of Gregory II. (715–731). The
church remained in its old form until the beginning of the last
century. I have found in the state archives a plan of the church

[1] Adolf Becker, *De muris*, p. 120; and *Topographie*, p. 556.
[2] Sangallo the younger, *Uffizi*, n. 899.

and cloisters taken on May 15, 1716, by the architect Melchior Passalacqua, full of interesting details. Benedict XIV. in 1744, with the assistance of Passalacqua and Gregorini, reduced the glorious monument to its present grotesque form, a work which Milizia justly condemns as "nefando." This was done at the expense of another hall of the palace, known in ordinary guide-books by the name of Tempio di Venere e Cupido. This beautiful hall, of which only the apse, standing in the garden north of the church, is left, was almost intact in the sixteenth century, with its columns of red granite, its portico and vestibule, etc. Benedict XIV. and his acolytes destroyed it for the sake of a few cartloads of bricks.

No student should omit to visit the Vigna di S. Croce in Gerusalemme.[1] The remains of the Claudian aqueduct which inclosed the Imperial gardens on the north, of the walls of Aurelian which run across them on the south side, of the "hall named Hierusalem," and of the so-called Temple of Venus and Cupid, make it one of the loveliest spots of Rome.

The statue of Sallustia Barbia Orbiana, wife of Severus Alexander, who was himself cousin of Heliogabalus (now in the Cortile di Belvedere, Vatican Museum, No. 42), is said to have been found in these gardens as early as the time of Julius II. Ligorio mentions another statuette of Venus cut in rock crystal (?); and Ficoroni describes the works of art found in 1741, when Benedict XIV. cut away a knoll called Monte Cipollaro, which rose in front of the church. They include the Boy struggling with a Goose, probably after Boëthos, now in the Capitoline Museum, room of the Faun, No. 16; a head of Caracalla; a second resembling the Carneades of the same museum; a third unknown; and a column of bianco e nero. Marchese Campana tried the ground again in 1855, but he found only a wine-cellar with rows of amphoræ of white clay.

The Thermæ Helenianæ and the reservoir which supplied them with water can be seen in what is now called the Vigna Conti (entered by the last gate on the left of the Via di S. Croce). I was able to give a careful plan of these thermæ in sheets xxxi., xxxii. of the "Forma Urbis," from unpublished drawings by Palladio (Devonshire Collect.) and Antonio da Sangallo the younger (Uffizi, 1439). The inscription, now in the Vatican Museum, sala della Croce greca (Corpus, vol. vi. n. 1136), says that "Helena the venerable, mother of Constantine, etc., etc., rebuilt the baths

[1] Ring at the first gate on the left of the church.

ARCVS NERONIANI

PORTA MAGGIORE

WALLS OF AVRELIAN

AQVA CLAVDIA

HORTI VARIANI

RESERVOIR

Fig. 152. — The Horti Variani, Vigna Conti, by S. Croce in Gerusalemme.

after a fire" — (thermas incendio destrvctas restitvit). This inscription was probably discovered in the excavations of Lelio Orsini, Duke of Bracciano, described by Bartoli (Mem. 12), in the course of which five "bellissime" statues were found in an underground room, with fragments and marbles of every description. It seems that after the fall of the Empire one or more rooms of these baths were adapted to Christian worship. Flaminio Vacca saw images of saints painted on their walls, and Cherubino Alberti adds that S. Helena was said to have been buried in one of them; he also gives a sketch of the place. I have myself seen traces of painting in some extensive apartments which run deep underground in front of the present church.

LITERATURE. — Alberti Giovanni, *Cod. san Sepolcro*, f. 7.—Alberti Cherubino, *ibid.*, vol. i. f. 37'. — Pirro Ligorio, *Cod. vatic.*, 3439, f. 32. — *Liber pontific.*, Duchesne, i. p. cxxvi. note C, and p. 196. — *Corpus Inscr.*, vol. vi. n. 781, 782, 2251, 2252. — Flaminio Vacca, *Mem.* 114 (in Fea's Miscell., vol. i. p. ci.). — Francesco Ficoroni, *Mem.* 71; *ibid.*, p. clii. — Ridolfino Venuti, *Roma antica*, vol. i. p. 130. — Carlo Fea, ad Winckelmann, *Storia dell' arte*, vol. iii. p. 44. — Henry Stevenson, *Annal. Inst.*, 1877, p. 371. — Rodolfo Lanciani, *Itin. di Einsiedlen*, p. 58. — Wolfgang Helbig, *Guide*, vol. i. p. 84, n. 142 ; and p. 382, n. 518.

XXII. HORTI LICINIANI, at the southern end of the Viale Principessa Margherita, between the church of S. Vibiana and the Porta Maggiore.

The Licinian family must have possessed property on the Esquiline from the time of the Republic. Cicero mentions certain *atria Licinia* outside the Esquiline gate, belonging to M. Licinius Crassus. A columbarium of freedmen of the same name was discovered at the time of Pope Barberini near the Church of S. Vibiana.[1] The "Vita Gallieni" (c. 17) calls the gardens "horti nominis sui," that is to say, "Horti Liciniani," that Emperor being a Licinius himself. The "Vita" says that Gallienus was very fond of residing in such a delightful place, that he was followed there by the whole Court, and that every officer of state was admitted to the Imperial table and baths. When one of these officers, named Aurelius Victor, determined to erect a standing testimonial of his devotion to Gallienus and to his Empress Salonina, he chose for its site the high street leading to the gardens, and changed the old Esquiline gate of Servius into a travertine arch inscribed with the name of his masters (see Corpus, n. 1106). Ecclesiastical

[1] Raffaele Fabretti, *Inscr. domest.*, pp. 13, 373. — Antonio Nibby, *Roma antica*, vol. ii. p. 330. — *Corpus Inscr.*, n. 9154.

documents place the church of S. Vibiana near the "Palatium Licinianum," viz., near the decagonal nymphæum of the gardens, the so-called *Minerva Medica* of the present day. The nymphæum, the first ruins to strike the eye of the stranger on his entering the walls of the Eternal City,[1] and the most conspicuous landmark of this district, were called Galluce, Galluccie, Caluce in the Middle Ages, and have been known as the Basilica Caii et Lucii since 1527. The name of Minerva Medica given to the ruins towards the beginning of the seventeenth century by Nardini and others is doubly wrong, because it belongs to a street and to a street-shrine half a mile distant (discovered in 1887 in the Via Curva, west of the Merulana), and because it is not true that the statue of the goddess (No. 114 Braccio Nuovo), with a serpent at her feet, was found among these ruins. The seicento archæologists supposed the harmless creature — the protector of olive gardens so dear to Minerva — to be the serpent of Æsculapius, and therefore to allude to Minerva's *medical* science. At all events the beautiful statue was discovered not on the Esquiline but near the church of S. Maria sopra Minerva, among the ruins of the temple raised to her by Pompey the Great.

LITERATURE. — P. Sante Bartoli, *Mem.* 112 (in Fea's Miscellanea, vol. i. p. ccliv.). — Emil Braun, *Ruins and Museums*, p. 153, n. 14. — *Galleria Giustiniana*, vol. i. p. 3. — Wolfgang Helbig, *Guide*, vol. i. p. 31, n. 51.

The nymphæum was once covered with mosaics and slabs of porphyry, and its dome incrusted with shells and enamel. The "vignettes" of the sixteenth and seventeenth centuries show it in a much better state of preservation. It has nine semicircular recesses and one door on the ground floor, and ten windows above. The greater part of the dome fell in 1828, and the rest was much shattered by a thunderbolt in the following year. It was first excavated, as far as we know, by Messer Cosmo Jacomelli "medico," at the time of Julius III. (1550–1555). The produce of the excavations is described by Ligorio, and his statements are substantially corroborated by Flaminio Vacca. Numbers of statues were discovered lying in pieces before their respective niches; they were thought to represent Pomona (in black marble with heads and hands of bronze), Æsculapius, Adonis, Venus, Hercules, Antinous, and several Fauns. Ligorio adds to the list a " Minerva with her dragon," and says that the Minerva, the Venus, the Æsculapius

---

[1] The nymphæum stands close to the *Tre archi*, by which all the railway lines enter the city.

were given to Pope Julius III, who was then collecting marbles for his Villa Giulia outside the Porta del Popolo ; and as the Pope was in need of a naked statue to pair with another already in his possession, he caused the God of Medicine to be deprived of his mantle and condemned to a state of nudity. Cosmo Jacomelli also found four columns of verde antico and ten fluted spiral

Fig. 153. — Statue of a Roman Magistrate of the Fourth Century giving the Signal for a Chariot Race.

columns of giallo. One of the Fauns, restored by Flaminio Vacca, was purchased by Cardinal Alessandro Farnese. In another portion of the gardens, owned by Francesco d' Aspra, treasurer to Julius III., many other statues were found, as well as bronze busts of Emperors ; medals, marbles, etc., removed likewise to the Villa Giulia. It is no wonder that, after so many finds, our own excavations in 1875–78 should have led to no results. The only objects recovered were the bust of Manlia Scantilla, wife of the Emperor Didius Julianus, now in the Palazzo dei Conservatori, Rotunda No. 44, some fanciful capitals and columns with Bacchic reliefs, and two statues of Roman magistrates of the fourth century (the two Symmachi ?) in the act of giving the signal to start the races in the circus by throwing into the arena a piece of cloth (*mappa*). One of these is here represented (Fig. 153). There was also a bas-relief representing the " Forge of Vulcan." (See Bull. com., 1874, p. 131; 1878, pp. 142, 199 ; 1879, p. 240; 1883, p. 17).

Fig. 154. — Columbaria discovered in 1872 on the Site of the Horti Liciniani.

The gardens of the Licinian family, like those of Mæcenas, were laid out on ground occupied by a number of tombs and columbaria of the last century of the Republic and of the Augustan age. The cemetery was buried under a mass of earth from four to eight metres high, and as religious respect for tombs was still deeply rooted among workmen, when the change took place, the tombs have been found intact and full of funeral "supellex." Between February 7 and May 27, 1871, in a space only a few hundred feet square, five columbaria were discovered, containing 204 inscriptions, 200 lamps, 2 marble and 40 terra-cotta cinerary urns, 195 coins, 150 glass perfume-bottles, 200 balsamaria of terra cotta, and a few gold rings and earrings. A complete description of this necropolis is to be found in vol. vi. part ii. of the "Corpus Inscr.," p. 976, under the title *Monumenta effossa in vinea Belardiorum prope portam Prænestinam.* The above illustration (Fig. 154) shows some of the columbaria [1] excavated in 1872 and the depth at which they lay buried under the level of the Licinian gardens.

LITERATURE. — Baldassarre Peruzzi, *Uffizi,* n. 498. — Sallustio Peruzzi, *ibid.,* n. 689. — Martin Heemskerk, *Berlin,* f. 49'. — Jean Jacques Lequeu, in Cabinet des Estampes, Paris, *Rome,* vol. Monti, n. G. — Louis Duchesne, *Liber pontif.,* i. p. 250, n. 1. — Antonio Nibby, *Roma antica,* vol. ii. p. 328. — Edoardo Brizio, *Pitture e sepolcri scoperti sull' Esquilino nell' anno 1875.* Rome, 1876. — Rodolfo Lanciani, *Bull. com.,* 1880, p. 51, pl. ii.

XXIII. HORTI TAURIANI. — The most important group of tombs described in the section of the "Corpus" just quoted are the columbaria of the servants and freedmen of the Statilian family, discovered partly in 1875, partly in 1880, in that part of the Licinian gardens now crossed by the Viale Principe Eugenio. They contained 427 inscriptions relating to 370 servants attached to the person of Statilius Taurus, consul in A. D. 11, and to his children. (See Ancient Rome, p. 132.) The presence of these family vaults in this special corner of the Esquiline indicates that the Statilii must have owned property of some kind in the neighborhood. The acts of SS. Faustus and Pigmenius discovered by the Bollandist fathers, in "Cod. lat." 5289 of the Bibliothèque nationale, Paris, mention a *forum* (Statilii) *Tauri* between the church of S. Vibiana and the Porta S. Lorenzo. This gate was called Porta *Taurina* in the Middle Ages, and the whole district Regio Tauri or Regio Caput Tauri. Lastly, there were two churches called S. Silvester de Tauro and S. Laurentius ad Taurellum. The origin of these names was explained by the discovery (made in 1874, in the Via Principe Amadeo behind the apse of S. Eusebio) of two terminal stones with the legend CIPPI · HI · FINIVNT · HORTOS ·

---

[1] Marked J, K, L, M in the plan of the *Corpus,* pp. 982 and 990.

CALYCLAN(OS) · ET · TAVRIANOS. "These cippi mark the boundary line between the gardens called Calyclanii and those of (Statilius) Taurus." A water-pipe discovered not far from the cippi, inscribed with the name of Vettius Agorius Prætextatus and of his wife Fabia Aconia Paullina, proves that the classical gardens of the Statilii had passed into the hands of the Vettii in the fourth century after Christ, and were embodied in the old Horti Scatoniani,

Fig. 155. — Statue of Shepherdess discovered in the Horti Vettiani.

so-called from the Vettii Scatones. Both families had enriched the grounds with works of art to such an extent that several thousand marble fragments were extracted, in March, 1874, from two walls alone, into which they had been built after the first barbaric inroads. A summary catalogue of these sculptures, now exhibited in the Palazzo dei Conservatori, is to be found in the "Bull. com.," 1873, p. 293, n. 58; 1874, p. 59; and 1875, p. 151. One of them, an old shepherdess with her pet lamb under the left arm, is here reproduced (Fig. 155). It was found in the Piazza Manfredo Fanti.

Literature. — Louis Duchesne, *Lib. pont.*, vol. i., pp. 123, 127, 258, note 2. — Gio. Battista de Rossi, *Il forum Tauri nella regione Esquilina*, in Bull. com., 1890, p. 280. — *Catalogus codicum hagiographicorum*, in Biblioth. nationale, Paris, Bruxelles, 1889, vol. i. pp. 520–523. — *Pianta dell' aula temporanea del Palazzo dei Conservatori*. Rome, Salviucci, 1876, n. 17, 30, 31, 40, A. 68, 72, 76, 107. — Christian Huelsen, *Nuove osservazioni*, etc., in Bull. com., 1893, p. 119; 1894, p. 101, etc. — *Ancient Rome*, p. 169. — *Corpus Inscr.*, vol. vi. n. 6241, 6281, 6282.

XXIV. Horti Lamiani et Maiani. — Valerius Maximus, praising the modesty and frugality of the Ælian family, says that a humble house near the "trophies of Marius" was sufficient to accommodate sixteen Ælii. The trophies of Marius stood near the present church of S. Eusebio on the Esquiline. The Ælii Lamia, the more illustrious branch of the family, which claimed descent from Lamus, king of the Lestrigonians, enlarged the property on the line of the Via Merulana, and laid out gardens, worthy rivals of those of Mæcenas on the other side of the same street. It is supposed that Lucius Ælius Lamia, consul in A. D. 3, must have bequeathed the park to Tiberius, as Mæcenas had done for Augustus, because we find it described as a part of the Imperial domain on the Esquiline, immediately after the death of Lamia, which took place in A. D. 33. Philon, who led the Jewish embassy to Caligula, and who was received in the Horti Lamiani, says they were next to those of Mæcenas and to the Servian walls; that they contained magnificent apartments, two stories high, with windows having panes of transparent marble instead of glass, besides avenues, woods, fountains, works of art, etc. The murdered body of Caligula was removed here from the Palatine, on January 24, A. D. 41, cremated and buried in haste, but some time later his sisters carried the ashes to the mausoleum of Augustus. However, as long as the ashes were kept in the gardens, the keepers were constantly harassed by the phantom of the murdered prince.

The halls of the palace were so large that a portrait of Nero one hundred and twenty feet high (35.64 metres) could be painted in one of them. The huge canvas, twice as large as the mainsail of a frigate, was set on fire by lightning, together with the palace : " pictura, accensa fulmine, cum optima hortorum parte conflagravit." [1] The damages must have been repaired at once. The staff of keepers is mentioned in several inscriptions (Corpus, n. 6152, 8668, 8669). At the time of Severus Alexander the park received improvements, especially in the waterworks.

A volume could be written on the exquisite works of art, paintings as well as sculptures, discovered in the Horti Lamiani since the beginning of the sixteenth century. The list comprises, besides objects of secondary interest, the Meleager of the Belvedere ; the pediment of a temple (?), with the slaughter of the Niobides, and the two Athletes, now in the Uffizi, Florence, found in the spring of 1582 ; the " Nozze aldobrandine," found at the time of Clement VIII. (1592–1605), now in the Vatican library ; the Discobolos of Myron, found March 14, 1781, now in the Lancellotti palace ; the Hercules, removed to England by Colonel Campbell ; the relief of Dancing Women, now in the Museo Chiaramonti, section xxvii. n. 644 ; and many other marbles lately in possession of the Massimi family.

LITERATURE. — Fabroni, *Dissert. sulle statue appartenenti alla favola di Niobe.* Florence, 1779. — Francesco Cancellieri, *Dissertazioni epistolari sopra la statua del Discobolo.* Rome, 1806. — Antonio Nibby, *Roma antica*, vol. ii. p: 324. — Wolfgang Helbig, *Guide*, vol. i. p. 66, n. 116, pp. 78, 133; and vol. ii. p. 184, n. 958. — Zuccato, *Idea dei Pittori*, book ii. p. 37. — Moreau de Mautours, *Mém. Acad. des Inscriptions*, Hist., vol. v. p. 297. — Visconti, *Catal. Villa Miollis*, p. 127.

The discoveries made in our own time may well challenge comparison with those described above. On Christmas eve, 1874, in one room only (at the corner of the Via Foscolo and the Via Emmanuele Filiberto), we found lying on the marble floor the bust of Commodus under the attributes of Hercules, reproduced in the following cut (Fig. 156) ; it was flanked by two Tritons or marine Centaurs and by two statues representing either two maiden daughters of Danaos (according to Helbig), or two Muses, Terpsichore and Polyhymnia (according to Visconti). There were also the " Venus Lamiana " (called by Helbig " A Girl binding a fillet round her head "), a portrait head of young Commodus, a head of Diana, a Bacchus of semi-colossal size, with drapery of gilt bronze (missing),

[1] Pliny, *Hist. Nat.*, xxxv. 7, 33.

and about twenty-five exquisite fragments, legs, arms, hands, feet, etc., belonging to statues whose drapery was likewise of bronze. These works of art are exhibited in the octagonal room of the

Fig. 156. — Bust of Commodus from the Horti Lamiani.

Palazzo dei Conservatori, and the fragments in Hall II. of the Museo Municipale al Celio. The graceful girlish statuette re-produced in the following cut (Fig. 157) discovered near the Vicolo di S. Matteo, is evidently modeled in imitation of the terra-cotta figurines which have made the names of Tanagra and Myrina famous over the world.

LITERATURE. — Carlo Ludovico Visconti, *Bull. com.*, vol. iii. (1875), pp. 3, 16, 57, 140, pls. i.–v., ix., x., xiv., xv.; vol. xviii. (1890) p. 68, pls. iii., iv. — Wolfgang Helbig, *Guide*, vol. i. p. 418, n. 558–560; p. 421, n. 564, 565; p. 422, n. 566. — *Forma Urbis Romæ*, pls. xxiii., xxx., xxxi.

Fig. 157. — Statuette of a Girl from the Horti Lamiani.

XXV. HORTI MÆCENATIS. — The old Esquiline cemetery was divided into two sections, one for the slaves, beggars, prisoners, and criminals who had undergone capital punishment, another for a better class of citizens who could afford to be buried apart in tombs or columbaria. This first section covered an area 1000 feet long and 300 deep (297 metres by 89.10), and contained many *puti-culi* or pits, into which men and beasts, bodies and carcasses, and all kinds of city refuse were thrown in a horrid confusion. About seventy-five puticuli were discovered and explored in the cutting of the Via Napoleone III., some containing a uniform mass of black, viscid, pestilent, unctuous matter, whilst in others the bones could in a measure be singled out and identified. The neighborhood of this field of death was set apart for the daily refuse of the city.

The suppression of this hotbed of pestilence, with the sanitary reform of public cemeteries, took place under Augustus at the suggestion of his prime minister C. Cilnius Mæcenas. The whole district, alongside the Agger of Servius Tullius, was buried under a mass of earth six to eight metres high, and gardens were laid out on the newly-made ground, which became the world-famous Horti Mæcenatiani. The event was sung by Horace (Sat. i. 8, 14) : —

> " Nunc licet Esquiliis habitare *salubribus,* atque
> Aggere in aprico spatiari, quo modo tristes
> Albis informem spectabant ossibus agrum."

The gardens contained a palace and a tower or " belvedere," which Horace describes as reaching the clouds : " molem propinquam nubibus." Nero is accused by Suetonius of having watched from this lofty observatory the progress of the flames in the fire of July, 64, while singing the capture and burning of Troy in a theatrical robe ; but the fact is contradicted by Tacitus. No further mention occurs of the gardens in classics. In the Middle Ages they took the name of Massa Iuliana, which has survived to our own times in the church and convent of S. Giuliano.[1] There are two groups of remains within the area of the horti : one in the Piazza Fanti, in the grounds of the Aquarium, consisting of a few rooms with mosaic pavements ; one at the corner of the vie Merulana and Leopardi, which deserves a visit. It is a noble hall built of reticulated work, half underground, with six niches on each of the side walls, and seven steps in the curve of the apse. The following cut (Fig. 158) shows the hall in the state in which it was found in March, 1874. The apse and the niches were covered with exquisite landscapes, in the style of those of Livia's villa at Prima Porta. These have since all faded away except a few bits under the shelter of the niches. Visconti gave the hall

---

[1] Louis Duchesne, *Liber pontif.,* vol. ii. p. 44, n. 84. — De Rossi, *Bull. crist.,* 1871, p. 28.

the name of auditorium or " sala de recitazioni," assuming that it could accommodate 334 spectators ; others believe it to have been a conservatory for rare and delicate plants. The hall is on view every Thursday, and permits are delivered at the Ufficio della Commissione Archeologica Municipale, Aracœli, Capitol.

The catalogue of the works of art discovered at various times in the gardens of Mæcenas is very copious. Hermæ or busts of

Fig. 158. — The Conservatory of the Gardens of Mæcenas.

eminent men come in the first place. Vacca calls them " portraits of philosophers . . . one of which is of Socrates." One of Homer was found in 1704 between S. Antonio and S. Vito, and a replica in the Via Merulana. A portrait statue of Euripides with the name of his tragedies engraved on a tablet came to light in the same district. Between 1872 and 1878 twelve more heads were found, and removed to the Palazzo dei Conservatori, together with a superb figure of a mastiff in verde ranocchia, a semi-colossal group of Hercules and (one of) the horses put together out of 137 pieces, a replica of the so-called " genius of the Vatican," a figure of Marsyas of pavonazzetto, a statue of Silenus, an exquisite head of an Amazon, several caryatides, and marble fountains of various shapes, one of which is here reproduced. This graceful object is

signed by ΠΟΝΤΙΟΣ, an Athenian artist, and presents the form of
a drinking-horn or rhyton placed on a group of lotus leaves.   The
mouth of the rhyton may have been used as a flower-pot, while
the water fell from the mouth of the winged monster.   All these
objects are exhibited in the octagonal hall and gallery of the
Palazzo dei Conservatori.   The epigram of Kallimachos painted

Fig. 159. — The Fountain of Pontios the Athenian, discovered in the Gardens of
Mæcenas.

on the walls of the greenhouse, illustrated by Visconti and Dressel,
is preserved in the Museo Municipale al Celio, Hall No. II.

LITERATURE. — Antonio Nibby, *Roma antica*, vol. ii. p. 339. — Carlo Ludo-
vico Visconti, in *Bull. com.*, 1874, p. 137, pls. xi.–xviii. — August Mau, *Bull.
Inst.*, 1875, p. 89; and *Ann. Inst.*, 1880, p. 137, note. — Heinrich Dressel,
Rivista di filologia, anno 111, April–June. — Ridolfino Venuti, *Cod. vatic.*,
9024, f. 232. — Flaminio Vacca, *Mem.* 39 (in Fea's Miscellanea, vol. i. p. lxxii).
— Francesco Ficoroni, *Vestigie di Roma antica*, vol. i. p. 10. — Winckelmann,
Storia delle arti, vol. ii. p. 63; and *Mem.* 2 (in Fea's Miscell., vol. i. p. clxxxiii).

XXVI. HORTI LOLLIANI. — In building the foundations of the
"Istituto Massimi," at the corner of the Via Principe Umberto
and the Piazza di Termini, some terminal stones were found inscribed with the words, " These stones mark the boundary line of
the gardens of Lollia [Horti Lolliani], which are now the property
of the Emperor Claudius."   Lollia Paulina was made an Empress

by Caligula in A. D. 37, in spite of the protests of her legal husband, Memmius Regulus; but Caligula soon grew tired of the alliance and Lollia was banished from the Imperial house. Eleven years later Claudius, being in quest of a wife after the death of Messalina, hesitated for a while between the two professional beauties of the age, Lollia and Agrippina. Agrippina won the day, and her first act was to obtain the banishment of her rival and the confiscation of her property. The Horti Lolliani thus became part of the great Imperial park on the Esquiline.

LITERATURE. — Raffaele Garrucci, in *Civiltà Cattolica*, serie xii. vol. iv. fasc. 800, p. 205. — *Ancient Rome*, p. 104. — *Notizie Scavi*, 1883, p. 339. — *Corpus Inscr.*, vol. vi. n. 31,284.

XXVII. HORTI SALLUSTIANI — originally laid out by the historian Sallust with the wealth acquired during his governorship of Numidia. After his death they passed into the hands of Q. Sallustius Crispus, to become crown property at the time of Tiberius. They were a favorite residence of many Emperors, who enlarged the domain with subsequent acquisitions, embellished it with the costliest works of art, and supplied it liberally with water. There were several reservoirs for the storage and distribution of the water over the grounds: one of them, two hundred metres long, runs parallel with the Via Venti Settembre under the Hôtel Royal and the houses facing the Ministero delle Finanze; another can still be seen in the riding-grounds of the king's corazzieri, Vicolo di S. Nicola da Tolentino; a third was discovered in 1888 right under the Casino dell' Aurora. The water-pipes bear the names of Claudius, Trajan, Severus Alexander, and of one of the Valentinians.

Among the historical events connected with Sallust's gardens are the attack made on them by Antony, one of the generals of Vespasian, in the campaign against the Vitellians in A. D. 70; the long residence of Vespasian, who ordered the gates of the park and of the palace to be kept open to every one and removed the sentinels from them; the death of Nerva in his seventy-second year, which took place A. D. 99; the long residence in them of Aurelian, who built a colonnade called *porticus Milliariensis*, because it was 1000 feet (297 metres) long. Under the shelter of it he would fatigue himself and his horses by constant riding, although already advanced in years. A curiosity was shown in the crypts of the palace: the bodies of two giants named Possion and Secundilla, each 10 feet 3 inches long (3.04 metres). Palace and

gardens were burnt down and devastated by Alaric on August
10, 410.

The principal ornament of the gardens was the Temple of
Venus Erycina, afterwards named Sallustiana, or else "Venus
hortorum Sallustianorum." Classics described it as standing at
the head of the valley between the Pincian and the Quirinal, outside the Porta Collina. Its construction had been promised by
the consul L. Porcius while engaged in the Ligurian war of 184
B. C., and its dedication had taken place two years later.

Fig. 160. — Part of the Marble Throne of the Venus Sallustiana, now in the Ludovisi
Museum.

The temple was discovered in the middle of the sixteenth century in the vineyard then belonging to Gabriel Vacca, father of
Flaminio, who describes it as round peripteral, with the peristyle
of fluted columns of giallo antico, and with four pairs of columns
of alabaster at the four entrances. The discovery aroused the
interest of antiquaries. Pirro Ligorio sketched and described it
in "Cod. vatic.," 3439, f. 28; "Cod. paris. (fonds St. Germain),"
86, etc.; and Panvinio wrote a brief comment on Ligorio's designs. The temple contained a statue of the goddess seated on a
throne; the upper part of the throne here reproduced (Fig. 160)
was discovered in the summer of 1887, near the junction of the
vie Boncompagni and Abruzzi; the head of the statue — a wonderful specimen of Greek archaic art — has formed part of the
Boncompagni-Ludovisi Museum since its first institution (n. 33,
Room III.).

Literature. — Carlo Ludovico Visconti, *Bull. com.*, 1887, p. 267, pls. xv., xvi. — Eugen Petersen, *Mittheilungen*, 1892, p. 32, pl. ii. — Wolfgang Helbig, *Guide*, vol. ii. p. 112, n. 882. — Rodolfo Lanciani, *Bull. com.*, 1888, p. 3. — Christian Huelsen, *Mittheilungen*, 1889, p. 270.

The gardens contained also a group of buildings of Egyptian style, so much in fashion in Rome at the time of Hadrian. To these structures belong the four statues, formerly in the Capitoline Museum and now in the Vatican, two of which were discovered in 1714, two in 1720. They are clever Roman copies of Egyptian originals, and are cut in red granite and gray basalt. The obelisk now in front of the Trinità de Monti formed part of the same group. Ligorio saw it lying in the vineyard of Messer Paulo Patella about 1550, and made a sketch of it in " Cod. vat.," 3439, f. 3. Sixtus V. had planned to raise it in front of the church of S. Maria degli Angeli, but he had not time to carry the project into execution. In 1733 one of the Ludovisi princesses made a present of it to Clement XII., who caused it to be removed to the Lateran, then in course of reconstruction. I have found in volume G, 1, of the Queen's Library at Windsor a sketch by Carlo Fontana, showing the exact place in which the two pieces of the obelisk were lying in 1706, when that architect was urging Pope Albani, Clement XI., to erect it in the niche of the Fountain of Trevi. It was ultimately set up at the top of the steps of the Trinità by Pius VI. in 1808. Its socle, of red granite, measuring 323 cubic feet, was discovered accidentally in 1843, near the gate of the villa. It now lies abandoned in the Piazza del Maccao, near the reservoir of the Acqua Marcia.

Literature. — Bottari, *Museo Capitol.*, vol. iii. n. 76, 77. — Braschi, *De tribus statuis*, i. 5. — Gio. Battista Cipriani, *Degli Obelischi*, p. 19. — Emiliano Sarti, *Archivio Società storia patria*, vol. ix. p. 436.

The only remains now visible in the Piazza Sallustiana, at a great depth under its level, belong to a nymphæum built over the springs of the river Petronia, which were originally called Catifons. The nymphæum is connected with a palace of very curious design, of which not less than four stories can still be traced. Excellent designs by Ligorio can be found in " Cod. parisin. (fonds St. Germain)," n. 1139, f. 311–314 ; and in " Cod. vatic.," 3439, f. 27, 30, 48. These gardens of Sallust had practically survived the shocks of time and lasted to our own days. I think that, as regards natural beauty and taste in the arrangement of their shady walks, open vistas, floral decorations, artificial ponds, etc., the Villa Ludovisi

and the Villa Massimo, which covered the same ground, were not
inferior to the old Roman park.   The Museo Ludovisi contained,
perhaps, more masterpieces of Greco-Roman art than Sallust and
his Imperial successors had been able to gather in the gardens.
Both villas, the pride of modern Rome, were mercilessly sacrificed
by their owners in 1886, and to no purpose whatever.   It is true

Fig. 161. — A Group of Pines in the Villa Ludovisi, cut down in 1887.

that the villas have disappeared, that their magnificent ilexes
have been burnt into charcoal, their great pines used for timber,
their hills and dales cut away or filled up to a dead level, and
their deliciously shady avenues destroyed to make room for broad,
straight, sun-beaten thoroughfares; yet no one seems to have
gained by it.   Those who sold and those who bought the grounds
have failed alike in their speculations, and the new quarter remains
still unfinished.

Besides the head and the throne of the Venus Sallustiana, many
works of art have passed from these gardens into our museums.
Ligorio mentions the discovery of life-size figures of Niobe and
the Niobides in full relief, belonging probably to the pediment of

a temple, of statues of Bacchus and of a Faun, together with several Nymphs of fountains. The celebrated Silenus with the infant Dionysos in his arms, formerly in the Villa Borghese and now in the Louvre (Fröhner, Catalogue, 1889, p. 265, n. 250), and the Bacchic Vase in the same museum (*ibid.*, p. 302, n. 311) were discovered about 1575 near the present Casino Massimo. The statue of Zeus, n. 326 Sala dei Busti, Vatican Museum, seems to have been discovered near the site of the obelisk, together with other works of art formerly in possession of the Verospi family. Winckelmann mentions a group of two young girls playing with the ἀστράγαλοι, discovered in 1765 and bought by General Walmoden.

There is no doubt that the Dying Gaul of the Capitoline Museum and the group of a Gaul and his wife of the Boncompagni Museum [1] belong to the same artistic composition, and to the same place, the Gardens of Sallust. Helbig contends that the composition, of which the group occupied the centre and the Dying Gaul the extreme right corner, cannot "have formed the sculptural decoration of a pediment, because the plinths are oval instead of rectangular. The life-like details of the works would also have been lost at so great a height. It is therefore probable that the group of the Villa Ludovisi, the Capitoline figure, and the other statues of the series were placed side by side on one or more pedestals of moderate elevation," like the Niobides of the Horti Lamiani. Helbig also thinks that the composition did not represent "Parnasi eiectos de vertice Gallos," a companion subject to the slaughter of Niobe's children, but a victory gained by King Attalos I. of Pergamos over the Gauls. We must remember, however, that Ligorio's account of the existence of statues of Niobides in these gardens is confirmed by the discovery of a fragment of one of the female figures made in 1887. The fragment is preserved in the Museo Municipale al Celio.

Another portion of the Gardens of Sallust, the beautiful valley in the shape of a circus, with the cliffs shaded by evergreens, disappeared in 1881–82, when Herr Spithoever, the librarian, who had bought the ground from the Barberini, filled up the valley with the materials of the Servian embankment which crowned the cliffs, and turned one of the most picturesque corners of the city into flat building lots.

No traces of the temple of Venus Erycina (Venus Hortorum Sallustianorum) were found ; but the foundations of that of one of the three Fortunes ad Portam Collinam came to light near the

---

[1] The so-called Dying Gladiator, and group of Arria and Pætus.

Fig. 162. — Cliffs on the South Side of the Vallis Sallustiana, before the Construction of the New Quarters.

junction of the Via Venti Settembre and Via Salaria. Many works of art were collected by Spithoever on this occasion. Twenty metres below the platform of the temple, at the bottom of the moat which protected the Servian embankment from the outside, a statue was found, life-size, and of good workmanship, representing Endymion asleep on the rocks of Mount Latmos. A few steps farther a statue of Leda and the Swan came to light, a good copy of a better original, and also the figure of a dog finely cut in rosso antico.

LITERATURE. — Antonio Nibby, *Roma antica*, vol. ii. pp. 281 and 348. — Wolfgang Helbig, *Guide*, vol. i. p. 164, n. 245 ; and p. 396, n. 533; vol. ii. p. 117, n. 884. — Rodolfo Lanciani, *I comentarii di Frontino*, p. 224, n. 87–94; and *Itinerario di Einsiedlen*, pp. 27, 28. — *Corpus Inscr.*, vol. vi. 122, 4327, 5863, 8670, 8671, 9005. — *Bull. com.*, 1880, p. 133; 1885, p. 165. — *Forma Urbis Romæ*, pl. iii. — Theodor Mommsen, *Corpus Inscr.*, vol. i. second edit. pp. 315, 319, 335.

XXVIII. HORTI LUCULLIANI, on the slope of the Pincian hill, now crossed by the vie Sistina, Gregoriana, due Macelli, and Capo le Case. These gardens, laid out by Lucullus and brought to perfection by Valerius Asiaticus, contained a palace, the favorite residence of Messalina ; porticoes and libraries in which Lucullus gathered the leading savants of his age ; and a banqueting-hall named from Apollo, where Cicero and Pompey the Great had been entertained at dinner. No traces remain of these buildings, except some mosaic pavements under the houses Via Sistina No. 57 and Via Gregoriana No. 46, and some walls under and near the Mignanelli palace. Two well-known works of art have been found on the site of these gardens : the so-called Arrotino, or Scythian sharpening his knife for the execution of Marsyas, now in the Tribuna degli Uffizi, Florence ; and the head of Ulysses, discovered in the foundations of the Colonna della Concezione, Piazza di Spagna, now in the Vatican Museum.

LITERATURE. — Antonio Nibby, *Roma antica*, vol. ii. p. 336. — Rodolfo Lanciani, *Bull. com.*, 1891, pp. 150–153.

XXIX. HORTI ACILIANI (Passeggiata del Pincio, Villa Medici). — The promenade of the Pincian is known to strangers and to most of the Romans as a simple pleasure-ground, giving opportunities for a pleasant walk in shade or sunshine, and for meeting friends. Its terraces overhanging the valley of the Tiber, and the plains crossed by the Via Flaminia, seem to have been created by the genius of Valadier for the enjoyment of our golden sunsets, when the opposite ridge of the Monte Mario appears fringed with a glowing halo of fire.   There is, moreover, another attraction unknown to the "vulgus profanum," the historical and archæological associations of the place.

Many suppositions had been made by topographers as to the former state of the hill, until the controversy was settled by an accidental discovery made in 1868.   Whilst new water-pipes were being laid in the avenue which leads from the Trinità de' Monti to the "rond point," where the Cairoli monument has lately been erected, a votive marble tablet was discovered at a depth of three feet, inscribed with the following dedication : *Tychicus freedman of* (Manius Acilius) *Glabrio, and intendant* (or keeper) *of his gardens, has dedicated* (this shrine) *to Silvanus.*   The tablet is of delicate workmanship, with edges cut sharply in the shape of a swallow's tail; and as these pointed edges were in perfect condition, it is evident that the tablet was found not far from its original place.   The family of the Acilii, of whose gardens Tychicus was intendant, may be called the noblest among the noble in ancient times.   It was divided into several branches, such as the Acilii Aviolæ and the Acilii Glabriones.   The latter is especially known in Roman history, from the time of the battle of Thermopylæ, in which Acilius Glabrio, consul 191 B. C., defeated King Antiochus.   His great-grandson and namesake, the consul of 67, and commander-in-chief in the Mithridatic war, is better known to students as the Prætor Urbanus who presided over the impeachment of Verres (70 B. C.).   In Imperial days the name of the family appears not less than eleven times in the *fasti consulares*, therefore it is not possible to determine who is the Glabrio mentioned in the tablet as owner of the Pincian villa.   The palæography of the inscription seems to pertain to the end of the second century, in which a Manius Acilius Glabrio twice obtained the consulship.

The discoveries made by De Rossi in the catacombs of Priscilla have thrown an unexpected light on the history of these Acilii Glabriones.   De Rossi had repeatedly expressed a doubt as to whether the Acilii had become Christians at a very early period. Thrice he has discussed the problem in his "Bullettino" (1863, p. 29; 1865, p. 20; 1869, p. 78), but the evidence he was able to collect was merely circumstantial.   The discovery of a beautiful hypogæum of the second century in the very heart of Priscilla's cemetery, containing the tombstone of Manius Acilius Verus and Acilia Priscilla, son and daughter of Manius Acilius Glabrio, consul A. D. 152, proves that the "noblest among the noble" had embraced our faith from the first announcement of the gospel in Rome.

To come back, however, to the Pincian Hill, we must remark that the gardens of the Acilian family were not confined to the narrow limits of the Promenade, but comprised within their present boundary line the Villa Medici, a portion of the Villa Borghese, and the convent and garden of the Trinità de' Monti. Many discoveries have taken place in this vast surface of ground, from the time of cardinals Riccio di Montepulciano and Ferdinando de' Medici to the present day. The accounts left by contemporary writers, compared with the existing ruins, enable us to reconstruct the general outline of the villa, as well as the detailed plans of some of its leading structures. These structures may be classified as follows. In the first place, there are the supporting walls of the terraces facing the north and the east, afterwards inclosed by Aurelian in his line of city walls; then come the buildings connected with the supply, storage, and distribution of water, such as nymphæa, reservoirs, aqueducts, fountains, etc.; thirdly, the palace of the Acilian family, and the residences of their servants, gardeners, gamekeepers, etc.; lastly, the wine-cellars, which form one of the most interesting features of the estate.

The substructures facing the east and the north side of the rectangle, towards the Villa Borghese, have been mostly concealed by modern buttresses, raised between 1850 and 1865 by Vescovali. They are built of reticulated work, with edges of small tufa blocks, a style of construction which is considered especially characteristic of the time of Sulla. Their surface is corrugated by a number of niches, with buttresses projecting between them, so as to give to the whole construction the look of an aqueduct. This is probably the reason why, in a document of 1026, edited by Tommasetti, the substructures are called *gli arcioni* (the arcades).

In the second decade of this century, Count Tournon, prefect of the Napoleonic department of the Tiber, aided by Valadier and other eminent artists, laid out the plans for turning the vineyards, then belonging to the Augustinian monks of S. Maria del Popolo,[1] into a public promenade. The works began in 1812, on the slope facing the Campus Martius, and were watched by Giuseppe Guattani, to whom the archæological interests of the enterprise had been intrusted.

---

[1] There are two relics left of this *vigna dei Frati del Popolo:* two old umbrella pines which mark the site of one of the gates opening on a side lane. They are to be seen not far from the fountain of Moses in the inner garden, and are conspicuous in the spring from the rich mass of climbing roses which covers their trunks.

He asserts that he saw remains of the same substructure walls all along this western slope, from S. Maria del Popolo to the Vicolo del Borghetto : there were two lines of them, one above the other ; the lower terrace contained no trace of buildings, the upper

Fig. 163. — The " Parnaso " or Nymphæum of the Villa Aldobrandini at Frascati.

one was covered by a network of reticulated walls. The best and most elaborate part, however, of these substructures has been seen and described, and can still be faintly traced, in the garden of the Sacro Cuore by the Trinità de' Monti, under the gardener's house. Lucio Fauno describes this part as a " gran fabbrica antica, a guisa d' un mezzo cerchio che è già per andare in rovina." Pirro Ligorio adds that the hemicycle opened toward the west, that it measured 1100 feet (326.70 metres) in diameter, and that it was profusely ornamented with colonnades, staircases, fountains, niches, and statuary. The nymphæum or " Parnaso " of the Villa Aldobrandini at Frascati, designed by Giacomo della Porta, although smaller in size, may give an idea of the magnificent hemicycle of the Acilian gardens (Fig. 163). Ligorio ends his description by saying, " questo luogo è rovinato e dal tempo e da li frati della Trinità."

A plan of these ruins, now concealed from view, has been given in the "Bull. com." of 1891, pl. v., vi. The best way of examining those left standing on the side of the Villa Borghese is to walk along the Via delle Mura from the Porta del Popolo to the Porta Pinciana. This lovely walk gives the student an opportunity of observing also that strange relic, called the " Muro Torto," which marks the northeast corner of the gardens. In the Middle

Fig. 164. — The Substructures of the Gardens of the Acilii Glabriones on the Pincian. A Sketch by Valadier.

Ages women of ill fame were buried at the foot of the Muro Torto, and in more recent times men and women who had refused religious help on the scaffold.

I have in my collection of drawings an original sketch by Valadier (here reproduced, Fig. 164) which shows how beautifully preserved the substructures were when he undertook to transform the Vigna dei Frati Agostiniani into the present Passeggiata. The walls were lined by masses of evergreens, an overhanging forest which was periodically leased or sold by the Camera Capitolina to dealers in charcoal or firewood. I have seen a lease dated September 11, 1716, by which the S. P. Q. R. allows a certain Francesco Battaglia " di cioccare, ripulire, e liberare tutte le mura da porta del Popolo sino a p. Pinciana, da radiche spine, licini, ellere, ed altro," on condition that the three largest ilex trees should be left to the Camera.

WATERWORKS. — The highest point of the Pincian hill is marked by a conical mound called Il Parnaso or Belvedere di Villa Medici, from which Karl Sprosse designed in 1847 his beautiful panorama of the city. The mound is an artificial one: it is the work of Cardinal Riccio da Montepulciano, who took advantage of some existing ruins to form a foundation for his belvedere. The ruins are marked in early maps of Rome under the name of "the Temple of the Sun." A drawing of Sallustio Peruzzi (Uffizi, n. 665) shows that the would-be Temple of the Sun was simply a nymphæum, like the one of the Sallustian gardens, and the so-called Minerva Medica of the Licinian park. It was ornamented with fourteen niches or fountains, and towered high above an extensive and elaborate system of waterworks. It stood on a line with the hemicycle the remains of which have been described above, and it is possible that, as in the case of the Villa Aldobrandini at Frascati, masses of water rushed down in graceful cascades from the nymphæum to the terraces below.

Other masses of water, for the irrigation of the estate, were carried by means of underground channels and leaden pipes to a reservoir, which is still partially in use. The reservoir is excavated in the rock, and consists of galleries six feet wide, and seven and a half high, intersecting each other at right angles. When I descended for the first time into these crypts, on June 12, 1876, only twenty-one galleries were accessible, of which ten ran from southwest to northeast, eleven in the opposite direction. Far more numerous are those made inaccessible by the crumbling down of the roof or by the hands of the monks. "On the Pincian hill," relates Pietro Sante Bartoli, "there was a large reservoir of water, half destroyed by certain monks (the Augustinians of S. Maria del Popolo) to turn it into a wine-cellar. The destruction proved to be useless, because the crypts are too warm for the preservation of wine." Two galleries, 80 metres long, connect this labyrinth with a piscina on which the modern Casino

is built. The piscina — now used as a storeroom for the tools of
the gardeners — is composed of two parts: one, 30 metres by 10,
which was capable of holding 1200 cubic metres of water; the
other held only 200.[1]

The palace of the owners occupied that portion of the modern
promenade which stretches between the "Viale dell' Obelisco"
and the northern boundary wall of the Villa Medici. Its centre
is marked by the piscina just described, viz., by Valadier's Casino,
where the gardeners are stationed, and which, of late years, has
partially been turned into a restaurant. The buildings faced the
southwest with a frontage line of 230 metres. The style of
masonry was the reticulated, with but little mixture of brickwork.
The plastering of the walls was of the finest quality, composed of
marble dust and lime. The pavements were inlaid with mosaic
either monochrome or in colors, and the apartments were painted
in the so-called Pompeian style, with polychrome figures on vermilion or black grounds. There were bathrooms, with hot-air
pipes radiating from the furnace or hypocaustum below; corridors
and galleries, the floors of which were not laid horizontally, but
inclined like the one which leads down to Mæcenas' hall in the
Via Merulana; rooms with cornices and panels elegantly carved
in gilt stucco; others with a dado inlaid in alabaster, porphyry,
serpentine, and other precious marbles; remains of porticoes, peristyles, and colonnades with pieces of columns of alabaster and
pavonazzetto; capitals of the composite order; a colossal head of
Niobe; and a torso of Cupid. All these things were found in
1812. In the spring of the following year the excavations were
continued near and behind the apse of S. Maria del Popolo; and
here also many apartments were excavated with painted walls,
mosaic pavements, marble incrustations, and ·so forth. One of
the leading features of this excavation was the large quantity
of seashells found among the rubbish which leveled up the
ground over the ruins. They were examined by Brocchi, who
decided that they had nothing to do with the geology of the
Pincian hill, but that they had simply been used as a decoration
for fountains and artificial grottoes.

WINE-CELLARS. — The Via delle Mura (between the Porta del
Popolo and the Muro Torto) is separated from the foot of the

---

[1] The entrance to these crypts (not accessible to the public) is on the east
side of the Casino, on the right of the little fountain. In February, 1881,
other galleries were discovered and destroyed right under the wall of the
Villa Medici.

substructures by a strip of land, which, I think, is now occupied by a nursery for trees and shrubs belonging to high latitudes, as the place is naturally cold and shaded from the sun even in the height of summer. This northern aspect of the slope made it especially suitable for the establishment of wine-cellars and caves, which, as every one knows, constituted one of the most important sections of a Roman villa. And here they have been found. The discovery took place more than a century ago, and was fortunately witnessed by a careful archæologist, Seroux d'Agincourt, who describes it in p. 45 of his " Recueil des fragments de sculpture antique en terre cuite."

Here is a free translation of his graphic account. " At the foot of the walls of Rome, between the Porta del Popolo and the gate of the Villa Borghese under the Muro Torto, a small staircase composed of eight or nine steps was discovered in 1789, in an excavation seven feet deep. This staircase led to a room eighteen feet long, five and a half feet wide, paved with a tessellated floor in black and white of a strange design. The walls and the ceiling were decorated with fresco paintings in arabesque style, representing festoons and birds of various kinds, with a tasteful cornice carved in stucco. Next to this chamber there was another of nearly the same size, but without ornaments. Opening on this second apartment was a crypt of the same height extending towards the Muro Torto for a length of eighty or ninety feet. The second room was not paved : its floor was covered with loose sand into which amphoræ of the largest size were fixed upright. I believe these terra-cotta jars to have been used for holding wine or even precious liqueurs. They stood round the walls in a single row. The long gallery, on the contrary, contained an infinite quantity of earthen jars, ranged in parallel lines, all in a standing position, as their peculiar shape required. Although they belonged to the class of wine amphoræ or *diotæ*, still the variety of their forms, and even more the variety of the objects found in them at the time of the discovery, leaves us rather perplexed as to their primitive use. One of the vases contained water in a sufficiently pure state. In another were found some little heads of terra-cotta, a hand carved in ivory, glass and terra-cotta perfume bottles shaped like (the so-called) lachrymatories. In a third, bones of oxen expressly cut and sawn to go through the narrow neck of these receptacles. In a fourth skeletons, heads, jaws, vertebræ, bones of different animals, such as lizards, serpents, small quadrupeds, and even scales of fish. Others contained needles

of ivory and metal, hairpins, medals, and coins. The initials
M. D. S. were impressed on the handle of several jars, and on the
neck of one the maker's name, MATVRI. I could not find on any
vase the names of consuls marking the date of the year in which
the liquid had been sealed into them. Nothing could throw any
light on their history, or tell me why and how these miscellaneous
objects should be found mixed together in such a manner as to
give an idea of those superstitious incantations and evocations of
infernal spirits which — under one form or another — have been
practiced by credulous people from remote times up to the present
day. On the floor of the crypt, and buried deep in the sand, an
object was found which looked like the top or handle of a walk-
ing-stick; it was made of glass or enamel, with that iridescent
patina which gives to such things the look of mother-of-pearl. I
would mention, lastly, fragments of terra-cotta lamps, dishes, and
cups, and some bricks bearing the mark EX OFFICINA DOMIT(*iae*)
LVC(*illae*), which seems to confirm the opinion of those antiquaries who place the gardens of the Domitian family on the
Pincian hill.[1]

"The destruction of this singular and interesting monument
should be put in the list of those due to the thoughtlessness and
rapacity of landowners, and to the indifference and avidity of
their workmen, a subject of everlasting regret in Rome."

Fresh excavations were opened in the same place, along the
northern slope, in 1813, and they led to the discovery of other
groups of amphoræ, set up against the walls of the caves in parallel lines. Other amphoræ came to light in 1868, together with
the inscription of Tychicus near the gate of the Trinità de' Monti.
This last find seems to indicate that wine-cellars were established
not only in a place naturally exposed to the tramontana and
shaded from the sun, but wherever the building of the substructures afforded an opportunity to create subterranean vaults under
the terraces of the villa.

LITERATURE. — *Corpus Inscr.*, vol. vi. n. 623. — Rodolfo Lanciani, *Bull.
Inst.*, 1868, p. 119.; *Bull. com.*, 1891, p. 132; and *Forma Urbis*, sheet i. —
Lovatelli Ersilia Caetani, *Il monte Pincio* (in Miscellanea Archeologica, p.
211. Rome, 1891).

XXX. I have remarked already that the public and private
parks on the hills of the left bank were intersected by roads, by

---

[1] The brick-stamps of Domitia Lucilla prove only that the crypt was built
towards the middle of the second century.

popular or aristocratic quarters, and by great public buildings. Three of these, belonging to the sixth region, Alta Semita, are partially left standing: the Temple of the Sun in the Villa Colonna, the baths of Diocletian, and the Prætorian Camp. (See map, Fig. 165.)*

XXXI. Templum Solis Aureliani. — Communication between the plains of the Via Flaminia and the Quirinal hill, the favorite abode of Roman patricians, had always been difficult, owing to the steepness and narrowness of the streets leading to the three Quirinal gates, the Salutaris (Via delle Quattro Fontane, Via del Giardino), the Sanqualis (Salita della Dateria), and the Fontinalis (Salita delle tre Cannelle). When Aurelian, after the conquest of Palmyra, determined to offer to the Romans a specimen of eastern architectural splendor, by raising a great temple to the Sun on the very hill on which it had been worshiped from time immemorial (soli indigeti in colle quirinali, feast day, August 9), and on the very site of the "Pulvinar Solis," which Quintilian places near the Temple of Quirinus, he combined architectural magnificence with public utility. The temple was placed at the top of great steps, which, like our Scalinata della Trinità de' Monti, were destined to afford a direct and easy communication from the Campus Martius to the plateau of the hill. The steps were designed so that great crowds could ascend or descend them, without meeting or crossing each other.

The temple itself was of immense size. It covered an area of 16.890 square metres, and towered to the height of thirty metres above the pavement of the sacred inclosure. The shafts of the columns were 17.66 metres high, the Corinthian capitals 2.47 metres, the entablature 4.83 metres. A fragment of the cornice lying in the Villa Colonna weighs a hundred tons, and measures 34.27 cubic metres. The fountain of Sixtus V., formerly in the Piazza del Popolo, has been cut out of one of the bases, and also the fountain of Piazza Giudea. The pavement of the Colonna gallery has been inlaid with marble, cut out of one piece only of the frieze. Such colossal proportions make clear the wish of the conqueror of Palmyra to give the Romans a taste of the wonders he had himself admired in the East, especially at Heliopolis, where stones 60 feet long and 13 thick were raised to a height of 21 feet at the northwest corner of the platform.

Classics and inscriptions give us very little information about this temple. The "Vita Aureliani" calls it "magnificentissi-

*Figure 165 faces page 429.

Fig. 150

PARKS AND GARDENS

OF

ANCIENT ROME.

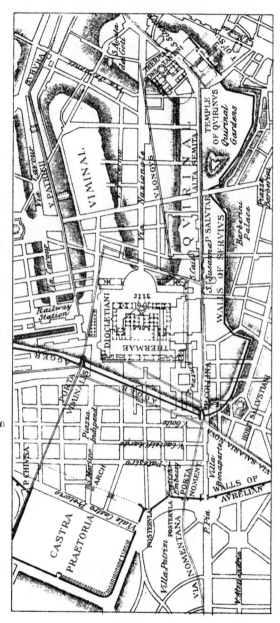

Fig. 165 MAP OF THE VIᵗʰ REGION "ALTA SEMITA".

mum," adding that the vaults and crypts of the temple were used
for storing the wine which some of the lands of the Peninsula
were wont to send to Rome as a "contribution en nature" to the
treasury. This is an instance of the practical good sense of the
Romans, which enabled them to seize every opportunity offered by
edifices of this kind, and to turn such buildings as were ostensibly
erected for the purpose of display to very practical purposes.

The destruction of the temple began at a very early age, if it
is true that eight of the porphyry pillars used by Justinian in the

Fig. 166. — The Ruins of the Temple of the Sun in the Sixteenth Century.

decoration of S. Sophia were removed from it. Towards the end
of the Middle Ages we find it already reduced to the state shown
in this view of 1575 by Etienne du Perac (Fig. 166). The ruin,
crowned by a battlemented tower, was called "Torre Mesa," or
"Torre di Mecenate," and more commonly the "Frontispizio di Nerone," and formed part of the fortified inclosure of the Colonnas.

It consisted of a portion of the cella, built of blocks of peperino,
and of the right corner of the pediment, the same which is now
lying in the Colonna gardens. The Torre Mesa was still standing

in 1616, when Alò Giovannoli made another — and the last known — sketch of it. It disappeared at the time of Urban VIII.

The destruction of the substructures of the temple began in January, 1549, and lasted at least up to February, 1555. In the first period of the works search was made for marbles alone. A regular lease had been signed between the Princess Giulia Colonna and the representatives of Pope Paul III., then engaged in finishing the Palazzo Farnese. From January 2 to November 9, 1549, 4131 scudi were spent simply in wages of men employed in the work of destruction. After the death of Paul III., Prince Ascanio Colonna made a present of what was left of the Temple to Julius III., then engaged in building his Villa Giulia. For three consecutive years hundreds of cartloads of stone were removed every month from the Colonna gardens. Besides the Palazzo Farnese and the Villa Giulia, the Cesi chapel in S. Maria Maggiore had its share of the spoils. Sixtus V. began in 1587 the destruction of the platform of concrete upon which the temple rested; Innocent XIII. in 1722, Pius IX. in 1866, and the municipality of Rome in 1878 blew up the rest to make room for the pontifical stables, for the new Salita della Dateria, and for the new Via del Quirinale. On this last occasion some crypts were discovered with Greek and Palmyrene inscriptions written with charcoal or red chalk on the white plaster of their walls. These interesting recollections of Queen Zenobia's fate are now exhibited in Hall VI. of the Museo Municipale al Celio.

The marble steps of the great staircase were removed to the Aracœli in 1348 by Lorenzo di Simone Andreozzo. One of the most remarkable facts connected with this temple is the respect shown by the semi-barbarian Romans of the Middle Ages for some works of statuary which adorned the steps in front of the propylaia. This museum of marbles, which may well compare with the museum of bronzes at the Lateran, comprised the two incomparable groups representing the Dioscuri in the act of making their fiery steeds feel the power of the bridle, now in front of the Royal Palace; the two River Gods now in the Piazza del Campidoglio; and a figure of Rome seated on the throne, which was bought by Cardinal d' Este. Later on the three statues of the Constantines, now in the Piazza del Campidoglio and in the vestibule of the Lateran, were added to this popular collection.

The following reproduction of an engraving by Lafrery, dated 1546, shows how the Dioscuri were then placed, and what damages they had suffered in the course of centuries. Sixtus V. and

Fig. 167. — The Dioscuri of the Quirinal, as they appeared in 1546.

Domenico Fontana removed them to their present position, after horsemen and steeds had undergone a thorough restoration. Bertolotti has published an account of the work full of useful information. It cost 2334 scudi.

LITERATURE. — *Corpus Inscr.*, vol. i², p. 324; and vol. vi. n. 726. — Flaminio Vacca, *Mem.*, 40, 78, 88, in Fea's Miscellanea, vol. i. — Francesco Ficoroni, *Mem.*, 115, *ibid.* — *Notizie Scavi*, 1878, p. 369. — A. Bertolotti, *Artisti lombardi a Roma*, vol. i. p. 75. — Christian Huelsen, *Rheinischen Museum f. Philologie*, 1894, p. 392; and *Bull. com.*, 1895, p. 39. — Rodolfo Lanciani, *Bull. com.*, 1894, p. 297; and 1895, p. 94.

XXXII. THERMÆ DIOCLETIANÆ, built by Diocletian and Maximian, and opened A. D. 306, [1] after their abdication from the throne. According to Olympiodorus, they contained about 3000 marble basins, besides a swimming piscina of 2400 square metres. They contained also a library, the Bibliotheca Ulpia, removed from the Forum of Trajan, gardens, gymnasia, and club-rooms. Together they covered an area of 130,000 square metres. The excavations made in the last twenty-five years for the building of the railway station, of the Grand Hôtel, of the Massimi palace, for the opening of new streets, and for the laying out of new gardens have enabled us to find out the names and the plans of some of the edifices destroyed by the two Emperors to obtain a site for the baths. Amongst them are the offices of a Collegium Fortunæ Felicis, a temple built on foundations of concrete; a portico or a shrine, rebuilt once by one of the Valerii Messallæ and again by Cn. Sentius Saturninus; pavements of streets; walls of private houses; and pieces of the largest and longest water-pipe ever found in Rome. It went from the Porta Viminalis to the Alta Semita, and through the Alta Semita to the Forum of Trajan. The tube, made of sheets of lead three centimetres thick, is inscribed with the name of the Emperor Hadrian, and of Petronius Sura, his *procurator aquarum*. The tube was at least 1750 metres long, and as it weighs 132 kilogrammes and 745 grammes for each metre, 231 tons, at least, of metal must have been used in its construction.

Inscriptions placed above the four principal gates described and praised the great work of Diocletian and of his colleague. The fate of these historic documents is truly remarkable: pieces of them have been found at various times in the Certosa, at S. Antonio on the Esquiline, at S. Alessio on the Aventine, at the Monte della Giustizia, in the foundations of the Treasury buildings,

[1] Between May 1, 305, and July 24, 306.

and in the Via Principe Umberto. The last piece came to light in June, 1890, from the foundations of the Grand Hôtel. The history of the baths is not known. Probably they suffered damage during the sack of Alaric, because a fragmentary inscription seen by Fra Giocondo da Verona on the spot (about 1495) speaks of repairs made in the course of the fifth century. They were still in use under King Theodoric; the collapse of the Marcian aqueduct must have soon brought about their abandonment. The compiler of the " Itinerary of Einsiedlen " saw one of the great inscriptions still fixed above one of the gates. In the year 1091 Pope Urban II. made a present of the ruins to S. Bruno and to Gavin, his friend, for the establishment of a Carthusian brotherhood. In 1450 Giovanni Ruccellai saw a great many columns of white or colored marble standing on their bases and crowned by finely cut entablatures. Francesco Albertino mentions the first discoveries of statues and pedestals made under Julius II. at the beginning of the sixteenth century. Jean du Bellay, ambassador of Francis I., created cardinal by Pope Paul III. in 1533, purchased the greater portion of the baths and laid out gardens among their picturesque ruins, known by the name of Horti Belleiani ; at his death, however, in 1560, creditors seized the estate and divided it among themselves. The Horti Belleiani fell to the lot of S. Carlo Borromeo, who sold them in his turn to his uncle Pope Pius IV. This pope took up the old project of Urban II. for the transformation of the baths into a Certosa, and of their tepidarium into a magnificent church. His bull of grant to the monks of S. Croce in Gerusalemme is dated July 27, 1561, and says among other things that the malaria raged so virulently at S. Croce that the abbot and his flock were in constant danger of life. The work of transformation, begun on April 24, 1563, and finished on June 5, 1566, cost 17,492 scudi. The state of the tepidarium, when Michelangelo entered it for the first time, is shown in the following sketch made by a contemporary artist. [1] Michelangelo converted the great hall into a Greek cross by adding to it the present vestibule and the choir, the entrance being from

---

[1] Photographed by Miss Dora Bulwer from f. 90 of the sketch-book of an unknown artist, now in the library of Trinity College, Cambridge (marked R, 17, 3ª). There are other valuable sketches by Du Perac (*I Vestigi*, f. 30); Dosio (*Ædificiorum reliquiæ*, 44, 45, 46; and *Uffizi*, 74, 76, 79, 2573); Jean Vander Wylt, in the Laing collection, Edinburgh; Lafrery (plate not numbered; very scarce; a copy in the Cabinet des Estampes). Volume " Rome, rione Monti A," of the same Cabinet des Estampes contains 72 views of the baths.

the southeast side, opposite the present railway station. Vanvitelli changed Michelangelo's plan: the nave was converted into a transept, and a new entrance made from the present Piazza di Termini. To avoid damp Michelangelo raised the low-lying pavement by three feet, so that the original bases of the columns remain buried to that depth. Of the sixteen columns of the church, the eight in the transept are antique, of red granite and of wonderful size. Those of the nave, of bricks, covered with painted stucco in imitation of granite, are an addition of 1740. One of the marble capitals comes from the temple of Claudius on the Cælian.

No discoveries seem to have been made in the course of the works; that of a bell with the name " Firmi Balneatoris " is said

Fig. 168. — The Tepidarium of the Baths of Diocletian, before its Transformation into the Church of S. M. degli Angeli.

by Doni to have taken place in 1548. Gregory XIII. in 1566 transformed a portion of the baths into grain stores; these " horrea Ecclesiæ " were afterwards enlarged by Paul V. in 1609, by Urban VIII. in 1630, and by Clement XI. in 1705.

Sixtus V., while engaged in building his beautiful Villa Peretti Montalto, as a present to his sister Donna Camilla, destroyed about one fifth of the baths. His books of accounts certify that between May 16, 1586, and May 15, 1589, not less than 94,482 cubic metres of Diocletian's masonry were demolished with the help of gunpowder. About the same time Flaminio Vacca registers the discovery of eighteen busts of "philosophers," sold first to Giuliano Cesarini, and by him to Cardinal Alessandro Farnese. They are now at Naples.

In January, 1594, Caterina Sforza, Countess of Santafiora, converted into a church and presented to the Cistercians the circular hall which formed the southwest corner of the outer circuit of the baths (S. Bernardo). In cleaning the cellars of their new abode the monks found great masses of lead, which, made into sheets, were sufficient to cover the whole dome of the rotunda. The fresco paintings of the same hall were whitewashed on account of their profane character.

No works of art of any consequence have been found in these baths, except, perhaps, a headless athletic statue, which appears in Lafrery's engraving, and a beautiful head of Venus discovered in January, 1805, by Petrini.

The present generation has not treated the remains of the thermæ kindly. A wide street, the Via Cernaia, has been cut right through the halls on the left of the tepidarium; a tunnel bored diagonally across the rectangle to convey the Acqua Felice to the Fountain of Moses; other halls destroyed in building the approaches to the railway station, the Massimi Palace, the Treasury, and the Grand Hôtel. The only redeeming point is the transformation of Michelangelo's portico into a museum in which objects of art and antiquities, discovered on government land and in government works, are exhibited. (See Helbig's Guide, vol. ii. p. 188, n. 964–1108.) The famous group of cypresses which shaded the fountain in the centre of the quadrangle was half destroyed by a tornado in the summer of 1886. The noble trees contemporary with the foundations of the Certosa are represented in the following illustration (Fig. 169), from a photograph taken in 1874.

LITERATURE. — *Corpus Inscr.*, vol. vi. n. 1124, 1130, 1131, 1131ᵃ, 31,242. — Ridolfino Venuti, *Antichità di Roma*, vol. i. p. 168. — *Beschreibung*, vol. iii², p. 351. — Theodor Mommsen, *Archæol. Zeitung*, 1846, p. 229. — Angelo Pellegrini, *Dissertazione sulle rovine delle terme diocleziane* (in Buonarroti, serie ii. vol. xi. August, 1876). — *Bull. com.*, vol. viii. 1880, p. 132. — *Notizie Scavi*, 1886, p. 36; 1890, pp. 185, 215. — Paulin, *Restauration des thermes de Dioclétien.* Paris, 1890. — Christian Huelsen, *Rheinische Museum f. Philologie*, 1894, p. 388. — Rodolfo Lanciani, *I comentarii di Frontino*, p. 96; and *Forma Urbis*, sheets n. x., xvii. — Henry de Geymuller, *Documents inédits sur les . . . thermes de Dioclétien.* Lausanne, 1883.

The designs, sketches, and plans of artists of the sixteenth and seventeenth centuries are innumerable. The best set, by far, is to be found in a portfolio of drawings, formerly in the possession of the architect Destailleurs, Paris, and now in the Kunstgewerbe Museum, Berlin (f. A, 377). The name of the artist (French) is not known. Cardinal Perrenot de Granvelle employed Sebastian

Fig. 169. — Group of Cypresses in the Cloisters of La Certosa.

de Oya, a Flemish architect, to design the baths, and his drawings were engraved on twenty-six copper plates by James Cock of Antwerp. The edition, dated 1558, has become very rare.

XXXIII. Castra Prætoria (fortified barracks of the Prætorian guard). — The name *prætorium*, used in a military sense, signifies the "commando," the headquarters, whether of a general commander-in-chief or of the Emperor himself. When Augustus reorganized the Roman army and navy, the legions and the auxiliary forces were quartered on the frontiers of the Empire, the fleet stationed partly at Misenum, partly at Ravenna, while Rome and his own person were intrusted to the protection of two or three thousand picked men, quartered in various districts of the city and of the suburbs, not in military barracks, but in houses of peaceful aspect — "nunquam plures quam tres cohortes in urbe esse passus est, eaque sine castris" (Sueton., Octav., 49). After the death of Augustus, Tiberius changed tactics at once, hardly appearing in public without an escort; and, with the excuse of keeping the Prætorians in stricter discipline, "procul urbis inlecebris," away from the seduction and corruption of the city, he built magnificent barracks in a field between the Via Nomentana and the Via Tiburtina, in imitation of a Roman fortified camp. This was done in A. D. 23, on the suggestion of Sejanus, then prefect of police. The chief power in the Roman state was thus placed practically in the hands of the Prætorians, and "the readers of the historians of the Empire will recall the many vivid pictures of their rapacity and violence. To go to the Prætorian camp and promise a largess to the guards was the first duty of a Roman Emperor." "Here occurred that memorable and most melancholy scene in Roman history, when the Prætorians shut themselves within their camp after the murder of Pertinax and put up the throne to auction. Julian and Sulpicianus . . . bid one against the other, and at last they ran up the price little by little to 5000 drachmas to each soldier. Julian then impatiently outbid his rival by offering at once 6250, and the Empire was knocked down to him. This was not by any means the first or only time that its fate had been decided here."[1]

The Prætorians furnished the guard of honor at the gates of the Imperial residence, on which occasions they wore the toga instead of the ordinary sagum. Their supreme commander was, of course, the Emperor, but practically they were under the rule of one or more "præfecti prætorio." The number of their cohorts varied

[1] See Burn, *Ancient Rome*, London, 1895, p. 189.

from a maximum of sixteen under Vitellius to a minimum of nine under Vespasian ; they were cohortes milliariæ equitatæ, viz., 1000 men strong, with a squadron of cavalry each.   Their term of service lasted sixteen years ; their pay was about 720 denarii a year.

Fig. 170. — Remains of the Castra Prætoria : Northeast Corner of the Quadrangle.

The Prætorians were recruited from volunteers from the more civilized provinces of the Empire; but Septimius Severus having dissolved the corps at the beginning of his reign, to reorganize it under a different system, the men were recruited henceforth from the most tried and trustworthy barbarians, and Rome was thus filled with bands of savage-looking Prætorians, speaking unknown languages, and of uncouth and barbarous manners.

Under Maximus and Balbinus, the citizens tried to put down

Fig. 171. — The Walls of the Prætorian Camp, with Aurelian's Superstructure.

their violence by cutting the water-pipes which supplied the castra from the reservoir by the Porta Viminalis, and thus to subjugate them by water famine. Aurelian and Probus included in their line of fortifications the north, east, and south side of the rectangle, and raised the height of the walls by ten to fifteen feet. The line of separation between the original walls, which were battlemented, and Aurelian's superstructure can still be traced on the north side. (See Fig. 171.)

The Prætorians were finally suppressed in 312 by Constantine, who caused the front or western wall of the camp to be demolished.

The camp is nearly square, being 430 metres wide by 371 deep. It was approached by a triumphal arch, — dedicated, it appears, to

Gordianus the younger, and to his Empress Tranquillina,—splendid remains of which have been found on three occasions: first in 1495, when Bramante was searching for marbles for the decoration of the Palazzo della Cancelleria, belonging to Cardinal Raffaele Riario; then in 1873, when the workshop was discovered in which the spoils of the arch were adapted to their new purpose (Via Gaeta, near the Villino della Somaglia); and again, in the winter of 1886–87, in the foundations of a house at the corner of the Via Solferino and the Viale Castro Pretorio. This last discovery took place while I was away from Rome on long leave. I am told that the winged Victory represented in the following cut, now in Copenhagen, was found on this occasion. It belongs to the left spandril above the middle archway.

Fig. 172. — One of the Victories from the Arch of Gordianus III.

THE PLAIN ON THE LEFT BANK OF THE TIBER.

REGIO IX. THE CAMPUS MARTIUS AND THE CIRCUS FLAMINIUS.

XXXIV. The plain which extends from the foot of the Pincian, Quirinal, and Capitoline hills to the left bank of the river was not changed from a grassy swamp into a region of architectural wonders by one man or at one time. The transformation was the work of centuries, and the result of the combined efforts of wealthy citizens and of enterprising Emperors, from the time of Pompey the Great to that of Severus Alexander. The architectural development of the Campus Martius, moreover, did not proceed at random, but by zones or districts, which follow each other in chronological order; and each of these groups was designed by one man according to his own piano regolatore, and generally with a different orientation from that of the neighboring districts. The fundamental lines for such orientation are the Via Flaminia (Corso) running 16° 30' west of the meridian; the Via Recta (Acquasanta, Coppelle, S. Agostino, Coronari), which runs due west; and a third street, name unknown (vie di Pescheria, del Pianto, de' Giubbonari, de' Cappellari), which runs from southeast to northwest. For a long time the natural aspect of the Campus Martius was not altered: the river Petronia continued to flow towards the "Goat's Pond" (*Capræ palus*), not yet transformed into the "Stagnum Agrippæ." Romans and foreigners continued to seek health at the springs of the Tarentum, not yet drawn into a canal around the Ara Ditis et Proserpinæ; the youth continued to race in the Trigarium, to bathe in the Tiber, to hold athletic sports in the Campus Martius, and to enjoy the shades of the Æsculetum.

The first impulse towards the transformation of the Campus was given by C. Flaminius, censor in 220, by the erection of a circus, and by the opening of the Via Flaminia. The Flaminian group, otherwise called "Ad Circum" or "In Circo," comprises the following structures: —

Circus Flaminius.	Ædes Kastoris.
(Stabula quatuor Factionum vi.)	Ædes Pietatis.
Columna bellica.	Ædes Volkani.
Ædes Bellonæ Pulvinensis.	Ædes Herculis Magni Custodis.
Ædes Martis.	Via Flaminia.

A commercial quarter had been formed in the meantime at the southern end of the plain, near the cattle and vegetable markets, the wharves of the Tiber, and the bridges (Sublician, Æmilian, Fabrician, Cæstian) through which provisions were brought in from the Etruscan or transtiberine orchards and farms. The group of the Forum Holitorium comprised in due time —

Forum Holitorium.	Ædes Spei.
(Porticus) Minucias duas, Veterem	Ædes Pietatis.
et Frumentariam.	Ædes Iunonis.
Porticus usque ad Elephantum.	Ædes Iani.

The building over of the plain, in accordance with a carefully studied project, began in the last century of the Republic, and was

the joint work of Julius Cæsar and Pompey the Great.   Cæsar
had planned to divert the course of the Tiber along the foot of the
Vatican ridge ("secundum montes Vaticanos"), so that the city
could expand over the Campus Martius, and to make a campus of
the present "Prati di Castello" (Cicero, Ad Attic., xiii. 33); but he
had no time to accomplish his scheme.   Pompey, on the contrary,
could see his idea carried into execution.   With the Pompeian
buildings, and with the additions made to them in later times, a
third group is formed, called "Ad Theatrum Lapideum" or
"Pompeianum."   It comprises the —

Theatrum Lapideum, with the Curia.	Ædes Honoris, Virtutis, Felicitatis.
Porticus Pompeianæ, with the Horti.	Ædes Fortunæ Equestris.
Hecatostylon.	Ædes Minervæ Campensis.
Ædes Veneris Victricis.	

We come now to the age of Augustus.   He may truly be said to
have found this region built of bricks and to have left it of marble.
Suetonius (Octav., 29) says: "He was fond of erecting costly
structures under the name of his wife, of his sisters and nephews,
like the Basilica of Caius and Lucius, the Portico of Livia, that
of Octavia, and the Theatre of Marcellus.   He would also urge
his wealthy friends to follow his example by raising new buildings, or by repairing and adorning old ones.   His call was re-
sponded to by Marcius Philippus, who built the Ædes Herculis
Musarum; by Lucius Cornificius, who rebuilt the Temple of Diana
on the Aventine; by Cornelius Balbus with his theatre; by Statilius Taurus with his amphitheatre.   Agrippa surpassed all of
them in the number and greatness of his constructions."   Strabo
the geographer gives the following account of the Campus Martius
as it appeared in the early part of the reign of Tiberius: "The
old Romans were so bent upon things and actions of more serious
consequence for the commonwealth, that they paid little or no attention to the beauty of their city; but the Romans of the present
day . . . have filled it with many and noble structures.   Pompey,
Cæsar, Augustus, his sons, his wife, his sister directed all their
energy and lavished great sums of money on the purpose.   Of this
we have ample evidence in the Campus Martius, which, in addition
to pleasantness of site and charms of landscape, has been vastly
improved by architectural beauty.   It affords at the same time
plenty of space for the multitudes who gather in its green fields to
train themselves in chariot and horse races, and in athletic sports
of all kinds.   The buildings of white marble, framed by masses

of green, the hills which inclose the plain on the opposite side of the river delight the eyes of the stranger. There is another campus, adjoining the one called Martius,[1] containing porticoes, sacred woods, three theatres, one amphitheatre, so close to each other that it appears to form part of the city itself. The campus being held sacred in the minds of the citizens, many illustrious men and women have selected it for their last resting-place. Conspicuous among all is the so-called Mausoleum, raised on a pedestal of white marble near the banks of the river, and shaded by evergreens to the summit of the mound, where a bronze statue of the founder of the Empire has been set up. His relatives are buried in the crypts below."

Three groups can be formed of the works of the Augustan and Tiberian age. The first, or Augustan, comprises the —

Ara Fortunæ reducis.	Ripæ Tiberis.
Ara Pacis Augustæ.	Porticus ad Nationes.
Solarium or Horologium.	Porticus Octaviæ.
⎰ Ustrinum.	Porticus Corinthia Cnei Octavii.
⎱ Mausoleum.	Theatrum Marcelli.
⎰ Silvæ et Ambulationes.	

The second, or Agrippianum, extended from the foot of the hills, by Capo le Case, to the Ponte Sisto. The Monumenta Agrippæ are —

Porticus Pollæ or P. Vipsania.	Porticus Eventus Boni.
Campus Agrippæ.	Horti.
Diribitorium.	⎰ Neptunium.
Ductus et Lacus Virginis.	⎱ Porticus Argonautarum.
(Ædes Juturnæ.)	Sæpta Iulia.
Pantheum.	Villa publica.
Thermæ.	Pons Agrippæ.
Stagnum, with the Euripus.	Cloacæ.

The third group may be called the "Spectacular Buildings" raised by Augustus, and by his friends and successors. It comprises the —

Theatrum Marcelli.	Amphitheatrum Tauri.
Theatrum Balbi.	Stadium.
Crypta Balbi.	Odeum.

No other constructions by zones or districts are recorded for the

[1] Strabo means the Prata Flaminia, at the south end of the plain.

space of over a century. Tiberius repaired the stage of Pompey's theatre ; Claudius the aqueduct of the Aqua Virgo. Nero built other great baths near those of Agrippa. In the conflagration of July, 65, the flames avoided, or were made to avoid, the Campus Martius, probably to save the newly built thermæ of Nero, so that the homeless multitudes could find shelter in the Monumenta Agrippæ. However, in the last days the fire got the better of those trying to keep it within the prescribed limits, and consumed some of the porticoes and gardens (porticus amœnitati dicatæ), some of the temples, the Æmilian gardens of Tigellinus (prædia Æmiliana Tigellini), and the Statilian amphitheatre.[1]

The fire of Titus, A. D. 80, damaged considerably the Diribitorium, the portico of Octavia, the Temple of Isis and Serapis, the Sæpta Iulia, the Admiralty (Neptunium), the Baths of Agrippa, the Pantheon, and, of course, the public and private buildings of secondary importance wedged in among the great ones. Some of them, like the Diribitorium, were abandoned forever ; others repaired by Domitian (the Temple of Isis and Serapis, the Pantheon, the Porticus Minucia Vetus, the Minervium of Pompey the Great), who added " de proprio " an odeum and a stadium ; others repaired by Hadrian (many temples, the Sæpta Iulia, the Thermæ Agrippianæ, and again the Pantheon and the Admiralty), who added also " de suo " a temple in honor of Marciana, sister of Trajan, and of Matidia his mother-in-law ; others finally repaired more than a century later (?) by Septimius Severus and Caracalla, like the stage of Pompey's theatre, the portico and the libraries of Octavia, and probably the theatre and the crypta of Balbus.

The district on the left of the Flaminia, between the " zone " of Augustus (Via in Lucina) and that of Agrippa (Piazza di Pietra), had been occupied in the meantime by the Antonines. This group, which we may call Antoninianum, comprises the —

(So-called) Arch of M. Aurelius and L. Verus.	Templum Antonini.
	Columna divi Pii.
Columna centenaria divi Marci, with the Hospitium of its keeper Adrastus.	Ustrinum et Ara Antoninorum.

If we take into consideration the object of some of the buildings mentioned above, instead of the name and epoch of those who raised them, and the age to which they belong, we can make up a last and most important group, the group of the Porticoes,

---

[1] Tacitus, *Ann.*, xv. 40.   Dion Cassius, *Hist.*, lxii. 18.

under the shelter of which it was possible to cross the plain from one end to the other.

Under the Republic they were comparatively rare, and the few that existed at that time were built not as places of pleasant resort, but with a definite and more practical aim. The Minucia served for the distribution of grain; the Æmilia for the storage of merchandise brought by river and by sea; those of the Forum Holitorium as a vegetable market; the Porticus Pompeianæ as a place of refuge in case of rain. Augustus made porticoes popular; under his rule the whole campus was covered with colonnades. He himself built that of Octavia, and a second called Ad Nationes on account of some colossal statues, representing the nations of the world, and rebuilt a third, named Corinthian from the capitals of its columns, cast in (gilt) Corinthian brass. Balbus added a crypta to his theatre; Marcius Philippus surrounded with a portico the Templum Herculis Musarum. To Agrippa the Romans owed the Porticus Vipsania, the Sæpta, used for electoral meetings under shelter, the Villa Publica, the Porticus Argonautarum, the Porticus Eventus Boni (and the Porticus Europæ ?). The example set by Augustus and his courtiers found imitators down to the very fall of the Empire, and even after it, as shown by the Horti Largiani, the Portico of Constantine, the Porticus Maximæ of Gratian, Valentinian, and Theodosius, and lastly by those which led from the Ælian bridge to S. Peter's, from the Porta Ostiensis to S. Paul's (and from the Porta Tiburtina to S. Lorenzo).

No attention has been paid by topographers to the special nature of these structures; they have been studied individually, as simple inclosures of temples, annexes to theatres, picture-galleries, museums of statuary, and places of meeting and resort; but if we consider them as successive manifestations of the same original plan, and part of a whole system, their importance increases tenfold. They were designed so that the citizens could walk in every season and at any hour under shelter from wind, rain, cold, and the heat of the sun. Needless to say this happened after the taste for luxury and comfort had superseded the previous austerity of Roman life. Whenever the poets, and Martial especially, speak of the porticoes, they allude to one idea, to the delight of enjoying there the warmth of sunshine in winter while outsiders were shivering from the blasts of the tramontana. The spaces between the colonnades were intersected in graceful designs by the *tepida buxeta*, walls of boxwood. Towards the end of the Empire it became possible to walk under shelter from the region of the Fora to the church of S. Peter, a distance of nearly two miles ; and the sight would have struck the least enthusiastic person in the world with wonder.   The development of the twelve larger colonnades of the Campus Martius amounts to 4600 metres; the sheltered surface to 28,000 square metres; the total area, central gardens included, to 100,000; the number of columns was about 2000.

These columns were of the rarest kinds of marble.   Their capitals were sometimes of gilt Corinthian metal, and their pavements were inlaid with jasper and porphyry.   Each portico contained a museum of sculpture and a gallery of pictures, and the space inclosed by them was laid out in gardens, with thickets of box, myrtle, laurel, arbutus, pine, and plane trees shading lakes, fountains, and waterfalls.   Each one offered to the visitor a special attraction.   In the Porticus Vipsania the maps of the Roman world surveyed at the time of the birth of our Lord were displayed. The Sæpta contained curiosity-shops, where antiquities and manufactures of the Far East, China included, were exhibited.   Lastly, in the portico of Philippus ladies could find the latest fashions in wigs and hairdressing that the fancy of Roman coiffeurs could contrive.

LITERATURE. — Rodolfo Lanciani, *I portici della regione ix.* (in Ann. Inst., 1883, pls. A, B).   *Ancient Rome*, p. 94. — Luigi Borsari, *Sui portici della regione vii.* (in Bull. com., 1887, p. 141). — Heinrich Jordan, *Forma*, p. 33.

My description of the existing remains of the ninth region will follow the division by chronological zones or groups, in this order : (*a*) Monuments illustrating the original state of the Campus Martius ; (*b*) Monuments ad Circum (Flaminium); (*c*) Monuments ad Forum Holitorium ; (*d*) Monuments ad Theatrum Lapideum (Pompeianum) ; (*e*) The Augustan Group; (*f*) The Monumenta Agrippæ; (*g*) The Spectacular Buildings; (*h*) The group of the Antonines ; (*i*) The Porticoes.

A. MONUMENTS ILLUSTRATING THE ORIGINAL STATE OF THE CAMPUS MARTIUS.

XXXV. THE TARENTUM. — In the early days of Rome the northwest section of the Campus Martius, bordering on the Tiber, was conspicuous for traces of volcanic activity.   There was a pool called Tarentum or Terentum, fed by hot sulphur (?) springs, the efficacy of which was attested by the cure of Volesus, the Sabine, and of his family.   Dark vapors hung over the springs, and tongues of flame sprang from the cracks of the earth. The place became known by the name of the Fiery Field (*campus ignifer*), and its connection with the infernal regions was soon an established fact in folk-lore. An altar was erected to the infernal gods on the borders of the pool, and games were held periodically in honor of Dis and Proserpina, the victims being a black bull and a black cow. The games, originally called *ludi Tarentini*, became in progress of time the *ludi Sæculares*, and their direction was intrusted to a college of priests named the " quindecemviri sacris faciundis." No other object of Roman topography, no other feature in Roman religious institutions, has been better illustrated by recent discoveries than have this famous altar and these famous games. We have found the altar itself and the basin of the spring, the residence of the Quindecemviri, and the official report of the celebration of the games under Augustus and under Septimius Severus and Caracalla.

The discovery of the Ara Ditis et Proserpinæ took place in the winter of 1886–87, while the new Corso Vittorio Emmanuele

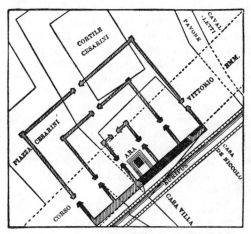

Fig. 174. — Plan of the Ara Ditis et Prosperinæ.

was being opened at the back of the Cesarini Palace. The position and shape of the monument are shown in the accompanying drawings. No traces of the altar and of its triple inclosure have been left visible, except two pieces of the *pulvini* of the altar removed to the court of the Palazzo dei Conservatori.

The *schola* or residence of the Quindecemviri was discovered on April 16, 1889, under and near the (now destroyed) oratorio di S. Giovanni de' Fiorentini, Via del Consolato. There were

Fig. 175. — Fragments of the Pulvini of the Ara Ditis.

remains of a hall of basilical type, built of red and yellow bricks, and divided into a nave and aisles by two lines of columns. These ruins were far more conspicuous in bygone days: the Mirabilia give them the name of " Secretarium Neronis." The drain of the Corso Vittorio Emmanuele cuts the apse of the hall in a slanting direction. I am sure that, if a proper search were made, historical documents of great value would be brought to light.

The official *compte rendu* of the celebration of the ludi sæculares was discovered on September 20, 1890, by the workmen employed in the construction of the sewer between the Ponte S. Angelo and that of S. Giovanni de' Fiorentini. The fragments of marble upon which the precious records were engraved lay embedded in a mediæval wall. There were one hundred and thirteen fragments in all; of which eight refer to the games celebrated by Augustus in 17 B. C., two to those of Domitian, the rest to those celebrated by Septimius Severus in A. D. 204. The fragments of the year 17 fit together so as to make a block three metres high, containing a hundred and sixty-eight lines. The others are in a more fragmentary state. They are all exhibited in the Museo delle Terme, first room, first floor.

LITERATURE. — Rodolfo Lanciani, *L' itinerario di Einsiedlen*, p. 108; and *Pagan and Christian Rome*, p. 73. — Theodor Mommsen, *I comentarii dei ludi secolari Augustei e Severiani* (in Mon. ant. Lincei, vol. i. 3, a. 1891); and in Ephemeris epigr., 1892, vol. viii. pp. 225–309. — Carlo Pascal, *Bull. com.* 1893, p. 195; and 1894, p. 54. — Giovanni Pinza, *ibid.*, 1896, p. 191.

XXXVI. CAMPUS MARTIUS. — The ninth region of Augustus, bordered by the Via Flaminia, the Servian walls, and the Tiber, was divided into two sections, one named (from the) *Circus Flaminius*, the other, *Campus Martius*. The latter, in its turn, was subdivided into a Campus Martius *maior* and a Campus Martius *minor*. The origin of these sections and denominations must be briefly explained, but the evidence to be gathered from classics is rather conflicting. Livy (ii. 5) says that the field on the left bank of the Tiber was dedicated to Mars, and obtained accordingly the name of Martius only after the expulsion of the Tarquins. Dionysius (iv. 22; v. 13) asserts that the field was consecrated to that deity before the time of Servius Tullius, but without saying when. It is certain that an "Ara Martis" existed from a very ancient date in the campus, and also an "Ædes Martis," distinct from and probably much older than that erected by Brutus Callaicus near the Circus Flaminius. Its ruins (?) were discovered by Baltard in 1837, and again by Vespignani in 1873, under the block of houses bounded by the Via and Piazza di S. Salvatore in Campo and the Via degli Specchi.[1] On the whole, we may conclude that the field had been set aside for public use, and placed under the protection of the gods, before the time of Tarquinius Priscus. Tarquinius Superbus appropriated and cultivated it for his own use; and when, after his flight, the consuls Brutus and Valerius proceeded to confiscate his estates, the campus was covered with standing corn. The crop, being deemed accursed, was thrown into the river, where it lodged on a mud-bank and formed the insula Tiberina (di S. Bartolomeo).

We hear for the first time of the *Prata Flaminia* as a section of the same plain about 445 B. C. It was at the time of the second secession, brought about by Virginius, when the tribunes, restored to power, held an assembly of the people in the above named meadows, situated under the Capitoline hill, at the southern end of the plain. The meadows, therefore, formerly owned by the Flaminii, must have become public property; and indeed they appear to have been, at least in part, consecrated to Apollo and called the *Apollinar* (Livy, iii. 63). Some time later a Temple of Apollo, voted in 433, in propitiation of a pestilence, was erected near this site, and dedicated by the consul Cnæus Julius in 439. The well-preserved remains of this venerable monument are to be seen in some caves that can be reached from the convent of S. Maria in Campitelli.

[1] LITERATURE on the Temple of Via degli Specchi, so little known to students. — Luigi Canina, *Annal. Inst.*, 1838, p. 1, pls. A, B; and *Edifizii di Roma antica*, vol. ii. pl. vi. — Urlichs, *Beschreibung*, iii³, p. 30. — Virginio Vespignani, *Bull. com.*, 1873, p. 212, pls. v., vi. — Brunn, in *Sitzungsberichte der Münchener Akad.*, 1876, p. 343, identifies these remains with the Templum Neptuni in Circo Flaminio.

LITERATURE on the Temple of Apollo, the *Ædes Apollinis Medici* of Livy, xl. 51. — Rodolfo Lanciani, *Bull. Inst.*, 1878, p. 218; and *Bull. com.*, 1883, p. 188. — Carlo Pascal, *Il più antico tempio d'Apollo a Roma* (in Bull. com., 1893, p. 46). — Gioacchino Corrado, *Memorie di S. Maria in portico*, pianta lett. S. Rome, 1871.

Besides the estate of the Flaminii, we hear of another field bequeathed to the people by the vestal Tarracia. Then comes the section set apart for the breaking in of horses (Trigarium), and another where horse races, said to have been instituted by Romulus in honor of Mars, were celebrated (Equirriorum Campus). The bank of the river was lined with bathing-houses, where the young men, tired of horse-riding, could refresh themselves with a plunge in the cool stream. There were also quays for the landing of wine (Portus Vinarius) and other merchandise brought in by barges from Etruria and Sabinâ.

At the time of Augustus the campus was already divided into the "greater" and the "lesser." (See Strabo, v. 3; and Catullus, lv. 3.) The origin and the scope of such division are not clear: one thing is certain, that in the first century of our era, while the name of Circus Flaminius had been extended to the whole ninth region, that of Campus Martius had been restricted to a very limited space, lined by stone cippi, one of which (Corpus Inscr., vol. vi. n. 874) was discovered in 1592 in the foundations of the Palazzo Serlupi Crescenzi, Via del Seminario. This fragment of the historical campus, as it were, destined to perpetuate the memory of a state of things which had long ceased to exist, is located in the region of the present Palazzo Serlupi, also by the "Vita Sev. Alex.," 26.

LITERATURE. — Rodolfo Lanciani, *La basilica Matidies et Marcianes* (in Bull. com., 1883, p. 11).

B. THE MONUMENTS OF THE PRATA FLAMINIA (AD CIRCUM FLAMINIUM).

The group comprises the Circus Flaminius, indirectly connected with the *stabula quatuor Factionum sex;* the Temple of Hercules, keeper of the Circus; those of Bellona (of Mars), of Castor, of Piety, of Volkan; and lastly, the Via Flaminia.

XXXVII. CIRCUS FLAMINIUS. — Among the important works undertaken for public convenience in the period between the first and second Punic wars, those of C. Flaminius Nepos, censor in 221 B. C., and killed at Lake Trasimenus in 217, hold a prominent place. He built a circus in that section of the campus which bore his family name, and opened a highroad between Rome and northern Italy. The proximity of the circus to the gates of the city and to the Capitol made it a favorite place for popular meetings, like the one of 211 B. C., in which Marcellus cleared himself of the accusations brought forward by his enemies; and the other of 189, in which Fulvius Nobilior, the conqueror of Ætolia, conferred the military rewards on his officers and men. The tribuni plebis used it constantly for meeting and addressing their constituents; and fairs (*nundinæ*) were held periodically under cover of its arcades. Augustus filled the race-course with water in 6 B. C., and gave the citizens a specimen of alligator-hunting, in which thirty of these monsters were killed.

The remains of the circus were very conspicuous in the Middle Ages, and disappeared from view only in the second half of the sixteenth century. Three documents describe them in detail : a bull of Celestin III. of 1192; a passage in Andrea Fulvio's " Antiqq. Urbis," book iii. p. lxv.; and another in Ligorio's " Circhi," p. 17'. The bull of Celestin calls the ruins " the golden castle " (*castellum aureum*); mentions the arcades which ran the whole length of the circus (*parietes altæ et antiquæ in circuitu positæ*); the principal doorway in the middle of the carceres opening towards the *campitello;* a garden near (or within?) the circus full of great remains; the slopes upon which the seats for the spectators were placed; and lastly, churches and houses built against and above the ruins.

Fulvio says : " The shape and the plan of the circus can still be easily made out; there are traces of the seats at S. Caterina de' Funari, so-called from the ropewalks established under the porticoes. The length of the circus is marked by the house of Pietro Margani and the church of S. Salvatore in Pensili at one end, and the palace of Ludovico Mattei at the other; the width runs between the street called le Botteghe Oscure on one side, and the Torre del Cetrangolo on the other. The head of the circus (viz., the curved end with the Porta Triumphalis) is to be seen by the Mattei Palace, in the region called Calcarara on account of the lime-burners who use the arcades for kilns."

Ligorio, while confirming Fulvio's statements as to the size and orientation of the circus, says that Ludovico Mattei is responsible for the destruction of its last remains. " Only a few years ago [about 1550] I was able to design the curved end, and measure its plan; but in laying the foundations of his house Messer Ludovico has uprooted its remains, made of great blocks of travertine; I have

seen the floor of the arena, made of concrete (*opus signinum*) very
hard and thick, covered here and there with patches of mosaic;
and also the channel (*euripus*) which separates the seats from the
arena.   Water still runs in the euripus, from a spring called il
Fonte di Calcarara, visible under the house of a dyer close by."
The Mattei Palace mentioned by Ligorio is not the present one
opposite the church of S. Caterina de' Funari, but the Palazzo
Paganica on the street and piazza of the same name, in the court
and in the cellars of which a few walls are still to be seen.   The
spring of which he speaks has been lately rediscovered by Narducci.[1]   Some of the marble ornaments brought to light in the
course of the excavations are to be seen in the cortile of the present
palace.   The name of le Botteghe Oscure given to the street which
skirts the circus on the south side is a recollection of the long line
of arcades which gave shelter to the rope-makers and lime-burners.

While the statements of Fulvio and Ligorio, and the existing
remains of the round end at Piazza Paganica, allow us to locate
the circus within well-defined limits, and to assign it a length of
about 297 metres, and a width of about 120, the drawings of
Antonio da Sangallo the elder, of Antonio the younger, of Vinandus
Pighius, and of Baldassare Peruzzi give us the means of restoring
its plan and elevation.

Peruzzi's sketch is to be found in sheet 408 of the "Uffizi."   The
intercolumniation (from centre to centre of the Doric semicolumns
of the lower portico) measured about 7 metres, the diameter of the
semicolumns 0.74 metre, the abacus of the capital 1.02 metre; the
direction of the circus diverged by 19° from the west.   Sangallo
the elder gives the sketch of the cornice of the lower order (Uffizi,
2050), while Sangallo the younger designs "uno basamento di uno
edifitio trouato in casa di messer Gregorio di Serlupis presso alla
torre del melangolo," the same tower where Fulvio places the carceres of the circus (Uffizi, 2087).   In the last place, Vinandus Pighius gives a sketch of an architrave with the inscription of Anicius
Faustus (Fig. 177, p. 454), discovered about 1550 (Cod. Berolin.,
f. 120′).

LITERATURE. — Antonio Nibby, *Roma antica*, vol. i. p. 607. — Giacomo
Lumbroso, *Memor. di Cassiano dal Pozzo*, p. 48. — C. Ludovico Visconti, *Bull.
com.*, 1873, p. 217.— *Notizie Scavi*, 1877, p. 80. — *Corpus Inscr.*, vol. vi. n. 1676,
8423, 9136. — Emiliano Sarti, *Archivio Società storia patria*, vol. ix. p. 484. —
Mariano Armellini, *Chiese*, pp. 552, 555, 558. — Heinrich Jordan, *Topogr.*, vol.
ii. p. 383.

[1] *Della Fognatura*, p. 38.

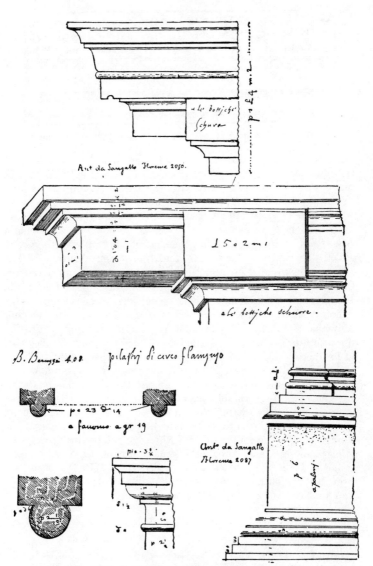

Fig. 176. — Architectural Details of the Circus Flaminius.

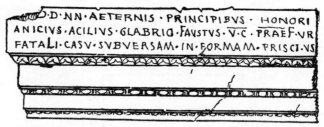

D·NN·AETERNIS · PRINCIPIBVS · HONORI
ANICIVS·ACILIVS·GLABRIO·FAVSTVS·V·C·PRAEF·VR
FATALI·CASV·SVBVERSAM·IN·FORMAM·PRISCINS

Fig. 177. — The Inscription of Anicius Faustus, from the Circus Flaminius (?).

XXXVIII. Stabula quatuor Factionum VI.: barracks of the four (six) squadrons of charioteers, connected with all Roman racing grounds, but especially with the Circus Flaminius by location and proximity. The factiones were distinguished by a color. At first there were only two, the red, "russata," and the white, "albata;" next came the blue, "veneta," probably in the time of Augustus; and soon after the green, "prasina." Lastly, Domitian added the purple, "purpurea," and the golden, "aurata." The barracks in which they and their race-horses were quartered are generally placed on the site of the present church of S. Lorenzo in Damaso and of the Palazzo della Cancelleria, because one of the denominations of the same church is *in prasino;* but the fact that only one of four (or six) factions is alluded to, coupled with the discovery of a pedestal dedicated to an *agitator factionis Prasinæ*, at la Cancelleria, and of a water-pipe on which the name "factionis prasinæ," and no other, is engraved,[1] proves in my opinion that there was not one great establishment for the four squadrons together, but four establishments, one for each. They covered approximately the space between the churches of S. Lucia della Chiavica, and S. Lorenzo in Prasino, and the English college, Via Monserrato, in the foundations of which an interesting inscription (Corpus, n. 621) and "una bellissima statua di un Fauno" were found in 1682. The blues are recorded in n. 9719 [Crescens, natione Bessus, (olearius) de portic(u) Pallantian(a) venetian(orum)]; and in No. 10,044, a pedestal erected in memory of one of their great victories, found at S. Lucia della chiavica. The cemetery of the charioteers was in the Vatican district, along the Via Triumphalis.

Literature. — Lovatelli Ersilia Caetani, *Bull. com.*, 1878, p. 164. — Rodolfo Lanciani, *Ancient Rome*, p. 213. — Friedländer, *Sittengeschichte*, fünfte Aufl.,

[1] *Corpus Inscr.*, vol. vi. n. 10,058 (and 10,063) ; *Bull. com.*, 1887, p. 10.

1881, vol. ii. p. 460. — *Corpus Inscr.*, vol. vi. part ii. pp. 1307–1321. — Pietro Sante Bartoli, *Mem.* 107 (in Fea's Miscellanea, vol. i. p. ccliii.).

XXXIX. TEMPLUM HERCULIS MAGNI CUSTODIS AD CIRCUM FLAMINIUM (Temple of Hercules, the great keeper of the Circus Flaminius). — In the garden of the small cloisters annexed to the church of S. Nicolò ai Cesarini there are remains of a circular temple with fluted columns of tufa coated with white plaster, and resting upon a basement of travertine. The church itself rests on the foundations of another temple, rectangular in shape, and built likewise of tufa coated with stucco. Both appear in fragment xvi. 110 of the "Forma Urbis," here reproduced. Three or four hundred years ago they were in a much better state of preservation. The round temple was named "Veneris in Calcarario," "calcararium" meaning the region of the lime-kilns and of the lime-burners, which extended from the Piazza dell' Olmo and S. Lucia dei Ginnasi to the church of the Stimmate, once called of SS. Quaranta in Calcarari. The name, however, was wrong : the elegant little structure belongs to Hercules the protector of the circus, to Hercules the oracular god, so much in favor with the charioteers. It stands in the same relation to the Circus Flaminius as the round Temple of Hercules Invictus of the eleventh region stood to the Circus Maximus. Speaking of the temples of Hercules in general, Vitruvius (i. 7, 1) contends that they must be raised near the gymnasium or the amphitheatre of each city; and in case there should be no gymnasium or amphitheatre, near the circus at least. Vitruvius therefore places the god in relation first to athletes, then to gladiators, lastly to charioteers; but in Rome the charioteers were his favorites. The birthday of the god, February 1, was celebrated with races (Corpus, vol. i. 336, 337), and other races were run on June 4, near the Porticus Minucia, before a colossal bronze statue of him.

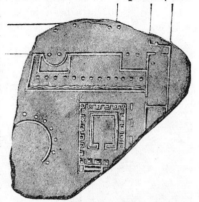

Fig. 178. — A Fragment of the Forma Urbis showing round Temple of Hercules.

LITERATURE. — Ludwig Preller, *Gr. Mythol.*, ii. 3, p. 276. — Theodor

Mommsen, *Gesch. d. röm. Munzwesens*, p. 619, n. 259. — Babelon, *Descript. des monnaies de la République*, ii. 565, gens Volteia, n. 1–5. — *Corpus Inscr.*, i. n. 1538, p. 561 (and p. 301); vi. 335; ix. 421. — Roscher, *Ausführliches Lexicon*, p. 2979.

By an almost inexplicable coincidence, which is certainly unique in the annals of the plunder and destruction of ancient Rome, the Hercules Invictus and the Hercules Magnus Custos, both cast in bronze, both of colossal size, both still glittering under their coating of gold, have been found concealed near their respective temples. We possess but scanty information about the finding

Fig. 179. — The Finding of the Bronze Statue of the Hercules Magnus Custos, August 8, 1864.

of the Hercules Invictus, *ad duodecim portas*, viz., near the carceres of the Circus Maximus, which took place under Sixtus IV. (1471–1484).[1] That of the Hercules Magnus Custos took place on August 8, 1864, near the Piazza di Campo de Fiori, in the foundations of the Palazzo Pio-Righetti, which stands on the ruins of Pompey's Theatre. The statue was lying in a deep cavity,

[1] Gio. Battista de Rossi, *L' ara massima di Ercole* (in Annal. Inst., 1854, p. 28). — Heinrich Jordan, *Topographie*, i2, 491. — *Corpus Inscr.*, vol. vi. pp. 313–319. — Rodolfo Lanciani, *Pagan and Christian Rome*, p. 69.

between two walls of peperino, and was carefully protected with
slabs of portasanta placed one against another like the tiles of a
roof. It is evident that the charioteers, still flourishing in Rome
at the time of the first barbarian invasions, exerted themselves
to save the valuable bronze images of their god from outrage and
plunder; and they succeeded so well that it took ten centuries to
rediscover the hiding-place of the Invictus, and fourteen and a
half that of the Magnus Custos.

The accompanying original sketch of 1864 represents this last
event. (Fig. 179.)

The statue, slightly restored by Tenerani, has been given a
place of honor in the rotunda of the Vatican Museum, No. 544.
That of the Invictus has been removed from the salone of the
Capitoline Museum to a hardly decent room in the Palazzo de'
Conservatori. (Compare Helbig's Guide, vol. i. p. 211, n. 299;
and p. 454, n. 613.)

LITERATURE. — Ovid, *Fasti*, vi. 209. — Fabio Gori, *Nuova dimostrazione che
la statua scoperta al Biscione*, etc. Rome, Chiassi, 1864. — Carlo Ludovico
Visconti, *Osservazioni sulla statua di bronzo*, etc. (in Giornale arcadico, vol.
xxxix., nuova serie, 1864). — Enrico Fabiani, *L' Ercole del palazzo Pio*, Rome,
Menicanti, 1864; and *Ancora dell' Ercole del palazzo Pio*, same year, Nov. 1.
— Ugo Koehler, *Bull. Inst.*, 1864, p. 227. — Rodolfo Lanciani, *Annal. Inst.*,
1883, p. 11, tav. A, B. — Gio. Battista de Rossi, *Bull. com.*, 1893, p. 191. —
Furtwaengler, *Masterpieces*, p. 296, n. 3.

A third centre of the worship of Hercules by the charioteers was discovered
in August, 1889, outside the Porta Portese, at the southwest end of the new
railway station. It consisted of a sacred cave hewn out of the live rock,
with a niche and an altar at the bottom, and dedicatory inscriptions stating
that the whole had been done by a certain L. Domitius Permissus by order
(*imperio*) of the god. There were two
arœ, a statuette of Hercules Victor, another of Hercules Cubans, architectural
fragments, fragments of pottery, and
above all a set of seven portrait-hermæ
of charioteers, in white marble. Helbig thinks that the seven hermæ, although by different sculptors, date from
the same period, that of the Julian Em-

Fig. 180. — The Shrine of the
Hercules Invictus, discovered
in 1889, on the Via Portuensis.

perors. This discovery must be compared with that (made in the same place, March, 1632, by Andrea Brugiotti) of an inscription describing how Plotius Romanus, a consul suffectus of uncertain date, had raised a temple to Hercules Invictus in this tract of the Via Portuensis.

This interesting group of monuments has been unhappily dispersed: the sacred cave and the altar covered with bas-reliefs of stucco was destroyed in 1889; the seven heads of charioteers are exhibited in the south wing of the quadrangle of the Museo delle Terme, somewhat apart from each other (n. 16, 18, 22, 24, 30, 34, 38). I do not know the fate of the stone statuettes and of the two aræ of Domitius Permissus.

LITERATURE. — *Notizie degli Scavi*, 1889, p. 223. — *Mittheilungen*, 1891, p. 149. — *Corpus Inscr.*, vol. vi. n. 332. — Wolfgang Helbig, *Guide*, vol. ii. p. 206, n. 1007, 1013.

C. THE MONUMENTS OF THE FORUM HOLITORIUM.

(See § lix. p. 511.)

XL. The Forum Holitorium (Piazza Montanara), the central market for vegetables, will be described in § lix., with other similar establishments lining the left bank of the Tiber " above and below bridge."

From a monumental point of view the Forum Holitorium was remarkable, on account of the many temples and porticoes by which it was inclosed on every side. The temples were four at least, viz. : —

A. ÆDES SPEI (Temple of Hope), vowed by M. Atilius Calatinus in 254 B. C., during the first Punic war, burnt to ashes several times, and rebuilt lastly by Germanicus.

B. ÆDES PIETATIS, vowed by Manius Acilius Glabrio at the battle of the Thermopylai, 191 B. C., and dedicated by his son ten years later.

C. ÆDES IUNONIS SOSPITÆ, built in 197 B. C., by C. Cornelius Cethegus.

D. TEMPLUM IANI, connected with the legend of the Fabii (Festus, Müll., p. 285), rebuilt first by C. Duilius in the third century before Christ, and secondly by Tiberius. The Roman calendars in mentioning the feast-days of this temple, August 17 and October 18, place it " ad theatrum Marcelli."

The porticoes were two at least, the MINUCIA VETUS and the FRUMENTARIA, the work of M. Minucius, consul in A. D. 110.

D. The Pompeian Buildings.

XLI. The group of buildings raised by Pompey the Great in the centre of the plain, known to topographers as the group *ad theatrum Lapideum*, presents this curious fact: that while it is known in every particular, from texts of classics, from plans and designs taken at various times, and from discoveries made to the present day, no trace of it exists above ground. The theatre, which contained 17,580 seats (*loca*); the curia, where Julius Cæsar was murdered on March 15, 44 b. c.; the Porticus Pompeiana, inclosing exquisite gardens; the portico of the hundred columns (hecatostylon); the Temple of Victory on the highest point of the cavea; and the Temple of Minerva Campensis, have all been leveled to the ground or have disappeared. The description, therefore, of the Theatrum Lapideum and of the monuments near it cannot find a place in a book which treats only of existing ruins.

Among the many works of art saved from the wreck of these buildings, two are deservedly popular among students: the Pompey of the Palazzo Spada and the Minerva of the Galleria Giustiniani.

The discovery of the colossal statue of the hero (so-called) is thus described by Flaminio Vacca: "I remember that in the Via de' Leutari, close to the Cancelleria, at the time of Julius III. (1553), a marble statue of Pompey, fifteen palms high, was found in a cellar. The parting wall with the next house happened to fall just across the neck, so that the owner of each house claimed it for his own: the first because the largest part of the statue was lying on his side of the wall, the second because the head, the noblest part, and that which gave a name to the statue, happened to be on the other side. After mature discussion the ignorant judge decided that the head should be severed from the body and each part handed over to its legitimate possessor. Poor Pompey! It was not enough that he should have suffered once the same evil fate at the hands of Ptolemy! When Cardinal Capodiferro [1] heard of this foolish arrangement, he made an appeal to the pope. Julius III. had the statue carefully excavated on his own account, leaving a sum of five hundred scudi to be divided among the two fighting neighbors, and made a present of it to the cardinal" (Mem., 57).

Modern art critics, who seem to delight in making us disbelieve

---

[1] Girolamo Capodiferro, a Roman patrician, born in 1502, legate to France and Portugal in 1541, bishop of Nice in 1542, cardinal of S. Giorgio in 1544, built a noble palace in the piazza which still bears his name. After his death in 1559 the palace passed into the hands of Cardinal Bernardino Spada.

what were once considered fundamental points in the history of ancient art, deny any connection between this noble portrait-statue and Pompey the Great.   Carlo Fea, in his "Osservazioni intorno alla celebre statua detta di Pompeo lette il 10 settembre [1812] nell' Accad. rom. d' Archeologia," called the attention of archæologists to the traces of a band or ribbon, visible on the sword-belt

Fig. 181. — The so-called Pompey the Great of the Palazzo Spada.

near the left shoulder, and on the cloak behind the clasp, which cannot possibly belong to the present head, but to an original one encircled by a garland or a tænia. Wolfgang Helbig, comparing in 1886 the Spada head with those on the family coins of Sextus Pompeïus, and with three portrait heads of the hero undoubtedly genuine, said it was needless to discuss a question already settled in the minds of most archæologists. Helbig has again taken up the controversy in vol. ii. p. 170 of the "Guide," concluding with these words: " The writer feels it utterly superfluous to waste more words on the point, since a head has recently been found which ... may be unreservedly recognized as a likeness of Pompey. The head placed on the statue is of an unknown individual ; ... the two neck pieces do not harmonize ; ... the head also differs from the body in the quality of the marble. ... The alien head had been placed on the body in ancient times."

LITERATURE. — Carlo Fea, *Notizie degli Scavi dell' anfiteatro Flavio*. Rome, 1813, p. 31. —Wolfgang Helbig, *Mittheilungen*, 1886, p. 37, pl. ii.; and *Guide*, vol. ii. p. 172. — Emil Braun, *Ruins and Museums*, p. 459.

The Minerva, formerly in the possession of the Giustiniani and Prince Lucien Bonaparte, and now one of the ornaments of the Braccio Nuovo in the Vatican (n. 114), was certainly found near the church named after her (S. Maria sopra Minerva), among the ruins of the temple erected by Pompey the Great in 62 B. C., injured by the fire of Titus, and restored by Domitian under the name of "Minerva Chalcidica." Pliny (vii. 27) gives a copy of the inscription probably engraved in front of the temple : " Cnæus Pompeius Magnus, triumphant general, having brought to a close a war of thirty years, having defeated and put to flight or death, or made prisoners, 1,201,803 men, taken 846 war vessels, conquered 1538 open or fortified towns, and occupied the lands between the Red Sea and the Palus Mæotis (Sea of Azov), offers this temple to Minerva." Andrea Fulvio describes the temple as nearly perfect in 1513. It seems to have been destroyed by Clement VIII. in 1527, except the inclosure wall of the sacred area which appears in one of Alò Giovannoli's sketches of 1619.

E. THE AUGUSTAN BUILDINGS.

There are remains of the Mausoleum, of the Sun-dial, of the Ara Pacis, of the portico of Octavia, and of the theatre of Marcellus.

XLII. MAUSOLEUM, USTRINUM, SILVÆ ET AMBULATIONES. — Of the mausoleum, built by Augustus in 27 B. C., forty-one years before his death, we have a description by Strabo, and ruins which substantiate that description in its main lines. It was composed of a circular basement of white marble, 88 metres in diameter, which supported a cone of earth, planted with cypresses and evergreens. The bronze statue of the Emperor towered above the trees. The vaults were approached from the south, the entrance being flanked by monuments of great interest, such as the two obelisks now in the Piazza del Quirinale and the Piazza dell' Esquilino; the copies (in marble or bronze) of the decrees of the Senate in honor of the personages buried within; and above all, the *Res gestœ divi Augusti*, a political will, autobiography, and apology, the importance of which surpasses that of any other epigraphic document relating to the history of the Roman Empire.

LITERATURE on the *Res gestœ.* — Theodor Mommsen, *Res gestœ divi Augusti,* 2d edit. Berlin, Weidmann, 1883. — Geppert, *Zum Monumentum Ancyranum.* Berlin, 1887. — Gaston Boissier, *Le Testament d'Auguste* (in Revue des deux mondes, xliv. (1863) p. 734). — Luigi Cantarelli, *L' iscrizione di Ancyra* (in Bull. com., 1889, pp. 3, 57).

The gates of the mausoleum were opened for the first time in 28 B. C. to receive the ashes of young Marcellus, whose premature death is so touchingly lamented by Virgil (vi. 872); for the last in A. D. 98, for the reception of the ashes of Nerva. We hear no more of it until 410, when the Goths must have ransacked the Imperial vaults. No harm, however, seems to have been done to the building itself. Like the mausoleum of Metella, of Severus Alexander, and of Hadrian, it was subsequently converted into a stronghold. Mausoleum and stronghold were nearly destroyed in 1167 by the populace, infuriated at the news of the defeat which the Roman army, led by the Colonnas, had suffered on Whit Monday of the same year in the territory of Tusculum. The shapeless ruins were again put into a state of defense by the Colonnas in 1241. The corpse of Cola di Rienzo was cremated here in October, 1354. Archæological exploration began in 1519. On July 14 of that year Baldassare Peruzzi discovered and copied some of the historical inscriptions *in situ*, and made drawings of the basement which I have reproduced in the " Bull. com." of 1882, p. 151, pls. xvi., xvii., from the originals in the " Uffizi," n. 393, 394, 2067, and 2068. The obelisk, now in the Piazza dell' Esquilino, was found also in 1519 near the church of S. Rocco. The Soderini family turned the place into a hanging garden about 1550, and filled it with remarkable works of statuary.

In the spring of 1777, while the corner house between the Via del Corso and the Via degli otto Cantoni was being built, the Ustrinum, or sacred inclosure for the cremation of the members of the Imperial family, came to light with many historical monuments. The first object to appear was the beautiful urn of alabastro cotognino now in the Galleria delle Statue, n. 421; then came several inscribed pedestals, some intended to indicate the

MAVSOLEVM AVGVSTI

Romæ collapsa Mausolei Imper. Augusti; quod elegantissimi fuit sepulchri a se constructi ad humandos consanguineos suos, in quo ipse et sui sepeliuntur. Imposuit autem illi nomen Mausolei, eo quod constructerit ad similitudinem illius inclyti sepulchri, quod Mausolo Regi Cariæ ab Artemisia sua conjuge erectum fuit; eius autem reliquiæ aliæ non egrmantur præterqua muru circularis ex cocto lapide, seu lateribus cæstructi; aliquot in quibus latebant duæ piramides fractæ, quaru una a Sixto V.PP. translata et erecta, iuxt ante Basilica S.Maria Maioris Mausolei autem isius structuræ uicina est Ecclesia S. Roschi ad emori Tiberis ripa, uocate uulgo ripetta adiuncta adibus DD Soderineis.

Fig. 182. — The Mausoleum of Augustus, turned into a Garden by the Soderini about 1550.

spot on which each prince had been cremated, others the places
where the ashes had been deposited, — the former end with the
formula "hic crematus [or cremata] est;" the latter with the
words "hic situs [or sita] est." The cippi mention the names of
Caius Cæsar; of Tiberius, d. 37; of Agrippina, wife of Germanicus,
d. 33, buried in the mausoleum 37; of Nero, Gaius, Gaius Tiberius,
and Livilla, sons and daughter of Germanicus; of Junia Silana,
first wife of Nero Cæsar; of Tiberius Cæsar, son of Drusus and
Livia, murdered 37; and of Vespasian, son of T. Flavius Clemens,
and nephew of the Emperor of that name. The mausoleum of
Augustus and its contents have not escaped the spoliation and
desecration which has raged in past times, and occasionally rages
still. The building, formerly a bull-ring, is now used as a circus;
its basement is concealed by mean houses; the two obelisks have
been removed, one by Sixtus V. in 1587 to the Esquiline, the other
by Pius VI. in 1786 to the Quirinal; the urn of Agrippina, used
as a grain measure in the Middle Ages, is kept in the Palazzo dei
Conservatori; six urns belong to the Vatican; three others have
been destroyed.

The shell of the mausoleum, built of reticulated masonry, can
be examined from the court of the Palazzo Correa, Via de' Ponte-
fici, and from that of the Palazzo Valdambrini, Via di Ripetta, n.
102.

LITERATURE. — *Corpus Inscr.*, vol. vi. p. 157, n. 884-895, 914, 8686. —
Strabo, v. 361. — *Res gestœ*, 2d edit. p. ix. — Pietro Sante Bartoli, *Gli antichi
sepolcri*, pl. 72. — Antonio Nibby, *Roma antica*, vol. ii. p. 520. — Otto Hirschfeld, *Die Kaiserlichen Grabstätten in Rom*, Sitzungsb. d. Berl. Akad., Dec. 9,
1886. — Luigi Borsari, *Bull. com.*, 1885, p. 89. — Flaminio Vacca, *Mem.* 97 (in
Fea's Miscellanea, vol. i. p. xciv).

XLIII. HOROLOGIUM or SOLARIUM (sun-dial). — Pliny (xxxvi.
10), speaking of the obelisks removed from Egypt to Rome by the
first Emperors, says that Augustus had turned to a practical purpose the one raised by him (in the year 10 B. C.) in the Campus
Martius south of the mausoleum. It served as a γνώμων or needle
to a great sun-dial, the lines of which were traced on a pavement
of white marble, with rules of gilt metal. Pliny says that thirty
years before he wrote the "Natural History" the sun-dial had
become defective, but he could not tell whether in consequence
of an earthquake or because the frequent floods of the Tiber had
made the foundations of the obelisk sink. The inscriptions of
the pedestal (Corpus, 702) are exactly like those of the obelisk of
the Circus Maximus now in the Piazza del Popolo: "imp. Cæsar

Augustus . . . Ægupto in potestatem populi romani redacta, Soli donum dedit." Both came from Heliopolis: the one of the Circus, 23.91 metres high, dates from the time of Ramses the Great; the one of the Horologium, 21.79 metres high, from the time of Psammetik I. The obelisk was still standing on its base in the eighth or ninth century, and the date and the circumstances attending its downfall are still a matter of speculation (Norman Fire of 1084?).

In the year 1463, while Cardinal Filippo Calandrino was laying the foundations of the chapel of SS. Philip and James in S. Lorenzo in Lucina (where he was buried in 1476), a considerable portion of the dial was laid bare. Another portion seems to have come to light from the foundations of the chapter-house, about the time of Sixtus IV. The lines of gilt metal were still set in their marble grooves; and on the border of the dial there were the images of the winds, accompanied by their names, AQVILO, SEPTENTRIO, BOREAS, etc. The discovery of the obelisk itself is thus related by Lælius Podager (the gouty) in a marginal note to Mazochio's "Vatic. cod.," f. 11: "In the time of Julius II. (1503–1513), while a certain barber was digging in the garden of his house between S. Lorenzo in Lucina and the house of Cardinal Grassi, he discovered the lower portion of an obelisk and its pedestal, the inscription of which mentioned the conquest of Egypt by Augustus. I recognized at once in this monolith the dial mentioned by Pliny, and I learned from people living in that neighborhood that, every time they had excavated the ground for their wine-cellars or drains, they had come across wonderful celestial signs, beautifully designed with lines of metal. Applications were made to Julius II. to have the pavement cleared and the obelisk set up in its former place, but he was too distracted by his wars to mind these things. The barber lost patience and buried the pedestal over again." Ligorio affirms having seen the obelisk under the house of the celebrated banker Spanocchi. Sixtus V. gave a commission to his architect Fontana to report on the possibility of raising it on its pedestal, but he found it too much damaged by fire to be of any use. It was examined for the third time about 1666, when Athanase Kircher proposed to Alexander VII. to set it up in front of S. Maria degli Angeli, in the Piazza di Termini, not yet incumbered by the granaries of Clement XI. (1705). At last Benedict XIV., in 1748, caused it to be brought to the surface, under the skillful guidance of Maestro Zabaglia. Pius VI. in 1792 restored the damaged portions with

the granite of the column of Antoninus Pius (p. 510), and set up
the obelisk in front of the Curia Innocenziana, now the House of
Parliament. While searching for the missing portions, Zabaglia
discovered a round stone 1.75 metre in diameter, with squares,
triangles, and other geometrical emblems engraved upon it. The
stone was removed to the Villa Valenti Conzaga, now Bonaparte.

LITERATURE. — *Corpus Inscr.*, vol. vi. n. 702. — Gio. Battista de Rossi, *Note
pomponiane di topogr. rom.* (in Studii e docum. di storia e diritto, 1882, p. 55).
— *Codex musei florent.*, 7ᵃ, f. 103′. — Baldassare Peruzzi, *Cod. vat.*, 3439, f. 2′.
— Giuliano da Sangallo, *Cod. Siena*, 8, iv. 5. — Ridolfino Venuti, *Cod. vat.*,
9024, f. 181. — Angelo Bandini, *Dell' obelisco di Cesare Augusto*. Rome, 1750.
— Francesco Cancellieri, *Il Mercato*, etc., p. 170 ; *Colonna antonina*, p. 24 ;
Descrizione delle carte cinesi della villa Valenti, p. 14.

XLIV. ARA PACIS AUGÙSTÆ. — Among the honors voted to
Augustus by the Senate in 13 B. C., on the occasion of his triumphal return from the Germanic and Gaulish campaigns, was the
erection of a votive altar in the Curia itself. Augustus refused
it, consenting at the same time to the erection of an altar in the
Campus Martius which should be offered to Peace. Its dedication took place on January 30 of the same year. Judging from
the fragments which have been brought to light at various times
from the foundations of the Palazzo Fiano Ottoboni, at the corner
of the Via del Corso and Via in Lucina, the Ara Pacis was one of
the most exquisite artistic productions of the Golden Age. The
discoveries were made in the second quarter of the sixteenth
century, in 1568, and in 1859. Three pieces were found on the
first occasion, and removed, first, to the Palazzo della Valle Capranica, later on (1584) to the villa of Cardinal Ferdinando de'
Medici ; fifteen or twenty on the second, which were purchased
by Cardinal Ricci di Montepulciano ; all the rest on September 7,
1859, in the recess which the Palazzo Fiano makes in the Via in
Lucina between n. 16 B and 16 C. All these fragments, dispersed
in Rome (Palazzo Fiano, Villa Medici, Museo Vaticano), Florence
(Uffizi), and Paris (Louvre), have been illustrated by Petersen
in the "Roemischen Mittheilungen" of 1894 ; he also proposes
a reconstruction of the monument from the designs of V. Rau-
scher.

LITERATURE. — *Res gestæ*, 2d edit. (Mommsen), p. 49. — Von Duhn, *Ann.
Inst.*, 1881, p. 302. — Eugen Petersen, *L' ara Pacis augustæ* (in Mittheil.
1894, p. 171, pl. vi).

XLV. OPERA S. PORTICUS OCTAVIÆ. — The portico was

originally built by Q. Cæcilius Metellus about 147 B. C. to inclose the temples of Jupiter Stator (?), the first marble structure of its kind in Rome, built by himself from the designs of Hermodoros; and that of Juno Regina, erected by Æmilius Lepidus in 178. In the year 32, both the temples and the colonnade which surrounded the sacred area were rebuilt on a scale of greater magnificence by

Fig. 183. — The Ara Pacis Augustæ — Details.

Augustus, under the name of his sister Octavia. Augustus availed himself of the " manubiæ " of the Dalmatic war, and of the skill of his favorite architects Sauros and Batrachos. Pliny says that, as they were denied the privilege of signing their work with their names, they hit upon the device of carving among the flutings of the columns their *armoiries parlantes*, a lizard, σαῦρος, and a frog, βάτραχος. The same writer has another anecdote regarding the statues of the two gods. When the temples were ready to receive the statues, the porters by mistake placed the statue of Jupiter in

Juno's cella, and that of Juno in the cella of Jupiter. The augurs to whom the case was submitted decided that it was the will of the gods that their images should remain as they were. There are exquisite remains of both temples in or under the houses Via di S. Angelo in Pescheria, n. 8 and n. 11 : those of Jupiter above ground, those of Juno below ; but they are allowed to remain in such a state of neglect and filth that it is hardly worth while to try to approach them.

Fig. 184. — The Ara Pacis Augustæ — Details.

The portico was in the form of a rectangular double colonnade, with "Iani," or four-faced archways, at the four corners, and beautiful propylaia on the side fronting the temples. It measured 135 metres in depth, 115 in breadth. On the side opposite the propylaia, viz., behind the temples, there were a "schola," a curia for the meeting of the Senate, and two libraries, one for Greek, one for Latin works. The whole group of buildings, the "Opera Octaviæ," as it was technically called, was crowded with masterpieces; and in the area in front of the temples were ranged the seventy-five bronze equestrian statues of the generals and friends of Alexander the Great who perished at the ford of the Granikos. They were the work of Lysippos, and had fallen a prey to Metellus at the close of the Macedonian war. It is not improbable that the beautiful bronze horse found in April, 1849, in the Vicolo delle Palme, Trastevere, and now in the hall of Bronzes of the Palazzo dei Conservatori, originally formed part of the herd exhibited in the portico of Octavia.

The temple of Jupiter contained the statue of Juno by Dionysios, the Pan and the Olympus wrestling, a marvelous group by Heliodoros, the Venus and the Dædalos by Polycharmos, and a Jupiter carved in ivory by Pasiteles. The temple of Juno contained the statue of Jupiter by Polykles and Dionysios, sons of Timarchides, the Æsculapius and the Diana by Praxiteles, the Juno by Polykles, and the Venus by Philiskos.

The schola or "conversation-hall," as Nibby calls it, contained pictures by Antiphilos representing Hesione, Alexander, Philippus, and Athena; four Fauns by an unknown artist; and a statue of Cupid with the thunderbolt, or rather of Alcibiades under the attributes of Cupid, a work attributed by some to Skopas, by others to Praxiteles. It was probably the same Cupid that was offered by Praxiteles to Phryne or Glycera, and by her to the city of Thespiæ. Caligula brought the precious work to Rome in spite of the remonstrances of the Thespians, who said they owned no other work of Greek sculpture. Claudius gave the masterpiece back to its legitimate owners, but Nero took it away for the second time. It was consumed by the flames in the fire of Titus. On April 13, 1878, traces of another Greek masterpiece were found between the propylaia and the temple of Jupiter: an oblong pedestal (now in the court of the Palazzo dei Conservatori) bearing the double inscription —

OPVS · TISICRATIS

CORNELIA · AFRICANI · F
GRACCORVM

The pedestal, which measures 1.76 by 1.20 metres, was made to support the sitting statue of Cornelia, daughter of Scipio Africanus, and mother of the Gracchi, a statue seen and described by Pliny, xxxiv. 31, — "in Octaviæ operibus." The fire of Titus destroyed all the works of art of the "opera," the statue of Cornelia included, as shown to the present day by the calcination of this pedestal. Septimius Severus and Caracalla, the restorers of the portico, placed upon the vacant and half-charred support a biga guided by a woman, a joint work of Piston and of Teisikrates from Sicyon, a distinguished pupil of Eutykrates. On the alleged discovery of the Venus of the Medici, now in Florence, see Bartoli, "Mem.," 108. The inscription on the entablature of the propylaia commemorates the restoration of the portico "incendio corruptam," made in 203. The portico, therefore, had been allowed to remain in a ruinous state for the space of one hundred and twenty-three years, which seems to me hardly credible.

LITERATURE. — Heinrich Jordan, *Forma*, p. 34, plate v. n. 33. — *Corpus Inscr.*, vol. vi. n. 1034, 2347. — Antonio Nibby, *Roma antica*, ii. p. 600. — Rodolfo Lanciani, *Scavi nel portico di Ottavia* (in Bull. Inst., 1878, p. 209). — Angelo Contigliozzi and Angelo Pellegrini, *Bull. Inst.*, 1861, p. 126; *Annal. Inst.*, 1868, p. 114; and *Buonarroti*, serie ii. vol. xi. — Wolfgang Helbig, *Guide*, vol. i. p. 452, n. 608; and p. 455, n. 615. — *Notizie Scavi*, 1878, p. 93; 1883, p. 420; 1888, p. 276. — *Bull. com.*, 1888, p. 132; 1890, p. 66. On the officers attached to the Greek and Latin libraries, see *Corpus Inscr.*, vol. vi. n. 4431–4433, 4435, 4461, 5192, 8708.

The description of the theatre of Marcellus will be found on p. 490, under the head of "Spectacular Buildings."

F. THE MONUMENTA AGRIPPÆ.

XLVI. This most important monumental group of the Campus Martius occupied the plain from the foot of the Pincian and of the Quirinal to the banks of the Tiber by the modern Ponte Sisto. It contained the Porticus Pollæ or Porticus Vipsania, the remains of which I discovered and identified in 1892 on the left of the Via Flaminia (Corso), between the Via di S. Claudio and the Piazza di Sciarra, under the (now destroyed) Palazzo Piombino;[1] the

[1] LITERATURE. — Rodolfo Lanciani, *Bull. com.*, 1892, p. 272; and *Itinerario di Einsiedlen*, p. 35. — Luigi Borsari, *Bull. com.*, 1889, p. 146.

Campus Agrippæ, which extended behind the portico, in the direction of the Quirinal;[1] and the Diribitorium, an edifice where the bulletins of voters on election days were verified and sorted by a committee of nine hundred delegates, — an operation described by the technical verb *diribire* (= dis-hibere). The Diribitorium was the largest "roofed" hall in Rome, the trusses being composed of larch-beams from 29.70 to 35.64 metres long. Its position is not known. Dion Cassius (lxvi. 24) mentions it among the edifices burnt to the ground in the fire of A. D. 80, after the Pantheon and before the theatre of Balbus, and as an absolutely independent building from the Sæpta Iulia (lv. 8). I believe it must have occupied a space on ground to the right (east) of the Via Flaminia opposite the Sæpta, the same on which the Catabulum, or office for parcel-post, was afterwards established.[2]

THE SÆPTA IULIA. — In a letter to Atticus dated September 30, 54 B. C., Cicero, speaking of the projects of Cæsar for the transformation of the campus, says: "We expect to build of marble, and to cover with a roof the space where the comitia tributa have been in the habit of meeting, surrounding it with a lofty portico one mile [1480 metres] long, and adding to it the Villa Publica." The space where the comitia tributa had assembled up to that time was a long strip of land on the left (west) of the Via Flaminia, divided by palisades or ropes into as many compartments as there were electoral sections: thirty for the comitia curiata, thirty-five for the comitia tributa, eighty or eighty-two for the comitia centuriata. On the side of the parallelogram opposite the one by which the electors entered there was a platform called "the bridge" (*pons*), with as many wooden stairs of access as there were electoral compartments. The president sat in the middle of the pons, while the voters, marching past one by one, handed over their voting paper to the rogator.

Cæsar did not live to see his projects accomplished; after his death the works were continued by M. Lepidus the triumvir, who built the portico parallel with the Via Flaminia. Agrippa finished it in 27 B. C., under the name of *Sœpta* or *Septa Iulia*. With the suppression of political liberties, the building lost its importance: it was used sometimes for the meeting of the Senate, more

---

[1] LITERATURE. — Adolf Becker, *Topographie*, p. 595. — Rodolfo Lanciani, *Bull. com.*, 1892, p. 276. — Christian Huelsen, *ibid.*, 1895, p. 45.

[2] LITERATURE. — Fedele Lampertico, *I Diribitores*, Venice, 1833. — Christian Huelsen, *Bull. com.*, 1893, p. 136. — Rodolfo Lanciani, *Itinerario di Einsiedlen*, p. 38.

frequently as a place where curiosities were exhibited for sale. It was restored twice after the fire of Titus, once by Domitian, once by Hadrian. Remains of the portico can be seen under the church of S. Maria in Via and under the Palazzo Doria-Pamfili. The Sæpta Julia began at the corner of the Via del Corso and the Via del Caravita, and ended precisely under the side door by which the church of S. Marco is entered from the Piazza di Venezia. An ancient well-paved street, running at right angles from the Via Flaminia westwards, was discovered under that side door in March, 1875.

Literature. — Gio. Battista Piranesi, *Campo Marzio*, pl. xxv.; and *Antichità di Roma*, vol. iv. p. 47. — Heinrich Jordan, *Forma Urbis*, p. 34, pl. vi. n. 34, 35, 36. — Rodolfo Lanciani, *Itinerario di Einsiedlen*, p. 39. — Christian Huelsen, *Bull. com.*, 1893, p. 119, pls. vi., vii.

Little or nothing is known of the Villa Publica. It was erected on the south border of the campus, between the (subsequent site of the) Sæpta, the Circus Flaminius, and the cliffs of the Capitoline hill, probably on the other side of the above-named street which runs across the Palazzo di Venezia. The villa was finished in 432 b. c., and used for taking the census in the same year. It served also for other public business, which could not be transacted within the walls, such as the levying of troops, the reception of foreign ambassadors before they obtained an audience from the Senate, and of victorious generals awaiting their decree for a triumph. Publius Fonteius Capito rebuilt it at the time of Augustus, to efface, perhaps, the memory of the wholesale slaughter of 8,000 prisoners of war, the "flos Hesperiæ, Latii iam sola iuventus" of Lucanus (ii. 197), perpetrated by order of Sulla on November 4, 82 b. c. The Villa Publica was not simply a field shaded by trees, but contained splendid edifices, which appear in the coins of the Didii and of the Pompeii. Varro, who came to vote in the Sæpta in the elections of 54 b. c., says that his friend Q. Axius and himself, to avoid the scorching sun while waiting for the results of the scrutiny, retired under the shade of the trees of the villa.

The villa and the Sæpta served also for the organization of triumphs, the pageant moving afterwards in the direction of the Portico of Octavia and of the Porta Triumphalis of the Servian walls, through which the victorious general was wont to enter the city. It seems that the portico under shelter of which the procession was organized took the name of Porticus Triumphi, and that it was exactly one mile long; but whether it is the same as that mentioned by Cicero in the Sæpta, or whether it belonged to the villa, it is not possible to say. At all events this Porticus Triumphi, one mile long, became the prototype of similar places in Roman villas for taking a " constitutional " on foot (*ambulatio*) or in a lectica (*gestatio*). However, as very few privileged ones could afford to have in their gardens or villas an avenue or a portico one mile long, it became the fashion to put at the entrance of such ambulationes or gestationes an advertisement to this effect : " If you go round ten times this [oval or circular] allée, you make exactly one thousand paces, or five thousand feet ; " or else, " If you go up and down five times in this apple yard, you will cover a mile." In progress of time these private walks or drives took the regular name of Porticus Triumphi. Three inscriptions relating to them have already been found : one by Ficoroni in Hadrian's villa,[1] one outside the Porta Metroni by Matranga, the third at Baiæ by de Petra. The last says : " This Porticus Triumphi is 556 feet long, 1112 if you go back and forth ; 1112 feet correspond to 222 (double) steps and a half ; therefore, if you go five times over the same length you will cover 556 (double) steps, over a mile." This practice explains the old proverb, " post cænam stabis aut passus mille meabis."

LITERATURE. — Antonio Nibby, *Roma antica*, vol. ii. p. 842. — Adolf Becker, *Topographie*, p. 624. — Gio. Battista de Rossi, *Notizie Scavi*, 1888, p. 709 ; and *Miscellanea di notizie . . . per la topografia*, etc., n. 24, 32. — Babelon, *Monn. de la Républ.*, Fonteia, n. 18.

The bridge of Agrippa, the cloacæ by which he drained the lowest and dampest district of the campus, and the aqueduct of the Virgo have been described in their proper places. I shall now give an account of the two great creations of that statesman, which still stand in their glory among so many ruins of the Campus Martius, — the Pantheon and the Neptunium.

XLVII. PANTHEON. — The Pantheon of Agrippa well deserves the name of the Sphinx of the Campus Martius, because, in spite of its preservation, it remains inexplicable from many points of view. This uncertainty relates to the general outline as well as to the details of the building. The rotunda is obviously disjointed from the portico, and their architectural lines are not in harmony with each other. On the other hand, it is evident that the Pantheon seen by Pliny the elder, in Vespasian's time, was not the one which has come down to us, because there is no place

---

[1] *Corpus Inscr.*, vol. xiv. n. 3695 *a*.

in the present building for the Caryatides of Diogenes the Athenian, and for the capitals of Syracusan bronze which he saw and described as crowning the columns of the temple. Therefore, when I was asked in 1881 to write an official account of the excavations undertaken by Guido Baccelli, the Minister of Public Instruction, who freed the Pantheon from its ignoble surroundings,[1] I began the report by stating that the veil of mystery in which the monument was shrouded had by no means been lifted by these last researches, and that perhaps it never would be. We were far from supposing that before a few years had elapsed we should discover another, nay, two more Pantheons under the existing one, and should be able to declare that Agrippa's name engraved on the epistyle of the pronaos is historically and artistically misleading.

To make the case clear, I must give a brief account of the fortunes of the building, from Agrippa's time to the last restoration by Septimius Severus and Caracalla.

There are two witnesses to the origin of its construction: the legend on the face of the building, M · AGRIPPA · L · F · COS · TERTIVM · FECIT ; and the record of Dion Cassius, liii. 27, "[Agrippa] finished the construction of the so-called Pantheon." The date of the inscription is 27 B. C., while Dion relates the events of the year 25. This discrepancy of dates may be reconciled if we suppose the inscription to commemorate the material completion of the structure, and the historian to be recording the solemn dedication of the Pantheon and of the Lakonikon, which stood close by.

The same historian relates that the Pantheon was dedicated to the ancestral gods of the Julian family, namely, Mars and Venus, and that "Agrippa wished to raise a statue to Augustus also, so that the temple might be placed under his protection. Augustus, however, declined the proposal. In consequence of his refusal, only the statue of Julius Cæsar was placed inside; those of Augustus and Agrippa outside in the pronaos."

From this passage we gather the evidence that Agrippa's temple was furnished with a portico or pronaos. Now, as I remarked at the beginning, between the present rotunda and the portico inscribed with the name of the founder there is no artistic or structural connection. The cornices of the round body are cut

---

[1] *Il Pantheon e le Terme di Agrippa.* Prima relazione a sua Eccellenza il Ministro della Istruzione pubblica. Rome, Salviucci, October, 1881. *Ibid.,* Seconda relazione, August, 1882.

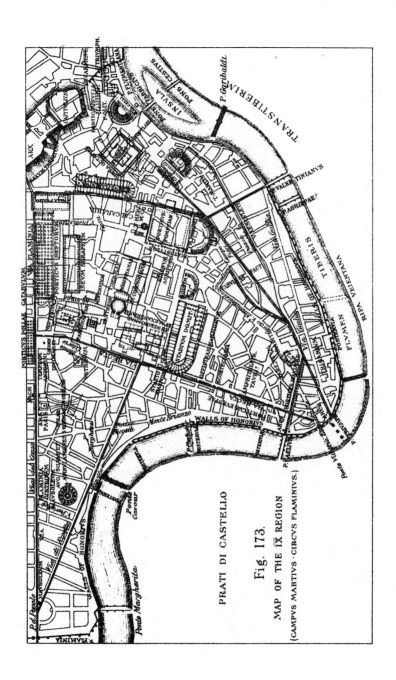

PRATI DI CASTELLO

Fig. 173.

MAP OF THE IX REGION

(CAMPVS MARTIVS - CIRCVS FLAMINIVS.)

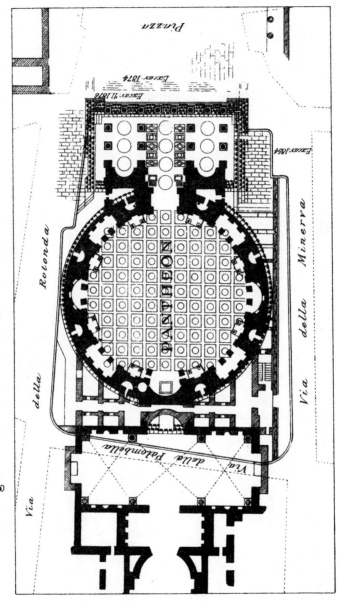

Fig. 185. PLAN OF THE FIRST (Red) AND OF THE THIRD (Black) PANTHEON

up by the portico, while those of the portico are intercepted by the round body. There is a break between the two, five and a half centimetres wide, through which the light shines. This state of things has been discussed by Milizia, Fontana, Piranesi, Lazzeri, Hirt, Fea, Piale, Nibby, and Canina. The majority believe, and I believed with them in 1881, that the portico was a later addition ; in other words, that before the refusal of Augustus to permit his statue to stand within the temple, Agrippa's architect had not thought of the portico, and that it was added by him when the Emperor selected for his own statue a site outside the rotunda.

No less debatable is the relation between the Pantheon and the Thermæ of Agrippa. Regarding this architects and archæologists are divided into two groups. Some believe that the rotunda belongs to the original plan of the baths, and that it was designed for a "caldarium ; " others deny any connection between the two. It is interesting, in view of the light now thrown on this subject, to recall what Emil Braun wrote forty-two years ago : " The incomparable circular edifice originally intended by Agrippa to form the termination of the Thermæ, with which it is intimately connected, is one of the noblest and most perfect productions of that style of architecture specifically denominated Roman. When the first wonderful creation of this species came into existence, the designer of this glorious dome appears to have himself shrunk back from it, and to have felt that it was not adapted to be the every-day residence of men, but to be a habitation for the gods. It is as difficult to reconcile the statements of different authors respecting the original idea of Agrippa as it is hazardous to attempt to prove the successive metamorphoses which the plan sketched by the artist has undergone. This much is, however, certain : that with respect to the modal transformation of the whole the consequences have been most melancholy and injurious. The combination of the circular edifice with the rectilinear masses of the vestibule . . . has been unsuccessful, and the original design of the Roman architect has lost much of its significance. . . . No one previously unacquainted with the edifice could form an idea, from the aspect of the portico, of that wonderful structure behind, which must ever be considered as one of the noblest triumphs of the human mind over matter in connection with the law of gravity."

Eheu, quantum mutatus ab illo ! How differently we are obliged to speak and write after these last discoveries. At the same time, the reader will notice that Emil Braun himself, in 1854, considered

it difficult, if not impossible, to wrest from the Sphinx of the
Campus Martius the secret of its existence and metamorphoses.
We know a great deal more now, but the difficulties remain the
same.

The Thermæ were built six years after the dedication of the
Pantheon and of the Lakonikon ; namely, in 19 B. C. It appears
also that in this second period of the great undertaking Agrippa
must have changed his mind more than once. At all events,
after the year 19 we hear no more of the Lakonikon, but only of
the Thermæ. Was the Pantheon connected directly or indirectly
with the baths, or did it stand by itself, alone, independent, at the
northern end of the quadrangle ? In other words, is it possible
that the Pantheon, originally dedicated to the gods, should have
been used, six years later, as a caldarium, and thus have been absorbed as an integral part of the great whole ? The question must
remain unanswered ; so many alterations have taken place at the
point of contact between the rotunda and the baths that nothing
is left of the first design. No other Roman structure, except the
temple of Jupiter Optimus Maximus, has been so unfortunate, and
has undergone so many trials.

In the year 80, during the fire of Titus, the baths and the
Pantheon were burnt down. Domitian restored both. In 110,
under the rule of Trajan, a thunderbolt set the building on fire,
and destroyed it to the level of the ground. How such a thing
could have happened is a mystery, to be added to the many others
connected with this structure. In the years 120–124 Hadrian
reconstructed the rotunda and the baths, as shown by his biographer, ch. 19. Some other dreadful accident must have happened
soon after, for Hadrian's successor, Antoninus Pius, is said to have
restored *templum Agrippæ*. In the year 202 Septimius Severus
and Caracalla PANTHEVM VETVSTATE CORRVPTVM RESTITVERVNT.
These words, engraved on the same entablature which is inscribed
with the name of the founder, are more than enigmatic. How is
it possible that a structure of immense solidity, only eighty years
old if we reckon from the restoration of Hadrian, fifty or sixty if
we reckon from the restoration of Antoninus, should have become
in so short a time " vetustate corrupta " ? It may help us to
explain the fact if we assume that, while the upper part of the
Pantheon was often struck by lightning and attacked by fire, the
lower part was submerged by the Tiber three or four times a year.
Fire and water must have increased tenfold the destructive power
of time.

Summing up the information supplied to us by writers and inscriptions, we had come to the following inferences, which were hypotheses rather than conclusions : first, that the present Pantheon, inscribed with the name of Agrippa, was substantially his work ; second, that the portico was a later addition to, or alteration of, the original plan ; third, that some details of the structure, especially the inner decoration, were the work of Hadrian and of Severus and Caracalla; fourth, that the Pantheon had never been used as a caldarium. Such were the current theories at the beginning of 1892.

At that time the Department of Antiquities was raising a movable scaffolding to repair the dome in two or three places, where rain-water had filtered in and damaged the coating of stucco. A distinguished pupil of the French Academy (Villa Medici), Louis

Fig. 186. — The Pantheon flooded by the Tiber.
(From a water-color by Pannini, in possession of the author.)

Chedanne, then engaged in the architectural study of the Pantheon, was allowed by the department to take advantage of the scaffolding and to examine the structure of the great dome. He was surprised to find it built of bricks stamped with a date (Agrippa's bricks are not dated) ; and the date was of the time of Hadrian. It was felt to be desirable to ascertain at once whether these bricks belonged to a local and unimportant restoration of the beginning of the second century, or whether they bore testimony to the chronology of the whole edifice.

The masonry of the rotunda, like that of Hadrian's mausoleum, is faced with small triangular bricks, and with rows of tegulæ bipedales at intervals of five feet, one above the other. (See p. 47.) Since these tegulæ bipedales are dated, as a rule, holes were bored

into them in about fifty places, and as many brick-stamps were
found; some on the outside facing, others in the thickness of the
wall, in the foundations, in the dome, in the staircases, in the
arches and vaults ; in short, wherever the search was made.

The dates vary from A. D. 115 to 125. I mean, they are the
dates of tilers who produced bricks between those dates. A
stricter chronological investigation, too minute and technical to
be recorded in these pages, has enabled us to ascertain that the
reconstruction of the Pantheon began in the year 120, and was
finished in 124. It was absolute, complete, from the lowest depths
of the foundations to the skylight of the dome; it included the
rotunda as well as the portico, whose foundations have also been
explored to a depth never reached before. In short, the present
Pantheon, the world-known masterpiece, — counted by Ammianus
Marcellinus among the wonders of Rome, considered by Michelangelo "disegno angelico e non umano," proclaimed by Urban
VIII. "ædificium toto terrarum orbe celeberrimum," [1] — is not the
work of Agrippa, whose name it bears, but the work of Hadrian.
The fact, however startling, is confirmed by other evidence, to
which little or no attention has been paid. In a pamphlet entitled
"Conclusione per la integrità del Pantheon," Rome, 1807, Carlo
Fea, then Commissioner of Antiquities, describes how, on September 13, 1804, he found three brick-stamps of the time of Hadrian, —
one in the thickness of the round wall, one under the flagstones
of the portico, one in the so-called Lakonikon. Piranesi, who witnessed the barbaric "restorations" of Benedict XIV. in 1747,
read likewise on the brick of the attic other names and dates of
the same period.

We must now meet the question which at once confronts us in
this new state of things. In rebuilding the Pantheon in its
entirety, from top to bottom, from the steps of the portico to the
small apse at the opposite end of the structure, did Hadrian
respect the architectural form of Agrippa's (and Domitian's)
building, or did he erect a new structure of his own design, altogether different in general outline and details? The following
considerations may help the student to unravel the tangle.

If we read on the face of the Pantheon the names of Agrippa,
the founder, and of Septimius Severus, the restorer in 202 B. C.,
and not that of Hadrian, the explanation is ready at hand. "Hadrian never inscribed his name on the monuments which he
designed and raised, with the exception only of the temple which

---

[1] See inscription on the vestibule.

he dedicated to Trajan," at the northern end of the Forum. So says his biographer in ch. 19. The omission of the name is thus easily explained. Some one, however, has succeeded in finding it inside the rotunda. In a paper read before the Archæological Academy by Stefano Piale, June 26, 1828,[1] I find the following passage : —

"I have been kindly informed by our secretary, Filippo Aurelio Visconti, that when the tribune (the main altar and apse) of the rotunda was restored, a short time ago, the name of Julia Sabina, the Empress of Hadrian, was found engraved on the columns of pavonazzetto. This confirms the theory which I have long held, that the apse does not belong to the original structure, but is the work of Hadrian. He made use of it as a bench, when he, together with other magistrates, sat in the Pantheon to administer justice and dictate the law, as we are told by Dion Cassius."

The inference to be drawn from these remarkable statements is that the inscription on the face of the building, which we had always supposed to be the "signature," as it were, of the first builder of the Pantheon, must be considered simply as homage paid to his memory by some one who did the work over a century and a half later. This unknown person was a great artist, in the true sense of the word, a worthy rival of the great Apollodoros, the builder of the Forum of Trajan. The Temples of Venus and Rome, of Matidia, of Trajan, of Neptune, designed and built by Hadrian, his own mausoleum, the bridge which leads to it, count among the architectural masterpieces of ancient Rome. To a man possessed of such genius the rebuilding of the Pantheon must have proved an almost irresistible temptation to show his power; it is more than probable, therefore, that the original design would have been changed, enlarged, improved. This supposition, namely, that the pre-Hadrianite structure was different in shape, size, material, etc., seems to be supported by the record of the two fires in the times of Titus and Trajan. The present building is absolutely fire-proof;[2] therefore the Pantheon of Agrippa and of Domitian, wrecked by fire in the years 80 and 110, must have been different from that of Hadrian and Septimius Severus, which does not contain one inch of inflammable matter.

To pass from theory to fact, from speculation to substantial evidence, there was but one way left open : to make a search under

[1] *Un monumento . . . della basilica di S. Paolo.* Rome, 1828.

[2] The wooden framework of the roof of the portico is an innovation of the seventeenth century; the original trusses were cast in bronze.

the rotunda and its portico. The work has been carefully carried
out by all concerned with it, but the results are rather disappoint-
ing : they have led only to greater confusion and uncertainty.

First as to the interior of the rotunda. The excavations made
in a line from the centre to the chapel of the Madonna del Sasso,
and also from the centre to the entrance gate, have shown the
existence of an earlier marble pavement at the average depth of
six feet under the present one (Hadrian's). The pavement is composed of a bed of concrete, over which are laid slabs of giallo antico
and pavonazzetto, marbles which were used in this form and for
such purpose only under the Empire. The pavement is not horizontal, but slopes from the centre towards the circumference, like
the lower floor of the arena of the Coliseum. The pavement,
therefore, belongs to a circular space open to rain ; and a circular
wall, built of reticulated masonry, has actually been discovered
around the present structure, to which it is concentric. It is
marked in red in Fig. 185. The same pavement has been found
running under the portico, at a depth of five feet. The bed of concrete is one foot thick ; the marble slabs from two to three inches.

As regards the portico itself — under and near which the excavations have been carried on with much more freedom than those
inside — it has been found to rest on a magnificent substructure of
travertine, much larger and of different design (marked also in red
in Fig. 185). The level of the platform is nearly eight feet lower
than the floor of Hadrian's portico, and between the two there are
traces of an intermediate one.

It is very difficult for me to make this account clear without the
help of plans and diagrams. However, summing up the facts
which I have tried to describe, and the results of the search made
by the Department of Antiquities, we reach the following conclusions.

(1) The present Pantheon, portico included, is not the work of
Agrippa, but of Hadrian, and dates from A. D. 120–124.

(2) The columns, capitals, and entablature of the portico inscribed with Agrippa's name may be original, and may date from
27–25 B. C.; but they were first removed and then put together
again by Hadrian. The original portico was decastyle, as shown
by the foundations of travertine, which project right and left of
the present octostyle portico enough to admit one more intercolumniation at each end (see plan).

(3) The original structure of Agrippa was rectangular instead
of round, and faced the south instead of the north. It resembled

in shape the Temple of Concord, that is to say, the façade was on one of the longer sides of the parallelogram, and not on one of the smaller. This shape is special to the Augustea, and the Pantheon belonged to this class of buildings.

(4) In front of the rectangular temple opened a round space, inclosed by a wall of reticulated work and paved with slabs of giallo and pavonazzetto. The wall can still be seen at the level of the foundations of Hadrian's rotunda, with which it is concentric.

(5) The platform, built of huge blocks of travertine, some eight feet below Hadrian's level, dates from the time of Agrippa.

(6) The intermediate marble floor (from two to three feet higher than Agrippa's, from five to six feet lower than Hadrian's) dates most likely from the time of Domitian.

(7) Septimius Severus and Caracalla did not alter the shape of the structure. Their restorations were only superficial, and relate mostly to the attic inside, which they incrusted with slabs of porphyry and serpentine. Their beautiful decorations were destroyed by Pope Benedict XIV. in 1747.

(8) If the outside architecture of Hadrian's rotunda is rather coarse, and not worthy the exquisite beauty of the interior, we must remember that the round body — the front excepted — was entirely concealed and made invisible by the thermæ.

The history of the building, from its last restoration in A. D. 202 to our own time, is too well known to be narrated again in these pages. I shall mention two episodes only: one relating to the destruction of the roof of the portico by Pope Barberini, the other to the discovery of Raphael's body in 1833.

Giacinto Gigli, a diarist contemporary with Urban VIII., thus describes his shameful action: " In 1625, while the war-cry was raised from one end of the peninsula to the other, Urban VIII. made a great provision of arms and ammunition, and more especially of artillery. To provide himself with a copious stock of ' materia prima,' he caused the portico of the Pantheon to be stripped of its bronze roof, a marvelous work, resting on the capitals of the columns. But no sooner was the destruction accomplished than he found the alloy of the metal not hard enough for casting guns.[1] Meanwhile, the population, who flocked in great numbers to see what was being done at the Pantheon, were deeply grieved, and urged that such a beautiful work of antiquity, the only one which had escaped plunder from the barbarians, should not now be dismantled. But the intention of the pope was not to destroy the

---

[1] Gigli affirms that the metal " was copiously mixed with silver and gold."

Pantheon: he gave orders for the construction of a new roof, and showed his willingness to make other improvements. The weight of the metal stored in the apostolic foundry was 450,251 pounds, of which 440,877 represented the weight of the beams, 9374 that of the nails alone. Besides the four columns of the baldacchino in S. Peter's, eighty guns were cast from it, and mounted on the bastions of Castel S. Angelo."

Fig. 187. — The Pantheon at the time of Urban VIII. (1625).

The story about the casting of the four columns of the baldacchino is not correct: the bronze, save a few thousand pounds, was all absorbed by the guns of Castello. Giano Nicio Eritreo, another eye-witness, thus speaks of the event: "Our good pontiff, Urban VIII., could not bear the idea that such a mass of metal, intended for loftier purposes, should humble itself to the office of keeping off forever the rain from the portico of the Pantheon. He raised it to worthier destinies, because it is becoming that such noble material should keep off the enemies of the Church rather than the rain. At all events, Agrippa's temple has gained more than it has lost, because Pope Urban VIII. has provided it with a much better roof" (*tectum multo quam antea elegantius*).

Carlo Fea has discovered among the accounts of the pope's treasury that concerning the fate of the bronze. The casting of the eighty guns (*bombarde*) used up 410,778 pounds, worth 67,260 scudi. The small fraction that was left was handed over to the Apostolic Chamber and used for other purposes. The metal for the baldacchino was supplied from Venice.

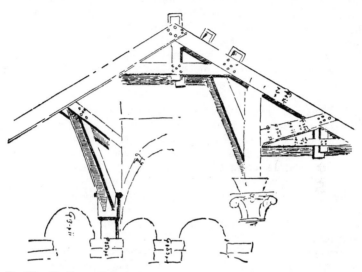

Fig. 188. — The Bronze Trusses of the Pronaos of the Pantheon, from a Sketch by Dosio.

I have found in the Uffizi in Florence, and in other private collections, a set of drawings by Sallustio Peruzzi, Sebastiano Serlio, Giovanni Antonio Dosio, Jacopo Sansovino, and Cherubino Alberti, which show the construction of the bronze trusses in their minutest details. The main beams were composed of three sheets, two vertical, one horizontal, riveted together in this shape. The beams as well as the heads of the nails were ornamented with gilt rosettes. One of the nails was presented as a souvenir to the Duke of Alcalá and was placed in the private museum of that distinguished statesman. I have also discovered documents which prove that the bronze doors, so often brought forward as a specimen of antique workmanship, were practically cast over at the time of Pius IV.

The second and latest episode in the history of the Pantheon is the discovery of the remains of Raphael, which took place on

September 14, 1833. The search began in the early morning of September 9, in the presence of a committee of eminent artists, prelates, and public notaries. It took five days to remove the massive masonry of the altar and to reach the *arcosolium* under the statue of the Madonna del Sasso, the place distinctly mentioned by Vasari in Raphael's biography as well as in Lorenzetto Lotti's. "Raphael provided in his will for the restoration of one of the antique tabernacles in the church of S. Maria Rotonda, and expressed the wish to be buried in it, under the new altar, and under a marble statue of Our Lady." In the "Life of Lorenzetto" he adds: "In execution of Raphael's will, he modeled a marble statue four cubits high, to be placed over his tomb in S. Maria Rotonda, in the tabernacle restored at his expense."

The arcosolium appears to have been built in a hurry, together with the wall which sealed its opening — a particular which agrees well with the account of the burial. Raphael died in the night between Good Friday and Easter Eve (1520). His remains were laid to rest on the following night, and the wall which seals the opening of the crypt must have been finished before dawn; that is to say, before the Easter office began. Every kind of material was used in it, bricks, tufa, travertine, and chips of porphyry and serpentine.

At noon of September 14, 1833, the last stone was removed, and the excited assembly beheld for the first time the remains of the "divine painter." They were lying in a coffin made of deal boards nailed with small iron nails. It seems that the waters of the Tiber, by which the Pantheon is periodically inundated, had filtered into the tomb, in spite of its being surrounded by a wall two feet thick, and had caused the wooden coffin to decay, and the bones to be covered by a layer of mud. The first bones to appear were the right scapula and the crest of the right ilium. At 2.25 P. M. Gaspare Servi announced the discovery of the skull, the leading feature of which was a double set of strong, healthy, shining teeth. At 2.30 Baron Camuccini, the painter, made a pencil sketch of the skeleton, which shows that the body had been laid to rest well composed, with hands crossed on the breast, and the face looking up towards the Madonna del Sasso, as if imploring from her the peace of the just. The size of the skeleton, from the vertex of the skull to the protuberance of the heel, was measured by means of a wooden compass of the kind used by marble-cutters: it was given at 1664 millimetres, exactly eight times the measure of the head. The *sceletognosis*, or expert examination of the bones,

was made by the "last of the Frangipani," the learned surgeon
Baron Antonio Trasmondo. Among the peculiarities described
in his report, there is a " great roughness of the thumb," which is
characteristic of painters.

The mud which filled the arcosolium was sifted most carefully,

Fig. 189. — The Remains of Raphael, discovered September 14, 1833.
(From a contemporary drawing.)

with no result worthy of notice. The missing tooth of the lower
jaw (the last molar on the left) was not found. There were, however, some tags and small rings for lacings, which proves that
Raphael was buried in his official robe of "cubicularius ponti-
ficis," a design of which is given by some contemporary painters.

After being exposed in a glass case for some days, Raphael's
remains were again buried under the Madonna del Sasso, near
those of Maria da Bibiena, his betrothed, the niece of the well-
known Cardinal Bernardo Divizio, as the inscription over the
girl's grave says: LÆTOS HYMENEOS MORTE PRÆVERTIT, ET ANTE
NUPTIALES FACES VIRGO EST ELATA.

The proposal to demolish the houses which surrounded the Pantheon on three sides, concealed its proportions, and destroyed its

architectural effect, dates from the age of Pomponius Letus, who complains of the state of things in his " Dialogues." Eugenius IV. lowered the rubbish accumulated against the portico, and paved the piazza and the adjoining streets.   Urban VIII., having stripped the roof of the portico of its bronze beams, restored the east corner of the colonnade, and destroyed the shops built between the granite pillars.   Alexander VII. put two columns from the baths of Nero (found in the Piazza di S. Luigi de' Francesi) in place of those missing, and pulled down some houses from which the canons of the Rotonda derived an income of 1500 scudi a year. Pius VII. demolished the booths of fishmongers which surrounded the fountain.   Pius IX. in 1854 carried the demolition of the houses as far as the Palazzo Vittori-Bianchi on the corner facing the Minerva.   The city of Rome in 1876 cut away one half of the Crescenzi and Aldobrandini palaces.   The minister of public instruction, Guido Baccelli, brought the matter to a close in 1882, at a cost of over £30,000.   The works were inaugurated on July 1, 1881, and completed in the following January.   Houses and palaces of 150 metres frontage were demolished, two thousand square metres of Agrippa's baths excavated, two thirds of the Pantheon restored to view, and many thousand metres of débris carted away.

The literature on the Pantheon up to 1881 is given by the *Notizie Scavi*, 1881, p. 256 ; after that date by Huelsen, *Nomenclator*, p. 49.   The latest work is Giovanni Eroli's *Raccolta generale delle iscrizioni nel Pantheon di Roma*.   Narni, Petrignani, 1895.

XLVIII.   The name of LAKONIKON has been given to the beautiful hall laid bare by Baccelli at the back of the Pantheon towards the Via della Palombella, but it is not certain whether we are right in applying it.   The hall, which extends under the street and under the Palazzo della Accademia Ecclesiastica for a length of 45 metres and a depth of 19, seems to me more a frigidarium of the baths of the time of Hadrian than an original work of Agrippa.   The hall has sixteen niches for statues, and a tribune for a group of great size, back to back with the apse of the Pantheon.   The ceiling was supported by four fluted columns of pavonazzetto and four of red granite.   The frieze, of which many fragments were found and replaced *in situ*, is a marvel of art, probably of the time of Agrippa.

This hall was excavated for the first time (?) during the stay in Rome of Giovanni Alberti, whose drawings are the best that we have. It seems that when the ceiling of this hall gave way, and thundered down with a sudden crash, some one who happened to be underneath was crushed to death. The bones of this poor fellow, who had probably selected the ruins of Agrippa's baths for his dwelling, were found in December, 1881, under a piece of the cornice weighing many tons. Not far from this strange grave an earthern vase was discovered containing about 2,000 coins of the thirteenth century. This is perhaps the date of the final collapse of Agrippa's baths. There are other indifferent remains visible in the Via dell' Arco della Ciambella and under the adjoining houses.

XLIX. BASILICA NEPTUNI, NEPTUNIUM, ΠΟΣΕΙΔΩΝΙΟΝ, PORTICUS ARGONAUTARUM (the Temple of Neptune and the portico of the Argonauts, the Admiralty of the Empire). — In commemoration of the naval victories against Sextus Pompeius at Mysæ and at Naulochos (36 B. C.), for which he received the naval crown, and of the share he had taken in the battle and victory of Actium (31), Agrippa erected in 26 a group of buildings in the Campus Martius, which comprised a square 108 metres long, and 98 metres wide, surrounded by a colonnade and by halls of various kinds, and a temple in the middle of the square dedicated to the God of the Seas. The group is called Ποσειδώνιον, *Neptunium*, by Dion Cassius, while the portico was named *Argonautarum*, from the paintings of naval subjects — like that of the "Sailors of the Argo" — which it contained. "If we inquire as to the object of so extensive a structure, having in its design so much in common with the fora of the Emperors, we must be satisfied with the answer that, according to all analogy, no other building of ancient Rome seems so suitable for the seat of the Admiralty as this sanctuary of Neptune."[1] Like the Iseum, the Sæpta, the Pantheon, the Thermæ Agrippianæ, and the Diribitorium, it was destroyed in the conflagration of A. D. 80, and restored by Hadrian. A considerable portion of the temple, including eleven columns of the north side, with the corresponding wall of the cella and of the richly decorated ceiling, stands in the Piazza "di Pietra," so called from the "petraia" or marble quarry established within its boundaries in mediæval times. The pillars and their heavy entablature are much injured by fire; the proportions of the order, although not so perfect as was usual at the time of Hadrian, are good, especially if we remember that its lofty substructure is buried deep

[1] Emil Braun, *Ruins and Museums*, p. 63.

under the modern soil. This substructure was decorated with figures of Roman provinces, one beneath each column, and with trophies and panoplies, one beneath each intercolumniation. Three provinces and two trophies were discovered under Paul III. (1534–50), and removed, first to the Palazzo Farnese, and then to the Museo Nazionale of Naples, except one fragment left in Rome. Under Innocent X. (1644–55) two more provinces were dug up and presented to the Capitoline Museum, where they were placed, one in the courtyard, one in the lower corridor of the museum. The trophy set in the wall on the first landing of the stairs of the Altieri Palace was probably discovered at the time of the Altieri pope, Clement X. (1670–76). Under Alexander VII. (1655–67) another couple of provinces were discovered *in situ*, viz., in the basement under two of the existing columns. The pope kept them for himself, and they are still to be seen in the staircase of the Chigi-Odescalchi Palace at SS. Apostoli. In 1876 our Archæological Commission found six bas-reliefs in the same Piazza di Pietra, placed upside down, in the pavement of a mediæval church called S. Stefano del Trullo (demolished by Innocent X.). On February 9, 1883, three more pieces were dug up from the same place, making a total of thirteen provinces and of six panels with panoplies. The peristyle of the temple numbered thirty-six columns, which is the number of the provinces of the Empire when the temple itself was restored by Hadrian. If the wishes of artists and archæologists had been listened to, provinces and panoplies would have been restored long ago to their original places, so as to make the remains of the Temple of Neptune one of the most beautiful and impressive monuments of Rome ; but the request made to this purpose in the year 1883 was negatived by the state, and the sculptured pieces were allowed to remain scattered in five palaces or museums, and in two cities, two hundred miles apart. The same thing may be said of the Forum, the 150 inscriptions of which, found at various times, are dispersed in eighteen different places, although it would be so easy to restore them to the Forum, if not in the original, at least in plaster casts. Theodor Mommsen, speaking of the " Hemerologium Allifanum," a fragment of which is kept in Naples, the other at Capua, justly exclaims, " Hoc enim voluerunt sive fatorum iniquitas, sive cæca hominum studia, ut eiusdem monumenti reliquiæ expositæ sint in duobus museis, publicis ambobus, et ambobus italis." The Neptunium, however, has gone, and quite recently, through other vicissitudes, which would appear grotesque if the interest of the

monument were not at stake. When Innocent XII. turned the
place into a "Dogana di terra" (the maritime custom-house was
then at the Ripa Grande), his architect plastered over the cornice,
not according to its old moulding, of which Palladio and others
had taken and left careful designs, but according to his own
imagination. In 1878, when the Italian government took down

Fig. 190. — The Temple of Neptune : an unfinished Study by Vespignani.

the "modernizations" of Innocent XII., it was decided to restore
the cornice to its original shape. The person intrusted with the
work, having read in Nardini (Nibby, vol. iii. p. 120, n. 1) that
a genuine piece of the cornice, discovered under Clement XII.
(1730–40) had been removed to the Capitol,[1] went there, took by
mistake the cast of the cornice of the Temple of Concord, and
applied it to that of Neptune — not to the whole of it, but to a

---

[1] The statement is groundless. The beautiful piece of carving was not
removed to the Capitol, but sawn into slabs and used in the restoration of
the Arch of Constantine.

space comprising five columns out of eleven. The student who looks at the entablature will find it sectioned in three parts, different in shape, size, style, and epoch.

The (unfinished) sketch of the front of the Neptunium (Fig. 190) is by Vespignani the elder, who in 1880 directed the works for transforming the cella of the God of the Seas into the Bourse of the capital of Italy.

A crucifix of a comparatively recent date is sculptured on the fourth column, counting from left to right, about 4.50 metres above ground. The upright piece of the cross falls into the first fluting on the right of the middle one.

A genuine piece of the entablature is to be seen in the garden of "la salita delle tre Pile," the winding street which leads from the Piazza dell' Aracœli to that of the Campidoglio.

Narducci, who in 1887 explored the network of drains connected with the temple and with the portico of the Argonauts, speaks of them with admiration. They are 2 metres high, 0.70 metre wide, and are covered with large tiles stamped with the names of Faustina the elder and of Annia Lucilla, wife of Lucius Verus.

The Neptunium was a favorite subject of study with the artists of the sixteenth century. The vignettes of G. A. Dosio (1569), of Etienne du Perac (1575), the drawing of Palladio (Archit., iv. c. 15), of Antonio da Sangallo (Uffizi, 1407), of Giovanni Alberti (Borgo S. Sepolcro, p. 38', 39), and of the "Cod. Barberin.," xlviii. 101, enable us to form a better idea of the monument than we can gather from the ruins in their actual state.

Literature. — Rodolfo Lanciani, *Bull. com.*, 1878, p. 10, pls. ii. to v. — Gio. Battista Piranesi, *Campo Marzio*, pl. (xxxiv.) xxxv. — Enrico Narducci, *Fognatura*, p. 28. — *Notizie Scavi*, 1878, pp. 64, 92; 1879, pp. 68, 240, 267, 314; 1880, p. 228.

G. The Spectacular Buildings.

L. Theatrum Marcelli (Theatre of Marcellus), begun by Julius Cæsar on the site of many public and private buildings; as, for example, the Temple of Piety, from the demolition of which he was suspected to have gathered large sums of money. He was also accused of having burnt many statues of gods, carved in wood. The work, unfinished at the time of the death of the dictator, was continued by Augustus, and dedicated in 13 b. c., under the name of his beloved son-in-law Marcellus, then recently deceased. The architecture of the semicircular part resembles that of the Coliseum, the arcades of the lower tier being of the Doric order, those of the upper, of the Ionic. Above the open porticoes was an attic pierced with rectangular windows, and ornamented with pilasters of the Corinthian order. The architect of the Coliseum has certainly designed its exterior in close accordance with the lines of this theatre. Both are built in travertine from the Cava del Barco.

On the dedication day the " Ludus Trojæ " was performed by the sons of illustrious patricians, led by Caius Cæsar, the nephew of Augustus; and six hundred wild beasts from Nubia were slain in the circus. The breaking down of the Sella Curulis, on which the Emperor sat to witness the performance, caused him to fall on his back; but the accident had no serious consequences. Vespasian restored the stage after the fire of Nero, and celebrated the event with scenic plays and musical concerts, in the course of which Apollinaris the tragedian received a gift of 400 sestertia; Terpnos and Diodoros, harpists, another of 200 each,[1] besides several crowns of gold. A passage in the Life of Severus Alexander, ch. 44, seems to indicate that the theatre was no more used in the first half of the third century (Theatrum Marcelli reficere voluit); but the almanacs of the fourth century and the poet Ausonius assert the contrary, and give the theatre a capacity of 20,500 seats (*loca*), which is reduced by Huelsen to about 13,400 by interpreting the word *loca* in the sense of *feet*.[2] When Avianius Symmachus restored the Cestian bridge (A. D. 365–370), under the rule of Gratianus, he laid his hands on the disused theatre, and made use of some of the travertine blocks belonging to the Doric arcade. After the death of Gregory VII. in 1086 it was turned into a stronghold by the Pierleoni, and for two centuries at least was subject to the same vicissitudes through which the Coliseum and other prominent edifices passed in the time of the barons of that turbulent period. The Pierleoni gave shelter in it to Pope Urban II. (1099), and in it that pope died in 1118. On May 24, 1368, Luca di Jacopo Savelli purchased " plures domus et palatia et *antiqua œdificia cum cryptis* posite in monte " (the Monte Savello of the present day), and after the extinction of that family in 1712, the property passed into the hands of the Orsini.

The section of the outside shell, visible at present, a magnificent ruin in outline and color, is buried fifteen feet in modern soil, and supports the Orsini palace erected upon its stage and ranges of seats. What stands above ground of the lower or Doric arcades is rented by the prince for the most squalid and ignoble class of shops. Other corridors and rooms are tolerably well preserved;

---

[1] £3200 and £1600 respectively.   [2] *Bull. com.*, 1894, p. 319.

but being now converted into offices belonging to the palace which has insinuated itself into these ruins, they are not accessible to strangers. The stage lay towards the Tiber, and being lower than half the belts of seats, afforded the spectators massed in the upper mæniana a fine view of the chain of hills on the right bank of the river.

The arcades which are seen from the Via del Teatro di Marcello are not the only remains accessible to the student. There are

Fig. 191. — Remains of the Hall of the Theatre of Marcellus, from a Sketch by Du Perac (1575).

walls in the cellars of the " Osteria della Campana " close by, described by Venuti as corridors leading to the vomitoria of the equestrian order, and to the orchestra where the senators had their seats. Other walls can be examined in the court of the house Via del Portico d' Ottavia, No. 22. The pillars and cornices of travertine which appear near the gate of the Palazzo Orsini belong to the " aula regia " or " curia " on the left of the stage. This beautiful hall was nearly intact three centuries ago, and the public street leading from the Piazza Montanara to the Ponte Quattro Capi passed through it, as shown in the above sketch by Etienne du Perac.

LITERATURE. — *Corpus Inscr.*, vol. i. p. 392 (April 27); vol. vi. n. 956, 1660, 9868, 10,028. — Heinrich Jordan, *Forma Urbis*, pl. iv. n. 29. — Theodor Mommsen, *Res gestæ*, iv. 22, p. 88. — Ridolfino Venuti, *Antich.*, vol. ii. p. 75. — Mariano Armellini, *Chiese*, p. 622. — Rodolfo Lanciani, *Bull. com.*, 1875, p. 173; 1886, p. 206. — Antonio da Sangallo the elder, *Barberin.*, 4, 37, 71'. — A. da Sangallo the younger, *Uffizi*, 930, 932, 1107, 1122, 1270. — Baldassare Peruzzi, *Uffizi*, 626. — Vincenzo Scamozzi, *Uffizi*, 1806.

LI. THEATRUM ET CRYPTA BALBI, built by L. Cornelius Balbus, a friend of Augustus, with the riches acquired during the

Fig. 192. — Arcades of the Theatre of Balbus, from a Sketch by Sangallo the Elder.

Garamantic war, and dedicated in the year 13, on the return of the Emperor from his campaigns beyond the Alps. An inundation of the Tiber obliged the distinguished company invited to attend the opening ceremony to reach their destination in boats. The fire of Titus did great damage to the structure, but we do not know by whom, or at what time, it was repaired. It could accommodate 11,600 spectators (7700 according to Huelsen).

Like the theatre of Marcellus, that of Balbus gave rise to a mound of ruins, called "Monte dei Cenci" from the family of that name who had occupied and fortified it. The name was accepted by the Renaissance in substitution for that of Theatrum Antonini used in the Middle Ages. The remains visible when Piranesi was preparing his magnificent plates of the Campus Martius were two walls once covered by the marble seats of the cavea; he saw them in the cellar of a wine-shop, right under the church of S. Tommaso à Cenci, in the Via di S. Bartolomeo de' Vaccinari.[1] Those two converging walls have allowed us to trace the exact location of the whole building, the curved part of which faced the Tiber, while the scena was parallel with our Via del Pianto. The want of existing ruins, however, is amply atoned for by a set of drawings taken by the elder Sangallo before the final collapse of the theatre, and by the discoveries made in 1888, when the Via Arenula was opened and drained at a great depth on the north side of the theatre. I have as yet had no opportunity of putting together the plans and notes which I took in 1888. To show, however, what valuable documents we possess in connection with this theatre, I reproduce in the above illustration (Fig. 192) a sketch taken by Sangallo at the beginning of the sixteenth century, representing a section of the portico behind the scene.

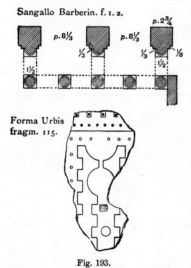

Sangallo Barberin. f. 1. 2.

p. 2¾ p. 8⅓ p. 8½ ⅓ ⅓ ⅛ 1½ 1½

Forma Urbis fragm. 115.

Fig. 193.

The sketch shows a particular quite unprecedented in the history of Roman architecture, that of columns cutting in two the space between the corresponding pilasters, and standing right in the middle of the passage, so that the number of columns on the outer line was

---

[1] More walls were visible under the church in the sixteenth century; in a deed of April 15, 1513, they are described as "arcus volti subtus ecclesiam Sancti Thomæ."

double that of the pilasters on the inner. The arrangement was really such, as we can gather from fragment n. 115, pl. xvii. of the marble plan, and from another drawing by Sangallo, here reproduced (Fig. 193).

THE CRYPTA BALBI. — The name of "crypta" is peculiar to underground porticoes, lighted from windows or skylights above, cooler in summer and warmer in winter than the ordinary open colonnades. We do not know why it was given to the portico built by Balbus behind the scene of his theatre (a portico entirely above ground), unless it was on account of the darkness or "dim religious light" into which the inner halls were plunged owing to the existence of an upper story.

The crypta, a parallelogram 148.50 metres long and 44.55 metres wide, occupied the space now bounded by the Via di S. Maria in Cacaberis, Via del Pianto, Via Arenula, and Piazza Giudea. Two pilasters with engaged columns with their entablature of bricks and travertine are visible on each side of the door No. 23 Via di S. Maria in Cacaberis ; but the whole block of houses rests on ancient foundations. Nibby explored these substructures in 1835 and saw traces of the round halls and exhedræ which occupied the middle of the portico. Its original name was preserved in the Middle Ages, under the diminutive form of *crypticula* or *craticula*. When Baldassare Peruzzi took its plan at the end of the fifteenth century the crypt was almost intact. The arcades were occupied by butchers, sellers of copper vessels (*caccabarii*), and candlemakers (*candelottari*), by the houses of the Santa-

Fig. 194. — Remains of the Crypta Balbi, designed by Sangallo the Elder.

croce, and by the church and cemetery of S. Salvatore in Cacabariis. The best plan is that of Palladio, in portfolio xi. sheet 1 of the Burlington-Devonshire collection. The best elevation is that of Sangallo the elder, in "Barberin.," f. 1, which I reproduce here at one fifth of the original.

The paved square around the theatre was ornamented with several fountains. One of the basins, of white and black granite, over twenty-two metres in circumference, discovered about 1750 in the Piazza di Branca (now Cairoli), was purchased by Cardinal Alessandro Albani, and removed to his villa on the Via Salaria. Another, smaller in size, was discovered on the same spot in 1887, and has been set up in the garden of the Piazza Cairoli in front of the Santacroce palace. Here also was found in the seventeenth century the beautiful statue of the sitting Ares now in the Ludovisi-Boncompagni museum, described by Helbig, "Guide," vol. ii. p. 115, n. 883.

LITERATURE. — Hochte, *De L. Cornelio Balbo,* 1882. — Antonio Nibby, *Roma antica,* vol. ii. p. 586. — *Beschreibung Roms,* vol. iii. 3, 60. — *Notizie Scavi,* 1887, pp. 114, 144, 236, 276, 327. — Antonio Sangallo the elder, *Barberin.,* f. 1, 2, 4′, 14′. — Baldassare Peruzzi, *Uffizi,* n. 486. — Fra Giocondo (?), *ibid.* 125. — Piranesi, *Antichità,* vol. iv. pl. 46; and *Campo Marzio,* pl. xv.

LII. ODEUM. — Becker refers the building of this theatrical hall, capable of containing 10,600 (7000) spectators, to the institution of the Agon Capitolinus, a competition for the world's championship in gymnastics, equestrian sports, music, and poetry, established by Domitian at the beginning of his reign. It was probably restored by Trajan. Ammianus Marcellinus numbers it among the most beautiful monuments of the Urbs Æterna. Topographers place it on the site of the present Palazzo Massimi, Corso Vittorio Emmanuele, on account of the discovery of great architectural fragments from a "curved" edifice made in its foundations. This surmise seems to be substantiated by quite recent finds of the same nature.

LITERATURE. — Suetonius, *Domitian,* 4. — Dion Cassius, lxix. 4. — Ammianus Marcellinus, xvi. 10. — Luigi Canina, *Indicaz. topogr.,* p. 394. — Ridolfino Venuti, *Antichità,* ii. 158. — Stefano Morcelli, *Sull' Agone capitolino.* Milan, 1816. — Joachim Marquardt, *Handbuch der römischen Alterthümer,* vol. iv. p. 453. — Rodolfo Lanciani, *Pagan and Christian Rome,* p. 280.

LIII. STADIUM. — The Romans were so insatiable for spectacular performances of every description that, in spite of the many buildings permanently erected for this purpose, temporary ones (*subitaria*) were very often raised to meet extraordinary emergencies. In ch. 39 of Cæsar's Life, Suetonius mentions a *stadium ad tempus extructum* in the Campus Martius, for athletic competitions which lasted three days; Dion Cassius (liii. 1) another, ξύλινον (wooden) erected in the same place under Augustus. A memento of this last was discovered in 1547 in the Piazza di S. Apollinare, opposite the palace of Cardinal Ridolfi, in the shape of two marble pedestals, commemorating the "votive games" performed in it in the years 13 and 7 B. C., on the return of Augustus from the Spanish and Gallic wars. There were also five scenic masks cut in marble, in the shape of those preserved in the theatre at Ostia.

Domitian built a permanent stadium, in which the gladiators fought whenever the amphitheatre was closed for repairs. The

Fig. 195. — Remains of the Stadium discovered in 1869, at the South End of the Piazza Navona.

stadium, capable of containing 30,088 spectators, was restored by Severus Alexander; hence the name of " Circus Alexandrinus " given to it in the Middle Ages. The stadium is now represented in size and shape by the Piazza Navona, on which the Roman municipality has imposed the doubly wrong name of " Circo Agonale." The houses, palaces, and churches by which the piazza is surrounded are all standing on the well-preserved ruins of the seats and corridors. The only part accessible to students is the "fornices" under the church of S. Agnese, where the lovely young martyr is said to have been publicly exposed after her torture, and to have struck with blindness the first person who saw her degradation. This account is substantiated in its main lines by the well-known passage in the "Vita Heliogab.," 26 — "omnes de circo, de theatro, de *stadio* . . . meretrices collegit." Another fragment of the substructures is to be seen in the court of the house No. 31 Via delle Cinque Lune.

The first accounts of excavations date from 1511, when some richly carved bases and friezes were found "under a church (S. Agnese de Cryptis Agonis) near the palace of the countess of Massa." Pius IV. is responsible for the destruction of the east side between the Piazza Navona and the Piazza Madonna, which he undertook in August, 1561, to provide building materials for his casino in the Vatican gardens. Other sections were demolished by Du Jardin, the architect of S. Nicolo dei Lorenesi; by Rainaldi, the architect of the Palazzo Pamfili; and by Morelli, the architect of the Palazzo Braschi. I have myself seen the remains of the Stadium excavated twice: on October 13, 1868, at the curved end, towards S. Apollinare; and on December 10, 1869, at the opposite or square end, by the Via della Cuccagna, when the photograph was taken which is here reproduced (Fig. 195).

The custom of flooding the Piazza Navona on Sundays in July and August, instituted in 1652, was given up in 1867.

LITERATURE.— *Corpus Inscr.*, vol. vi. n. 385, 386. — *Cod. Vatic.*, 5253, f. 362; and 6039, f. 246, 247. — Antonio Sangallo, *Uffizi*, n. 1321. — Sangallo il Gobbo, *ibid.*, 1552. — Francesco Cancellieri, *Il mercato, il lago*, etc. Rome, 1811. — Gio. Battista Piranesi, *Camp. Mart.*, tav. xxxvii. — Bianconi, *Dei Circhi*, pp. 8, 18, 84. — Emiliano Sarti, *Arch. Società storia patria*, vol. ix. p. 478.

H. The Buildings of Nero, Domitian, and Hadrian.

LIV. THERMÆ NERONIANÆ ET ALEXANDRIANÆ. — While restoring the Stadium about A. D. 228, Severus Alexander rebuilt and considerably enlarged the adjoining thermæ which Nero had constructed, together with a gymnasium, in the year preceding the great fire (64). They occupied the space now covered by the palazzi Madama (Senate-house), Giustiniani, Patrizi, by the houses on the Piazza Rondinini, and by the church and palace of S. Luigi dei Francesi. There are no remains above ground except a few walls in the Senate-house concealed under the modern plastering; but the site of the thermæ has been and is still a mine of marbles, especially of columns of red granite. When Alexander VII. excavated the Piazza di S. Luigi in 1666, besides the two columns with which he restored the left corner of the pronaos of the Pantheon, he found capitals with Victories in the place of the volutes. Two more columns were discovered in the time of Innocent X., lying across the street which separates the Palazzo Madama from the church of S. Luigi, and several others under the Giustiniani Palace. A piece of a column of the most beautiful granite, 1.44 metre in diameter, lies in the cellar of the Palazzo Patrizi. Another found in the Piazza di S. Eustachio has been made use of in the restoration of the steps of S. Peter's. Several have been brought to light in my own time. The one erected last year opposite the "breccia di Porta Pia" in the Corso d' Italia, in commemoration of the twenty-fifth anniversary of the reunion of Rome to Italy, was found in the Salita dei Crescenzi in the spring of 1875.

No less remarkable is the abundance of basins for fountains cut out of a single block of granite. The first, 6.70 metres in diameter, found in the Piazza di S. Eustachio, was given by Pius IV. to Rutilio Alberini, commissioner of streets; the second and the third, found on the same occasion, were abandoned in consideration of their fragmentary state. The fourth came to light in 1706 from the foundations of the Seminario Romano; the fifth towards 1750 from those of the Palazzo Cenci at S. Eustachio. An inscription (Corpus, n. 8676) mentions a *vilicus* or intendant *thermar*(um) *N*(eronis) of the time of the Flavians; another (n. 3052), scratched on the wall of the guard-house of the Vigiles at the Monte de' Fiori, Trastevere, seems to prove that the name of Nero had survived through the restoration of Severus Alexander.

Two other buildings belonging to this period, viz., the Stadium and the Odeum, have been described above.

LITERATURE. — Powath, *Der Kaiser Alexander Severus*. Halle, 1876. — Lanciani, *Notizie Scavi*, 1881, p. 270; 1882, pl. xxi.; and *Forma Urbis Romæ*, pl. xv. — *Notizie Scavi*, 1876, p. 12; 1882, pp. 412, 433; 1883, pp. 15, 81, 130; 1892, p. 265. — Antonio Sangallo the younger, *Uffizi*, 949, 1634. — *Cod. Barberin.*, xlviii. 101, f. 13', 14', 28, 29. — Alò Giovannoli, *Roma antica*, l. iii. pl. 10.

LV. The short reign of Titus was saddened by three public calamities: the eruption of Mount Vesuvius, the plague, and a fire in Rome (A. D. 80) which lasted three days and three nights, damaging or destroying two thirds of the buildings of the Campus

Martius. Dion Cassius mentions as destroyed the Diribitorium, the Temple of Isis and Serapis, the Sæpta Julia, the Admiralty, the Baths of Agrippa, and the Pantheon. The damages were so great that it took many years and the efforts of four Emperors to repair them. Titus himself, a passionate collector of works of art (the Laocoon, for instance, belonged to his private mansion on the Oppian), gave them up to replace those that had perished in the flames. Domitian began and Hadrian finished the reconstruction of the various buildings, except that of the Portico of Octavia, which remained in its ruinous state until the reign of Septimius Severus. Of these buildings, the only one which I have not yet mentioned or described is the

ISIUM ET SERAPIUM, the great sanctuary of Isis and Serapis, which occupied the space between the Sæpta, the Minervium, and the Baths of Agrippa, on the line of the present Via del Collegio Romano. The sanctuary contained the propylaia, or pyramidal towers, with a gateway flanked by obelisks at each end of the *dromos* (one near the present church of S. Stefano del Cacco, one near the church of S. Macuto); the dromos or sacred avenue leading to the double temple, lined with masterpieces of Egyptian sculpture; a peristyle inclosing the sacred area, built (or rebuilt) by Domitian, exactly like the inclosure wall of his Forum Transitorium, in the purest Greco-Roman style prevailing in his time; and the double cella of the temple of pure Egyptian architecture, built with materials of an old sanctuary brought over, piece by piece, from the banks of the Nile to those of the Tiber, except a few accessory parts which seem to be of Roman imitation. Whatever may be left standing of this great structure is concealed by the modern houses of the Via di S. Ignazio and di S. Stefano del Cacco; but the archæological and artistic treasures discovered among the ruins from 1374 to 1833 are innumerable and mostly preserved in Rome.

In 1374, the first obelisk, now in the Piazza della Rotonda, was found under the apse of S. Maria sopra Minerva; it is possible that the other, now in the Villa Mattei (von Hoffmann) may have come to light at the same time. In 1435, Eugenius IV. discovered the two lions of Nektaneb I. which are now in the Vatican (hall of monuments, Museo Egizio), and the two of black basalt now in the Capitoline Museum (vestibule, ground floor). In 1440, the colossal reclining figure of a River God was found and buried again. The Tiber of the Louvre (Froehner's Catalogue, p. 411, n. 449) and the Nile of the Braccio Nuovo seem to have come to

light during the pontificate of Leo X.; at all events it was he who
caused them to be removed to the Vatican. These two masterpieces (L'art romain, qui se plaisait à imposer par les masses, n'a
rien produit de supérieur à ces deux colosses) were stolen by the
French invaders in the month of Messidor, an X. (July, 1803).
The Nile was given back, however, after the fall of Napoleon.
This last event, an act of plain justice if ever there was one, is

Fig. 196. — The Nile of the Braccio Nuovo — A Fragment.

thus alluded to by Froehner : " Le group du Nil, qui formait pendant avec *notre* Tibre, *a été enlevé* du musée Napoléon le 18 octobre
1815." In 1556, Giovanni de Fabi found and sold to Cardinal
Farnese the reclining statue of the Ocean, now in Naples; in 1719,
the Isiac altar, now in the Capitol (Corpus Inscr., vol. vi. n. 344),
was found under the Casanatense library. The date of the find
of the obelisks of the sphæristerion at Urbino, of the Villa Albani,
and of La Minerva is not known. In 1858, Pietro Tranquilli, in
restoring his house, the nearest to the apse of La Minerva, discovered the following objects : a Sphinx of green granite, with
the portrait head of Queen Haths'epu, sister of Thothmes III.,
now in the collection of Baron Barracco, Via del Corso, 160 ; a

group of the cow Hathor, the living symbol of Isis, nursing the young Pharaoh Horemheb; a portrait statue of the grand dignitary Uahábra, now in the Museo Archeologico, Florence; a column of the temple, with high reliefs representing an Isiac procession; a capital carved with papyrus leaves and lotus flowers, now in the Museo Capitolino; and a fragment of an Egyptian bas-relief in red granite, now in the Museo delle Terme.

In 1859, Augusto Silvestrelli, the owner of the next house on the same side of the Via di S. Ignazio, found five capitals of the same style and size, which, I believe, are now in the Museo Etrusco Vaticano. In 1883, I asked the Archæological Commission to search the ground in front of the Silvestrelli and Tranquilli houses, where I knew that many other works of art were lying. My request was kindly complied with, and the work began on Monday, June 11. The first thing to appear was a magnificent Sphinx of black basalt, the portrait of King Amasis; then came the obelisk inscribed with the name of Rameses the Great, set up in 1887 in the Piazza dei Cinquecento opposite the railway station, in memory of the brave soldiers who fell at the battle of Dogali; two Kynokephaloi, with the cartouches of King Necthorheb, carved in black porphyry; a crocodile in red granite; the pedestal of a candelabrum; another column of the temple covered with bas-reliefs; and a portion of the capital. All these objects are exhibited in the vestibule and court of the Museo Capitolino.

LITERATURE.— Rodolfo Lanciani, *Le reconti scoperte dell' Iseo Campense* (in Bull. com., 1883, p. 33).— Ernesto Schiaparelli, *ibid.*, p. 61. — Giovanni Barracco, *ibid.* p. 104.— Orazio Marucchi, *ibid.*, n. 112, and plates i. to vii. — Wolfgang Helbig, *Guide*, vol. i. p. 28, n. 47. (Compare also *Bull. com.*, 1887, p. 377; and 1890, p. 307.) — Kaibel, *Inscr. grœcæ Italiæ*, n. 961, 1031.

LVI. TEMPLUM MATIDIÆ. — After restoring the Baths of Agrippa, the Sæpta, and the Portico of the Argonauts, and after rebuilding the Pantheon and the Neptunium, Hadrian filled up the vacant space between these last two edifices with a construction of his own, viz., with a temple (and a portico?) in honor of Marciana, sister of Trajan, and of Matidia, his sister-in-law. The seven large columns of cipollino, one of which is visible in the Via della Spada d' Orlando, the others under the adjoining houses, are the only existing remains of the temple. In the "album" of archæological views of Rome published in 1619 by Alò Giovannoli, plate 7 represents a round hall which he calls "tempio di Siepe" and places within the "pallazzo di SS^{rl} Capranici inverso Mezzogiorno." If he means the palace now occupied by the Collegio Capranica,

A. B. Templum Septarum ubi Vienne feruabantur unigo Capranua um ació Ad Meridiem fiscat Fulmen in Pantheon illapsa complures tegulas argenteas liquefecit
bi a i Tempio di Mezzo doue le Vienne si conferuauano Hora e Palazzo di SS. Capranica Inuerio Mezzogiorno Il Fulgore percuoti il Pantheone lessa molte delle sue tegole d'argento

Fig. 197. — A Round Temple or Hall sketched by Giovannoli in 1619, near the Palazzo Capranica.

in the piazza of that name, this noble relic must have formed part of Hadrian's architectural group. If we may believe a statement of Canina, worded in a very obscure way, the relic was discovered again in 1889.

LITERATURE. — Luigi Canina, *Indicazione topografica*, p. 399, n. 61. — Antonio Sangallo the younger, *Uffizi*, n. 1154. — Baldassare Peruzzi, *ibid.*, n. 632. — Rodolfo Lanciani, *La basilica Matidies et Marcianes* (in Bull. com., 1883, p. 6, pls. i., ii.).

I. THE OPERA ANTONINORUM.

LVII. The strip of land built and decorated by the first Antonines "marches" on the north with that built by Augustus, on the south with that built by Agrippa. Referring to the present state of the ground, it began at the corner of the Corso and the Via in Lucina, and ended with the Palazzo Ferraioli in the Piazza Colonna. The group comprised a temple in honor of (M. Aurelius) Antoninus, on the site of the Palazzo Chigi (?); a square in front of the temple, corresponding within certain limits with our Piazza Colonna, in the middle of which stood the celebrated spiral column of Marcus Aurelius; the house of Adrastus, the custodian of the same column; a portico; the column of Antoninus Pius; and the Ustrinum, where the bodies of the princes of this dynasty were cremated.

The entrance to this monumental group by the Via Flaminia was marked by a triumphal arch which stood at the corner of the Via della Vite, and was destroyed in 1662 by Pope Alexander VII. The arch was a patchwork of the third or fourth century (fatto di qualche reliquia di altri archi più antichi). We cannot therefore trust to the evidence of its bas-reliefs, — alleged to represent, the one on the right, the apotheosis of Faustina the younger, the one on the left, the Emperor M. Aurelius proclaiming a decree, — because they may have been borrowed from some other monument, like the panels of Constantine's arch; and because the heads of the Empress and the Emperor are modern. The two bas-reliefs were removed at first to the Capitoline Museum, and later on were placed in the upper landing of the stairs of the Conservatori Palace (1815). There is a third bas-relief of exactly the same size and style in the Palazzo Torlonia, Piazza di Venezia, which was formerly in the possession of Maria Felice Peretti Savelli; but Matz and von Duhn deny its connection with the arch on the Corso. Two of its columns of verde antico were bought by the Pamfili for two thousand scudi and placed on each side of the high altar at S. Agnese; two others ended in the Corsini Chapel at the Lateran. The key of the arch is to be found in the vestibule of the university, at the foot of the stairs. The arch is known in topographical books as the "Arco di Portogallo," because the Portuguese ambassadors lived in the adjacent Palazzo Ottoboni-Fiano. In the Middle Ages it was called *ad tres faccicelas,* — an extraordinary name, which seems to allude to "three faces," — and also "Arch of Tripolis," in allusion to three figures of cities. No clue to the origin of these strange denominations was obtained until 1891, when I discovered in a MS. note to an edition of Fulvio's "Antichità" of 1588, now in possession of Professor Hartmann Grisar, S. J., the statement by an eye-witness that in 1740, fifty palms from the northeast corner of the arch, a pillar had been found, "with *three figures* around it, of draped women in a mournful attitude, representing perhaps three cities conquered by the one to whom the triumphal arch belonged." The account is perfectly genuine: the pillar with the "three faces" is still in existence, and can be seen in the second compartment at the end of the Galleria delle Statue, Museo Vaticano. No mention of this highly interesting group is made in Helbig's "Guide." The following illustration of the arch was made from a photograph of an original sketch by Ligorio in "Cod. Torin.," xiv.

LITERATURE. — Antonio Sangallo the elder, *Cod. Barberin.*, f. 22'. *Cod. Barberin.*, xlviii. f. 3. Drawing in the Kunstgewerbe Museum, Berlin. — Marcello Severoli, *Atti accad. Cortona*, vol. i. p. 109. — Rodolfo Lanciani, *L' arco di Portogallo* (in Bull. com., 1891, p. 18). — Matz and von Duhn, *Antike Bildwerke in Rom*, vol. iii. n. 3526. — Wolfgang Helbig, *Guide*, vol. i. p. 409, n. 549, 550.

Fig. 198. — The so-called Arch of M. Aurelius on the Corso, sketched by Ligorio.

The TEMPLUM DIVI MARCI, which may also be called the Augusteum of his dynasty, has disappeared so completely that topographers are still discussing where to place it. Nibby believes it to be represented in the third bas-relief of the arch now in the Torlonia Palace.

The COLUMNA DIVI MARCI ET DIVÆ FAUSTINÆ, also called

Columna Centenaria (one hundred feet high) and "Column of Marcus Aurelius," was raised in or about the year a. d. 176 in commemoration of the satisfactory issue of the Germanic and Sarmatian wars fought by the Roman army under M. Aurelius. This monument, designed in imitation of Trajan's Column, has been lately cast, photographed, and minutely studied by Professor Petersen of the German Institute, who has already given us a foretaste of the results of his work in the "Beiblatt zum Jahrbuch des Archäologischen Instituts," vol. xi. 1896, pp. 2–18. Professor Petersen treats the various points of the subject in the following order : the history of the column, the history of the double war, the erection of the column, its structure, the chronology of its historical reliefs (bellum Germanicum and bellum Sarmaticum), the ornaments of the pedestal. The whole artistic and archæological apparatus will be published shortly in a magnificent and richly illustrated volume.

There are two (?) other monuments in Rome commemorating the wars in which Marcus Aurelius was engaged during the last fourteen years of his reign, against the Germanic Marcomanni or Quadi and against the Sarmatian Jazygi : the panels from the triumphal arch raised to him between the Curia and the Carcer, at the entrance to the Clivus Argentarius (which may be called the beginning of the Via Flaminia) from the Forum ; and the sarcophagus from the Vigna Ammendola, now in the Museo Capitolino, ground floor, second room on the right, No. 5. The panels are now set up in the walls of the first landing of the staircase of the Conservatori Palace. (See Helbig's Guide, vol. i. p. 406, n. 544–546; and Lanciani's L' aula e gli uffici del senato Romano, p. 15.) The bas-reliefs of the sarcophagus, discovered in the Vigna Ammendola in 1830, were identified by Dr. Blackie in 1831 as representing a battle-scene of the same wars. The workmanship, he said, was necessarily different from that of the column, because the reliefs of the coffin were to be seen quite near to the pavement of the square, those of the pillar at a great height from it. The figures, therefore, are naked and anatomically perfect in the first case, whilst in the other they are draped and "sketchy." Dr. Blackie thinks that one of the leading officers of M. Aurelius may have been buried in the sarcophagus. His statements, however, have not been accepted by archæologists, who believe the barbarians to be Gauls and not Germans.[1]

---

[1] Literature. — *Annal. Inst.*, 1831, p. 287, pls. 30, 31. — *Revue archéologique*, vol. iii. 1889, p. 331, n. 4. — Wolfgang Helbig, *Guide*, vol. i. p. 304, n. 422.

The column stood in the middle of a square probably inclosed by a portico. Ligorio (Cod. Torin., xv. f. 101') sketched a beautiful base as belonging to one of the "edifices of the Corinthian order bordering on the square, in which many marbles and blocks of stone have been dug up and destroyed by stonecutters." The columns were probably of pavonazzetto. The pavement of the square, 4.75 metres lower than the present one, was of slabs of travertine resting on a bed of concrete 0.33 metre thick. A bronze finger, probably from the statue of the Emperor on the top of the pillar, was discovered by Marchese Ferraioli in 1872 in the foundations of his palace on the south side of the piazza. It is now exhibited in the Room of Bronzes of the Conservatori Palace.

In the Middle Ages the column became the property of the monks of S. Silvestro (SS. Dionysii et Silvestri in Catapauli). An inscription in the vestibule of the present church, dated 1119, states that both the column and the little church of S. Nicholai de Columna, which stood close to it, were leased to the highest bidder by the monks, probably from year to year. The column was evidently rented on account of the profit which could be derived from pilgrims or tourists wishing to ascend it. For a similar reason (rather than for taking care of and watching the monument) an application was addressed to the Emperor Septimius Severus in 193 by a freedman named Adrastus, for the right of building a lodge in its neighborhood — "in contermiuis locis" — where he and his successors could more easily attend to their duty. The application was granted, and Adrastus received also a free supply of bricks and tiles, and ten cartloads of timber from the Imperial administration. Like a wise and cautious man, he caused the official correspondence about this business to be engraved, word by word, on the door-posts of his lodge. These valuable documents, dated from August 6 to September 9, A. D. 193 — a remarkably short period for such a transaction — were discovered *in situ* in 1777 in the Piazza di Monte Citorio on the right of the obelisk, and removed to the Museo Pio-Clementino. (See Corpus Inscr., vol. vi. n. 1585, *a, b.*)

The abacus of the capital of the column and the "loggia" on the outside of it can be reached by a spiral staircase, now entered from the south side, and formerly from the (east) side facing the Via Flaminia. There are 203 steps (185 in that of Trajan) and 56 loopholes (46 in Trajan's), each looking towards the cardinal points. The existence of so many openings makes the pillar weaker, so that the cracks of the great rings of marble run mostly through them.

Sixtus V. spent 9284 scudi in repairing the column, injured by
time, fire, lightning, and earthquakes. The vignettes of Lafreri
(1550), Gamucci (1565), du Perac (1573), Cavalieri (1585), and the
frescoes in the Vatican library, show to what an insecure state
it was reduced towards the end of the sixteenth century (1589).
The accounts of Domenico Fontana, the architect of Pope Sixtus,
who directed the repairs, are full of valuable information, especially as regards the restoration of part of the bas-reliefs. The
marble was taken from the Septizonium.

LITERATURE. — Antonio Bertolotti, *Artisti lombardi a Roma*, vol. i. p. 80. —
Carlo Fea, *Miscellanea*, vol. ii. p. 8, n. 2 ; and p. 254. — *Notizie del Giorno*,
March, 1820 ; and *Dissertazione sulle rovine di Roma*, pp. 332, 348 (in Winckel-
mann's *Storia*, vol. iii.). — *Bull. Inst.*, 1831, p. 198. — Bernardo Gamucci, *Anti-
chità*, p. 154. — Antonio Nibby, *Roma antica*, vol. ii. p. 635. — Gio. Battista
Piranesi, *Campus Martius*, p. 69 ; and, *Colonna Antonina*, in 16 sheets. — Pietro
Sante Bartoli, *Colonna eretta in onore di Marco Aurelio*, in 77 sheets.

The COLUMNA DIVI PII (of Antoninus) and the USTRINUM
and ARA ANTONINORUM were excavated in 1703–1704 under the
garden of the Cavaliere Eustachio, now occupied by the ex-convent
of the "Signori della Missione," west of the Curia Innocenziana
(House of Parliament). The excavations and discoveries have
been described by Professor Huelsen in a memoir on the "Antichità di Monte Citorio," published and profusely illustrated in vol.
iv. 1889, of the "Mittheilungen," p. 41. The column, raised in
memory of Antoninus Pius by his sons M. Aurelius and L. Verus,
was of red granite, 14.75 metres high, and rested on a marble
pedestal with high reliefs representing the apotheosis of Antoninus
and Faustina and a military "decursio." The pedestal and the
column were removed to the Piazza di Monte Citorio, to be re-
erected in front of the Curia Innocenziana; but the project was
given up after a fire which consumed the wooden shed under which
the shaft was lying. Pieces of the half-charred shaft were used
in the restoration of the obelisk of Augustus raised by Pius VI.
in the same piazza, and the pedestal, restored by de Fabris, was
placed in the middle of the Giardino della Pigna in the Vatican.
Leo XIII. has caused it to be removed to the hemicycle of Pius
IV., at the north end of the same gardens.

LITERATURE. — Giovanni Vignoli, *De columna Antonini*. Rome, 1705. —
Francesco Cancellieri, *Della colonna di Antonino*. Rome, 1821. — *Journal des
Savants*, vol. xxxii. p. 542 ; vol. xxxiii. p. 785. — *Giornale dei Letterati*, vol.
v. p. 12. — *Cod. vatic.*, 8091, f. 41; 9023, f. 224. — Francesco Ficoroni, *Piombi
antichi*. Rome, 1740, p. 6. — Francesco Posterla, *Ragguaglio di quanto si

operato per l' innalzamento della colonna Antonina. Rome, 1705. — Carlo Fea, *Miscellanea*, vol. i. p. cxxiii. — *Corpus Inscr.*, vol. i. n. 1004. — De Fabris, *Il piedistallo della colonna Antonina.* Rome, 1846. — Luigi Bruzza, *Annal. Inst.*, 1870, p. 131, pl. G, 3. — Gio. Battista Piranesi, *Campus Martius*, p. 53, tav. xxxii.

THE HARBOR OF ROME AND THE COMMERCIAL QUARTERS
ON THE LEFT BANK OF THE TIBER.*

LVIII. The commercial quarters occupied a considerable space of the city ground on the left of the Tiber, reaching inland as far as the cliffs of the Capitoline and of the Aventine, and down stream from the Theatre of Marcellus (Piazza Montanara) to the neighborhood of S. Paolo fuori le Mura. The places of interest in this region were —

The *Forum Holitorium.*
Several porticoes.
The temples of *Juno, Hope,* and *Piety.*
The *Forum Boarium.*

The temples of *Ceres, Mater Matuta,* and *Fortuna Virilis.*
The *Statio Annonæ.*
The wharves and warehouses for grain, marble, salt, lead, bricks, etc.

The pool of the Tiber began with the last of the city bridges and extended as far as the reach of the Vicus Alexandri, 2500 metres below the Porta Ostiensis, where the larger sea-going vessels were obliged to take to the moorings to avoid the sand-banks and the exceedingly sharp turns of the upper channel. As the Pons Sublicius can be compared to a certain extent with London Bridge, so the Vicus Alexandri may be called the Gravesend of ancient Rome. The Pons Sublicius, by preventing vessels furnished with masts from reaching the wharves up stream, divided the navigation of the noble river into two sections, the maritime and the fluvial. Bargees, porters, lightermen, pilots, sailors, skippers, underwriters, etc., connected with the maritime section were probably called *infernates,* an adjective which is better explained in the " Corpus Inscr.," vi. n. 1639, by the phrase "infra pontem sublicium," below bridges; those connected with the section above bridges were probably called *supernates.*

These rowdy crowds lived mostly in the slums of the Trastevere, under the watch of the vigiles. Sailors from foreign lands placed their interests in the hands of their respective consuls or πρόξενοι, of whom many records have been found at Porto, at Ostia, and in Rome itself. These foreigners were also allowed to worship their own gods, θεοὶ πατρῷοι, in places appointed by the Harbor and

*See Figure 199 facing page 532.

Docks Commissioner. We find, therefore, some of the consuls in-
vested at the same time with commercial and religious functions.
The copious and highly interesting epigraphic material collected
in vols. vi. and xiv. of the " Corpus " on the subject of the harbor
of Rome, and of the motley crowd which thronged its quays, has
not yet been examined synthetically. Such a study would make
us acquainted with many details regarding the various lines of
navigation, the quantity and quality of merchandise imported and
exported, the corporations of tradesmen haunting the wharves
(*portus, ripæ*) and the warehouses (*horrea*), the police of the river,
etc.[1]

From the point of view of topography and of existing remains,
we must confine ourselves to the following brief considerations : —

The left bank of the river, within the limits above stated, was
divided into sections or wharves, called *portus* or harbors. The
wharves did not protrude into the river : they were simply sections
of the quay or embankment, provided with landings, stairs, or
inclines, and mooring-rings, parallel with the stream, and destined
for a particular kind of trade, — for marbles, wine, oil, lead, pottery, building-materials, fish, fuel, timber, iron, and so forth.
They were named from their special appropriation, as the Portus
vinarius, lignarius, etc. ; or from the owner of the wharf, as the Portus Licinii, Portus Vargæ ; or from the seaport with which the
trade was carried on, such as the Portus Neapolitanus, etc. The
name *portus* for a wharf has survived to the present day, although
their number has been reduced to two (Porto della Legna and
Porto della Pozzolana). The classic name of *ripa* for a quay or
embankment would also have survived, had it not been officially

---

[1] Inscriptions speak of "mercatores frumentarii et olearii Afrarii," importers of wheat and oil from Northern Africa (n. 1620); of "negotiatores
olearii ex Bætica," importers of oil from Andalusia (n. 1625, *b*), also called
"mercatores olei hispani ex provincia Bætica " (n. 1934); of "negotiantes
vini Ariminensis," importers of wine from the Northern Adriatic coast (n.
1101); of "negotiantes boarii qui invehent," importers of cattle (n. 1035), and
so on. Engaged in the river trade and in harbor operations were the " codicarii," also called "codicarii navicularii," forming the crew of light ships employed in transporting the corn from Ostia to Rome (Marquardt, *Staatsverw.*,
ii. 110); the "curatores navium amnalium et marinarum," whose duties in reference to river barges and sea-going vessels are not well defined; the "lenuncularii," patrons of skiffs; the "lenuncularii traiectuum," specially engaged
in ferrying men and merchandise from one bank to the other; the "fabri
navales," shipbuilders or repairers ; the "stuppatores " or calkers ; the
"saburrarii," loaders and unloaders of ballast; the "scapharii," boatmen and
bargees; the "urinatores," divers, etc. See *Corpus*, vol. xiv. p. 581.

substituted by that of "Lungo Tevere." And we have come to
the point of having a section of the embankment called "Lungo
Tevere Ripa"!

Vegetables, imported by land or water, were put for sale in a
special market called the —

LIX. FORUM HOLITORIUM (see p. 458). — Its site corresponds
with that of the Piazza Montanara. It was surrounded by stately
buildings, like the Theatre of Marcellus, the Temple of Apollo,
the Porticus Minucia, and the four temples of Juno (Sospita?), of
Janus, of Spes, and of Pietas. Remains of the Porticus Minucia
can be seen under the houses Nos. 27 and 34 on the east side of the
piazza, and also in the Via della Bufola, under the house No. 35,
belonging to Augusto Castellani. Others were discovered and
destroyed in December, 1879, during the demolition of a block of
houses at the south end of the Piazza Montanara. The Porticus
Minucia is built of travertine, and its pilasters are crowned with
Doric capitals.

Opposite the portico and in a parallel line with it, under, within,
and around the church of S. Nicola in Carcere — so named from
the Byzantine state prison of Rome, which opened on the adjoining street of Porta Leone (Pierleoni) — are the remains of three
temples of the time of the Republic — two of the Ionic, one of the
Doric order.

The Temple of Hope, built about 253 B. C. by Aulus Atilius
Calatinus, in fulfillment of a vow made during the Spanish campaign, is the nearest to the Theatre of Marcellus. The middle
temple, the largest of the three, of Ionic architecture like the preceding one,[1] is considered to be the Templum Pietatis vowed by
Manius Acilius Glabrio at the battle of Thermopylæ, and built
and dedicated by his son in 181 B. C. The question has been asked
whether or not the name of Piety was connected with the legend
of the pious daughter who, with the milk of her breast, kept alive
her father, sentenced to death by starvation in the prison built by
Appius the decemvir. The legend, however, is much later than
the temple itself. In the excavations made in 1808 by the architect Valadier the pedestal of an equestrian statue was found at the
foot of the stairs in front of the temple; the same, most likely, as
that mentioned by Livy.

[1] The volutes of the capitals of the columns differ from the ordinary type,
and attracted the attention of Raphael by their singularity. Compare Winckelmann's *Storia delle Arti*, vol. iii. p. 59.

The third and smallest temple, of the Doric order, is considered to be the one vowed to Juno Sospita by Cnæus Cornelius Cethegus during his encounter with the Insubrian Gauls in 197 B. C.   To study these interesting remains, it is necessary to make the tour of the block of houses within which the church of S. Nicola is confined, and also to descend into the crypt, where some interesting details can be seen.   (Apply to the sacristan.)

When Byron was in Rome, the crypt was shown to him as the real prison of Appius the decemvir, and to it he dedicated the well-known stanza commencing with the verse, " There is a dungeon in whose dim drear light."   The name of S. Pietro in Carcere appears for the first time in the Life of Urban II. (1088–99), but it is of earlier origin.   Compare Duchesne, " Liber pontificalis," vol. i. p. 515, n. 13 ; and vol. ii. p. 295, n. 12, 13.

The area of the Forum Holitorium between the three temples and the Porticus Minucia is paved with slabs of travertine. Valadier saw the pavement in 1808, and I traced it myself for a length of 30 or 40 metres on November 20, 1875.   In the middle of it stood the Columna Lactaria, where infants were exposed and abandoned to public charity.   Here also auctions were held.   No traces are left of the " Templum Jani apud Forum Holitorium " built by C. Duilius, reconstructed by Tiberius, the anniversary feast of which fell on August 17.

LITERATURE.— Pietro Bellori, *Vestig. vet. Romæ*, p. 1.— *Corpus Inscr.*, vol. vi. n. 562, 979, 1113, 29,830.— Adolf Becker, *Topographie*, pp. 259, 602.— Antonio Nibby, *Roma antica*, vol. ii. p. 17.— *Notizie degli Scavi*, 1876, p. 138; 1879, p. 314. The fundamental designs for the whole group are by Baldassare Peruzzi, marked 477, 478, 536, 537, 573, 631 in the Uffizi collection. See also Piranesi, *Camp. Mart.*, pl. xiv.— *Beschreibung*, vol. iii. 3 (6–13).— Rodolfo Lanciani, *Bull. com.*, 1875, p. 173.— Otto Hirschfeld, *Verwaltungsgeschichte*, p. 134; and *Philologus*, xxix. 63.— Theodor Mommsen, *Staatsrecht*, ii³, p. 1053.

LX. FORUM BOARIUM (the cattle wharves and cattle market). — A remarkable inscription discovered in 1892 on the Via Prænestina speaks of a cattle-dealer as one of the celebrated men of the age : " To the memory of M. Antonius Terens, from Misenum, elected to the highest offices in his native city, a most famous importer of pigs and sheep " (*negotiatori celeberrimo suariæ et pecuariæ*), etc.[1] The supplies for the daily maintenance of the population of Rome were not brought in and sold promiscuously in one or more markets (the Macella were used for retail trade only), but each whole-

[1] The tombstone is exhibited in the Museo delle Terme, on the east wing of the cloisters. See *Bull. com.*, 1891, p. 318.

sale trade had its own special place. The Forum Boarium was set apart for dealers in horned cattle, the Vinarium for wine merchants, the Piscarium for fishmongers, the Holitorium for green-grocers, the Pistorium for importers of grain; candles, paper, spices were sold in the Horrea Candelaria, Chartaria, Piperataria; the trade in boots and shoes had its centre in the Vicus Sandaliarius; that of perfumes in the Vicus Tuscus. Goldsmiths had taken possession of the Porticus Margaritaria on the Sacra Via, booksellers of the Argiletum, copyists or antiquaries of the Forum Julium. The streets, or vici, Lorarius, Vitrarius, Argentarius; the squares, or areæ, Pannaria, Lanataria, had probably been so named from the saddlers, glaziers, money-changers, and dry-goods merchants who had their shops in them. M. Antonius Terens must have become celebrated in the pig market, Forum Suarium, the place of which is still marked by the church of S. Nicolao in Porcilibus, Via dei Lucchesi; and in the sheep market, Campus Pecuarius, the site of which is not known. Both places were subject to the jurisdiction of the prefect of the city. Dealings were regulated by strict rules engraved on marble in a double copy: one was posted in the Porticus Tellurensis, the official advertising place of the Præfectura Urbis; the other on the market itself. We possess the original regulations issued in A. D. 339 by the Prefect Apronianus: one concerning the dealers in pigs, one the dealers in sheep. (See *Corpus Inscr.*, vol. vi. n. 1770, 1771.) The situation of these two markets in or near the centre of the city gives rise to this question, Were they really destined to actual trade in cattle? and if so, how was the daily passage of cattle through the city regulated?

The inscription on the so-called " Arco degli Argentieri " at S. Giorgio in Velabro leaves no doubt that cattle were actually bought and sold on the spot — " negotiantes Boarii HVIVS LOCI qui invehent." [1] Contracts are usually made in such places in the presence of the live animal, which is touched and felt and valued at a glance by the importer, the butcher, and the mediator. The same practice must have been followed in the Forum Suarium. Now it seems impossible that some of the main thoroughfares of the Imperial city, and three or four bridges, should have been periodically closed to traffic, for the accommodation of importers of cattle driving their stock from one market to the other. I believe that the oxen came to the Forum Boarium by the river, by barge-loads, but for the other animals I can make no suggestion.

[1] *Corpus Inscr.*, vol. vi. n. 1035.

The Roman fora and campi of this kind differed from modern shambles and slaughter-houses in this respect, that cattle were only bought and sold in their precincts, not slaughtered. The slaughter took place in the premises of each butcher, a habit which lasted up to Gregory XVI. (1838). Roman inscriptions speak of a Corpus Confectuariorum,[1] makers and packers of sausages and pig's meat, spread all over the city. Butchers also had no special quarters, except perhaps in the region of the Piscina publica, where the " lanii piscinenses " formed a powerful corporation.[2] It is probable that the wholesale slaughter of oxen may have taken place in this remote district.

The Forum Boarium is very interesting from a monumental point of view. It was surrounded by stately buildings, most of which exist still in a tolerable state of repair. These buildings are the temples of Fortuna Virilis, of Mater Matuta, of Ceres, Liber, and Libera (of Pudicitia Patricia, of Hercules Victor destroyed by Sixtus IV.), the Janus, the so-called " Arco degli Argentieri," and the " Loggia dei Mercanti " of ancient Rome.

LXI. TEMPLUM FORTUNÆ, miscalled VIRILIS, built of stone coated with stucco, in the Ionic style, on the gradient leading from the Forum Boarium to the Æmilian bridge. Antiquaries agree in identifying it with the temple originally built by Servius Tullius about 557 B. C., and reconstructed after a fire in 214. If they are not mistaken, this would be one of the most ancient of the Roman temples existing, at the same time the best preserved of all. It shows the manner in which such edifices were constructed of the native stone of the country, before marble was introduced. Not only, therefore, have we evidence of the date given by the material; but the style, the purest and simplest example of the Ionic order in Rome, proves the edifice to have been built at a time when the Romans had not commenced to debase the fair proportions of Greek orders by attempting to improve or to embellish them. It was converted into a church in 872 by a certain Stephen, who walled up the open intercolumniations of the pronaos to increase its size. In the time of Pius V. (1566-72) it was given to the Armenians, and from that time has been called Santa Maria Egiziaca. The temple was excavated for the first (?) time in 1551, when the inscriptions given in "Corpus," vol. vi. n. 897, 898, came to light. The best-known

---

[1] *Corpus Inscr.*, vol. vi. n. 1690.
[2] Wilhelm Henzen, *Scavi nel bosco degli Arvali.* Rome, 1868, p. 103.

Fig. 200. — Temple of Fortuna; Details of the Order.

ornament of the ancient sanctuary was a wooden statue of king
Servius Tullius, dressed in a double toga, held in great veneration
by the Romans.

LITERATURE. — Antonio Nibby, *Roma antica*, vol. ii. p. 17. — *Corpus Inscr.*,
vol. vi. n. 897, 898. — Sallustio Peruzzi, *Uffizi*, 664. — Antonio Dosio, *ibid.*,
2027. — Giovanni Alberti, *Cod. S. Sepolcro*, f. 67′, 68; and Cherubino Alberti,
ibid., f. 26, 27, 42. — *Kunstgewerbe Museum*, Berlin, f. A, 376, C.

LXII. TEMPLUM MATRIS MATUTÆ (the so-called Temple of
Vesta). — No less than ten names have been attributed to this
graceful round temple, on the west side of the Forum Boarium.
The most acceptable of all seems to be that of Mater Matuta, an
old Italic goddess of the dawn (*mane, matutina*), also worshiped
as a goddess of the sea and of harbors, like Ino Leucothea, with
whom she was identified. No better location could have been
selected by Servius, the supposed builder of this temple, on the
bank of the Tiber, and at the head of its harbor and quays. The
temple was rebuilt by the dictator Camillus after the capture of
Veii; but the one the picturesque remains of which form the leading landmark of the present Piazza della Bocca della Verità dates

probably from the time of Augustus. It is peripteral, formed by twenty Corinthian columns, of which only one is wanting. As in the case of the Temple of Fortune, we owe its preservation to its having been dedicated to Christian uses. The Savelli, by whom it was offered to S. Stefano (delle Carrozze), walled up the spaces between the columns. In 1560 the name was changed to that of S. Maria del Sole. At the beginning of this century the inter-columniations were reopened, the building was restored and pro-tected by railings, and the roof was repaired. At the same time the accumulation of soil between the two temples (of Matuta and For-tuna) was removed, and the steps were exposed to view. These excavations are described by Guattani in "Roma antica," vol. i. p. 93, note. It was then ascertained that the Augustan marble temple rests on the Republican structure, the foundations and steps of which were not removed or taken away, but simply covered by the new superstructure of marble. No better example of such a con-tingency, I mean, of the chronological vicissitudes and of the archi-tectural transformation of a temple, can be found within the walls.

The temple ran a certain risk in 1827 when a visionary — repre-sentative of a race which is not yet extinct — obtained from the government of Leo XII. permission to cut a deep hole inside the cella to discover a buried treasure of the Savelli. The following illustration of this extraordinary search is taken from a sketch made by Valadier while it was going on (Fig. 201). Needless to add, no treasure was found.

The Temple of the Mater Matuta is often mentioned by Livy: first in 394 B. C., when Camillus "ædem Matutæ matri refectam dedicavit" (v. 19, 23); again in 215, when the whole quarter "inter salinas et portam Carmentalem" was destroyed by fire, its damages being repaired the following year (xxiv. 47 to xxv. 7); and lastly in 198, when L. Stertinius raised two arches in the Forum Boarium with the spoil of the Spanish war: one opposite the Temple of Fortune, one opposite that of Mater Matuta. The cella of this last contained among other things the "elogium" of Tiberius Sempronius Gracchus, and a plan of the island of Sardinia.

LITERATURE. — Adolf Becker, *Topographie*, p. 483. — Heinrich Jordan, *To-pographie*, vol. i. part ii. p. 484. — Antonio Sangallo, *Cod. Barberin.*, f. 37. — Sallustio Peruzzi, *Uffizi*, 655, 689. — Antonio Dosio, *ibid.*, 2024. — Palladio, *Vatican.*, 9838, p. 3. — *Notizie Scavi*, 1895, p. 458.

LXIII. TEMPLUM CERERIS LIBERI LIBERÆQUE (Temple of Ceres, Bacchus, and Proserpina), vowed by A. Postumius, dictator

Fig. 201. — The Excavations of 1827 in the Temple of Mater Matuta, from a Sketch by Valadier.

497 B. C., while pressed by famine in the Latin war, and dedicated by Spurius Cassius, consul 494 B. C. It was designed in Tuscan style, and built mostly of painted terra-cotta panels nailed on a wooden frame, the joint work of Damophilos and Gorgasos. Tacitus includes it among the sacred edifices the restoration of which, begun by Augustus, was finished by Tiberius in A. D. 17. Vitruvius says it was areostyle, with wooden architraves resting on columns of the Tuscan order. It was destroyed by Pope Hadrian I. to please the Greek colony settled in the neighborhood (Schola Græca, 772–795), as it threatened to crush in its fall their national church of S. Maria in Cosmedin. There are only two fragments of the walls of the cella left standing : one in the crypt of the church just mentioned, one in the courtyard of the sacristy. (See Fig. 203.)

LITERATURE. — *Corpus Inscr.*, 2181, 2182. — Pliny, *Hist. Nat.*, xxxv. 45. — Mario Crescimbeni, *Diaconia di S. Maria in Cosmedin.* Rome, 1715. — *Bull. com.*, 1876, p. 181. — Antonio Nibby, *Roma antica*, vol. ii. p. 654. — Gio. Battista Giovenale, *Annuario*, 1895, *dell' associazione artistica fra i cultori di architettura in Roma*, p. 13.

LXIV. THE JANUS AND THE ARCH OF SEVERUS AND CARACALLA. — Near the church of S. Giorgio in Velabro stands a four-faced arch of considerable size, entirely built of marble in the style of the decadence prevailing at the beginning of the fourth century, believed by the common people to be that of the four-headed Janus represented on the coins of Nero. Each of the four piers is decorated with twelve niches, apparently intended for the reception of statues. Of these niches eight are complete, four left unfinished. In one of these is a doorway leading up a narrow staircase to a suite of chambers and corridors, scientifically explored for the first time by Angelo Uggeri at the time of the French invasion. The brick part of the structure is very bad, and in the thickness of the vault there are earthen vases (*pignatte*) to lessen its weight, like those in the circus of Romulus and in the mausoleum of Helena, called for this reason Torre Pignattara.. This singular building belongs to a class rather common in Rome, that of places of shelter raised in public markets for the convenience of money-lenders and changers, merchants, scribes, etc. That this forum was actually used for transactions in the horned cattle trade is proved by the inscription engraved on the frieze of the graceful little arch near by, upon one pier of which the campanile of S. Giorgio in Velabro is raised. The inscription states that it was built in the year 204, in honor of Septimius Severus, Caracalla, Geta, and Julia Domna, by the "argentarii et negotiantes boarii *huius loci* qui invehent."

(See Corpus, vol. v. n. 1035.) The architects of the Renaissance gave the most curious names to this structure. Cherubino Alberti calls it " l' arco di la vacha el toro," the arch of the cow and the bull, presumably because of the figures of these animals which

Fig. 202. — The Janus of the Forum Boarium, the Arch of Severus, and the Church of S. Giorgio, from a Sketch by M. Heemskerk.

appear in the bas-relief; and Giuliano da S. Gallo "larcho didecio," the arch of Decius, a title which remains inexplicable. The accompanying view of both structures (Fig. 202) was taken in 1536 by Martin Heemskerk.

LITERATURE. — Emiliano Sarti, in *Archiv. Società storia patria*, vol. ix. p. 500. — Heinrich Jordan, *Topographie*, vol. i², p. 470. — Rodolfo Lanciani, *Ancient Rome*, p. 295; and *Bull. Inst.*, 1871, p. 9.

LXV. STATIO ANNONÆ, the residence of the præfectus Annonæ, the headquarters of the administration of public supplies, and the "loggia dei Mercanti" of ancient Rome. Discoveries made at various times had already indicated the neighborhood of S. Maria in Cosmedin as the probable seat of this department. When the Piazza della Bocca della Verità was lowered in 1715, a pedestal dedicated to Constantine by Madalianus, præfectus Annonæ, was discovered in front of the church. The banks of the Tiber on either side of the piazza were occupied by public buildings connected with, and dependent on, the statio, which must have been a great edifice in itself, with a large staff of officials of the "fiscus frumentarius," of the "tabularium," etc. The statio must have been established here in the remotest period of Roman history, at least since the famine of 437 B. C., when L. Minucius was created præfectus Annonæ (Livy, iv. 13), because the monument commemorating his services was erected precisely in this neighborhood. The monument took the characteristic shape of a column, made

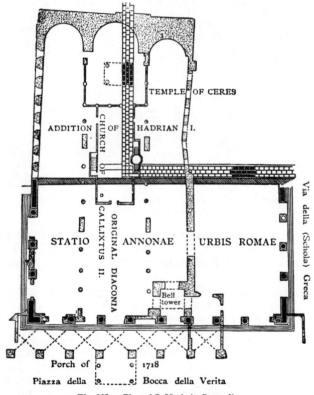

Fig. 203. — Plan of S. Maria in Cosmedin.

with stone mortars for grinding corn, placed one above the other. The same motive of decoration is to be found in the tomb of the prince of Roman bakers, M. Vergilius Eurysaces, discovered in 1838 outside the Porta Maggiore. The remains of the statio An-

nonæ were brought to light in 1893 under rather curious circumstances. Architects and topographers were unanimous in admitting
that the church of S. Maria in Cosmedin occupied the site of the
Temple of Ceres, described above. A committee of the Society of
Roman Architects having been asked to inquire into the possibility
of restoring the church to its original type, doing away with the
barbarous restorations of the eighteenth century, the most careful
search was made to ascertain the age of the various parts of the
building. The result of the search is illustrated by the following
plan, which proves that the building contains — (*a*) Remains of
the foundations of the temple, two thousand four hundred years
old. (*b*) A hall of the fourth century after Christ, with an open
colonnade on three sides, resembling the "loggie dei Mercanti" of

Fig. 204. — S. Maria in Cosmedin in the Sixteenth Century.

our mediæval cities. This was probably the corn exchange of
ancient Rome, forming part of the offices of the prefect of the An-
nona. The columns and their capitals and bases are of uneven
size; the style of the stucco decorations, in the arches above the
columns, is exactly like that of the Christian structures of the
fourth century; and so is the style of masonry, made up of bricks
and chips of stone with no regularity in the lines of the layers.
(*c*) Remains of the original Diaconia, believed to be contemporary

with the reigns of Theodoric and Athalaric. The Diaconia occupied part of the corn exchange, without trespassing on the area of the temple. (d) Remains of the church rebuilt and enlarged by Pope Hadrian I. about A. D. 780. The colony of the *schola græca* (the name is still attached to the street parallel with the south side of the church) having increased in number after the outbreak of the iconoclastic persecution of 725, their national church "in Cosmedin" became insufficient for their use. The "Liber pontificalis" describes it as "dudum brevis, in ædificiis existens, sub ruinis posita," a small oratory nestled among ruined edifices. ◦Hadrian I. spent one year in demolishing the Temple of Ceres, which is called "maximum monumentum de tiburtino tufo super eam (diaconiam) dependens," and doubled the size of the church. Calixtus II. (1119–24) connected in better style the two halves of the fifth and the eighth centuries. Under Boniface VIII. (1294–1303) Cardinal Francesco Caetani, nephew of the pope, repaired the edifice, reducing it to the form which appears in the above sketch of the sixteenth century, which I found in the Kupferstich Kabinet at Stuttgart (Grosse Sammlung, f. 81, n. 209).

Clement XI., between 1715 and 1719, leveled the piazza and built the curious fountain from the designs of Carlo Bizzaccheri. The pope's nephew, Annibale Albani, built the present façade and spoilt the beautiful bell-tower by concealing some of the finely cut windows with an enormous clock. The last damages done to the building date from 1758.

LITERATURE. — *Corpus Inscr.*, vi. 1151 (xiv. 135). — Gio. Battista de Rossi, *Le horrea sotto l' Aventino e la statio Annonæ urbis Romæ*, Ann. Inst., 1885, p. 223. — Theodor Mommsen, *Staatsrecht*, 2d ed., vol. ii[1], p. 468. — Marquardt, *Staatsverw.*, ii. p. 132. — Mario Crescimbeni, *L' istoria . . . di S. Maria in Cosmedin.* Rome, 1715. — Sallustio Peruzzi, *Uffizi*, n. 660. — *Annuario dell' associazione fra i cultori di architettura in Roma*, anno v., 1895, pp. 13–36. — Huelsen, in *Dissert. accad. arch. pont.*, 1896, p. 231.

LXVI. THE HORREA PUBLICA POPULI ROMANI (the grain wharves and warehouses). — The provinces bound to contribute to the maintenance of Rome with their staple products were Sicily, Africa, Mauretania, Egypt, Mœsia, and Spain. Aurelian extended the same charge (*canon urbicarium*) to some regions of the Peninsula, and to wine, oil, and wheat added the contribution of porkmeat. The præfectus Annonæ in charge of this great branch of Roman administration was represented in every centre of production by one or more officers, like the "adiutor præfecti Annonæ ad oleum afrum et hispanum recensendum" stationed at Hispalis,

Sevilla (Corpus Inscr., ii. 1180), to collect the oil from Andalusia and from the coast of Mauretania. The receiving officers stored these "contributions en nature" in cellars and granaries until the fleets hired or kept for this purpose were ready to sail. These provincial storehouses are called "horrea populo Romano destinata" by Ammianus (xxviii. i. 7). Rusicade (Stora, near Philippeville), the harbor of Cirta (Constantina), was one of the great collecting ports, with extensive "horrea ad securitatem," or "ad utilitatem populi Romani," and with a statue symbolizing the Genius Annonæ sacræ Urbis. (See Corpus Inscr., viii. 7960, 7975, etc.) Among the fleets employed to convey the contributions to the harbor of Rome (see Pingonneau, De convectione urbanæ annonæ, Paris, 1877), the best known is the Egyptian or Alexandrine, which carried a yearly tribute of 7,000,000 hectolitres, or 144,000,000 bushels, the approach of which was anxiously watched from the heights of Misenum and signaled at once to Rome.[1] Second in importance to it was the classis Africana Commodiana Herculea. With favorable winds and smooth sea, the crossing from Alexandria would require but eleven days, from the ports of Bætica seven, from the straits of Messina five, from the gulf of Lyons three, from the nearest coast of Africa two.

Grain-laden vessels were of large tonnage, like the one mentioned in the Acts of the Apostles as having on board, besides its cargo, two hundred and fifty souls. We may judge of their number from the fact that during a fierce gale in the time of Nero not less than two hundred vessels were lost in the roads of Ostia. It seems that wheat was not transported in bulk, for fear of the cargo shifting to one side or the other, but in amphoræ or earthen jars.

A bas-relief of the Torlonia Museum, discovered in my presence at Porto, and described in "Ancient Rome," p. 253, represents the unloading of one of these ships. "There is a plank connecting the ship with the quay, and upon the plank a line of sailors and porters each carrying an amphora on the left shoulder, and a tessera or ticket in the right hand. The tesseræ are collected by a customs officer or a scribe, sitting at a desk with the account-book before him."

The length of the warehouses around Trajan's dock at Porto amounts to two miles and a half. At Ostia they cover one third

---

[1] LITERATURE. — Ferrero, *L' ordinamento delle armate Romane*, p. 160. — Marquardt, *Handbuch*, vol. v², p. 489. — *Corpus Inscr. Gr.*, 5973, etc. — Lanciani, *Bull. Inst.*, 1868, p. 234. — Visconti, *Bull. com.*, 1881, p. 52. — *Vita Commod.*, 17.

of the area of the city. In Rome the horrea Galbana alone occupied a space of 200 by 155 metres, and of these public warehouses there were two hundred and ninety in Rome. They were named either from their builder or owner, like the horrea Galbana, Petroniana, Leoniana, Seiana, Agrippiana, etc., or from their contents, like candelaria, chartaria, piperataria, etc. In progress of time others had to be built in the suburbs, like the horrea Nervæ in the farm now called Della Nunziatella, between the Via Ardeatina and the Via Ostiensis, the " fundum orrea via Ardeatina " of the " Liber pontificalis." [1]

No traces of the horrea remain above ground in the region of Testaccio, between the cliffs of the Aventine and the river; but many have been found in constructing the drains of the new quarters. With the help of these discoveries I have been able to reconstruct the complete plan of the horrea Galbæ in sheet n. xl. of the Forma Urbis. The tomb of Sulpicius Galba, an ancestor of the Emperor of that name, and probably the founder of the horrea, discovered *in situ* in 1885, has been removed bodily to the Museo Municipale al Celio.

LITERATURE. — Preller, *Die Regionen*, p. 101. — Luigi Bruzza, *Bull. Inst.*, 1872, p. 140. — Heinrich Jordan, *Archæol. Zeitung*, xxvi. p. 18; and *Topographie*, ii. pp. 68, 104. — *Forma Urbis*, pl. xliii. — Mommsen, *Ephem. Epigr.*, vol. iv. p. 260. — Enrico Stevenson, *Iscrizione relativa alle horrea Galbiana* (Bull. Inst., 1880, p. 98). — Gio. Battista de Rossi, *Le horrea sotto l' Aventino e la statio Annonæ* (Ann. Inst., 1885, p. 223, *sq.*). — Giuseppe Gatti, *Alcune osservazioni sugli orrei Galbiani* (Mittheil., 1886, pp. 62, 65); and *Frammento d' iscrizione contenente la lex horreorum* (Bull. com., 1885, p. 110). — Wilhelm Henzen, *Iscrizione relativa alle horrea Galbiana* (Mittheil., 1886, p. 42). — Rodolfo Lanciani, *Iscrizione del sepolcro di Galba* (in Bull. com., 1885, p. 166); *Pagan and Christian Rome*, p. 44; *Ancient Rome*, p. 250; *Forma Urbis Romæ*, pl. xl.

LXVII. THE MARBLE WHARF AND SHEDS, MARMORATA. — To the commercial transactions in the necessaries of life, we must add the trade in marbles, so brisk and active that, as Tibullus says, the streets of the city were always obstructed by carts laden with transmarine columns and blocks, — columns measuring sometimes 1.97 metre in diameter and 17.66 metres in length, like those of Trajan's temple; or blocks weighing sometimes 27 tons, like those belonging to the pediment of the Temple of the Sun in the Villa Colonna. When Marcus Scaurus was collecting in 84 B. C. the three hundred and sixty columns of Lucullean marble required for

---

[1] Vol. i. p. 202, ed. Duchesne. — Tommasetti, *Archivio Società storia patria*, vol. iii. p. 143.

the decoration of his theatre, the contractor for the maintenance of public sewers sued him before the magistrates for damages which would eventually be done to streets and drains.

There were two quays for the landing and for the storage of marble, — one on the bank under the Aventine, which still retains the old name of *Marmorata*, another on the banks of the Campus Martius, a little above the Ælian bridge.

The first was rediscovered and completely excavated by Baron Visconti in 1868–70.

LITERATURE. — Gio. Battista de Rossi, *Bull. arch. crist.*, 1868, pp. 17, 47; 1870, p. 7; 1873, p. 147; 1876, p. 113; 1883, p. 81. — Leone Nardoni, *Bull. Inst.*, 1872, p. 72. — Luigi Bruzza, *ibid.*, 1870, pp. 9, 37; 1871, p. 68; 1872, p. 134; 1873, p. 108; *Sui marmi Lunensi* (in Dissertaz. accad. arch., p. 389). — Rodolfo Lanciani, *Ancient Rome*, p. 250. — Arthur Schneider, *Das Alte Rom*, Leipzig, 1896, taf. x. n. 18.

The second marble wharf — directly connected with the government office for the administration of quarries and for the sale of their products — was discovered in April, 1891, 160 metres above the bridge of S. Angelo, in demolishing the teatro di Torre di Nona, which stood above it. The structure looked like a raised causeway, fourteen metres wide, protruding into the river for twenty-six metres, at an angle of 40° with the direction of the stream. On each side of the causeway there are spacious landings built of concrete and faced with a palisade. This palisade, a perfect specimen of Roman hydraulic engineering, is made of square beams of quercus robur from six to eight metres long, ending in a point protected by a four-pronged cap of iron. The beams are fifty-five centimetres square, and fit into each other by means of a groove on one side and a projection on the other, shaped like a swallow's tail. Sheets of lead are nailed against the inner face of the palisade, so as to make it thoroughly water-tight. A line of piles runs in front of it, to protect it from the friction of vessels moored alongside the pier. This wharf answered a double purpose : for the landing of the great monoliths used in the buildings of the Campus Martius, of the Pincian and Quirinal hills, and for the supply of statuary marble to the many artists' studios which had sprung up in Imperial times in the vicinity of the government marble office (*statio rationis marmorum*) at S. Apollinare.

During the transformation of Rome and the building of the Campus Martius accomplished by Augustus and his wealthy friends, the old marble wharf, at the other end of the city, could not have been used for the purpose of landing the materials destined for these constructions, because the transportation of columns, pillars, and obelisks through the narrow and tortuous streets of the ninth, eleventh, and thirteenth regions would have been impossible in some cases, difficult in others, and always costly to excess.   And besides, there was no reason why preference should be given to transportation by land, when the vessels loaded with transmarine marbles could easily be brought within a short distance of the buildings in course of construction.   The blocks were evidently discharged on the side landings, level with the water's

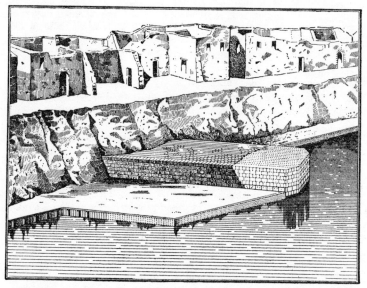

Fig. 205. — The Wharf for Landing Marbles on the Banks of the Campus Martius.

edge, which have a water frontage of a hundred metres, and then raised by means of cranes (such as the one represented in the basrelief of the Haterii, published, among others, by Parker in part iv. of the "Archæology of Rome," plate xxiii.) to the level of the causeway, and pushed on rollers (*chamulci*) towards their destination.

LITERATURE. — Domenico Marchetti, *Di un' antico molo per lo sbarco dei marmi* (in Bull. com., 1891, p. 45, pl. iii). — Christian Huelsen, *Mittheilungen*, 1892, p. 322. — Francesco Azzurri, *Bull. com.*, 1892, p. 175, pl. ix. — *Notizie degli Scavi*, May, 1890. — Rodolfo Lanciani, *Bull. com.*, 1890, p. 23.

The discovery of this new topographic feature of ancient Rome

fits remarkably well with others previously made in connection
with the sale, trade, and working of marbles in this portion of the
Campus Martius. When the church of S. Apollinaris was modernized and disfigured in 1737–40 by Popes Clement XII. and Benedict XIV., ruins and inscriptions were discovered proving that
there stood in old times the Statio Rationis Marmorum, that is to
say, the central office for the administration of marble quarries,
which were the private property and a monopoly of the crown.
Around this office, and on each side of the avenue connecting it
with the pier just discovered by the Tor di Nona, stone-cutters and
sculptors had settled in large numbers. Wherever the ground is
excavated between S. Andrea della Valle and the left bank of the
river we are sure to find traces of these workshops and artists'
studios, the site of which is marked by a layer either of marble
chips or of that yellowish crystalline sand which is used to the
present day for sawing the blocks. Pietro Sante Bartoli, Flaminio
Vacca, Ficoroni, and Braun describe many such shops found under
the Monte Giordano, S. Maria dell' Anima, the Collegio Clementino, the Chiesa Nuova, etc. It is difficult to explain why many
of these should have been abandoned so suddenly that works of
sculpture in an unfinished state have been found, together with
the tools of the trade, — hammers, chisels, and files. A fact still
more difficult of explanation is that, in the majority of cases, the
unfinished statues represent Dacian kings or Dacian prisoners, in
the same characteristic attitude of sad resignation which we notice
in the prototypes removed from the triumphal arch of Trajan to
that of Constantine (p. 194). One of these figures of Dacians,
discovered in the reign of Clement X. in the Via del Governo
Vecchio, is now placed on the staircase of the Altieri palace; a
second was found in July, 1841, under the house No. 211 Via de'
Coronari ; a third in January, 1859, under the house of Luigi
Vannutelli, near the Via del Pellegrino; a fourth in 1870, under
the house of Paolo Massoli in the same Via de' Coronari. These
curious facts lead us to believe that the production of the article
in fashion under the rule of Trajan, the conqueror of Dacia, must
have been in excess of the demand.

LXVIII. SALINÆ (the salt-warehouses). — The oldest account
we have of salt-works near the mouth of the Tiber precedes that
of the foundation of Rome. The people of Veii had adapted to
the production of salt one of the shallow inlets west of the mouth,
and the quantity obtained — by natural evaporation — was enough

to meet the wants of the southern Etruscans as well as of the Sabines. Romulus gained temporary possession of the works. Ancus Marcius conquered the whole coast, and to insure the monopoly to the Romans, he founded Ostia, on the opposite bank of the river, and opened near it new works, surrounded and protected by water from possible hostile inroads. The event was celebrated by a popular distribution of 52,520 litres of salt in the form of a bounty. The Salinæ Ostienses supplied for a time the demand of the Romans and of the Sabines, the trade being so brisk that the main road uniting the two territories was named Salaria. Later on a larger supply became necessary, and the old salinæ of Veii were again brought into use, only they changed their name and became the Salinæ Romanæ. From about 500 B. C. to the tenth century after Christ no mention occurs of either works, except in a marble plinth of a statuette which a boatman of the marshes of Campo Salino had used for years for mooring his canoe, until a sportsman noticed its inscription in the winter of 1887. The valuable document, now exhibited in Hall I. of the Museo Municipale al Celio, mentions the corporation of the porters (*saccarii salarii*), who carried the salt in sacks from the Campus Salinarum Romanarum (Campo Salino) to Porto and Rome; besides some of their officers, and the two intendants of the Emperor who had the management of the monopoly. It dates from the time of Septimius Severus. The exact position of the salt-warehouses on the left bank of the Tiber in Rome is indicated by Frontinus (i. 5), " at the foot of the Clivus Publicius near the Porta Trigemina, which place is called Salinæ." It is not difficult to identify the place. The warehouses — repaired from time to time — were kept there from the time of Ancus Marcius to the spring of 1888. The glorious though unpretending edifice was pulled down to connect the new Quartiere di Testaccio with the city by a convenient thoroughfare. The same fate has befallen the salt-works at the mouth of the Tiber. Those of Campo Salino were abandoned in the sixteenth century ; those of Ostia in 1874.

LITERATURE. — Marquardt, *Staatsverwaltung*, vol. ii. p. 154. — Antonio Nibby, *Analisi della . . . campagna romana*, vol. ii. p. 368. — Lanciani, *Bull. arch. com.*, 1888, p. 83.

LXIX. THE LEAD-WAREHOUSES. — In November, 1887, a mass of pig-lead, shaped like a punt, and weighing thirty-three kilos., was discovered in the bed of the river, near the place called " Porta Leone," opposite the Ripa Grande. It bore the stamp of the

company of the argentiferous mine of Mount ILVCR (*sic*), probably
a mistake for ILVRCO, and also the word GALENA, which indicates
the kind of lead obtained from the smelting of silver ore. The
discovery of this object is of topographical interest. The mass
must have fallen overboard when the ship was unloading alongside the "lead" wharf. This, and the corresponding warehouses,
both the property of the Crown, were therefore situated on the
left bank, between the "marble" wharf and the Forum Boarium.
A find, already mentioned, p. 432, gives an idea of the activity
which prevailed under the Empire in the lead business, and which
must have called into the harbor of Rome or Porto hundreds of
Spanish vessels. The lead pipe which conveyed the water to the
Forum of Trajan from a reservoir by the Porta Viminalis (fragments of which were found in 1877 in the Piazza del Quirinale,
and in 1879 in the Piazza di Termini) was 1750 metres long, and
weighed 133 kilos. per metre. The whole pipe must have required 232,750 kilos. of metal, nearly 233 tons; and of these
conduits there were thousands in Rome. The one which brought
the water to the Baths of Agrippa, discovered about 1626 in the
foundations of S. Ignazio, is compared by Donati with the largest
guns (*maiores bombardæ*) of the age. Another, discovered in 1650
by the Borghese in their farm at Acqua Traversa, measured 67
centimetres in diameter, and must have weighed 300 kilos. per
metre.

LXX. THE BRICK-WAREHOUSES. — A curious document concerning the trade in the excellent products of Roman brick-kilns
was discovered in 1877 in the catacombs of S. Sebastiano. It was
written with a nail or a sharp stick on a tile — before the clay
was dried and baked — and the tile was afterwards used in wall-
ing up a *loculus* of the fourth century. The inscription says,
"Beneventus has ordered of Julius 400 tiles, to be consigned,
ready for shipment, at the Neapolitan quay." Other sheds, set
apart for the same trade, were called Portus Licini, Portus Parræ,
Portus Cornelii, etc. (See Corpus Inscr., vol. xv. 1, 408, 409, 412;
and Notizie Scavi, 1892, p. 347.)

LXXI. THE MONTE TESTACCIO. — The student wishing to
survey the ground formerly occupied by these great establishments
connected with the harbor of Rome must make the ascent of the
Monte Testaccio, which rises to the height of 115 feet in the very
heart of the region of the Horrea. The hill itself may be called a

monument of the greatness and activity of the harbor of Rome. The investigations of Reiffersheid and Bruzza, completed in 1878 by Heinrich Dressel, prove that the mound is exclusively formed of fragments of earthen jars (amphoræ, diotæ), used in ancient times for conveying to the capital the agricultural products of the provinces, especially of Bætica and Mauretania. Bætica supplied not only Rome, but many parts of the western Empire, with oil, wine, wax, pitch, linseed, salt, honey, sauces, and olives prepared in a manner greatly praised by Pliny. Potters' stamps and painted or scratched inscriptions of Spanish origin, identical with those of Monte Testaccio, have been discovered in France, Germany, and the British Islands. It appears that the harbor regulations obliged the owners of vessels or the keepers of warehouses to dump in a space marked by the Commissioners the earthen jars which happened to be broken in the act of unloading, or while on their way to the sheds. The space was at first very limited; in progress of time part of a public cemetery, containing, among others, the tomb of the Rusticelii (Corpus, vi², 11,534), was added to it. At the beginning of the fourth century the rubbish heap had gained a circumference of half a mile, and a height of over a hundred feet. After the fall of the Empire masses of fragments were washed down the hill, and spread over a considerable part of the plain. In the sixteenth century quarries were opened on the north side, the material (coccio pesto) being used for macadamizing the roads. In the same century the south side was used by the Bombardieri of the pope as butts for gun-practice. The first wine-cellars, — the Grotte di Testaccio, — known for their aptitude to improve the quality of the stock, were excavated through the heart of the mound about 1650.

The consular dates discovered by Dressel on the handles and on the body of the amphoræ range between A. D. 140 and 255. The upper strata, near the wooden cross (Croce del Testaccio), date from the first half of the fourth century.

Another mound of the same nature, but much smaller in size, has been lately explored on the right bank of the river, above the Ponte Margherita, at a place called Monte Secco.

LITERATURE. — Heinrich Dressel, *Ricerche sul monte Testaccio* (in Annal. Inst., 1878, p. 118; and *Bull. com.*, 1893). — Otto Richter, *Topographie*, p. 129.

Another place well worth a visit before leaving this commercial quarter of ancient Rome is the " Sponda della Marmorata," where there are still traces left of the great excavations of 1868–70.

Many blocks of marble discovered by Visconti are to be seen near the cottage of the Custode. Some are roughly squared, others roughly shaped (*abbozzati*) into columns or architectural pieces and even into statues and bas-reliefs. Their finishing must have been given up either on account of a defect discovered in the marble, or because it was found too hard or crystalline for the chisel or the saw. Sculptors' or stone-cutters' tools abound in the vicinity of the wharf. (See Venuti, Descrizione topogr., vol. ii. p. 45.)

The blocks are all distinguished by one or more marks referring to the quarry from which they were extracted (e. g., *ex metallis novis Cæsaris nostri*); to the Emperor who owned the quarry at the time (e. g., *imperatorum Cæsarum Antonini et Veri augustorum*); to the department to which the blocks were addressed (e. g., *rationi urbicæ*); to the number of blocks of a special kind of marble quarried during the fiscal year; to the date of the year; and so forth.

It seems that the crown did not own all the quarries of the Empire, but only those which could yield the great blocks and the great columns (of red and gray granite, africano, cipollino, pavonazzetto, portasanta, white marble, etc.) that were necessary for the decoration of Imperial buildings. Quarries of rare and peculiar marbles or breccias were opened and worked by private speculators. The Imperial "procurator marmorum" had representatives (*curam agentes*, μεταλλάρχαι) on the coasts of Asia, Greece, Egypt, Numidia, Mauretania, in the Ægean Islands, etc. Their duty was to direct the shipment of the product of the local quarries to the harbor of Rome, where it was received by a "tabularius Portuensis rationis marmorum." The transportation, in ordinary cases, was effected by means of "naves lapidariæ," specially constructed by the administration for this kind of trade; in extraordinary cases the ship was built in accordance with the size of the columns or obelisks which had to be landed at Rome. Such were the wonderful crafts constructed under Augustus and Caligula for the shipping of the obelisks of the Circus Maximus and of the Circus Vaticanus respectively; such, and even larger, the one built under Constantius for the transportation of the obelisk now in the Piazza di S. Giovanni. Caligula's ship, which carried 120,000 "modii" of lentils for ballast, was sunk at the entrance of the Claudian harbor at Porto, to serve as foundation for the breakwater (*antemurale*) and lighthouse.

Quarries were usually worked by convicts, the "damnatio ad

opus metalli" being one of the ordinary punishments sanctioned by the Roman code. The jails connected with the single quarries were intrusted to the care of a body of warders under special officers, independent of the military comando of the province. Letronne quotes the inscription of an Annius Rufus, captain of the XV Legio Apollinaris, detailed to act as "præpositus operis marmorum monti Claudiano" (superintendent of the quarries of the Claudian mountain). The same archæologist found in the chapel attached to the mining works of Khardasy, Nubia, an inscription which seems to prove that chaplains were attached to these penal establishments, and that divine service was occasionally celebrated for the benefit of the convicts.

The Roman Marmorata has been excavated, almost without intermission, for four hundred and fifty years, and yet its wealth in blocks and columns of the rarest kinds of breccias seems to have hardly diminished. There is another marmorata on the banks of the Canale di Fiumicino, the ancient "Fossa Traiana." Blocks were landed here when the river was too shallow for the "naves lapidariæ" to reach the harbor of Rome. The unloading of these ships, and the transferment of their cargo to barges and pontoons of lighter draught, and the navigation up the river was (probably) the privilege of a powerful corporation called "corpus traiectus marmorum."

LITERATURE. — Garofalo, *De antiquis marmoribus*. 1743. — Faustino Corsi, *Delle pietre antiche*. Rome, 1843. — Letronne, *Recherches pour servir à l'histoire de l'Egypte*, pp. 429-482. -- Luigi Bruzza, *Iscrizioni dei marmi grezzi*, in Ann. Inst., 1870.

THE AVENTINE.

(REGIONS XII AND XIII.)

The Aventine, and its southeastern appendix called the "pseudo or smaller Aventine" (Monte di S. Balbina), count among the few regions of ancient Rome which have escaped "modernization." The panorama of the hill from the terrace of the so-called "Castello di Costantino" (a popular restaurant, Via di S. Prisca), from the belfry of S. Alessio, from the tower of S. Balbina, or from the upper portico of S. Saba, is perhaps the freshest and loveliest within the walls. Yet, with the exception of churches of monumental interest, there is very little left above ground to attract the classic student. The baths of Caracalla by SS. Nereo and Achilleo and those of the Decii in the Vigna Torlonia are the only ancient buildings which have escaped total destruction.

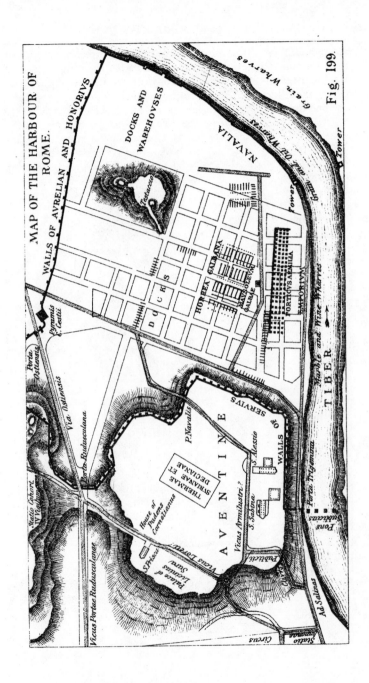

MAP OF THE HARBOUR OF ROME.

Fig. 199.

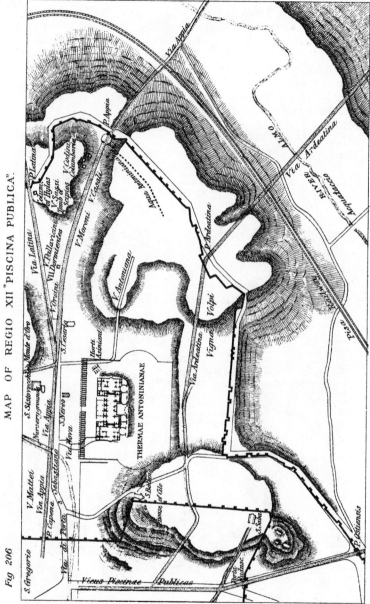

Fig 206

MAP OF REGIO XII "PISCINA PUBLICA".

LXXII. Thermæ Antoninianæ. — Baths of Caracalla (Fig. 206), begun about a. d. 212, and opened for public use in the early spring of 216. Part of the ground which they cover probably belonged to the gardens of Asinius Pollio, the " Horti Asiniani " of Frontinus. As the level of the baths is higher than that of the gardens, these, and the buildings connected with them, were not destroyed, but made use of to support the new platform in the same way as the remains of the Golden House of Nero were made

Fig. 207. — Part of the Building discovered by Guidi under the Baths of Caracalla.

to support the platform of the baths of Trajan. A portion of the Asinian buildings was discovered by G. B. Guidi in 1860–67, under the southeast corner of the baths, and described by Angelo Pellegrini, Orti di Asinie Pollione, in Bull. Inst., 1867, p. 109. (See Fig. 39, p. 101.) The excavations can still be seen by applying at Via di Porta S. Sebastiano, No. 29. They belong to a noble house, the upper floor of which was demolished by Caracalla, while the ground apartments were left almost untouched. The rooms, opening on three sides of a square peristylium, show traces of fresco-paintings; their pavements are of white and black mosaic, with figures of sea-nymphs, tritons, marine monsters, etc. (Fig.

207.) The best preserved room is the lararium, or domestic chapel, with figures of Arpokras and Anubis on each side of the door, and of three Capitoline deities above the altar.

Guidi, however, was not the first explorer of this house: previous excavations are recorded by Ficoroni (Mem. 111) as having taken place towards the middle of last century. The terra-cotta panels representing the three Capitoline gods, the labors of Hercules, a triumphal arch, etc., now in the Kircherian museum, are described among the finds.

Ancient writers give the most enthusiastic accounts of Caracalla's baths, which were completed by Heliogabalus and Severus Alexander. Like those of Trajan and Diocletian, they consist of a central building with halls of great size, surrounded by a belt of gardens, the whole space being inclosed by an outer quadrangle of smaller buildings. The central block measures 216 metres by 112, the outer quadrangle 353 metres by 335; the area amounts to 118,255 square metres. (Baths of Diocletian, 130,000 sq. m.)

The present entrance to the baths is by the hall next to the north peristyle (Via Antoniana). No description can be given in detail of this magnificent suite of halls, nor can the object of each one be specified, except as regards the frigidarium, the tepidarium, and the caldarium, which occupy the central line; and the peristyles, which occupy the two ends.

The frigidarium seems to correspond to the "cella soliaris" described by the biographer of Caracalla, ch. ix., the ceiling of which was the largest flat ceiling in the world. The biographer says that the architects of his own (Constantine's) time could not explain such a miracle of engineering, except by supposing that the whole roof was supported by girders of metal dexterously concealed in the thickness of the masonry. No trace of these girders of brass or copper (*cancelli ex aere vel cupro*) was found in the

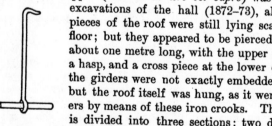

excavations of the hall (1872–73), although many pieces of the roof were still lying scattered on the floor; but they appeared to be pierced by iron bars, about one metre long, with the upper end bent like a hasp, and a cross piece at the lower end. Perhaps the girders were not exactly embedded in the roof, but the roof itself was hung, as it were, to the girders by means of these iron crooks. The frigidarium is divided into three sections: two dressing-rooms at each end, and a swimming-basin in the centre; the pool, 53 metres long and 24 wide, was flooded by 1430 cubic metres of

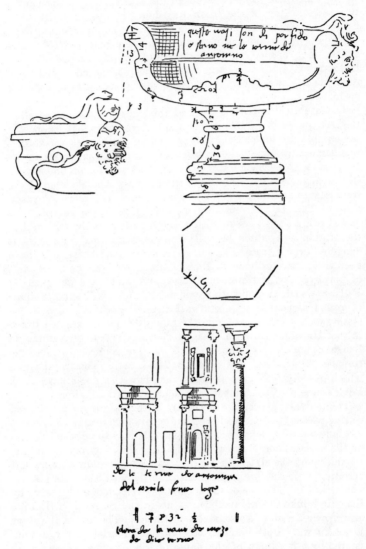

Fig. 208. — A Leaf from Palladio's Sketch-book (Baths of Caracalla).

water, which had to be renewed several times a day. The empty-ing and refilling of the basin was done in a wonderfully short time. The floor is inclined towards a sluice communicating with an emissarium which slopes down at an angle of about 15°. The sluice being opened, all the water could run off in a few minutes. In the reservoir of the baths were stored 33,000 cubic metres of water, nearly twenty-two times the quantity necessary to flood the basin.

The architectural decoration of this hall was rather peculiar. Besides the eight large pillars of gray granite, which supported the entablature under the flat roof, each of the niches for statues was flanked by two smaller columns, supporting a pediment in the shape of a " tabernacolino." The student can better understand this arrangement by referring to the drawings and sketches of the Renaissance architects, who saw the building before the devasta-tions of Paul III. I reproduce here (Fig. 208) a p ge from one of Palladio's sketch-books, with a rough outline of the east wall of the frigidarium, which he calls "cortile senza loge," viz., without "loggie" or porticoes. The preservation of the baths must have been truly extraordinary in those days, when even precious vases of porphyry lay scattered on the ground. The one designed by Palladio was decorated with scenic masks, and handles in the shape of coiled serpents. " Queste vasi sono di porfido," he says, " e stanno ne le terme di antonino." Equally valuable are the draw-ings of Giovanni Antonio Dosio (Uffizi, 2563); and of Antonio da Sangallo the elder (Siena, 8, iv. 5, f. 7′, reproduced in Memorie romane per le Belle Arti, 1786, p. 242, n. iv.). The frigidarium, which is only 2.23 metres narrower than the great nave of S. Peter's, was used last century for the "giuoco del Pallone."

The tepidarium occupies the centre of the building. Its vaulted ceiling was supported by eight granite columns, nearly two metres in diameter, of which but one fragment is now to be seen. It lies on the mosaic floor of one of the adjoining dressing-rooms. At the beginning of the sixteenth century two whole columns were left standing, viz., the first and the third on the northeast side (Dosio, Uffizi, 2563). The one at the corner was removed to Florence by the grand duke Cosimo in 1564, set up in the Piazza di S. Trinità, and crowned with a bronze statue of Justice. The fate of the other is not known. Both bore the label of the Imperial quarry, admin-istered by a freedman of the name of Diadumenus. (See Codex Vatic., 6039, p. 242.) The weight of the ceiling had been consid-erably lessened by the architect, by making use of pumice-stone,

instead of bricks or chips of tufa. The tepidarium has three recesses on each of the longer sides, two of which contain a piscina
set deep in the pavement. These basins, incrusted with precious
marbles, were divided from the main hall by a line of columns of
porphyry, many fragments of which were discovered by Guidi in
1868. One of their capitals, of ultra-composite invention, is represented below (Fig. 209).

Ficoroni mentions four bases, also of red porphyry, as belonging
to the same decorations. They measured 4.68 metres in circumference. One of them was to be seen opposite the door of SS.

Fig. 209. — Capital of the Composite Order from the Tepidarium of Caracalla's Baths.

Nereo ed Achilleo; the second within the same church; the third
near the shop of a certain de Marchis in the Vicolo Scanderbeg.
The last was purchased by Ficoroni himself for forty sequins, cut
into slabs to serve for tables, and sold or given to the king of
Poland. Fra Giocondo da Verona (Uffizi, 1538) asserts that he saw
and sketched part of the entablature of the tepidarium, " a gustin
gissi," in the garden of the wealthy banker Agostino Chigi.

The caldarium was a noble circular hall projecting halfway into the inner garden. Its dome rested on eight pilasters of great size, each pierced by a narrow staircase. There are only two left standing: the basements of the others were excavated partly in November, 1878, partly in the spring of the present year. At the foot of one of the stairs several bricks were found, inscribed with the motto + *reg*(nante) *d*(omino) *n*(ostro) *Theoderico, bono Rom*(a)*e*, the first intimation of repairs having been made in the baths by that provident king.

The peristyles or palestræ at each end of the tepidarium contained a portico of precious columns, paved with polychrome mosaic, and opening on a court; and a hemicycle or tribune, the pavement of which was divided into squares and parallelograms, each containing a full-sized figure or bust of an athlete. These valuable mosaics, discovered by Count Velo in 1824, were removed to the Lateran Museum by Gregory XVI. Consult Pietro Secchi, "Il musaico antoniniano rappresentante la Scuola degli Atleti," Rome, 1843; Helbig's "Guide," vol. i. p. 507, n. 704; and the "Corpus Inscr.," vol. vi. n. 10,155.

A marble frieze in bold relief, with festoons and hunting scenes, ran the whole length of both peristyles. Of this frieze, once over a thousand feet long, one fragment alone remains (north side of south peristyle) to tell the tale of destruction: the lime-kilns have absorbed the rest. Another piece with the figures of two gladiators must be preserved in the Villa Albani, where it was removed by Cardinal Alessandro about 1767. Piranesi claims to have seen (in the course of the Albani excavations?) pieces of the gates of gilt bronze, which still clung to the posts of the passages leading to the frigidarium.

To appreciate the number and the value of the works of art with which Caracalla, Alexander, Heliogabalus, Valentinian and Valens, King Theoderic, and several prefects of the city in the fourth century lavishly decorated these baths, we must consult the accounts of the excavations made at the time of Paul III. (1546), and also the catalogues of the Museo Farnese, the contents of which were removed to the Museo Borbonico (Naples) in the second half of last century. "The search made in the Antoniana at the time of Paul III.," says Bartoli (Mem. 78), "turned out so rich in statues, columns, bas-reliefs, architectural marbles, cameos, intaglios, bronzes, medals, lamps, that a museum (the Farnesiano) was formed with them. The enormous quantity of heads, busts, and bas-reliefs, which fill two large rooms in the ground floor of the palace, were also found at the Antoniana." And yet the excavations of Paul III. were preceded and have been followed by many others, the product of which was always considerable. In the "Storia degli Scavi di Roma," the first volume of which will be published, I hope, early next year, forty excavations at least are recorded in the "Antignano," from the time of Paschal I. (817–824) to the present day. Among the Farnese finds Ulisse Aldovrandi mentions the group of Dirce tied to the horns of the bull, the colossal Hercules of Glycon, Atreus with the son of Thyestes, the so-called Vestal Tuccia, a colossal Pallas, a Flora, a Diana, four other figures of Herakles, a Venus, an Hermaphrodite, some busts of Antoninus Pius, and many torsos and heads not identified, a pedestal (" Corpus," n. 749), and one of the two large granite basins which now adorn the fountains of the Piazza Farnese. The other, seen by Ruccellai in 1450, " in una vigna presso alle terme," was first removed by Pius II. to the Piazza di Venezia and again to its present location by Cardinal Odoardo Farnese in 1612. Another dilettante, Messer Mario Maccarone, whose house still exists by the Macel de' Corvi, found pieces of an equestrian group and a statue of Caracalla, which was destroyed by his own workmen. Flaminio Vacca mentions the discovery of a large block of marble representing an island on the surface of which were left the footprints of several human figures (*molti piè di figure attaccate nell' istessa isola*) ; a ship laden with passengers appeared to be steering for the island. This curious piece was probably placed in the middle of the swimming-pond. Towards the end of last century two precious basins were discovered in the direction of S. Cesario, one of green, one of reddish basalt; both had been used for coffins in the Middle Ages. They are now placed in the Cortile de Belvedere. The three cathedræ or armchairs, also, of red marble, formerly in the cloisters of Vassallectus at the Lateran, are said to have been discovered in these baths. The last excavations of the present century were made by Count Velo in 1824, by Guidi in 1868, by Rosa in 1872, and by Fiorelli in 1879. These last led to the discovery of one of the furnaces or hypocausts, still filled with charcoal, and also of brick-stamps, with the legend OPVS · DO-LIARE · EX · PRÆDIS · AVG ☐ N · FIG · TERTI, remarkable for its allusion to the murder of Geta, brother of Caracalla (see p. 41).

The service of this mighty establishment, which could accommodate 1600 bathers at one time, was carried out underground by means of cryptoporticoes, lighted from glass-covered skylights. These subterranean corridors, many thousand feet long, are not accessible at present, except for a small section under the Vigna Bernabó. Those within the government grounds were filled with rubbish at the time of Piranesi.

A branch aqueduct of the Marcia (Marcia Antoniniana, Marcia Iovia after the restoration by Diocletian) supplied the reservoir of the baths. The aqueduct crossed the Appian Way over the so-called Arch of Drusus. Its arcades in the Vigna Casali were destroyed during last century.

LITERATURE. — *Corpus Inscr.*, vol. vi. n. 749, 1088, 1170–73, 9232, 10,155. — A. da Sangallo the elder, *Cod. Barberin.*, f. 66', 67. — A. da Sangallo the younger, *Uffizi*, n. 1093, 1133, 1206, 1381, 1411, 1656 (?). —Aristotile da Sangallo, n. 1554, 1555. — Baldassare Peruzzi, n. 476. — Fra Giocondo, n. 1538. — Alberti Cherubino, *Cod. Borgo S. Sepolcro*, vol. i. pp. 3', 4, 5. *Codex Berolin.*, f. 43. — Heemskerk, *Berlin*, i. f. 59, 59'; and ii. f. 7. — Seventeen large drawings (by Simon Travail?) of much importance are preserved in the Kunstgewerbe Museum in the same city (large portfolio, A, p. 377, f. 20–46). — Etienne du Perac, *Vedute*, pls. 19–22. — Gio. Battista Piranesi, *Antichità*, vol. i. p. 23, n. 199. — Abel Blouet, *Restaur. des thermes de Caracalla.* Paris, 1823. — Luigi Canina, *Edifizi*, vol. iv. pls. 207–214. — Pietro Rosa, *Relazione*, pp. 83, 85. — *Notizie degli Scavi*, 1878, p. 346; 1879, pp. 15, 40, 114, 141, 314; 1881, p. 57. — Rodolfo Lanciani, *Bull. Inst.*, 1869, p. 236; and *Ancient Rome*, pp. 90–94.

LXXIII. The churches of the Aventine — S. Balbina, S. Saba, S. Sabina, S. Prisca — vie in archæological interest with the remains of classic monuments. S. Balbina occupies the site of the Domus Cilonis; S. Saba that of the Statio Cohortis IV. Vigilum; S. Sabina stands close to the Templum Iunonis Reginæ; while S. Prisca represents the Domus Aquilæ et Priscæ of the Acts, between the Domus Licinii Suræ and the Domus Gai Marii Pudentis Corneliani.

The Domus Cilonis is mentioned in the Imperial almanacs of the fourth century as one of the prominent buildings of the twelfth region. It was reconstructed at the time of Septimius Severus, and presented by that Emperor to Lucius Fabius Cilo, consul A. D. 204, prefect of the city, and an intimate friend. The remains consist of some walls of reticulated work, which serve as foundations to the monastery (now a house of refuge for women), and of a hall, 23 metres long, and 16.44 wide, which forms the shell of the church of S. Balbina. The Servian walls run across the building and can be examined in the refectory as well as in the garden on the east side. S. Balbina, a unique specimen of a mediæval fortified monastery, was modernized and whitewashed in 1884. The Domus Cilonis was excavated at the beginning of the sixteenth century. Two pedestals of statues dedicated to him by the cities of Ancyra and

Mediolanum were removed to the Museo Cesi; two perished in the "Calcarara" at le Botteghe oscure. Other excavations were opened by Pius IX. (December, 1858, to November, 1859), an account of which is given by Carlo Ludovico Visconti in the "Bull. Inst.," 1859. They led to the discovery of nine marble heads and busts, two of which, alleged to represent Caius and Lucius, nephews of Augustus, are exhibited in Compartment XVII. of the Museo Chiaramonti, n. 417, 419; and of a water-pipe inscribed with the name of the owner (*Lucii f*)ABI CHILONIS PRAEF(*ecti*) VRB(*i*).

LITERATURE. — *Corpus Inscr. Lat.*, vol. vi. 1408–1410. — *Corpus Inscr. Græc.*, n. 5896. — C. Ludovico Visconti, *Bull. Inst.*, 1859, p. 164. — Heinrich Jordan, *Forma*, p. 43. — Rodolfo Lanciani, *Notizie Scavi*, 1884, p. 223.

Nothing is left above ground of the statio of the fourth battalion of the vigiles at S. Saba; but many of the marbles used in the decoration of the church must pertain to it. A visit to this delightful spot and to the secluded mediæval cloisters, shaded by orange groves, cannot fail to please the student. The loggia above the vestibule of the church affords a good point of survey over the southwestern quarters of ancient Rome.

LITERATURE. — Gio. Battista de Rossi, *Annal. Inst.*, 1858, p. 285. — Mariano Armellini, *Chiese*, 2d edit. p. 589.

The church of S. Sabina, built in 425 by Peter, an Illyrian priest, with the spoils of some neighboring classic edifice, stands very near the site of the Templum Iunonis Reginæ, erected by Camillus after the capture of Veii. Livy (xxvii. 37) places it at the top of the Clivus Publicius, a steep lane still in existence, which leads from the church of S. Anna (Via della Salara) to the Via di S. Sabina (Vicus Armilustri?). Further south stood the Temple of Jupiter Libertas, erected by Gracchus and restored by Augustus. Asinius Pollio added to it an atrium in which a library, formerly belonging to Varro, was placed for public use in 36 B. C. On these sites a fortress was raised by the Savelli at the beginning of the thirteenth century, part of which was made over to the newly established Dominican brotherhood by Honorius III. (1216–27). The fortress is still in good condition, and can be visited by applying to the gardener (Via di S. Sabina), first gate on the right.

The remains of the palace of Licinius Sura, a friend of Trajan, occupy the tableland of the Vigna Cavalletti by S. Prisca. There is a magnificent view from the terrace of the so-called "Castello di Costantino," a hostelry dear to the archæological brotherhood, which occupies the centre of the old palace. Other walls appear under and close to the apse of the church just named. The place is closely connected with the first preaching of the gospel in Rome. (See Pagan and Christian Rome, p. 110.)

LXXIV. THE THERMÆ DECIANÆ. — Trajan built for public use baths of great magnificence, which he named Balneæ Suræ or Thermæ Suranæ, from the friend to whose residence they were contiguous. No trace is left of them above ground. Considerable remains, on the contrary, exist of another bathing-establishment of the Aventine, named Thermæ Decianæ, from the family of the Cæcinæ *Decii* Albini, who also resided on this aristocratic hill. The farmhouse and the casino of the Vigna Torlonia (formerly Massimi, Maccarani, and of the Casa professa dei Gesuiti) are built over and within some of the halls. The place is entered from the gate opposite the church of S. Prisca, and the gardener generally allows students to visit the painted rooms in the cellars of his house.

The Thermæ Decianæ, the plan of which I have lately discovered in one of Palladio's portfolios, and now publish for the first time (Fig. 210), have proved to their first explorers a mine of works of art. Bartoli mentions "nobilissime stufe e bagni" and "stanzoni immensi" adorned with paintings and stucco-reliefs of delicate workmanship. Their pavements lay very deep under the present level of the ground. The statue of the "Infant Hercules" in green basalt, now in the "salone" of the Capitoline Museum, and the bas-relief of Endymion in the "sala degli imperatori" were discovered among the ruins, as well as many inscriptions, marked in the "Corpus Inscr." with n. 1159–60, 1165, 1167, 1192, 1651, 1671, 1672, *a*, *b*, and 1703. We gather from them that the Emperors Constantius and Constans "thermas vetustate labefactatas restauraverunt;" that statues were erected to them in memory of the event by Vitrasius Orfitus, prefect of the city in 353, and by his successor Flavius Leontius; that the baths were profusely decorated with Greek works of sculpture removed from the semi-abandoned temples by Anicius Paulinus, Tanaucius Isfalangius, Pomponius Ammonius, and Fabius Titianus, all city magistrates about the middle of the fourth century; and lastly, that in 414, Honorius and Theodosius being Emperors, an illustrious descendant of the founders of the baths, Cæcina Decius Acinatius Albinus, restored the "cella tepidaria," the fall of which would have caused the ruin of the whole building.

The baths have been excavated thrice within my recollection:

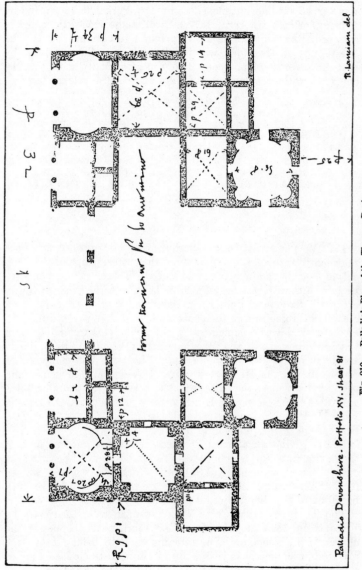

Fig. 210. — Palladio's Plan of the Thermæ Decianæ.

by General Lamoricière in 1867, when the plateau of the Aventine was turned into an intrenched camp; by Parker in 1869; and by Prince Torlonia in April, 1877. In all these excavations, brick-stamps of the time of Trajan were found in vast numbers. The question rises, therefore, whether the Thermæ Suranæ built by that Emperor were not connected topographically with the De-cianæ, as in the case of those of Nero and Severus Alexander.

LITERATURE. — Heinrich Jordan, *Forma,* n. 41, p. 59; and *Topographie,* vol. ii. p. 104. — Pietro Bartoli, *Memorie,* n. 125, 127, 129 (in Fea's Miscell., vol. i.). Angelo Pellegrini, *Le terme Suriane e Deciane* (in Bull. Inst., 1868, p. 177). — Rodolfo Lanciani, *Bull. Inst.,* 1870, p. 74; and *Bull. com.,* 1877, p. 266.

THE GREAT PARKS ON THE WEST SIDE OF THE CITY.

(REGIO XIV — TRANSTIBERIM.)

(Compare Map, Fig. 150, p. 394.)

LXXV. The transtiberine quarter, of which Augustus made the fourteenth ward of the city, covered the eastern slope of the Jani-culum, and the plain between it and the Tiber. The plain, with its labyrinth of tortuous and narrow lanes, was the abode of rowdy crowds of bargemen, lightermen, fishermen, porters, tanners, Jews, etc. The Janiculum, on the contrary, one of the "seven wonders" of the capital, was occupied by a great public park extending from the first milestone of the Via Portuensis (Pozzo Pantaléo), north-wards as far as the Vatican ridge. The park was composed of four sections: the HORTI CÆSARIS, between the Portuensis and the Aurelia Vetus; the HORTI GETÆ, between the Aurelia Vetus and the Aurelia Nova; the HORTI AGRIPPINÆ, between the Aurelia Nova and the Triumphalis; and lastly, the HORTI DOMITIÆ, between the Triumphalis and the Tiber.

Before giving an account of these delightful gardens and of the monuments for which they were famous, I must describe the only place of archæological interest which the student can see in the Trastevere, the guard-house or outposts of the seventh battalion of the City Police, at the Monte de' Fiori.

The ESCUBITORIUM COH · VII · VIGILUM was discovered by Visconti in 1866 at the Monte de' Fiori, nearly opposite the church of S. Crisogono. The remains seem to belong to a large private house, bought or leased by the Administration as a police station for the fourteenth region. Such stations, called *escubitoria,* were distributed all over the city, one for each region, as "dependences" of the central barracks or *stationes*, of which there were only seven. The headquarters, the Scotland Yard of ancient Rome, were with the statio of the first battalion, under the church of S. Marcello and the Palazzo Muti-Balestra.

The escubitorium of Monte de' Fiori was garrisoned by the men of the seventh cohort, to which the care of the ninth and fourteenth wards of the city was intrusted. The main barracks have been located in the neighborhood of the transtiberine church of S. Salvatore in Corte (*in cohorte*), on no sufficient evidence, however, as the name *curtis* (court-yard) has been connected with other churches in mediæval Rome. The other escubitorium of the same cohort was at the Thermæ Neronianæ in the ninth region.

The ruins at the Monte de' Fiori are made attractive by the excellent preservation of some of the apartments and by the graffiti with which the walls are covered. These last number about one hundred, and have been published and illustrated by Henzen. They begin as a rule with a date; then follow the number and name of the cohort, the name of the captain of the company to which the writer of the graffito belonged, the name of the writer, his special rank in the company, — if he had one, — and lastly, the reason which prompted him to scratch his sentences on the wall.

The dates begin with A. D. 215, and end with 245, a lapse of thirty years. The Emperors named are Severus, Caracalla, Macrinus, Severus Alexander (Mammæa, his mother), and Gordianus III. In token of loyalty towards their sovereigns, the men call their cohorts Severiana, Antoniniana, Mamiana, Alexandriana, and Gordiana. Twenty-five names of captains are recorded. The writers are mostly common soldiers: a few sub-officers call themselves *adiutores centurionis*, adjutants of the captains; *quæstionarii*, examiners of prisoners; *carcerarii*, warders of the prison; *aquarii*, plumbers and keepers of fire-engines (siphones ?); *balnearii*, keepers of the baths attached to the barracks; *horrearii*, attached to the commissariat, and so forth.

The reasons given for the writing of the graffiti are mainly two: the first is to express feelings of loyalty, and wishes of welfare and long life for the reigning Emperor (*vota decennalia, vicennalia,* etc.); the second is to thank the gods, the Genius of the Escubitorium, and the fellow soldiers, and to congratulate one's self on having finished the sebaciaria. What were these sebaciaria?

I shall not tire the reader by summing up all the conjectures
advanced on this subject; three points are certain: first, that the
men intrusted with the sebaciaria were on duty for one whole
month: " sevaciaria fecit ex Kalendas Iulias in Ka(lendas) Augu-
(stas);" secondly, that the sebaciaria were not exempt from
a certain amount of danger, so much so that the men accompany
very often their statement with the congratulatory "omnia tuta!"
"everything safe!" thirdly, that the sebaciaria were a heavy and
tiresome work: "Lassus sum: successorem date!" "I am tired:
let some one else take my place!" Professor Henzen thinks
that the mysterious words "sebaciaria facere" mean to take care
of the torches, lamps, and candles made of tallow (sebum) used
by the policemen to light their barracks and to carry about in
their night rounds. The explanation is not satisfactory.

The part of the Escubitorihm now accessible contains a court
paved with mosaics in chiaroscuro, with a fountain in the centre;
and a chapel or lararium, one of the most perfect specimens of
ornamental brickwork of the time of Severus and Caracalla. (See
Ancient Rome, p. 231.) Some of the walls reach the height of
the second floor of the modern houses of the Monte de' Fiori.

LITERATURE. — Wilhelm Henzen, *Bull. Inst.*, 1867, p. 12; and *Annali Inst.*,
1874, p. 111. — Pietro Ercole Visconti, *La coorte settima dei Vigili.* Rome,
1868. — *Corpus Inscr. Latin.*, vol. vi. n. 2998–3091. — Carlo Nocella, *Sebaciaria Emitularius.* Rome, Forzani, 1887. — Alessandro Capannari, *Bull. com.*,
1886, p. 253. — Compare *Bull. com.*, 1887, pp. 31, 77.

LXXVI. HORTI CÆSARIS, laid out by the Dictator, and bequeathed to the people by a codicil in his will (*novissimo testamento*).
They occupied the sites of the present Villa Sciarra, vigne Mattei,
della Missione, and di S. Michele, reaching south to the tufa
quarries of Pozzo Pantaleo, and the beautiful uplands of the
Monteverde. The view from these uplands over the harbor, the
city, the campagna, the hills, the Apennines was, and is now,
celebrated: —

> "Hinc septem dominos videre montes
> et totam licet æstimare Romam."

The slope of the hill was cut into terraces supported by porticoes
and colonnades, with shady glens and waterfalls to break the
symmetry of the architectural masses. The low land at the foot
of the slope was not all included in the park, a strip along the
Via Portuensis being occupied by temples (of the Fors Fortuna, of
the Sun), by tombs, by granaries and warehouses, and by private

gardens. One of these last is described in a document of the sixth century (A. D. 577–78) as the "Horti Transtiberini Eugenii notarii, foras muros iuxta portam Portuensem qui fuerunt ex iure quondam Micini cancellarii inlustris urbanæ sedis patris eius" (Corpus Inscr., vol. vi. n. 8401). Although no remains of the Horti Cæsaris appear above ground, works of art are occasionally discovered within their boundary line even after four centuries of plunder.

The first excavations of which we have a written account took place about 1550 in the Vigna Vittori, opposite the Marmorata. Several statues, busts, and heads of poets, philosophers, and Emperors were found concealed in two rooms. Some were bought by Cardinal Alessandro Farnese, others were placed in the Museo Vittori. About the same time the celebrated group of Menelaos and Patroklos, known as "il Pasquino," came to light from the Vigna of Antonio Velli, half a mile outside the Porta Portese. Duke Cosimo, who happened to be in Rome at the time, bought it for 500 scudi, and placed it in the Loggia de' Lanzi.[1]

In 1822 the following works of art were dug up in the Vigna della Missione: an exquisite polychrome mosaic pavement with masks, fish, fruit, and flowers (it was cut into squares and sold partly to Earl Russell, partly to Lord Kinnaird); a statue of Diana; another of Neptune, which stood in the niche of a fountain; a Cupid; and the figure of a stag in nero antico, larger than life-size. Some of these marbles are exhibited at present in the Lateran Museum. The search was resumed in the year 1825, the only work of art recovered being the statue of Æsculapius kept until late years in the "Casa dei Signori della Missione" at the Monte Citorio.

Giovanni Battista Guidi excavated in 1860 the palmyrene temple of Helios, discovering among its ruins the Venus now in the Hermitage at St. Petersburg. Schnetz, then president of the French Academy in Rome, and Visconti, then director of the excavations, proclaimed the statue superior to the Venus of the Medici; but their judgment, expressed under the excitement of the find, has not been sanctioned by experts.

In the following year a precious vase of porphyry, with handles in the shape of snakes, was discovered in building the Civitavecchia

---

[1] Flaminio Vacca, *Mem.* 96, 97 (in Fea's Miscell., vol. i. p. xciv.). — Francesco Cancellieri, *Notizie sulle statue di . . . Pasquino.* Rome, 1779. — Winckelmann, *Storia delle Arti,* vol. i. p. xxvi. — Urlichs, *Ueber die Gruppe des Pasquino.* Bonn, 1867.

railway station, outside the Porta Portese. Baron Pontalba, one of the railway officials, made a present of it to Señor Solar. It is now in Spain. The Archæological Commission again searched the slope of the Vigna della Missione in 1884, and found a bust of Anakreon, inscribed with his name (ΑΝΑΚΡΕΩΝ ΛΥΡΙΚΟΣ), which is now on exhibition in the Palazzo dei Conservatori.

Students can get access to the upper plateau of the Horti Cæsaris on the occasion of the annual feast celebrated in the catacombs of Pontianus in the Vigna della Missione.

LITERATURE. — *Corpus Inscr.*, vol. vi. n. 642, 817, 8401. — C. Ludovico Visconti, *Annal. Inst.*, 1860, pp. 415–450, pl. R. — Rodolfo Lanciani, *Bull. com.*, 1884, p. 25; and *Notizie Scavi*, 1866, p. 52. — Luigi Borsari, *Bull. com.*, 1887, p. 90. — Helbig, *Guide*, vol. i. p. 443, n. 599; p. 479, n. 646.

LXXVII. HORTI GETÆ, laid out by Septimius Severus under the name of his youngest son, on the plateau and on the slope of the Janiculum, in the space now occupied by the Villa Corsini, the convent of S. Onofrio, and the Villa Lante. There are remains of a reservoir on the left of the gate of the modern park, under the wall of the Villa Heyland. A bronze statue of Septimius Severus was found here by Pope Urban VIII., while building the new walls of the city. Three halls with beautiful marble pavements were discovered by Prince Corsini in January, 1857 ; columns of cipollino, Corinthian capitals, and part of a sitting female statue, by the Commissioners of the Hospital of S. Spirito in 1883.

LITERATURE. — Pietro Bartoli, *Mem.* 117 (in Fea's Miscell., vol. i.). — Maffei, *Raccolta di statue*, pl. 92.

LXXVIII. THE HORTI AGRIPPINÆ. — The early history and topography of the Vatican district have been beautifully illustrated by Prof. Anton Elter, in the " Rheinisch. Museum " of 1891, p. 112. There were four roads departing from the transtiberine end of the Pons Neronianus or Vaticanus by S. Spirito : the Aurelia Nova on the extreme left, the Cornelia and the Triumphalis in the middle, and the Via di Porta Castello (classic name unknown) on the right. (See plan, Fig. 150, p. 394.) The space between the first two roads was occupied by the gardens laid out by Agrippina the elder, mother of Caligula, which became in due course of time crown property, and a favorite resort with young profligate Emperors, like Caligula himself, Nero, and Heliogabalus. The gardens contained a portico on the river-side, and a circus, named "Gaianum" from its founder (Gaius Cæsar, Caligula), the north side of which was made use of by Constantine as a foundation to the south half of S. Peter's basilica. (Compare plan and description in "Pagan and Christian Rome," p. 128.) The obelisk which once marked the middle line of the Circus and now stands in front of the basilica is the only relic left of the Horti Agrippinæ. It is a monolith of red granite, without hieroglyphs, brought over from Heliopolis, the only one which was not thrown down after the fall of the Empire. Its close proximity to the tomb of the Apostle, and to the mausoleum of the Christian Emperors of the fourth century (Mosileos, S. Petronilla), saved it from sharing the fate of the others. It measures 25.36 metres in height, without the pedestal, made of four blocks of the same granite. The name *agulia* (*guglia, aiguille,* needle) is given to it for the first time in a bull of Leo IX., A. D. 1053, in which the pope calls it also the tomb of Julius Cæsar. The belief that the bronze globe on the pinnacle contained the ashes of the Dictator was widespread in the Middle Ages; in fact, a whole cycle of legends was formed about the obelisk in the early dawn of the Renaissance. Giovanni Dondi dell' Orologio († 1389) asserts having seen engraved in the middle of the monolith the distich —

> "ingenio, Buzeta, tuo bis quinque puellæ
> appositis manibus, hanc erexere columnam."

Another even more absurd inscription is given by Giambullari ap. Mercati, "Obelischi," p. 139. A third appears in the early epigraphic manuals of Metello, Lilius the gouty, Ferrarino, etc. —

> "orbe sub hoc parvo conditur orbis Herus.
> si lapis est unus, dic qua fuit arte levatus,
> et si sunt plures, dic ubi contigui."

Mercati thinks that the lower portion of the obelisk was covered with sheets of gilt bronze, described by Petrarch (?), and that they were stolen during the Sacco del Borbone. There seems to be no doubt that those brutal lansquenets fired several shots and hit the globe in more than one place. The removal, accomplished by order of Sixtus V., by his architect Domenico Fontana, is an event too well known to be described in these pages. The official minutes of the religious ceremony of September 26, 1586, which preceded it, are to be found in Grimaldi's Diary, p. 212' of the Barberinian copy. Thirty-seven thousand scudi were spent on the operation, nearly 7000 being for ropes alone. The timber for the scaffoldings erected to lower and then raise it into its new position was cut in the woods of Nettuno and Campomorto, each beam being drawn by fourteen buffaloes. The metal ornaments were cast by

G. B. Laurenziano and Francesco Censori, the brass-founders of the "Fabbrica." The four lions were modeled by Prospero Bresciano and Cecchino da Pietra Santa, cast and gilt by Ludovico Torrigiani. Altogether, 5694 pounds of bronze and 10,802 of iron were made use of in the operation. The lowering took place on May 7, 1586, the removal on June 13, the reërection on September 10, the same day on which the Duke of Luxembourg and De Pisany, ambassadors of Henry III., made their solemn entry through the Porta Angelica. The successful architect was serenaded by all the trumpeters of Rome; the pope made him a nobleman, and offered him the insignia of knighthood, a magnificent work of the goldsmith Ottavio Vanni, also a pension of 2400 scudi, and all the material used in the transportation. The best description of the event is to be found in vol. ii. p. 128 of Baron Hübner's "Sixte-Quint," and the best representation in a copper plate designed by Fontana and engraved by Natale Bonifazio da Sebenico.

The reconstruction of the Basilica of S. Peter, begun by Julius II. and finished by Paul V., led to the discovery of important remains of the Circus, the foundations of which were built on palisades of a hard kind of wood which had become fossilized. Grimaldi says that in digging the foundations of the southeast corner of the façade the masons discovered those of the Circus at the depth of 6.69 metres, the pavement of the Via Cornelia at 11.15, a bed of loose ground at 20.07, and lastly a bed of clay at 30.01. The southeast corner, therefore, is sunk to the depth of over a hundred feet. Grimaldi also tells us that the shell of the Circus was composed of six parallel walls of reticulated masonry, three on each side, upon which the seats were placed, the width of the arena being 51.29, while the Circus itself was 73.59 wide, and 323 long.

The name Gaianum was transferred in the Middle Ages to another circus-like edifice of the gardens of Domitia, the remains of which were dug up in 1743 a little to the north of the Mausoleum of Hadrian.

In a deed of April 6, 1506, which I have found in the Capitoline Archives (vol. xxii. f. 103), Matteo di Bartolomeo sells to Domenico da Sutri, a goldsmith, a vineyard and a cane-field located " extra portam Castelli in loco qui dicitur Gaiano." Another deed, of August 12, 1512 (vol. dccxciv.), mentions a vineyard of Sisto de' Mellini " extra portam Castelli in loco dicto Gaiano."

The Via Cornelia, bordering on the north side of the Horti Agrippinæ, was lined with pagan and Christian tombs. To the

pagan group belong the sarcophagus of Claudia Hermione Archi-
mima, discovered in 1612 under the atrium of S. Peter's; the
tombstones of Ælius Eutacius and Ælia Valeria, discovered in
1611 under the front steps; those of Mæsia Titiana and Pomponia
Fadiula, discovered in 1615 in the foundations of the "Confes-
sione;" and many others described in "Pagan and Christian
Rome," p. 129. The early Christian tombs were clustered around
the grave of the Apostle; those of a later age were scattered also
under the church and its neighborhood. The most important
bore the exact indication of the spot to which they belonged; for
instance, "ad sanctum Apostolum Petrum, ante regia(m portam)
in porticu, columna secunda quo modo intramus, sinistra parte
virorum." Parallel with the north side of the Circus, and under
the clay cliffs of the Vatican hill, was a portico, resting on square
brick pilasters painted with flowers, birds, and vines on a white
ground. These arcades, discovered in 1607, ran from the Altare
del Sacramento to the end of the atrium, a distance of 250 feet.

LITERATURE. — On the Obelisk. — Domenico Fontana, *Della transportatione
dell' obelisco vatic.* Rome, 1590. — Michele Mercati, *Degli obelischi di Roma,*
pp. 239, 365. — Gio. Battista Cipriani, *Sui dodici obelischi egizi,* Rome, 1823,
p. 13. — Platner, *Beschreibung,* vol. ii¹, p. 156. — Francesco Cancellieri, *De
Secretariis,* vol. ii. p. 926. — Hübner, *Sixte-Quint,* vol. ii. ch. vi. p. 128. —
Enrico Stevenson, *Dipinti di Sisto V.,* p. 9, n. 2, pl. iii. — Andrea Busiri,
L' obelisco vat. Rome, 1886. — Carlo Fea, in Winckelmann's *Storia delle Arti,*
vol. iii. p. 291; and *Miscellanea,* vol. ii. p. 5. — *Corpus Inscr.,* vol. vi. n. 882.
— Sangallo, *Cod. Barber.,* xlix. 33, pl. 28; and *Cod. Siena,* 8, iv. 5, pl. 9'. —
Heemskerk, *Berol.,* pls. 7, 9, 22. — Dosio, *Uffizi,* 2535, 2536, 2555, 2580. —
Baldassare Peruzzi, *Uffizi,* 631. — Giacomo Grimaldi, *Cod. Barber.,* passim.

On the tombs of the Via Cornelia. — Rodolfo Lanciani, *Pagan and Christian
Rome,* p. 270. — Flaminio Vacca, *Mem.* 61 (in Fea's Miscellanea, vol. i.). —
Giacomo Lombroso, *Mem. di Cassiano dal Pozzo,* p. 48. — *Corpus Inscr.,* vol.
vi. n. 9797, 9971, 10,048, 10,052–10,054, 10,056, 10,106, 10,215, etc.

On the Circus near Hadrian's Mausoleum. — Procopius, *Goth.,* ii. 1. —
Revillas, *Atti accad. pontif. arch.,* vol. x. p. 455. — *Beschreibung,* vol. ii¹, p.
17. — Luigi Canina, *Atti accad. pontif. arch.,* vol. x. p. 433; and *Edifizi,* vol.
iv. pls. 191, 192. — Gio. Battista de Rossi, *Piante di Roma,* p. 85.

LXXIX. The gardens of Domitia extended from the Via di
Porta Castello eastward as far as the Palazzo di Giustizia and
the Ponte Umberto.[1] The only monument left standing is the
Mausoleum seu Moles Hadriani (Hadrianium, Antonineum, Mole
Adriana, Castel S. Angelo).

Nerva was the last Emperor buried in the mausoleum of

---

[1] LITERATURE. — Rodolfo Lanciani, *Bull. com.,* 1889, p. 173.

Augustus. Trajan's ashes were laid to rest in an urn of gold under his monumental column (?). Hadrian determined to raise a new tomb for himself and his successors, and, like Augustus, selected a site on the green and shady banks of the Tiber, not on the city side, however, but in the gardens of Domitia, which, with those of Agrippina, formed a crown property called by Tacitus (Annal., xv. 39) "Horti Neronis." The mausoleum and the bridge which gave access to it were substantially finished in A. D. 136.

Fig. 211. — Capital from the Basement of Hadrian's Tomb.

Antoninus Pius, after completing the ornamental part in 139, transferred to it Hadrian's ashes from their temporary burial-place in the former villa of Cicero at Puteoli, and was himself afterwards interred there.

It has been conjectured that the porphyry sarcophagus which contained the remains of Hadrian, and was placed in the recess of the sepulchral chamber opposite the entrance door, is the one removed by Pope Innocent II. to the Lateran in order that it might serve as his own tomb, and destroyed there by fire in 1360. The cover, however, was saved, if we care to believe the same tradition, and made use of for the tomb of the Emperor Otho II., in the atrium of S. Peter, until Pope Albani removed it to the first chapel on the left of that church and turned it into a baptismal font. This story is groundless : that porphyry coffin, of colossal size, may have been placed in the mausoleum by a late Emperor, but cannot have contained the remains of Hadrian, because this prince was cremated and not inhumated.

Besides the passages of the "Vita Hadriani," 19; and of Dion Cassius, lxxvi. 15; lxxviii. 9, 24, two descriptions of the monument have come down to us, one by Procopius, the other by Leo I. From these we learn that it was composed of a square basement of moderate height, each side of which measured 247 feet. It was faced with blocks of Parian marble, with pilasters at the corners, crowned by a capital of which I give a reproduction from the original now in the Museo delle Terme. (Fig. 211.)

Above the pilasters were groups of men and horses in bronze, of admirable workmanship. The basement was protected around by a sidewalk and a railing of gilt bronze, supported by marble pillars crowned with gilded peacocks, two of which are in the Giardino della Pigna, in the Vatican. A grand circular mole, nearly a thousand feet in circumference, and also faced with blocks of Parian marble, stood on the square basement and supported in its turn a cone of earth covered with evergreens, like the mausoleum of Augustus. Of this magnificent decoration nothing now remains except a few blocks of the coating of marble, on the east side of the quadrangle, near the Bastione di S. Giovanni. All that is visible of the ancient work from the outside are the blocks of peperino of the mole which once supported the outer casing. The rest, both above and below, is covered by the works of fortification constructed at various periods, from the time of Honorius (393–403) to our own days. In no other monument of ancient and mediæval Rome is our history written, moulded, as it were, so vividly, as upon the battered remains of this castle-tomb. Within and around it took place all the faction fights for dominion with which popes, Emperors, barons, barbarians, Romans have distracted the city for fifteen hundred years. I must refer the reader on this point of history to Gregorovius, "Geschichte d. Stadt Rom;" [1] to Nibby's excellent article in vol. ii. of the "Roma antica," p. 488; and to Mariano Borgatti's "Castel Sant' Angelo," 1890. Of the internal arrangement of the monument nothing was known until 1825, when the principal door was discovered in the middle of the square basement facing the bridge. It opens

[1] P. 67 of index of Italian edition, Venice. 1876.

upon a corridor leading to a large niche, which, it is conjectured, contained a statue of Hadrian. The walls of this vestibule, by which modern visitors generally begin their inspection, are built of travertine, and bear evidence of having been paneled with Numidian marble. The pavement is of white mosaic. On the right side of this vestibule, near the niche, begins an inclined spiral way, 30 feet high and 11 wide, leading up to the central chamber, which is in the form of a Greek cross.

The inscriptions of the members of the Imperial family buried in the mausoleum, of which we have a copy, were set in the front of the basement towards the bridge, in the following order (see Huelsen in Mittheilungen, 1891, p. 142) : —

I. Inscription of Hadrian and Sabina put up in A. D. 139 above the entrance door (Corpus, n. 984). II. Of Antoninus Pius, d. 161 (n. 986). III. Of Faustina the elder, d. 141 (n. 987). IV.–VI. Of

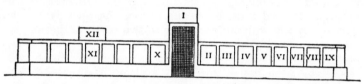

Fig. 212. — Diagram showing the Order in which the Imperial Tombstones were placed in the Mausoleum.

M. Aurelius Fulvus (n. 988), of M. Galerius Aurelius Antoninus (n. 989), and of Aurelia Fadilla (n. 990), sons and daughter of Antoninus Pius. VII.–IX. Of T. Aurelius Antoninus (n. 993), of T. Ælius Aurelius (n. 994), and of Domitia Faustina (n. 995), sons and daughter of M. Aurelius. X. Of L. Ælius Cæsar, d. 138 (n. 985). XI. Of L. Verus, d. 169 (n. 991). And lastly, XII., of Commodus, d. 192 (n. 992), placed above it. The position of this last shows that the panels destined by the designer for the reception of funeral tablets were all filled before the death of Commodus, and that a new line of epitaphs was begun at a higher level. When Bernardo Gamucci described the Castello towards 1565, inscriptions XI. and XII., as well as part of the frieze ornamented with bucranii and festoons, were still to be seen *in situ*. Gregory XIII. laid his hands on these historic marbles, and cut them in slabs for the decoration of his "cappella Gregoriana" in S. Peter's. The date of this wanton act of destruction is July, 1579. Giovanni Alberti, who happened to be in Rome in those days, wrote the following memorandum in his sketch-book (f. 25′, 26):

"This frieze with wreaths and bulls' heads (marked A), this architrave (marked B), and this basement (marked C) are being extracted at the present moment from the mausoleum of Hadrian,
and precisely from the front which faces the river, where there is
a great inscription above the door. They were all large pieces
of marble, wrenched from their sockets by order of our lord pope
Gregory XIII. and worked anew for the Gregorian chapel in S.
Peter's. (I took these drawings) on July 20, 1579." We know
from other sources that the demolition had begun in the month of
February of the preceding year.[1]

There is no doubt that the tomb was adorned with statues.
Procopius distinctly says that, during the siege laid by the Goths
to the castle in 537, many of them were hurled down from the
battlements upon the assailants. On the strength of this passage
topographers have been in the habit of attributing to the mausoleum all the works of statuary discovered in the neighborhood :
like the Barberini Faun now in Munich, the exquisite statue of a
River God described by Cassiano dal Pozzo,[2] etc., as if such subjects were becoming a house of death. The statues must have
represented the Ælian and the Aurelian princes and princesses ;
and I believe that the only two marbles which may be attributed
to the series are the colossal head of Hadrian now in the Rotunda
of the Vatican, No. 543, and that of Antoninus which stood by it
before they were removed from the Castel S. Angelo. (See Helbig,
Guide, vol. i. p. 211, n. 298.)

The mausoleum is crowned by the statue of the angel sheath-
ing the sword. He seems to protect it with his outspread wings.
The figure appears for the first time in a miniature of Nicolò
Polani of 1459, discovered by Geffroy in MSS. CC, 12 of the Bibliothèque de Sainte Geneviève in Paris.[3] Next in chronological
order comes the fresco of Benozzo Gozzoli at S. Geminiano (1465),
published by Stevenson, which also represents the angel in his
typical attitude ; and both as a statue, not as an allusion to the
legend of Gregory the Great (A. D. 590). The statue — of gilt
wood with a framework of copper — had been set up on the pinnacle of the castle in January, 1453, by order of Nicholas V. A
restoration is mentioned in 1475. Sigismondo de' Conti (Raphael's

---

[1] See Laurentius Frixolius, *Sacellum Gregorianum.* Rome, 1581.

[2] Lombroso, *Mem. di Cassiano dal Pozzo*, p. 49.

[3] REFERENCES FOR THE ANGEL'S STATUE. — Auguste Geffroy, *Mélanges
de l'Ecole française*, vol. xii. (*Une vue inédite de Rome en* 1459.) — Eugène
Müntz, *Les Antiquités de la ville de Rome*, Paris, 1886, p. 60, n. 1.

Fig. 213. — The Girandola at the Castle of S. Angelo, from an Engraving by Lauro (1624).

friend, from whom the divine painter received the order in 1511 for the celebrated Madonna di Foligno) says that under Pope Borgia (1497) the statue was blown up by the explosion of the powder-magazine, "cuius frusta etiam in Exquiliis sunt inventa!" A new one was substituted in 1499, stolen in 1527 by the lansquenets of Charles V., and a fourth in the time of Paul III., which is now set up in a niche at the last turn of the stairs. It is the work of Raffaello da Montelupo. The present bronze statue, modeled by Wenschefeld, dates from the time of Benedict XIV.

Among the other duties to which the mausoleum has been condemned, that of serving as a framework for the Girandola (a world-known display of fireworks on Easter Sunday and S. Peter's day) was certainly a picturesque one. See Fig. 213.

The mausoleum of Hadrian formed part of one of the largest and noblest cemeteries of ancient Rome, crossed by the Via Triumphalis. (See Pagan and Christian Rome, p. 270.) The tomb next in importance to it was the so-called "Meta," or "sepulcrum

Fig. 214. — The Mausoleum of Hadrian and the Meta in Raphael's "Vision of Constantine."

Romuli," or "sepulcrum Neronis," a pyramid of great size, which stood on the site of the church of S. Maria Transpontina, and was destroyed by Alexander VI. in 1499. There are many representations of the pyramid in works of art of the early Renaissance connected with the martyrdom of S. Peter and with his basilica; such as Giotto's fresco in the sacristy, Antonio Filarete's bronze doors, a panel of a ciborum in the sacre grotte Vaticane, and a vignette of the "Liber ystoriarum romanarum," recently published at the

215. — The Prati di Castello in 1870.

216. — The Prati di Castello in 1890.

expense of the city of Rome from the original of the thirteenth century.[1] I reproduce on page 557 the view of these tombs, which forms the background of Raphael's fresco, the " Vision of Constantine " (Fig. 214).

The " Prati di Castello," the modern representatives of the classic " Horti Neronis," have suffered more than other districts of the city from its transformation since 1870. The two preceding views represent the "prati" as they appeared twenty-five years ago (Fig. 215) and as they appear now (Fig. 216).

LITERATURE. — *Beschreibung*, vol. ii[1], p. 404. Luigi Canina, *Edifizii*, vol. iv. pls. 284–286. — Rodolfo Lanciani, *Bull. com.*, 1888, p. 129. — Christian Huelsen, *Mittheil.*, 1890, p. 137; 1893, p. 321. — Luigi Borsari, *Notizie Scavi*, 1892, p. 411.

[1] Ernesto Monaci, in *Archiv. Società rom. storia patria*, vol. xii.

CONCLUSION

WE have seen that buildings for the habitation of citizens in ancient Rome were of two kinds, private houses or palaces for the residence of one family, with a more or less copious retinue of servants (*domus*), and lodging houses or tenement houses many stories high, and adapted to the reception of several families and of single individuals (*insulæ*). We have seen, furthermore, that at the time of its greatest development the city numbered 1790 palaces and 46,602 lodging houses, the population being about 1,000,000 souls. These statistics refer to the city limits only, marked approximately by the walls of Aurelian; but the habitations extended beyond the walls for a radius of three miles at least. This suburban belt of houses and lodgings, with gardens and orchards between them, was called the belt of *expatiantia tecta*.

Tenement houses, unknown in villages, very rare in provincial towns (like Pompeii, Herculaneum, Ostia, and Velleia, considerable portions of which have been excavated), were introduced in Rome in 455 B. C., as related by Dionysius : "The Plebeians agreed to divide among themselves *bona fide* the building lots on the Aventine, each family selecting a space in proportion with the means at its disposal; but it happened also that families, not able to build independently, joined in groups of two, three, and more, and raised a house in common, one family occupying the ground floor, others the floors above."

This passage throws considerable light on the history of human habitations in Rome, about which such scanty information has been left by classics. It seems that, from the time the city was built on the Palatine hill to the reign of the Tarquins, the Romans dwelt in huts, not unlike those which to the present day give shelter to the shepherds of the Campagna. They are composed of a framework of timber, or boughs, with thatched walls and conical roofs, and a ring of stones. A piece of ground, called the ancestral field or the family estate, was attached to each hut, its limits being marked by trees sacred to Terminus or Silvanus. It measured 54,285 square feet, namely, one acre and thirty-nine perches, a space obviously insufficient to support and nourish the family, but very useful as a domestic garden or orchard. It contained also the family tomb.

In spite of the extension of the city limits under Servius Tullius, in consequence of which the whole circuit of the seven hills was included in the new line of walls, space began very soon to have a marketable value. Wealthier citizens built extensions to their houses, like shops furnished with bedrooms, and small apartments for the use of the poorer ones. These groups, composed of the mansion of the landlord and of the cottages and small buildings around them rented to outsiders, were called *insulæ* (islands) because, according to the ancient law, they were surrounded by a narrow strip of free ground, called *ambitus*, isolating them from the neighboring estates.

As long as the prehistoric system of habitations lasted, houses were restricted to the ground floor ; but when stones and tiles began to take the place of boughs and boards and thatched roofs, the height of buildings increased. Livy describes Tanaquil addressing the people through the windows from the upper part of the house, but she was a lady of royal birth and the style in which she lived was exceptional.

No better evidence can we get of the fatal law which divides men assembled in cities into a few who possess a large property and many who possess nothing, than the manner in which the few and the many are lodged. There were hardly eighteen hundred families of wealth and rank in old Rome enjoying the luxuries of a palace and of a private mansion, while about one hundred thousand families were massed in lodgings or tenement houses hardly fit for human habitation. We know that the tenement houses were not well built : their foundations were not sunk to the proper depth on account of the swampy nature of the subsoil; their front walls were only a foot and a half thick, and patched up with sun-dried bricks. Such houses were only capable of one story above the ground floor. At the time of Vitruvius, about 15 B. C., their construction had undergone some improvement, thanks to the energetic action of Augustus, and thanks also to the increase in the value of space which compelled builders to gain in height what they were losing in surface. Vitruvius describes the new tenement houses as composed of a framework of solid stone with partition walls of brick or concrete, attaining a considerable height, and capable of accommodating as many families of tenants as they had floors. Yet, even in the golden age of Augustus, cheap building was not given up altogether. In the inundation of 54 B. C. many houses collapsed because the waters had dissolved the sun-dried bricks of their walls. Augustus was compelled to dredge and clear out the bed of the river because it was choked up by the buildings which had fallen. The inundation of A. D. 69 undermined hundreds of houses even in inland quarters; and the Emperor Otho, who was then marching against Vitellius, found his way barred for over twenty miles by the ruins of buildings on either side of the Via Flaminia. The spontaneous collapse of the tenement houses was such a common occurrence that nobody paid attention to it, although it is an event which would fill our newspapers with a thrilling subject for days. The fall of some cottages, attended with loss of life, is related by Cicero as an item hardly worthy of serious remark. Seneca depicts the tenants of popular dens as fearing at the same time to be buried or burnt alive. There were companies formed for the purpose of propping and sustaining " in the air " houses, the foundations of which had to be strengthened.

Jordan, Richter, De Marchi, and others have tried to discover in more than one way what was the average size of a Roman insula, and how many tenants it was capable of containing. Supposing the population to have been 1,000,000, and supposing that a private palace counted 100 inmates, including master, servants, and slaves, we find that 179,000 people lived in palaces, 821,000 in tenement houses. This would give about 18 tenants for each of the 46,602 houses. As regards their size, Jordan suggests 350 square metres, Richter 282, while De Marchi reminds us that in the oldest quarters of Milan, which have as yet resisted civilization, the area of such houses varies from a minimum of 112 to a maximum of 270 square metres. We must be very careful, however, in forming our judgment by comparing modern with ancient cities, as the consequences may be misleading. Many points which we consider now as absolutely necessary to the health and welfare, nay, to the very existence of a city, were considered in by-gone days a matter of luxury, or were perhaps utterly ignored. It is not so very long ago since a municipal law of the city of Milan ordered that no more than fourteen people should sleep in the same room ! The problem is very complex, and the figures obtained by comparing our own municipal statistics with those of the Curiosum and Notitia mean little or nothing. My opinion is that the ignoble quarters which disfigured, and partly disfigure still, the neighborhood of the Ponte Sant-Angelo, of the Ghetto, of the Regola, may be taken as the nearest representatives of the old plebeian quarters of the Subura and of the Trastevere, and I agree with Niebuhr (Vorträge über Römische Alterthumer, p. 628) when he contends that the houses built three or four hundred years ago in the above-named quarters are good specimens of an old Roman insula. The comparison is proved correct, first, by the number of inmates, which varies from 15 to 20; secondly, by their surface not exceeding 200 square metres; thirdly, by their great height in comparison with their width ; fourthly, by the fact that they contain as many families as there are floors; in the last place, by their resemblance to the celebrated view of a Roman popular street, discovered by Rosa in the house of Germanicus on the Palatine (p. 149). The fragments of the plan of the city, engraved on marble under Septimius Severus and Caracalla, show many blocks composed entirely of insulæ and surrounded by narrow and tortuous streets.

Archæologists have collected the following information as regards house rents in Athens and Rome. In Athens, lodging houses were let mostly to foreigners who came there on business. Pasion, the banker, had one valued at 100 minas, or $2000. City property, yielding a return of rather more than $8\frac{1}{2}$ per cent on the purchase money, is mentioned by Isæus. Boeckh says that rents varied from a minimum of 3 minas, or $60, to a maximum of 120 minas, or $2400, according to size, location, and comfort of house. Rents were commonly paid by the month. Lodgings were frequently hired on speculation by persons called ναύκληροι, who made a profit by underletting them, and sometimes for not very reputable purposes. Rents in Rome were equally high, even for a miserable garret. Persons in the lowest conditions of life appear to have paid 2000 sesterces, or $85, at the time of Julius Cæsar. Cœlius is said to have paid 30,000 sesterces, or $1330, for a third floor in the insula of Publius Clodius. Hence, it became a profitable speculation to build or to hire a whole insula, or a whole block, and to sublet the *cenacula*, single rooms, or suites, to different tenants, the whole establishment being placed under the care of a manager and collector of rents, called *insularius*. Noblemen, owning a large town property, counted among their clerks a *procurator insularum*.

We come now to the question of the height of buildings. We must divide them into three classes : insulæ, palaces, and public buildings. The excessive height of tenement houses is noticed for the first time, I believe, in Cicero, who compares Rome "suspended in the air" to Capua lying comfortably down in the plains of Campania Felix. Seneca complains of the impunity which builders of tall tenement houses were allowed to enjoy, because the poor tenants, perched in those heights, had no possible escape from fire or from the collapse of the building itself. We know from Suetonius that Rutilius Lupus, who died after 77 B. C., had written an oration " on the height of public and private buildings," a fact which proves that excesses in this line of speculation had already aroused the suspicions and fears of persons intrusted with the care of public interests. There is no doubt that towards the end of the Republic Rome had higher houses than some large modern cities. While the Building Act promulgated in Berlin in 1860 admits a maximum height of 36 feet only — provided the street is of the same width — and a greater height only in case the street should be considerably broader; while the Viennese Building Act allows 45 feet (four stories at the utmost), and the Parisian 63½ feet, if such or more is the breadth of the thoroughfare, in ancient Rome higher figures were allowed with no consideration whatever for the width of the street. Augustus, to obviate disaster, limited the height of new houses to 70 Roman feet (20.79 metres), at least on the street side, and recited on this occasion the oration of Rutilius Lupus to prove that such a momentous question for the welfare of the city had been taken into consideration since the time of the Republic. This fact proves, first, that the height of 20 metres had been generally surpassed before the time of Augustus; secondly, that the new regulations concerned street fronts only, and not the back part of houses opening on yards, alleys, or narrow lanes; thirdly, that they concerned new structures alone, and not those already existing.

In spite of the boast attributed to the founder of the Empire, that he would leave built of marble the city which he had found built of bricks, there is no doubt that the crowding, the unhealthiness, the congestion of popular quarters, and their want of air, light, and space, remained very much as they had been before. The merit of having put an end to this wretched state of things, of having renewed the aspect of the metropolis, altering its plan in accordance with the principles of sanitation and art, belongs to Nero. He set the whole city into a blaze of fire, and did it so cleverly that, of the fourteen wards into which Rome had been divided by Augustus, three were annihilated, seven for the greater part destroyed, and yet not a single life was lost in the monstrous conflagration. Severus and Celer, the Imperial architects charged with the reconstruction of the city, showed themselves equal to their task. In tracing the new streets and avenues through the smoking ruins, they followed the straight line and the right angle, as far as could be done in a hilly and deeply furrowed region. Hasty and irregular constructions were forbidden ; large squares were opened, in place of filthy and densely inhabited quarters, and the height of private houses was limited, it seems, to double the width of the street. Porticoes were to be built in front of each dwelling to give the passer-by protection from rain and from heat ; lastly, wooden ceilings were excluded, at least from the lower stories, and isolation of houses on every side was made compulsory.

A new building act fixing the height of tenement houses at 60 feet (17.83 metres) was issued by Trajan. This incessant renewal of regulation after regulation shows how little respect speculators paid to them ; and, besides, the Imperial ordinances concerned, as I said, only the front of houses, not their interior parts opening on courtyards or alleys. No doubt these back sections attained a greater height. Martial speaks of a poor man, a neighbor, who had to mount two hundred steps (*ducentas scalas,* viz. *gradus*) to reach his garret. Giving to each step 0.15 metre, that garret must have been perched 30 metres, or 100 feet, above the level of the street ; but Martial uses perhaps a hyperbolic expression. The same poet says in another place, " *scalis habito tribus, sed altis,*" " I live in the third floor, *but* high above ground," which seems to indicate that ceilings must have hung very low in ordinary lodging houses (rooms have been found at Pompeii only 1.95 metre high). Juvenal mentions the case of a fire which had already attained the third floor of a building, without being noticed by the poor tenants living in the topmost stories under the roof. Tertullian compares the numberless stories of a tenement house to the " zones " of heaven imagined by the Gnostics. An inscription discovered on October 8, 1819, opposite the church of S. Eligio dei Ferrari (near the Piazza della Consolazione) describes a tenement house belonging to a Sertorius, as composed of ten shops and six floors above. We must remember, furthermore, that the maximum height was allowed by law independently from the breadth of the street, so that in this respect Rome must be placed far behind the large modern cities. While in Berlin the medium width of all the streets is 22 metres, that of the principal living streets in Rome reached only from 5 to 6 metres, inferior to the Parisian minimum of 7.80 metres; yet while in such cases the Parisians can raise their structures only 11.90 metres above the level of the street, the Romans were permitted to reach three times that height.

We must not wonder too much at such a state of things. There are actually in Rome — in Rome, the rejuvenated capital of the kingdom of Italy — two important thoroughfares, the Via degli Astalli and the Via delle Colonnelle, one measuring *eight feet*, between the Palazzo Muti and the Palazzo della Fabbrica di S. Pietro, so that hardly a ray of light can force its way between the eaves of their roofs; the other *ten feet*, between the church of la Maddalena and the opposite tenement houses. Pliny says that no city in the world surpasses Rome if the height of houses be also taken into consideration. Juvenal calls the housetops "sublime," and says that the windows are apt to make one giddy. In justice to Rome, we must also remark that houses three and four stories high are mentioned in Babylon by Herodotus, four to five in Naples by Philostratos, six in Carthage by Appianus, eight in Motya by Diodorus. The houses of Tyre were higher than those of Rome. The Emperor Zeno, referring to an older building act of Leo, which fixed at 100 feet the maximum height of houses in course of reconstruction after a fire, extended the privilege to all new structures, provided they should be separated one from the other in every direction by an interval of 100 feet. The law admitted, however, one exception, that no one could take away from his neighbor the view of the sea. So far as regards the tenement houses.

Palaces and private mansions may be left aside, because, as a rule, they were but two stories high. The Imperial palace makes an exception. The wing built by Caligula at the north corner of the Palatine hill, overlooking the Forum, rose 150 feet above the level of the Nova Via, which street was only 12 feet across! The palace of Septimius Severus, at the opposite corner of the hill, rose 180 feet above the level of the Via Triumphalis.

Public edifices were built on an equally grand scale. Let me mention again the Temple of the Sun, erected by Aurelian, after his conquest of Palmyra, in that part of the Quirinal which is now occupied by the Villa Colonna (see p. 428). Its columns measured 1.95 metre in diameter, and 17.66 metres in height, not including the capital, which alone measured 2.47 metres. The entablature measured 4.83, and was composed of blocks of marble 5 metres long: total height of order, 26 metres; of temple, including steps, pediment, and acroteria, 35 metres; to which we must add the height of the cliff on the edge of which the temple rose. The Cælii Saturnini, who lived at the foot of the cliff in a noble mansion discovered in 1854 (under the Palazzo Filippani, Piazza della Pilotta), must have seen the chariot of the god glittering in the morning sun 200 feet above their heads.

The reader may ask at this point why, in treating the subject, I bring forward only the evidence of classics, and not that of personal experience, and of actual discoveries made in Rome in the course of the last quarter of a century. The fact is that no insulæ have been found which could be excavated systematically; and even if they had been found, we could have studied only their ground plan, not their elevation. The Insula Sertoriana, opposite the church of S. Eligio dei Ferrari, has never been excavated, the only portion discovered being two shop doors opening on the public street. The Insula Bolaniana, discovered in March, 1743, in the foundations of the monastery of S. Pasquale Baylon, Trastevere, was also left unexplored, the only part described being the well which occupied the centre of the court. A third insula named Vitaliana was found in the spring of last year near the apse of S. Pietro in Vincoli, under circumstances that made a search impossible without damage to the houses above. The only fact that I can point out to specialists interested in the question is this: In describing the attack made by the partisans of Vitellius on those of Vespasian, who had intrenched themselves in the Capitolium, Tacitus distinctly affirms that the roofs of houses which surrounded the sacred hill were level with the platform of the temple of Jupiter Optimus Maximus. The platform of the temple, still visible in the gardens of the Caffarelli palace, now occupied by the German Embassy, rises 31 metres above the level of the ancient street which skirts the foot of the cliffs on the north side; therefore, the houses built against the cliffs were at least 31 metres high. The account of Tacitus is confirmed by existing ruins. Near the apse of the church of La Beata Rita, Via Giulio Romano, there are remains of an insula, of which only four stories are left standing, one half perhaps of the original number. That insula when perfect must have reached the level of the Arx now represented by the church of the Aracœli.

Such are the facts connected with the question of the general aspect of the city of the Cæsars. The Romans went undoubtedly beyond the line; but they had at least two excuses in their favor. The first is alluded to by Tacitus — in describing the reconstruction of the city after the fire of Nero, with large avenues, and large streets crossing each other at right angles, lined with houses of moderate height — when he says that in cities of southern latitudes (and subject to malaria) shade is more agreeable and desirable than the fiery rays of the sun; and that the health of the inhabitants in malarious regions is favored by agglomeration more than by dissemination over a large area.[1] The second excuse lies in the want of proper means of locomotion from one part of the city to another. It makes very little difference to a Londoner to lodge miles away from his club, from his office, from his shop, because he can reach his destination quickly, comfortably, and cheaply at all hours of the day and night. The old Romans, on the contrary, had no means of contending with distances; therefore they increased the height of their insulæ in the central quarters instead of building new ones in the outlying districts.

[1] In the city of the popes the healthiest district was the overcrowded and overbuilt Ghetto, in which six thousand Jews were massed in houses of exceptional height.

APPENDIX

A. Comparison between Years of the Christian and of the Roman Eras.

(V. C.) Anni ab Urbe Condita.	(B. C.) Anni Ante Christum.	(V. C.) Anni ab Urbe Condita.	(B. C.) Anni Ante Christum.	(A. D.) Anni a Christo Nato.	(V. C.) Anni ab Urbe Condita.	(A.D.) Anni a Christo Nato.	(V. C.) Anni ab Urbe Condita.
1	753	325	429	1	754	325	1078
10	744	350	404	10	763	350	1103
20	734	375	379	20	773	375	1128
30	724	400	354	30	783	400	1153
40	714	425	329	40	793	425	1178
50	704	450	304	50	803	450	1203
60	694	475	279	60	813	475	1228
70	684	500	254	70	823	500	1253
80	674	525	229	80	833	...	...
90	664	550	204	90	843	...	...
100	654	575	179	100	853	...	...
125	629	600	154	125	878	...	...
150	604	625	129	150	903	...	...
175	579	650	104	175	928	...	...
200	554	675	79	200	953	...	...
225	529	700	54	225	978	...	...
250	504	725	29	250	1003	...	...
275	479	750	4	275	1028	...	...
300	454	753	1	300	1053	...	...

B. Chronological List of Roman Emperors.

B. C.

48. *Caius Julius* Cæsar,

   son of C. Cæsar and of Aurelia, born 100 B. C., pont. max. 63, dictator 48, assassinated March 15th, 44. His wife —

   Cornelia, dau. of L. Cinna, d. 68.

27. *Caius Octavius Cæsar* Augustus (*Octavianus*),

   son of C. Octavius (died 58) and Atia, niece of Julius Cæsar, b. 63, declared Emperor 29, obtained the name of Augustus 27, d. Aug. 29th, A. D. 14. His wives —

   1. *Clodia*, dau. of Clodius and Fulvia.
   2. *Scribonia*, married 40 B. C., divorced 38.
   3. *Livia* Drusilla, first married to Tib. Claudius, b. 57 B. C., d. A. D. 29.

B. C.

27.   *Octavia*, his sister, married C. Marcellus, 50 B. C., M. Antony, 40 B. C.,
     d. 11.   Her son by Marcellus —
     Marcellus, m. Julia, dau. of Augustus, adopted successor, d. 23 B. C.
     Julia's children by Marcus Agrippa —
      1. *Caius Cæsar*, b. 20 B. C., d. 4.
      2. *Lucius Cæsar*, b. 17 B. C., d. 2.
      3. *Julia*, m. L. Æmilius Paulus, d. A. D. 28.

A. D.

14.   TIBERIUS *Claudius Nero Cæsar*,
     b. Nov. 16th, 42 B. C., Caesar A. D. 4, smothered March 16th, 37.   Married
      1. *Vipsania Agrippina*.   Their son, *Drusus* Junior, b. 13, poisoned
       A. D. 23.
      2. *Julia*, dau. of Augustus, d. A. D. 14.
     Drusus Senior, his brother, b. 38 B. C., d. A. D. 9.   Married —
     Antonia, b. 38 B. C., poisoned A. D. 38.   Their son —
     Germanicus, b. 15 B. C., Cæsar A. D. 4, poisoned A. D. 9.   Married —
     Agrippina Senior, dau. of M. Agrippa and of Julia, dau. of Augustus,
      b. 15 B. C., starved to death A. D. 33.   Their sixth child —

37.   *Gaius Cæsar* CALIGULA,
     b. A. D. 12, murdered Jan. 24th, 41.   Married —
      1. *Claudia*, d. 36.
      2. *Orestilla*, consort of Cn. Piso.
      3. *Lollia Paulina*.
      4. *Cæsonia*, killed 41.

41.   *Tiberius* CLAUDIUS *Drusus Nero Germanicus*,
     son of Drusus Senior and Antonia, b. 10 B. C., poisoned A. D. 54.   Mar-
     ried —
      1. *Plætia Urgulanilla*.
      2. *Ælia Pætina*.
      3. *Valeria Messallina*, killed 48.   Their son —
       Britannicus, b. 42, poisoned 55.
      4. *Agrippina* Junior, dau. of Germanicus and Agrippina Senior, m.,
       first Cn. Domitius Ahenobarbus, secondly Crispus Passienus,
       thirdly Claudius.

54.   NERO *Claudius Cæsar Drusus Germanicus*,
     son of Cn. Domitius Ahenobarbus and Agrippina Junior, b. 37, Cæsar
     50, killed himself 68.   Married —
      1. *Octavia*, dau. of Claudius and Messallina, b. about 42, killed her-
      self 62.
      2. *Poppæa Sabina*, wife of Otho, d. 66.
      3. *Statilia Messallina*.

68.   *Ser. Sulpicius* GALBA,
     b. Dec. 24th, 3, murdered 69.

69.   *M. Salvius* OTHO,
     b. 32, Emperor Jan. 15th, 69, killed himself April 16th, 69.

69.   A. VITELLIUS,
     son of L. Vitellius (d. 49), b. 15, Emperor Jan. 2d, 69, killed Dec. 22d,
     69.   His brother —
     L. Vitellius.

A. D.

69. *T. Flavius Sabinus* VESPASIANUS,
  b. Nov. 17th, 9, d. June 24th, 79. Married —
  Flavia Domitilla. Their dau. —
  Domitilla, m. Flavius Clemens.

79. TITUS *Flavius Sabinus Vespasianus,*
  son of Vespasian, b. Dec. 30th, 40, Cæsar 69, Emperor with his father
  71, d. Sept. 13th, 81. Married —
   1. *Arrecina Tertulla.*
   2. *Marcia Furnilla.* Their dau. *Julia* married Flavius Sabinus,
   nephew of Vespasian.

81. *T. Flavius* DOMITIANUS,
  son of Vespasian, b. 51, Cæsar 69, assassinated Sept. 18th, 96. Married —
  Domitia, dau. of Domitius Corbulo, d. 140. Their son —
  Anonymus.

96. *M. Cocceius* NERVA,
  b. 32, d. Jan. 27th, 98.

98. *Marcus Ulpius* TRAJANUS,
  b. Sept. 18th, 52 or 53, associated in Empire with Nerva, 97, d. Aug.
  117. Married —
  Pompeia Plotina, d. 100.
  Marciana, his sister, mother of —
  Matidia.

117. *P. Ælius* HADRIANUS,
  b. 76, adopted by Trajan 117, d. July 138. Married —
  Julia Sabina, dau. of Matidia, killed herself 137.

138. *T. Ælius Hadrianus* ANTONINUS PIUS,
  b. Sept. 19th, 86, adopted by Hadrian 138, d. March 7th, 161. Married —
  Annia Galeria Faustina Senior, b. 105, d. 141. Their son —
  Galerius Antoninus.

161. M. AURELIUS *Antoninus,*
  son of Hadrian's sister Paulina, b. April 20th, 121, adopted by Antoninus 138, d. March 17th, 180. Married, 138 —
  Annia Faustina Junior, dau. of Antoninus Pius and Faustina, d. 175.
  Their children —
   1. *Annius Verus,* b. 163, Cæsar 166, d. 170.
   2. *Annia Lucilla.* Married —
   Lucius Aurelius Verus, son of L. Ceionius Commodus, adopted by
   Antoninus 138, associated in Empire 151, d. 169.

180. *L. Aurelius* COMMODUS,
  b. 161, Cæsar 166, Emperor 176, strangled Dec. 31st, 192. Married —
  Bruttia Crispina, d. 183.

193. *P. Helvius* PERTINAX,
  b. 126, murdered March 28th, 193. Married —
  Flavia Titiana. Their son —
  P. Helvius PERTINAX.

A. D.

193. *M.* DIDIUS *Salvius* IULIANUS,
> b. 133, Emperor March 28th, 193, murdered June 1st, 193. Married —
> *Manlia Scantilla.* Their dau. —
> *Didia Clara.*

193. *C. Pescennius* NIGER,
> saluted Emperor by the legions in the East 193, killed 194.

193. *Clodius* ALBINUS,
> named Cæsar by Septimius Severus 193, took title of Emperor 196,
> killed 197.

193. L. SEPTIMIUS SEVERUS,
> b. 146, d. Feb. 4th, 211. Married —
> *Julia Domna,* starved herself to death 217. Their son —
> *Septimius Geta,* b. 189, Cæsar 198, Emperor with Caracalla 211, assas-
> sinated 212.

211. *Marcus Aurelius Antoninus* CARACALLA,
> son of Severus, b. 188, Cæsar 196, Augustus 198, sole Emperor 212.
> Married —
> *Fulvia Plautilla,* dau. of *Fulvius Plautianus.*
> Murdered 217 by —

217. *M. Opellius* MACRINUS,
> b. 164, killed 218, with his son —
> *M. Opellius* DIADUMENIANUS.

218. *Marcus Aurelius Antoninus* ELAGABALUS, or HELIOGABALUS,
> son of Varius Marcellus and Julia Sœmias *Bassiana,* and grandson of
> Julia Mæsa (sister of Julia Domna), b. 205, killed 222. Married —
> 1. *Julia Cornelia Paula,* divorced 200.
> 2. *Aquilia Severa.*
> 3. *Annia Faustina.*

222. *M. Aurelius* SEVERUS ALEXANDER,
> son of Gessius Marcianus and *Julia Mammœa,* dau. of Julia Mæsa,
> b. Oct. 1st, 205, adopted by Elagabalus'as Cæsar 221, murdered 235.
> Married —
> 2. *Memmia.*
> 3. *Herennia Sallustia Barbia Orbiana.*

235. *C. Julius Verus* MAXIMINUS,
> b. 173, assassinated 238. Married —
> *Paulina.* Their son —
> C. Julius Verus MAXIMUS, Cæsar 238, killed 238. Married —
> *Junia Fadilla.*

238. *M. Antonius* GORDIANUS AFRICANUS I.,
> son of Metius Marullus and Ulpia Gordiana, b. 158, killed himself 238
> Married —
> *Fabia Orestilla.* Their son —
> GORDIANUS AFRICANUS II.,
> b. 192, Emperor with his father for forty days, killed 238.

238. *D. Cœlius* BALBINUS,
> b. 178, and
> *Maximus Clodius* PUPIENUS,
> b. 164, joint Emperors for three months, murdered June, 238.

A. D.

238. GORDIANUS *Pius* III.,
     grandson of Gordianus I., b. 222, Cæsar 238, assassinated 244.   Married —
       Furia Sabinia Tranquillina, dau. of Temesitheus.

244. *M. Julius* PHILIPPUS,
     b. 204, killed 249.   Married —
       Marcia Otacilia Severa.   Their son —
     M. Julius PHILIPPUS,
       b. 237, Cæsar 244, Augustus 247, killed 249.

249. *C. Messius Quintus Trajanus* DECIUS,
     b. 201, drowned 251.   Married —
       Herennia Cupressenia Etruscilla.   Their sons —
     1.   *Q. Herennius* ETRUSCUS, Cæsar 249, Augustus 251, killed 251.
     2.   *C. Valens* HOSTILIANUS, Cæsar 249, Emperor with Galius 251, d. same
         year.

251. *C. Vibius Trebonianus* GALLUS,
     killed 254.   Married —
       Afinia Gemina Bebiana.   Their son —
     C. Vibius VOLUSIANUS, Cæsar 251, Emperor 252, killed 254.
       Æmilius ÆMILIANUS, b. 208, Emperor in Mœsia 253, killed 254.
       Married —
       Cornelia Supera.

253. *P. Licinius* VALERIANUS,
     b. 190, taken prisoner by the Persians 260, d. 263.
       Mariniana, his second wife, mother of —
       Valerianus junior, killed 268.
     P. Licinius Valerianus Egnatius GALLIENUS,
       son of Valerianus by his first wife, Emperor 253, assassinated 268.
       Married —
       Cornelia Salonina.
     TETRICUS pater, Emperor in Gaul 267, defeated by Aurelian 274.   His
     son —
       Tetricus filius, Cæsar in Gaul 267.

268. *M. Aurelius* CLAUDIUS GOTHICUS,
     b. 214, d. 270.   His brother —
       Quintıllus, Emperor at Aquileia, 270.

270. *L. Domitius* AURELIANUS,
     b. 207, assassinated 275.   Married —
       Ulpia Severina.

275. *M. Claudius* TACITUS,
     assassinated April, 276.   His brother —

276. *M. Annius* FLORIANUS,
     b. 232, Emperor for two months, killed 276.

276. *M. Aurelius* PROBUS,
     b. 232, massacred 282.

282. *M. Aurelius* CARUS,
     b. 230, killed by lightning 283.   His sons —
     M. Aurelius CARINUS,
       b. 249, Cæsar 282, Emperor 283, killed 284.   His son —
       Nigrinianus.

A. D.

282. *M. Aurelius* NUMERIANUS,
    b. 254, Cæsar 282, Augustus 283, d. 284.

284. *C. Aurelius Valerius* DIOCLETIANUS,
    b. 245, abdicated 305, d. 313. Married —
    Prisca, executed by order of Licinius, 315.
    M. Aurelius Valerius MAXIMIANUS I.,
        styled Herculius, associated in the Empire with Diocletian 286, abdicated 305, retook the Empire 306, abdicated again 308, Emperor again 309, strangled himself 310. Married —
        Eutropia. Their son —
    M. Aurelius Valerius MAXENTIUS,
        b. 282, Emperor of Rome 306, drowned in the Tiber 312. Married —
        Valeria Maximilla. Their son —
        Romulus, b. 306, Cæsar 307, d. 309.

305. *Constantius* CHLORUS,
    b. 250, Cæsar 292, d. 306. His wives —
      1. *Helena,* d. 328.
      2. *Theodora.* His children —
    Constantia, d. 330. Married —
        Licinius senior, b. 263, associated in the Empire with Galerius Maximianus 307, put to death by Constantine 323.
    Eutropia.
    Julius Constantius. Married —
      1. *Galla.*
      2. *Basilina.*
  GALERIUS *Valerius Maximianus Armentarius,*
    adopted and named Cæsar by Diocletian 292, Augustus and Emperor 305, d. 311. His second wife was —
    Galeria Valeria, dau. of Diocletian and Prisca, executed by order of Licinius 315.

306. *Flavius Valerius* CONSTANTINUS *Magnus,*
    son of C. Chlorus and Helena, b. 274, named Cæsar and Augustus 306, converted to Christianity 311, sole Emperor 311, changed the seat of Government to Byzantium (Constantinople) 336, d. 337. Married —
      1. *Minervina.* Their son —
        Flavius Julius Crispus, b. 300, Cæsar 317, put to death by order of his father 326. Married —
        Helena.
      2. *Fausta,* dau. of Maximian, smothered by order of her husband 326. Their son —

337. *Flavius Julius* CONSTANTINUS II.,
    b. 316, Cæsar 317, killed 340. His brother —
  CONSTANS I.,
    b. 320, Cæsar 333, Emperor of the East 346, assassinated 350. His brother —
  CONSTANTIUS II.,
    b. 317, Cæsar 323, Augustus 327, Master of all the Empire 350, d. 361.

A. D.

337. *Flavius Popilius* MAGNENTIUS,
  b. 303, Emperor at Autun 350, killed himself 353. His brother —
    Decentius, Cæsar 351, killed himself 353.

Constantius GALLUS,
  son of Julius Constantius and Galla, b. 325, Cæsar 351, executed 354.
  Married —
    Constantina, wife first of Hannibalianus, d. 354.

360. *Flavius Claudius* JULIANUS,
  surnamed the Apostate, son of Julius Constantius and Basilina, b. 331,
  Cæsar 355, Emperor at Paris 360, sole Emperor 361, killed in battle
  against the Persians 363. Married —
    Helena, dau. of Constantine.

363. *Flavius Claudius* JOVIANUS,
  b. 331, d. Feb. 17th, 364.

364. VALENTINIANUS II.,
  son of Gratianus, b. 321, d. 375. Married —
    1. *Valeria Severa,* mother of —
  GRATIANUS,
    b. 350, Augustus at Amiens 361, Emperor 375, slain 389. Married —
    1. *Constantia,* dau. of Constantinus II., d. 383.
    2. *Justina,* mother of —

383. VALENTINIANUS II.,
  b. 371, Augustus 375, Emperor of the West 383, assassinated 392.

VALENS (East),
  brother of Valentinianus I., b. 328, associated in the Empire and Augustus 364, burnt alive 378.

379. THEODOSIUS Magnus I. (East),
  b. 346, Augustus and associated in the Empire by Gratian 379, d. Jan.
  17th, 395. Married —
    1. *Flaccilla,* d. 388.
    2. *Galla,* dau. of Valentinian I.
    Eugenius, rhetorician, proclaimed Emperor by Arbogastes 392, de-
      feated and slain by Theodosius 394.
    Arcadius, son of Theodosius, b. 377, Augustus 383, Emperor of the
      East 395, d. 408. Married —
    Eudoxia, d. 404. Their son —
    Theodosius II., b. 401, Augustus 402, Emperor of the East 418, d. 450.

395. *Flavius* HONORIUS,
  youngest son of Theodosius and Flaccilla, b. 384, Augustus 393, d.
  423. Married —
    Maria, dau. of Stilicho.

CONSTANTIUS III.,
  Augustus and associated in Empire of the West 421, d. the same year.
  Married 417 —
    Galla Placidia, sister of Honorius, widow of Ataulf, king of the
      Goths, died 423.
    Priscus Attalus, made Emperor by Alaric at Rome 409, deprived of
      that title, reassumed it in Gaul 410, died in the island of Lipari.

A. D.

425. *Placidus* VALENTINIANUS III.,
son of Constantius III. and Galla Placidia, b. 419, slain by Petronius Maximus 455. Married —
Licinia Eudoxia, dau. of Theodosius II. Their dau. —
Eudocia, married Hunneric, son of Genseric, king of the Vandals.

455. *Petronius* MAXIMUS,
b. 395, slain after a reign of three months. Married —
Licinia Eudoxia, widow of Valentinianus III.

455. *Flavius Cæcilius* AVITUS,
deposed 456.

457. *Julius* MAJORIANUS,
compelled to abdicate 461, died five days after.

461. *Libius* SEVERUS,
d. 465.

467. ANTHEMIUS,
son of Procopius, slain by his son-in-law Ricimer 467. Married —
Euphemia, dau. of the Emperor Marcianus.

472. OLYBRIUS, *Anicius*,
a Roman Senator, d. 472. Married —
Placidia, dau. of Valentinian III. and Eudoxia.

474. JULIUS NEPOS,
retired to Dalmatia 475, assassinated by Glycerius 480, married a niece of the Empress Verina.

475. ROMULUS AUGUSTULUS,
son of Orestes, a patrician, dethroned by *Odoacer*, king of the Heruli, 476, who assumes the title of King of Italy.

C. CHRONOLOGICAL LIST OF THE FIRST KINGS OF ITALY.

476	Odoacer	540	Theodebald
493	Theodoric	541	Eraric
526	Athalaric	541	Totila or Badiula
534	Theodatus	552	Theias
536	Vitiges		

D. CHRONOLOGICAL LIST OF THE POPES.

ST. PETER TO HADRIAN I.

(From Duchesne — *Liber Pontificalis*, vol. i. p. cclx.)

Date of Election.	Date of Death.	Name.
? Feb. 22	67 June 29	Petrus
*67		Linus
*78		Anencletus (Cletus)
*91		Clemens I.
*96		Evarestus

* Approximate dates.

Date of Election.	Date of Death.	Name.
*109		Alexander
*119		Xystus I.
*127		Telesphorus
*139		Hyginus
*142		Pius
*157		Anicetus
*168		Soter
*177		Eleutherus
*193		Victor I.
*202		Zephyrinus
*219		Callistus I.
*223		Urbanus I.
230 July 21 discinctus	235 Sept. 28	Pontianus
235 Nov. 21	236 Jan. 3	Anteros
236 Jan. 10	250 Jan. 20	Fabianus
251 Mar.	253 June	Cornelius
253 June 25	254 Mar. 5	Lucius
254 May 12	257 Aug. 2	Stephanus I.
257 Aug. 30	258 Aug. 6	Xystus II.
259 July 22	268 Dec. 26	Dionysius
269 Jan. 5	274 Dec. 30	Felix
275 Jan. 4	283 Dec. 7	Eutychianus
283 Dec. 17	296 April 22	Gaius
296 June 30	304 Oct. 25	Marcellinus
308 May 27 (or June 26)	309 Jan. 16	Marcellus
309 or 310 April 18	309 or 310 Aug. 17	Eusebius
311 July 2	314 Jan. 11	Miltiades
314 Jan. 31	335 Dec. 31	Silvester
336 Jan. 18	336 Oct. 7	Marcus
337 Feb. 6	352 April 12	Julius
352 May 17	366 Sept. 24	Liberius
366 Oct. 1	384 Dec. 11	Damasus
384 Dec. 15 or 22 or 29	399 Nov. 26	Siricius
399 Nov. 27	401 Dec. 19	Anastasius I.
401 Dec. 22	417 Mar. 12	Innocentius I
417 Mar. 18	418 Dec. 26	Zosimus
418 Dec. 29	422 Sept. 4	Bonifatius I.
422 Sept. 10	432 July 27	Cælestinus I.
432 July 31	440 Aug. 19	Xystus III.
440 Sept. 29	461 Nov. 10	Leo I.
461 Nov. 19	468 Feb. 29	Hilarius
468 Mar. 3	483 Mar. 10	Simplicius
483 Mar. 13	492 Mar. 1	Felix III.
492 Mar. 1	496 Nov. 21	Gelasius
496 Nov. 24	498 Nov. 19	Anastasius II.

* Approximate dates.

Date of Election.	Date of Death.	Name.
996	999	Gregorius V. (Bruno), Saxony.
999	1003	Silvester II. (Gerbert), Auvergne.
1003	1003	Johannes XVI., Rome.
1003	1009	Johannes XVII., Rome.
1009	1021	Sergius IV., Rome.
1021	1024	Benedictus VIII., Tusculum.
1024	1033	Johannes XVIII., Tusculum.
1033	1046	Benedictus IX., Tusculum.
1046	1047	Gregorius VI., Rome.
1047	1048	Clemens II. (Snidger), Saxony.
1048	1049	Damasus II. (Boppa) Bavaria.
1049	1055	Leo IX. (Bruno), Alsace.
1055	1057	Victor II. (Gebhard), Bavaria.
1057	1058	Stephanus X., Lorraine.
1058	1061	Nicholaus II. (Gerard), Burgundy.
1061	1073	Alexander II. (Badagio), Milan.
1073	1086	Gregorius VII. (Hildebrand or Aldobrandeschi), Soana, Tuscany.
1086	1088	Victor III. (Epifani), Benevento.
1088	1099	Urbanus II., Reims.
1099	1118	Paschalis II., Bieda.
1118	1119	Gelasius II. (Giovanni Caetani), Gaeta.
1119	1124	Calixtus II., Burgundy.
1124	1130	Honorius II., Bologna.
1130	1143	Innocentius (Papareschi), Rome.
1143	1144	Cælestinus II., Città di Castello.
1144	1145	Lucius II., Bologna.
1145	1150	Eugenius III. (Paganelli), Pisa.
1150	1154	Anastasius IV., Rome.
1154	1159	Hadrianus IV. (Nicholas Breakspeare), Langley, England.
1159	1181	Alexander III. (Bandinelli), Siena.
1181	1185	Lucius III., Lucca.
1185	1187	Urbanus III. (Crivelli), Milan.
1187	1187	Gregorius VIII. (Di Morra), Benevento.
1187	1191	Clemens III. (Scolari), Rome.
1191	1198	Cælestinus III. (Buboni), Rome.
1198	1216	Innocentius III. (Conti), Anagni.
1216	1227	Honorius III. (Savelli), Rome.
1227	1241	Gregorius IX. (Conti), Anagni.
1241	1243	Cælestinus IV. (Castiglioni), Milan.
1243	1254	Innocentius IV. (Fieschi), Genoa.
1254	1261	Alexander IV. (Conti), Anagni.
1261	1264	Urbanus IV. (Pantaleo), Troyes.
1264	1271	Clemens IV. (Foucauld), Narbonne.
1271	1276	Gregorius X. (Visconti), Piacenza.
1276	1276	Innocentius V., Savoy.
1276	1276	Hadrianus V. (Fieschi), Genoa.

Date of Election.	Date of Death.	Name.
1276	1277	Johannes XIX. or XX. or XXI. (Giuliano), Lisbon.
1277	1281	Nicholaus III. (Orsini), Rome.
1281	1285	Martinus IV., Champagne, Montpitié.
1285	1287	Honorius IV. (Savelli), Rome.
1287	1292	Nicholaus IV. (Masci), Ascoli.
1292	1294	Cælestinus V. (Pietro da Morrone), Isernia.
1294	1303	Bonifatius VIII. (Benedetto Caetani), Anagni.
1303	1305	Benedictus XI. (Boccasini), Treviso.
1305	1316	Clemens V. (de Gouth), Bordeaux.
1316	1334	Johannes XXII. (Jacques d'Euse), Cahors.
1334	1342	Benedictus XII. (Jacques Fournier), Foix.
1342	1352	Clemens VI. (Pierre Roger de Beaufort), Limoges.
1352	1362	Innocentius VI. (Etienne Aubert), Limoges.
1362	1370	Urbanus V. (Guillaume de Grimoard), Mende.
1370	1378	Gregorius XI. (Roger de Beaufort), Limoges.
1378	138ǝ	Urbanus VI. (Bartolommeo Prignani), Naples.
1389	1404	Bonifatius IX. (Pietro Tomacelli), Naples.
1404	1406	Innocentius VII. (Migliorati), Sulmona.
1406	1409	Gregorius XII. (Angelo Correr), Venice.
1409	1410	Alexander V. (Petrus Phylargius), Candia.
1410	1417	Johannes XXIII. (Baldassare Cossa), Naples.
1417	1431	Martinus V. (Oddone Colonna), Rome.
1431	1447	Eugenius IV. (Gabriele Condolmiere), Venice.
1447	1455	Nicholaus V. (Tommaso Parentucelli), Sarzana.
1455	1458	Calixtus III. (Alfonso Borgia), Valencia.
1458	1464	Pius II. (Æneas Sylvius Piccolomini), Pienza.
1464	1471	Paulus II. (Pietro Barbo), Venice.
1471	1484	Sixtus IV. (Francesco della Rovere), Savona.
1484	1492	Innocentius VIII. (Giovanni Battista Cibo), Genoa.
1492	1503	Alexander VI. (Roderigo Lenzoli Borgia), Spain.
1503	1503	Pius III. (Antonio Todeschini Piccolomini), Siena.
1503	1513	Julius II. (Giuliano della Rovere), Savona.
1513	1522	Leo X. (Giovanni de' Medici), Florence.
1522	1523	Hadrianus VI. (Adrian Florent), Utrecht.
1523	1534	Clemens VII. (Giulio de' Medici), Florence.
1534	1550	Paulus III. (Alessandro Farnese), Rome.
1550	1555	Julius III. (Giovanni Maria Ciocchi del Monte), Rome.
1555	1555	Marcellus II. (Marcello Cervini), Montepulciano.
1555	1559	Paulus IV. (Giovanni Pietro Caraffa), Naples.
1559	1566	Pius IV. (Giovanni Angelo de' Medici), Milan.
1566	1572	Pius V. (Michele Ghislieri), Bosco Ligure.
1572	1585	Gregorius XIII. (Ugo Boncompagni), Bologna.
1585	1590	Sixtus V. (Felice Peretti), Montalto.
1590	1590	Urbanus VII. (Giovanni Battista Castagna), Rome.
1590	1591	Gregorius XIV. (Nicolò Sfrondati), Cremona.
1591	1592	Innocentius IX. (Giovanni Antonio Facchinetti), Bologna.
1592	1605	Clemens VIII. (Ippolito Aldobrandini), Fano.

Date of Election.	Date of Death.	Name.
1605	1605	Leo XI. (Alessandro Ottaviano de' Medici), Florence.
1605	1621	Paulus V. (Camillo Borghese), Rome.
1621	1623	Gregorius XV. (Alessandro Ludovisi), Bologna.
1623	1644	Urbanus VIII. (Matteo Barberini), Florence.
1644	1655	Innocentius X. (Giovanni Battista Pamfili), Rome.
1655	1667	Alexander VII. (Fabio Chigi), Siena.
1667	1670	Clemens IX. (Giulio Rospigliosi), Pistoja.
1670	1676	Clemens X. (Giovanni Battista Altieri), Rome.
1676	1689	Innocentius XI. (Benedetto Odescalchi), Como.
1689	1691	Alexander VIII. (Pietro Ottoboni), Venice.
1691	1700	Innocentius XII. (Antonio Pignatelli), Naples.
1700	1721	Clemens XI. (Giovanni Francesco Albani), Urbino.
1721	1724	Innocentius XIII. (Michelangelo Conti), Rome.
1724	1730	Benedictus XIII. (Pietro Francesco Orsini), Rome.
1730	1740	Clemens XII. (Lorenzo Corsini), Florence.
1740	1758	Benedictus XIV. (Prospero Lambertini), Bologna.
1758	1769	Clemens XIII. (Carlo Rezzonico), Venice.
1769	1775	Clemens XIV. (Lorenzo Francesco Ganganelli), S. Angelo in Vado.
1775	1800	Pius VI. (Angelo Braschi), Cesena.
1800	1823	Pius VII. (Gregorio Barnaba Chiaramonti), Cesena.
1823	1829	Leo XII. (Annibale della Genga), Spoleto.
1829	1831	Pius VIII. (Francesco Saverio Castiglioni), Cingoli.
1831	1846	Gregorius XVI. (Mauro Cappellari), Belluno.
1846	1878	Pius IX. (Giovanni Maria Mastai-Ferretti), Sinigaglia.
1878		Leo XIII. (Gioachino Pecci), Carpineto.

E. Alphabetical List of Painters, Sculptors, and Architects mentioned in this Book.

PAINTERS.

Albani, Francesco, of Bologna	1578–1660
Alberti, Cherubino	1552–1615
Alberti, Giovanni	1558–1601
Allegri, Antonio da Correggio	1494–1534
Barbieri, Gio. Francesco da Cento	1590–1666
Battoni, Pompeo, of Lucca	1708–1787
Berettini, Pietro da Cortona	1596–1669
Bril, Paul, of Antwerp	1556–1626
Buonarroti, Michelangelo	1474–1564
Caldari, Polidoro, da Caravaggio	1495–1542
Caliari, Paolo, Veronese	1532–1588
Caracci, Agostino, of Bologna	1558–1601
Cesari, Giuseppe, of Arpino	1560–1640
Clovio, Giulio, of Grisone, Croatia	1498–1578
Duguet, Gaspard (Poussin)	1613–1675

Gelée, Claude, called Lorraine	1600–1682
Giotto di Bondone, of Vespignano	1276–1336
Peruzzi, Baldassare, of Siena	1480–1536
Pierin del Vaga (Buonaccorsi)	1500–1547
Pinturicchio, Bernardino, of Perugia	1454–1513
Piombo, Sebastiano del (Luciano), of Venice	1485–1547
Pippi, Giulio, of Rome	1492–1546
Poussin, Niccolò, of Andelys	1574–1665
Reni, Guido, of Bologna	1575–1642
Ricciarelli, Daniele da Volterra	1500–1557
Roncalli, Cristoforo delle Pomarance	1553–1626
Rosa, Salvatore, of Naples	1615–1673
Sanzio, Raffaele, of Urbino	1483–1520
Sarto, Andrea del (Vanucchi), of Florence	1488–1530
Van Dyck, Antonio, of Antwerp	1599–1641
Vanni, Francesco, of Siena	1565–1609
Vasari, Giorgio, of Arezzo	1512–1574
Vecellio, Tiziano (Cadore)	1477–1576
Venusti, Marcello, of Mantova	1580
Vinci, Leonardo da, Tuscan	1452–1519
Zampieri, Domenico, of Bologna	1581–1641
Zuccari, Federico, of Urbino	1543–1609
Zuccari, Taddeo, of Urbino	1529–1566

SCULPTORS.

Algardi, Alessandro, of Bologna	1602–1654
Bernini, Gio. Lorenzo	1598–1680
Buonarroti, Michelangelo, Florentine	1474–1564
Canova, Antonio, of Possagno	1757–1822
Cellini, Benvenuto, Florentine	1500–1570
Cordieri, Niccolò	1612
Donatello (Donato Bardi), Florentine	1466
Ferrata, Ercole, of Pelsotto	1610–1686
Gros, Pietro le, of Paris	1666–1719
Houdon, of Paris	1740–1820
Lorenzo detto il Lorenzetto, Florentine	1530
Oliviero, Pietro Paolo, Roman	1551–1599
Porta, Guglielmo della, Milanese	
Porta, Gio. Battista della, Milanese	1542–1597
Quesnoy, Francesco, Belgian	1594–1643
Sanzio, Raffaelle, of Urbino	1483–1520
Vacca, Flaminio, Roman	1600

ARCHITECTS.

Alberti, Leon Battista, Florentine	1392–
Algardi, Alessandro, of Bologna	1602–1654
Ammanati, Bartolommeo, Florentine	1511–1586
Barozzi, Giacomo, of Vignola	1507–1573

Berettini, Pietro, of Cortona	1596–1669
Bernini, Gio. Lorenzo	1598–1680
Bibbiena, Galli Francesco, of Bologna	1659–1739
Borromini, Francesco, of Bissone	1599–1667
Buonarroti, Michelangelo, Florentine	1474–1564
Desgodetz, Antonio, of Paris	1653–1728
Fontana, Carlo, of Bruciato	1634–1714
Fontana, Domenico, of Mili	1543–1607
Fuga, Ferdinando, Florentine	1699–1780
Galilei, Alessandro, Florentine	1691–1737
Giamberti, Giuliano, Sangallo il Vecchio	1443–1517
Giocondo, fr., of Verona	1435–
Lazzari, Bramante, of Urbino	1444–1514
Ligorio, Pirro, Neapolitan	1580
Lunghi, Onorio, Milanese	1569–1619
Maderno, Carlo, of Bissone	1556–1629
Maiano, Giuliano da, Florentine	1407–1477
Olivieri, Pietro Paolo, Roman	1551–1599
Palladio, Andrea, of Vicenza	1518–1580
Peruzzi, Baldassare, of Siena	1481–1536
Picconi, Antonio, da Sangallo	1546–
Pintelli, Baccio, Florentine	1420–1480
Ponzio, Flaminio, Lombard	1555–1610
Porta, Giacomo della, Roman	1539–1604
Posi, Paolo, of Siena	1708–1776
Rainaldi, Carlo, Roman	1611–1691
Sanzio, Raffaelle, of Urbino	1483–1520
Serlio, Sebastiano, of Bologna	1552
Vanvitelli, Luigi, Roman	1700–1773

F. Roman Coins.

Copper Coinage of the Republic.

For nearly five hundred years after the foundation of the city the Romans coined no metal except copper. If any gold or silver pieces were in circulation, they must have been of foreign stamp.

The ordinary copper coins of the Republic were six in number, each being distinguished by a particular device, which is preserved with almost perfect uniformity. The names of these coins were : —

	On the Obverse a Head of
1. As	Janus.
2. Semis, the half As	Jupiter.
3. Triens, one third of the As	Minerva.
4. Quadrans, the quarter As	Hercules.
5. Sextans, the half Triens	Mercury.
6. Uncia, one twelfth of the As	Minerva.

The device on the reverse is the same in all, being a rude representation of the prow of a ship. On the As we find the numeral I, on the Semis the Letter S, while on the rest round dots indicate the number of Unciæ ; thus the Triens is marked oooo, the Quadrans ooo, the Sextans oo, the Uncia o. Many of them have the word ROMA, and it gradually became common for the magistrate under whose inspection they were struck to add his name.

SILVER COINAGE.

According to Pliny, silver was first coined at Rome in 269 B. C., five years before the commencement of the first Punic War, in pieces of three denominations : —

        1. The Denarius, equivalent to 10 Asses.
        2. The Quinarius   "   "   5   "
        3. The Sestertius   "   " $2\frac{1}{2}$ "

But when the weight of the As was reduced in 217 B. C. to one ounce, it was ordained at the same time that —

        The Denarius should be equivalent to 16 Asses.
        The Quinarius   "   "   8   "
        The Sestertius   "   "   4   "

and this relation subsisted ever after between the silver coins bearing the above names and the As.

The Denarius and the Quinarius continued to be the ordinary silver currency down to the age of Septimius Severus and his sons, by whom pieces composed of a base alloy were introduced, and for several reigns entirely superseded the pure metal.

GOLD COINAGE.

Pliny asserts that gold was first coined in 207 B. C., and a few pieces are still extant which correspond with his description, but they are now generally regarded as having been struck in Magna Græcia. The number of gold coins, undoubtedly Roman, belonging to the Republican period is so small that the best numismatists are of opinion that this metal did not form part of the ordinary and regular currency until the age of Julius Cæsar, the want having been supplied by Greek Philippi. The principal gold coin of the Empire was the Denarius Aureus, which is generally termed simply Aureus, but by Pliny uniformly Denarius. The Denarius Aureus always passed for 25 silver Denarii. Half Aurei were also minted, but these are comparatively rare.

COMPARISON OF ROMAN WITH AMERICAN MONEY.

According to accurate calculations, based upon the weight and assay of the most perfect specimens of Denarii, the value of the silver Sestertius at the close of the Republic may be fixed at four cents. After the reign of Augustus the coinage underwent a sensible deterioration, both in weight and in purity, and we cannot reckon the Sestertius higher than three and a half cents from the age of Tiberius down to Septimius Severus. Taking the higher value the following table may be useful in converting sums from Roman into American currency : —

1 Sestertius	=	$ .04
10 Sestertii	=	.40
100 "	=	4.00
1000 "	=	40.00
10,000 "	=	400.00
100,000 "	=	4000.00
1,000,000 "	=	40,000.00
10,000,000 "	=	400,000.00

G. Roman Measures of Length.

	Decimals of a Metre.	Feet.	Inches.
Digitus	.0185	0	0.7281
1⅓ Digiti = Uncia or Pollex	.0247	0	0.9708
4 " = Palmus	.0740	0	2.9124
12 " = Palmus Major (of late times)	.222	0	8.7372
16 " = Pes	.296	0	11.6496
20 " = Palmipes	.370	1	2.562
24 " = Cubitus	.444	1	5.4744
2½ Pes = Gradus or Pes Sestertius	.740	2	5.124
5 " = Passus	1.48	4	10.248
10 " = Decempeda or Pertica	2.96	9	8.496
120 " = Actus (in length)	35.32	116	5.952
5000 " = Mille Passuum	1480.00	4854	0.000

A metre is 39.37 English inches. An English foot is 0.3048 metre.

H. Roman Weights.

	Grammes.	Avoirdupois Weight. Oz.	Grs.
Uncia	27.288	0	430.83⅓
1½ Unciæ = Sesuncia or Sescunx	40.932	1	203.75
2 " = Sextans	54.576	1	404.16⅔
3 " = Quadrans or Teruncius	81.864	2	168.75
4 " = Triens	109.152	3	270.83⅓
5 " = Quincunx	136.440	4	354.16⅔
6 " = Semis or Semissis	163.728	5	337.5
7 " = Septunx	191.016	6	320.33⅓
8 " = Bes or Bessis	218.304	7	104.16⅔
9 " = Dodrans	245.592	8	277.5
10 " = Dextans	272.880	9	270.83⅓
11 " = Deunx	300.168	10	260.83⅓
12 " = As or Libra	327.456	11	237.5

I. The Roman Calendar.

At the period when Julius Cæsar attained to supreme power the Calendar had fallen into great confusion. The Dictator, therefore, resolved to reform the whole system, and being himself versed in astronomy, with the aid of Sosigenes, a peripatetic philosopher of Alexandria, introduced, 45 B. C., that division of time which, with a few modifications, is still employed by all Christian nations, and received from its author the name of the Julian year.

The solar year, or the period between two vernal equinoxes, was supposed to contain 365¼ days ; but to prevent the inconvenience which would have arisen from the use of fractional parts, three years out of four were regarded as consisting of 365 days, while every fourth year had 366.

The year had been of old divided into twelve months. This number and the ancient names were retained, but the distribution of the days was changed. By the new arrangement Januarius, the first month, had 31 days, Februarius 28 in ordinary years, and every fourth year 29, Martius 31, Aprilis 30, Maius 31, Junius 30, Quintilis 31, Sextilis 31, September 30, October 31, November 30, December 31.

Julius Cæsar retained also the ancient divisions of the month by Calendæ, Nonæ, and Idus. The Calendæ fell uniformly on the first day of each month; the Idus on the 13th, except in March, May, July, and October, when they fell on the 15th ; the Nonæ were always eight (according to the Roman computation nine) days before the Idus, and therefore on the 5th, except in March, May, July, and October, when they fell on the 7th.

When an event did not happen exactly on the Calends, Nones, or Ides of any month, the day was calculated by reckoning backwards from the next division of the month. Thus, if it happened between the Calends and the Nones, it was said to take place so many days before the Nones ; if it happened between the Nones and the Ides, it was said to take place so many days before the Ides ; if it happened after the Ides, it was said to take place so many days before the Calends of the ensuing month.

In the second place, these computations always included the day *from* which the reckoning was made, as well as the day *to* which it extended. Thus the 3d of January was called the third day before the Nones of January, the 10th of March the sixth day before the Ides of March, the 14th of Jun' the eighteenth day before the Calends of July.

J. A List of Ancient Marbles.

(From H. W. Pullen's *Handbook of Roman Marbles.* London, 1894.)

I. White or Statuary Marbles.

Modern Name.	Ancient Name.	Quarries.
Pario (greco duro)	Marmor parium	Island of Paros
Porino (grechetto duro)	" porium	Neighborhood of Olympia
Pentelico (greco fino)	" pentelicum	Mount Pentelikos
Tasio (greco livido)	" thasium	Island of Thasos
Lunense (carrara antico)	" lunense	Fantiscritti, Carrara
Imezio (greco rigato)	" hymettium	Mount Hymettus
Palombino	" coraliticum	Coralio, Phrygia

II. Colored Marbles.

Modern Name.	Ancient Name.	Quarries.
Bianco e nero	M. proconnesium	Proconnesos
Nero antico	" tænarium	Tænarum, Laconia
Bigio	" batthium	Probably North Africa
" lumachellato		
" venato		
" morato	" luculleum	Island of Melos
Bardiglio		Carrara and Massa
Giallo antico	" numidicum	Supposed in Numidia, Algeria
" e nero antico	" rhodium	Island of Rhodes
Rosso antico	" tænarium	Tænarum, Laconia

III. Veined or Variegated Marbles.

Cipollino	M. carystium	Eubœa (Negroponte)
" verde		
" rosso		
" mandolato		Pyrenees and Cannes
Cottanello		Moricone (Sabine Hills)
Fior di persico	M. molossium	Epirus
Pavonazzetto	" synnadicum	Synnada, Phrygia
Porta santa	" jassense	Island of Jasos

IV. Shell Marbles.

Lumachella		
Astracane		Agra (supposed)
Broccatello	M. schiston	Tortosa, Spain
Occhio di pavone		

V. Breccie.

Br. di Aleppo		Aleppo
" " Villa Casali		
" dorata		
" traccagnina		
" Quintilina		
" rossa brecciata	M. lydium	Lydia, Asia Minor
" Serravezza		
" d' Egitto		Near Hamamat, Egypt
" corallina		
" Sette Basi		
" Semesanto		
" Africana	" chium	Island of Chios

VI. Alabasters.

Bianco	M. alabastrum	Egypt
Fiorito		
A. giaccione		

Modern Name.	Ancient Name.	Quarries.
Marino		
Rosa		
Cotognino		
A. pecorella		

VII. Miscellaneous.

Lapislazuli	Lapis cyanus	Scythia and China
Malachite	Molochites	Arabia, China, Sweden, Siberia
Spato fluore	Murrha	Parthia
Pietra di paragone	Lapis lydius	Lydia

VIII. Serpentines.

S. commune	M. ligusticum	Liguria
" rosso di Levanto		Between Spezia and Chiavari
" verde ranocchio	Lapis ophites	Egypt and French Riviera
" " antico	" atracius	Atrax, Thessaly

IX. Porphyries.

P. rosso	Lapis porphyrites	Egypt
" pavonazzo		
" verde		
" bigio		
" nero		
" serpentino	" lacedæmonius	Laconia, Peloponnesus

X. Granites.

G. rosso	Lapis pyrrhopœcilus	Syene (Assouan)
" del foro	" psaronius	" "
" bigio	" syenites	" "
" nero	" hethiopicus	Ethiopia
" verde		
" della sedia		

XI. Basalts.

B. bronzino	Lapis basanites	Ethiopia
" nero		
" ferrigno		
" bigio		
" verde		

INDEXES

I. The Existing Remains of Ancient Rome described alphabetically in Architectural Groups

II. The Existing Remains of Ancient Rome described in Chronological Order

I. Recollections of Prehistoric Times.

II. Monuments of the Kings (753–509 b. c.).

III. From the Expulsion of the Kings to the Age of Sulla (509–138 b. c.).

IV. THE LAST CENTURY OF THE REPUBLIC (128–29 B. C.).

The Monuments of the Empire (29 b. c.–608 a. d.).

V. Augustus (29 b. c.–14 a. d.).

VI. Agrippa.

VII. Tiberius (A. D. 14–37).

VIII. Caligula (A. D. 37–41).

IX. Claudius (A. D. 41-54).

X. Nero (A. D. 54–68).

Buildings of the Flavians (a. d. 69-96).

XI. Vespasian (a. d. 69-79).

XII. Titus (a. d. 79-81).

XIII. Domitian (a. d. 81-96).

XIV. Trajan (a. d. 98-117).